Freedom of Religion under Bills of Rights

For our families

Freedom of Religion under Bills of Rights

Edited by
Paul Babie and Neville Rochow

Published in Adelaide by

University of Adelaide Press
Barr Smith Library
The University of Adelaide
South Australia
5005
press@adelaide.edu.au
www.adelaide.edu.au/press

The University of Adelaide Press publishes externally refereed scholarly books by staff of the University of Adelaide. It aims to maximise the accessibility to its best research by publishing works through the internet as free downloads and as high quality printed volumes on demand.

Electronic Index: this book is available from the website as a down-loadable PDF with fully searchable text. Please use the electronic version to serve as the index.

© 2012 The Authors

This book is copyright. Apart from any fair dealing for the purposes of private study, research, criticism or review as permitted under the Copyright Act, no part may be reproduced, stored in a retrieval system, or transmitted, in any form or by any means, electronic, mechanical, photocopying, recording or otherwise without the prior written permission. Address all inquiries to the Director at the above address.

For the full Cataloguing-in-Publication data please contact National Library of Australia

ISBN (electronic) 978-0-9871718-1-8
ISBN (paperback) 978-0-9871718-0-1

Book design: Midland Typesetters
Cover design: Emma Spoehr, John Emerson, Paul Babie

Contents

Acknowledgments	vii
List of Contributors	ix
Foreword by *The Hon Sir Anthony Mason AC KBE*: Human Rights and Courts	xi

INTRODUCTION

1. Protecting Religious Freedom under Bills of Rights: Australia as Microcosm — 1
   Paul Babie and Neville Rochow

SETTING THE SCENE

2. How Religion Constrains Law and the Idea of Choice — 12
   Ngaire Naffine
3. Is the Emperor Wearing the Wrong Clothes? Human Rights and Social Good in the Context of Australian Secularity: Theological Perspectives — 29
   Bruce Kaye
4. Anniversary Overlap: Or What happens when St Paul Meets the Universal Declaration of Human Rights — 51
   Alan Cadwallader

CONTEMPORARY FREEDOM OF RELIGION ISSUES

5. Defamation and Vilification: Rights to Reputation, Free Speech and Freedom of Religion at Common Law and under Human Rights Laws — 63
   Neil Foster
6. Should an Australian Bill of Rights Address Emerging International Human Rights Norms? The Challenge of 'Defamation of Religion' — 86
   Robert C Blitt
7. Christian Concerns about an Australian Charter of Rights — 117
   Patrick Parkinson
8. Apostasy in Islam and the Freedom of Religion in International Law — 152
   Asmi Wood

COMPARATIVE EXPERIENCE WITH FREEDOM OF RELIGION

Europe

9 Political Culture and Freedom of Conscience: A Case Study of Austria 172
   David M Kirkham

10 The Sky is Falling if Judges Decide Religious Controversies! –
    Or is it? The German Experience of Religious Freedom Under a Bill of Rights 190
    Cornelia Koch

11 Religious Freedom in a Secular Society: The Case of the Islamic Headscarf
    in France 216
    Nicky Jones

12 Religious Freedom in the UK after the *Human Rights Act 1998* 239
    Ian Leigh

North America

13 Judicial Interpretation, Neutrality and the US Bill of Rights 253
    Frank S Ravitch

14 Protecting Religious Freedom: Two Counterintuitive Dialectics in
    US Free Exercise Jurisprudence 285
    Brett G Scharffs

15 Walking the Tightrope: The Struggle of Canadian Courts to Define
    Freedom of Religion under the Canadian Charter of Rights and Freedoms 321
    Barbara Billingsley

16 *Quo Vadis* The Free Exercise of Religion? The Diminishment of Student
    Religious Expression in US Public Schools 349
    Charles J Russo

Australia and New Zealand

17 Freedom from Discrimination on the Basis of Religion 365
    Kris Hanna

18 Ruminations from the Shaky Isles on Religious Freedom in the Bill of
    Rights Era 371
    Rex Tauati Ahdar

19 Indigenous Peoples and Bills of Rights 393
    Paul Rishworth

TABLE OF LEGISLATION AND INTERNATIONAL INSTRUMENTS 422

INDEX 437

Acknowledgments

It goes without saying that a volume such as this would not have been possible without the contributions and assistance of many people. The book had its genesis in the 'Cultural and Religious Freedom under a bill of rights' Conference held 13-15 August 2009 at Old Parliament House in Canberra, Australia. Many of the chapters in this volume had their first airing at that conference and we express our gratitude to all of those who presented and participated.

The organisation of the conference was a substantial undertaking, and Stephen Webster deserves special mention for directing the work of the Organising Committee. Of course, that organisation could not have happened without significant support from a number of sources, to each of which we express our sincere thanks: the International Center for Law and Religion Studies at Brigham Young University Law School and its sponsor, the Church of Jesus Christ of Latter-day Saints, the Adelaide Law School, The University of Adelaide Research Unit for the Study of Society, Law and Religion (RUSSLR), the University of Auckland, the University of Otago, Durham University, The Group of Eight Universities, ATF Press, and the Australian Human Rights Commission.

A number of valued contributors both to the conference and to the book deserve special mention: the former Chief Justice of Australia, Sir Anthony Mason AC, KBE, whose conference keynote address appears in revised form in this volume; Professors W Cole Durham, Jr, and Brett G Scharffs from Brigham Young University Law School; Dean Rosemary Owens and Dean John Williams of the Adelaide Law School; the Archbishop of Adelaide, the Most Rev Philip Wilson; Dean Carolyn Evans of the Melbourne Law School; Dean Bruce P Elman of the University of Windsor Faculty of Law; Nigel Wilson and Peter Burdon of the Adelaide Law School and RUSSLR, and; Hilary Regan of ATF Press.

We are, of course, indebted to Ben Mylius (LLB candidate, Adelaide, 2012) for research and editorial assistance, and to our publisher, The University of Adelaide Press, and its Director, Dr John Emerson, and its Commissioning Editor, Dr Patrick

Allington, for their confidence in this project, and for their unstinting patience and guidance in bringing the book to fruition. Dr Allington has been untiring in working with the manuscript and the finished product has benefited enormously from his efforts.

Finally, we are indebted to our families. Paul thanks his wife, Rachael, for being a partner in all that he does, and his two young children, Catherine and Luke, just for being themselves. Neville thanks his wife, Penny, for her unending support in this project (as in everything) and his daughters Jacquie (for her patience) and Kelly (without whose organisation and on-the-ground support, the conference that formed the basis for the book may never have taken place). Both of us recognise that without our families' kindness, generosity and patience we could not be what we are and we certainly could not have produced this book.

Paul Babie and Neville Rochow
Canada Day 2011
Calgary, Canada, and Adelaide, Australia

List of Contributors

Rex Tauati Ahdar is Professor, Faculty of Law, University of Otago and Visiting Professor, National University of Samoa and Piula Theological College, Lufilufi, Samoa (2011).

Paul Babie is Associate Professor, Adelaide Law School, at The University of Adelaide, and Founder and Director of the University of Adelaide Research Unit for the Study of Society, Law and Religion (RUSSLR).

Barbara Billingsley is Professor in the Faculty of Law, University of Alberta.

Robert C Blitt is Associate Professor of Law, University of Tennessee College of Law.

Alan Cadwallader is Senior Lecturer in Biblical Studies, Australian Catholic University, Canberra.

Neil Foster is a Senior Lecturer at the Newcastle Law School, University of Newcastle, NSW.

Kris Hanna recently resumed general legal practice in Adelaide after serving in the South Australian House of Assembly 1997-2010.

Nicky Jones is a Lecturer in Law, University of Southern Queensland.

Bruce Kaye is the foundation editor of the Journal of Anglican Studies, a Professorial Associate at the School of Theology, Charles Sturt University and a Visiting Faculty member at UNSW. Widely published, he has taught in universities in England and Australia and was General Secretary of the Anglican Church of Australia from 1994 to 2004.

David M Kirkham is Senior Fellow for Comparative Law and International Policy, Brigham Young University Law School.

Cornelia Koch is a Senior Lecturer, Adelaide Law School, at The University of Adelaide.

Ian Leigh has been a Professor of Law at the University of Durham since 1997.

The Hon Sir Anthony Mason AC KBE sat on the High Court of Australia from 1972 to 1995. He was the ninth Chief Justice of the High Court (1987–1995).

Ngaire Naffine is a Professor of Law at Adelaide Law School, The University of Adelaide. She has published in the areas of criminology, criminal law, jurisprudence, feminist legal theory and medical law.

Patrick Parkinson AM is Professor in the Faculty of Law, the University of Sydney. He is a specialist in family law, child protection and the law of equity and trusts.

Frank S Ravitch is Professor of Law and Walter H Stowers Chair of Law and Religion at Michigan State University College of Law.

Paul Rishworth is Professor of Law at the University of Auckland, where he was Faculty Dean and the Head of the Department of Law 2005-2010.

Neville Rochow SC is a Barrister at Howard Zelling Chambers in Adelaide, South Australia.

Charles J Russo is Professor and Panzer Chair in Education, University of Dayton.

Brett G Scharffs is Professor of Law, Brigham Young University Law School and Associate Director, International Center for Law and Religion Studies.

Asmi Wood is a Barrister and Solicitor (Supreme Court of the ACT). He teaches at the Australian National University.

Foreword

Human Rights and Courts

The Hon Sir Anthony Mason AC, KBE

The Australian Constitution contains no guarantee of freedom of religion or freedom of conscience. Indeed, it contains very few provisions dealing with rights — in essence, it is a Constitution that confines itself mainly to prescribing a framework for federal government, setting out the various powers of government and limiting them as between federal and state governments and the three branches of government without attempting to define the rights of citizens except in minor respects.

Section 116 of the Constitution merits mention not only because it has been wrongly said, during the course of debate, that properly understood it guarantees freedom of religion. Properly understood, it does no such thing. It prohibits the Commonwealth from:

- establishing any religion
- imposing any religious observance
- prohibiting the free exercise of any religion
- requiring any religious test as a qualification for any office or public trust under the Commonwealth.

Because s 116 does not apply to state laws, it provides no protection against state laws interfering with religion. Further, the High Court of Australia has interpreted the provision narrowly. While it is distinctly possible that the High Court could revise its view that s 116 is *not* infringed by a Commonwealth law whose *effect*, as distinct from its *purpose*, is to establish or prohibit a religion or impose a religious observance, there is nothing at this time to support the view that the other shortcomings of the section can or will be overcome.

The major criticism of the High Court's principal decision on s 116[1] is that the decision wrongly held that the section does not prohibit Commonwealth financial aid to Church schools. There is no sign that the Court will revise this decision, which is of vital importance to religious schools in Australia.

The significance of the absence of a guarantee of religious freedom, except for that contained in the Victorian *Charter of Rights and Responsibilities 2006* (the 'Victorian Charter'), is that state and territory (save the ACT, which has a charter) laws can interfere with freedom of religion. This is not an academic question. State laws prohibiting vilification of religion and religious beliefs would seem to interfere with freedom of religious expression unless it is otherwise protected. Overseas decisions indicate that such laws would have this effect. A guarantee of freedom of religion (including freedom of religious expression) would inhibit such laws from having this effect.

Section 8 of the *Racial and Religious Tolerance Act 2000* (Vic) is an example. It prohibits a person from engaging in conduct that incites hatred against, serious contempt for, revulsion for, or severe ridicule of another or a class of persons on the ground of their religious beliefs or activities. Section 11 of that Act provides a defence when a person engages in the conduct reasonably and in good faith. The presence of a guarantee of freedom of religious expression would strengthen a defendant's prospects of making out this defence,[2] or, alternatively, provide a basis for interpreting the offence to raise the bar as to what constitutes the prohibited conduct.[3]

It follows that the adoption by a federal law of art 18 of the International Covenant on Civil and Political Rights ('ICCPR') would not only guarantee freedom of religion, it would also strengthen the position of a person exercising his freedom of religious expression from the impact of vilification laws. Article 18(3) of the ICCPR provides that the freedom may be subject only to 'such limitations as prescribed by law and are necessary to protect public safety, order, health or morals or the fundamental rights and freedoms of others'. There is much to be said for the view that art 18(3) maintains a correct balance.

The history of the Australian bill of rights debate

Whether Australia should have a national bill of rights has been a controversial issue for quite some time. This is despite the fact that Australia has acceded to the ICCPR, as well as the First Optional Protocol to the ICCPR, thereby accepting an international obligation to bring Australian law into line with the ICCPR, an

---

[1] *Attorney-General (Vic) ex rel Black v Commonwealth* (1981) 146 CLR 559 ('*DOGS Case*').
[2] *Hammond v DPP* [2004] EWHC 69.
[3] See, eg, *Brooker v Police* [2007] 3 NZLR 91.

obligation that Australia has not discharged. Australia is the only country in the Western world without a national bill of rights.[4] The chapters that follow in this book debate the situation in Australia and in various other Western jurisdictions.

There has always been strong opposition to an Australian bill of rights on the part of persons in authority, including politicians, retired politicians, political commentators, judges (including retired judges) and religious leaders. They mainly represent the voice of authority. In essence, they say that a bill of rights will weaken the democratic process and transfer power to unelected judges. It may well be, however, that their real concern is that a bill of rights will expose the exercise of power to greater scrutiny and lead to a possible erosion of authority. They also say that rights adjudication will involve judges in deciding issues that are political in character, thereby eroding parliamentary sovereignty and politicising judges. These and other arguments led to three unsuccessful attempts to introduce a federal statutory bill of rights, each initiated when the Australian Labor Party was in government.

There has also been strong opposition from the Australian media, notably the Murdoch press (which has a dominating presence in Australia). The Australian media has been waging a self-serving campaign for increased recognition of freedom of expression and freedom of information while concurrently opposing recognition of a right of privacy.

The dialogue model of a bill of rights

It is therefore not surprising that the present political climate is opposed to a constitutionally entrenched bill of rights. It would require a constitutional amendment under s 128 of the Australian Constitution that requires approval by a majority of electors and a majority of electors in a majority of States. This high hurdle has only been surmounted in the case of eight amendment proposals out of forty-four submitted to the people.

Nor is it surprising that the statutory model, which may have the most support, is the so-called weak 'dialogue model' confined to civil and political rights. New Zealand,[5] the ACT[6] and the State of Victoria[7] have enacted the dialogue model based on civil and political rights. The United Kingdom *Human Rights Act 1998*

---

[4] As I will note, there are statutory Bills of Rights in the Australian Capital Territory (*Human Rights Act 2004* (ACT)) and the State of Victoria (*Charter of Human Rights & Responsibilities Act 2006* (Vic) ('the Victorian Charter')).
[5] *Bill of Rights Act 1990* (NZ).
[6] *Human Rights Act 2004* (ACT).
[7] *Charter of Human Rights & Responsibilities Act 2006* (Vic).

is a stronger example of the dialogue model. It is based on, and backed by, the *European Convention on Human Rights and Fundamental Freedoms* (the 'European Convention') rather than provisions of the ICCPR on which the New Zealand, ACT and Victorian legislation is based.

The dialogue model is a weak bill of rights model because it is interpretive only, requiring the courts to interpret legislation consistently with the bill of rights as far as they can do so legitimately. The dialogue model does not enable the courts to strike down legislation that it finds to be inconsistent with the bill, as courts in other jurisdictions under stronger models, such as Hong Kong, can do. The dialogue model respects the doctrine of parliamentary sovereignty because it accords full force and effect to the legislation and leaves Parliament free to amend it as it chooses.

The argument about parliamentary sovereignty

There has been constant repetition of the argument that the dialogue model will frustrate the democratic will by transferring power to unelected judges from elected politicians, an argument that might have force when applied to a constitutionally entrenched model but has no application when applied to the weak dialogue model. A mutant of this argument was the suggestion that the debate was about 'who is the master?' The suggestion seems to have been inspired by a misreading of *Alice's Adventures in Wonderland* or *Through the Looking Glass and what Alice Found There*. The suggestion, so extreme that one might well think it was the brainchild of Humpty Dumpty or the Mad Hatter, was that the debate is whether the judges or Parliament exercise power. How this imagined struggle for mastery can be reconciled with the Australian Constitution defies any attempt at rational explanation.

Underlying the democratic deficit argument as applied to the weak dialogue model is the assumption that Parliament will not override a judicial interpretation of legislation that renders it bill of rights-compliant, even if it is in the public interest to do so. Why not? If an override has public support, why would the politicians not support an override? Surely not out of respect for the judges. Even if there is some doubt about public support, what about the capacity of our politicians to lead and persuade the electorate? And if the courts make a finding of inconsistency, it has no legal impact on the legislation, which remains of full force and effect. The democratic deficit argument is without a foundation.

The argument about politicising the judges

There has been a resurrection of the old argument that a bill of rights will politicise the judges, an argument contradicted by the United Kingdom, New Zealand and Hong

Kong experiences. I mention Hong Kong specifically because if this argument had any substance, I suggest it would arise frequently in Hong Kong. Yet I can say that, in my 12 years experience as a Non-Permanent Judge of the Hong Kong Court of Final Appeal, this is not the position. There was the occasion in 1999 when the Standing Committee of the National People's Congress overruled the Court's decisions in the two rights of abode cases under art 158 of Hong Kong's Basic Law, as the Standing Committee was entitled to do. No such event has occurred since, despite the fact that the Court of Final Appeal has upheld human rights and fundamental freedoms in many cases, including the right of the Falun Gong (an organization banned in mainland China) to protest outside the mainland Government's Liaison Office in Hong Kong.[8]

The risk of judges being politicised by the dialogue model of a bill of rights is far less than the risk that has always existed, and still exists, under the Australian Constitution when the High Court of Australia decides politically divisive constitutional disputes about the extent of Commonwealth and State powers. These disputes go to the very heart of the powers of government in this country and they have generated both calls for changes in the mode of appointment of Justices of the High Court of Australia and media branding in the past of particular Justices as 'centralists', 'States righters', 'Neanderthalers' or 'troglodytes', as the case may be. Remember also the politically inspired ferocious attacks on the High Court over its decisions recognising Indigenous title to land in the *Mabo*[9] and *Wik*[10] decisions, which did no more — indeed not as much — than bring the common law relating to Indigenous land rights in Australia approximately into line with the common law in North America and New Zealand? With its emphasis on individual rights rather than the existence or absence of government power, the weak dialogue model will not subject the judges to the level of controversy to which High Court Justices are already exposed.

The 'floodgates' and the 'villains' charter' arguments

The notion that the dialogue model will open the floodgates to a deluge of 'rights' litigation — 'government by litigation' was the shrill shriek of one critic — has been refuted by reports made after surveys in the United Kingdom and the ACT of the legislative regimes in operation in those jurisdiction.[11] Likewise, the emotive

---

[8] *Ng Ka Ling and Chan Kam Nga v Director of Immigration* (1999) 2 HKCFAR 82, and *Yeung May Wan v HKSAR* (2005) 8 HKSAR 137.
[9] *Mabo v Queensland (No 2)* (1992) 175 CLR 1.
[10] *Wik Peoples v Queensland* (1996) 187 CLR 1.
[11] Public Law Project, *The Impact of the Human Rights Act on Judicial Review — an Empirical Study* (2003) 31; Department of Justice and Community Safety (ACT), *Twelve Months Review of the Human Rights Act 2004* (2006) 11–3.

description 'villains' charter' is inaccurate. Criminal cases represent a substantial proportion of cases in which Charter issues arise and there are cases in which a defendant in a criminal case successfully relies on a bill of rights defence, just as there are instances of such a defendant successfully relying on a common law or statutory defence. But to suggest that, in some way or other, the criminal class is the real beneficiary of such a regime is a frolic in fantasyland.

A considered perspective of the United Kingdom experience

What is striking about the debate has been the absence in the mainstream media of any discussion of the important contribution to the Australian debate made by Lord Bingham of Cornhill, until very recently England's senior judge and one of the world's great jurists, in his address 'Dignity, fairness and good governance: The role of a Human Rights Act'.[12] What his Lordship says about the operation of the *Human Rights Act 1998* (UK) and his response to media criticism made of that Act (similar to the criticisms made here) is a convincing answer to the arguments voiced recently in Australia.

After reviewing the main criticisms directed at the *Human Rights Act 1998* and the European Convention, Lord Bingham said:

> [A]s will be obvious, they do not, in my opinion, amount to very much. They do not begin to outweigh the very real benefit which the Act confers by empowering the courts to uphold certain very basic safeguards even — indeed, particularly — for those members of society who are most disadvantaged, most vulnerable and least well-represented in any democratic representative assembly.[13]

He went on to say:

> Decisions have undoubtedly been made in the UK which have, in my view, been beneficial and which would not — in some cases could not — have been made without the mandate given by the Act.[14]

---

[12] Lord Bingham of Cornwall, 'Dignity, fairness and good governance: The role of a Human Rights Act' (Speech delivered at the Human Rights Law Resource Centre, Sydney, 11 December 2008); also published as Lord Bingham of Cornwall, 'Dignity, fairness and good governance: The role of a Human Rights Act' (Winter 2009) *NSW Bar News* 42.
[13] Ibid 47.
[14] Ibid.

After giving examples of such decisions, he added:

> These examples ... could be multiplied. I do not for my part doubt that such decisions enhance the fairness, decency and cohesiveness of the society in which we live in the United Kingdom.[15]

The case for a bill of rights

The first point to be made in favour of a national bill of rights — protecting civil and political rights — is that it would substantially enhance our democratic system of government, and respect for the rights and dignity of the individual, by promoting a culture of respect for human rights and human dignity. To insist that the protection of human rights is best left to politicians rather than judges is not only to forget the lessons of history but also to ignore the contemporary disenchantment with the political process that prevails in countries such as Australia and the United Kingdom today. There is a popular perception that politicians are disconnected from the concerns of the people, that politics is all about gaining and maintaining power at all costs and that powerful lobby groups and stakeholders exploit the political process for their own interests. In addition, many people perceive an unhealthy relationship between the media and politics, a relationship in which politicians vie with each other for media attention and the media sensationalises and trivialises politics.[16] In such a climate, there is little or no incentive for politicians to take action to protect the disadvantaged minority or the individual, unless to do so offers the prospect of political mileage. Unfortunately, very often that may be no more than a remote prospect.

John Lloyd, in an opinion piece published in the *Financial Times*[17] following the recent British MP's expenses claim scandal, quoted the views of well-known political scientists on the condition of modern democracy. The views were disturbing. Colin Crouch, who wrote the book *Post-Democracy* in 2004, argued that politics was 'increasingly slipping back into the control of privileged elites, in the manner characteristic of pre-democratic times' and that 'the consumer has triumphed over the citizen'.[18] John Keane, who published *The Life and Death of Democracy* in 2009, wrote that there is a 'sense that official politics [are] irrelevant, or at least they poorly represented the interests of the citizens'.[19]

---

[15] Ibid 48.
[16] The sorry saga of the so-called 'Ozcar affair' is just one of many examples that might be given.
[17] John Lloyd, 'Politicians must listen, learn and level with citizens', *Financial Times* (London), 3–4 July 2009, 7.
[18] Ibid (quoting Colin Crouch).
[19] Ibid (quoting John Keane).

Lloyd also discussed Margit van Wessel, the Dutch political scientist, who tested a small sample of Dutch voters to find out what they thought of parliamentary democracy. According to Lloyd's summary, she concluded that 'Many saw parliamentarians as self-interested, prone to compromise, unable to connect with citizens' concerns, immured in their own world'.[20]

This view, strikingly captured in that phrase 'immured in their own world', resonates widely, not least in Australia. For example, in 2009 Tony Fitzgerald QC called our attention to the soggy side of the Queensland political world, with donations paving the way to access to government ministers and very large 'success fees' paid to former ministers who act as unregulated lobbyists.[21]

This is not to say that the general public does not support democracy. Disenchantment with its present condition shows no present sign of citizens deserting democracy for some other form of government. Rather, disenchantment leads citizens to hope that democracy can undergo reforms so that it will achieve the lofty aspirations claimed for it by politicians. One way of contributing to that goal is to focus more attention on the protection of human rights and fundamental freedoms.

A dispassionate view of the political process in Australia does not reveal a landscape dedicated to the protection of human rights. One only has to look at the situation of Indigenous peoples, ethnic minorities, disabled persons, the mentally ill, abused children, the aged, the incarcerated boat people, asylum seekers and, most recently, the situation of Indian and Asian students in Australia who have been the victims of assaults, robbery and reported educational exploitation. The way in which the then Australian Government dealt with David Hicks[22] and Dr Haneef highlights the inadequacies of human rights protection in Australia. There has been a systemic failure to protect human rights and human dignity, due to lack of public consensus and political inertia.

Another concern is the fact that over many years there has been a steady increase in the growth of executive power, authorised by legislation, to the detriment of individual rights and interests. Subject only to such oversight as the Senate is from time to time capable of providing, the executive dominates the parliamentary process. The inroads made into the traditional principles of due process, initially justified as necessary in

---

[20] Ibid.
[21] *Tony Fitzgerald Lecture Slams Queensland Corruption* (2009) Lawyers' Weekly <http://www.lawyersweekly.com.au/blogs/slide_show/archive/2009/07/29/tony-fitzgerald-lecture-slams-queensland-corruption.aspx> at 12 September 2011.
[22] The then Australian Government did not object to his detention for more than three years in Guantanamo Bay and his trial by a military commission, despite a statement by five independent UN Special Rapporteurs calling on the United States Government to bring all detainees before an independent and competent tribunal or release them.

order to deal with the threat of terrorism, are now being repeated in other situations, ostensibly to protect criminal information and to enable us to deal with bikie gangs. Why discard traditional principles when for so long in the past they were a defining point of our claim to be a just, fair and ordered society?

The political process is an inadequate safeguard

The argument that judicial enforcement of a bill of rights is on its own an antidote to our problems is not compelling. What we need to bring about is a dramatic change in the political and bureaucratic culture, in particular by reform of the parliamentary process, modelled on the United Kingdom system of parliamentary reviews. But on its own it will not be a sufficient protection of civil and political human rights in Australia. This was the view taken in both the United Kingdom and in New Zealand. In both places, the enhanced parliamentary system of review sits alongside the *Human Rights Act 1998* (UK) and the *Bill of Rights Act 1990* (NZ) respectively.

In this respect, if one thing is abundantly clear it is that a political review of human rights, unaccompanied by a statutory bill of rights interpreted and applied by judges, will not adequately protect civil and political human rights. The political process has failed to deliver in the past. What reason now is there to think that, left to its own devices, it will deliver in the future? Although the parliamentary system of review certainly offers advantages in relation to economic and social rights, it is not sufficient on its own as a safeguard for civil and political rights, though, in combination with a statutory bill of rights interpreted and applied by judges, it will mark a significant step forward. In time — and it may take quite a long time — the combination of the two should bring about a change in our political and bureaucratic culture.

An illustration of what can be achieved by a bill of rights in Australia is the decision in *Kracke v Mental Health Review Board*[23], where a mentally ill man was required to take psychotropic medication without his consent. The drugs had adverse side effects. He tried without success to persuade the medical authorities to let him stop taking the drugs. The *Mental Health Act 1986* (Vic) allows the making of treatment orders without consent calling for the administration of drugs. But the Act requires periodic reviews by the Board within stipulated time limits. In this case, the authorities did not observe the limits. The failure was substantial and systemic. The declaration under the Victorian Charter that Mr Kracke's human rights were violated and the judgment setting out the circumstances of the case drew attention to an injustice suffered by a minority group, an injustice that the political process failed to remedy.

---

[23] [2009] VCAT 646 (23 April 2009).

Other advantages of a bill of rights

In the United Kingdom, the *Human Rights Act 1998* is leading to a reformation of English administrative law. Thomas Poole of the London School of Economics and Political Science has pointed out that the core concerns of traditional English administrative law were (as they currently are in Australia) the examination of powers and procedures of authorities, according to the notion that the community should be protected from abuses of public power, a notion more suited to a collectivist age than an individualist age. The focal point of the legal analysis was not the individual and his interest, whatever it might be.[24]

In the UK, the old administrative law is giving way to a new approach in which the rights of the individual are becoming the focal point of the legal analysis, accompanied by an application of the proportionality principle as a standard by which courts and other tribunals judge administrative decisions. This development leads to a stronger element of substance-based judicial review of administrative decision.[25] In turn, this exposes the decision-making processes of government to publicity and review, enhancing modern democratic governance in two ways. It enables the public to form a judgment on the question of whether the executive government is respecting human rights in its decision-making processes.

In time, the new approach to administrative law will have an impact on the political and bureaucratic culture by way of encouraging a greater respect for human rights. An Australian bill of rights would hopefully have a similar impact. What is happening in the United Kingdom, however, has been influenced by the European Convention and the jurisprudence of the European Court of Human Rights which, practically speaking, binds the courts of the United Kingdom.

Neither a bill of rights nor a Parliamentary review of legislation would set to right all the existing shortcomings of the political process. But the two together would be a step in the right direction. It would encourage our politicians to think about the people rather than the preservation of their power and the pursuit of party and personal interests, and to focus on how they can protect the rights and freedoms of individuals, upon which our very society depends.

One very disturbing illustration of a continuing trend in modern politics is the increasing marginalisation of the rule of law and of respect for the traditional principles of due process. The emergence of the so-called 'War on Terror' marked the beginning of a movement to dispense with the requirements that the law imposed before detention and punishment could be justified in law. In the long saga in

---

[24] Thomas Poole, 'The Reformation of English Administrative Law' [2009] 68 *Cambridge Law Journal* 142.
[25] Ibid 143–5.

which David Hicks was involved, he was detained for more than four years before a conviction was recorded against him — and even then, by consent — and for most of that time no charge was preferred against him. The US imprisoned him because he was a suspected terrorist. Australian authorities detained Dr Haneef in circumstances in which, as it transpired, there was no evidence to support the proposition that he was linked to terrorism or a terrorist organisation.

Other objections to the dialogue model

Another possible objection to the dialogue model or, indeed, any model based on the ICCPR, is that it would involve the courts in deciding whether particular permitted restrictions on protected rights and freedoms are 'necessary'. I take as an example the limitations permitted by art 22(2) of the ICCPR on freedom of association, namely,

> restrictions which are prescribed by law and which are necessary in a democratic society in the interests of national security or public safety, public order ... the protection of public health or morals or the protection of the rights and freedoms of others ...

The determination of the legitimacy of such a restriction under this formulation, according to the criterion 'necessary in a democratic society in the interests of', is a formulation interpreted and applied by courts in various parts of the world, including the United Kingdom, European and other courts, pursuant to international and regional conventions. Qualifications of this kind, applied by the courts, are essential if we are to protect the rule of law and due process from the exercise of arbitrary power by an executive government under the cover of statutory authority.

Perhaps the strongest objection to the dialogue model — an argument that has so far attracted little attention — is that the dialogue model may not add much to the existing common law principle of legality. According to this principle of statutory interpretation, a court will not interpret a statute in such a way that it abrogates or curtails rights recognised by the common law and, arguably, human rights and fundamental freedoms, unless the statute exhibits an unambiguous intention to do so.[26]

The interpretive provision in the dialogue model seeks to achieve a stronger pro-rights interpretation than the common law principle of legality would achieve.

---

[26] See *Coco v The Queen* (1984) 179 CLR 427.

There is a question as to how effective the dialogue model will be in this respect.[27] The common law principle of legality has its shortcomings. One is that there is uncertainty about the rights to which it applies. A bill of rights would remove that uncertainty by identifying all the rights and freedoms that the bill is to protect.

Another shortcoming is that the common law principle of legality is just one of many common law principles of statutory interpretation. It has no special focus on human rights. The absence of that focus is one reason why some Australian lawyers are opposed to any kind of bill of rights. They are accustomed to think in terms of common law rules based on precedents; they are not attuned to thinking about the law in terms of the substance of its impact upon human rights and human dignity. That is the central thrust of a bill of rights. Its objective is to provide a new focus and induce all of us, including judges, politicians and administrators, to think positively about human rights and human dignity, as it is doing in the United Kingdom.[28]

Although I support the dialogue model, I think that some issues, such as abortion and euthanasia, are better left to the political process and should be carved out. For my part, I do not think that compelling answers to these questions can be judicially articulated from 'the right to life'.

The constitutional argument

Opponents of a bill of rights continue to refer to a constitutional objection to a federal bill of rights. The argument was that a judicial declaration of incompatibility would be unconstitutional because it does not amount to an exercise of federal judicial power. A roundtable of constitutional experts convened by the Australian Human Rights Commission unanimously rejected this argument. The roundtable pointed out that a bill that provided for a 'finding of inconsistency' in the event that a particular statute was inconsistent with the bill was no more than a conclusion reached on an issue that arises in a case brought by or against a litigant who relies on a right or freedom protected by the bill.[29]

Despite this, the Attorney-General for Western Australia, Christian Porter, has reportedly said: 'I personally would have no hesitation in advocating to my cabinet

---

[27] See *RJE v The Secretary to the Department of Justice* [2008] VSCA 265, [117–119]) (Nettle JA) (where his Honour applied the interpretive provision to an expression which was capable of two interpretations, although on ordinary principles of interpretation he would have favoured the alternative meaning).

[28] See above.

[29] Australian Human Rights Commission, *Constitutional validity of an Australian Human Rights Act* (2009).

a challenge to any declaratory bill of rights'.[30] What he meant by the words 'any declaratory bill of rights' is by no means clear. According to the report, the Attorney-General acknowledged that he did not 'claim to be a constitutional lawyer' and went on to say that he had not yet sought legal advice on the issue. You might wonder how, in these circumstances, a Law Officer could contemplate giving advice to his Cabinet along the lines he proposed. The answer is that, in Australia, politicians think that governments are reluctant to initiate proposals for reform if they are likely to sink into a Serbonian bog of constitutional litigation. Consequently, the tactic here is to 'talk up' a supposed constitutional problem in order to discourage government from proceeding with any proposal.

Future prospects

While there did seem some prospect that the Rudd Labor government would make a legislative response to the enforcement of human rights norms, this did not eventuate. After receipt of the National Human Rights Consultation Committee (the Brennan Committee) recommendations, the federal government moved entirely away from any legislative response. Instead, on 21 April 2010, the federal Attorney-General launched Australia's Human Rights Framework as an executive approach to human rights at the federal level.

The government indicated that the Framework was based on five key principles and focuses:

- reaffirming a commitment to our human rights obligations;
- the importance of human rights education;
- enhancing our domestic and international engagement on human rights issues;
- improving human rights protections including greater parliamentary scrutiny; and
- achieving greater respect for human rights principles within the community.[31]

It now seems that the possibility of a federal bill of rights will remain in limbo for some time to come.[32]

---

[30] 'WA to challenge bill of rights', *Australian Financial Review* (Sydney), 26 June 2009, 54.
[31] *Australia's Human Rights Framework* (2010) Attorney-General's Department <http://www.ag.gov.au/humanrightsframework> at 18 April 2011.
[32] See Babie and Rochow in this volume, 7–9.

1

Protecting Religious Freedom under Bills of Rights: Australia as Microcosm

Paul Babie and Neville Rochow

While the world undergoes a religious revival,[1] the protection of religious freedom, particularly of minority religious groups, seems increasingly under threat.[2] Most religious scholars report that religious liberty is 'treading water at best, retreating at worst'.[3] According to the Pew Forum on Religion & Public Life, nearly 70 per cent of the world's 6.8 billion people live in countries with high restrictions on religion.[4] Religious constraints take two forms: 'official curbs on faith and ... hostility that believers endure at the hands of fellow citizens'.[5] All of this is troubling, especially in light of the fact that the Universal Declaration of Human Rights (UDHR),[6] one of the great international breakthroughs in the protection of human rights, came only in the last century. From any perspective, human rights, and especially religious

---

[1] William Twining, *General Jurisprudence: Understanding Law from a Global Perspective* (2009) 6–7, 125.
[2] The mainstream media continues to demonstrate this threat: see, eg, Joshua Kurlantzick, 'The Downfall of Human Rights', *Newsweek* (New York), 1 March 2010, 30. Religious leaders have also drawn attention to this threat: see, eg, Denis Hart, 'The Right to Religious Freedom', *The Swag* (Belmont), Summer 2009, 26. And it has received recent scholarly attention: see, eg, Elizabeth H Prodromou, 'International Religious Freedom and the Challenge of Proselytism' in Aristotle Papanikolaou and Elizabeth H Prodromou (eds), *Thinking Through Faith: New Perspectives from Orthodox Christian Scholars* (2008) 247.
[3] 'Religious Freedom: Too Many Chains', *Economist* (London), 19 December 2009, 111–2.
[4] Pew Forum on Religion & Public Life, *Global Restrictions on Religion* (2009) 1 (available at http://pewforum.org/uploadedFiles/Topics/Issues/Government/restrictions-fullreport.pdf).
[5] 'Religious Freedom: Too Many Chains', above n 3, 111.
[6] See *Universal Declaration of Human Rights*, GA Res 217A, UN GAOR, 3rd sess, 1st plen mtg, UN Doc A/810 (1948) (available at http://www.un.org/en/documents/udhr/).

freedom, appear to be under threat,[7] making current both its international status and domestic protection through constitutional or other legislative means.

While many do, not every democratic state provides the comprehensive protection for human rights — including religious freedom — found at the international level. Australia's record, for instance, serves as a microcosm of the international debate about protecting religious freedom using constitutional or legislative instruments in an attempt to balance the collective, the community, the society, against the individual, the group, the minority. And the Australian experience demonstrates, perhaps most dramatically, the discordance that can exist between domestic and international protection. While successive federal governments have made it a matter of policy to be critical of what are considered to be human rights abuses and denial of due process in other countries, even ratifying several international covenants relating to human rights and freedoms, Australia has implemented few of these covenants as part of its domestic law. Indeed, it may surprise many people to learn that Australia is the only Western liberal democracy still lacking, at a minimum, a legislated bill or charter of human rights and freedoms.[8] Yet, as we know, many countries do provide, in their domestic laws, the protections found in international covenants for the protection of fundamental rights and freedoms, including that of religion — how do they accomplish that? Australia's story, while one of failure (or disinclination) to provide domestic protection in anything like a comprehensive fashion, can nonetheless tell us much about what other democracies have done to protect fundamental rights and freedoms.

Australia as Microcosm

Bill of Rights as Dialogue

Unlike the constitutional protections found in countries like the United States[9] or Canada,[10] or of the legislative but still quasi-constitutional protections found in nations like the United Kingdom[11] or New Zealand,[12] Australians enjoy no comprehensive protection of rights and freedoms — either at the federal constitutional or at the state legislative level — and any protections that are afforded are on the narrowest of

---

[7] Kurlantzick, above n 2, 30.
[8] The terms 'bill' or 'charter' of human rights and freedoms tend to be used interchangeably in the Australian debate. This Article uses 'bill of rights' or 'bill' in reference to either a bill or a charter of human rights and freedoms.
[9] *United States Constitution*, amends I–X.
[10] *Canada Act 1982* (UK) c 11, sch B pt 1 ('*Canadian Charter of Rights and Freedoms*').
[11] *Human Rights Act 1998* (UK) c 42.
[12] *New Zealand Bill of Rights Act 1990* (NZ).

bases.[13] Still, from the moment of its Federation in 1901, the 'bill of rights question' — whether to adopt one and, if so, what rights it should protect and how they should be enforced — looms large in Australia's constitutional history, oscillating between periods of wild enthusiasm, on the one hand, to apathy coupled with a lack of sophisticated discussion, on the other. Yet, while it has yet to provide the comprehensive protection found in other jurisdictions, the ongoing debate itself serves as a guide to the contours of protecting rights and freedoms, and especially religious freedom, in liberal democratic systems. The Australian experience provides, in short, a microcosm of the broader international debate about the protection of individual and group rights.

The story is revealed most clearly in the recent attempt of the federal government to breathe new life into the effort to provide comprehensive human rights protection in Australia. In late 2008 (in fact, on the sixtieth anniversary of the UDHR), the Attorney-General of Australia launched the National Human Rights Consultation,[14] which empowered a National Human Rights Consultation Committee to seek the views of the Australian community on how human rights and responsibilities should be protected in the future and to promote a broad discussion on the range of available options. For many, this meant a renewed but by no means new discussion about whether or not Australia should adopt a national bill of rights.[15] On 30 September 2009, the Committee, having received more than 35,000 submissions and conducted over sixty-five community roundtables and public hearings in more than fifty urban, regional and remote locations across the country, delivered its Consultation Report to the Attorney-General.[16] Two aspects of the Consultation Report concern us here: the notion of a bill of rights as setting the parameters for a 'dialogue' between the judicial and legislative branches of government concerning human rights, and the place of religion itself within such a dialogue.

---

[13] See, eg, *Australian Constitution* s 116, *Racial Discrimination Act 1975* (Cth), the *Human Rights Act 2004* (ACT) and the *Charter of Human Rights and Responsibilities Act 2006* (Vic).

[14] This was an outcome of an election promise made by the Labor Party in 2007. See also Andrew Byrnes, Hilary Charlesworth and Gabrielle McKinnon, *Bills of Rights in Australia: History, Politics and Law* (2009) 146–7.

[15] Robert McClelland, *A Message from the Attorney-General the Hon Robert McClelland MP* (2010) National Human Rights Consultation <http://www.humanrightsconsultation.gov.au/www/nhrcc/nhrcc.nsf/Page/Who_AMessagefromtheAttorney-GeneraltheHonRobertMcClelland> at 26 July 2011.

[16] National Human Rights Consultation Committee, *National Human Rights Consultation Report* (2009) (available at http://www.humanrightsconsultation.gov.au/www/nhrcc/nhrcc.nsf/Page/Report_NationalHumanRightsConsultationReportDownloads). See also *Australia Releases National Human Rights Consultation Report* (2009) Gov Monitor <http://thegovmonitor.com/world_news/asia/australia-releases-national-human-rights-consultation-report-7855.html> at 26 July 2011.

The Consultation Report contained an extensive comparative discussion of 'dialogue' models found in other jurisdictions — especially the United Kingdom and New Zealand[17] — and recommended a 'weak' dialogue model federal Human Rights Act (bill of rights).[18] All legislation in some way affects the distribution of power between the three branches of government. In that sense, 'dialogue' or 'institutional interaction'[19] is not new. First introduced as a metaphor by Peter Hogg and Allison Bushell for interaction between the three branches in response to criticisms that judicial review under constitutional bills of rights was anti-democratic or anti-majoritarian,[20] dialogue has always occurred in all Australian jurisdictions between the legislature and the judiciary and, to a lesser extent, the executive. Moreover, it comprises a feature of many constitutional systems, even those in Canada and the US, where the judiciary has the power to invalidate legislation, seemingly giving it the last word on human rights issues.[21]

Because human rights protection, whether constitutional or legislative, directs the executive and the judiciary to conduct their business in certain ways, dialogue models for bills of rights encourage 'conversation' between the three branches,[22] allowing the judiciary to comment upon the adequacy of legislation or to be critical of the actions of the executive. The legislature can respond in turn by amending legislation or administrative practices or the bill might even leave open the possibility of allowing for an explicit rejection of the judicial decision, all of which is generally seen as a desirable outcome of the implementation of a bill of rights.[23]

Dialogue has generally taken two forms. First, in its 'strong' form, as in the US, it may redistribute powers to such an extent that the judiciary is given the power to invalidate acts of the legislature for the infringement of enumerated rights. How strong the dialogue is depends on whether the legislature has any recourse to respond once the courts have spoken. Strong dialogue has received extensive

---

[17] *Consultation Report*, above n 16, 241–62.

[18] Ibid 361–4, 371–9. This recommendation may be regrettable, as it is not clear that either Constitutional amendment or legislative enactment as a weak dialogue model is the only way forward: see Neville G Rochow, *Paying for Human Rights Until the Bill Comes* (Legal Studies Research Paper Series, University of Adelaide Law School, 2009) (available at <http://papers.ssrn.com/sol3/papers.cfm?abstract_id=1356382>).

[19] Leighton McDonald, 'Rights, "Dialogue" and Democratic Objections to Judicial Review' (2004) 32 *Federal Law Review* 1.

[20] Peter W Hogg and Allison A Bushell, 'The Charter Dialogue Between Courts and Legislatures (or Perhaps the Charter of Rights Isn't Such a Bad Thing After All)' (1997) 35 *Osgoode Hall Law Journal* 75.

[21] Australian Capital Territory, *Towards an ACT Human Rights Act: Report of the ACT Bill of Rights Consultative Committee* (2003) 61.

[22] Byrnes, Charlesworth and McKinnon, above n 14, 51.

[23] Australian Capital Territory, above n 21, 61–2.

academic scrutiny in Canada, where section 33 of the Canadian Charter of Rights and Freedoms constitutionally entrenches this model.[24] The focus of debate in Canada turns on whether in practice the Charter involves genuine dialogue or simply allows the judiciary's view of the meaning of human rights to supersede those of the other branches.[25] Some in fact argue that rather than true dialogue, the outcome of the process mandated under the Charter is in fact judicial 'monologue' or even 'ventriloquism'.[26]

Dialogue may, however, take a 'weak' form, allowing the judiciary to play a role in the enforcement of human rights short of invalidation of legislation.[27] This form permits institutional interaction amongst the three branches of government and the community while conferring on the legislature the 'final say' in relation to human rights issues. Under such a scheme, the judiciary is not given the power to invalidate legislation (although it could do so in relation to executive acts, including subordinate legislation) but rather may express its opinion that a law is incompatible with enumerated rights. It is then up to the legislature to determine whether or not to amend the legislation in question so as to bring it into conformity with the protected rights.[28] The United Kingdom *Human Rights Act 1998* and the New Zealand *Bill of Rights Act 1990* are weak dialogue models,[29] reflecting the current trend in national legal systems to move away from the American strong dialogue model, which gives substantial power — or at least the courts have arrogated that power to themselves[30] — to have the final say in matters of human rights protection and towards a model preserving to the legislature its democratic function to decide how best to protect human rights.[31]

As part of its weak dialogue package, the Consultation Report recommended that only federal 'public authorities' should be required to comply with enumerated human rights — this would include Ministers, public servants, and government departments. In the case of legislation, however, the bill of rights would require that other laws be interpreted consistently with enumerated rights, provided that this was consistent with Parliament's intent. Where incompatible, no invalidation

---

[24] See Byrnes, Charlesworth and McKinnon, above n 14, 52.
[25] Peter W Hogg, Allison A Bushell Thornton and Wade K Wright, 'Charter Dialogue Revisited—or "Much Ado About Metaphors"' (2007) 45 *Osgoode Hall Law Journal* 1.
[26] Christopher Manfredi and James Kelly, 'Six Degrees of Dialogue: A Response to Hogg and Bushell' (2009) 37 *Osgoode Hall Law Journal* 513, 520–1.
[27] Australian Capital Territory, above n 21, 61.
[28] Ibid 61–2.
[29] Byrnes, Charlesworth and McKinnon, above n 14, 52–4.
[30] *Marbury v Madison*, 5 US 137 (1803).
[31] Byrnes, Charlesworth and McKinnon, above n 14, 51.

would be possible; rather, only the High Court would have the power to issue a 'declaration of incompatibility'. Such declarations would notify the government of the incompatibility while leaving Parliament the final word in the dialogue between the two branches of government as to whether to amend the law.[32]

Once a nation determines to protect human rights through a bill of rights, and once the procedural decision is taken to do so through either a strong or weak dialogue document, it becomes necessary to consider the substantive content of the rights that the bill will protect. That is no easy task, and perhaps nowhere is this truer than in the case of freedom of religion. The Australian story is again instructive.

Protecting Religious Freedom

In addition to a weak dialogue model,[33] the Consultation Committee recommended the inclusion of a non-derogable freedom from coercion or restraint in relation to religion and belief. The Committee recommended that under this right no person could be coerced or impaired in their freedom to have or to adopt a religion or belief of their choice. While free to adopt a religion or belief, however, the Consultation Report also included a list of enumerated derogable rights, including the freedom of thought, conscience, and belief, the freedom to manifest one's religion or beliefs, and the freedom of expression. Thus, while protecting the right to choose a religion, the Consultation Committee's recommendations would allow limitations to be placed on the practice of that religion.

Yet, this rather placid treatment of religious freedom belies a much stronger undercurrent of views and positions. In establishing the Consultation, the Australian Government unleashed, perhaps unwittingly, a torrent of national concern amongst religious communities regarding the protection of religious freedom should a bill of rights be enacted. Many religious groups made formal submissions to the Committee.[34] And while some supported a bill, those voices were drowned out in large part by those who were opposed to one of any kind, strong or weak dialogue. Two themes emerged from this opposition: (i) a concern with the protection of

---

[32] Consultation Report, above n 16, 361–4, 372–9; see also Edward Santow and George Williams, *National Human Rights Consultation Report: A Brief Summary* (2009) (Gilbert + Tobin Centre of Public Law <http://www.gtcentre.unsw.edu.au/Resources/docs/cohr/Brennan_Committee_Report_Summary.pdf>.

[33] The Terms of Reference for its consultation required the Committee not to pursue options inconsistent with a 'weak dialogue' model: National Human Rights Consultation Committee, *Terms of Reference* (2010), <http://www.humanrightsconsultation.gov.au/www/nhrcc/nhrcc.nsf/Page/Terms_of_Reference> at 26 July 2011.

[34] See, eg, Australian Christian Lobby, *Submission to the National Human Rights Consultation* (2009) (available at www.humanrightsconsultation.gov.au/www/nhrcc/submissions.nsf/list/7C16C13B8A6F2E21CA257607001AF3A9/$file/ACL_AGWW-7T28ZS.pdf).

equality in a document that also attempted, or worse, did not attempt, to protect religious freedom, and (ii) a concern that a bill would confer powers on the judiciary to override the will of the executive and legislative branches of government. From a summary review of these themes, we can learn much about the place of religion and its protection within bills of rights.

Those religious groups which made submissions to the Committee opposing a bill of rights both perceived an antipathy among many Australians towards exemptions under anti-discrimination legislation for faith–based organizations[35] and believed that vague and poorly drafted anti-vilification legislation has a chilling effect on freedom of religious expression.[36] The central concern was that courts use bills of rights generally, and the protection of equality rights specifically, for illegitimate, undemocratic, and anti-majoritarian purposes. This, these opponents argued, places the judiciary in a paramount position relative to the other branches of government, allowing that branch to 'create' new rights, not unlike the right to privacy in the United States,[37] the major consequence of which will be to weaken community.

The Government's Response to the Consultation Report

In the end, religious groups opposed to a bill of rights need not have worried. The day after the release of the Committee's report, 1 October 2009, the Attorney-General issued a press release announcing that the government intended to withhold public release of the Committee's recommendations until the final months of 2009 when it, too, would issue a formal response,[38] which the Attorney-General did in October 2009.[39] While lauding Australia's human rights record and the government's commitment to human rights, the Attorney-General stopped short of endorsing the enactment of a bill of rights,[40] giving instead a general commitment to respecting the human rights that underpin Australian society and a safe and inclusive democracy. Yet, the Attorney-General's response suggested that there are other ways in which to protect human rights short of enacting a bill of rights, including fostering a culture where the fundamental human rights of all people are respected and protected, and

---

[35] Patrick Parkinson, 'Christian Concerns about an Australian Charter of Rights', Ch 7 in this volume.
[36] Ibid 3.
[37] *Griswold v Connecticut*, 381 US 479 (1965). The background to this decision included *Tileston v Ullman*, 318 US 44 (1943), and *Poe v Ullman*, 367 US 497 (1961). Subsequent cases citing and extending the right to privacy include *Eisenstadt v Baird*, 405 US 438 (1972), *Roe v Wade*, 410 US 113 (1973), *Bowers v Hardwick*, 478 US 186 (1986), and *Lawrence v Texas*, 539 US 558 (2003).
[38] See *Australia Releases*, above n 16.
[39] Hon Robert McClelland, *The Protection and Promotion of Human Rights in Australia* (2009) (available at http://www.ag.gov.au/www/agd/agd.nsf/Page/Publications_NationalHumanRightsConsultationReport).
[40] Ibid 1–3.

ensuring that a range of mechanisms are made available to promote and protect those rights[41] in conjunction with ensuring the sovereignty of Parliament.[42]

By early 2010, it was increasingly apparent that this latest comprehensive Australian attempt to protect human rights was unravelling. The mainstream media published negative editorials indicating significant unease about a bill of rights. In February, one commentator argued that a weak dialogue bill of rights that gave the legislative branch the final say about human rights would allow lobbyists and the interest groups they represent to affect the way government does business, resulting in the legislative fashioning of narrow, interest-group specific rights.[43] Father Frank Brennan, Chair of the National Human Rights Consultation, even entered the fray to urge churches to back a bill of rights.[44]

Still, the negative pressure exerted by the media seemed to work. As members of Parliament returned for the 2010 sitting, reports emerged of widespread opposition to a bill of rights within federal cabinet.[45] Opposition took the now familiar mantra that a bill would place too much power in the hands of unelected judges.[46] The Attorney-General was said to be considering a 'Framework Approach' containing two options that, while falling far short of a bill of rights, would offer some human rights protection: (i) a Senate committee that would be given a test of compatibility with human rights against which it could measure proposed legislation, and (ii) an education awareness campaign about human rights.[47] As of March 2010, the then Prime Minister's ongoing silence on the government's official response, however, only fuelled the fire of speculation that a bill of rights of any kind was a non-starter.[48]

The political climate in Australia has shifted. It now seems clear that there is little likelihood of the enactment of a bill of rights of any kind; the Framework Approach

---

[41] Ibid 3.
[42] Ibid.
[43] Elise Parham, 'Rights charter would empower only lobbyists', *The Australian* (Sydney), 4 February 2010 (available at http://www.theaustralian.com.au/news/opinion/rights-charter-would-empower-only-lobbyists/story-e6frg6zo-1225826508311).
[44] Susanna Dunkerley, 'Churches Urged to Back Charter of Rights', *Sydney Morning Herald* (Sydney), 8 February 2010 (available at http://news.smh.com.au/breaking-news-national/churches-urged-to-back-charter-of-rights-20100208-nn5g.html).
[45] James Allan, 'Kevin Rudd's Good Job on Opposing Rights Bill', *The Australian* (Sydney), 19 February 2010 (available at http://www.theaustralian.com.au/business/legal-affairs/kevin-rudds-good-job-on-opposing-rights-bill/story-e6frg97x-1225831948151).
[46] 'Rudd Government Mum on Rights Charter Report', *WA Today* (Perth) 18 February 2010 (available at http://www.watoday.com.au/breaking-news-national/rudd-govt-mum-on-rights-charter-report-20100218-og0n.html).
[47] Allan, above n 45.
[48] 'Rudd Government Mum', above n 46.

has removed any such legislation from the political agenda for the foreseeable future. And only time will tell whether the two options contained in the Framework Approach will have the effect of conferring upon the judiciary greater power in the review of legislation for its effect on human rights than had been proposed under the now all but defunct bill of rights proposals.

Yet the Australian story itself serves to highlight, in a concrete way, what is involved in protecting human rights in bills of rights, both procedurally (the notion of dialogue between branches of government) and substantively (the place of rights such as religion within a dialogue). Exploring and assessing the different ways that nations have done that represents the goal of the essays collected in this volume.

The Goal

How, then, can a nation protect fundamental rights and freedoms, including religious freedom, within a liberal democratic context? The objective of the essays presented in this volume, taken as a whole, is to provide an overview of the principal models used to protect fundamental freedoms, and especially the right to freedom of belief, expression and practice of one's religion, in major liberal democratic systems. While there is no effort made to be comprehensive about this, the book is clearly not simply about Australia — the chapters cover the range of methods typically used to protect such freedoms. This represents the significance of the volume: it prioritises no one approach. Rather, a range of viewpoints are presented in a comparative way in order to obtain insights, reveal strengths, weaknesses and differences of opinion, and to learn from the lessons of others, how religion might be and has been protected.

The means of protection explored here include the fully entrenched constitutional model — both those forms of it that provide the courts with a great deal of power, as in the US, and those that provide a strong dialogue model, giving the judicial and legislative branches of government more or less equal power to determine the nature and content of the freedom of religion, such as that found in Canada. It also includes consideration of those efforts that are legislative yet recognised as quasi-constitutional documents, adopting a weak dialogue approach, such as those found in the European Union, the United Kingdom, and New Zealand. In addition, it includes a consideration of the status of such rights in Australia.

We intend an overview of approaches, demonstrating the strengths and weaknesses of each system, without descending into the detail that one might expect of a study of any one alone of the systems studied here. Still, while avoiding the detail, this book nonetheless provides some of the debate *within* systems as well, both in relation to the meaning of religious freedom and its protection. Those authors who consider the US Constitution, for instance, take quite different approaches to the now well-known tripartite Establishment Clause test in *Lemon v Kurtzman* 403 US 602 (1971).[49] Thus, there is, in one volume, a resource for use in exploring specific types of protection, specific jurisdictions, or particular regions. Alternatively, the volume as a whole offers an overview of the range of approaches.

It is worth remembering, though, that in protecting such freedoms, there is more to consider than simply the political-legal approaches that nations might use. If nothing else, the Australian experience outlined in this chapter demonstrates that in protecting fundamental rights and freedoms, one must also understand something about the substantive content of what one seeks to protect. In the case of religious freedom, that means understanding something about religion itself. This volume attempts, albeit in an attenuated way, to enter that debate. The chapters contained in Setting the Scene seek to provide some background to the role of liberalism, as political theory, in its treatment of religion, and to an understanding of the approach taken by Christian theologians to the question of religious freedom.

What one finds is that liberalism itself, while positing a place and role for religion in a robust society, demands that in protecting religious freedom for religious adherents, there must also be a protection of freedom *from* religion for those who choose, quite legitimately, to live life according to secular principles. One also finds that Christianity, at least, says much about the protection of religious freedom. The emphasis in this book is on Christianity but the book is not wholly about Christianity and freedom of religion. Other religious traditions, and particularly Judaism, Islam, Buddhism, Sikhism, Hinduism, and the Indigenous spiritual traditions of countries like the US, Canada, Australia and New Zealand, and many others, reach the same conclusions that Christianity reaches regarding religious freedom. Chapters in other parts of this volume bear this out in the case of Islam and the Māori of New Zealand. This is significant, for while one might have chosen in a volume such as this to focus on specific political-legal questions pertaining only to the operation of those documents that protect fundamental rights, such an approach is an impoverished one if we seek a full, procedural and substantive picture of religious freedom and its protection.

Some parting words: although the subject of 'religious liberty' evokes deeply held responses, it defies any agreed definition. Varying definitions commonly say as much about the source of the definition as they do about the subject. For example, in societies where there is a dominant or state-endorsed religion, the definition may amount to a freedom to believe and practise in only one accepted way. A secularist in a Western society, on the other hand, may choose to define that liberty as a freedom *from* religion in the public square. Because societies and people can differ, then, a book such as this one is sure to arouse disagreement. Clearly, religion is a topic that can do

---

[49] *Lemon v Kurtzman*, 403 US 602 (1971).

that — some consider religion itself to be divisive and, indeed, perhaps 'poisonous' in a modern, secular society,[50] while others see religion (and specifically theology) as the 'Queen of Sciences', alone capable of answering the deepest metaphysical and ontological questions facing humankind.[51] And this book offers no exception. Indeed, modestly, it hopes to contribute to the ongoing dialogue, or perhaps debate, so central to our own age yet so ageless. Within its pages you will find authors who disagree strongly, even vehemently, with one another. Far from a disadvantage, this is our goal: firmly held positions and vigorous debate. Yet, in producing heat, we hope also to shed some light.

---

[50] See, eg, Richard Dawkins, *The God Delusion* (2006).
[51] See, eg, Thomas Albert Howard, *Protestant Theology and the Making of the Modern German University* (2006).

2

How Religion Constrains Law and the Idea of Choice

Ngaire Naffine

Render unto Caesar the things which are Caesar's, and unto God the things that are God's.
Matthew: 22

In its broadest sense, this chapter is about the exercise of religious influence on and within law. Its focus is on the Christian religion and especially those parts of the Christian faithful that seek to influence law: who proselytise. Specifically, it concentrates on the ideas of the Roman Catholic Church. It considers the nature, the desirability and legitimacy of such influence, especially in the light of liberal Enlightenment principles that entail a commitment to human reason, equality and choice.

Inevitably, it begins with certain preoccupations, beliefs and presuppositions and with certain expectations. Always one needs a reason to engage with an intellectual enterprise and a set of triggering interests. Its particular interest is in the way religious believers declare their authority over some of the most fundamental human matters — life, sex and death — and seek to make law conform to their beliefs, and the degree of legal receptivity and susceptibility to these interventions. It is critical of such interventions, regarding them as constraining of human choice and against human interests, and tends to be critical of jurists who permit them.[1] It is polemical in style: it seeks to kindle debate between the secular and the religious about the role religion does and should play in the shaping of laws, especially those that limit human choice in the most personal spheres of life.

---

[1] This is not to say that religion invariably plays a destructive legal role. Compassion, altruism, helping the weak, respecting humanity, are all beneficial Christian principles.

Two Stories

I begin with the classical liberal understanding of law, the individual and the church and their respective roles in determining life's meaning. In this official liberal story, our liberal law permits us to find our own meaning of life and assiduously guards our right to do so. It respects freedom of belief (and non-belief); it does not impose religious doctrine.

I then consider what I believe is the truer story: that law, in many ways, dictates the meaning of life, tells us what has value and how we are to live in the most intimate parts of our lives, and that it does so with the assistance of its spiritual advisor, the Church.

The Official Liberal Story

I tell the official liberal story in a stark and simple manner, in order to accentuate its central message.[2] My intention is to draw out of the story what seems to matter most. I acknowledge that many contemporary liberal legal thinkers have introduced subtleties, refinements, qualifications and complications to their accounts of liberalism, often in response to their critics. In telling the official story, I do not wish to caricature what has emerged as a rich liberal legal scholarship. Rather, my intention is to simplify the liberal story in order to draw out what I believe is its most important moral proposition: that human beings are most honoured and respected as persons when they are permitted to exercise maximum choice and control over their lives: to decide for themselves how to live their lives.

The official story is infused with Enlightenment values and derives from liberal political theory. It tells of a formal commitment to the importance of human agency and autonomy and a correspondingly constrained state that respects the autonomy of the individual. This is a dignifying theory of society made up of persons who are creatures of reason, who are engaged in rational arms-length *public* relations of choice and who are entitled to their *private* beliefs, free from state intervention.

According to this official liberal story, law respects and preserves human choice by constructing two sectors of life: the public sector and the private sector and this division is thought to be vital for the preservation of individual freedom, *especially* the individual right to determine life's deepest meaning.

---

[2] We might regard the official liberal story as a type of heuristic device, designed to stimulate further intellectual inquiry and dialogue.

The public sector

In the public sector, power is ceded to the state for the purpose of securing the conditions of public order (including orderly market transactions) and personal security, while preserving a private sector, ostensibly free from state intervention. In the public sector, the market is permitted to operate and is notionally given a loose rein as it is guided by the decisions of market individuals. Law enables and regulates the commercial decisions of these economic actors through its laws of agreement, largely respecting their individual choices. People relate at arms length as market actors, for these are not intimate relations.

The state also adopts and imposes the harm principle for its duty is to provide a safe setting for these public relations: it instructs public persons that they must respect the bodily integrity of each other and that they must not harm one another as they engage with one another, and, further, that they will be held accountable for their harmful actions. They will be treated as rational agents who chose their harmful conduct and hence punishable as choosing agents by the state.

In the public sector, people therefore relate to one another in a limited human capacity: as economic actors and as human agents respecting the agency and the boundaries of all others.

The liberal (secular rationalist) private sector

By contrast, in the private sector[3] the individual is permitted to flourish as a whole person. Here individuals devise their personal conception of the good; they exercise their religious beliefs, their deepest convictions. Here they also come together in loving and altruistic relations *of choice*. They become authors of their own biographies, to invoke an idea of personal autonomy developed by Ronald Dworkin.[4] The private sector of the liberal story is importantly an arena of rich *personal freedoms*: spiritual, of the heart, of personal creativity, of conviction. This is the sector of deep belief and also of personal intimacy, where the person is meant to be able to live out *their individual* conception of the good and to determine the meaning of their own life.

The principles of respect for autonomy (relations of choice) and bodily integrity are therefore carried over into the private sector. We touch by choice;[5] we love by choice; we are intimate by choice; we procreate by choice. As the court said in *Malette v Shulman*:

---

[3] Or what Charles Reich terms 'the individual sector', 'the zone of individual power': Charles Reich, 'The Individual Sector' (1991) 100 *Yale Law Journal* 1442.
[4] See Ronald Dworkin, *Life's Dominion* (1993).
[5] *Collins v Willcox* [1984] 3 All ER 374.

> The right to determine what shall be done with one's own body is a fundamental right in our society. The concepts inherent in this right are the bedrock upon which the principles of self-determination and individual autonomy are based.[6]

We therefore exercise sovereignty over ourselves, to invoke the words of John Stuart Mill.[7]

We also form and exercise our own beliefs, by choice, and this idea of the free exercise of belief is at the heart of the various constitutionally-secured freedoms of religion. But as this is also the place of the heart, of the spirit, of intimacy, the market is notionally excluded. We do not do it for money.

Respect for religious belief is therefore part of liberal respect for the private sector: the place where the individual has an absolute right to devise their conception of the good, of the meaning of life. Religious belief must not be imposed but it must be permitted. The state must not impose its own religion or favour one set of religious convictions over another. Thus, the law treats religion and the religious with deep respect, with 'solicitude'.[8]

In the private sector, each person is treated as an *individual* centre of belief and as a little sovereign, over their bodies and over their personal lives and therefore over their intimate relations and over their spirituality. They must determine what is to give their own life value.

In this liberal understanding of the place and nature of religious belief, they are deep personal matters that are to be taken utterly seriously because they are matters of profound conviction. It is acknowledged that, to many, religion defines life's meaning. Religious commitment is most importantly to be based on personal choice and it is to be respected once chosen. It is not for the state to judge the relative value of different religious belief systems.

Choice is therefore at the centre of the idea of the private sector, in the liberal story, for it is here that we are meant to make and exercise our deepest, most significant and life-defining choices. The state is therefore to abstain from criticising and limiting private conceptions of these goods, precisely because they are the values that most define us.

The private sector, in the liberal account, is therefore the place (mental, physical, spiritual, emotional) of critical freedoms — of intimacy, of belief — and it is a place

---

[6] (1990) 67 DLR (4th) 321, 336.
[7] See J S Mill, *On Liberty* (1869).
[8] Denise Meyerson, 'Religion' in Peter Cane and Joanne Conaghan (eds), *The New Oxford Companion to Law* (2008) 1002.

of state-secured personal security and safety. To exercise freedom of intimacy and of belief, one must be safe. There must be 'a haven in a heartless (economic) world', to quote Christopher Lasch.[9]

This is the liberal ideal, schematically presented: it is the official story. It describes a metaphysically *thin* individual operating in the public sector, a metaphysically *rich* individual operating in the private sector, but an individual of her own making, who determines her own meaning of life. It describes a state that secures the freedoms of the two lives of the person as they operate in both sectors. I now want to describe what I think is really happening and why it means that the state is strongly implicated in the imposition of religion — that the state is behaving in ways which undermine its own avowed liberal ideals for the public and private sector.

The real story: The coexistence of a liberal secular and illiberal religious sector

I suggest that, in truth, the private sector comprises the individual sector of the liberal story (the place of personal freedoms) as well as a religious sector, of imposed belief. In other words, law also subscribes to some basic religious tenets that stand in tension with the principles of assiduous liberalism. I have mentioned the liberal legal principles of *autonomy* and *bodily integrity*, which *both* public and private sectors strongly endorse. But there are two other cross-cutting legal principles, which stand in direct tension with these supposedly basic liberal rights and can serve to undermine them.

The first is the principle of *human sanctity*, usually referred to as the sanctity of life, which is also considered a fundamental legal principle. The legal-religious *principle of human sanctity* is that life is a blessing, a gift from God, something of inestimable value; it is distinct from the personal capacities or inclinations of the individual. It is independent of human choice, and it is independent of personal achievement or personal abilities. Human beings cannot help but have it, even if they do not want it; animals cannot help but not have it. It has nothing to do with what one chooses to do or be. Being human is enough. The corollary, which normally follows from the principle, is that it is wrong to end human life, whether or not the individual wants or chooses the end.[10]

---

[9] Christopher Lasch, *Haven in a Heartless World* (1977).
[10] Reverence for human life does not always have a religious basis. Secular rationalists can be said to revere in human beings the capacity for reason and so be said to revere life. However, secular rationalists are likely also to respect human choice: to allow the individual to decide for herself how best to honour her life. On the religious and rationalist bases of respect for human life, see Ngaire Naffine, *Law's Meaning of Life: Philosophy, Religion, Darwin and the Legal Person* (2009).

The second (illiberal) principle, the second piece of theology, that I suggest is firmly embedded within law of the private sector is *the sanctity or sacrament of marriage*. This is less often explicitly endorsed as a fundamental legal principle, but nevertheless it is basic to, and structures, intimate institutions of the private sector and it is powerfully endorsed by both law and religion. According to the Catholic Catechism, 'God himself is the author of marriage'[11] and it is to be between one man and one woman. Here the guiding idea is that the sexes have a correlative nature. Rather than functioning as distinct choosing individuals, forming intimate associations unrelated to our sex, the Catholic church expects us to form intimate relations only across the sexes and then, ideally, to reproduce naturally and so produce a family. In other words, there is a wholesome and honourable God-given form to the heterosexual family. It is paradoxically both the natural and required unit of being: the man, his woman, and their offspring.

The principles of the sanctity of life and the sacrament of marriage tend not to be understood as religious principles. Nor are they necessarily seen as constraining of choice. Rather, they are thought to be simply the natural setting or natural order against which human choices are exercised, indeed naturally directed.[12] In other words, it is taken as a given, just part of the background and the horizon, that human life has sanctity and that human intimacy will assume a heterosexual form: that choices will naturally be made in conformity to these principles. And yet both principles are fundamental to Christian theology, are matters of great concern to the Church and perceived departures from these principles are often associated with strong political lobbying and church intervention in legal matters.

If we consider the type of cases in which the Catholic Church has intervened in Australia, they demonstrate a clear concern for both principles: for the sanctity of life and the sacrament of marriage. In *CES v Superclinics*,[13] for example, which was about a negligent failure to diagnose a pregnancy therefore excluding the opportunity of a safe and early termination, the Catholic Church intervened and argued that termination was not a lawful option. Implicitly, it was declaring the sanctity of life before birth. In *Gardner; Re BVW*,[14] the Catholic Church intervened to argue the unlawfulness of withdrawal of nutrition and hydration (by PEG tube) from a woman suffering profound dementia. Implicitly, it was declaring the sanctity of life in the absence of all cognition. In *McBain v Victoria*[15] and *Re McBain*, the Catholic Church

---

[11] Society of St Paul, *Catechism of the Catholic Church* (1994) [1603].
[12] On our background of assumed meanings that can be invisible to us, see Susanne K Langer, *Philosophy in a New Key* (1957).
[13] (1995) 38 NSWLR 47.
[14] (2003) 7 VR 487.
[15] (2000) 99 FCR 116.

intervened and argued against the availability of IVF to a single woman. Implicitly it was supporting the sanctity of marriage and the traditional family unit.

It is true that the number of cases in which the Church has pushed hard for a right to intervene is small. However, this may be because the principles of sanctity of life and heterosexual marriage are already internal to law and so usually do not need to be imposed from without. Indeed, the life, sex and death matters are in important ways legal repositories of pre-Enlightenment religious values, infused with religious thinking (rather than based on modern contractual principles) and they are also the matters which the religious seek to influence further (to further diminish choice) when there is a straying from this principle.

Catholic theology

Christian doctrine, especially Catholic doctrine, is particularly concerned about matters of life, sex and death, indeed the very meaning of life, and the Catholic Church positively seeks to influence law in these areas. The Church asserts its particular competence and authority in these areas of life.[16] They relate to important parts of Christian theology. In these parts of life, the religious story is particularly rich. Indeed, as Ian McEwan says of our culture generally, it lacks a simple story of life, death, and the meaning of life that is anywhere near as satisfying and digestible as that offered by religion.[17]

It is perhaps within the very nature of religion that it should present itself as expert in these matters. As John Haldane observes, 'religion is best characterised as a system of beliefs and practices directed towards a transcendent reality in relation to which persons seek solutions to the observed facts of moral and physical evil, limitation and vulnerability, particularity and especially death'.[18]

The Catholic religious doctrinal attitude, as I understand it, is that life is a blessing (a Gift from God and subject to his giving and taking away), that chosen or inflicted death is an evil, and that the sexes are correlative, by nature and by God, and therefore non-conformist sex and reproduction represent a perversion of nature. In each of

---

[16] One might have thought that religious intervention into law would be triggered by perceived human rights abuses, perhaps by the ill-treatment of the vulnerable, by poverty and social inequality, or the use of armed force. But these are not the 'bads' at which religion tends to be directed when it moves into law.

[17] Ian McEwan, 'End of the World Blues' in Christopher Hitchens (ed), *The Portable Atheist* (2007) 351.

[18] John Haldane, *An Intelligent Person's Guide to Religion* (2005) 17 (quoted in Tamas Pataki, *Against Religion* (2007) 3).

these three areas, religion dictates that there should be conformity with God's choice, not human choice, and there is legal collusion with these views. These departures from the liberal legal principle of human choice entail paternalism, patriarchy and homophobia.

The cash value

So, what is the cash value of this legal complex of secular and religious principles, to borrow from William James? In practical terms, often the individual secular sector and the religious sector coexist without obvious tension and therefore we may not notice that both are operating in tandem. In other words, the secular principle of autonomy and the religious principle of the sanctity of life do not compete. But there is also a well-known catalogue of matters which are religiously sensitive and which typically trigger religious interest, and for which the religious typically seek to restrain choice. This generates cross-strains between legal principles. The fundamental secular legal principles of *autonomy* and *bodily integrity* become tensed against the other fundamental religious principles of *human sanctity* and the *sacrament of marriage*. Freedom of individual belief and individual choice are typically compromised.

These internal tensions are apparent in a range of laws governing a broad range of human activities, human choices and agreements. They encompass decisions about the use of human eggs, the decision to terminate a pregnancy, the refusal of medical treatment by pregnant women (life); saying 'no' to (heterosexual) marital sex, saying 'yes' to homosexual sex and marriage, or to change of sex (sex); refusal of life support, the request to end life, and even decisions about the use of organs after death (death). Indeed, they are evident across the private sector, notionally the site of maximum freedom.

The cross-cutting principles

In the cases that follow, we will see the secular principles of respect for autonomy and bodily integrity directly in tension with the legal-religious principles of human sanctity and the sacrament of marriage.

The sanctity of life v bodily integrity and autonomy: Anthony Bland

In *Airdale NHS Trust v Bland*,[19] the English Law Lords considered the legality of withdrawal of nutrition and hydration from Anthony Bland, who was diagnosed as

---

[19] [1993] AC 789.

permanently comatose. Lord Hoffman (Court of Appeal) explicitly contrasted the secular and sacred principles and held them in tension. He said:

> the sanctity of life is only one of a cluster of ethical principles ... Another is respect for the individual human being and in particular his right to choose how he should live his own life. We call this individual autonomy or the right of self determination.[20]

By contrast, Munby QC, who acted for the Official Solicitor as guardian *ad litem* (and who argued that it would be murder or manslaughter to withdraw treatment), asserted the primacy of the religious principle. He said that 'It is fundamental that all human life is sacred and that it should be preserved if at all possible'.[21] He maintained that the court was incompetent to judge on such a matter. It was 'unable to evaluate the consequence of death, that is, non-existence' and thus 'the question of life as against death is one wholly outside the competence of judicial determination'.[22] Neither the Court of Appeal nor the House of Lords agreed. They declared that Anthony Bland had a dignity interest in the cessation of the invasion of his bodily integrity, that what he would have wanted as an autonomous self-determining being was legally relevant, that he had no interest left in being alive and that the sanctity of life did not trump, though it was a highly relevant consideration.

However, the sanctity of life principle still exerted a powerful influence. It ensured that the life of Anthony Bland could not be ended quickly and deliberately but that nature must take its course. Clearly, this entailed a compromise to dignity. As Lord Mustill observed at the end of his judgment:

> Finally, the conclusion I have reached will appear to some to be almost irrational. How can it be lawful to allow a patient to die slowly, though painlessly, over a period of weeks from lack of food but unlawful to produce his immediate death by a lethal injection, thereby saving his family from yet another ordeal to add to the tragedy that has already struck them? I find it difficult to find a moral answer to that question. But it is undoubtedly the law and nothing I have said casts doubt on the proposition that the doing of a positive act with the intent of ending life is and remains murder.[23]

---

[20] Ibid 826.
[21] Ibid 836.
[22] Ibid 837.
[23] Ibid 885.

Reproductive autonomy v life as a blessing, a gift from God: Mrs Melchior

Cattanach v Melchior[24] is a decision of the Full Court of the High Court of Australia concerning a doctor's failure to advise about the continuing prospects of a pregnancy after a sterilisation procedure. The woman in question had a third child because of this failure and sued for the costs of the child's upbringing. The Defence conceded that the doctor had breached his duty to his patient in that he should have informed her of the possibility that she could still reproduce; he was negligent in his failure to do so and his negligence caused direct loss. At trial, it was found that the woman could therefore recover. Her right of reproductive autonomy had been breached because of the doctor's failure to advise her about the possibilities that she could still conceive a child. She had decided not to reproduce and because of the doctor's negligence, she had reproduced.

The doctor and the state appealed. The judges divided on the question of whether relatively straightforward principles of tort law should apply concerning the negligent infliction of damages and their quantification (here the costs of raising the child) or whether, as the doctor said, the case gave rise to special metaphysical considerations concerning the value of human life which made it exceptional, perhaps inherently religious in nature, and not actionable. In this latter view, life was a blessing and a birth could not form the basis of an actionable wrong.

In *Cattanach* we can see the strain between the secular liberal principles of autonomy, and the religious principle of the sanctity of human life and the view that life is always a blessing. Gleeson CJ, in dissent, allowed the appeal. He asserted, *inter alia*, that

> The common law has always attached fundamental value to human life; a value originally based upon religious ideas which, in a secular society, no longer command universal assent. Blackstone, in his *Commentaries*, referred to human life as 'the immediate gift of God, a right inherent by nature in every individual'.[25]

He observed that 'Many people who now respect the same value, do so upon different grounds' but did not say what those grounds might be.[26] He went on to declare that 'The value of human life' was 'universal and beyond measurement' — an assertion that is more religious than empirical or legal — but then conceded that 'the problem to be addressed [was] legal' and that 'it may be doubted that theology provides the answer to a financial dispute, between a provider of sterilisation services and aggrieved parents, concerning the extent of the damages to be awarded on account

---

[24] [2003] HCA 38.
[25] Ibid [6].
[26] Ibid.

of the birth of a child'.[27] Nevertheless, he found the damages too difficult to quantify and was opposed to 'treating, as actionable damage, and as a matter to be regarded in exclusively financial terms, the creation of a human relationship that is socially fundamental'.[28]

Heydon J, also in dissent, agreed that 'human life is invaluable — incapable of effective or useful valuation.'[29] He cited approvingly the view of Meagher J in *CES v Superclinics* that: '[O]ur law has always proceeded on the premise that human life is sacred. That is so despite an occasional acknowledgement that existence is a "vale of tears"'.[30]

McHugh and Gummow JJ, for the majority, said that it was inappropriate to think of this as a case of a 'wrongful birth', which might thereby undermine respect for human life; rather, it was one of wrongful negligence. In effect, the matter was legal rather than religious or metaphysical, and there was law to cover the relevant action: 'To suggest that the birth of a child is always a blessing, and that the benefits to be derived there from always outweigh the burdens, denies the first category of damages awarded in this case; it also denies the widespread use of contraception'.[31]

Kirby J was more openly critical of what he saw as the religious basis for disallowing recovery in such a clear case of negligence and consequent damage. Observing that 'many of the judicial opinions' from other jurisdictions (disallowing recovery in similar cases) were supported by 'Biblical citations' about the value of human life,[32] he insisted that judges

> have no authority to adopt arbitrary departures from basic doctrine. Least of all may they do so, in our secular society, on the footing of their personal religious beliefs or 'moral' assessments concealed in an inarticulate premise dressed up, and described as legal principle or legal policy.[33]

It was not for the judges to become theologians, he said: 'If there is any area where the law has no business in intruding, it is in the enforcement of judicial interpretations of Scripture and in giving legal effect to judicial assertions about "blessings"'.[34] Such religious argument, he believed, was divorced from the modern social realities of

---

[27] Ibid.
[28] Ibid [39].
[29] Ibid 353.
[30] Ibid 355.
[31] Ibid [79].
[32] Ibid 135.
[33] Ibid [137].
[34] Ibid [151].

Australia and other 'like countries' where 'millions of people use contraceptives daily to avoid the very result which the appellants would have the Court say is always to be viewed by the law as a benefit (except perhaps where the parent or child is disabled)'.[35] Moreover, the law was quite capable of quantifying the costs of such 'nebulous items such as pain and suffering and loss of reputation'.[36] It could therefore quantify the costs of raising a child.

As Bernadette Richards[37] has argued, the dissenting judges in *Cattanach* felt unable to apply quite straightforward principles of tort law concerning duty of care, its breach and occasioned loss, all of which were present, because they felt they were being asked to see human life as a loss rather than as a blessing and, worse still, to quantify the amount of loss occasioned by the birth of a child. In short, they believed they were being asked to challenge the principle of the sanctity of life, and they were unwilling to do this. To Richards, this was a wholly inappropriate framing of the legal question: it was not about whether the child, as human life, had value but whether the parents in question, who were not well off, were now further out of pocket as a consequence of the doctor's negligence, and clearly they were. A third and unplanned child would prove very costly to them. Indeed, we may see the willingness of High Court judges to depart from such settled legal principle as evidence of the strength of the sanctity of life principle — as a strong concession to openly religious thinking with the repeated invocation of life as 'a blessing'.

The correlativity of the sexes and the sacrament of marriage

The most dramatic tension between the secular principles of autonomy and bodily integrity and the sacrament of marriage is to be found in the criminal legal principle that the husband is immune from prosecution for the rape of his wife — a principle that persisted in Australia until 1991. The principle, of course, did not compromise the autonomy and bodily integrity of men, only women. It was clear evidence of a patriarchal religious order: rape was then in most common law jurisdictions a crime that could only be committed by a man against a woman and then there was the marital exemption, which, in essence, deemed the wishes of the woman irrelevant. The husband and wife were not to be thought of as separate individuals but as a single unit in which there was no room for consent or refusal in intimate relations.

The continuing exclusion of people of the same sex from marriage shows a perfect unity between law and religion in their understanding of the sacrament. The

---

[35] Ibid [165].
[36] Ibid [144].
[37] Bernadette Richards, 'Life as Loss?' in Vic Pfitzner and Bernadette Richards (eds), *Issues at the Borders of Life* (2011).

emergence of rights to register a legally-recognised non-marital union suggest a tempering of this approach and a movement towards the principle of autonomy. But it is clear that marriage is still not for gay people.

It is difficult to find areas of life more personal, more life-defining, as these. And yet they are regulated according to religious principles, despite the liberal legal theory of the inviolability of the private sector and the secular principles of autonomy and bodily self-determination. They positively impose a meaning of intimate life that is in conformity with religious precepts.

We could say that there has been a failure to make the move to contract, to a law based on personal choice, in certain areas of law that are (not-coincidentally) matters of strong concern to the Church (for example, family law and same-sex rights and the spousal immunity, and euthanasia). These are areas of life arguably left behind in a pre-contractual state: where legal principle is based on religious principle.

We must question the assertion that these supposedly difficult metaphysical areas strain the law's conceptual and doctrinal competence. (This was the suggestion of the minority in *Cattanach*.) Perhaps there is a case for saying that the orientation of law towards the able, rational, autonomous chooser weakens doctrine in areas of human vulnerability. But it can also be argued, as many judges do (witness Kirby J), that legal principle is generally competent and apposite and it is legally inappropriate to stray from it in a bid to pronounce on the metaphysical meaning of life and death.

Imposition of dogma

The imposition of Church doctrine is troubling because of its potentially illiberal nature. By definition, the efforts of the religious to impose their views on law, to make it conform to their view of religious doctrine, are illiberal as they are endeavouring to inhibit or override the contrary views of others. Typically, these religious views are against individual choice.[38] They are therefore also in conflict with the legal principle of autonomy which, is perhaps the most fundamental principle in legal thinking and in our liberal culture. They are also anti-Enlightenment because they are not based on reason and discovery or on human choice and representative democracy but on revelation and religious dogma.

But religion comes from the inside of law, as well as from the outside. And so we need to reflect on, and be willing to criticise, religious views already interior to law that are accorded great respect. These religious views dictate (rather than negotiate) ways of

---

[38] Witness the intense religious debates about the legality of abortion between those who are pro 'life' and those who are pro 'choice'.

coming into existence, of reproducing, of being a sex, of having sex (with whom and even how), of sexuality, of being or forming a family, of dying and treating the dead. They cover the entire human life cycle. They may be expressed tacitly, explicitly, and sometimes by force.

They tend to impose rigid, doctrinal, dogmatic, moral measures of what is good, bad and taboo. Life is sacred, a blessing, a gift from God; death is bad,[39] possibly a form of punishment for human sin; single women should not be mothers; homosexual couples seeking legal recognition of their relationships offer a perversion of the sacrament of marriage. These measures are typically patriarchal and homophobic. They down play the competence of law; they also attack its liberal foundations (which are based on human choice). The embedded religiosity of law tends to reproduce the gender order of religion. The religious worldview is highly patriarchal. The Catholic order is explicitly patriarchal; the Anglican order more subtly so. Marriage ordered in a certain gendered way is at the heart of it.[40]

State restraint and respect for the religious

A persistent problem is that the very liberal legal ideals that demand state restraint when it comes to our private lives and our deepest beliefs are likely to muffle and inhibit criticisms of religious principles as they operate within law. Indeed, it may be said that law treats Christian religious principles and Christian representatives with respect, even reverence, with positive 'solicitude'. There is preparedness to find good in religion, to find moral authority, to assume that the Church offers ethical expertise;[41] to assume that the religious are experts at being good, as if the secular were not;[42] to slide between morality and the Church.[43]

Therefore, there is, paradoxically, a secular liberal humanist reason for the thin metaphysics of law in the public sector and the simultaneous respect for the thick

---

[39] For an analysis of the medico-legal attitude to death, as a 'bad', see Robert A Byrt, *Death is that Man Taking Names: Intersections of American Medicine, Law, and Culture* (2002).

[40] This is a well-rehearsed feminist point and is dealt with in Carol Pateman's *The Sexual Contract* (1988).

[41] In *A Children* [2000] 4 All ER 148, eg, the Archbishop's submissions were rejected, yet Walker LJ said that the Archbishop's points were 'entitled to profound respect'.

[42] See Jeremy Webber, 'Understanding the Religion in Freedom of Religion' in Peter Cane, Carolyn Evans and Zoe Robinson (eds), *Law and Religion in Theoretical Context* (2008) 3.

[43] Religion is treated as a good, as ethically sound, and the religious as thoughtful, as nicer, even as ethical experts. (Webber suggests that the principle of freedom of religion and the protection of it as a right carries this necessary implication — it endorses a religious principle: ibid.) This is a view of the religious that Richard Dawkins, for one, has explicitly refuted. See Richard Dawkins, *The God Delusion* (2006).

metaphysics of the religious or at least a reluctance to take issue with religious metaphysics. As Pataki observes, 'religious tolerance is largely a creature of secular humanism, and in its spirit the majority of critics manqué have simply declined to fire'.[44] Thus, law, in liberal spirit, out of respect for the religious, has often declined to criticise the contents of religious belief and indeed has treated such belief as intellectually respectable and has been willing to draw upon it when need is thought to arise.

There is certainly a great legal reluctance to challenge directly what are taken by the religious to be truths. There may well be a judicial or scholarly recognition that what once had a Biblical justification (say the principle of the sanctity of life) now has a secular justification (humanism). But judges and lawmakers — and even legal scholars — are reluctant to go further and say, in true atheistic humanistic spirit, that there is no basis for belief in God and that its tenets can be positively harmful.

The situation is complex. Liberal law purports to respect, even to display solicitude for, the fact of personal religious belief and it explicitly protects the right to believe. It therefore endeavours to forbear from offering a rich conception of the meaning of life, of the good, so that each individual can form their own conception. Autonomy, choice and bodily self-determination are perhaps the strongest guiding liberal legal principles reflecting this position of metaphysical forbearance. Respect for these principles means that these life choices are ceded to the individual and their protection is regarded as vital to liberal freedom.

At the same time, the Catholic Church offers a strong defined dogmatic metaphysics, especially in relation to the intimate sphere of life and at the edges of life. Moreover, it does not hesitate in coming forward because it is a proselytising faith offering a universal conception of the good. Liberal legal restraint and respect for religious belief countenances a respectful, even forbearant attitude, to such interventions. But in truth, the concessions to faith are greater than this. For our liberal law has already accepted some of the most fundamental religious tenets as simply the natural, almost invisible, moral setting of personal choice. In other words, our liberal law takes it as given that personal choices will be for life and for intimate union understood in a largely religious manner. Already it presupposes the contents of religious belief (life is sacred, death is bad, wrong sex is misguided if not perverted).

If modern, liberal law is a product of secular, rationalist, Enlightenment, liberal thinking, surely it should be, in the first instance, sceptical of positions based on faith not on evidence (i.e. rationalist). Surely it should always affirm personal choice, as the starting position, in all relations and also be sceptical of hierarchical religious institutions that purport to speak for all believers (but which suppress or ignore internal dissent and plurality).

---

[44] Tamas Pataki, above n 18, 11.

Judicial willingness to treat the religious as existential experts and to accord its representatives particular respect — this referral of life, sex and death matters to the Church or to God or to conscience, treating them as exceptional, deep, mysterious and metaphysically difficult or obscure — can entail, I suggest, a renunciation of legal responsibility when law is actually fully up to the task (as Kirby J argues explicitly in *Cattanach v Melchior*, the legal principles are there).[45]

A thought experiment: A fully realised Enlightenment, secular, rationalist, contractual world

What if we engage in the thought experiment[46] of carrying through contract, that is self and other relations of choice, into all parts of life: of applying it in a thorough-going manner; in a comprehensive way? This may let us see more clearly the departures from secular principles that otherwise we can take as a given; to render the unthought of thinkable; to bring prohibited or suppressed or unacknowledged relations into the realm of possibility. It can render mindless automatic habits of thinking mindful and apparent. It can make explicit what is currently fuzzy thinking about what we take to be natural, beyond law, beyond contract. It can reveal the repositories of religion within law.

If motherhood (whether to become one), sexual intercourse (how and with whom), family formation (how we form a legal family unit), life and death decisions (such as voluntary euthanasia) were all a matter of choice, how different would our world be? If Enlightenment rationalism and liberal choice, based on the idea that we are creatures of reason who can govern our own lives, were carried through, what then? Would we be in a very different world? And who would be the main objectors to this world?

Or to put this in terms of permissible contractual relations, we need to consider contracts between mother and foetus, mother and baby, mother and doctor, human and animal, man and man, woman and woman, brother and sister, adult and child, and person to self. Who should have the right to contract, to be a party to relations? What sort of choices do we enable and prohibit?

---

[45] Birth, death and sex can signify lack of control over being human (see, eg, Burt, above n 39) and lead to fear, irrationalism, disgust and religious deference. Thus, the Church is brought in to bury people and to conduct the final rites, to offer explanation, security and solace. The Church baptises and marries. It provides authority and certainty, comfort and assurance.

[46] A thought experiment is just that. It is an experiment conducted within the imagination rather than in a laboratory. See David C Gooding, 'Thought Experiments' in Edward Craig (ed), *The Shorter Routledge Encyclopedia of Philosophy* (2005) 1018.

We must keep reminding ourselves that law is capable of conceptualising and contractualising all or any of these relations. It is omnicompetent. Think of the inheriting embryo and the personified corporation. It is limited only by imagination and by the acceptable.[47]

And having isolated the areas where contract is disallowed or inhibited, we can then consider the reasons for these departures. We can then also consider the role religion plays in securing and defending these prohibitions on human choice. And if, as a consequence of this experiment, we now see more clearly the deviations from this contractual ideal, then what do we think of them? Do we regard them as legitimate? Do we want them? In other words, we are in a position to make informed decisions about the legal relations we should be permitted to make and to have, especially when they concern the most intimate aspects of our lives.

---

[47] See Ngaire Naffine, above n 10, esp the chapter on Legalism.

3

Is the Emperor Wearing the Wrong Clothes? Human Rights and Social Good in the Context of Australian Secularity: Theological Perspectives

Bruce Kaye

This chapter suggests that a theological perspective born out of belonging to Jesus' kingdom, which he told Pilate was not of this world, might help us in understanding something about human flourishing and sociality in Australia. Such a perspective may provide some distance to help us to see that Australia has its own particular version of secularity and consequently an approach to sociality that is not entirely sympathetic to modern notions of human rights as a way of approaching human flourishing in society. Other ways exist to approach questions of fairness and human well-being in Australia. As with human rights regimes, those ways have not always been successful but in general the pattern has been more than notably defensible in the broad range of human societies. We clearly need to address failures. The question is, in what way? In this chapter I argue that working with the grain of the national story makes more sense than cutting across it.

The horrors of World War II created understandable revulsion among many and fuelled an interest in human rights as a strategy for dealing with abuse and corruption in human sociality. Theologians have responded in various ways to this movement. Nicholas Wolterstorff has tried to read back into the Hebrew Scriptures and the New Testament such notions of human rights, but he runs into significant tracts of this biblical material pointing in a different direction.[1] Roman Catholic theologians

---

[1] Nicholas Wolterstorff, *Justice: Rights and Wrongs* (2008) ('*Justice*').

have used their long tradition of natural law to argue for a moral universe and human rights as part of that world created by God.

The difficulty is that Jesus seems consistently to have resisted a political path and to have pointed rather to a kingdom, which, he said, was not of this world. This theme is littered all over the New Testament and Christian history, and in the twentieth century found sharp expression in the early writing of the Swiss theologian Karl Barth.[2] The enduring theme has pointed theologians to the importance of social connection in the life of faith and to the formative significance of the story of the Christian community. Narrative and connection are central to Christian understanding. Even that relatively conservative body, the Anglican Church of Australia, has them written into the recitals of its constitution.

These two themes of narrative and social connection are also crucial in the wider society, not least in Australia. The identity of discrete communities is shaped by the narrative of its origins and formation. The modern nation-state is no exception. The Australian pattern can be highlighted by setting it alongside that of the United States. The contrast between the origins of the US and Australia could not be more stark. The US Declaration of Independence in 1776 began with universal claims about the nature of the human condition:

> We hold these truths to be self-evident, that all men are created equal, that they are endowed by their Creator with certain unalienable Rights, that among these are Life, Liberty and the pursuit of Happiness. — That to secure these rights, Governments are instituted among Men, deriving their just powers from the consent of the governed.

It carried its claim to start a new nation on the basis of 28 complaints against George III, concluding 'A Prince, whose character is thus marked by every act which may define a Tyrant, is unfit to be the ruler of a free people'.[3] These were actions taken by the independent settlers in nine colonies.

In 1788, a motley crew of convicts and military settled in what was essentially a jail in New South Wales. Free settlers did not arrive until 1793 and so in stages and by concessions from the British government, what began as a jail with its virtual Anglican establishment, acquired political and legal freedoms and protections. That particular history has affected the character of Australian secularity and plurality and,

---

[2] The main statement of Barth's approach to ethics can be found in Karl Barth, *The Doctrine of Creation: Church Dogmatics, Volume III* (1961) 4, but see also John Webster, *Karl Barth* (2000) and Joseph L Mangina, *Karl Barth: Theologian of Christian Witness* (2004).
[3] *US Declaration of Independence*, 4 July 1776.

not surprisingly, has left in its train very significant differences from what emerged in the excitement and conflict of the War of Independence and the high drama of framing a constitution by the newly liberated colonies in the US.

During the last fifty years, the role of religion in Western societies has been revisited and is now being dramatically recast. The older secularisation thesis that, with the progress of the eighteenth century Enlightenment, religion would fade away and have no role in public life is giving way to a more pluralist version of religion and public life. More than that, both historians and sociologists now point to the different forms of secularity that the diverse narratives of modern societies have created.[4] Just as study of the Enlightenment has fractured the perception of its coherent generality and drawn attention to its significant local diversities, so also are scholars identifying the varied character of secularity in different national stories.[5]

That scholarly recasting has focussed on Europe and the US, but Australia invites the same kind of investigation and re-examination. Enlightenment attitudes have influenced Australian culture and social life in a variety of ways, but by no means always in anti-religious ways. More significantly, the Australian version of secularity has quite distinctive features that stand in some sharp contrast to the US experience. We can see this in our educational institutions. For example, in the foundational legislation of 1880, infant and secondary schooling in New South Wales was described as secular but the legislation provided for religious observances, general teaching in religion and for released time during the school week for teaching the beliefs and practices of specific religious traditions by their representatives. The University of Sydney retains to this day in its charter that it exists, amongst other things, for the advancement of religion and morality. The judicial interpretation of Section 116 of the Commonwealth constitution gives no basis for any idea of a separation of church and state, or, rather, institutional religion and the state.

Australia possesses a form of secularity that has emerged out of a monopoly Anglican state into a plural democratic nation by a gradual process of change with its own developing pattern of social relations. This narrative of Australia as an evolving society with commitments and social values is an important framework for any theologian approaching the issue of individual rights in this context. It reinforces the theologian's awareness of the contingent character of the

---

[4] See, eg, Hugh McLeod and Werner Ustorf, *The Decline of Christendom in Western Europe, 1750–2000* (2003) and Callum G Brown and M F Snape, *Secularisation in the Christian World: Essays in Honour of Hugh Mcleod* (2010).

[5] Roy Porter and Mikulas Teich, *The Enlightenment in National Context* (1981) and Roy Porter, *The Enlightenment* (2nd ed, 2001).

human condition in the light of the kingdom of Jesus. Far from diminishing the theologian's concern with social life, it underlines the enduring question of how the Christian is to be neighbour in this kind of society and thus to testify to the nature of the kingdom of God? Such a question applies not just to individuals within society but also to the institutions and frameworks that shape the lives of people in that society.

Any question of the appropriate form of protections and freedoms for individuals and groups in Australia needs to be considered in the light of its quite particular form of secularity and assumptions about social values embedded in its constitution, laws and social institutions. The notion of inalienable individual human rights that has so shaped that very differently structured society of the US has not been a central or powerful force in shaping the structure of Australian society. Indeed, despite many practical commonalities, the two societies are founded upon significantly different assumptions. Any question about the structures of human sociality in Australia must deal in the particulars of the existing arrangements. It would therefore make sense in the first instance to build on the existing narrative before resorting to novelty from elsewhere.

Human rights and Christian theologians

Speaking of social and political life in terms of human rights has only recently come into prominence, but like all similar traditions it looks to a long history of discourse as one of its powerful legitimating warrants in the present. Depending on how the question is configured, we can trace hints of some of the ideas attaching to rights back to antiquity, though these tend to refer to conceptions of office and duties.

Thomas Hobbes, writing out of the disorder and confusion of the Commonwealth period in seventeenth century England, asserted that the people were the source of authority in the body politic on the basis of a natural almost total right belonging to the individual that would be given up to the sovereign for the sake of peace and security.[6] Forty years later John Locke set natural rights within the framework of a moral order deriving from a divine creator. In this respect, Locke formulated his thought in relation to a sense of natural law, which also provided a framework for the reasonableness of Christianity.[7] A nest of theologians used a

---

[6] Thomas Hobbes, Karl Schuhmann and G A J Rogers, *Thomas Hobbes Leviathan* (2003).
[7] See, eg, John Locke and John C Higgins-Biddle, *The Reasonableness of Christianity: As Delivered in the Scriptures* (1999). (The book was first published in 1695.)

tradition of natural law in political discourse that favoured contract theory, and thus the rights of individuals, to limit notions of tyrannical government.[8]

Interest in rights did not slide effortlessly from the eighteenth into the twentieth-century world. It rather vacated the public stage during the nineteenth century, and in the twentieth century, rights language was subjected to a radical Marxist critique. But World War II changed all that. It involved mass suffering of non-combatant citizens and it was the arena for the ultimate horrors of the mass murder of Jewish people as well as the persecution of homosexuals, gypsies and some other minority groups. Haunting the post-war world was not just the personal grief of loss but the frightening thought that civilisation could have brought forth such violence. It is no wonder that a new world order was sought and it is no wonder that the perspective of the sufferers was crucial in the way that order was conceived.[9] This meant that the individualism of the eighteenth century was enhanced to include a wider understanding of the application of rights. Although rights for groups and categories of people and the right of self-determination for groups was incorporated into the universe of rights that belong in the human condition, the rights language had special force in the aftermath of World War II because it penetrated the borders of nation-states to assert the rights of individuals. Even where a nation-state appeared to have the trappings of legitimate processes, rights could reach beyond the state to the individual. The example of Nazi Germany was a powerful example of just this problem of state legitimacy.

Christian philosophers and theologians responded in different ways to this movement. In a recent book, Nicholas Wolterstorff[10] argued that human rights, far from being new, belonged in the foundational texts of the Hebrew Bible and the New Testament: 'Not only inherent natural rights but inherent natural human rights were implicitly recognized in the moral vision of the writers of the Hebrew

---

[8] See, eg, Richard Hooker, in *The Folger Library of the Works of Richard Hooker* (1995) and also Damien Grace, 'Natural Law in Hooker's *of Laws of Ecclesiastical Polity*' (1997) 21 *Journal of Religious History* 1, 10–22. The issue had been important in relation to the Glorious Revolution of 1689 in whose defence Benjamin Hoadly, later bishop of Bangor, wrote with polemical force. A century later, Hoadly's writing, particularly *The Original and Institution of Civil Government, Discuss'd* informed the legitimation of the American rebellion against the English crown and the establishment of the new republic. See, eg, Benjamin Hoadly and William Gibson, *The Original and Institution of Civil Government, Discuss'd* (2007), which includes an introduction setting out the influence of Hoadly's writing in America, and the extensive biography in William Gibson, *Enlightenment Prelate: Benjamin Hoadly, 1676–1761* (2004).

[9] For a background to the role of pity in the formation of social connection see Jean-Jacques Rousseau and Maurice Cranston, *A Discourse on Inequality* (1984).

[10] Wolterstorff, above n 1. It is itself somewhat surprising that he finds this recognition at the end of World War II quite surprising.

and Christian scriptures, as they were by the Church Fathers; in the writings of the canon lawyers of the twelfth century they were finally not only recognized but given explicit conceptualization'.[11] General recognition of these rights was slow and halting until 'quite surprisingly, it burst forth after the horrors of World War II in the UN declaration'.[12] Wolterstorff argues that justice is constituted of rights: 'A society is just insofar as its members enjoy the goods to which they have a right. And I think of rights as ultimately grounded in what respect for the worth of persons and human beings requires'.[13] For example, he says, the Biblical 'prescription against murder is grounded not in God's law but in the worth of the human being. All who bear God's image possess, on that account, an inherent right not to be murdered'.[14]

Christians and Jesus' kingdom, which is not of this world

Wolterstorff's account of the biblical material is highly contentious. From the point of view of the kinds of warrants that apply in the Christian tradition, the appeal to scripture is clearly crucial. His reading of the command not to murder illustrates the difficulties of interpreting 'classic texts' such as scripture when the interest is in some historically subsequent question that is formulated in terms or categories that may not belong in the era of the text and may not share the same framework of tacit assumptions.[15] His reference to the command not to murder also provides a way into another view of the theological account of the human condition.

The classic text for the command on murder is Exodus 20. The story is set in the context of the Israelites in the desert of Sinai three months after they had fled from Egypt. They camped at the foot of Mount Horeb and Moses went up the mountain to converse with God. He received words to deliver to the Israelites:

> Then Moses went up to God, and the LORD called to him from the mountain and said, 'This is what you are to say to the house of Jacob and what you are to tell the people of Israel: "You yourselves have seen what I did to Egypt, and how I carried

---

[11] Ibid 361.
[12] Ibid.
[13] Ibid xii.
[14] Ibid 95 (underlining in original).
[15] There is a long history of this challenge in text interpretation generally. See, eg, Conal Condren, *The Status and Appraisal of Classic Texts: An Essay on Political Theory, Its Inheritance, and on the History of Ideas* (1985). On the specific question of the biblical texts, see Ernst Troeltsch, *The Absoluteness of Christianity: And the History of the Religions* (1972), Anthony C Thiselton, *Two Horizons: New Testament Hermeneutics and Philosophical Description with Special Reference to Heidegger, Bultmann, Gadamer and Wittgenstein* (1980) and Anthony C Thiselton, *New Horizons in Hermeneutics* (1992).

you on eagles' wings and brought you to myself. Now if you obey me fully and keep my covenant, then out of all nations you will be my treasured possession. Although the whole earth is mine, you will be for me a kingdom of priests and a holy nation." These are the words you are to speak to the Israelites'. (Exodus 19.1–6)

The people accepted these words and after detailed preparation, Moses again went up the mountain to God and came back to the Israelites with what we know as the Ten Commandments. These commandments were introduced with very specific words that refer back to the words from God on the previous day; 'I am the LORD your God, who brought you out of Egypt, out of the land of slavery'.

The whole story is framed in the style of an ancient Near East suzerainty treaty where Israel is the vassal nation. The crucial theological issue is that obedience to the commandments is based on the deliverance of the Israelites from slavery in Egypt. This account of the giving of the Commandments occurs also in Deuteronomy 5 in anticipation of the Israelites crossing into the promised land of Canaan. They were to keep the commandments because they were God's people. The Ten Commandments set out the character of the redeemed people of God, or rather that character to which they are now committed.[16] There is nothing here about the image of God, even though that idea appears in the creation stories. There is no focus on the individual in any separated sense. The commandments, though referring to individual actions such as murder, are addressed to the people of Israel.

These issues have drawn theologians to a more sceptical or detached view of human rights. Rather than seeing human society as made up of individuals with inherent rights, they see societies and individuals as existing under the providence of God and their moral obligations as arising out of the revelation of the character of God in Jesus Christ who is seen as the fulfilment of the Hebrew scriptures, now seen as an Old Testament. Moreover, that revelation points to a final end, an eschatological vision of the kingdom of God. This orientation can be seen in the claim of Paul the apostle that the Philippian Christians to whom he was writing had their citizenship in heaven rather than in the Roman colonial city where they resided.[17]

An early Christian document describing the martyrdom of Polycarp, bishop of Smyrna, vividly illustrates this detached view of political life. Polycarp was brought

---

[16] Indirectly these commandments also point to the character God. The commands of God are a statement of how this chosen people are to behave because they belong to God and because they are called to honour God in the way they live. This implies that this kind of god has a moral character at least consistent with this human pattern of behaviour. Stanley Hauerwas and William H Willimon, *The Truth About God: The Ten Commandments in Christian Life* (1999) and Scott Cowdell, *The Ten Commandments and Ethics Today* (2008).

[17] Philippians 3:20.

before the Roman Pro-Consul and told to swear by the genius of Caesar. He declined and was threatened with wild beasts and being burned alive, to which he responded, 'You threaten me with the fire that burns for a time, and is quickly quenched, for you do not know the fire which awaits the wicked in the judgement to come and in everlasting punishment'.[18] Just as he was about to be burned at the stake, Polycarp prayed, 'O Lord God Almighty, Father of thy beloved and blessed child, Jesus Christ, through whom we have received full knowledge of thee, the God of angels and powers, and of all creation, and of the whole family of the righteous who live before thee!'.[19] This is just one of a multitude of examples of the enduring power of Jesus' statement that his kingdom is not of this world. Jesus' statement was made in the first instance in a political context to Pilate, the representative of Roman imperial rule. Expressions of this central character of the gospel recur all over the history of Christianity, even when the empirical church seems to ignore or forget them.

Polycarp did not interpret this truth to mean that there were not moral obligations for Christians in the world of politics or of daily social life. On the contrary, he told the Pro Consul that Christians have been 'taught to render honour, as is meet, if it hurts us not, to princes and authorities appointed by God'.[20]

This aspect of the Christian tradition has led some theologians to embrace a notion of divine inter penetration of the religious and the political and in that context to see a theological basis for affirming claims to rights. This line of argument is usually based on the idea of divine creation and the development from that to a notion of inherent value in the creation and thus to traditions of natural law. Thus, those Christian traditions that see a key role in theology for natural law are found to assert the place of human rights as things given by God and thus to be supported and affirmed. This line of thought inevitably makes these rights universal because of their cosmic divine origin.

Wolterstorff writes out of a philosophical background and a reformed theological tradition, but a Roman Catholic tradition of theology also affirms human rights. In addressing the United Nations General Assembly on the occasion of its fiftieth anniversary celebrations, Pope John Paul II referred to the Universal Declaration of Human Rights as 'one of the highest expressions of the human conscience of our time'. He went on to relate rights to a universal conception of human nature and a universal moral law embedded in the world itself. Then, calling on his own central European background, he focused on the right of nations to exist. The universal quest for freedom, he said,

---

[18] Kirsopp Lake (ed), *The Apostolic Fathers with an English Translation by Kirsopp Lake* (1965) 327.
[19] Ibid 331.
[20] Ibid 327.

confirms that there are indeed universal human rights, rooted in the nature of the person, rights which reflect the objective and inviolable demands of a *universal moral law*. These are not abstract points; rather, these rights tell us something important about the actual life of every individual and of every social group. *They also remind us that we do not live in an irrational or meaningless world*. On the contrary, there is a *moral logic* which is built into human life and which makes possible dialogue between individuals and peoples. If we want a *century of violent coercion* to be succeeded by a *century of persuasion*, we must find a way to discuss the human future intelligibly. The universal moral law written on the human heart is precisely that kind of 'grammar' which is needed if the world is to engage this discussion of its future.

In this sense, it is a matter for serious concern that some people today deny the universality of human rights, just as they deny that there is a human nature shared by everyone. To be sure, there is no single model for organizing the politics and economics of human freedom; different cultures and different historical experiences give rise to different institutional forms of public life in a free and responsible society. But it is one thing to affirm a legitimate pluralism of 'forms of freedom', and another to deny any universality or intelligibility to the nature of man or to the human experience. The latter makes the international politics of persuasion extremely difficult, if not impossible.[21]

This address not only reflects Pope John Paul II's philosophical background, it also neatly states a long tradition of Roman Catholic teaching on natural law applied to the modern assertion of human rights.[22] There is a crucial connection here between the notion of a universal moral order, the creator as the one who has given that order, and the claim that rights are not simply individualistic. Rights play a part in the symphony of considerations that go to make up a just and moral humanity that is both individual and social. This framing of the matter overcomes the somewhat artificial antithesis in Wolterstorff between notions of society based on inherent human rights and one based on right order.[23] It creates the basis for a real analogy (*analogia entis*) to operate between the creation and the creator, rather than an analogy based on and expressed in faith (*analogia fidei*). It concerns the crucial question: in what sense is Jesus' kingdom, which is not of this world, actually and really represented in some form in this world? Here John Paul II makes that connection in terms of moral values

---

[21] His Holiness John Paul II, *Address*, (Speech delivered at the United Nations, New York, 5 October 1995), italics in original.

[22] Compare the formulation in Vatican II, *Dignitatis humanae:, Declaration on Religious Liberty* (1965) ch 1; Austin Flannery, *Vatican Council II : The Conciliar and Post Conciliar Documents* (1992).

[23] See Wolsterstorff, above n 1, 11.

and draws the nation into that arena through a principle of self-determination. Not only is there real correlation of the divine, it is expressible in terms of values that can be embodied in institutions of sociality such as the nation.

Karl Barth, especially in his early volumes of the Church Dogmatics,[24] represents a polar alternative to this *analogia entis*. Whereas John Paul II's approach provides the basis for the essential immanence of God in the natural order, Barth came to represent a quite different approach to the nature of the knowledge of God and in consequence the relation between Jesus' kingdom, which is not of this world, and the social and political life of the Christian. That question about the kingdom of Jesus to which his disciples belong goes back elementally to the crucial issue of how Jesus of Nazareth is the true and adequate revelation of God in the here and now. How is the distinction between God and humankind to be seriously sustained while yet holding to the reality of the humanity of Jesus Christ who is also the revelation of God?[25] Barth's response was to place the divine initiative in Jesus at the forefront of his approach. Thus, true humanity is to be understood in terms of Jesus of Nazareth and others share his humanity. Such a divine initiative is an act of divine grace to which all and each are called to respond in faith.

It is hard to overstate the implications of this approach for any consideration of human rights and the nature of human sociality. At once it sets the whole life of the Christian in a context that is defined first and foremost by grace and the kingdom that is not of this world, and it makes Jesus' crucifixion the central reality of this kingdom. Belonging to this kingdom gives rise to a vocation to witness to the truth that is in Jesus. This certainly does not annihilate ethics or serious moral endeavour — or, yet, political engagements. On the contrary, it demands it because of the nature of the gospel through which this new relationship has come. That demand arises from, and takes its mode of working from, the same grace and love that is manifested in the action of God in Christ. This means that ethics and politics are about how to be neighbourly for and to the other. It also means that concepts such as rights have no role in the motivation of ethical action or the content of that action. The narrative of grace moves and shapes action.

Narrative and social identity

In this line of argument two dimensions become important in providing for an approach to the visible identity of this grace: some sense of sociality amongst believers,

---

[24] For Karl Barth's rejection of this *analogia entis* see Karl Barth, Geoffrey William Bromiley and Thomas F Torrance, *Church Dogmatics* (1977) I/1:x: 'I regard the *analogia entis* as the invention of the antichrist, and think that because of it one cannot become Catholic.'

[25] For an account of Barth's recognition of this issue see S Hauerwas, *With the Grain of the Universe: The Church's Witness and Natural Theology* (2001) 159ff.

and a narrative that constitutes and sustains the life of that community. Christians have talked about these lines of continuity in a variety of terms, probably the most common of which is catholicity. Catholicity points to the connection between the local community and a wider fellowship with which it interacts. In the Anglican tradition of Christian faith, this notion of catholicity as dynamic connection with a wider circle of the church community is held in check by a strongly inherited notion of the power and importance of proximity in ecclesial relationships. Richard Hooker put the point famously in his Ecclesiastical Laws in relation to political power and in relation to the nature of a national church: 'Yea the very deitie it self both keepeth and requireth for ever this to be kept as a law, that wheresoever there is a coagmentation of many, the lowest be knitt to the highest by that which being interjacent may cause each to cleave unto the other and so all to continue one'.[26] This history has left Anglicans with a tradition of ecclesiology that is basically regional and relational, rather than universal and institutional.[27] Sometimes the universal and institutional is spoken of as if there is a universal church to which local churches belong. The Anglican model moves rather in the opposite direction.[28]

There is a second, diachronic, sense of connection often spoken of in terms of tradition, in particular a tradition that goes back to the apostles and to Jesus himself. This tradition is constituted not just by content of ideas or beliefs but also as a process of connection between generations. Tradition is the process of handing over from one generation to another, from one situation to another, the practices and beliefs that define the community.[29] That process of tradition is the foundation out

---

[26] W E Speed Hill (ed), *The Folger Library Edition of the Works of Richard Hooker Vol 3* (1993) 331. See also Bruce Kaye, *Conflict and the Practice of Church: The Anglican Experiment* (2009).

[27] See the report of the international doctrine commission of the Anglican Communion, Inter Anglican Theological and Doctrinal Commission, *Communion, Conflict and Hope* (2008).

[28] See the strong statement on this in a report from the Lambent Conference which puts this Anglican model as the one that ultimately can be seen to be the truly Christian view. 'There are two prevailing types of ecclesiastical organisation: that of centralised government, and that of regional autonomy within one fellowship. Of the former the Church of Rome is the great historical example. The latter type, which we share with the Orthodox Churches of the East and others, was that upon which the Church of the first centuries was developing until the claims of the Roman church and other tendencies confused the issue. The Provinces and Patriarchates of the first four centuries were bound together by no administrative bond: the real nexus was a common life resting upon a common faith, common Sacraments, and a common allegiance to an Unseen Head.' Committee on the Anglican Communion, 'The Anglican Communion', in (Committee on the Anglican Communion ed), *The Lambeth Conference 1930: Encyclical Letter from the Bishops with Resolutions and Reports* (1930) 152–63.

[29] See Alasdair C MacIntyre, *Whose Justice? Which Rationality?* (1988) and E Shils, *Tradition* (1989).

of which the continuing narrative is available. That very process of receiving and passing means that the continuity provided by the narrative cannot be univocal in the details present in the tradition at different points in the narrative. The foundational narrative of the apostolic age and the life and death of Jesus of Nazareth provides the point of reference for testing the adequacy of any given part of the narrative.[30] If we think in terms of tradition then we can more easily recognise that sub-traditions emerge as the narrative moves to new situations and is transformed to gain expression and life in those new situations.[31] This process of differentiation feeds into the overall picture rather than distorting it.

In an Australian context, we can see this in the constitutional recitals of the Anglican Church of Australia (ACA). The constitution has two parts: Part I, the Fundamental Declarations and the Ruling Principles, and Part II, the Government of the church. The fundamental Declarations say three things: the ACA is part of the One Holy Catholic and Apostolic Church, it receives the scriptures of OT and NT as 'the ultimate rule and standard' of Christian life and belief, and it will obey the commands of Christ. In other words, this church is part of mainline Christianity and will act accordingly. The Ruling Principles, which are of somewhat lesser constitutional weight,[32] declare the church to be derived from the Church of England and that it retains key elements of that tradition, including communion with the Church of England, so long as that is consistent with the Fundamental Declarations. On the other hand, the church has authority to conduct its own affairs according to the provisions of the constitution. Part II of the constitution sets out in twelve chapters how the church is to be governed. The narrative of this church is thus clear. It is part of historic Christianity, it derives from the sub-tradition of English Anglicanism and within that framework it is an independent entity to act appropriately in its Australian context according to certain agreed procedures.

---

[30] See, eg, S L Greenslade, 'The Authority of the Tradition of the Early Church in Early Anglican Thought' in GGaVV (ed.), *Tradition in Lutheranism and Anglicanism* (1972) 9-33; R P C Hanson, *Tradition in the Early Church* (1962). For a discussion of this point more generally see Condren, *The Status and Appraisal of Classic Texts* (1985).

[31] See Bruce Kaye, *Reinventing Anglicanism: A Vision of Confidence, Community and Engagement in Anglican Christianity* (2004) ('*Reinventing Anglicanism*') and Bruce Kaye, *An Introduction to World Anglicanism* (2008) ('*An Introduction*').

[32] There is no provision to alter the Fundamental Declarations, save in the matter of the name of the church. The rest of the constitutions can be amended according to varying levels of requirements. See Anglican Church of Australia, *The Constitution Canons and Rules of the Anglican Church of Australia* (2004).

This example of a church constitution also shows that the kind of tradition we are discussing sustains its continuity through a commitment in its community life to the originating narrative[33] of the Christian scriptures and the early church creeds not only by means of certain beliefs but also by means of certain persistent practices in the life of the community.[34] The constitution specifies how decisions are made in synods, how the community exists within dioceses and how there are certain classes of people who have ministerial responsibilities and privileges and how they are to be held accountable. These arrangements exist to provide for an ordered ministry of word and sacrament in the local communities of Anglicans. These procedures assume not only the spiritual value of practices of word and sacrament, but also the necessity to provide for these through institutional arrangements. These institutional arrangements carry within them tacit assumptions about the beliefs and values of the community they serve.[35]

In the ACA, these beliefs and practices shape the life of the ongoing community of Anglicans and provide the resources that enable the life and faith of the individuals that belong to this community to flourish. Within the terms of this narrative, these resources are means of grace. Framing the sacraments and the ministry of the word is the persistent response to the energising and creative activity of God in the community. The church community lives and dies by its openness to this divine initiative. Within this framework, the church is a community of responsible agents shaped by a gospel of grace and forgiveness, marked by a story of continuity and by institutions that exist not only to house memory but to shape the virtues in the community.[36] The organisational aspects of the institutions are secondary to the primary practices in the community and the growth of faith and Christian

---

[33] On the role of origins in contemporary Christian faith and practice see Bruce Kaye, *Web of Meaning: The Role of Origins in Christian Faith* (2000) ('*Web of Meaning*'). A different model arising from a different conception of the character of institutional continuity through time is evident in the exposition of continuity and renewal in Roman Catholic moral teaching can be seen in John Paul II, *Solicitudo Rei Socialis: On Social Concerns* (1988), esp ch 2.

[34] For this way of understanding Anglicanism generally, see Kaye, *An Introduction*, above n 31.

[35] For example, the General Synod has updated the inherited Canons of the Church of England so that they fit the current Australian context. Similarly, they have revised the disciplinary procedures for clergy and bishops in the light of institutional failure in the area of sexual abuse in the church.

[36] See Kaye, *Reinventing Anglicanism*, above n 31, *A Vision of Confidence, Community and Engagement in Anglican Christianity* (Adelaide: Openbook, 2004) and Kaye, *Web of Meaning*, above n 33.

character in the community.[37] It is this local setting that has led Anglicans worldwide to recognise that the ministerial offices may be adapted to local needs.[38]

The social and political narrative of Australia

Similar questions about the nature of human society apply more broadly in the general political arena. It is customary to describe Australia as secular as if that settled a number of questions about religion in public activity and the nature and configuration of our public institutions. It is easy to assume that other terms such as plural or multicultural always carry the same meaning. Even within Australia the meaning of multiculturalism has changed over time. Multicultural has generally been the term used to describe the move since the middle of the twentieth century to a more mixed population and recognition of ethnic diversity after the demise of the White Australia Policy.[39] The contemporary hegemonic role of the US can easily suggest that plural societies are societies like the US. However, even a cursory reading of the pluralist literature of the second half of the twentieth century makes it clear

---

[37] Notice the interesting decision of the New South Wales Supreme Court as to whether the administrative investment arm of the diocese of Sydney was a religious institution for certain taxation purposes. The court found it not to be so on the grounds that it did not directly engage in religious activities: *Glebe Administration Board v Commissioner of Pay-Roll Tax* (1987) 10 NSWLR 352. In this context it is interesting to notice the recent changes in the ordination service. The 1662 BCP ordinal defined the task of the priest in terms of the result in the life of the congregation it was to produce. The recent Australian Prayer Book defines it simply in terms of the activities clergy are to do.

[38] See the famous Lambeth Quadrilateral and its reference to the local adaptation of episcopacy in ecumenical dialogue: 'That, in the opinion of this Conference, the following Articles supply a basis on which approach may be by God's blessing made towards Home Reunion:
  (a) The Holy Scriptures of the Old and New Testaments, as "containing all things necessary to salvation," and as being the rule and ultimate standard of faith.
  (b) The Apostles' Creed, as the Baptismal Symbol; and the Nicene Creed, as the sufficient statement of the Christian faith.
  (c) The two Sacraments ordained by Christ Himself — Baptism and the Supper of the Lord — ministered with unfailing use of Christ's words of Institution, and of the elements ordained by Him.
  (d) The Historic Episcopate, locally adapted in the methods of its administration to the varying needs of the nations and peoples called of God into the Unity of His Church.'
Lambeth Conference of 1888 Resolution 11 (2011) Lambeth Conference <http://www.lambethconference.org/index.cfm> at 1 September 2011.

[39] See Mark Lopez, *The Origins of Multiculturalism in Australian Politics, 1945-1975* (2001) and Geoffrey Brahm Levey and Tariq Modood, *Secularism, Religion, and Multicultural Citizenship* (2008).

that the underlying assumptions pluralists hold are quite varied.[40] One difference relevant to our present question is that in general British pluralists tended to be more open to the idea of plurality of groups within the body politic, whereas US pluralists focussed more on the individual as the fundamental entity in their pluralist conceptions of the state.

In one sense, this should not be surprising. The foundations of the US Republic were conceived in terms of the freedom of the individual. The Declaration of Independence makes this clear,[41] and the Virginia Statute, written by Jefferson and promoted by Madison, also makes the point in relation to religion and the state.[42] This foundational element in the US political and cultural tradition has had an influence on the values accepted in US public life and those tacit in the shape and operation of public institutions.[43]

These differences arise from the history of the community. Even when modern society is seen in bureaucratised terms, the impact of the past on the character of the society is not removed. The modern nation-state did not emerge onto the stage of history without parentage or pedigree. While Madison and Hamilton may have wanted to create something entirely new at the Constitutional Congress in the summer of 1787 it remains the case that this most dramatic Enlightenment-inspired modern nation, the US, created institutions and developed cultural habits that had significant traces of the past from which they imagined themselves to be separating. In his later reflections on Madisonian democratic thought, Robert Dahl pointed out that the strong assertion of the political power of the people still left open choices about the structures of society.[44] Those choices were in the terms available at the time. Some precedents were available, such as the extent of the franchise and the

---

[40] See, eg, P Q Hirst (ed), *The Pluralist Theory of the State: Select Writings of GDH Cole, JN Figgis, and HJ Laski* (1989); D Nicholls, *The Pluralist State* (2nd ed, 1975) and William E Connolly, Samuel Allen Chambers and Terrell Carver, *William E. Connolly: Democracy, Pluralism and Political Theory* (2007).

[41] 'We hold these truths to be self-evident, that all men are created equal, that they are endowed by their Creator with certain unalienable Rights, that among these are Life, Liberty and the pursuit of Happiness. — That to secure these rights, Governments are instituted among Men, deriving their just powers from the consent of the governed': *US Declaration of Independence*, 4 July 1776.

[42] See Merrill D Peterson, Robert C Vaughan et al, *The Virginia Statute for Religious Freedom: Its Evolution and Consequences in American History* (1988) and Kaye, above n 26, ch 3.

[43] Simple things like the emerging agreement to incorporation with limited liability came readily in the US, for example in the New Jersey Acts, as compared with Europe and the United Kingdom. The difference was in no small degree because such incorporation was seen as part of the right of the individual citizen, whereas in the United Kingdom it was thought of in terms of Crown prerogative and grant.

[44] Robert Alan Dahl, *A Preface to Democratic Theory* (2006) 152-72.

relation between private property and personal freedom. On the other hand the phenomenon of a large-scale mass democratic state was a new challenge.

As noted, the contrast between the origins of the US and Australia is stark. The final vestiges of British legal and political power in the Commonwealth and States of Australia did not disappear until well into the twentieth century. Any response to the application of notions of rights in the Australian context needs to be set within the framework of the story of the nation and the social values that have been shaped by that story, especially those values that point to the ways in which individual and social flourishing have been enabled or diminished. From the point of view of Christian theology, these are the particularities of divine providence with which a theologian must grapple.

I have already noted not only that the notion of rights is complex within its own history but also that theologians view the status of rights quite differently. Some see a foundation for rights as given in the creative and redemptive action of God. They arise because humans are created in the image of God and are the subject of God's redeeming work in Jesus Christ. Such views are often built upon notions of natural law. Others see rights as a distraction from the real story of Christianity, which points to a gospel of divine grace and initiative that reaches out to a fallen humanity. This second view of the matter nonetheless can come to rights as practical mechanisms that might restrain evil and enable freedom of action and belief. However, when rights are approached on this basis they have a very different status and character. They are not fundamental principles that are intrinsic in the human condition. They are not the inalienable rights found in the US proclamation tradition, which has found an echo in the UN declarations. Rather they are mechanisms and ways of talking about social relations in order to address intractable power imbalances.

These two different approaches to rights language will generally lead to different ways of approaching the shaping of social relations. The former will have a more crusading ideological approach, though it will inevitably be combined with a realpolitik sense of what is possible, even for what is suitable for those whose power is necessary for the viability of a political unit. The most obvious case of such a pragmatic approach is the US when the founding fathers allowed slavery to stand outside the practical reach of their constitutional rhetoric. Given the second order sense of rights in the second approach, it is obvious that practicalities will be a critical element in the deployment of rights language for political and social argument. In either sense the application of rights is set in the context of a particular society with its own story and developed social values and institutions. That means that we must now notice the particularities of the Australian context and in doing so focus on the place of religion in Australian social thinking. For the contemporary issues in Australia that means in particular addressing the character of Australian secularity and the narrative of the nation within which that secularity has been formed and gains meaning.

The particular Australian secularity and social change

Despite recent criticism and disturbing discontinuities for it, the broad secularization theory retains a residual hold for many people in Western countries, especially in Europe.[45] That theory asserts that in the progress of modernity, humanity has outgrown the need for religion and as a result belief must wither away. Modernisation meant the inevitable decline in religious faith. Hugh McLeod underlines the role of human agency in this, rather than seeing it as some kind of impersonal process. It was a contest between rival points of view: 'Secularization happened at least in part because there were large numbers of people who were trying their hardest to bring it about'.[46] However, sociologists and especially historians are increasingly dismantling the secularization theory. One of its most prominent advocates in the middle of the twentieth century, Peter Berger now says that

> what I and most other sociologists of religion wrote in the 1960s about secularization was a mistake. Our basic argument was that secularization and modernity go hand in hand. With more modernization came more secularization. It wasn't a crazy theory. There was some evidence for it. But I think it is basically wrong. Most of the world today is certainly not secular. It is very religious.[47]

This reconsideration has led to some very different interpretations of the place of religion in public life in some countries. Callum Brown sees Christianity in Britain as having entered terminal decline in the 1960s,[48] and Philip Jenkins sees a new Christendom emerging in the southern hemisphere and potentially including the US.[49] This new approach has not done away with the older view entirely but it has shown that secularization is not a universal phenomenon affecting all societies in the same way. It has demonstrated that secularity is a way of speaking about the religious character of societies, or more particularly the place of religion, in the life of societies, including its public and private institutions.

---

[45] See Jeffrey Cox, 'Master Narratives of Long-Term Religious Language', in McLeod and Ustorf (ed), above n 4, 201–17.

[46] Hugh McLeod, *Secularisation in Western Europe, 1848-1914* (2000) 28. One might compare the market analogy used to similar effect in Rodney Stark and Roger Finke, *Acts of Faith: Explaining the Human Side of Religion* (2000).

[47] Peter Berger, 'Epistemological Modesty: An Interview with Peter Berger', *Christian Century* 114 (1997) 972, 974. Criticism of the secularization theory in this form began as early as 1965 with the writings of David Martin, but it has now reached a point of significant generality. See Stark and Finke, above n 46, esp ch 3.

[48] Callum G Brown, *The Death of Christian Britain: Understanding Secularisation 1800—000* (2009).

[49] Philip Jenkins, *The Next Christendom: The Rise of Global Christianity* (2002).

One aspect of this reconsideration of religion in public life has been the closer identification of the different patterns of secularity in different countries. Following the Treaty of Westphalia and the operation of the principle of *cuius regio, eius religio* toleration came gradually and in different forms in Europe. The separation of church and state has been changing in different countries right up until the present day. The dramatic effect of the revocation in 1685 of the Edict of Nantes removed any semblance of toleration for Protestants in France, while a concordat between church and state still exists in Switzerland and Germany that directly affects major social institutions such as universities. Hugh McLeod, who has written extensively on this theme, concludes that 'In questions to do with church and state and the role of religion in public institutions, there is no single European pattern, but there have been wide differences from country to country'.[50] France represents a dramatic legislative separation in this process, and in the US separation was affected by the new revolutionary constitution and its bill of rights.[51] England and Germany stand in some contrast to these with a gradual change that left remnants of the earlier pattern in place.[52]

In this framework, Australia represents a gradualist move to secularity in the institutions of public life with distinct residual public values in those institutions. There was no fundamental separation of church and state at any stage of constitutional development in Australia.[53] During the nineteenth century there was certainly a great deal of suspicion about competition for social power from the churches, especially the Anglican Church.[54] After all, the colony of NSW had begun as an Anglican jail, the creation of what was still in the late eighteenth century an Anglican state. Arthur Philip took oaths of loyalty as Governor of the new colony that included the very particular and, at the time very Anglican form of religious polemic, 'that I do believe that there is not any Transubstantiation in the Sacrament of the Lord's Supper or in the elements of Bread and Wine at or after the consecration thereof by any person

---

[50] McLeod and Ustorf (ed), above n 4, 9.

[51] For the variety of arrangements around the world see the recent survey, Jonathan Fox, *A World Survey of Religion and the State* (Cambridge: Cambridge University Press, Cambridge Studies in Social Theory, Religion, and Politics, 2008).

[52] See David Hempton, 'Established Churches and the Growth of Religious Pluralism: A Case Study of Christianisation and Secularisation in England since 1700', in McLeod and Ustorf (ed), above n 4.

[53] See T R Frame, *Church and State: Australia's Imaginary Wall* (2006).

[54] When the Church of England in NSW sought a constitution through an act of the state parliament a committee of enquiry was established and heard evidence. Almost all the objections to the proposal reflected a fear that the Church of England was seeking some preferential position in the life of the state. New South Wales Select Committee, *Report from the Select Committee on the Church of England Synods Bill: Together with the Proceedings of the Committee, Minutes of Evidence and Appendix* (1860).

whatsoever'.[55] Only Anglican chaplains were allowed to work in the colony and when an ecclesiastical structure was established it was Anglican. The archdeacon had a monopoly on the registration of marriages, and in due course one seventh of the land in the colony was ceded over to the Church of England Church and Schools Corporation.[56]

All this began to change under governor Richard Bourke with his church acts of 1836, which shared state financial support between the main Christian churches: Presbyterian, Roman Catholic and Anglican. The Anglican bishop, William Grant Broughton, opposed these moves on the grounds that it was against the constitution of England, which gave preference to the Church of England. He failed, and soon the Anglican monopoly on state funds for education was lost. The Church and Schools Corporation had already been dissolved and by mid-century state funding for churches through education and directly to clergy was related to numbers of registered members of each church. Direct aid to churches in NSW was abolished in 1862 and in 1880 in NSW all state funding for church schools was abolished and a state system of free compulsory and secular schools was established.

But secular did not mean irreligious, or even lacking any religious content. The 1880 Act provided for worship assemblies, the teaching of general Christianity in the school curriculum and released time for clergy to teach their particular doctrines of Christian faith. Those obligations remain to this day, and church representatives regularly visit schools to give Christian education.

When the University of Sydney was established there was much controversy about the nature of its secularity, or as it was expressed at the time, the presence in the university of the 'religious principle'.[57] A compromise was agreed principally with the Anglican Church, which required all graduands to provide a certificate that they had received religious instruction from an authorized person from their church, often from one of the church colleges in the university.[58] The correspondence at the time makes it clear that the principle of secularity fought for by the first provost and the members

---

[55] See F Watson, *Historical Records of Australia: Series IV Legal Papers, Sn A, Volume 1* (1914) 19–22. See also Bruce Kaye, 'Descended From An Anglican Jail: Anglicans and Church and State in Twenty First century Australia', forthcoming in Hilary Carey and John Gascoigne (eds), *Church and State from Old to New Worlds* (2012).

[56] The corporation was established in 1826 but abandoned in 1833 as being impractical. The action was subsequently explained as being a contradiction of the plurality of religious bodies that had come to recognition in the Bourke Acts of 1836.

[57] See the memorandum by Bishop Tyrell, *Sydney Morning Herald* (Sydney), 18 December 1852.

[58] See Bruce Kaye, 'George Augustus Selwyn in Australia', forthcoming in Alan Davidson (ed), *Essays to Celebrate the G A Selwyn* (2012); K J Cable, 'The University of Sydney and Its Affiliated College, 1850-1880', (1964) 2 *The Australian University* 183 and C Turney, U Bygott and P Chippendale, *Australia's First: A History of the University of Sydney Volume I 1850–1939* (1991).

of the Senate of the university was that there should be no teaching of divinity in the university. Nonetheless, the speeches at the inauguration of the university make it clear that the chief protagonists in the establishment and shaping of the university saw the new institution as serving to promote the Christian religion and morality. Furthermore, this sentiment was inscribed in the charter of the university and it remains there to this day.[59] There were church representatives on the first senate and the first principal was an Anglican priest as is the present vice chancellor, though there are no church representatives on the Senate now.

These two important areas of education and the place of religion in public life in Australia do not comprehend the whole story, but they illustrate that Australian secularity is made up of a series of arrangements that may differ in detail but which set out a pattern that retains religion as a critical issue in the public life of the society.

A similar pattern can be seen in the judicial tradition of interpretation of clause 116 of the Commonwealth constitution.[60] That tradition sets out the matter in terms that are significantly different from the strict separation that has developed in the US. Instead of the wall of separation in the US, the Australian pattern provides for equitable support for religions from the state. Instead of a doctrine of non-entanglement in the US, the Australian tradition has a doctrine of equitable entanglement. The question of what constitutes a religion so as to bring it within this catchment is thus a real question in interpreting the constitution in Australia,[61] as, also, is the question of what makes an institution religious.[62]

---

[59] It reads: 'for the advancement of religion and morality and the promotion of useful knowledge to hold forth to all classes and denominations of our faithful subjects, without any distinction whatsoever, throughout our dominions encouragement for pursuing a regular and liberal course of education'. University of Sydney, *Charter* (2008).

[60] See especially R Ely, *Unto God and Caesar: Religious Issues in the Emerging Commonwealth 1891–1906* (1976).

[61] 'The differing approaches of the judgements in the Full Court in this case, however, manifest the need for an authoritative Australian exposition of the concept of religion': *Church of the New Faith v Commissioner for Pay Roll Tax (Vic)* (1983) 154 CLR 120, 131 (Mason ACJ and Brennan J). See also Bruce Kaye, 'An Australian Definition of Religion' (1992) 14 UNSWLJ 332.

[62] The question before the High Court in *Church of the New Faith v Commissioner for Pay Roll Tax (Vic)* (1983) 154 CLR 120 was on appeal from the Supreme Court of Victoria in relation to exemption from pay-roll tax by the Church of the New Faith. The relevant Victorian law provided for exemption from pay-roll tax for 'religious organisations'. The High Court addressed the question of whether the members of the church had a religion that fell within an appropriate Australian legal definition, found that they did have such a religion, and upheld their appeal. The court did not clarify the concept of a 'religious organisation', which might actually be different from an organisation whose members all happened to share a common religion. That question of what is a religious organisation was addressed in the New South Wales Court of Appeal in *Glebe Administration Board v Commissioner of Pay-Roll Tax* (1987) 10 NSWLR 352.

The changes in the pattern of this secularity in Australia were not done in the name of atheism, nor of irreligion, nor yet in the name of a secular Enlightenment notion of the state or human sociality. Some of the protagonists in making changes may have acted out of such motives, but they were not the rationale or the main arguments. These changes were done in different ways for a variety of reasons — sometimes to manage religious conflict and sometimes to promote institutions that could operate more strictly in the terms of their own activity, such as a university. They were done within the framework of a notion of the human condition that was essentially social and in terms of the interests and values of the society as a society, which they assumed to be religious and, in a long early period, Christian.

That approach did not preclude concern for individuals. On the contrary, the weak were to be assisted, and the disadvantaged were to be given a fair go. Such arrangements did not always succeed in their aims and modifications were demanded. The values of one generation did not always succeed unchanged into the next. Attitudes to race, foreigners, and Indigenous people are glaring examples. The position of tenants, creditors and employees are others. The Australian form of multiculturalism represents a form of inclusive group pluralism not found in many comparable nations.[63]

Australia presents a form of secularity that has emerged out of a monopoly Anglican state into a plural democratic nation with its own ongoing development of the pattern of its social relations and the success and failures of its public institutions. Its public institutions are subject to forms of scrutiny that differ in their style and effectiveness in different areas of public life. Several states have independent corruption commissions, independent auditors examine state and commonwealth government activity, Royal Commissions and other forms of enquiry examine egregious failures and a range of legislation addresses issues such as discrimination. Amongst these instruments can be included the various international agreements about the treatment of individuals and certain classes of people and certain kinds of actions such as torture to which Australia is a signatory. These various instruments constitute an inventory of methods for dealing with institutional failure and the protection of the social values embedded in and developing within this Australian story.

This ongoing narrative of Australian existence as an evolving society with commitments and social values is an important framework for anyone approaching the issue of individual rights in this context. Given the contingent character of the human condition in the light of the kingdom of Jesus, which is not of this world, the theologian's question becomes how in this particular context is the Christian to

---

[63] See Lopez, above n 39.

be neighbour in this kind of society. How are they thus to testify to the nature of the kingdom of God? Such a question is addressed not just to individuals within society but also, and fundamentally, to the institutions and frameworks that shape the lives of those who engage with them and inhabit them.

Yet any question of the appropriate form of protections and freedoms for individuals and groups in Australia needs to be considered in the light of its quite particular form of secularity and assumptions about social values. The notion of inalienable individual human rights that has so shaped that very differently structured society of the US has not been a central or powerful force in shaping the structure of Australian society. Indeed, despite many practical commonalities, the two societies are founded upon significantly different assumptions.

Perhaps trying to live as one who belongs to a kingdom not of this world suggests a greater awareness of the importance of narrative and the shaping influence of institutions. It seems to me that it would make more sense to build with the bricks and mortar drawn from that narrative rather than introduce principles that imply a significantly different understanding of society.

There are various mechanisms currently in place in state and federal levels that regulate and audit the operation of public institutions and their agents, including the parliaments. A more coherent and, if necessary, more extensive set of such auditing and regulating mechanisms for public institutions would be more consonant with the Australian social and political narrative than the introduction of rights instruments that ill-fit the social traditions and particularities of the Australian story.

4

Anniversary Overlap: Or What Happens When St Paul Meets the Universal Declaration of Human Rights

Alan Cadwallader

In 2007, Paul Gray, a columnist for the Melbourne *Herald Sun*, vented his spleen against the Australian Catholic Film Office and the Australian Film Institute for the awards given to Rolf de Heer's film *Ten Canoes*.[1] His reason: the film's subtitles. Australian money, he argued, was fritted away on a film that was not in the 'national language'. He went on to claim that this made the film 'elitist', 'baffling', 'high-minded', its awards being a case of 'the unsociable rushing to laud the unwatchable'. The Jesuit Father Richard Leonard's rationale for the ACFO award was that it 'can only be a useful instrument for reconciliation'. In contrast, Gray queried whether any reconciliation was possible. For him, reconciliation was tied to the universality of English at least as defined with an Australian frame of reference, or even broader, movies as 'the business of the masses'. Drew Roberts, from the Adult Multicultural Education Services in Melbourne, underscored the significance of Australia's first Indigenous language (Ganalbingu) film in a context where only 18 of 128 extant Indigenous languages are currently exempt from the threat of extinction.[2] Death and loss have already severely decimated the 500 dialects and 250 languages estimated to have layered the great southern land before white settlement. Gray at least acknowledged that he was a 'white guy' but what he did not acknowledge was that white guys who speak English are presumably the measure of universality. The loss

---

[1] 'Paddling a new canoe', *Herald Sun* (Sydney), 8 Jan 2007.
[2] ABC Radio National, 'Lingua Franca', *Lingua franca*, 1 August 2009.

of bilingual education in the Northern Territory is but one structural parallel to this attitude.[3]

This concrete example highlights one of the ongoing conflicts over human rights: that between the universal and the particular. It plays out in issues of identity framed within ethnicity, culture, gender, sexual orientation and a host of other parameters where the particular is frequently sacrificed to the universal, even though the universal is itself tainted as particularly Western and Judeo-Christian.[4] In this sense, given that the universal, in Gray's terms, is tied to the linkage of art with business so that worth is defined in terms of the box office, '"human rights" is nothing other than the ideology of modern liberal capitalism'. At least, this is the assessment of the French Marxist philosopher, Alain Badiou.[5]

Badiou's revised quest for the universal

Badiou does not want to jettison universality. Rather, he wants to re-position universality in an ethics of truth not in morality. Rights defined by morality, he finds, are always undermined by an often Western capitalist particular determination masquerading as the universal when it is in fact replete with obscurantism, commercial academicism, the politics of profit and inequality and sexual barbarism.[6] Truth is reduced to a linguistic form, an instrument in the exercise of power. For Badiou, the universal has nothing to do with either dominator or victim.[7] These are the frequent indicators that competition and/or moral relativism is alive and well, even over the 'universality' of rights.

To assist Badiou in the construction of a universalism that is built on truth rather than competition, he turns, like all good recent Marxists,[8] to the apostle, St Paul. Badiou is not interested in any metaphysical or theological reading of Paul's letters — he remains

---

[3] See J Simpson, J Caffrey and P McConvell, 'Gaps in Australia's Indigenous Language Policy: Dismantling bilingual education in the Northern Territory'(2009) *AIATSIS Research Discussion Paper* 24.
[4] See C R Fontaine, *With Eyes of Flesh: The Bible, Gender and Human Rights* (2008) 11.
[5] See J Barker, *Alain Badiou: A critical introduction* (2002) 135.
[6] Alain Badiou, Christoph Cox, et al, *On Evil: An Interview with Alain Badiou* (2002) Cabinet Magazine Online <http://www.cabinetmagazine.org/issues/5/alainbadiou.php> at 9 September 2011..
[7] A Badiou, *Saint Paul: The Foundation of Universalism* (R Brassier trans) (2003), 6.
[8] Cf S Žižek, *The Ticklish Subject: The Absent Centre of Political Ontology* (1999), 127–70, S Žižek, *The Parallax View* (2006), G Agamben, *The Time That Remains: A Commentary on the Letter to the Romans* (P Dailey trans) (2005). For the recognition of the importance of Paul in contemporary Marxism, see R Boer, *Criticism of Heaven: On Marxism and Theology* (2009) 343–60.

an avowed materialist.[9] Badiou's main Marxist interlocutor, Slavoj Žižek, agrees, arguing that it is only the materialist who can give expression to the 'subversive kernel of Christianity'.[10] But Badiou is fascinated by the power of Paul to rise above the constraints of his age and by the power of Paul's unreal fable (the 'fabulous') — that is, the resurrection of the crucified — to expose the paralyzing falsity of the past age in which he lived. In this sense, Badiou is completely at ease with a fable. It is the integral germination of an imaginary alternate construction that initiates the 'truth process' that extracts truth and its possibility from a communitarian stranglehold resisting its emergence. He calls this 'the fabulous forcing of the real'.[11] Paul's militant commitment to this emergent truth arises as an antiphilosophical and antilegal declaration (Cf Rom 2:10, 1 Cor 1:18f, Gal 2:20–21)[12] called forth by the totally new moment of the encounter with the resurrected crucified one. The emergent truth may retain, for a time, strategic negotiations of the philosophy and law of the previous dominant and dominating masters, as part of the process of release from the stranglehold. These negotiations utilise the word 'Christ/Messiah' of Jesus, make frequent references to the Hebrew scriptures, even uses Greek as the language of discourse, although under the powerful influence of the imaginary alternate construction are given a totally new amalgam. But the primary faithfulness to the declaration of the fabulous truth event is part of the very truth process that prevents it from being 'subsumed back into the prevailing order', through the contingent use of such language.[13]

Paul is prized as a subject. He is one who was able to rise, like the prophets that framed his upbringing, above the constraints of previous monolithic, immutable and self-justifying systems — whether that be Judaic law observance or Greek privileging of the logos. Badiou's prized texts are Romans 12:2, which he translates as 'Do not be conformed to the present century, but be transformed by the renewal of your thought'[14] and Galatians 3:28 — 'neither Jew nor Greek, slave nor free, male nor female'[15] — for Badiou the fundamental affirmation about Truth and the condition of universality.[16] The new, emerging universal lies beyond and must not be constrained by any particularism, whether that be the particularism

---

[9] Badiou, above n 7, 2; A Badiou, *Metapolitics* (J Baker trans) (2005) 60, 68–77.
[10] S Žižek, *The Puppet and the Dwarf: The Perverse Core of Christianity* (2003) 6.
[11] Badiou, 5 Cf 56. For Badiou, the fable itself (resurrection of the crucified) is dispensable even though the subject's enunciation and its initiation of a universal truth process remain as testimony, precisely to that possibility amidst the otherwise despairing impossibility of truth or justice in and arising from a 'preconstituted historical aggregate' (6).
[12] Badiou, above n 7, 9, 14, 41–2.
[13] M Pound, *Žižek: A (Very) Critical Introduction* (2008) 80.
[14] Badiou, above n 7, 110.
[15] Ibid 9, 109. Cf Romans 10:12 (57).
[16] Badiou, above n 7, 57, 109. See M de Kesel, 'Truth as Formal Catholicism — On Alain Badiou, Saint Paul: La fondation de l'universalisme' (2007) 1 *International Journal of Žižek Studies* 8.

of identity politics (gays, disabled, feminist etc) or the particularism of law and wisdom posturing as a universal, especially as they respectively enforce and espouse a particular morality as universally binding. Paul's epistles themselves are prized over against other literary forms (including gospels and acts along with the texts of law and wisdom). The occasional, critical, nonsystematic form of the authentic letters is crucial to the 'forceful extraction of an essential core of thought'.[17] The contingency of the letters — what Nils Dahl calls the 'problem' of the particularity of Paul's letters[18] — is not for Badiou a problem at all. Their value can and must never become a frozen substitute for the central, dynamic, unfolding and fabulous resistance to the hegemonic dominance of institutions and systems in the present. Everything returns to and is inspired by the event that stands against both law and philosophy — the resurrection of the crucified one. The truth of this event enters into the process of emerging revelation through Paul's conviction and faithfulness to it. As Nick Hewlett observes, 'It is not possible to prove (in an empirical, positivist sense) that an event has taken place, as the truth process associated with the event only exists through the active commitment of those who declare its existence and importance'.[19] This is why there is almost nothing of Jesus' life, sayings and work in Paul's letters — they simply do not matter; indeed, they cloud the revelation.

Truth is a process that gathers momentum, adherence and memory and is tied to a subject that constantly fights against conformity to some monolithic pretender. Badiou, like Slavoj Žižek (another Marxist rescuer of Paul),[20] is critically concerned not merely with the ability of a subject to make a break with the past but with the subject's ability to resist and overcome the 'McDonaldsisation' of language and thought — the inability of thinking other than the status quo, the freezing over of any imaginative conception of an alternative.[21] This notion of process is important because it will help to save Badiou's universalism from the very charge that threatens to undermine it, as in all Marxist systems: the displacement of one monolith by another. Badiou is careful to say, though, that it is not the removal of differences but rather the rendering of them as insignificant, that is critical to this universalism. He

---

[17] Badiou, above n 7, 33. See R Boer, 'The Perpetual Allure of the Bible for Marxism' (2007) 15 *Historical Materialism* 62.

[18] N Dahl, 'The Particularity of the Pauline Epistles as a Problem in the Ancient Church' in O Cullman (ed), *Neotestamentica et Patristica (NovTs 6)* (1962), 261-71.

[19] N Hewlett, 'Engagement and transcendence: the militant philosophy of Alain Badiou' (2004) 12 *Modern & Contemporary France* 343.

[20] See S Žižek, *The Fragile Absolute or, Why is the Christian Legacy worth fighting for?* (2000).

[21] See A Cadwallader, 'In Go(l)d we Trust: Literary and Economic Exchange in the Debate over Caesar's Coin (Mk 12:13–17)' (2007) 14 *Biblical Interpretation* 486, 486–507.

has no wish to offer any solace to fascist tendencies.[22]

Although Badiou claims that his reading of Paul is independent,[23] there is much in his portrayal and even in his very assertion of independence that reveals Badiou as a surrogate protestant individualist.[24] He admits that Paul is a 'cultural revolution on which we all depend'[25] and there is regular reference to biblical scholars and their consensus.[26] Badiou speaks of Paul's conversion and 'Damascus convocation'[27] and ignores the current scholarly consensus that Paul's experience constituted a 'call' not a 'conversion'.[28] 'Conversion' accents discontinuity, the very fracturing with the past that Badiou favours. 'Call' accents continuity, even though it is possible to see the prophetic nature of Paul's call as itself equally radical in its vision and practice of a break-through reconfiguration of the past inheritance.[29] The danger is always that a mere transgression of the law will negate the possibility of a new society and social vision precisely because it draws its energy, its violence from that very law.[30]

Badiou also reiterates the traditional emphasis on the displacement of the way of the flesh for the way of the spirit,[31] though, in Badiou's case, without sacrifice of a

---

[22] References to contemporary and past French politics run through his work. Note especially his critique of Le Pens: Badiou, above n 7, 8–9, Cf 44.

[23] What he calls a 'direct reading' of the text. He wants to avoid all obscurantism, frequently the bane of hermeneutics. See A S Miller, 'An Interview with Alain Badiou: 'Universal Truths and the Question of Religion'' (2005) *Journal of Philosophy and Scripture* 3.

[24] This in a curious way accompanies his 'formal Catholicism', understood as universality: see de Kesel, above n 16, 2.

[25] Badiou, above n 7, 15.

[26] He is, however, prepared to make significant contributions of his own, such as the reframing of translation equivalents for key technical terms — eg, *pistis* as conviction rather than 'faith' — so as to remove the mouldy layers of religiously constraining and distorting meanings: Badiou, above n 7, 15 Cf 41.

[27] Badiou, above n 7, 17, 20. In this, he uncritically adopts the Lukan Acts framing of Paul, even though he recognises Acts as 'the Hollywood version', harbouring a 'pro-Roman benevolence' (at 27, 30).

[28] The seminal essay is that of Krister Stendahl, 'Call Rather than Conversion' in K Stendahl, *Paul among Jews and Gentiles* (1976) 7–23. See also J Munck, *Paul and the Salvation of Mankind* (1959). J D G Dunn, "A Light to the Gentiles', or 'The End of the Law'? The Significance of the Damascus Road Christophany for Paul' in L D Hurst and N T Wright (eds), *The Glory of Christ in the New Testament* (1987) 251–66. Some try to have it both ways: Cf F J Matera, *Galatians (Sacra Pagina)* (2007) 62–4.

[29] Badiou may contest this given that, for him, the prophet in Judaism is the archetypal expositor of signs, which Paul set himself against. Badiou, above n 7, 41.

[30] See C Packman, 'Towards a Violent Absolute: Some Reflections on Žižekian Theology and Violence' (2009) *IJŽS* 3, 3–5.

[31] K Jackson, 'The Great Temptation of 'Religion': Why Badiou has been so important to Žižek' (2007) 1 *IJŽS* 11.

materialist foundation. He rejects all law as the antipathy of truth and accents the radical newness of the idea and the bearer.[32] Greek and Jew are constructed not as ethnic but as monolithic systems, almost ciphers, much like they became signs of Renaissance philosophy on the one hand and Catholic legalism on the other in Martin Luther's reformational rhetoric.[33] The very prizing of letters[34] is reminiscent of the preference for essays, one of the key instruments of the *action* of the reformation. The sheer privileging of Paul even over the Gospels, Badiou himself recognises is found in Luther.[35] In this sense, there is, as Žižek has noted,[36] a legacy of idealism in Badiou's work, that is, a trace of the metaphysical reification of the subject and the program/vision. In the overarching accent on the radical newness of the event — its declaration and adherence to it (ALL, it should be noted, comprising the emergent truth) — the influence from and importance of the past are discounted. The problem here is that historical materiality, for all Badiou's commitment, is eviscerated if not evaporated. Consequently, Badiou, ironically, is inured to the influences that have facilitated *his* reading of Paul — what Biblical scholars today call 'the old perspective',[37] even if Badiou's reading is leached of any metaphysic. Moreover, it induces, even requires, a minimization of both historical and literary influence, so that, for example, Badiou reads the 'I' refrain of Romans 7 ('the thing I hate I do') as biographical.[38] There is no acquaintance with the ancient rhetorical form of *prosopopoion* — the adoption of a generic role, a 'speech-in-character' — that would see Paul adopting a generic character, which may include himself but is certainly designed to a self-identification among his addressees.[39] Consequently, the universalism that Badiou extracts from his heroic subject, as new and vibrant and open as he may claim, can only be secured by an erasure not merely a denial[40] of the influence of past particulars. Such an erasure, threatens the real — the truth he is eager to declare — far more than his overt denial, of the material reality of the resurrection of the crucified one. In this

---

[32] Badiou, above n 7, 13–15.
[33] See, eg, Luther's *A Commentary on St Paul's Epistle to the Galatians* (P S Watson trans) (1953), 129–31.
[34] Badiou, above n 7, 31.
[35] Badiou, above n 7, 33. Interestingly, Roland Boer forges a link with Calvin: Boer, above n 17, 64.
[36] S Žižek, *On Belief* (2001), 125; Žižek, above n 8, 56, 326.
[37] See D Boyarin, *A Radical Jew: Paul and the Politics of Identity* (1994), 41–2.
[38] Badiou, above n 7, 79–81. Badiou in fact pits Paul against rhetoric which he sees as nothing but an arm of the very philosophy that has built one ideological expression of the masterly monolith from which Paul is extracting himself and others (at 27, 36). This is where Badiou's subjective use of Paul staggers against the valid claims of history and exegesis (Cf at 2).
[39] See S Stowers, *A Rereading of Romans: Justice, Jews and Gentiles* (1994), 264–72; see, by contrast, A Kotsko, 'Politics and Perversion: Situating Žižek's Paul' (2008) 9 *Journal for Cultural and Religious Theory* 51.
[40] Badiou overtly denies any influence from past particulars, previous differences: Badiou, above n 7, 2.

he comes dangerously close to the obscurantist phenomena of capitalist imperialism he abhors.

From Marxist universal to Jewish particular

A radically alternate appreciation of Paul comes from the Jewish scholar of the New Testament, Mark Nanos. If, for Badiou, 'the production of equality and the casting off, in thought, of differences are the material signs of the universal',[41] for Nanos the continuing Jewishness of Saint Saul[42] is manifest as fundamental in his writings and even the Acts of the Apostles. Paul remained a Torah-observant Jew and was recognized as such by those around him.[43] The offensive particularism of Paul's hereditary and personal commitment has of course been submerged beneath a 'universal' Gentile church that has rationalised its own historical accidence as a supercessionist sign of God's providence. Part of Nanos's project is the removal of the anti-Jewish bias from commentary on particular key texts of the Pauline corpus.[44] But his overarching theme is Paul's construction of a major new narrative of Jewish negotiation of the Gentile world. The cipher of religious/philosophical typology is removed here as Nanos pushes Paul back into his heritage (claiming he never left it!) and the battles for that heritage that command so much of first century Jewish life.

For Nanos, Paul's remarkable but highly disputed achievement is to reconfigure the way in which Gentiles and Jews can relate in the worship of the one God and in the social interactions that flow from that monotheistic base. His addressees are equally Jewish and Gentile. Paul, according to Nanos, takes seriously the vision of the incoming of the Gentiles as part of Jewish election and hope. The critical issue is how that would happen. Nanos sees Paul as historically particularist in the extreme in that the fundamental confirmation of the incoming of the Gentiles does not lie in

---

[41] Ibid 109.

[42] See D H Akenson, *Saint Saul: A Skeleton Key to the Historical Jesus* (2002), who not only accents the Jewishness of both Paul (Saul) and Jesus (Yeshua) but who adopts such a maximalist position on the Jesus references in Paul's writings that far more than the crucifixion-resurrection is rendered critical to the apostle.

[43] M Nanos, *The Irony of Galatians: Paul's Letter in First Century Context* (2002) 3.

[44] See, eg, his assertion of a polytheistic calendar in Gal 4:10: ibid 267-268. See also his timely reminder that 'dogs' is a ubiquitous term of derision throughout the Mediterranean world: M Nanos, *Paul's Reversal of Jews Calling Gentiles 'Dogs' (Phillipians 3:2): 1600 Years of an Ideological Tale Wagging an Exegetical Dog?* (2008) <http://www.marknanos.com/Phil3Dogs-Reverse-1-17-08.pdf> at 9 September 2011. I have explored the gendered elements of the use of 'dogs' as insult at length, arguing that gender, not ethnicity, is foundational to its use: see A Cadwallader, *Beyond the Word of a Woman: Recovering the Bodies of the Syrophoenician Women* (2008).

Gentiles going through the ritual process of circumcision in order to be full members of the community of God worshippers.[45] This, quite literally, would remove their identity and identification *as Gentiles*. In other words, any hope of the universal for Paul does not lie in the obliteration of, or indifference to, the distinctions between Jew and Gentile, but in full knowledge and recognition of them. Here universalism, catholicity, is constructed not through a revolutionary new humanity but by an equally revolutionary new conception of appreciation of the particular distinctions within humanity.

For this reading to gain traction and to be faithful to it, Nanos takes the historical and rhetorical context as critical both to Paul and to the interpretation of Paul. Both history and rhetoric inextricably shape Paul's discourse and cannot be ignored. One example will suffice. In Paul's letter to the Romans, the metaphor of grafting is taken into the argument of trying to explain the historical process of Gentile inclusion (Rom 11:17–24). Gentile commentators and translators through to the present day have taken the metaphor of grafting to read some branches are 'broken off' and replaced by others.[46] This goes completely against the gardening techniques known in the ancient world.[47] Rather, branches were incised but not severed and other branches were sutured into the gap. Hence, Nanos favours the translation 'dislocated' or 'sprained'.[48] They are still identified as wild even though they are now part of the natural, even if grafted in 'against nature' (Rom 11:24). Nanos affirms that 'Paul maintains the proposition that those from the nations who respond to this good news of Christ remain members of the other nations thereafter, joining alongside of Israelites in the worship of the One God of *all* the nations'.[49]

Here one can see the obverse of Badiou's accent on universalism as a rupture from the particulars of the past. Rather, the particulars are regarded as absolutely critical to universalism precisely *in* their particularity. The crucial work of achievement of a universal that embraces the particular is a combination of continuity with the heritage of all parts with the dialogical imagination that produces a revolutionary

---

[45] Nanos, above n 43, 6.

[46] See, recently, de Kesel, above n 16, 17.

[47] See Columella, *De re rustica* 5.9.16; Theophrastus, *De causis plantarum* 3.7.5–12; Theophrastus, *De historia plantarum* 2.7.12. For exposition see M Nanos, *'Broken Branches': A Pauline Metaphor Gone Awry?* (Romans 11:11-24) (2008) <www.marknanos.com/BrokenBranches-8-1-08.pdf> at 9 September 2011; P E Esler, 'Ancient Oleiculture and Ethnic Differentiation: The Meaning of the Olive-Tree Image in Romans 11' (2003) 26 *JSNT* 103.

[48] M Nanos, 'Romans 9-11 from a Jewish perspective on Christian-Jewish Relations', *Paulus Magazine* (Italy), 10 June 2009, 3. He recognizes that the language in Romans 11: 22–24 does indicate severance, but that this operates as an *a fortiori* argument for the sake of Gentile Christ-believers.

[49] Ibid 272.

new engagement. For biblical scholars, Nanos's work is a significant innovation on what is called 'the new perspective' on Paul.

Finding the universal and particular in the Creator

A revolutionary new engagement, I would like to suggest, can actually be achieved by a return to theology — Paul's theology or at least as informed by Paul. This in no way is to escape from the materialist commitments, upon which our Marxist brothers and sisters rightly insist, into some metaphysical flight from the world. And I hope that it will make possible a measure of dialogue between Badiou and Nanos — not a synthesis which would be anathema to both, for the one obscurantist and for the other a deficit.

I would like to suggest that for Paul the fundamental issue at stake in the Christ event has to do with what Badiou somewhat dismissively terms the Father. In theological terminology it is the problem of theodicy — the justification of God. This is not to do with the old chestnut of the problem of suffering and evil and its reconciliation with a powerful, caring God. Rather, it is the conundrum of trying to hold together God's justice and God's faithfulness in regard to creation. In reductionist terms, this seeks to resolve the fundamental tension between a holy God reacting against a creation that has defiled itself along with God's own intentions and a faithful God who has persevered in forbearance to seek out relationship with that creation.[50]

The key determinative image of God for Paul is God as Creator. For Paul, God as Creator cannot be untrue to God's own self. This requires that God remain as Creator. To be Creator requires creation, requires creatures. Creation is necessary if God is to be and is to remain Creator — in short, if God is to be God. This understanding of God dominates Romans from its opening (see Rom 1:19-25). God therefore must take responsibility for the continuing relationship with creation. God's justice and faithfulness are both determined by and subject to this basic affirmation.

Here is the contribution and part resolution to the fundamental issue of the universal and the particular raised thus far. Because God is Creator — not an immovable absolutist but a dynamic ongoing relational and relating subject, then God, for Paul, *must* be in relation, seeking relation. This does not require some anachronistic,

---

[50] In recent Pauline scholarship, for the accent on the righteousness of God, see E Käsemann, *Perspectives on Paul* (1971); J Fitzmyer, *Romans* (1992); for the accent on the faithfulness of God, see B Byrne, *Reckoning with Romans* (1986), J D G Dunn, *The Theology of Paul the Apostle* (1998). Along with the dialogue with Badiou and Nanos, my approach owes some of its inspiration to R B Hays, *Echoes of Scripture in the Letters of Paul* (1989) and L E Keck, *Paul and His Letters* (2nd ed, 1988).

static Trinitarian sense[51] but rather needs to be understood as a consequence of the fundamental characteristic of Creator. For Paul, any exposition of incarnation or resurrection must be predicated on the human-divine relationship. Either category as fundamental truth event (to fall back on Badiou's terminology) must be grounded in a dynamic process of creator-creature relationality.

Here, oddly enough, is not merely the theodicy that Paul is committed to establishing (that is, how God can be both faithful and just in the light of God's promise to the world through the historic accidence of Israel) but a justification of God that is predicated on the affirmation of God as Creator. If God as Creator requires an ongoing relationship with that which is created, so the theological reasoning of Paul unfolds with particular reference to the faithfulness of both God and Jesus (Creator and representative creature: see Rom 5), then *here is the model to be imitated between creatures*, whether that be ethnically-culturally based or even ecologically grounded.

This, for Paul, sacrifices neither truth nor difference. Jew and Greek remain Jew and Greek. Both are, of necessity, critical both to God and to one another, even when, in the necessary dialogical engagement, there are elements of the mediocre in the one and the militarist in the other. In this sense, Paul's theological agenda is not idealist but fundamentally processual and materialist, precisely because God as creator requires creation in ongoing dynamic relation if God's fundamental subjectivity is to be preserved. The quality of that subjectivity and relationality demands constant engagement with the truth of that relationship — what in jargonistic biblical discourse would be called justification and sanctification — but which is now predicated not on a final *telos* but on a constant engagement and generation of truth.

The qualification therefore that exists over all relationality is the 'not-finishedness' that Levinas recognizes for dialogue, that Badiou asserts for ontology and that Žižek perceives in materialist discourse.[52] We must resile from sounding as if, in the 'not-finished', we have an inkling of what we do not know and confer a completed ontology to that which has yet to be. In this sense, multiplicity is the very fabric of existence *even in the limitations of description*. Thus, the difference between subjects, whether creator and creature or Jew and Greek, cannot and must not be eradicated even as it cannot be completely described — this preserves the difference or qualitative distinction of both God *and* creature. At the same time, attention to this distinction is what generates the truth process and the organic relational quality and unpredictability of subjectivity: 'The subject does not sustain the universal order of Being but is a product of the event'.[53]

---

[51] Rightly criticized by Badiou, above n 7, 59, Cf 42–4.
[52] Compare Jackson, above n 31, 6.
[53] Ibid 11.

What I have done here is turn the event of the resurrection of the crucified one to its proper purpose: the justification of God as creator-in-relation-with-creation. In this sense, the resurrection event itself is a participation in and a restoration of the relationships of creation. A materialist view therefore asserts the fundamental unity of creation in all its diversity, just as the ecologists have been trying to get through to us. This is not an idealist conception that would remove being from material reality — as Badiou and others have rightly warned us against[54] — but rather the means to hold and to see unity and diversity really together *as a political process* not (merely) a religious or humanist doctrine. A theological view embraces this materialistic witness as the fundamental testimony to the being-in-relation of the creator God just as Paul asserted (Rom 1:19–20) and to which Paul tied the Christ-crucified-resurrected event. Reapplying Badiou's terms, *creation* is the prime fabulous event.

Hence, we can see, I trust, both the limitations and the possibilities of an engagement between Paul and the Universal Declaration of Human Rights. Paul, I suggest, is not just about the subject's ability to rise above or break through the differences in a particular historical epoch masquerading as a universal monolith, to a universalism which discounts difference in commitment to some larger Truth. Rather, he is about justifying a God who is Creator, a descriptor that, in Paul's terms, fundamentally predicates a relationship that is characterized materially and organically. The truth of the relationship is therefore something that must be worked at, constantly processed, constantly made in a relationship which is variegated and mutable, and, allowing a trace of Badiou's great concern, constantly constructed in the freedom of the respective subjects in dialogue. It can become neither a law nor a philosophy, and it cannot be used as an instrument of control nor an advancement of academically-insinuated superiority. It must remain organically in process as a declaration calling forth the ongoing dialogue between particulars, even as it constantly seeks and establishes the Truth and Truths in the process of initiative and response. And this, Paul suggests, is what characterizes the relationship between creatures of difference. In this sense, universality must be predicated on constant engagement with the particular, a constant making rather than an imposition or a competition.

An inaugural conclusion …

In this chapter, I hope to have demonstrated in method as well as content how particulars must be included in any discussion of the universal. To do otherwise would be immediately to destroy any hope of the universal before we have begun. By bringing Marxist, Jewish and Christian voices into dialogue, albeit under my own

---

[54] Ibid 5.

(decidedly contingent) univocality,[55] particular accents have all made a contribution to an understanding and a possibility of the viability of universality. Any truth that may be recognised and prized can only be recognised as an outcome of the necessarily dialogical, open and 'in-formation' engagement between those of significant and particular difference. Any talk of the universality of rights (for creation in general as much as for human creatures in particular) can only ever be a processual striving after the truth of those rights as an expression of relationship (itself in process of articulation). Accordingly, any articulation can only be understood as a Pauline-style 'letter', tenacious and inspirational in its faithfulness to the Truth which itself relies upon just that faithful commitment even as it recognises that it remains unfolding, a 'being-in-becoming'. For a bill of rights to have any claim on the 'evental'[56] nature of Truth in this understanding, it must avoid any monolithic inscription. It must incorporate openness to as yet undiscovered aspects of Truth in relationship and cultivate the dialogue between particulars as the necessary lifeblood of its ongoing viability for, and expression in, acts of 'making right'.

---

[55] Badiou celebrates being in a triangular exchange with a Catholic (Stanislas Breton) and a Protestant (Günther Bornkamm) in his portrayal of Paul and his ideas: Badiou, above n 7, 3.
[56] Badiou's term: Ibid 14 ff.

5

Defamation and Vilification: Rights to Reputation, Free Speech and Freedom of Religion at Common Law and under Human Rights Laws

Neil Foster

Laws prohibiting religious vilification (or religious 'hate speech') are controversial and often criticised. On the one hand, it seems obviously wrong that someone should be insulted and humiliated on the basis of his or her religious commitments. But how far should the law go in putting controls on freedom of speech? Critics charge that religious vilification laws amount to an undue restriction of freedom of speech, and in fact may generate, rather than reduce, acrimonious religious debate in multicultural and multi-faith societies.

This chapter is sympathetic to those critiques. But the particular angle it addresses is this: are religious vilification laws really necessary? The common law has dealt with verbal attacks on others for many years through the law of the tort of defamation. I suggest that many of the aims of those who propose religious vilification laws can be met by noting the remedies that are available under the ordinary law of defamation. In addition, I suggest that some of the concerns raised by opponents of the laws are met by the various defences and qualifications that have developed in the defamation area.

This chapter serves as a preliminary study, but I hope that it may at least open the way for further research on a topic that will become increasingly contentious. At the very least, I hope that the chapter illustrates that the adoption of further protection for human rights in Australia, including for freedom of religion, does not assume the adoption of religious vilification laws, and indeed, may be a further reason not to introduce such laws.[1]

Overview of laws on religious vilification

There are now a number of important overviews of the developing law of 'religious vilification' or 'religious hate speech', to which this chapter is indebted.[2] Here, I offer a brief summary. Gerber and Stone offer a good working definition of the type of law at issue here, sometimes referred to as 'hate speech':

> Hate speech is speech or expression which is capable of instilling or inciting hatred of, or prejudice towards, a person or group of people on a specified ground ...[3]

In particular, religious vilification laws aim to prohibit certain types of speech, which attack others based on their religion.

---

[1] See the remarks by Frank Brennan: 'It is very doubtful that the broad Victorian religious vilification law... would be passed by a Parliament constrained by a legislative human rights act'. Frank Brennan, *Vilification laws fuel disharmony* (2009) *Eureka Street* <http://www.eurekastreet.com.au/article.aspx?aeid=13572> at 26 August 2011.

[2] See Lawrence McNamara, 'Salvation and the State: Religious Vilification Laws and Religious Speech' in K Gelber and A Stone (eds), *Hate Speech and Freedom of Speech in Australia* (2007) 145, esp ch 8, and see other chapters in Gelber and Stone (eds); N Aroney, 'The Constitutional (In) Validity of Religious Vilification Laws: Implications for their Interpretation' (2006) 34 *Federal Law Review* 287; I Hare, 'Crosses, Crescents and Sacred Cows: Criminalising Incitement to Religious Hatred' [2006] *Public Law* 521; G Holland, 'Drawing the Line - Balancing Religious Vilification Laws and Freedom of Speech' (2006) 8 *University of Technology Sydney Law Review* 9; R T Ahdar 'Religious Vilification: Confused Policy, Unsound Principle and Unfortunate Law' (2007) 26 *University of Queensland Law Journal* 293; G Blake, 'Promoting religious tolerance in a multifaith society: Religious vilification legislation in Australia and the UK' (2007) 81 *Alternative Law Journal* 386; P Parkinson, 'Religious vilification, anti-discrimination laws and religious minorities in Australia: The freedom to be different' (2007) 81 *Alternative Law Journal* 954; I Hare and J Weinstein (eds), *Extreme Speech and Democracy* (2009) esp ch 2 and Part III (chs 15-17). In a related context, see J Temperman, 'Blasphemy, Defamation of Religions and Human Rights Law' (2008) 26 *Netherlands Quarterly of Human Rights* 517, and S Parmar, 'The Challenge of "Defamation of Religions" to Freedom of Expression and International Human Rights' (2009) 3 *European Human Rights Law Rev* 353, warning of the dangers to freedom of speech rights occasioned by repeated calls for an international convention prohibiting so-called 'defamation of religion'. This chapter will not address the international law issues in any detail.

[3] Gelber and Stone, above n 2, xiii.

In Australia, three jurisdictions have introduced such laws: Queensland, Tasmania and Victoria.[4] There is an important 'defence' provision in the Victorian legislation:

11. Exceptions-public conduct

(1) A person does not contravene section 7 or 8 if the person establishes that the person's conduct was engaged in reasonably and in good faith-

(a) in the performance, exhibition or distribution of an artistic work; or

(b) in the course of any statement, publication, discussion or debate made or held, or any other conduct engaged in, for–

(i) any genuine academic, artistic, religious or scientific purpose; or

(ii) any purpose that is in the public interest; or

(c) in making or publishing a fair and accurate report of any event or matter of public interest.

(2) For the purpose of subsection (1)(b)(i), a religious purpose includes, but is not limited to, conveying or teaching a religion or proselytising.[5]

In *Deen v Lamb* [2001] QADT 20, publication of a pamphlet inferring that all Muslims were obliged to disobey the law of Australia, which would otherwise have contravened the section, was said to have been allowable under the exception in s 124A(2)(c) as it was done 'in good faith' for political purposes.

The most controversial application of these laws so far, however, was in the litigation involving the 'Catch the Fire' organisation.[6] McNamara, Ahdar, Blake and Parkinson all offer cogent critiques of the way that the original decision finding the organisation guilty of vilification was made, and comment on the overturning of the decision by the Victorian Court of Appeal.[7] A brief summary, however, may be appropriate.

The original decision was *Islamic Council of Victoria v Catch the Fire Ministries Inc* [2004] VCAT 2510. In short, a Christian religious group advertised to a Christian

---

[4] See for an overview McNamara, above n 2, 146. The provisions are the *Anti-Discrimination Act 1991* (Qld) s 124A, the *Anti-Discrimination Act 1998* (Tas) ss 19, 55, and s 8 of the *Racial and Religious Tolerance Act 2001* (Vic).

[5] Ss (2) was added to the Act in 2006 partly in response to the *Catch the Fire* litigation discussed below.

[6] See also the other main case decided under the Victorian provisions, *Fletcher v Salvation Army Australia* [2005] VCAT 1523 (discussed in Blake, above n 2, 396–7).

[7] See the articles noted in above n 2.

audience that it was proposing to run a seminar that would critique Islam and help its listeners understand how to reach out to Muslims. Representatives of the Islamic Council of Victoria knew the nature of the seminar, chose to attend, and then took action against the group on the basis of statements that were made critiquing Islam. While some untrue and unhelpful statements may have been made in the course of the lengthy seminar (and in some related material published on a website), most of the comments made were sourced from multiple Islamic authors. Initially, the court found the pastors involved to be guilty of vilification and ordered them to publish retractions. On appeal the Victorian Court of Appeal in *Catch the Fire Ministries Inc & Ors v Islamic Council of Victoria Inc* [2006] VSCA 284 overturned the Tribunal's findings of vilification. The matter was referred back to the Tribunal, but the parties entered into a settlement of the proceedings that affirmed their mutual right to 'criticise the religious beliefs of another, in a free, open and democratic society'.[8]

Nettle JA, in particular, in the Court of Appeal noted that the Tribunal had failed to distinguish between criticisms of the *doctrines* of Islam and 'incitement to hatred' of *persons*:

> s.8 does not prohibit statements about religious beliefs per se or even statements which are critical or destructive of religious beliefs. Nor does it prohibit statements concerning the religious beliefs of a person or group of persons simply because they may offend or insult the person or group of persons. The proscription is limited to that which incites hatred or other relevant emotion and s.8 must be applied so as to give it that effect.[9]

While to some extent the decision of the Court of Appeal draws an appropriate line, the fact remains that the Victorian legislation seems to have been used in a way unintended by the framers of the legislation.[10] In general it seems far preferable for debate about religion to be 'untrammelled' by fear of legal intervention.

The UK has also introduced legislation prohibiting religious vilification. There, the *Racial and Religious Hatred Act 2006* (UK) added Part 3A to the *Public Order Act 1986* (headed 'Hatred against persons on religious grounds'), which now prohibits what in Australia would be called 'religious vilification'. Consistent with the comments of Nettle JA above, the UK prohibition on stirring up 'religious hatred'

---

[8] See, eg, the summary in Ahdar, above n 2, 305.
[9] [2006] VSCA 284, [15].
[10] And Ahdar, above n 2, in his perceptive analysis of the judgments in the Court of Appeal, points out how many uncertainties still remain, due not least to failure to agree on some issues among the judges in the Court of Appeal.

can only be breached by acts that stir up hatred against *believers*, rather than by attacks on *beliefs*.[11]

Addison, in a very useful study of the UK law, sums up the history of these provisions.[12] He notes that the offences apply to words that are 'threatening' (not simply insulting or abusive, as commentators had suggested about a previous version of the legislation), and that the offender has to 'intend' to stir up religious hatred. Interestingly, he notes that the Government's original proposals to make the offences wider were partly defeated in the House of Lords because of concerns that the UK law would end up like the law in Victoria that gave rise to the *Catch the Fire* litigation.[13]

In addition, there is a general provision protecting freedom of speech in s 29J of the *Public Order Act 1986*:

> **29J Protection of freedom of expression**
>
> Nothing in this Part shall be read or given effect in a way which prohibits or restricts discussion, criticism or expressions of antipathy, dislike, ridicule, insult or abuse of particular religions or the beliefs or practices of their adherents, or of any other belief system or the beliefs or practices of its adherents, or proselytising or urging adherents of a different religion or belief system to cease practising their religion or belief system.

This is a vital safeguard if this sort of legislation is to be introduced. It recognises among other things the importance of freedom of speech and freedom of religion, and the right noted under Art 18 of the Universal Declaration of Human Rights (UDHR), 'freedom to change his religion or belief' (as freedom to change clearly involves the freedom to hear the arguments for change).

Problems with religious vilification laws

The commentators previously cited have also noted the problems with such laws. Perhaps the most obvious and major problem is that these provisions amount to a severe restriction on freedom of speech. The right of freedom of speech, of course, is a right protected by international human rights instruments such as the UDHR, Art 19. But it is perhaps not so commonly noticed that, even in a jurisdiction such as Australia where there is currently no formal, broad-reaching protection of freedom of speech, the courts have regularly noted that the common law itself provides such a protection as a fundamental value.

---

[11] *Public Order Act 1986* (UK) ss 29A, 29B.
[12] Neil Addison, *Religious Discrimination and Hatred Law* (2007), esp ch 8.
[13] Addison, above n 12, 140.

In the High Court of Australia decision in *Australian Broadcasting Corporation v O'Neill* (2006) 227 CLR 57, the Court was wrestling with, among other things, the right of a person who was a convicted prisoner to prevent the broadcast of allegations that he had committed other crimes. In refusing to authorise the 'prior restraint' of publication, the majority in the High Court referred to the 'public interest in free communication of information and opinion'.[14]

Another example of the strength of the common law protection of freedom of speech is in the litigation generated by the 'World Youth Day' event in Sydney in 2008. In *Evans v NSW* [2008] FCAFC 130 a major ground for overturning restrictive regulations that had prohibited the 'annoying' of WYD participants was that they interfered (without explicit Parliamentary authority) with the fundamental common law right of freedom of speech.

In the Full Court of the Federal Court French, Branson and Stone JJ commented:

> Freedom of speech and of the press has long enjoyed **special recognition at common law**. Blackstone described it as 'essential to the nature of a free State': *Commentaries on the Laws of England*, Vol 4 at 151–152. …

> In its 1988 decision in *Davis v Commonwealth* (1988) 166 CLR 79, the High Court applied a principle supporting freedom of expression to the process of constitutional characterisation of a Commonwealth law. … In their joint judgment Mason CJ, Deane and Gaudron JJ (Wilson, Dawson and Toohey JJ agreeing) said (at 100):

> Here the framework of regulation … reaches far beyond the legitimate objects sought to be achieved and **impinges on freedom of expression** by enabling the Authority to regulate the use of common expressions and by making unauthorised use a criminal offence. Although the statutory regime may be related to a constitutionally legitimate end, the provisions in question reach too far. This extraordinary intrusion into freedom of expression is not reasonably and appropriately adapted to achieve the ends that lie within the limits of constitutional power …

> The present case is not about characterisation of a law for the purpose of assessing its validity under the Constitution of the Commonwealth. The judgments in *Davis* 166 CLR 79 however support the general proposition that **freedom of expression in Australia is a powerful consideration** favouring restraint in the construction of broad statutory power when the terms in which that power is conferred so allow.[15] [emphases added]

---

[14] *Australian Broadcasting Corporation v O'Neill* (2006) 227 CLR 57, [30] (Gleeson CJ and Crennan J).
[15] *Evans v NSW* [2008] FCAFC 130, [74–8].

The evidence in that case disclosed that Evans and other members of the public were planning to demonstrate against what they perceived to be bad policies and doctrines taught by the Roman Catholic Church. The challenged regulations would have restricted their right to do so by requiring them not to 'annoy' participants. The Federal Court held that these regulations should be struck down on the principle that the head legislation enacted by the NSW Parliament should not be interpreted, in the absence of express words, as allowing regulations to be made which interfered with this fundamental common law right.

The Court also incidentally referred to the fact that 'another important freedom generally accepted in Australian society is freedom of religious belief and expression',[16] supporting this by reference to the general terms of s 116 of the *Constitution*, and to Art 18 of the UDHR. This is a reminder that another problem with laws prohibiting religious vilification is that, where there is a danger that they may be interpreted as hampering the liberty to say that one's own religion is right and that others are wrong, then they also constitute impairment of the speaker's freedom of religion.

When these factors are coupled with pragmatic considerations concerning the enforcement of such laws, the case against the laws is particularly strong. A law that on its face seems designed to protect freedom of religious choice, may allow abuse of the law to attack others who are seeking to express their religion. Indeed, as Parkinson has pointed out, not only the precise terms of the legislation are important, but also the way that they are perceived:

> The law that impacts upon people's lives is not the law as enacted by parliaments, and not even the law as interpreted by the courts. What matters is the law as people believe it to be. This 'folklaw' may have only a tenuous connection with the law as enacted or applied in the courts. There is often a distorted effect as the perceived meaning of laws is spread through general communities of people who may not have a copy of the law itself or know the outcomes of cases they have heard are going through the courts.[17]

If speakers think that any public speech criticising other religious views is in danger of being prosecuted, then they will effectively 'self-censor', and public debate about important religious issues will shrink. Such debate, in the end, may be 'forced underground', where the lack of light being shone from the glare of publicity may end up entrenching prejudice and ignorance.

---

[16] Ibid [79].
[17] Parkinson, above n 2, 960.

There are a number of important philosophical questions about laws that impose restrictions on freedom of speech, as any law that prohibits certain types of speech will do. Some speech can clearly be regulated and penalised — classic examples include someone who shouts 'Fire!' in a crowded hall or someone who tells a lie that attacks an individual's reputation. But should the law go further and address speech that attacks others' beliefs?

The arguments of those who state that it would be best not to have anti-vilification laws based on religion at all are persuasive. Religion, unlike race or sex, is a matter that is fundamentally based on a person's acceptance of certain *propositions* about the universe. (The view that religious matters, being questions of 'faith', are beyond rational debate, is clearly wrong. Anyone who puts forward such a view needs to spend some time in dialogue with representatives of actual religions, which almost all argue that there are good *reasons* to adopt their position as opposed to others. This is certainly the case with religions such as Christianity and Islam.) In any serious religious debate there will be a challenge to the worldview of the hearers. To penalise speech connected with religion runs the grave risk that rational debate on religious matters will be 'driven underground', and hence that where there are disagreements they will be resolved in less rational ways.[18]

But is there any way of preventing those who would insult and verbally attack others on the basis of their religion? One possibility not often considered in the literature on this area is the tort of defamation.

Overview of the law of defamation

The law of defamation protects a person's reputation — in short, the interest that a person has in the views that others have of him or her. It has a long and chequered history, and has been the subject of lengthy development at common law, as well as various attempts over the years to codify or modify it by statute.[19]

---

[18] 'If Western nations do not defend free speech and religious freedom, then the open discourse required for a deliberative democracy will be choked off. As long as full religious freedom is absent, religious groups — including moderate Muslims — will face the threat of punishment for what is essentially a prohibition on blasphemy. This creates an atmosphere of fear that is never conducive to open, democratic debate. And if you don't have open, deliberative democracy, you can't peel off and correct the disaffected, i.e., those who turn to the world of the violent Islamists as an alternative': letter from Prof Carl H Esbeck, School of Law, University of Missouri, to author, 1 August 2009.

[19] For an overview of the history of the action in England and Australia, see P George, *Defamation Law in Australia* (2006) chs 2 and 3. There is also much helpful material in R P Balkin and J L R Davis, *Law of Torts* (4th ed, 2009) chs 17–19, with a brief historical overview at 519–22. For a more extensive historical study see P Mitchell, *The making of the modern law of defamation* (2005).

Currently, after a long period of debate, Australia has something resembling a uniform law of defamation after agreement by the various States. This (mostly) uniform legislation has generally been in operation since the beginning of 2006.[20] Here, I refer mainly to the NSW version, the *Defamation Act 2005* (NSW).[21]

The law of defamation is complex and controversial; it seeks to strike a balance between interests that are often competing: freedom of speech and protection of reputation. International human rights instruments recognise the importance of reputation and privacy, and of freedom of expression (for example, in Articles 17 and 19 of the *International Covenant on Civil and Political Rights* (ICCPR)).

The tort of defamation, then, gives people a right of action when their reputation has been diminished. However, some of the defences to the tort support freedom of speech, for those defences can override the plaintiff's claim of diminished reputation. The appropriate balance between these competing interests is not easy to achieve:

> If the balance is tilted too far in favour of protecting personal reputation, the danger is that the dissemination of information and public discourse will be stifled to an unhealthy degree. Conversely, if it is tilted too far in favour of freedom of expression there will be little to constrain people from lying, or exaggerating and distorting facts, and causing irreparable harm to the reputations of individuals.[22]

Interestingly, Gillooly argues that there is a 'third man' involved in cases where the defendant has made a statement to someone else about the plaintiff, whose interests *also* need to be considered: the recipient or potential recipient of the alleged defamatory statement.[23] He suggests to subsume the interests of recipients into the overall heading of 'public interest' is confusing, as the specifically intended recipient may have interests that weigh more than the 'general public'.

---

[20] For a brief overview of the changes made by the uniform legislation see Richard Potter, 'Defamation law goes national' (2006) 44 (1) (February) *Law Society Journal* 70.

[21] Note however that the Act is not a complete 'code'; a number of areas are left to be decided under principles developed by the courts at common law. These include, eg, what amounts to 'publication'; whether a meaning is conveyed by that publication; what constitutes defamatory character in a meaning. In addition, some defences available at common law may be relied upon by a defendant, although some are supplemented by provisions of the legislation, and the common law in relation to damages also remains largely applicable.

[22] SCAG Working Group of State and Territory Officers, 'Proposal for Uniform Defamation Laws' (Discussion Paper published by the Legislation and Policy Dvision of the NSW Attorney General's Department, July 2004) 6.

[23] M Gillooly, *The Third Man: Reform of the Australasian Defamation Defences* (2004).

The tort of defamation, like other tort actions, is defined by certain elements that need to be made out by the plaintiff to show a *prima facie* claim. In common with other actions, the law also provides a number of specific defences, the onus of establishing which lie on the defendant. Unlike many other torts, however, in defamation actions the defences are often the main point of dispute in the case.

This is because the elements of a *prima facie* case in defamation are in many cases not difficult to make out. Essentially, there are usually acknowledged to be three elements in a claim: that the plaintiff has been **defamed**, in the sense that their reputation has been attacked, that the plaintiff was **identified** clearly as the target of the attack, and that the defamatory material was **published** by the defendant, in the sense of it having been made available to someone else other than the plaintiff.[24]

Many of these areas raise complex issues that this chapter cannot address. But it is worth noting what makes a statement 'defamatory' at common law.[25] Many members of the community are familiar with the test developed in *Parmiter v Coupland* (1840) 6 M&W 105 at 108; 151 ER 340 at 342 that published matter is defamatory if it exposes the plaintiff to 'hatred, contempt or ridicule'.

More recently, however, it is common to refer to a statement made by Jordan CJ in *Consolidated Trust Co Ltd v Browne* (1948) 49 SR (NSW) 86 at 88:

> In NSW as a general rule it is illegal, under the law of defamation, to publish about a person anything which is likely to cause ordinary decent folk in the community, taken in general, to think the less of him.[26]

The common law test that has evolved now provides greater protection for people when disparaging statements are made about them. It is clearly easier to prove that published matter causes ordinary reasonable people to think less of the plaintiff, or to shun or avoid him or her,[27] than it is to prove that the plaintiff is the victim of hatred, contempt or ridicule.

---

[24] For example, see C Sappideen and P Vines (eds) *Fleming's Law of Torts* (10th ed, 2011) [25.160]: 'If a plaintiff establishes that defamatory matter has been published about him or her, he or she has established a prina facie claim for defamation.'

[25] For a recent detailed analysis of the notion of 'reputation' in defamation law, see L McNamara, *Reputation and Defamation* (2007).

[26] See also Beaumont J in the more recent decision of *Random House Australia Pty Ltd v Abbott* [1999] FCA 1538, (1999) 94 FCR 296, [22].

[27] Old cases establish that the 'shunning' effect may be relevant even if no-one would cast personal blame on the subject of the statement — eg, *Youssoupoff v Metro-Goldwyn-Mayer Pictures Ltd* (1934) 50 TLR 581 where it was defamatory to say that the plaintiff had been raped, as at that stage it would have led to her being 'shunned' by others.

It is not entirely clear whether simply exposing someone to 'ridicule' is defamatory or not.[28] One principle often cited is that words that are simply 'vulgar abuse' will not normally be defamatory. To make outrageously insulting remarks that no one listening to would take seriously, will usually not be defamatory, however much they may hurt someone's feelings.[29]

In the UK in the case of *Berkoff v Burchill and anor* [1997] EMLR 139 it was held to be defamatory to state that an actor was 'horrendously ugly', but there has been much debate about whether this decision was correct or not. However, some cases in Australia have suggested that exposing someone to ridicule (for example, by publishing an embarrassing photograph of them)[30] may be defamatory, so the question may still be open.

If the above three elements of the tort have been made out, it is then up to the defendant to make out one of the defences that are provided by the law. In broad terms, and simplifying somewhat, the main defences that can be relied on today under the uniform legislation are:

(1) ***truth***: that the matter which was published is either wholly or substantially true[31]

(2) ***honest opinion***: that the matter was the honest expression of opinion by the defendant, not a statement of fact[32]

(3) ***privilege***: that the matter was published either in a forum where the law provides complete protection of free speech (under ***absolute privilege***, such as in Parliament or a court room) or was published in circumstances where the law recognises what is called a ***'qualified' privilege***. Such a privilege arises either where the defendant had a duty to make a statement for some reason, and

---

[28] For a detailed analysis see McNamara, above n 25, ch 7.
[29] See *Mundey v Askin* [1982] 2 NSWLR 369, where the plaintiffs were called 'vermin', and comments by Bryson JA on the issue of 'vulgar abuse' in *Bennette v Cohen* (2005) 64 NSWLR 81, [46–56]. As noted there, words 'might injure a man's pride without injuring his reputation'.
[30] See *Ettingshausen v Australian Consolidated Press* (1991) 23 NSWLR 443, where the court accepted that a photograph of the plaintiff football player which showed him naked could be regarded as defamatory on the basis that it had exposed him to ridicule; the case was followed in *Obermann v ACP Publishing Pty Limited* [2001] NSWSC 1022.
[31] See *Defamation Act 2005* (NSW) s 25. There is also a related defence of 'contextual truth' in s 26, where statements which are made on the same occasion as those complained of are true, and given their truth the statements that are complained of do no further harm to the plaintiff's reputation.
[32] See *Defamation Act 2005* (NSW) s 31. The defence was previously called 'fair comment'. It will be defeated if the statement in context would be understood as a statement of fact, rather than an expression of opinion; if it is not on a matter of 'public interest'; if it is not based on 'proper material'; or if it is shown not to be an opinion honestly held by the defendant.

the recipients had a duty or interest to hear it; or under statutory provisions, where the recipients had an 'interest' in receiving the communication, and it was published 'reasonably'.[33] In addition, under current Australian law there is a further situation where 'qualified privilege' arises, where the communication is on a matter of political interest[34]

(4) *triviality*: that the matter in the context in which it was published is not likely to have caused any harm (where, for example, it was a statement made in a private social context to a small group of people).[35]

In addition to these formal defences, the legislation now contains a provision whereby a defendant may avoid liability by an appropriately speedy 'offer to make amends', which will usually include some sort of published correction or apology.[36]

Defamation on the basis of religion

The above commentary is only a superficial overview of the law of defamation, but it deals with a number of issues that are mentioned by the vilification provisions referred to previously. The similarities and differences between the provisions are worth noting.

Defamation and religious vilification compared

Areas of *similarity* between the two are that both are concerned with words that 'inspire hatred or contempt'. The classic definition of 'defamation', as noted above, refers to 'hatred, contempt or ridicule'. The Australian legislative provisions refer to 'hatred towards, serious contempt for, or severe ridicule of' persons (the Victorian provisions add 'revulsion', which seems not to be very different from the other concepts).[37]

In fact, the law of civil defamation sets a lower barrier than the vilification provisions. Requiring more recently that a statement simply 'cause ordinary decent folk in the community, taken in general, to think the less of' the plaintiff allows a wider range of speech acts to be taken into account. The addition of words like 'serious' and 'severe' in the legislation seems to clearly signal that it will be harder to make out a case of vilification than it will be to succeed in a defamation action.

---

[33] See *Defamation Act 2005* (NSW) s 30.
[34] Implementing the implied freedom of political communication spelled out by the High Court in *Lange v Australian Broadcasting Corporation* (1997) 189 CLR 520.
[35] See *Defamation Act 2005* (NSW) s 33.
[36] See *Defamation Act 2005* (NSW) Pt 3, Div 1.
[37] See the legislation noted at above n 4.

Another similarity is that both the common law of defamation and the statutory provisions about religious vilification provide a civil legal remedy to someone who is the subject of remarks by a defendant. A civil remedy allows the award of damages. The amount of damages, and the basis on which damages are assessed, may not be the same, but usually some amount of money can be ordered by the court to be paid by the defendant, an order that will not only provide some material compensation for the harm suffered but will also mark the community's disapproval of the defendant's behaviour.

There are, however, a number of important *differences* between the action for defamation and an action for religious vilification. One that I have noted already is that an action for defamation will be available in relation to a range of what might be called 'less offensive' speech than the vilification action.

But the most obvious difference is that, in an action for defamation, the plaintiff must be able to demonstrate that he or she, *in particular*, was identified as the subject of the defamatory statement. By contrast, an action for religious vilification seems to be available to anyone who belongs to a particular 'class of persons' or 'group of persons'. Each of these aspects of the two actions warrants further examination.

In Australia the High Court laid down the following some years ago about a statement that does not specifically name someone, in *David Syme & Co v Canavan* (1918) 25 CLR 234:

> The test of whether words that do not specifically name the respondent refer to him or not is this: Are they such as reasonably in the circumstances would lead persons acquainted with the plaintiff to believe he was the person referred to?[38]

The decision of the House of Lords in *Knupffer v London Express Newspaper, Ltd* [1944] AC 116 held that a plaintiff who was a member of a 'Young Russia' group could not sue for defamation in relation to a newspaper article that referred generally to the group around the world. In that case the class was so large that it was not possible for the particular plaintiff to claim that he personally had been defamed. However, the House of Lords was careful to say that there was no general rule about 'defamation of a class' — it was a question in each case, as Lord Atkin in particular emphasised, whether 'the defamatory words must be understood to be published of and concerning the plaintiff' (at 121). If the words were spoken 'of a large or indeterminate number of persons described by some general name', then it will usually be difficult to show that they refer to the plaintiff (at 122). But there may be cases where even words spoken of a large number might sufficiently identify the plaintiff. There is a fascinating aside by Lord Porter near the end of his judgment:

---

[38] *David Syme & Co v Canavan* (1918) 25 CLR 234, 238.

In deciding this question the size of the class, the generality of the charge and the extravagance of the accusation may all be elements to be taken into consideration, but none of them is conclusive. Each case must be considered according to its own circumstances. I can imagine it being said that each member of a body, however large, was defamed where the libel consisted in the assertion that no one of the members of a community was elected as a member unless he had committed a murder.[39]

It is interesting to speculate on what makes the difference in this last example. Is it the seriousness of the allegation? The judgment gives no further guidance.

Other cases based on defamation of a large group have failed for this reason of failing to 'identify' the specific plaintiff. In *Mann v Medicine Group Pty Ltd* (1992) 38 FCR 400, an attack on 'all bulk-billing doctors' was found not to be specific enough to be sued on by one doctor. The case is interesting for its careful discussion of the principles relating to defamation of a group, and for the strong dissent in the Full Court of the Federal Court by Miles J. But it illustrates that the principles spelled out in *Knupffer* are still applied in Australia.

In *Gauthier v Toronto Star Daily Newspapers Ltd* (2004) 245 D.L.R. (4th) 169, the Ontario Court of Appeal upheld a trial judge's striking out of a defamation action brought by members of the Toronto Police Force in response to newspaper articles referring to 'Toronto police' as 'racist'. The articles were general in nature and could not be read as referring to any individual member of the force.

But in other cases, actions by unnamed group members have succeeded. In *Jackson v TCN Channel 9* [2001] NSWCA 108, a statement that referred to 'outlaw motorcycle gangs' was held to be actionable at the instance of a member of the 'Rebels' motorcycle club, where it was broadcast on television accompanied by a picture of the plaintiff. This seems to be a clear example of the principle that a plaintiff may sue where specifically identified. But it is interesting to note the further comments of Handley JA, on the common example given in the cases that the statement 'all lawyers are thieves' would not be actionable by any one lawyer:

> While 'all lawyers' are members of the same profession, they are not members of a cohesive and disciplined group with a command structure such as a gang. The statement about 'all lawyers' is an obvious over-generalisation which no reasonable reader or listener would understand applied or was intended to apply literally to every single member of the group.

---

[39] *Knupffer v London Express Newspaper, Ltd* [1944] AC 116, 124.

On the other hand outlaw bikie gangs of the type described in the programme would only attract and retain members who accepted and were willing to conform to the prevailing culture and ethos of the gang. In my judgment the statements made in this programme are akin to statements about organised groups such as the SS, the Klu Klux Klan or the Mafia, rather than statements such as: 'all lawyers are thieves'. It would be well open to a jury to conclude that general statements made about groups such as those applied, and would be understood to apply, to every member of those groups.[40]

The question, in other words, may be resolved in favour of a member of a group being able to sue if the nature of the group is such that one would expect all members to strictly conform to some standard said to apply to the group as a whole. It must be said, however, that other members of the Court did not specifically adopt these views.

The application of these general principles to members of a religious group can be seen in the Canadian decision of *Bai v Sing Tao Daily Ltd* (2003) 226 DLR (4th) 477. In that case, a defamation action brought by a number of members of the 'Falun Gong' religious group failed, where the newspaper articles in question did not refer to them individually. McMurty CJO in the Ontario Court of Appeal commented:

There is nothing to distinguish the appellants from the class of all Falun Gong practitioners throughout the world. In this context, I am of the view that, the succinct endorsement of Justice Zuber in *Sun Tanner's Image v. White* (September 12, 2000), Doc. Windsor 00-GD-4893 (Ont. S.C.J.), affirmed at (Ont. C.A.), provides a helpful approach:

'It is necessary that the plaintiffs show that they are identified or singled out. The words clearly do not identify the plaintiffs. Further it is not pleaded that the class is so small that the plaintiffs are necessarily identified and would lead one to believe that the plaintiffs are the target of the words. As a result this action must fail and the claim is dismissed.'[41]

This may be seen, then, as an example of a 'gap' in the law that the law of religious vilification may fill. But the fundamental question is whether there is indeed such a gap.

---

[40] *Jackson v TCN Channel 9* [2001] NSWCA 108, 23–4.
[41] *Bai v Sing Tao Daily Ltd* (2003) 226 DLR (4th) 477, 14.

When an individual's reputation is attacked, then it seems perfectly fair that they should have an action to defend themselves, and to seek damages. But where an attack is made on a wide group, then the 'sting' of the attack is dissipated across that group. The question that needs to be asked is whether, given that there are strong competing values of freedom of speech involved, the harm that is occasioned in such a weakened form is one that the law should provide a remedy for?

The ancient Romans used to attack Christians on the basis that they committed incest (as they said that they 'loved' those they called 'brother' and 'sister'), or that they were guilty of cannibalism (in that they participated in meetings where Jesus' words about 'eating my body' and 'drinking my blood' were repeated).[42] If such an attack occurred today, should a Christian have a remedy?

I would support a criminal remedy where a speaker got up in a public square and said 'Neilus Fosterius is a follower of the Nazarene, is a cannibal and we should go to his house and kill him now!' That, under Australian law, would be an unlawful incitement to violence. I would support the availability of an action for defamation where the speaker simply said, 'Neilus Fosterius is a follower of the Nazarene, and is a cannibal', because I could demonstrate that the allegation of cannibalism (which would be untrue) would lead my Roman neighbours to 'think less of me' at the very least, and because the attack is targeted at me alone.

But if a speaker in a public square said 'All followers of the Nazarene are cannibals', I do not think I ought to have a *legal* remedy. I will then be able to go into the same public square and argue against him, and I will have the support of my fellow believers. And the opportunity for dialogue will hopefully provide an opportunity for proclamation of the gospel about Jesus.

The only qualification one might want to add is that it would perhaps be best if there were a legal remedy when the religious group was very small, with very little opportunity or resources to respond to insult or denigration. But it is interesting to note that in the cases on 'defamation of a group' the courts continue to assert that there is no 'bright line' rule, and that the size of a group is one of the relevant factors. The principle is simply that there is a defamatory statement about the plaintiff where the words are be 'published of and concerning the plaintiff' (*Knupffer*), and where there are only a few members of a group, and the plaintiff is known to be one of the members, then an allegation (particularly a highly damaging allegation) concerning the whole group, could not unreasonably be seen specifically to apply to the plaintiff for the purposes of the law of defamation.

---

[42] See Minucius Felix, 'Octavius' in *The Ante-Nicene Fathers Volume 4* (R E Wallis trans, 1887) 177–8.

It is also interesting to compare the defences that are available in the two causes of action. Perhaps the most glaring difference, and the most objectionable, is that there is no defence of 'truth' available under the vilification legislation. Neave JA commented in the *Catch the Fire* appeal that:

> Section 11 of the Racial and Religious Tolerance Act ... does not provide that the fact that words are true takes them outside s.8 of the Act.[43]

Under the vilification legislation, the available defences (which differ between the States) may be summarised as 'fair report', 'absolute privilege', 'public interest discussion', or 'artistic exhibition':

- 'publication of a fair report of a public act' (Qld, s 124A(2)(a)); 'fair report of a public act' (Tas, s 55(a)); something done 'reasonably and in good faith', 'in making or publishing a fair and accurate report of any event or matter of public interest' (Vic, s 11(1)(c))

- 'publication of material in circumstances in which the publication would be subject to a defence of absolute privilege in proceedings for defamation' (Qld, s 124A(2)(b)); 'a communication or dissemination of a matter that is subject to a defence of absolute privilege in proceedings for defamation' (Tas, s 55(b))

- a 'public act, done reasonably and in good faith, for academic, artistic, scientific or research purposes or for other purposes in the public interest, including public discussion or debate about, and expositions of, any act or matter' (Qld, s 124A(2)(c)); 'a public act done in good faith for – (i) academic, artistic, scientific or research purposes; or (ii) any purpose in the public interest' (Tas, s 55(c)); something done 'reasonably and in good faith', 'in the course of any statement, publication, discussion or debate made or held, or any other conduct engaged in, for – (i) any genuine academic, artistic, religious or scientific purpose; or (ii) any purpose that is in the public interest (Vic, s 11(1)(b))

- something done 'reasonably and in good faith', 'in the performance, exhibition or distribution of an artistic work' (Vic, s 11(1)(a)).

Note the obvious point that at least some of these defences are merely a repetition of those available under the law of defamation — those relating to occasions of 'absolute privilege', for example (where statements are made in parliament or before certain courts and tribunals). The defence of 'fair report' also parallels very closely the defence available under the uniform defamation legislation that allows a defence of a 'fair report

---

[43] [2006] VSCA 284, [178].

of proceedings of public concern'.[44] The vilification defence is actually wider than that available under the defamation laws; the 'public act' that can be the subject of a 'fair report' in Queensland and Tasmania seems to be the act which itself incites hatred, and so on. So it seems, though there are no cases on the matter, that a speaker at a rally who says vilificatory words can be sued, but the newspaper or TV station that repeats those words the next day cannot be sued. Indeed, it would seem that another speaker who prefaced their remarks by 'this is what was said yesterday' could also avoid liability.

Victoria also has a specific defence relating to artistic works. It seems likely that this reflects the sensitivities involved by the exhibition of a controversial exhibition in Victoria, and action that was taken to stop the exhibition.[45] The result, however, is an interesting illustration of the weighing of public values by the Victorian Parliament. A believer may have hatred, serious contempt, revulsion or ridicule incited against them or their group without legal recourse, so long as it is done in the name of 'art'. For some reason, freedom of speech applies to artists, but not to authors, preachers, or public speakers.

The final broad category of defence in all the jurisdictions almost defies summary. Common themes are that the purposes that are seen as legitimate include academic and scientific 'research' — and 'research' generally. But they extend to 'other purposes in the public interest', or 'public discussion or debate about, and expositions of, any act or matter'. The Queensland provision in particular is so broad that it seems hard to find any occasion for speech or writing that will not fall within the defence. For this reason, the important operative words in all the provisions seem to be 'reasonably and in good faith'.

But the *Catch the Fire* litigation illustrates the difficulty with such a broad discretion being left to the courts. Is it acting 'reasonably and in good faith' for a religious speaker, when urging the truth of their own beliefs, to present an 'unbalanced' account of another faith? Does a speaker depart from this standard when in some other context they have exaggerated their own qualifications or the extent of their publications? As Ahdar notes, these matters counted against the pastor in that case and led the original tribunal to find that the comments made in the seminar were not made 'in good faith'. Ahdar comments:

> It is troubling that a preacher's misleading characterisation of works he had authored should somehow lead to the conclusion that his beliefs about a religion were not his real beliefs. Even more disquieting is a secular tribunal's determination that where a religious leader had misconstrued and misrepresented another religion's sacred writings,

---

[44] See, eg, *Defamation Act 2005* (NSW) s 29.
[45] See *Pell v Council of Trustees of the National Gallery of Victoria* [1997] VSC 52.

this also indicated an absence of honest belief. A wrong interpretation of scripture does not necessarily point to dishonest intent and, moreover, a secular body ought not to be trying to rule on what are correct and honest representations of sacred writings.[46]

In short, this defence and others like it are so unclear, and so difficult to interpret in advance of litigation, that they will have the effect of 'chilling' religious speech in many cases.

Examples of defamation and religion cases

It is worth noting briefly that the law of defamation is already used in the context of religious bodies and persons. Where a plaintiff has been clearly identified and attacked in a way that causes other persons to think less of them, then they have a chance to sue for damages. In response, the defendant has an opportunity to argue that what they said was true, or that it was legitimate expression of an honest opinion, or that it was made on an occasion where free speech should be encouraged because there is a duty to speak, or that one of the other available defences is applicable. Just by way of illustration, and without any necessary comment on whether or not these decisions are correct, I cite three recent cases.

Plenty v Dickson [2009] SASC 9 (19 January 2009) was part of the most recent stage of long-lasting litigation generated by the 'disfellowshipping' of Mr and Mrs Plenty from their Seventh Day Adventist congregation in 1979. These proceedings were the conclusion of defamation proceedings, where the court awarded the Plentys $10,000 in damages based on a letter published in a newspaper referring to the events. The letter referred to 'continuing attitudes and actions which were felt contrary to church standards of behaviour'. The judge concluded that this was defamatory:

> Members of the church are committed to a strict code of behaviour and the plaintiffs were disfellowshipped for an alleged failure to abide by that code. However, Mr Dickson's letter has to be judged from the position of the average reasonable reader. To such a reader, the phrase 'continuing attitudes and actions which were felt contrary to church standards of behaviour' could well imply conduct more serious than the allegations that led to the disfellowshipping. It is relevant to take into account the circulation of the newspaper and the effect that the publication appears to have had on the plaintiffs.[47]

---

[46] Ahdar, above n 2, 313.
[47] *Plenty v Dickson* [2009] SASC 9 (19 January 2009), [8].

The Court of Appeal rejected appeals against the amount of damages made by the Plentys, holding that the amount of damages awarded was reasonable.

In *Ayan v Islamic Co-ordinating Council of Victoria Pty Ltd and ors* [2009] VSC 119 (3 April 2009), the ICCV were involved in 'halal' certification of abattoirs (that animals had been killed in accordance with Islamic law), and were in dispute with the plaintiff. They published a letter to various abattoirs alleging that Mr Ayan was claiming to be authorised by the Australian Quarantine Service to provide Halal certificates. In fact, the plaintiff was authorised to carry out various procedures but did not claim to be authorised by AQIS.

The Court ruled that the letters were defamatory, that no defence of truth was available, and that no defence of qualified privilege was available. The defendants relied on the defence of 'qualified privilege' partly on the basis that their aim was to communicate the results of an independent report into the Halal industry. But in fact, the report did not support the claims in the letter, and Beach J commented that:

> It is well settled that an occasion of qualified privilege must not be used for some purpose or motive foreign to the interest that protects the making of the statement. Further, there must be a significant connection between the defamatory material and the privileged occasion.[48]

Perhaps the issues being discussed here are raised most sharply in *Trad v Harbour Radio Pty Ltd* [2009] NSWSC 750. The plaintiff, who had been seen as a spokesman for the Muslim community in Sydney at some stages, sued the proprietors of radio station 2GB for comments made about him on a talkback radio show. The comments arose out of a 'peace rally' that the plaintiff had addressed following the infamous 'Cronulla riots', which, as McClellan CJ noted, 'were perceived by many people as a confrontation between adherents to the Muslim faith and persons of Caucasian heritage'.[49] Part of the thrust of the remarks made by the plaintiff was an attack on 2GB as in part responsible for stirring up ill feeling against Muslims and contributing to the violence. The comments upon which the plaintiffs sued were made in response to that general attack, and partly in response to the fact that when a 2GB reporter was present at the rally, there was what seemed a very direct attempt to incite the crowd to ill feeling against 2GB.

---

[48] *Ayan v Islamic Co-ordinating Council of Victoria Pty Ltd and ors* [2009] VSC 119 (3 April 2009), [42]. See generally *Andreyevich v Kosovich and Publicity Press (1938) Pty Ltd* (1947) 47 SR(NSW) 357, *Roberts v Bass* (2002) 212 CLR 1, *Bashford v Information Australia (Newsletter) Pty Ltd* (2004) 218 CLR 366 and *Bennette v Cohen* [2009] NSWCA 60.

[49] *Trad v Harbour Radio Pty Ltd* [2009] NSWSC 750, [6].

The judgment is lengthy and raises a number of important issues. Briefly, a jury had been impanelled under the then-applicable procedure in NSW,[50] and had found that the comments of the announcer had contained imputations that the plaintiff was guilty of a number of things (including 'inciting people to acts of violence' and 'inciting people to have racist attitudes'), and also that 'the plaintiff [was] a dangerous individual' and 'a disgraceful individual'.[51]

The defence of truth used by the defendant meant that the court had to assess the truth or otherwise of the comment that the plaintiff was 'disgraceful'. McClellan CJ noted that this raised issues of 'some complexity'.[52] His Honour ruled that this required him to apply 'general community standards' to the proved behaviour of the plaintiff.[53] However, he also noted that he could take into account legislation prohibiting discrimination and racism in determining the content of those community standards.[54]

His Honour then referred to a number of matters that had been brought forward by the defendant to support their allegation that the plaintiff was 'disgraceful' by community standards. Many of those matters were not related to the specific words that had been uttered at the rally, but were drawn from statements made by the plaintiff on other occasions in the past, and in particular from statements made by Sheikh Taj el-Din al-Hilali who had held the position of 'Mufti of Australia', and whose spokesman the plaintiff had been for some years. In effect, his Honour noted a number of highly controversial statements made by Sheikh al-Hilali, and the fact that the plaintiff had associated himself with, or not dissociated himself from, those statements was taken into account. Statements made by the Sheikh of this sort included comments associating unveiled women with 'cat's meat' (and implying that some women bear responsibility for their own rape),[55] statements arguably expressing support for the stoning of a woman for adultery in Nigeria,[56] and statements made in a sermon at a mosque in Lebanon arguably supporting the September 11 2001 attacks and the use of children as martyrs in the cause of Islam.[57] Material either referred to with approval on the plaintiff's website, or directly written by him, was

---

[50] *Defamation Act* 1974 (NSW) s 7A (applicable because the events occurred before the commencement of the uniform legislation). While this specific procedure is no longer applicable, on the whole the law as to what amounts to defamation, and the relevant defences, has not changed from that being considered by the judge.
[51] *Trad v Harbour Radio Pty Ltd* [2009] NSWSC 750, [2].
[52] Ibid [13].
[53] See ibid [16–17].
[54] Ibid [20].
[55] See ibid [27–42].
[56] See ibid [43–51].
[57] See ibid [52–58].

also used by the court. In the end, the court ruled that most of the imputations made against the plaintiff by 2GB, including that of being a 'disgraceful' and 'dangerous' individual, were proven to be true.

The court found some of the imputations made were untrue (such as the specific claim that 'the plaintiff stirred up hatred against a 2GB reporter' or 'the plaintiff is widely perceived as a pest'). But the court found that the defence of 'contextual truth' applied, so that even though these remarks were not true, given that they were made in a context where much more serious allegations were made out, they did not further harm the plaintiff's reputation.[58]

While not necessary given the success of the other defences, the court also held that the defendant would have been able to make out a defence of 'qualified privilege', which applies when someone is responding to a prior attack that has been made by the plaintiff.[59]

On later appeal, in *Trad v Harbour Radio Pty Ltd* [2011] NSWCA 61 (22 March 2011) the Court of Appeal (Tobias, McColl & Basten JJA) overturned the lower findings on a number of points. The main point they relied on was that even if Mr Trad held views that many other Australians would disagree with, the judge had not asked whether 'a right-thinking member of the Australian community' would consider him to be 'disgraceful' or the other terms that were applied.[60]

Nevertheless, the case illustrates the common law courts are able, when required, to enter the arena of robust comment about religious issues. None of the issues in the case precisely raise the question of vilification on the grounds of religion — indeed, the radio commentator was very careful to say that Mr Trad in his view was not representative of the Muslim community and was responsible for 'misinformation about the Islamic community'. But the court was able to deal with, and make reasoned judgments on, specific claims about someone who spoke on religious issues.[61]

---

[58] See discussion, ibid [125-30]. The defence of contextual truth is also available under s 26 of the *Defamation Act 2005* (NSW).
[59] See [132-47], also holding that the defence was not defeated by any allegation of 'malice'. A further defence of 'fair comment' was upheld but with more hesitation.
[60] See, eg, [2011] NSWCA 61, [84].
[61] For a more recent decision raising important issues about the law of defamation and religious communities, see *Haddon v Forsythe* [2011] NSWSC 123 (8 March 2011), where a defence of 'qualified privilege' was upheld in relation to an email sent by the rector of a church (and copied in to other church leaders) asking a member of the congregation not to continue harassing female members of the church, based on past patterns of behaviour.

Conclusion

This chapter has only been able to raise the issues here in a limited way. It would be worthwhile, for example, to conduct further research on other situations that are analogous to religious vilification that have come before courts in defamation actions in the past.

But I hope that it has at least raised the possibility that what is seen as a 'gap' in the legal protection of rights may not be as broad as some have suggested. Where speech is aimed at producing violence it ought to be punished by the criminal law. Where speech attacks the reputation of individuals and can be shown to do so falsely and without the protection provided by the law of defamation for free speech, then an action should lie. But I argue that further protection of 'religious sensibilities' by the enactment of general 'religious vilification' laws is not only unnecessary, but may positively impair both freedom of speech and freedom of religion.

6

Should an Australian Bill of Rights Address Emerging International Human Rights Norms? The Challenge of 'Defamation of Religion'

Robert C Blitt*

The decision to draft a bill of rights heralds a momentous event in any country's history. In the latter half of the twentieth century, crafting a document that addresses the fundamental rights of individuals and groups and their relationship to the state has typically involved a flurry of public consultations, negotiations, drafting, and rewrites. Increasingly, however, such endeavours remain incomplete without some effort to observe, understand, and account for comparative trends related to human rights on the international level as well as in other states. Although writing about constitutions specifically, A E Dick Howard's observations are equally relevant to standalone bills of rights:

> The international human rights revolution has had undeniable impact upon comparative constitutionalism. It is hard to imagine drafters of a new constitution going about their task unconcerned about human rights standards ... For half a century, the Universal Declaration of Human Rights has served as a model for constitution makers. Countless constitutions written since 1948 contain guarantees that either mirror or draw upon the Declaration.[1]

---

* This chapter is a revised and updated version of an earlier previously published article, 'Should New Bills of Rights Address Emerging International Human Rights Norms? The Challenge of "Defamation of Religion"' 9 *North Western University Journal of International Human Rights* 1.

[1] A E Dick Howard, 'A Traveler from an Antique Land: the Modern Renaissance of Comparative Constitutionalism' (2009) 50 *Virginia Journal of International Law* 18.

Numerous examples across a wide range of states confirm this tilt in favour of consulting international norms.[2] Recent drafting efforts in Iraq,[3] Afghanistan,[4] New Zealand,[5] South Africa,[6] and all the states of the former Soviet Union and Warsaw Pact[7] leap to mind, to name but a few. In each of these cases — and with varying degrees of success — national drafters held their country's unique cultural, historical, and political experiences up against the collective database of international experiences to divine commonalities, mutual priorities, shared aspirations, and points of divergence. Although no bright line rule has emerged requiring states drafting new bills of rights to undertake such a comparative assessment or import wholesale the standards contained in the major international human rights instruments, the pattern of consultation and endorsement is undeniable, and may even signal an emerging international customary norm.[8] Indeed, in the past, the European Union has made diplomatic recognition of states conditional on their willingness to pledge

---

[2] The majority of these states integrated bills of rights into their new constitutional documents. New Zealand focused exclusively on drafting a standalone bill of rights.

[3] Though ultimately deleted from Iraq's 2005 constitution, a draft version contained a provision that would have explicitly provided individuals 'the rights contained in international human rights agreements to which Iraq is a party as long as those rights did not contradict the provisions of the constitution': Ashley S Deeks and Matthew D Burton, 'Iraq's Constitution: a Drafting History' (2007) 40 *Cornell International Law Journal* 32. The final constitutional text specifies that Iraq 'shall observe the principles of good neighborliness ... and respect its international obligations': *Iraq Constitution* art 8.

[4] Afghanistan's constitution requires the state to 'abide by the UN charter, international treaties, international conventions that Afghanistan has signed, and the Universal Declaration of Human Rights': *Afghanistan Constitution* art 7.

[5] New Zealand's 1990 Bill of Rights stipulates that one of its purposes is to 'affirm New Zealand's commitment to the International Covenant on Civil and Political Rights': *New Zealand Bill of Rights Act 1990* (NZ).

[6] It is widely acknowledged that South Africa's constitution drafting process borrowed from international treaties, national constitutions and international and foreign jurisprudence: Jeremy Sarkin, 'The Effect of Constitutional Borrowings on the Drafting of South Africa's Bill of Rights and Interpretation of Human Rights Provisions' (1998) 1 *University of Pennsylvania Journal of Constitutional Law* 176, 177.

[7] In central and eastern Europe generally, international law, including the Universal Declaration of Human Rights (UDHR) and the International Covenant on Civil and Political Rights (ICCPR), was 'universally perceived' as one of the most important sources of human rights used for modelling new constitutional regulations: Wiktor Osiatynski, 'Rights In New Constitutions of East Central Europe' (1994) 26 *Columbia Human Rights Law Review* 111, 161.

[8] This chapter is limited to exploring the relevancy of one potentially emerging international human rights norm on a possible future bill of rights for Australia. The larger question of whether states may be obligated to incorporate international human rights standards under customary international law when drafting a bill of rights is set aside for another occasion.

respect for human rights and provide legal 'guarantees for the rights of ethnic and national groups and minorities'.[9]

Along this line of reasoning, a further issue arises as to whether established international standards represent the normative ceiling or only the floor. Should states engaged in a bill of rights drafting process aspire to adopt not only minimalist existing norms but also emerging ones that arguably embody the natural normative extension of human rights but have yet to become entrenched? As Jacek Kurczewski and Barry Sullivan point out, the notion of minimum standards in human rights law 'dialectically entails as well the notion of something more demanding than the minimum — that is, the possible expansion of rights to which people are entitled'.[10] From this perspective, many additional questions follow: How much further should a state go? What is the international status of cutting-edge issues such as intersex and transsexual rights, the right to an adequate standard of living,[11] and migrant rights? What, if anything, should a newly drafted bill of rights say on these issues?

At least in part, these questions can be addressed procedurally within the discussion over whether the bill of rights will be a succinctly worded statement that takes a general approach, or a longer document that engages specificities. Substantively, however, drafters also have a duty to inform themselves of what, if any, emerging human rights issues are relevant, and how they should be addressed.

Using this understanding as a point of departure, this chapter posits that beginning the arduous task of drafting a bill of rights from a standpoint of openness toward comparativism and engagement with international norms affords the process several advantages. First, it informs the public at large that the discussion over the nature and scope of rights does not occur in the vacuum of domestic politics alone, but rather implicates larger ideas relevant to humanity as a whole.[12] Second, it allows a state the ability to consciously check any drafted domestic standards against its pre-existing international obligations under treaty or customary law. This in turn affords drafters an opportunity from the outset to furnish clear answers for basic

---

[9] *Declaration on the 'Guidelines on the Recognition of New States in Eastern Europe and in the Soviet Union'* (Extraordinary EPC Ministerial Meeting, Brussels, 16 December 1991) (1992) 31 ILM 1485, 1487.

[10] Jacek Kurczewski and Barry Sullivan, 'The Bill of Rights and the Emerging Democracies' (2002) 65 *Law and Contemporary Problems* 251, 259.

[11] Australia's National Human Rights Consultation Report has recommended that 'if economic and social rights are listed in a federal Human Rights Act, those rights not be justiciable and that complaints be heard by the Australian Human Rights Commission': National Human Rights Consultation, Commonwealth of Australia, *National Human Rights Consultation Report* (2009), xxxv ('National Human Rights Consultation').

[12] By this, I simply mean that one state's drafting process and resulting bill of rights may in the future inform the drafting process of the next state contemplating a new or revised bill of rights.

questions such as whether international or regional human rights treaty obligations will be directly enforceable on the municipal level. Even where existing treaty rights are determined to be non-justiciable, drafters can still test to what extent proposed domestic standards measure up against international norms.[13] Finally, exploring comparative and international experiences situates the debate in a broader context that is necessarily more diverse, more informative, and more comprehensive. By plugging into this fecund ideascape, drafters can build up a robust domestic understanding of the content of rights and their related limitations, the dynamics of public-private and individual-group relationships, and the existing mechanisms for balancing competing interests where inevitable conflicts may arise. Related to this, exploring comparative and international sources affords the benefit of alerting drafters to emerging rights or norms that otherwise might not figure in the domestic debate, providing additional opportunity to tweak the proposed language. Ultimately, such efforts — although more time-consuming and complex — can challenge pre-existing ideas and limitations, resulting in a more vibrant drafting process and more thoroughly 'beta-tested' final product.

With these advantages in mind, the following chapter considers the emerging norm of 'defamation of religion' — one recent flashpoint in the international human rights dialogue — in the context of a hypothetical bill of rights drafting process in Australia. Incorporating an earnest assessment of comparative experiences and benchmarks into a bill of rights drafting process is a natural and worthy step for the government of Australia, particularly in light of the country's long history of international engagement[14] and its ongoing commitment to international human rights.[15] This approach also respects the stated desire of many Australians to ensure their government 'protect[s] and promote[s] all the human rights reflected in its obligations under

---

[13] This advantage comports with the Australian Human Rights Commission's existing mandate, which includes 'making human rights values part of everyday life and language' and 'keeping government accountable to national and international human rights standards': *About the Commission* (2010) Australian Human Rights Commission <http://www.hreoc.gov.au/about/index.html> at 22 March 2011.

[14] For example, H V Evatt, an Australian, served as President of the UN General Assembly during the adoption and proclamation of the Universal Declaration of Human Rights. Australia was an original signatory to that Declaration: *Doc Evatt: A brilliant & controversial character* (2009) The Evatt Foundation <http://evatt.labor.net.au/about_evatt/> at 22 March 2011.

[15] Australia is a state party to all but two of the nine main human rights treaties, and it regularly reports to each of the bodies responsible for overseeing the implementation of these treaties. Australia has not signed or ratified the *International Convention on the Protection of the Rights of All Migrant Workers and Members of their Families*, opened for signature 18 December 1990, A/RES/45/158 (entered into force on 1 July 2003) or the *International Convention for the Protection of All Persons from Enforced Disappearance*, opened for signature 20 December 2006, A/RES/61/177 (entered into force on 1 December 2010).

international human rights law'.[16] Indeed, the Australian government has identified the advancement of human rights as every nation's responsibility:

> [T]he function of government is to safeguard the dignity and rights of individuals, whose lives should be free of violence, discrimination, vilification, and hatred. ... *[W]e do not rest on our laurels. We continue to strive to protect and promote human rights and to address disadvantage.*[17]

Given this firm commitment to an expansive understanding of rights, Australia can and should aspire to adopt not only minimalist existing norms but also the emerging ones that embody the natural normative extension of human rights. Indeed, as the Law Council of Australia suggested during the 2009–2010 National Human Rights Consultation process, 'Australia should actively engage with the process of developing new human rights principles through its interaction with international human rights bodies'.[18] Obviously, this responsibility does not begin and end with the international bodies. Rather, it logically entails that Australia adopt the same position vis-à-vis the process of developing new human rights principles on the home front as well.

This said, the notion of defamation of religion poses a challenge to the presumed desire to incorporate and strengthen domestic and international human rights regimes. As I argue below, this putative norm has the effect of attenuating rather than reinforcing the traditional scope of freedom of expression and freedom of religion or belief. Yet it has consistently garnered strong support on the international level, and therefore may be trending in the direction of an emerging customary norm.[19] Faced with this possibility, the question arises as to whether an Australian bill of rights process should account for defamation of religion, and, if so, how.

---

[16] National Human Rights Consultation, above n 11, 73.
[17] *Human Rights*, Attorney-General's Department (2010) <http://www.ag.gov.au/www/agd/agd.nsf/Page/Humanrightsandanti-discrimination_Humanrights> at 22 March 2011 (emphasis added).
[18] National Human Rights Consultation, above n 11, 72.
[19] As this chapter goes to print, there are signs the campaign to enshrine a prohibition against defamation of religion may be waning or shifting to alternate formulations. In 2011, the UN Human Rights Council abstained from passing its annual resolution addressing defamation, opting instead for a consensus resolution directed at combating intolerance, negative stereotyping and stigmatisation of, and discrimination, incitement to violence and violence against, persons based on religion or belief: *Combating intolerance, negative stereotyping and stigmatization of, and discrimination, incitement to violence and violence against, persons based on religion or belief*, HRC Res 16/18, Human Rights Council, 16th sess, UN Doc A/HRC/RES/16/18 (2011). As noted below, there are still a number of parallel worrying trends developing within the UN that attempt to prioritise protection for and influence of religion and religious beliefs over existing universal human rights.

In the next section, I offer a brief comparative history of the offence of blasphemy to help contextualize the intended meaning of defamation of religion. This chapter's third part discusses how defamation of religion became the focus of dozens of United Nations (UN) resolutions, assesses the challenges associated with grafting the legal concept of defamation onto the mercurial notion of religion and its potential implications for existing international law, and finally takes stock of the ongoing debate. This chapter's fourth part draws some preliminary conclusions concerning the possible impact of enforcing a norm against defamation of religion, and addresses to what extent — if at all — Australia should incorporate a response to this emerging norm in any future bill of rights.

A comparative overview of the offence of blasphemy: A foundation for understanding defamation of religion

Blasphemy in the West

In theological terms, blasphemy is equated with 'a direct criticism of God and sacred objects'.[20] The legal definition of blasphemy 'developed historically to meet various, primarily political rather than religious, perceptions of a need for the law to protect institutions, originally the State itself'.[21] In other words, the challenge posed by alleged heretics and blasphemers represented nothing less than an act of state treason threatening the very foundation of a society held together with the brick and mortar of an exclusive unassailable religious conviction.[22] The state could level blasphemy-related charges against an individual to protect the social or ideological underpinnings of society, or more specifically, use such charges to 'suppress the expression of religious beliefs or opinions' the dominant group believed to be false.[23]

---

[20] Reid Mortensen, 'Blasphemy In A Secular State: A Pardonable Sin?' (1994) 17 *UNSW Law Journal* 409, 409.

[21] Select Committee on Religious Offences in England and Wales, Parliament of England and Wales, *First Report: Appendix 3: Blasphemy* (2003) [7].

[22] For example, in recognising blasphemy as a common law offence in seventeenth century England, the court held that 'to say, religion is a cheat, is to dissolve all those obligations whereby the civil societies are preserved, and that Christianity is parcel of the laws of England; and therefore to reproach the Christian religion is to speak in subversion of the law': *R v Taylor* (1676) 1 Vent 293; 86 ER 189. In this brief quote, the court made plain the linkage between safeguarding the dominant faith and preserving the social and political order of the day.

[23] Tad Stahnke, 'Proselytism and the Freedom to Change Religion in International Human Rights Law' (1999) *Brigham Young University Law Review* 251, 289. Consequently, any nonconformist criticism of the dominant church — whether real or perceived — was not only dangerous, but considered 'necessarily wrong when emanating from inferior subjects against their masters': Leonard W Levy, *Emergence of a Free Press* (1985) 5.

As US Justice Felix Frankfurter famously observed, 'Blasphemy was the chameleon phrase which meant the criticism of whatever the ruling authority of the moment established as orthodox religious doctrine'.[24]

In many states today, the offences of blasphemy and heresy are viewed as antiquated tools for protecting a given ruler's religious worldview at the expense of all other differing opinions. Indeed, as religion and state gradually decoupled in the West,[25] charges of blasphemy grew more infrequent. While prosecutions for blasphemy in the US became 'no more frequent than the sightings of snarks',[26] the common law offence persisted in England until its abolition in 2008.[27] Prior to this, UK courts concluded that blasphemy required little in the way of intent,[28] could result in a sentence of hard labour,[29] and only operated to protect the Church of England

---

[24] *Joseph Burstyn, Inc v Wilson*, 343 US 495, 529 (1952).

[25] This trend may be linked to broader conditions of modernity leading to secularisation of society, wherein religion 'becomes increasingly a private concern of the individual and thus loses much of its public relevance and influence': Riaz Hassan, 'Expressions of religiosity and blasphemy in modern societies' in Elizabeth Burns Coleman and Kevin White (eds), *Negotiating the Sacred: Blasphemy and Sacrilege in a Multicultural Society* (2006) 119.

[26] Leonard W Levy, *Treason Against God* (1981) x (referring to the fictional animal introduced in Lewis Carroll, *The Hunting of the Snark: An Agony in Eight Fits* (1876)).

[27] *Criminal Justice and Immigration Act 2008* (UK) s 79. The *Racial and Religious Hatred Act 2006* (UK) arguably prohibits some acts that may have previously constituted blasphemy; however, its provisions apply equally to all religions. Part 3A of the *Racial and Religious Hatred Act 2006* (UK) addresses '[h]atred against persons on religious grounds': under s 29B(1), '[a] person who uses threatening words or behaviour, or displays any written material which is threatening, is guilty of an offense if he intends thereby to stir up religious hatred' (where 'religious hatred' is defined as 'hatred against a group of persons defined by reference to religious belief or lack of religious belief'). In addition to the offence requiring the impugned communication to constitute a threat, s 29J provides detailed protection for freedom of expression:
> Nothing in this Part shall be read or given effect in a way which prohibits or restricts discussion, criticism or expressions of antipathy, dislike, ridicule, insult or abuse of particular religions or the beliefs or practices of their adherents, or of any other belief system or the beliefs or practices of its adherents, or proselytising or urging adherents of a different religion or belief system to cease practising their religion or belief system.

The issue of incitement is discussed at greater length below.

[28] In 1979, the House of Lords affirmed a minimal threshold of intent for the offense of blasphemy, endorsing the trial judge's direction that 'guilt of the offence of publishing a blasphemous libel did not depend on the accused having an intent to blaspheme, but that it was sufficient for the prosecution to prove that the publication had been intentional and that the matter published was blasphemous': *R v Lemon (Denis)* [1979] AC 617, 618 (also known as *Whitehouse v Lemon*).

[29] William Gott, the last individual in the UK sentenced to a prison term for blasphemy, served nine months hard labour for distributing pamphlets describing Jesus Christ entering Jerusalem 'like a circus clown on the back of two donkeys': *R v Gott* [1922] 16 Cr App R 87, 89.

and its adherents rather than all religious beliefs.³⁰ In other states where blasphemy was not abolished outright, alleged violations were left unprosecuted or became unenforceable 'either through stricter intent requirements or judicial attempts to strike a balance between conflicting rights'.³¹

In Australia, the last successful prosecution for blasphemy occurred in 1871.³² The 1990s ushered in an era of renewed interest related to the common law offence of blasphemy, in part triggered by the Salman Rushdie affair in the United Kingdom.³³ In 1991, the New South Wales (NSW) parliament requested that the Law Reform Commission explore 'whether the present law relating to the offence of blasphemy is adequate and appropriate to current conditions'.³⁴ In undertaking its mandate, the Commission acknowledged two key questions: first, 'whether the offence [of blasphemy] is anachronistic in a modern society … which is multicultural, pluralistic, and secular, and maintains a strict separation between Church and State', and, second, 'whether the offence of blasphemy improperly impinges upon the fundamental right of freedom of speech'.³⁵ Because the offence of blasphemy had not been successfully prosecuted in over a century, the Commission also observed that there was 'a real question whether blasphemy still exists in the criminal law of New South Wales, even if it was "received" as law in colonial times'.³⁶

As part of its findings, the Commission identified 'several pieces of legislation in New South Wales … [that] assume[d] the existence of the crime' despite uncertainties regarding its reception from England.³⁷ Surveying the status of blasphemy in

---

30 In *Choudhury v UK* (1991) 12 HRLJ 172, members of Britain's Muslim community sought unsuccessfully to prosecute author Salman Rushdie for allegedly blaspheming against Islam in his novel *The Satanic Verses*; see also BBC, *Q & A: Blasphemy Law*' (2004) BBC News Online <http://news.bbc.co.uk/2/hi/uk_news/3753108.stm> at 24 August 2011.

31 Osama Siddique and Zahra Hayat, 'Unholy Speech and Holy Laws: Blasphemy Laws in Pakistan — Controversial Origins, Design Defects, and Free Speech Implications' (2008) 17 *Minnesota Journal of International Law* 303, 354: eg, Germany's criminal code forbids insulting religion publicly or by dissemination of publications, but successful prosecution requires 'the manner and content' of the insult to rise to such a level that an objective onlooker could reasonably conclude it would disturb the peace of those targeted (at 355–6).

32 *R v Jones* (Unreported, NSW Supreme Court Quarter Sessions, Simpson J, 18 February 1871) in Butterworths, *Halsbury's Laws of Australia*, vol 23 (at 23 March 2011) 365 Religion, '9(B) Blasphemy' [365–695].

33 Siddique and Hayat, above n 31.

34 Law Reform Commission, *Blasphemy*, Report No 74 (1994) Terms of Reference ('NSW Blasphemy Report').

35 Ibid [1.2–1.3].

36 Ibid [1.4].

37 Ibid [2.14].

Australia's other states and territories, the Commission also found that apart from section 574 of the *Crimes Act 1900* (NSW), only the Tasmanian Criminal Code contained another express statutory reference to blasphemy.[38] In contrast, other Australian jurisdictions had either abolished the offence altogether or maintained it only as a common law crime.

After weighing various options regarding the common law offence of blasphemy, including retention, progressive codification, selective replacement, and outright abolition, the Commission endorsed abolition without a substitute offence as the best option for NSW.[39] The Commission's recommendation stemmed from the status of the offence in NSW, its finding that there had been 'no prosecutions for blasphemy in other Australian states, Scotland, Ireland, New Zealand or other comparable jurisdictions for over 50 years, and … the fact that every law reform commission which [had] considered blasphemy law reform … recommended abolition of the offence'.[40] As a potential alternative, the Commission also found that anti-discrimination statutes were:

> better designed to preserve public order and social cohesion in a modern democratic society, given several important considerations: the emphasis on education and conciliation in the first instance; the clarity of the elements of the offences, and the protection of debate or discussion carried out in good faith; the more realistic penalties; and the requirement of the consent of the Attorney General before criminal proceedings may be instituted.[41]

On the federal level, Australia's early legislation revealed several efforts to enforce anti-blasphemy measures, particularly in literature, television, and film.[42] However, in 1992 the federal Law Reform Commission recommended that 'All references to blasphemy in federal legislation … be removed. Offences that protect personal and religious sensibilities should be recast in terms of "offensive material"'.[43] This recommendation stemmed from the Commission's opposition to extending the law of blasphemy for the purpose of covering religions other than Christianity. In the Commission's view it 'would be very difficult to devise a satisfactory definition of religion [to encompass faiths other than Christianity] and would be an unreasonable interference with freedom of expression' to perpetuate the offence of blasphemy.[44]

---

[38] Ibid [3.2].
[39] Ibid [4.3, 4.81].
[40] Ibid [4.80].
[41] Ibid [4.31].
[42] Ibid [3.12].
[43] Australian Law Reform Commission, *Multiculturalism and the Law*, Report No 57 (1992) [7.59].
[44] Ibid.

In the wake of these findings, Australia's federal government acted to repeal much of the legislation containing blasphemy-related offences.[45]

More recently, in the 'Piss Christ' case,[46] Melbourne's Catholic Archdiocese sought an injunction against the display of an allegedly blasphemous photograph by artist Andres Serrano. The photo, to be exhibited at the National Gallery of Victoria, depicted a crucified Jesus Christ the artist had immersed in urine. The Supreme Court of Victoria, noting that there was 'no evidence ... of any unrest of any kind following or likely to follow the showing of the photograph in question', held against the plaintiff, and also stated the need to contextualize the dispute with 'regard to contemporary standards in a multicultural, partly secular and largely tolerant, if not permissive, society'.[47] The Court concluded that if it were to 'grant the relief sought by the plaintiff, [it] might thereby use the force of the law to prevent that which, by the same law, is lawful'.[48]

Blasphemy in Muslim States

As noted above, blasphemy at its origin represented an ecclesiastical offence. In the Christian West, government implementation and enforcement of blasphemy laws through the common law often protected only specific iterations of the Christian faith. All other comers — including Muslims, Jews, and Hindus — had no means of bringing the wrath of the law to bear against the perceived disparagement of their respective religions.

Governments in the Muslim world similarly sought to outlaw offences equivalent to blasphemous conduct. Authorities invoked religious or statutory law to impose a variety of penalties against blasphemy, apostasy, and other related acts.[49] Like their

---

[45] The *Classification (Publications, Films and Computer Games) Act 1995* (Cth) repealed the previous *Customs (Cinematograph Films) Regulations 1979* (Cth). The prohibition against blasphemous works or articles contained in the *Customs (Prohibited Imports) Regulations 1956* (Cth) was discarded by amendment. Section 118 of the *Broadcasting Act 1942* (Cth), prohibiting the broadcast of blasphemous material, was similarly excised by virtue of being replaced with the *Broadcasting Services (Transitional Provisions and Consequential Amendments) Act 1992* (Cth).

[46] *Pell v Council of Trustees of the National Gallery of Victoria* (1998) 2 VR 391. For a discussion of this case, see Bede Harris, '*Pell v Council of Trustees of the National Gallery of Victoria*: Should Blasphemy Be A Crime? The 'Piss Christ' Case and Freedom of Expression' (1998) 2 *Melbourne University Law Review* 217.

[47] *Pell v Council of Trustees of the National Gallery of Victoria* (1998) 2 VR 391.

[48] Ibid.

[49] See, eg, Anthony Chase, 'Legal Guardians: Islamic Law, International Law, Human Rights Law, and the Salman Rushdie Affair' (1995–6) 11 *American University Journal of International Law and Policy* 375; Perry S Smith, 'Speak No Evil: Apostasy, Blasphemy and Heresy in Malaysian Syariah Law' (2003–4) 10 *University of California Davis Journal of International Law and Policy* 357.

Western counterparts, these offences[50] also shared a clearly identifiable connection with notions of treason or sedition against the state. This resulted in part due to the absence of any bright line separation between religion and state under the banner of Islam.[51] As Cherif Bassiouni has remarked, Islam provides a 'holistic conception of life, government, law and hereafter. There is no division of church and state; there is no division between matters temporal and religious, and between different aspects of law'.[52]

While the current trend in the West indicates a tendency to discard blasphemy offences into the trash bin of history,[53] there appears to be no parallel movement within Muslim states. For example, in Pakistan, a declared Islamic state,[54] existing blasphemy laws continue to result in miscarriages of justice and 'exacerbate a growing environment of dogma and intolerance — spawning a culture of extremism and violence'.[55] The US Department of State has observed that Pakistani authorities 'routinely used the blasphemy laws to harass religious minorities and vulnerable Muslims and to settle

---

[50] Although no exact offence parallel to the Judeo-Christian offence of blasphemy exists under Islam, insulting God, Mohammed or any other aspect of divine revelation amounts to an offence under Sharia: see Donna E Arzt, 'Heroes or Heretics: Religious Dissidents Under Islamic Law' (1995–6) 14 *Wisconsin International Law Journal* 349, 351–352. The article provides a long list of examples of blasphemy-type offences prosecuted in the Muslim world. See also Hassan, above n 25.

[51] See, eg, Ann Elizabeth Mayer, *Islam and Human Rights: Tradition and Politics* (2007) 167–8; Donna E Arzt, 'The Treatment of Religious Dissidents under Classical and Contemporary Islamic Law' in Johan D van der Wyver and John Witte (eds), *Religious Human Rights in Global Perspective: Religious Perspectives* (1996) 387.

[52] M Cherif Bassiouni, 'Speech, Religious Discrimination, and Blasphemy' (Speech delivered at the American Society of International Law Proceedings, Washington, 7 April 1989) (also (1989) 83 *American Society of International Law Proceedings* 433).

[53] An exception to this trend is evident in Ireland's recently passed *Defamation Act* 2009 (Ireland), which includes provisions covering the offence of blasphemy. See below 'Defamation of Religion and Drafting Australia's Bill of Rights'.

[54] For a closer examination of how the constitutional systems of Muslim States address religion-state relations, see Tad Stahnke and Robert C Blitt, 'The Religion-State Relationship and the Right to Freedom of Religion or Belief: A Comparative Textual Analysis of the Constitutions of Predominantly Muslim Countries' (2005) 36 *Georgia Journal of International Law* 947.

[55] Siddique and Hayat, above n 31, 384. For example, consider the 14-year imprisonment of a mentally ill woman suspected of blasphemy and the Pakistani government's failure to protect the Ahmadi community from threats against it, as well as its lackadaisical response in the face of violence targeting that community: see Mubasher Bukhari, *Pakistan Court Frees Mentally Ill Blasphemy Suspect After 14 Years* (2010) Reuters FaithWorld < http://blogs.reuters.com/faithworld/2010/07/23/pakistan-court-frees-mentally-ill-blasphemy-suspect-after-14-years/> at 23 March 2011; *Attackers target Lahore's Ahmadi worshippers; 70 dead* (2010) Dawn <http://www.dawn.com/wps/wcm/connect/dawn-content-library/dawn/news/pakistan/metropolitan/04-lahore-blasts-qs-07> at 23 March 2011.

personal scores or business rivalries'.[56] Most recently, gunmen in Pakistan's Punjab province shot and killed two Christian brothers as they returned to prison after a court appearance on blasphemy charges,[57] and several other Christians faced jail sentences[58] for violating Pakistan's Penal Code ordinances against blasphemy. Under the Code, any individual who 'directly or indirectly, defiles the sacred name of the Holy Prophet Muhammad' is subject to 'death, or imprisonment for life'.[59]

In Malaysia, the federal constitution declares Islam as the official religion, but authorizes states rather than the federal government to legislate in the area of Islamic law.[60] Within the Federal Territories (Kuala Lumpur, Putrajaya and Labuan), Part III of the *Syariah [Sharia] Criminal Offences (Federal Territories) Act 1997* enumerates 'Offences Relating to the Sanctity of the Religion of Islam and its Institution', which include '[i]nsulting, or bringing into contempt … the religion of Islam'.[61]

This Act also proscribes 'acts in contempt of religious authority' and 'def[ying], disobey[ing] or disput[ing] the orders or directions [of the *Majlis Agama Islam Wilayah Persekutuan* (Federal Territory Islamic Council)] expressed or given by way of fatwa'.[62] Upon conviction of either insulting Islam or defying an Islamic Council fatwa (a decision based on Islamic law), an individual is liable for a fine, prison

---

[56] Department of State, US Government, *International Religious Freedom Report* (2009). During the previous reporting period, Pakistani authorities 'arrested at least 25 Ahmadis, 11 Christians, and 17 Muslims on blasphemy charges' (*Pakistan: International Religious Freedom Report 2008* (2008) Department of State <http://www.state.gov/g/drl/rls/irf/2008/108505.htm> at 24 August 2011). See also below n 78.

[57] Fareed Khan, *On Trial for Blasphemy, Two Christian Brothers Murdered in Faisalabad* (2010) Asia News <http://www.asianews.it/news-en/On-trial-for-blasphemy,-two-Christian-brothers-murdered-in-Faisalabad-18977.html> at 23 March 2011. See also below n 78.

[58] See, eg, Fareed Khan, *Karachi, A Christian Sentenced to Life Imprisonment for Blasphemy*, Asia News (2010) <http://www.asianews.it/news-en/Karachi,-a-Christian-sentenced-to-life-imprisonment-for-blasphemy-17749.html> at 23 March 2011; Brian Sharma, *Pakistan's 'Blasphemy' Laws Claim 3 More Christians* (2010) The Christian Post <http://www.christianpost.com/article/20100311/pakistan-s-blasphemy-laws-claim-three-more-christians/index.html> at 23 March 2011.

[59] See, eg, *Pakistan Penal Code 1860* (Pakistan) art 295-C. The code also establishes punishments for other blasphemy-related offences including '[d]eliberate and malicious acts intended to outrage religious feelings', and for anyone who 'defiles, damages or desecrates a copy of the Holy Qur'an' (arts 295-A, 295-B).

[60] Under art 3(1) of Malaysia's Federal Constitution, 'Islam is the religion of the Federation': however, List II of the Constitution assigns significant legislative powers to the states pertaining to Islam (with certain limitations), including the creation and punishment of offences against precepts of Islam, as well as the constitution, organisation and procedure of Sharia courts: *Malaysia Constitution* (1994) arts 3(1), 367 (incorporating all amendments up to August 1994).

[61] *Syariah Criminal Offences (Federal Territories) Act 1997* (Malaysia) [7]. For an overview of the situation related to blasphemy in Malaysia, See Smith, above n 49.

[62] Ibid [9].

sentence of up to two years, or both.[63] According to the *Administration of Islamic Law (Federal Territories) Act 1993*, once a fatwa is issued by the Islamic Council and published in the official Gazette, it gains the status of enforceable law in the Federal Territories.[64] In turn, such fatwas are binding on every Muslim resident in the Federal Territories, each of whom is obligated by a 'religious duty to abide by and uphold the fatwa'.[65] The *Administration of Islamic Law (Federal Territories) Act 1993* further mandates that all courts in the Federal Territories recognize gazetted fatwas 'as authoritative of all matters laid down therein'.[66] Even in the event that a fatwa is not published, at least one former high-level government advisor has contended that the ruling demands respect as a religious decree.[67]

The influence of Malaysia's various fatwa councils is far-reaching. On the federal level, the National Fatwa Council, a body intended to harmonize state-issued fatwas, has sought to: prohibit Muslims from practicing yoga on the grounds that it risked 'destroy[ing] a Muslim's faith';[68] ban the '"unacceptable"' practice of women 'dressing in the clothes men wear';[69] and prohibit exhibitions pertaining to ghosts.[70] In a similar

---

[63] Ibid [7, 9].
[64] *Administration Of Islamic Law (Federal Territories) Act 1993* (Malaysia) [34(3)].
[65] *Administration Of Islamic Law (Federal Territories) Act 1993* (Malaysia) [34(3)]. According to Dr Abdul Hamid Othman, a prime ministerial adviser on religious affairs, 'The National Fatwa Council has been entrusted to deliberate on [questions of Islamic law] in depth and come out with edicts on them. And in an evolved world like ours, he adds, such a council plays an important role in providing 'guidelines' for these grey areas to Muslims': Hariati Azizan, *In a Twist Over Fatwa Ruling* (2008) The Star Online <http://thestar.com.my/news/story.asp?file=/2008/11/30/focus/2683235&sec=focus> at 23 March 2011.
[66] *Administration of Islamic Law (Federal Territories) Act 1993* (Malaysia).
[67] Azizan, above n 65.
[68] Niluksi Koswanage, *Muslims Warned to Avoid Blasphemous Yoga* (2008) Welt Online <http://www.welt.de/english-news/article2766685/Muslims-warned-to-avoid-blasphemous-yoga.html> at 23 March 2011; see also Robin Brant, *Malaysia Clerics Issue Yoga Fatwa* (2008) BBC News <http://news.bbc.co.uk/2/hi/asia-pacific/7743312.stm> at 23 March 2011. Ultimately, Malaysia's Prime Minister intervened to assure Muslims that yoga was still permissible, despite the fatwa's stated prohibition: *Malaysia Backs Down From Yoga Ban Amid Backlash* (2008) Reuters <http://www.reuters.com/article/idUSTRE4AP2CA20081126> at 23 March 2011.
[69] *Malaysian Religious Council Issues Ban on Lesbian Sex* (2008) AFP <http://afp.google.com/article/ALeqM5izKo_RKkF40cfljjibbi3Yai-5Tw> at 23 March 2011.
[70] According to the National Fatwa Council chair, the decision was taken to avoid undermining the faith of Muslims by exposing them 'to supernatural and superstitious beliefs': *Malaysia Issues Fatwa on Ghosts* (2007) Al Jazeera <http://english.aljazeera.net/news/asia-pacific/2007/04/200852513106697452.html> at 23 March 2011.

vein, the Islamic Religious Council in the central state of Selangor threatened to sue the Malaysian Bar Association for using the word 'Allah' on its website.[71]

In Indonesia, where the constitution is silent with regard to favouring secularism or Islam, the government actively invokes criminal ordinances to prosecute alleged blasphemy-related offences. Under the Criminal Code, publicly 'giving expression to feelings of hostility, hatred or contempt against one or more groups of the population of Indonesia' is punishable by a maximum imprisonment of four years or a fine.[72] While the Indonesian law is admirable for its attempt to move away from protecting the majority faith exclusively, the US Department of State has concluded that enforcement actions in practice 'have almost always involved blasphemy and heresy against Islam'.[73] Human Rights Watch likewise has concluded, 'Indonesian laws prohibiting blasphemy are primarily applied to practices perceived to deviate from mainstream Islam'.[74] Blasphemy charges have been invoked in a variety of situations, including an art exhibit containing photographic representations of fig leaf-covered Adam and Eve,[75] and against various individuals claiming to be reincarnations of the Prophet Muhammad[76] and the archangel Gabriel,[77] among others. On a much broader scale, the government has severely restricted and even banned certain activities of the Ahmadi community,[78] including public religious worship, as part of a larger clamp-down pattern targeting groups deemed '"heretical"', '"deviant"', or

---

[71] Becket Fund for Religious Liberty, *Malaysia: Legal Body Faces Lawsuit for Using Word 'Allah'* (2009) International Religious Freedom News Blog <http://becketinternational.wordpress.com/2009/03/23/malaysia-legal-body-faces-lawsuit-for-using-word-%E2%80%98allah%E2%80%99/> at 23 March 2011.

[72] *Penal Code 1952* (Indonesia) arts 156–56(a).

[73] Department of State, US Government, *International Religious Freedom Report* (2009). This report notes dozens of individuals charged and convicted under Indonesia's criminal code.

[74] Human Rights Watch, *World Report 2009* (2009) 261.

[75] *Indonesia: Blasphemy case against Adam and Eve photo exhibit* (2006) Indo-Asian News Service <http://religion.info/english/articles/article_227.shtml> at 23 March 2011.

[76] Peter Gelling, *Indonesia Bans Sects It Deems Blasphemous* (2007) New York Times <http://www.nytimes.com/2007/11/16/world/asia/16indo.html> at 23 March 2011.

[77] Andra Wisnu, *Lia Eden sentenced to prison, again* (2009) Jakarta Post <http://www.thejakartapost.com/news/2009/06/03/lia-eden-sentenced-prison-again.html> at 23 March 2011.

[78] The primary differentiation between Ahmadis and Muslims relates to the Ahmadi belief in the prophethood of Mirza Ghulam Ahmad (founder of the Ahmadiyya faith). Recognition of this designation by Ahmadis contravenes the basic teaching under Islam that Mohammed was the final prophet. However, Ahmadis consider themselves devout Muslims faithful to the teachings of Islam. See M Nadeem Ahmad Siddiq, 'Enforced Apostasy: Zaheeruddin v. State and the Official Persecution of the Ahmadiyya Community in Pakistan' (1995–6) 14 *Law and Inequality Journal* 275, 279–82; see also Amjad Mahmood Khan, 'Persecution of the Ahmadiyya Community in Pakistan: An Analysis Under International Law and International Relations' (2002–3) 16 *Harvard Human Rights Law Journal* 217.

heterodox.[79] Following Malaysia's lead, Indonesia's Ulema Council issued a similar fatwa prohibiting Muslims from practicing yoga for fear it might corrupt their faith.[80]

From this brief overview — and in contrast to the present situation in most Western countries — snark sightings remain quite a common occurrence in the Muslim world. Many Muslim states continue to shield Islam from even minor criticism, and in certain instances use anti-blasphemy measures as an offensive tool to stifle the free exercise of religious belief for minority faiths and Muslim dissidents alike. As illustrated, such practices are not exclusive to religious regimes but rather may be observed across the spectrum of Muslim constitutional models — including in states that make no declaration regarding Islam as the official religion.[81] It is from this milieu that the movement to prohibit 'defamation of religion' (originally expressed in the more specific and decidedly less ecumenical slogan 'defamation of Islam') emerged a decade ago to begin its journey in search of international legitimacy.

Defamation of religion: Blasphemy goes international

Origins of defamation of religion at the United Nations

The Organization of the Islamic Conference (OIC), whose 57 member states represent 'the collective voice of the Muslim world',[82] is responsible for spearheading the effort to secure international condemnation of acts deemed defamatory of religion — and, more precisely, defamatory of Islam. In addition to its own reporting and resolutions on the issue,[83] the OIC — working through its individual member states — has focused for the past 10 years on adding the creation of a norm prohibiting defamation of religion to the agendas of various UN bodies. The first step in this effort came in 1999 when Pakistan, acting on behalf of the OIC, submitted a draft resolution entitled 'Defamation of Islam' to the now defunct Commission on Human

---

[79] US Commission on International Religious Freedom, US Government, *Annual Report* (2009) 171.

[80] Niniek Karmini, *Indonesian Muslims Banned From Practicing Yoga* (2009) Associated Press <http://www.kilil5.com/news/19970_indonesian-muslims-banned-from-p> at 23 March 2011.

[81] Because of space constraints, examples on anti-blasphemy measures in Turkey, a declared secular Muslim state, have been omitted. See Robert C Blitt, 'The Bottom up Journey of "Defamation of Religion" from Muslim States to the United Nations: A Case Study of the Migration of Anti-Constitutional Ideas' (2011) 56 *Studies in Law, Politics and Society* 1, 121–211. See also above n 25.

[82] *About OIC* (2010) Organization of the Islamic Conference <http://www.oic-oci.org/page_detail.asp?p_id=52> at 23 March 2011.

[83] For a more detailed account of these activities, see Blitt, above n 81.

Rights (UNCHR).[84] This proposed resolution sought to combat perceived negative international media coverage of '"Islam as a religion hostile to human rights"'.[85] In the view of Pakistan's UN ambassador, this negative media coverage amounted to a 'defamation campaign' against the religion and its adherents to which the UNCHR had to react.[86] The draft of the resolution sought to have the UNCHR both express 'concern at the ... spread [of] intolerance against Islam',[87] and call upon the Special Rapporteur on religious intolerance to 'continue to devote attention to attacks against Islam and attempts to defame it'.[88]

In response to Pakistan's draft, Western governments proposed amendments to de-specify Islam and approach the challenge of discrimination from a more general perspective inclusive of all religions.[89] Subsequent Pakistani sub-amendments sought to preserve specificity relating to 'defamatory attacks against [Islam]'[90] and stressed that removing the resolution's focus on Islam 'would defeat the purpose of the text, which was to bring a problem relating specifically to that religion to the attention of the international community'.[91] Following additional negotiations, a compromise resolution emerged expressing concern over the stereotyping of all religions rather than Islam alone, and which retained the term 'defamation' in the resolution title only.[92] The representative from Pakistan hailed the OIC member states' 'considerable flexibility' in agreeing to a compromise resolution.[93] At the same time, Germany's representative, speaking on behalf of the European Union (EU), stressed the EU's collective 'wish to make it clear that they did not attach any legal meaning to the term "defamation" as used in the title'.[94]

---

[84] The first reference to defamation of Islam at the UN may be traced back to 1997. Rene Wadlow and David Littman, 'Blasphemy at the United Nations?' (1997) 4 *Middle East Quarterly* 4, 85–6.

[85] *Summary Record of the 61st Meeting*, [1], Human Rights Commission, 55th sess, 61st plen mtg, UN Doc E/CN.4/1999/SR.61 (1999) (quoting Ambassador Zamir Akram of Pakistan).

[86] Ibid [1–2].

[87] *Draft resolution E/CN.4/1999/L.40 (Defamation of Islam)*, [2], Human Rights Commission, 55th sess, 61st plen mtg, UN Doc E/CN.4/1999/L.40 (1999). The Draft Resolution was submitted by Pakistan on behalf of members of the OIC.

[88] Ibid.

[89] Ibid [8].

[90] *Proposed sub-amendments to the amendments to draft resolution E/CN.4/1999/L.40 contained in document E/CN.4/1999/L.90*, [1], Human Rights Commission, 55th sess, 61st plen mtg, UN Doc E/CN.4/1999/L.104 (1999).

[91] *Summary Record of the 61st Meeting*, above n 85, [8].

[92] *Defamation of Religions*, Human Rights Commission, 55th sess, 61st plen mtg, UN Doc E/CN.4/RES/1999/82 (1999) (adopted without a vote).

[93] *Summary Record of the 62nd Meeting*, [1], Human Rights Commission, 55th sess, 61st plen mtg, UN Doc E/CN.4/1999/SR.62 (1999).

[94] Ibid [9].

This seemingly insignificant resolution served as defamation's proverbial foot in the door at the UN for two reasons: first, it tasked two UN special rapporteurs with taking into account provisions of the resolution in future reports to the UNCHR, and, second, it expressed the UNCHR's intent 'to remain seized of the matter'.[95] Consequently, the effort to install a prohibition on defamation of religion became systematized and integrated not only into the UNCHR agenda, but also into the mandates of the Special Rapporteur on religious intolerance and the Special Rapporteur on racism, racial discrimination, xenophobia and related intolerance.

Over the relatively short time span of 10 years, the UNCHR, its successor the Human Rights Council (HRC), and even the UN General Assembly (UNGA) proceeded to pass regular resolutions dedicated to combating 'Defamation of Religion'. A review of these resolutions demonstrates that invocation of the term 'defamation' skyrocketed, from a solitary reference in 1999, to 23 references in 2009. Furthermore, placement of the term defamation within the resolution also shifted dramatically, from no references within the body of the resolution to up to eight preambulatory references coupled with eight additional operative references in 2009.[96] The repeated use of defamation in the operative clauses of these resolutions necessarily gives its meaning new significance. To understand this significance, it is helpful to start with the legal definition of defamation and explore the implications of efforts to graft this concept onto protection of religion within the framework of international law.

Defining defamation of religion: Challenges to existing principles of defamation law and international human rights law

Understanding defamation law

Although specifics vary from state to state, defamation is classically defined as the 'act of harming the reputation of another by making a false statement to a third person'[97] or as an intentional false communication that injures another person's reputation.[98] From this, several important elements are obvious: first, the offence must be directed

---

[95] *Defamation of Religions*, above n 92, [6].
[96] Operative paragraphs of UN resolutions are typically action-oriented statements intended to create or advance policy. In contrast, preambulatory text is explanatory in purpose, and provides justifications for action undertaken in the resolution's operative part. For a more detailed discussion of the evolution of defamation of religion at the UN, see Blitt, above n 81.
[97] Thomson Reuters, *Black's Law Dictionary* (2004), 'Defamation'.
[98] Special Rapporteur on Civil and Political Rights, Including the Question of Freedom of Expression, *The Right to Freedom of Opinion and Expression*, Economic and Social Council, 62nd sess, UN Doc E/CN.4/2006/55 (2005). This applies to individuals and corporations alike.

at individuals (or in certain potential instances, at groups[99]) rather than at an idea, concept, or set of beliefs, and, second, if the statement is merely an opinion, rather than an assertion of fact, a claim for defamation typically cannot be supported. In addition to the existing common law defence of fair comment,[100] under Australia's unified defamation law, a statutory defence to alleged defamation arises, *inter alia*, where the defendant proves that:

(a) the matter was an expression of opinion of the defendant rather than a statement of fact, and

(b) the opinion related to a matter of public interest, and

(c) the opinion is based on proper material.[101]

The US Supreme Court has ruled that the distinction between fact and opinion remains relevant in establishing whether a defamation claim is actionable. In *Milkovich v Lorain Journal Co.*,[102] the Court held communication in the form of an opinion may be considered defamatory, but only if the statement of the opinion implies that the speaker has knowledge of provably false (that is, defamatory) but undisclosed facts.[103] In other words, the opinion may be defamatory only if it is premised on some precursory and provably false statement of fact. However, the plaintiff must still show that the false implications of the communication were made with some level of fault to support recovery. As this practice indicates, a showing of intent may be required in certain instances.

Although the decision in *Milkovich* represented a more nuanced elaboration on the US Supreme Court's decision in *Gertz v Robert Welch*, it preserved the core principle that 'there is no such thing as a false idea' under the First Amendment of the US Constitution.[104] Moreover, *Milkovich* reaffirmed that statements that could not

---

[99] In *Beauharnais v Illinois*, 343 US 250, 258 (1952), a majority of the US Supreme Court seemed to endorse the notion of group libel claims. However, the Ninth Circuit US Court of Appeals has observed that 'cases decided since *Beauharnais*…have substantially undercut this support. To the extent that *Beauharnais* can be read as endorsing group libel claims, it has been so weakened by subsequent cases such as *New York Times* that the Seventh Circuit has stated that these cases "had so washed away the foundations of *Beauharnais* that it cannot be considered authoritative" …We agree with the Seventh Circuit that the permissibility of group libel claims is highly questionable at best': *Dworkin v Hustler Magazine Inc* 867 F 2d 1188, 1200 (9th Cir App) (1989).

[100] David Rolph, 'A Critique of the National, Uniform Defamation Laws' (2008) 16 *Torts Law Journal* 207, 237.

[101] *Defamation Act 2005* (NSW) s 31(1).

[102] *Milkovich v Lorain Journal Co*, 497 US 1 (1990).

[103] See *Restatement (Second) of Torts 1977* s 566.

[104] *Gertz v Robert Welch, Inc*, 418 US 323, 339 (1974).

'reasonably [be] interpreted as stating actual facts' about an individual would fail to satisfy the test for defamation.[105] In the majority's view, this protection served as 'assurance that public debate will not suffer for lack of "imaginative expression" or the "rhetorical hyperbole" which has traditionally added much to the discourse of our Nation'.[106]

Enforcing a prohibition on defamation of religion: Definitional and legal impediments

With this overview in mind, the problem of relying on defamation as a legal framework for protecting religion becomes evident. First, enforcement of, and limitations on, defamation vary from jurisdiction to jurisdiction, making it virtually impossible to extract clear, consistent rules regarding its application to individuals. Beyond this, applying defamation to various systems of belief that come with their own sets of unique but unprovable truth claims further complicates the effort. These claims often may be directly at odds with the competing claims of another religious group. Indeed, the latter group may even consider such rival views 'defamatory'. However, because these scenarios do not deal in provable statements of fact, defamation law cannot effectively address them. The problem of providing a workable definition of 'defamation of religion' is so apparent that after 10 years of passing resolutions, neither the HRC nor the UNGA has ventured to undertake the task.[107]

The conceptual challenge of defamation of religion is exacerbated further when considering the nature and purpose of international human rights law. To begin, international human rights law, and specifically the right to freedom of religion or belief, 'does not include the right to have a religion or belief that is free from criticism or ridicule'.[108] This same body of law also recognizes individuals' right to freedom of expression, and while that right may be limited in certain narrowly tailored contexts, hurt feelings alone do not rise to the level of a violation of rights that would justify such a limitation.[109] Recognizing such a limitation under international human rights

---

[105] *Milkovich v Lorain Journal Co*, 497 US 1, 2706 (1990).
[106] Ibid 2697 (1990).
[107] Instead, there is a new emphasis on blurring the boundary between defamation and the concept of incitement.
[108] Asma Jahangir and Doudou Diène, *Report of the Special Rapporteur on Freedom of Religion or Belief and the Special Rapporteur on Contemporary Forms of Racism on the incitement to racial and religious hatred and the promotion of tolerance*, Human Rights Council, 2nd sess, UN Doc A/HRC/2/3 (2006) ('Jahangir and Diène').
[109] *International Covenant on Civil and Political Rights*, opened for signature 16 December 1966, 999 UNTS 171, art 19.3 (entered into force 23 March 1976): 'Restrictions must be provided by law, and be necessary: (a) For respect of the rights or reputations of others; [and] (b) For the protection of national security or of public order (order public), or of public health or morals'.

law would entail nothing less than a reordering of rights resulting in the censoring of free expression by limiting, *inter alia*, 'scholarship on religious issues and ... [by] asphyxiat[ing] honest debate or research'.[110]

This reordering would also undermine freedom of religion, the very right supporters of outlawing defamation argue requires greater protection. The history associated with protecting religious freedom is intimately tied to the protection of minority rights.[111] However, blasphemy charges typically are used to stifle the freedom of religion or belief of minority groups disfavoured by the dominant faith. Granting the charge of defamation an international imprimatur allows it to be used not as a shield, but rather as a sword to silence those deemed to have religious or political beliefs at odds with the faith supported by the ruling party. Perhaps in response to this risk, the UN Human Rights Committee, the body of independent experts tasked with interpreting the provisions of the International Covenant on Civil and Political Rights (ICCPR) and monitoring its implementation,[112] concluded almost 20 years ago that:

> If a set of beliefs is treated as official ideology in constitutions, statutes, proclamations of ruling parties, etc., or in actual practice, this shall not result in any impairment of the freedoms under article 18 [freedom of thought, conscience and religion] or any other rights recognized under the Covenant nor in any discrimination against persons who do not accept the official ideology or who oppose it.[113]

Further, establishing defamation of religion as a legitimate basis for suppressing speech would essentially ascribe greater priority to the protection of a set of ideas rather than to individuals, an outcome antithetical to the very impetus for international *human rights law*.[114]

Despite these red flags — and in contradiction to the recommendations of at least one UN special rapporteur at the time — the HRC and the UNGA in 2007 proceeded with efforts to modify the longstanding consensus surrounding human

---

[110] Jahangir and Diène, above n 108, [42].
[111] See, eg, *Little Treaty of Versailles*, opened for signature 28 June 1919 (entered into force 10 January 1920) (the treaty between Poland and the League of Nations addressing minority rights in the newly created Polish state).
[112] *Human Rights Committee: Monitoring Civil and Political Rights* (2010) Office of the United Nations High Commissioner for Human Rights (OHCHR) <http://www2.ohchr.org/english/bodies/hrc/index.htm> at 23 March 2011.
[113] *General Comment 22 (Freedom of Thought, Conscience or Religion)*, [18], OHCHR, UN Doc CCPR/C/21/Rev1/Add4 (1993).
[114] *Universal Declaration of Human Rights*, GA Res 217 A (III), UN GAOR, 3rd sess, UN Doc A/810 (1948).

rights norms. In similar resolutions, both UN bodies asserted 'that everyone has the right to freedom of expression, which should be exercised with responsibility and may therefore be subject to limitations as provided by law and necessary for respect of the rights or reputations of others, protection of national security or of public order, public health or morals and *respect for religions and beliefs*'.[115]

This language signals surreptitious efforts by the UNGA and the HRC — the body 'responsible for strengthening the promotion and protection of human rights around the globe'[116] — to amend the longstanding legal consensus enshrined under the ICCPR. Using the limitations agreed upon in ICCPR article 19 as a jumping-off point, both resolutions unilaterally *add* a limitation on the right of freedom of expression, namely 'respect for religions and beliefs'. In other words, in the minds of the voting majorities within the UNGA and HRC, speech labelled defamatory (or blasphemous) of religion is no longer worthy of protection, regardless of contrary views expressed by the Special Rapporteur on freedom of religion or belief or in the ICCPR text.

The steady effort on the part of OIC member states to entrench defamation of religion as an international norm again bore fruit in 2008, when the UNGA passed a similar resolution, calling, *inter alia*, for increased restrictions on freedom of expression.[117] During voting in the Third Committee on the draft resolution submitted by Pakistan (again acting on behalf of OIC member states),[118] the European Union maintained its position that it 'did not see the concept of defamation of religions as valid in a human rights discourse; international human rights law protected primarily

---

[115] See GA Res 61/164, UNGAOR, 61st sess, UN doc A/RES/61/164 (Feb. 21, 2007) (emphasis added); see also Human Rights Council Res 4/9, Human Rights Council, 4th sess, UN Doc A/HRC/Res/4/9 (2007). (The vote in the General Assembly was 111 votes to 54, with 18 abstentions; in the Council, the recorded vote was 24 to 14 with nine abstentions).

[116] *The Human Rights Council* (2010) OCHRC <http://www2.ohchr.org/english/bodies/hrcouncil/> at 26 March 2011.

[117] GA Res 62/154, UN GAOR, 62nd sess, [10] UN Doc A/RES/62/154 (2008) (The resolution passed with a recorded vote of 108 to 51, with 25 abstentions). See also GA Res 10678 (X), UN GAOR, 62nd sess, UN Doc GA/10678 (2007).

[118] GA Draft Res (Pakistan), 62nd sess, UN Doc A/C.3/62/L.35 (2007). Subsequently, Belarus and Venezuela joined in sponsoring the draft resolution: Third Committee, *Promotion and protection of human rights: human rights questions, including alternative approaches for improving the effective enjoyment of human rights and fundamental freedoms*, UN Doc A/62/439/Add.2. The Third Committee endorsed the draft by a vote of 95 in favour to 52 against, with 30 abstentions. For the voting record, see UN Department of Public Information, *Third Committee Approves Three Country-Specific Texts On Human Rights: Despite Opposition Led By Developing Countries*, [Annex III], UN Doc GA/SHC/3909 (2007).

individuals, rather than religions as such, and religions or beliefs in most States did not enjoy legal personality'.[119]

Which way forward: Defamation of religion as customary international law or as a form of incitement?

Although some states continue to claim that 'defamation of religion' is an unworkable chimera, consistent majorities in the HRC and UNGA beg to differ. And yet, despite this majority, UNGA resolutions are arguably only a representation of that body's opinion and therefore not legally binding. In accordance with the UN Charter, the UNGA is not intended to serve as a legislative body:

> The General Assembly may discuss any questions or any matters within the scope of the present Charter or relating to the powers and functions of any organs provided for in the present Charter, and ... *may make recommendations* to the Members of the United Nations or to the Security Council or to both on any such questions or matters.[120]

However, it is also generally recognized that over time and under certain circumstances, UNGA resolutions may come to reflect and have the binding force of customary international law. The classic example of such practice is embodied in UNGA Resolution 217A (1948), more commonly known as the Universal Declaration on Human Rights (UDHR).[121] Over time, a variety of authorities have come to acknowledge this landmark Declaration as reflective of customary international law norms.[122]

Most recently at the end of 2009, the UNGA again endorsed a resolution on combating defamation of religion.[123] The resolution received a record 61 'no' votes[124]

---

[119] UN Department of Public Information, *Third Committee Approves Three Country-Specific Texts On Human Rights: Despite Opposition Led By Developing Countries*, UN Doc GA/SHC/3909 (2007).

[120] *Charter of the United Nations* 10 (emphasis added).

[121] *Universal Declaration of Human Rights*, above n 114.

[122] See, eg, *Filartiga v Pena-Irala*, 630 F.2d 876, 882 (2d Cir App 1980). See also Hurst Hannum, 'The UDHR In National and International Law' (1998) 3 *Health and Human Rights* 145, 145.

[123] GA Res 64/156, UN GAOR, 64th sess, UN Doc A/RES/64/156 (2010). (Note that the *Combating defamation of religions* resolution as passed in the Third Committee is referenced as UN Doc A/64/439/Add.2 (Part II)).

[124] UN Department of Public Information, *General Assembly Adopts 56 Resolutions, 9 Decisions Recommended by Third Committee on Broad Range of Human Rights, Social, Cultural Issues*, UN Doc GA/10905 (2009).

at the Assembly's 64th session.[125] Although the endorsement of a limitation on freedom of expression based on *'respect for religions and beliefs'* was conspicuously missing from the text,[126] the resolution continued to express 'deep concern' over 'the intensification of the overall campaign of the defamation of religions' despite offering nothing to substantiate the finding.[127]

At this point, a growing rift between the Special Rapporteur on freedom of expression, the Special Rapporteur on freedom of religion or belief (and possibly the Office of the High Commissioner on Human Rights) on the one hand, and certain UN member states on the other, has become evident.[128] Most of the early reports prepared by Doudou Diène, the Special Rapporteur on contemporary forms of racism, racial discrimination, xenophobia and related intolerance, signal strident support for prohibiting defamation of religion. For example, Diène urged 'the Commission to invite the Special Rapporteur to submit a regular report on all manifestations of defamation of religion, stressing the strength and seriousness of Islamophobia at the present time'.[129] In contrast, Diène's predecessor Abdelfattah Amor early on stressed that 'very frequently, prohibitions against acts of defamation or blasphemy are misused for the purposes of outright censorship of the right to criticism and discussion of religion and related questions', and that in 'many

---

[125] The resolution (GA Res 64/439, UN GAOR, 64th sess, UN Doc A/64/439/Add.2, part II) was adopted by a recorded vote of 80 in favour to 61 against, with 42 abstentions. One could make the case that the vote actually reflected a plurality rather than a majority since over 100 states either voted against or abstained.

[126] The provision is stricken from the paragraph addressing freedom of expression. It was also absent in 2008. See UN Doc A/64/439/Add.2 (Part II), above n 123 [10], and GA Res 63/171, 63rd sess, UN Doc A/RES/63/171 (2009) (emphasis added). The Human Rights Council in 2009 and 2011 passed an equally ominous resolution advancing the function of 'traditional values' in shaping universal human rights norms. Though some of the problems raised by these resolutions are related, they fall outside the immediate scope of this chapter. See *Promoting human rights and fundamental freedoms through a better understanding of traditional values of humankind*, HRC Res 12/21, Human Rights Council, 12th sess, UN Doc A/HRC/12/21 (2009) and *Promoting human rights and fundamental freedoms through a better understanding of traditional values of humankind*, HRC Res 16/3, Human Rights Council, 16th sess, UN Doc A/HRC/RES/16/3 (2011).

[127] UN Doc A/64/439/Add.2 (Part II), above n 123.

[128] The US described the voting over the most recent defamation resolution as evidencing an 'increasingly splintered view' within the General Assembly: UN Department of Public Information, *Third Committee Approves Resolution Aimed at 'Combating Defamation of Religions', One of 16 Draft Texts Recommended to General Assembly*, UN Doc GA/SHC/3966 (2009).

[129] Doudou Diène, *Report by the Special Rapporteur on Contemporary Forms of Racism, Racial Discrimination, Xenophobia and Related Intolerance*, [37], UN Doc E/CN.4/2006/17 (2006).

cases, defamation becomes the tool of extremists in censoring and maintaining or propagating obscurantism'.[130]

Despite these sharp disagreements, a survey of the reporting by the UN special rapporteurs and the OHCHR over 10 years indicates a recent about-face away from the defamation concept and in favour of addressing issues of concern through the offence of incitement. This sea change in attitude is particularly evident in 2008, even in Diène's reporting. Although non-existent as a concern over nearly 10 years, Diène suddenly argues that, 'With a view to promoting this change of paradigm, translating religious defamation from a sociological notion into a legal human rights concept, namely incitement to racial and religious hatred' will show 'that combating incitement to hatred is not a North-South ideological question but a reality present in a large majority of national legislations in all regions'.[131]

This concerted effort to redirect the defamation debate away from its sociological overtones in favour of a protection regime grounded in the more palatable — and arguably legally definable — notion of incitement finds dramatic expression in a joint statement released by three special rapporteurs during the 2009 Durban Review Conference. Oddly, however, this important document lacks an official UN Document number and is virtually buried on the UN's website.[132] According to the special rapporteurs who endorsed this statement, the concept of defamation of religion suffers from significant underlying problems:

> the difficulties in providing an objective definition of the term 'defamation of religions' at the international level make the whole concept open to abuse. At the national level, domestic blasphemy laws can prove counter-productive, since this could result in the de facto censure of all inter-religious and intra-religious criticism.

---

[130] Abdelfattah Amor, *Interim Report by the Special Rapporteur of the Commission on Human Rights on the Elimination of All Forms of Intolerance and of Discrimination Based on Religion or Belief*, [97], UN Doc A/55/280 (2000). Still, Amor also maintained that the issue of defamation reflected one of his 'major concerns … because it is an intrinsic violation of the freedom of religion or belief': Abdelfattah Amor, *Report by the Special Rapporteur on Freedom of Religion or Belief*, [137], UN Doc E/CN.4/2004/63 (2004).

[131] *Racism, Racial Discrimination, Xenophobia and Related Forms of Intolerance: Follow-up to and Implementation of the Durban Declaration and Program of Action*, [45], UN Doc A/HRC/9/12 (2008).

[132] Githu Muigai, Asma Jahangir and Frank LaRue, *Joint statement by Mr. Githu Muigai, Special Rapporteur on Contemporary Forms of Racism, Racial Discrimination, Xenophobia and Related Intolerance; Ms. Asma Jahangir, Special Rapporteur on Freedom of Religion or Belief; and Mr. Frank La Rue, Special Rapporteur on the Promotion and Protection of the Right to Freedom of Opinion and Expression, Freedom of Expression and Incitement to Racial or Religious Hatred* (Statement made at OHCHR side event during Durban Review Conference, Geneva, (April 22, 2009)) [1] ('Joint Statement').

Many of these laws afford different levels of protection to different religions and have often proved to be applied in a discriminatory manner. There are numerous examples of persecution of religious minorities or dissenters, but also of atheists and non-theists, as a result of legislation on religious offences or overzealous application of laws that are fairly neutral.[133]

Even as certain individual and institutional voices have begun endorsing this position, it remains likely that the debate will continue to spill over to future UNGA sessions. The reality remains that a majority of states at the UN continue to favour promulgating a new norm prohibiting defamation of religion, even if means fitting it in under a more consensual rubric of incitement. As Masood Khan, Pakistan's UN ambassador, reminded the HRC in 2008, the ultimate objective of OIC member states is nothing less than a 'new instrument or convention' addressing defamation.[134] The OIC already considers defamation a legitimate and existing norm: 'The succession of UNGA and UNHRC [UN Human Rights Council] resolutions on the defamation of religions *makes it a standalone concept with international legitimacy*'.[135]

In light of these views, the paradigm shift advocated by the special rapporteurs remains uncertain at best. Even if the UNGA and the HRC drop the effort to entrench a norm built around the specific language of defamation, there is little indication that a compromise based on 'incitement to religious hatred' would function any differently in practice. In other words, OIC member states and other governments may still invoke the incitement model to establish a justification under international law for outlawing speech, religious practice, and other actions deemed blasphemous. It is worthwhile to recall here that support for a defamation of religion norm transcends OIC member states. Countries such as Russia and China continue to be strong proponents of the norm. For example, former Russian Orthodox Church Patriarch Alexy II latched onto the concept of defamation of religion as a basis for building Christian-Muslim cooperation: 'In the framework of international organizations, it seems useful to create mechanisms that make it possible to be more sensitive to the spiritual and cultural traditions of various peoples'.[136]

---

[133] Joint Statement, above n 132, [2].
[134] Steven Edwards, *UN anti-blasphemy measures have sinister goals, observers say* (2008) Canwest News Service <http://www2.canada.com/theprovince/news/story.html?id=9b8e3a6d-795d-440f-a5de-6ff6e78c78d5> at 26 March 2011.
[135] *2nd OIC Observatory Report on Islamophobia, June 2008 to April 2009*, Council of Foreign Ministers, 36th council (Damascus, Syrian Arab Republic, 2009) 4 (emphasis added).
[136] *'Response from His Holiness Patriarchy Alexy II of Moscow and all Russia [to the open letter of 138 Muslim Theologians]* (2008), A Common Word <http://acommonword.com/en/a-common-word/6-christian-responses/202-response-from-his-holiness-patriarchy-alexy-ii-of-moscow-and-all-russia.html> at 26 March 2011.

Defamation of religion and drafting Australia's bill of rights

In the context of recent efforts to better protect and promote human rights in Australia through the development of a bill of rights,[137] the issue of defamation of religion merits consideration for a number of reasons. First, accounting for current international human rights debates in any final instrument may better position that document to meet potential future challenges. For example, by exploring the issue of defamation, drafters of a bill of rights can address the scope and priority to be assigned to freedom of expression and freedom of religion or belief, including what limitations may be applicable and when. Such a step can be a useful part of the process of determining where Australia wants to situate itself and its citizens vis-à-vis emerging human rights norms. This approach is also in sync with the Australian Human Rights Consultation Committee's finding that 'newly emerging rights in international law — such as the right to a clean and sustainable environment — are constantly in the Australian public's gaze'.[138] In other words, Australians arguably favour an open-minded and exploratory approach that enables consideration of unsettled questions related to rights. Such an approach should necessarily consider *lex lata*, but also *lex ferenda* and other sources of potential norms that offer a more expansive interpretation of emerging human rights principles.

Second, a robust upfront discussion on defamation of religion can help resolve potential inconsistencies between Australian foreign policy and national law. This is particularly important given Australia's ambivalent position regarding the protection of religion under defamation-based offences. Although Australia's international voting record at the UN reveals a national distaste for defamation of religion resolutions, domestic legislative initiatives indicate the possibility of allowing prosecution of such offences in the name of fostering tolerance. For example, Victoria's controversial *Racial and Religious Tolerance Act 2001* ('the Act') specifically prohibits 'conduct that incites hatred against, serious contempt for, or revulsion or severe ridicule' of persons 'on the ground of religious belief or activity'.[139] The Act also provides various exceptions, including where conduct of the accused is deemed to have occurred reasonably and in good faith:

(a) in the performance, exhibition or distribution of an artistic work; or

(b) in the course of any statement, publication, discussion or debate made or held, or any other conduct engaged in, for –

---

[137] This is in fact one of the objectives of Australia's National Human Rights Consultation: see *Terms of Reference*, National Human Rights Consultation <http://www.humanrightsconsultation.gov.au/www/nhrcc/nhrcc.nsf/Page/Terms_of_Reference> at 26 March 2011.

[138] National Human Rights Consultation, above n 11, 346.

[139] *Racial and Religious Tolerance Act 2001* (Vic) art 8 (incorporating amendments as at 1 October 2009).

(i) any genuine academic, artistic, religious[140] or scientific purpose; or

(ii) any purpose that is in the public interest; or

(c) in making or publishing a fair and accurate report of any event or matter of public interest.[141]

Disturbingly, the Act renders motive irrelevant in determining whether an offence has occurred[142] and boasts an extra-territorial effect covering conduct that may have transpired outside of Victoria proper.[143] Nevertheless, it would appear that the law does not afford protection to religious beliefs *per se*, but rather only to adherents as individuals or as a class of persons. In *Fletcher v Salvation Army Australia*, the administrative tribunal found that the Act

> is not concerned with the vilification of a religious belief or activity as such. Rather it is concerned with the vilification of a person, or a class of persons, on the ground of the religious belief or activity of the person or class ... The law does not stop a person from engaging in conduct that involves contempt for, or severe ridicule of, a religious belief or activity, provided this does not incite hatred against, serious contempt for, or revulsion or severe ridicule of another person or a class of persons on the ground of such belief or activity. The law recognises that you can hate the idea without hating the person.[144]

Beyond this, other constituencies in Australia have expressed support for a prohibition on defamation of religion. During a government-sponsored inquiry into revising the existing law on blasphemy in NSW,[145] the New South Wales Council of Churches (NSWCC) offered detailed submissions in favour of a new codification of the offence of blasphemy. As part of this re-codification effort, the NSWCC expressed support for retaining the offence but replacing the term 'blasphemy' with either 'religious vilification' or 'religious defamation', labels the NSWCC argued would avoid any misunderstanding or misconstruing of the offence while preserving its

---

[140] An amendment added in 2006 provides that 'a religious purpose includes, but is not limited to, conveying or teaching a religion or proselytizing': *Racial and Religious Tolerance Act 2001* (Vic) art 11(2).

[141] *Racial and Religious Tolerance Act 2001* (Vic) art 11(1). Article 12 addresses exceptions for private conduct 'in circumstances that may reasonably be taken to indicate that the parties to the conduct desire it to be heard or seen only by themselves'.

[142] *Racial and Religious Tolerance Act 2001* (Vic) art 9(1).

[143] *Racial and Religious Tolerance Act 2001* (Vic) art 8(2)(b).

[144] *Fletcher v Salvation Army Australia* [2005] VCAT 1523 [7].

[145] For a discussion of the Commission's findings.

essence (namely, the prohibition of criticism of religious beliefs and symbols).[146] Drafters of any bill of rights should be cognizant of such domestic expressions of support for retaining a blasphemy offence for two reasons: first, they mirror efforts on the international level to package an old offence in new, less 'offensive' terms, and, second, because such supporters still deserve a thoughtful explanation as to why reviving blasphemy may be at odds with other rights and values contemplated as worthy of protection under any future rights instrument.

The importance of having drafters clarify Australia's position therefore cannot be overstated. This becomes particularly evident when considering the emerging law in Ireland. Like Australia, Ireland has consistently voted against defamation of religion resolutions at the UN. Following the December 2008 vote on 'Combating Defamation of Religion', Ireland's Minister for Foreign Affairs Micheál Martin explained:

> We believe that the concept of defamation of religion is not consistent with the promotion and protection of human rights. It can be used to justify arbitrary limitations on, or the denial of, freedom of expression. Indeed, Ireland considers that freedom of expression is a key and inherent element in the manifestation of freedom of thought and conscience and as such is complementary to freedom of religion or belief.[147]

However, Ireland's constitution has long provided that the 'publication or utterance of blasphemous, seditious, or indecent matter is an offence which shall be punishable in accordance with law'.[148] To this end, a 2009 law enacted by the Oireachtas[149] has made it a fineable offence for anyone to publish or utter 'blasphemous matter'.[150] Under the new law, in force since January 2010, a blasphemous communication 'is grossly abusive or insulting in relation to matters held sacred by any religion, thereby causing outrage among a substantial number of the adherents of that religion'.[151]

---

[146] NSW Blasphemy Report, above n 34, [4.40].

[147] *New Blasphemy Laws—Free Speech is Not Up For Discussion* (2009) Irish Examiner <http://www.examiner.ie/opinion/editorial/new-blasphemy-laws-free-speech-is-not-up-for-discussion-90664.html#ixzz0LGSB9SNr&C> at 26 March 2011.

[148] *Ireland Constitution* art 40.

[149] A strict time limit, known as a guillotine, was imposed on the debate in the Dáil. Following the lower house vote, Ireland's Seanad passed the bill in a nail-biting 23–22 vote, with the Green Party voting in favour: *Libel law revisions pass the Dáil* (2009) RTE <http://www.rte.ie/news/2009/0708/libel.html> at 26 March 2011. Stephen Collins, *Defamation Bill stumbles through Seanad after lost vote* (2009) Irish Times <http://www.irishtimes.com/newspaper/frontpage/2009/0710/1224250388598.html> at 26 March 2011.

[150] Defamation Bill 2006 (Ireland), art 36(1). A fine may run up to 25,000 euro. Prior drafts of the law originally called for a maximum 100,000 euro fine for the offence.

[151] Defamation Bill 2006 (Ireland), art 36(2)(a).

Unlike Victoria's *Racial and Religious Tolerance Act 2001*, the Irish law establishes a *mens rea* threshold: prosecutors must demonstrate the accused intended 'by the publication or utterance of the matter concerned, to cause such outrage'.[152] The law also affords a defence to the charges if the defendant can prove 'that a reasonable person would find genuine literary, artistic, political, scientific, or academic value in the matter to which the offence relates'.[153] However, these grounds are arguably narrower than Victoria's since it makes no reference to the legitimacy of religious or public interest purposes. More problematic still, Ireland's law explicitly protects 'matters held sacred by any religion'. It therefore appears to track more closely with the push to outlaw defamation of religion at the UN, giving rise to an apparent inconsistency — if not outright conflict — between the law itself and statements of Foreign Affairs Minister Martin. As it stands, Ireland's *Defamation Act* potentially may run afoul of that country's obligations under international law and the European Convention on Human Rights.[154] Indeed, at least one group has already taken steps to challenge the legality of the Irish law's provisions on 'blasphemous matter',[155] and there is some speculation that the government will hold a public referendum to address the issue.[156]

By encouraging the drafters of a potential Australian bill of rights to confront questions related to religious defamation and vilification directly, Australia may avoid potential inconsistencies in law and foreign policy similar to those arising in Ireland. There is already some guidance on this issue emerging from the Australian judiciary, including expression of a narrow definition of incitement,[157] as well as a

---

[152] Defamation Bill 2006 (Ireland), art 36(2)(b).
[153] Defamation Bill 2006 (Ireland), art 36(3).
[154] In part as a consequence of the Defamation Act, Ireland's ranking dropped nine places from the top of Reporters Without Borders' international press freedom index: *2010 World Press Freedom Index* (2010) Reporters Without Borders <http://en.rsf.org/press-freedom-index-2010,1034.html> at 24 August 2011.
[155] For example, an Irish atheist group published a series of 'blasphemous' quotations by personalities including Jesus Christ, Mohammed, Mark Twain, Salman Rushdie and Bjork in an effort to challenge the law in court: *Irish Atheists Use Bjork, Mark Twain to Challenge Blasphemy Law* (2010) CNN <http://www.cnn.com/2010/WORLD/europe/01/02/ireland.blasphemy.law/index.html> at 26 March 2011.
[156] Cf Michael O'Regan, *Now Not the Time For Referendum on Blasphemy, Says Ahern* (2010) Irish Times <http://www.irishtimes.com/newspaper/ireland/2010/0326/1224267097750.html> at 24 August 2011, and Henry McDonald, *Ireland to Hold Referendum on Blasphemy Law* (2010) The Guardian (UK) <http://www.guardian.co.uk/world/2010/mar/15/ireland-referendum-blasphemy-law> at 26 March 2011.
[157] For example, in *Fletcher v Salvation Army Australia*, the tribunal focused on the meaning of 'incite' under the *Racial and Religious Tolerance Act*: 'In its context, this does not mean "causes". Rather it carries the connotation of "inflame" or "set alight". The section is not concerned with conduct that provokes thought': *Fletcher v Salvation Army Australia* [2005] VCAT 1523 [5].

directive to avoid conflating hatred of a given belief and hatred of adherents of that belief in the legal context. In *Catch the Fire Ministries v Islamic Council of Victoria*, the Victoria Court of Appeal found that the lower tribunal failed to consider that distinction, and held that the *Racial and Religious Tolerance Act 2001* does not 'purport to mandate religious tolerance'.[158] According to the Court, the Act 'goes no further in restricting freedom to criticise the religious beliefs of others than to prohibit criticism so extreme as to incite hatred or other relevant emotion of or towards those others. It is essential to keep the distinction between the hatred of beliefs and the hatred of their adherents steadily in view'.[159]

Finally, even if the drafters of an Australian bill of rights reject the defamation norm or its offspring, the process of reaching this decision will help establish the legal justifications for such a position. Within the context of a comprehensive evaluation of the proposed norm, this would position the bill of rights to address, either head-on or implicitly, any possible future gaps or inconsistencies between international human rights law and Australia's domestic implementation of rights. Similarly, in the context of the emergence of a related customary international law norm, Australia will be able to point to its internal bill of rights debate as evidence of its status as a persistent objector opposed to such a norm. In short, drafters can enshrine a more long-term vision of which rights are germane to Australia and how these rights will operate by evaluating not only norms expressed in the relevant treaty law but also the emerging and potential norms on or just beyond the horizon. This process would also have the benefit of strengthening Australia's prestige on the international level by 'limit[ing] future criticism for non-compliance [and] bolster[ing] Australia's credibility when [it comments] on human rights abuses in other jurisdictions'.[160]

Conclusion

This chapter has argued that there is much value and benefit to opening the drafting process surrounding a bill of rights to outside ideas and comparative data. Beyond increasing awareness and challenging preconceptions, such an approach provides a more robust and grounded domestic debate, and can facilitate an outcome that provides reasons and justifications for decisions. Taken together, these measures ultimately can help establish the foundation for fewer surprises down the road.

---

[158] *Catch the Fire Ministries v Islamic Council of Victoria* [2006] VSCA 284 [34].
[159] Ibid.
[160] Australia's National Human Rights Consultation Report has observed that passage of a Human Rights Act would result in improved international standing for Australia: National Human Rights Consultation, above n 11, xxv.

As the last Western democracy without some form of a bill of rights, Australia finds itself in an awkward, but potentially enviable, position. On the one hand, its citizens lack a clear understanding and expression of their rights and freedoms,[161] and the country itself risks being isolated from developments in similar legal systems and may suffer diminished stature during human rights discussions within international fora.[162] On the other hand, a future decision to draft a genuinely Australian human rights instrument holds significant promise: to empower citizens through a participatory drafting model, meaningfully engage with a body of international law that has advanced dramatically in the short span of 60 years, and create a document that not only adopts existing minimum standards but also contemplates and accounts for emerging human rights norms. Based on Australia's long history of support for international human rights and the findings of the National Human Rights Commission, it appears that Australians will not settle for an instrument that merely reflects the floor without consideration of the ceiling as well.

In the context of defamation of religion, a significant number of UN member states continue to support greater protection of religious symbols and beliefs, even if it comes at the expense of freedom of expression and freedom of thought, conscience, and religion or belief. This phenomenon — regardless of whether it is labelled 'defamation of religion' or 'incitement to religious hatred' — is part of an ongoing debate over the substance of international human rights. Therefore, it should figure in any future deliberations over the content and scope of rights in Australia. By recognizing this issue and accounting for it during a future drafting process, Australians can measure their vision of domestic rights against the one emerging on the international level and, if disparities arise, provide the necessary justifications in advance rather than post facto.

To be certain, the concept of defamation of religion is fraught with difficulties. However, navigating through these difficulties will ensure an open and participatory process, shine greater light on Australia's national values and identity, and result in a more durable final instrument capable of addressing future challenges. Undertaking this exercise has the added benefits of helping to flesh out and test more general positions relating to issues including balancing of rights and limitations, and of clarifying potential inconsistencies in Australia's domestic law and foreign policy. Importantly, these advantages should be reproducible regarding assessments of other similarly emerging human rights norms drafters may choose to investigate in the future.

---

[161] The National Human Rights Consultation Committee 'found a lack of understanding among Australians of what human rights are': ibid xvii.

[162] Ibid xxv.

7

Christian Concerns about an Australian Charter of Rights

Patrick Parkinson*

At the end of September 2009, the Report of the National Human Rights Consultation was published.[1] As the consultations leading to this report indicated, the issue of whether Australia should have a charter of rights, or some equivalent, is one on which opinions are sharply divided. The extent of the divisions amongst Australians on this issue led the Government to decide not to pursue the path of a human rights Act.[2]

The divisions about a charter of rights were seen in all parts of the community. There was significant opposition, for example, from leading figures in the Labor Party such as former premier of New South Wales, Bob Carr. There is, nonetheless, one quite prominent sector of Australian society in which opposition to a charter has been rather more evident than support for it. That is in the churches. The Australian Christian Lobby, a group with a significant level of support across the country, mostly from evangelical Christians, ran a strong campaign against having a charter.[3] Reservations about a charter are to be found not only in submissions by churches and Christian organizations to the National Human Rights Consultation

---

* The author wishes to thank Prof Rex Ahdar and Dr Paul Taylor for their helpful comments on an earlier draft of this chapter. A version of this chapter first appeared in (2010) 15 *Australian Journal of Human Rights* 83, and is reproduced here with permission.
[1] National Human Rights Consulation Committee, *National Human Rights Consultation Report* (2009).
[2] The announcement was made by the Attorney-General on 21 April 2010 in launching the National Human Rights Framework. See Attorney-General's Department, *Australia's Human Rights Framework* (2010) <http://www.ag.gov.au/humanrightsframework> at 9 September 2011.
[3] The ACL presented a petition to government with 21,000 signatures in November 2009.

itself, ('the NHRC') but also in submissions to the Australian Human Rights Commission's project on Freedom of Religion and Belief in Australia ('the AHRC project').

The spectrum of views among churches

Submissions to the NHRC that are critical of a charter, apart from the Australian Christian Lobby, include those from the Presbyterian Church of Australia, the Baptist Union of Australia, the Anglican Diocese of Sydney, the Life, Marriage and Family Centre of the Catholic Archdiocese of Sydney, and the Ambrose Centre for Religious Liberty (a body that has an advisory council that includes senior figures from a number of different faiths). In submissions to the AHRC inquiry, the NSW Council of Churches[4] and the Association of Christian Schools also expressed reservations about a charter.[5] In its submission to the NHRC, the Australian Catholic Bishops Conference decided not to take a stand either for or against a charter of rights. It considered that attention should first be given to the prior questions of what human rights should be protected and then to an examination of the extent to which protection of those rights could be improved. It suggested that 'seeking better coordination of existing protections and services should be considered prior to more substantial change. If such better coordination is unachievable or inadequate then more substantial change should be considered'.[6]

While the Catholic Bishops collectively did not take a stand either way, Cardinal George Pell, the church's most prominent leader, has been an outspoken critic of a charter.[7] He was part of a delegation of top leaders from across the spectrum of churches that met with the Attorney-General and Shadow Attorney in October 2009 to express opposition to a human rights Act.[8]

The opposition among the churches is not universal. The General Synod Standing Committee of the Anglican Church of Australia came out in support of human rights legislation, but only if strong provisions concerning freedom of religion were included, consistent with article 18 of the International Covenant on Civil and

---

[4] NSW Council of Churches, *Submission to Australian Human Rights Inquiry, Freedom of Religion and Belief in the 21st Century Project* (2009) 3.

[5] Australian Association of Christian Schools, *Submission to Australian Human Rights Inquiry, Freedom of Religion and Belief in the 21st Century Project* (2009) 14.

[6] Australian Catholic Bishops Conference, *Submission to the National Human Rights Consultation* (2009) 20.

[7] See 'Pell says no to bill of rights' *CathNews Online* (2008) <http://www.cathnews.com/article.aspx?aeid=6892> at 9 September 2011.

[8] Nicola Berkovic, 'Clergy unite over charter', *The Australian* (Sydney), 23 October 2009. The author accompanied the delegation.

Political Rights ('the ICCPR'). The submission was critical of the level of protection for freedom of religion in the Victorian and Australian Capital Territory charters. The submission also noted that within the Anglican Church there is 'a diversity of opinion around which human rights should be recognized and how they should be protected'.[9] The dissenting view is particularly evident in the submission of the Sydney Diocese (which has by far the largest active membership base of any diocese in Australia). It came out strongly against a charter of rights. By way of contrast, only the Uniting Church submission, and the submission of the Peace and Legislation Committee of the Religious Society of Friends, gave unqualified support to an Australian human rights Act or charter.

The church groups opposed to a charter are not at all against recognition of human rights — far from it.[10] Most church submissions emphasised the Christian foundations for the recognition of human rights and the extensive involvement of Christians both in advocating for human rights and in giving practical effect to the promotion of those rights through humanitarian services. What many of these submissions oppose, or have doubts about, is the means of promoting human rights, not the end. The churches are not alone, of course, in questioning whether the only effective means to stiffen respect for human rights is through the law.[11]

The paradox: Christian concerns about freedom of religion

What emerges, in particular, from submissions to the AHRC inquiry, is that there is a widespread, if not universal, view across Christian denominations and organisations that religious freedom is under threat in Australia. This threat is seen to come in particular from the growing antipathy among secular liberals towards exemptions under anti-discrimination legislation for faith-based organizations, and from the chilling effect upon freedom of speech arising from vague and poorly drafted

---

[9] General Synod Standing Committee of the Anglican Church of Australia, *Submission to the National Human Rights Consultation* (2009) 1.

[10] For example, the Australian Christian Lobby states: 'ACL is committed to the promotion and protection of the fundamental human rights of all persons. It is a large part of our motivation'; *Submission to the National Human Rights Consultation* (2009) 1 (available at <http://australianchristianlobby.org.au/2009/06/acl-submission-to-the-national-human-rights-consultation/>).

[11] David Kinley, 'Human Rights Fundamentalisms' (2007) 29 *Sydney Law Review* 545, 562–3. Kinley cites rights sceptics such as Jim Allen, Tom Campbell, Marie-Bénédicte Dembour, Keith Ewing, Mark Tushnet and Jeremy Waldron.

'anti-vilification' laws concerning religion.[12] There are also concerns about the respect being given in Australia to freedom of conscience.

One might think that organizations that perceive their fundamental human rights are under threat, rights guaranteed in very strong and clear terms by article 18 of the Universal Declaration of Human Rights ('the UDHR'), article 18 of the ICCPR and a number of other human rights' instruments, would be in favour of a charter of rights to provide some protection. Yet many of the same church submissions that raise concerns about religious freedom argue very cogently against a charter.

Understanding the churches' opposition

This chapter examines the submissions of various groups that are opposed to a charter of rights, drawing both on submissions to the NHRC and to the AHRC inquiry and explains the reasons for concerns about a charter from the perspective of one who has been actively involved with church leaders in the 'no' campaign. The views of church leaders are important, irrespective of what people may think about whether their concerns are justified, because they represent such a large body of educated and informed opinion in the Australian community, and because of the influence that their views have had in the charter debate. The concerns of the churches also raise important implications for the future of human rights discourse in Australia, since one of the primary issues for the churches is about the way in which freedom of religion and conscience has been seemingly disregarded by statutory bodies responsible for protecting human rights, and by other human rights advocates.

General arguments against a charter

Some of the submissions opposed to a charter of rights reflected concerns expressed much more widely in the Australian community. The submission of the Australian Christian Lobby, for example, articulated the general case against a charter of rights, and chose not to focus only on the particular interests and concerns of the Christian community. Many similar points concerning the respective roles of parliament and the courts in a democratic society were made by the Anglican Diocese of Sydney, the Presbyterian Church of Australia and the Baptist Union of Australia. The Anglican Diocese of Sydney, for example, argued that the courts were inappropriate fora

---

[12] Nicholas Aroney, 'The constitutional (in)validity of religious vilification laws: implications for their interpretation' (2006) 34 *Federal Law Review* 287; Patrick Parkinson, 'The freedom to be different: religious vilification, anti-discrimination laws and religious minorities in Australia' (2007) 81 *Australian Law Journal* 954; Rex Ahdar, 'Religious vilification: confused policy, unsound principle and unfortunate law' (2007) 26 *University of Queensland Law Journal* 293.

for the resolution of what were essentially competing moral claims.[13] It pointed to the advantage of the political process in allowing discussions on important moral questions to continue to be discussed and debated.[14] Through the political process, the compromises that are reached in one generation can be revisited in the next if those compromises prove unworkable or unsatisfactory.

This focus upon how to resolve competing claims of rights was, in my view, central to the concerns of many Christian leaders about a charter, particularly when claims to a right are made in absolute terms. As the Presbyterian Church of Victoria submission noted, 'it is absurd to speak of rights in the abstract, absolute way in which they are usually framed in human rights instruments, particularly when even those instruments themselves recognise that they are capable of legitimate abridgement'.[15]

The problem is when absolutist claims about the moral requirements of a charter are used to mask and provide some special authority for the policy positions of people with particular agendas. At the heart of Christian concerns about the development of a charter is that secular liberal interpretations of human rights charters will tend to relegate religious freedom to the lowest place in an implicit hierarchy of rights established not by international law but by the intellectual fashions of the day.

The issue of anti-discrimination law

Central to Christian concerns about religious freedom in Australia is the potential impact of anti-discrimination law. These concerns do not arise from a discomfort with anti-discrimination provisions generally. Most grounds of discrimination in the laws of Australian jurisdictions would attract widespread support from a Christian perspective. However, Christianity involves adherence to a moral code. Christians insist on the importance of being able to discriminate between right and wrong, and to have freedom of conscience, when it comes to moral issues.[16]

The problem, in particular, arises from an emerging and almost absolutist view of the requirement of non-discrimination in the workplace. There can be a dogmatism about such matters as powerful and rigid as any belief system of fundamentalist religious groups. That fundamentalism inheres in two aspects. The first is a belief that all limitations on who is eligible to apply for particular jobs should be abolished or severely restricted in the name of one conceptualisation of 'equality', even if 99.9 per

---

[13] Standing Committee of the Synod of the Anglican Church Diocese of Sydney, *Submission to National Human Rights Consultation* (2009) [28]-[29].
[14] Similar points were made by the Australian Christian Lobby, above n 10, 6–8.
[15] Presbyterian Church of Victoria, *Submission to National Human Rights Consultation* (2009) 8.
[16] Ibid [23].

cent of all the other jobs in the community were open to that person. This position involves taking a very restrictive approach to 'genuine occupational requirements' as a ground for exceptions to general anti-discrimination provisions.[17] The second fundamentalist aspect of the anti-discrimination movement arises from a belief that the only human rights that should be given any real significance are individual ones and not group rights. This can make adherents disregard the competing claims of groups that would justify a right of positive selection in order to enhance the cohesion and identity of the group.

Fundamentalism about non-discrimination

The view that any selection of a person for employment that takes account of characteristics other than merit is discriminatory reflects one particular understanding of what a commitment to equality requires.[18] This view is gaining ground in Western countries, and challenges the rights of faith communities to include and exclude based upon compatibility with the worldview and beliefs of that faith community. As Evans and Gaze note, 'there is an increasingly powerful movement to subject religions to the full scope of discrimination laws, with some scholars now suggesting that even core religious practices (such as the ordination of clergy) can be regulated in the name of equality'.[19]

This view was, for example, reflected in a statement of the Human Rights and Equal Opportunities Commission, as it was then known, questioning the exemption provided by s 37 of the *Sex Discrimination Act 1984* (Cth) and proposing a three-year sunset clause on its continued operation.[20] The Commission argued that 'the rights to religious freedom and to gender equality must be appropriately balanced in accordance with human rights principles' and that 'the permanent exemption does not provide support for women of faith who are promoting gender equality within their religious body'.

Not all proponents of this view are so extreme as to argue that government can regulate the ordination of clergy. Cass Sunstein, for example, argues that while there is no compelling argument for saying that religious institutions should be exempted

---

[17] For a discussion see Rex Ahdar and Ian Leigh, 'Chapter 10: Employment' in Rex Ahdar and Ian Leigh (eds), *Religious Freedom in the Liberal State* (2005).
[18] For a critique of the use of equality rhetoric as devoid of meaning, see Peter Westen, 'The empty idea of equality' (1982) 95 *Harvard Law Review* 537.
[19] Carolyn Evans and Beth Gaze, 'Between religious freedom and equality: complexity and context' (2008) 49 *Harvard International Law Journal Online* 40, 41.
[20] Human Rights and Equal Opportunity Commission, *Submission to the Senate Legal and Constitutional Affairs Committee Inquiry into the Effectiveness of the Sex Discrimination Act 1984 (Cth) in Eliminating Discrimination and Promoting Gender Equality* (September 2008) 166 (available at <http://www.hreoc.gov.au/legal/submissions/2008/20080901_SDA.pdf>).

from sex discrimination laws, at least some legislative restraint is justified.[21] He would protect religious autonomy when a law, whatever its nature and purpose, interferes with religious practices and is not supported by a legitimate and sufficiently strong justification. However, even that view leaves plenty of scope for regulating religious practice, since it is ultimately a value judgment whether interference with freedom of religion is 'strongly justified'. Adherents to a cause — whether it be women's ordination, gay and lesbian equality or another such movement — would no doubt be convinced that interference with religious freedom is strongly justified if it promotes that agenda. As Stanley Fish once put it, 'tolerance is exercised in an inverse proportion to there being anything at stake'.[22]

Genuine occupational requirements

Religious freedom is particularly under attack from a very narrow approach to the idea of genuine occupational qualifications. This was, for example, seen in the Equality Bill 2009 in Britain. Schedule 9, cl 2, provided various exemptions to religious bodies. If 'the employment is for the purposes of an organised religion' the organisation was to be permitted to have:

- a requirement to be of a particular sex
- a requirement not to be a transsexual person
- a requirement not to be married or a civil partner
- a requirement not to be married to, or the civil partner of, a person who has a living former spouse or civil partner
- a requirement relating to circumstances in which a marriage or civil partnership came to an end
- a requirement related to sexual orientation.

The original version of the Bill stated that the exemption would apply as long as the requirement is a proportionate means of complying with the doctrines of the religion or avoiding conflict with the strongly held religious convictions of a significant number of the religion's followers. Further, according to the original version of subparagraph (8), employment would be 'for the purposes of an organised religion' only if it wholly or mainly involves:

---

[21] Cass Sunstein, 'On the tension between sex equality and religious freedom' in Debra Satz and Rob Reich (eds), *Toward a Humanist Justice: The Political Philosophy of Susan Moller Okin* (2009) 129.
[22] Stanley Fish, 'Almost Pragmatism: Richard Posner's Jurisprudence' (1990) 57 *University of Chicago Law Review* 1447, 1466.

a) leading or assisting in the observation of liturgical or ritualistic practices of the religion, or

b) promoting or explaining the doctrines of the religion (whether to followers of the religion or others).

As the Archbishop of York pointed out, even he would not be included within this definition, as the majority of his working week, like most clergy, was spent doing work other than preaching and conducting services.[23]

The Government, which affirmed the Bill's compliance with the European Convention on Human Rights,[24] was quite clear about its intention to curtail religious freedom significantly if it clashed with the goal of equal access to employment opportunities. While clergy (at least those who mainly work on Sundays) would be exempted, the Explanatory Memorandum stated that the otherwise prohibited requirement 'must be crucial to the post, and not merely one of several important factors' and that the exemption would be unlikely to apply in relation to a non-celibate gay or lesbian church youth worker unless he or she 'mainly' teaches bible classes.[25] It followed that churches would not be allowed to insist that staff, other than those who mainly conduct services or teach the doctrines of the faith, exemplify Christian values in terms of family life and sexual practice.[26] The issue is not only about homosexual practice. Christians — and other faiths — have traditionally taught a disciplined sexual ethic in relation to heterosexual conduct as well.

The Government's provisions were defeated at Committee stage in the House of Lords,[27] with amendments returning the law to the status quo as it had been since 2003.[28] However, the British Government's Bill indicates clearly how narrowly the scope of 'genuine occupational requirements' may be drawn when it comes to matters of faith and sexual morality. As was pointed out in the debate, there would be no similar attempt to force a rape crisis centre to have male staff.

---

[23] House of Lords, *Parliamentary Debates*, 15 December 2009, Column 1433 (John Sentamu, Archbishop of York) (available at <http://www.publications.parliament.uk/pa/ld200910/ldhansrd/text/91215-0007.htm#09121563000195>).

[24] The requirement to certify this is contained in s 19(1)(a) of the *Human Rights Act 1998* (UK) and the certification was on the front page of the Bill.

[25] Explanatory Notes, Equality Bill 2009 (UK) 774–8. It appears also that the Government was under pressure from the European Commission to narrow the religious exemptions. See the House of Lords debate (available at <http://www.publications.parliament.uk/pa/ld200910/ldhansrd/text/100125-0004.htm#10012510000178>).

[26] Daniel Boucher, *A Little Bit Against Discrimination?* (2010).

[27] Avril Ormsby, *Government loses Equality Bill faith proposals* (2010) Reuters <http://uk.reuters.com/article/idUKTRE60P1KJ20100126> at 9 September 2011.

[28] See amendments moved in House of Lords debate, above n 23.

This reach of government into the way in which churches run themselves reflects a major shift from what John Rawls called 'political liberalism' to the promotion of 'comprehensive liberalism' that addresses the non-political aspects of life as well.[29] Michael McConnell explains that in political liberalism:

> Elements of this liberal polity were state neutrality, tolerance and the guarantee of equality before the law. 'Neutrality' meant, fundamentally, that the government would not take sides in religious and philosophical differences among the people ... Tolerance meant something like 'live and let live'.[30]

In contrast, he writes that 'Today there is a widespread sense not only that the government should be neutral, tolerant and egalitarian, but so should all of us, and so should our private associations'.[31]

The new version of liberalism involves a rejection of traditional ideas about the separation of church and state. Meyerson, for example, has offered an eloquent defence of the Rawlsian position concerning religion and the public square by emphasising that the principle of governmental neutrality that this entails preserves a large degree of autonomy for faith communities. She writes:

> in placing religion largely beyond the state's reach, it confers maximum autonomy on churches to regulate their own affairs, free of liberal constraints if they wish. It also provides the strongest possible protection for religious freedom, a protection which it extends even to those who would deny it to others.[32]

If only that were so. By way of contrast, the comprehensive liberalism evident in the British Government's Equality Bill, reflecting also a view within the European bureaucracy,[33] offers to churches and other faith communities only the most minimal level of autonomy to regulate their own affairs, and only very limited freedom from 'liberal constraints'.

Comprehensive liberalism uses law as a tool to impose a particular notion of the good by coercion, denying people the freedom to act upon dissenting moral views, and largely rejecting pluralism in relation to moral values. The issue is most acute in relation

---

[29] John Rawls, *Political Liberalism* (1993) 11–3.
[30] Michael McConnell, 'Why is Religious Freedom the First Freedom?' (2000) 21 *Cardozo Law Review* 1243, 1258–9.
[31] Ibid 1259.
[32] Denise Meyerson, 'Why Religion Belongs in the Private Sphere, not the Public Square' in Peter Cane, Carolyn Evans and Zoe Robinson (eds), *Law and Religion in Theoretical and Historical Context* (2008) 44, 61.
[33] See above n 25.

to sexual orientation, for here traditional Christian moral teaching collides, perhaps irreconcilably, with the equality agenda for gay and lesbian people.[34] Noted gay and lesbian rights scholar Carl Stychin observes that what is happening is now a public policy reversal that mirrors the historic closeting of gay and lesbian people to the realm of the private.[35] This is occurring through the utilisation of the public/private dichotomy:

> Ironically, supporters of sexuality equality at times fall back on the public–private, belief–conduct distinctions as the justification for curtailing religious freedom — relegating those of faith to the closet from which they themselves have emerged. In so doing, equality itself becomes a world view which monopolizes the public sphere …[36]

This monopolisation of the public sphere, which includes the world of work outside very narrow confines, represents the essence of the threat to religious freedom, for it impacts not only upon the individual's freedom of conscience when living in the general community — for example when providing goods and services to the general public[37] — but also in the communal life of faith communities and organisations. Churches and other faith communities are now being denied the very autonomy to regulate their own affairs that, in its earlier manifestations, liberalism was anxious to protect.

The liberal retreat from support of multiculturalism

This hostility towards exemptions to anti-discrimination law has been reinforced by another tendency. Whereas once a commitment to multiculturalism was one of the hallmarks of progressive liberalism, now there is an emerging trend in liberal thought to see respect for other cultures as a roadblock in the way of advancing the freedom and dignity of people and the promotion of individual rights.[38] This

---

[34] Chai Feldblum, 'Moral Conflict and Liberty: Gay Rights and Religion' (2006) 72 *Brooklyn Law Review* 61.

[35] Carl Stychin, 'Faith in the Future: Sexuality, Religion and the Public Sphere' (2009) 29 *Oxford Journal of Legal Studies* 727, 733.

[36] Ibid.

[37] See, eg, *Human Rights Commission v Eric Sides Motors Co Ltd* (1981) 2 NZAR 447; *Re The Christian Institute's and others' Application for Judicial Review* [2008] NI 86; *London Borough of Islington v Ladele and Liberty* [2009] IRLR 154; *Members of the Board of the Wesley Mission Council v OV and OW (No 2)* [2009] NSW ADTAP 57.

[38] Susan Moller Okin, for example, gave voice to these sentiments in her influential essay, 'Is Multiculturalism Bad for Women?' (1997) 22 *Boston Review* 8 (first publication) and Susan Moller Okin, 'Is Multiculturalism Bad for Women?' in Joshua Cohen et al (eds), *Is Multiculturalism Bad for Women?* (1999) (republication). For another view, see Will Kymlicka, *Multicultural Citizenship: A Liberal Theory of Minority Rights* (1995).

changing attitude towards multiculturalism is, for example, expressed by American philosopher H E Baber, who puts the case succinctly:

> Liberals value individual freedom. Multiculturalism restricts individual freedom. That is the liberal case against multiculturalism.[39]

Baber argues that liberals should discourage practices that promote cultural diversity and, instead, encourage assimilation. In a return to traditional American values espoused by conservatives, she argues for the promotion of a melting pot society in which only individual rights, and not the rights of groups, are recognized.[40]

This change in liberal thought is not confined to the US. Tensions over multiculturalism have been particularly marked in European countries, such as France, affected by mass immigration from Muslim societies.[41] The hostility to multiculturalism has gathered pace since 9/11, and the present climate in many Western nations is not at all hospitable to policies that permit or encourage a separate identity for Muslims.[42]

The combination of an almost absolutist attitude towards non-discrimination with the retreat from support for multiculturalism has led to a view of equality that has little or no place for the rights of discrete minorities to maintain their identity as groups if that conflicts with equality agendas based upon any of the standard grounds for non-discrimination, including religious belief or the lack of it. That is, there is little recognition of the importance to faith-based communities of being able to maintain the boundaries of the group by religiously-based rules of inclusion and exclusion. This has particular implications for faith-based schools and other religious organisations.

The issue of faith-based schools

From the earliest time in European-Australian history, churches have established schools. Many of the most well-known and prestigious private schools in Australia have such associations with churches. The Catholic Church also has a very well developed network of 'systemic' schools, both primary schools and high schools, in

---

[39] H E Baber, *The Multicultural Mystique: The Liberal Case Against Diversity* (2008) 17.
[40] Ibid 244.
[41] John Bowen, 'Recognising Islam in France after 9/11' (2009) 35 *Journal of Ethnic and Migration Studies* 439.
[42] Abdullah Ahmed An-Na'im, 'Global Citizenship and Human Rights; from Muslims in Europe to European Muslims' in M L P Loenen and J E Goldschmidt (eds), *Religious Pluralism and Human Rights in Europe: Where to Draw the Line?* (2007) 13; Dominic McGoldrick, 'Accommodating Muslims in Europe: From Adopting Sharia Law to Religiously Based Opt Outs from Generally Applicable Laws' (2009) 9 *Human Rights Law Review* 603.

which fees are modest and which give to parents an alternative to the State school system within a reasonable distance of their home.

These church-based schools vary in the extent to which they give importance to their Christian foundations.[43] Some of these faith-based schools, particularly some of the more prestigious, expensive and long-established private schools, no longer maintain a strong religious tradition beyond having a chaplain and religious services as part of school life. They do not insist upon adherence to the Christian faith as a condition for a teaching appointment. Other church-based schools endeavour to maintain a Christian ethos even if not all teaching staff are committed adherents to the faith.

However, there are other schools that have been established to provide an explicitly Christian environment for children and young people. These tend to be schools within the evangelical tradition of the Christian faith, and have a strong view of the authority of the Bible as central to life. Sometimes they are founded by one local church; more commonly, an independent association runs them. These schools have flourished in recent years. Typically, these schools have an inclusive employment policy in the sense that Christians from any denominational background are welcome, but adherence to the fundamentals of the Christian faith — belief in the divinity of Jesus Christ, his atonement for sins and his bodily resurrection from the dead — are regarded as essential for employment. Some Christian schools require adherence to the Christian faith from all staff, not just teaching staff. This includes administrators and maintenance personnel. The reason for this is that they see the school as being a community of faith, and all staff interact with parents and children.

The right of positive selection

The issue for Christian schools is not the right to 'discriminate'. That puts the issue in negative and pejorative terms. The core claim is a right of positive selection. The Australian Association of Christian Schools puts it this way:

> We also claim the right to employ only those persons who have a thorough understanding of and commitment to the school's Christian worldview and Statement of Faith and who, in their personal lives, are able and willing to model consistently a personal standard of conduct and lifestyle choices that aligns to the worldview and Statement of Faith of the school in which they have applied to teach/work.[44]

---

[43] Carolyn Evans and Beth Gaze, 'Discrimination by Religious Schools: Views from the Coal Face' (2010) 34 *Melbourne University Law Review* 392.

[44] Australian Association of Christian Schools, above n 5.

In this, Christian schools and organizations only ask to be treated equally with other employers that may have legitimate reasons for wanting to appoint only those with certain characteristics relevant to the identity of the organisation. It is quite understandable that gay bars might prefer to appoint only gay staff, that Thai restaurants might prefer to have Thai employees, and that government ministers would want to staff their offices with people sympathetic to the values of their political party. Recognition of minority group rights on an equal footing is another version of equality. A right of positive selection is rather different from discrimination. It is easy to see the problem if a restaurant advertised for staff of any nationality so long as they were not Thai. That would be discriminatory. However, it is quite different if a Thai restaurant advertises for Thai staff. Selection based in part on a characteristic that is relevant to the employment is not discriminatory.

The right of positive selection in relation to faith-based schools is supported by the foundational international covenants and declarations on human rights. Article 18(4) of the ICCPR provides:

> The States Parties to the present Covenant undertake to have respect for the liberty of parents and, when applicable, legal guardians to ensure the religious and moral education of their children in conformity with their own convictions.

In the interpretative documents such as the Human Rights Committee's General Comment 22, article 18 (1993), it is clear that international human rights law protects the right to run schools on a religious foundation. That is supported also, for example, by article 5 of the UN Declaration on the Elimination of All Forms of Intolerance and of Discrimination Based on Religion or Belief. The article 18(4) rights and similar international law provisions are abrogated if schools that are established for the purposes of providing a religious context for a child's education are deprived of the right to choose staff who adhere to the precepts of the faith and abide by the codes of conduct of that faith. What is true of Christian schools is no doubt true of Jewish and Islamic schools as well.

Similar issues also arise for many faith-based charitable and humanitarian organizations. These organizations are not only faith-based, but faith-motivated. Around the world, they do an enormous amount in practical terms to promote the human rights, dignity and well-being of the world's poor and disadvantaged. Destroying the faith-based character of these organizations so that they no longer have a reason for existence may well diminish the human rights of those they serve.

This issue of the right of positive selection of staff to Christian schools and organizations is perhaps the strongest theme running through all the church submissions to the National Human Rights Consultation and to the AHRC's freedom of religion and belief inquiry, and has affected their submissions on the charter of Rights. The Australian Catholic Bishops Conference, for example, wrote:

> Catholics will judge any proposed amendment to existing laws or any future human rights legislation by reference to the extent to which it will protect the right to religious freedom, not only for themselves but for all religions ...

> Does the law comprehensively protect the right of the Catholic Church, its institutions and agencies, such as parishes, schools, universities, hospitals, aged care facilities and welfare agencies, to employ their staff by reference to religious affiliation and commitment for such intrinsically religious purposes as religious instruction, formation and pastoral care, but more widely for the purpose of supporting and promoting the relevant entity's Catholic mission and identity?[45]

The Anglican Primate, Archbishop Phillip Aspinall, has also taken up the concerns of churches about a right of positive selection, in a letter to the then Prime Minister urging support for human rights legislation. He wrote:

> We believe that the right to freedom of religion should include the right of a religious body to determine the requisite qualifications, including religious belief, for employees and volunteers who carry out its work, in accordance with its religious doctrine and practices.

> We also support the right of religious bodies to determine whether, and in what circumstances, they will provide particular services in accordance with their beliefs. Governments should not coerce religious bodies to provide services contrary to their religious beliefs. This would be a fundamental denial of freedom of religion.[46]

Anti-discrimination and multiculturalism

Far from being antithetical to multiculturalism, a right of positive selection is essential to it. Multiculturalism involves respecting the rights of minority communities to maintain their identity as groups, for example, through cultural and religious organizations. It involves acknowledgement of diversity and allowing some degree of separateness within the wider community. There has been a widespread acceptance that respect for different beliefs and cultures requires acceptance of faith-based schools in order to promote that diversity. Schools provide a context in which faith

---

[45] Australian Catholic Bishops Conference, above n 6.
[46] Letter from the Most Rev'd Dr Phillip Aspinall, Primate, to the Prime Minister, 18 November 2009. Copy on file with author.

is taught and nurtured. They also support the article 27 rights of ethnic minorities to promote identity and cohesion within the community. Faith-based schools are very important to multiculturalism, for faith and culture are often closely intertwined, and a multicultural society needs to respect all faiths, as well as non-belief.

Paradoxically, one of the most effective ways to crush diversity is to insist on it. By requiring diversity in the employment of teaching staff within the faith-based school, its distinctive character as a faith-based school is undermined.

Anti-discrimination law and the right of positive selection

One solution to the 'problem' of religious organizations is to narrow the meaning of 'manifesting' to a very narrow set of activities — conducting religious rituals or engaging in teaching of religion. This is the narrow definition that lies behind the original version of the Equality Bill in the UK, for example. On this approach, equality legislation does not interfere with religious freedom because it does not impact upon 'core' religious activity, and that solves the problem when it comes to staffing of religious schools. The secular liberal may accept that the religious studies teacher should be an adherent of the faith because that person is engaging in a 'religious' activity. However, on this view there is no reason why the maths teacher, the office administrator or the gardener needs to be a believer. For example, Evans and Gaze argue:

> The hiring of staff in religiously run hospitals, schools and other institutions may well be important to many religions, but it usually does not have the central place of activities such as the selection and training of clergy, the language and symbolism of ritual, and the determination of membership of the religious community. Such core religious activities have a greater claim for freedom from regulation (including from the imposition of non-discrimination laws) than activities that are more peripheral.[47]

However, it is a *non-Christian* view of the Christian faith that supposes that religion can be confined to a particular set of beliefs taught in religious studies classes or in chapel. That is not how Christians understand their faith, as numerous submissions to the NHRC and AHRC made clear. Modelling Christianity within a faith community is as important as teaching Christianity within a classroom or from a pulpit. Indeed, it may well be more important and have more impact on people's lives.

A prominent gay and lesbian rights scholar, Chai Feldblum, who is now an equal opportunity commissioner in the Obama administration, acknowledges that the manifestation of religious belief cannot be confined to conducting services and teaching. She accepts that faith affects how people choose to live, and that

---

[47] Evans and Gaze, above n 19, 47.

anti-discrimination laws burden the liberty of people of faith to the extent that they prevent people acting in accordance with their convictions. However, while acknowledging this impact, she considers that a right of positive selection for faith-based organisations that provide social services should be limited to leadership positions on the basis that people in leadership ought to be able to articulate the beliefs and values of the enterprise. Even this rather modest proposal is offered hesitantly.[48] Even a preference for people of faith would be prohibited on Feldblum's proposal. This falls well short of respecting the fact that some organizations providing education or health care see themselves as faith communities, rather than being just educational or health care providers who happen to have had a religious foundation.

Why do many church organizations not want a charter?

Christian concerns about the freedom to run faith-based schools and organizations might logically lead them to support a charter of rights, given the non-derogable nature of religious freedom in international human rights instruments. That would act as a constraint upon parliament. The Australian Christian Lobby certainly supports more parliamentary scrutiny of legislation in terms of Australia's international human rights obligations. It recommends that the Senate Scrutiny of Bills Committee be strengthened to examine proposed and existing legislation in the light of international human rights instruments.[49] This maintains the primacy of elected representatives in protecting human rights. It also ensures the focus is on Australia's international human rights commitments.

One of the problems, though, as perceived by some churches, is that the two charters currently in existence in Australia do not adequately give effect to Australia's international human rights obligations, and there is a lack of confidence, based on international precedents, that a charter will do much to protect the freedoms that churches want to preserve.

Failures of jurisdictions with charter to properly enact article 18 of the ICCPR

One of the major concerns of the churches is about the weak protection for religious freedom in the Victorian and ACT charters. A number of submissions comment on this aspect of the *Charter of Rights and Responsibilities Act 2006* (Vic). The inadequate protection of freedom of religion is noted, for example, by the national Presbyterian[50]

---

[48] Feldblum, above n 34, 122.
[49] Australian Christian Lobby, above n 10, 16.
[50] Presbyterian Church of Australia, *Submission to the National Human Rights Consultation* (11 June 2009) [34]-[39].

and Anglican Church[51] submissions. They point out that the charters in the ACT and Victoria do not give proper application to article 18(3) of the ICCPR.[52] That article provides:

> Freedom to manifest one's religion or beliefs may be subject only to such limitations as are prescribed by law and are necessary to protect public safety, order, health, or morals or the fundamental rights and freedoms of others.

This may be compared with s 7(2) of the Victorian *Charter of Rights and Responsibilities Act 2006*, which provides:

> A human right may be subject under law only to such reasonable limits as can be demonstrably justified in a free and democratic society based on human dignity, equality and freedom, and taking into account all relevant factors including—
>
> (a) the nature of the right; and
>
> (b) the importance of the purpose of the limitation; and
>
> (c) the nature and extent of the limitation; and
>
> (d) the relationship between the limitation and its purpose; and
>
> (e) any less restrictive means reasonably available to achieve the purpose that the limitation seeks to achieve.

The Presbyterian Church of Australia submission offers a particularly incisive critique. It notes that the 'limitation provisions in Section 7 bear little resemblance to ICCPR Article 18(3) in their practical and legal effect'.[53] The submission goes on to note that there is no boundary to the grounds on which freedom of religion may be restricted. Furthermore, the charter introduces the concept of *reasonable* limitations, which finds no parallel in article 18(3) of the ICCPR. The Church also draws attention to the subsequently enunciated Siracusa Principles[54], which

---

[51] Above n 9, [15].

[52] For an overview of the art 18 jurisprudence, see Peter Radan, 'International law and religion: Article 18 of the International Covenant on Civil and Political Rights' in Peter Radan, Denise Meyerson and Rosalind Croucher (eds), *Law and Religion: God, the State and the Common Law* (2005) 9.

[53] Presbyterian Church of Australia, above n 50.

[54] United Nations, Economic and Social Council, UN Sub-Commission on Prevention of Discrimination and Protection of Minorities, *Siracusa Principles on the Limitation and Derogation of Provisions in the International Covenant on Civil and Political Rights*, Annex, UN Doc E/CN.4/1984/4 (1984).

define the conditions for permissible limitations and derogations enunciated in the ICCPR. It argues that section 7(2) of the Victorian charter fails to comply with three of those principles.

The Presbyterian Church also notes that while the *Charter of Rights and Responsibilities Act 2006* requires other Victorian legislation to be interpreted as far as possible in a way compatible with 'human rights',[55] judges have an unfettered discretion whether or not to take any account of international law in carrying out that work of interpretation.[56] If international human rights law is not the body of law that should guide judges, what should inform and constrain their interpretations of what 'human rights' require? The Victorian Act, like the ACT legislation, gives enormous discretion to whoever is the decision-maker about compatibility with the charter.

The argument of the Presbyterian Church that the Victorian charter, while purporting to gain its moral authority from international human rights law, in fact does not comply with that body of law, deserves serious consideration. The Victorian charter actually provides people of faith with far fewer rights than the ICCPR gives to them so far as the law of Victoria is concerned. Section 7 does not even state, as one might have expected consistent with article 18(3), that rights can only be limited in specified circumstances. The Act merely requires that the limits be reasonable and that they can be 'demonstrably justified in a free and democratic society based on human dignity, equality and freedom'. Similar criticisms could be levelled at the limitation provisions in certain other jurisdictions, notably that administered through the European Convention and those countries that adopt models which are similar to the European Convention, either through incorporation of Convention principles (such as the UK) or the adoption of a list of rights coupled with a single omnibus limitation provision (UK, Canada, ACT). This approach is in contrast to the ICCPR in which limitation provisions are sometimes specific and are contained within the article that defines the scope of that right.

The practical and legal difference is perhaps illustrated by the stark contrast in outcomes resulting from decisions reached within four months of each other in 2004 by the European Court (under article 9 of the European Convention) and the Human Rights Committee (under article 18 of the ICCPR) on the single issue of religious dress. In *Leyla Sahin v Turkey*[57] the European Court supported restrictions at a secular university on women students wearing the hijab, because of the impact it would have on other women students who might feel pressure to conform. The Grand Chamber upheld the decision of no violation. In *Raihon Hudoyberganova v*

---

[55] *Charter of Rights and Responsibilities Act 2006* (Vic) s 32(1).
[56] Ibid s 32(2).
[57] Application No. 44774/98, 29 June 2004.

Uzbekistan[58], a violation of article 18 was found when deterrence against university students wearing a headscarf took the form of an invitation to attend a different institution. The Human Rights Committee affirmed that the freedom to manifest religion encompasses the right to wear clothes in public in conformity with the individual's faith or religion. While there are many jurisprudential differences between the two systems of law, and the facts underlying the two cases were not identical, at the end of the day the manner of deployment of limitation provisions was decisive.

Section 7(2) has been interpreted by Warren CJ in *Re an application under the Major Crime (Investigative Powers) Act 2004*.[59] She said that the onus of justifying a limitation rests with the party seeking to uphold it, and that the standard of proof is high. She went on to say, quoting Canadian Supreme Court authority,[60] that the evidence required to prove the elements contained in s 7 should be 'cogent and persuasive and make clear to the Court the consequences of imposing or not imposing the limit'.[61] Her Honour also indicated that the 'more severe the deleterious effects of a measure, the more important the objective must be if the measure is to be reasonable and demonstrably justifiable'.[62]

This goes some way towards indicating that, when subject to judicial scrutiny, at least, the requirements of s 7(2) will not lightly be satisfied. It remains the case, nonetheless, that those limitations are drafted in very much broader terms that can be justified by reference to article 18 of the ICCPR and the Siracusa Principles. It follows that many enactments which might pass scrutiny under the terms of s 7(2) of the *Charter of Rights and Responsibilities Act 2006* could well breach Australia's obligations under international human rights law.

Article 18(3) of the ICCPR, and similar provisions in international human rights documents, require much more of the Victorian Parliament, precisely because the ICCPR places such a very high value on freedom of religion and belief. The ICCPR offers no justification for a hierarchy of human rights in which non-discrimination provisions are at the pinnacle and the rights to freedom of religion and conscience are on the bottom. Nor does it offer any justification for limiting fundamental human rights so long as those limitations are 'justified in a free and democratic society based on human dignity, equality and freedom' according to the values of the person appointed to make such a judgment. The ICCPR insists that human rights be given

---

[58] Communication No 931/2000. Views adopted on 5 November 2004.
[59] [2009] VSC 381 (7 September 2009).
[60] *R v Oakes* [1986] 1 SCR 103, 42.
[61] *Re an application under the Major Crime (Investigative Powers) Act 2004* [2009] VSC 381 (7 September 2009) [147].
[62] Ibid [150] (citing *R v Oakes* [1986] 1 SCR 103, 44).

much greater protection than this. Article 18 is indeed, one of the few rights in the Covenant that cannot be derogated from even in a time of public emergency that threatens the life of the nation (article 4(2)).

It is no doubt for this reason that the submission of the Standing Committee of the General Synod of the Anglican Church of Australia qualified its support for human rights legislation by insisting on guarantees for religious freedom that properly reflect the requirements of international human rights instruments, an insistence recently reiterated by the Primate in a letter to the then Prime Minister.[63]

Proper implementation of the ICCPR is also important because aspects of multiculturalism are so strongly endorsed by the ICCPR — not only article 18 but also article 27 on the preservation of ethnic and cultural identity.[64] Article 27 is, at least, replicated in section 19 of the Victorian charter.

It is troubling that the report of the Brennan Committee also fails to address these concerns despite the unanimous view of the Churches, including those that supported a human rights Act, that article 18 needed to be replicated properly in any charter. The Committee recommended that freedom from coercion or restraint in relation to religion and belief should be non-derogable,[65] but that freedom to manifest one's religion or beliefs should be subject to a limitation clause modelled upon the Victorian and ACT charter provisions.[66]

Proper enactment of the protections for religious freedom contained in the ICCPR would certainly assuage some Christian concerns. However there is scepticism that even this would do much to protect religious freedom. The concern is that in a situation where the prevailing intellectual fashions of the day tend towards a disregard for religious freedom, a narrow interpretation may be given to what it means to practice religion, confining it to private belief and worship. In communist countries of the old Soviet bloc, that amount of respect for freedom of religion was given as well.

Would a charter protect freedom of religion and conscience?

A further argument that appears in a number of submissions is that charters are no guarantee of protection for religious freedom.

---

[63] Above n 46.
[64] This provides: 'In those States in which ethnic, religious or linguistic minorities exist, persons belonging to such minorities shall not be denied the right, in community with the other members of their group, to enjoy their own culture, to profess and practise their own religion, or to use their own language.'
[65] Brennan Committee, above n 1, 372.
[66] Ibid.

Foreign experience

The Australian Christian Lobby, the Ambrose Centre for Religious Liberty in its submissions to both the NHRC and AHRC inquiries, and the Presbyterian Church of Victoria all provide examples from North America and Britain of failures by courts applying human rights charters to give adequate protection to religious belief and conscience.

In terms of anti-discrimination law, the position of charters is largely untested. A charter of rights would only properly be tested if first a legislature in a country with such a charter were to pass an anti-discrimination law that did not provide any exemptions on the grounds of religious belief. However, the signs are not promising that, given the intellectual fashions of the day, a charter would provide much protection. New Zealand scholar Rex Ahdar points to the limited protection given to religious freedom by courts applying charters of rights, particularly in the US.[67]

The US jurisprudence on religious freedom exemplifies the problem particularly well. Human rights are meant to represent enduring values. The case law may well develop, and interpretation may adapt to changing circumstances, but one would not expect major shifts in the meaning attributed to values that have been entrenched precisely because they are supposed to be unchanging precepts for human liberty, equality and dignity. Yet the US case law on religious freedom demonstrates compellingly how malleable at least some human rights provisions are, and how much interpretations can alter in accordance with the prevailing intellectual fashions, beliefs or social values of the day.

This is well illustrated by Michael McConnell.[68] He shows how the interpretation of the establishment and free exercise clauses has shifted in different eras. The religious freedom provision of the First Amendment has been the chameleon clause of the US Constitution, its meaning changing quite dramatically in the light of changing values, concerns and perspectives in the period after World War Two. McConnell writes that 'Arguably, the court's interpretation of these Clauses has changed more often, and more dramatically, than of any other provision of the Constitution'.[69] Of course, over that period of more than 60 years, there have been decisions supportive of religious freedom and others less supportive of it in competition with other values. Christians who oppose a charter of rights in Australia have not argued that freedom of religion clauses have never yielded positive decisions. They have. There is a concern, however, that protections for religious freedom, far from being a bulwark protecting

---

[67] Rex Ahdar, 'Slow Train Coming: Religious Liberty in the Last Days' (2009) 12 *Otago Law Review* 37, 51–2.
[68] Michael McConnell, 'The Influence of Cultural Conflict on the Jurisprudence of the Religion Clauses of the First Amendment' in Peter Cane, Carolyn Evans and Zoe Robinson (eds) *Law and Religion in Theoretical and Historical Context* (2008) 100.
[69] Ibid.

people's liberties from the changing intellectual and political fashions of the day, have proved to be hostage to those fashions, as McConnell so clearly demonstrates.

There is a view, for that reason, that a charter of rights will offer little protection from the secularising tendencies, and comprehensive liberalism, that is currently in vogue. The human rights scholar, Mary Ann Glendon, has observed this trend in the US jurisprudence:

> The current [US Supreme] Court majority has pressed forward with a six-decade-long trend of cabining religion in the private sphere while eroding protections of the associations and institutions where religious beliefs and practices are generated, regenerated, nurtured, and transmitted from one generation to the next.[70]

Similar trends may be observed in Canada. Canadian scholar Margaret Ogilvie observes that the Canadian 'courts have "protected" religious freedom by the erasure of religion from public institutions, public spaces and the public law ... Effectively, no religion now enjoys protection in Canada'.[71] This is not exactly a ringing endorsement of the benefits of a charter of rights.

There are certainly decisions of the European Court of Human Rights that offer some encouragement for freedom of religion,[72] as there are in the US and Canada. However, the decisions are somewhat mixed and the dominance of a narrow approach to freedom of religion is evident.[73] Cases that raise issues both of freedom of religion and of expression have tended to be dealt with under the freedom of expression provisions, leaving unclear how the issues would have been analysed as a religious freedom problem.[74] Most applications brought under article 9 of the European Convention have failed.[75] One of the causes is the doctrine of a 'margin of appreciation', which is frequently criticized for allowing excessive discretion to European state parties in restricting religious freedom in reliance on limitation

---

[70] Mary Ann Glendon, 'The Naked Public Square Now: A Symposium' (2004) 147 *First Things* 12, 13.
[71] M H Ogilvie, 'Between Liberté and Egalité: Religion and the State in Canada', in Peter Radan, Denise Meyerson and Rosalind Croucher (eds), *Law and Religion: God, the State and the Common Law* (2005) 134, 160.
[72] See, eg, *Kokkinakis v Greece* [1993] ECHR 20.
[73] Paul Taylor, *Freedom of Religion: UN and European Human Rights Law and Practice* (2005); Julian Rivers, 'Law, Religion and Gender Equality' (2007) 9 *Ecclesiastical Law Journal* 24.
[74] Mark Evans (2009), 'The Freedom of Religion or Belief and the Freedom of Expression' (2009) 4 *Religion and Human Rights* 197.
[75] Robin Hopkins and Can Yeginsu, 'Religious Liberty in British Courts: A Critique and Some Guidance' (2008) 49 *Harvard International Law Journal Online* 28.

provisions.[76] This itself obscures the essential gravamen of Strasbourg decisions. As Fenwick, Masterman and Phillipson comment:

> Strasbourg's jurisprudence is often notably under theorized. The reasoning is frequently brief, and lacking in rigour. In particular, the effects of the doctrine of the margin of appreciation result in some decisions in an almost complete failure to examine in any meaningful way the proportionality of restrictions upon individual rights adopted by states. Great variation in the intensity of review may be discerned; indeed, no single account of proportionality can be derived from the Strasbourg jurisprudence.[77]

This in turn has serious ramifications for the UK *Human Rights Act 1998*, which requires interpretation of European Convention rights and legislative compatibility with those rights. The interpretation of freedom of religion under the *Human Rights Act 1998* imposes significant hurdles in the way of applicants, particularly in being able to demonstrate an interference with their right to manifest their religion.[78] Julian Rivers comments on the jurisprudence of the Act, stating that 'there is a tendency to deal with clashes of ideology by denying the religious character of the impugned behaviour'.[79] One way, of course, to solve a dilemma is to pretend it does not exist, but as gay and lesbian rights scholars have acknowledged, this unreasonably limits religion to belief without conduct in a way that is difficult to defend as a coherent application of human rights principles.[80] It is also noteworthy that within 10 years of enacting the *Human Rights Act 1998*, it became a source of frustration to Tony Blair, whose government introduced it.[81]

Freedom of conscience and the Victorian charter

But what about Australia? A major issue referred to in many church submissions is the failure of the Victorian Parliament to protect doctors' freedom of conscience in relation to abortion, despite the charter in that State, and even though the human

---

[76] See Carolyn Evans, *Freedom of Religion under the European Convention on Human Rights* (2001).
[77] Helen Fenwick, Gavin Phillipson and Roger Masterman, 'The Human Rights Act in Contemporary Context' in Helen Fenwick, Gavin Phillipson and Roger Masterman (eds), *Judicial Reasoning under the UK Human Rights Act* (2007) 6.
[78] Hopkins and Yeginsu, above n 75.
[79] Rivers, above n 73, 37.
[80] See Feldblum, above n 34; Stychin, above n 35. See also Andrew Koppelman, 'You Can't Hurry Love: Why Anti-discrimination Protections for Gay People Should Have Religious Exemptions' (2006) 72 *Brooklyn Law Review* 125.
[81] Fenwick, Phillipson and Masterman, above n 77, 3.

rights issues were presented to it very clearly and publicly. This was interpreted as an indication that in the current climate, a charter of rights will do little for freedom of conscience.

Section 8 of the *Abortion Law Reform Act 2008* imposes upon doctors who have a conscientious objection to carrying out an abortion, a duty to refer the patient to another practitioner who does not have such a conscientious objection. The Victorian Parliament's Scrutiny of Acts and Regulations Committee drew the attention of the Parliament to the possible breach of the charter provision on freedom of belief, although the charter excluded abortion itself from coverage.[82]

The provision encountered very strong and sustained opposition not only from Churches but also from the Australian Medical Association (AMA) in Victoria.[83] The AMA pointed out that it already had a very clear and workable ethical code for dealing with conscientious objections to carrying out medical procedures, and that there was no need for a mandatory duty of referral. The AMA's ethical code had been supported by the Victorian Law Reform Commission as providing a reasonable balance between the rights of doctor and patient. Abortion is a procedure that needs no referral from a medical practitioner, unlike, for example, going to a specialist. Furthermore, access to information is hardly difficult. A woman need only go to the nearest public hospital or to contact a pregnancy advice service. Information is available everywhere through phone services, internet websites and other readily accessible sources of advice. The notion that the rights of women would in practical reality be prejudiced if a doctor did not have a duty of referral[84] in this context seems surreal. Modern Victoria is not nineteenth century Ireland.

The requirement for mandatory referral thus seemed like an unnecessary and gratuitous attack on freedom of conscience. Yet the right to an abortion is not guaranteed specifically in any of the foundational international human rights instruments such as the Universal Declaration of Human Rights (UDHR, 1948) or the ICCPR, although arguments have been put that other provisions of international law support it.[85] Still less is there any internationally recognized human right to

---

[82] *Charter of Rights and Responsibilities Act 2006* (Vic) s 48.
[83] The history of this is told in Frank Brennan, 'The place of the religious viewpoint in shaping law and policy in a pluralistic democratic society: a case study on rights and conscience' (Paper presented at Values and Public Policy Conference: Fairness, Diversity and Social Change, Centre for Public Policy, University of Melbourne, 26 February 2009).
[84] Rachel Ball, 'Victoria's Abortion Law Reform Act' (2008) 33(4) *Alternative Law Journal* 237.
[85] Christina Zampas and Jaime Gher, 'Abortion as a Human Right — International and Regional Standards' (2008) 8 *Human Rights Law Review* 249.

full information about accessing an abortion.[86] It appears that the mere possibility, however remote, that a woman's access to a lawful abortion could be inhibited by a lack of referral information seems to have been sufficient to overcome the very real and tangible concerns about freedom of conscience for doctors. It provides an example of how even the non-derogable rights contained in the ICCPR seem in practice to give way when there is even the slightest concern that a derogable or even non-recognised 'right' could be impaired. Certainly, human rights are limited when they interfere with the rights of others, but that is a two-way street. If all other rights are regarded as inherently of higher value than the rights of freedom of religion and conscience, then there is a hierarchy of rights in practice that no talk of 'balancing' can mask.

Frank Brennan's critique of the human rights 'lobby' concerning this issue was scathing:

> In my opinion, this was the first real test of the Victorian Charter of Human Rights and Responsibilities and it failed spectacularly to protect a core non-derogable ICCPR human right which fell hostage to a broader social and political agenda for abortion law reform and a prevailing fad in bioethics which asserts that doctors should leave their consciences at the door … Groups such as Liberty Victoria provided no coherent answers. Academic experts on the Charter largely remained silent. The Equal Opportunity and Human Rights Commission simplistically dismissed freedom of conscience.[87]

He concluded:

> We need to do better if faith communities and minorities are to be assured that a Victorian style charter of rights is anything but a piece of legislative window dressing which rarely changes legislative or policy outcomes, being perceived as a device for the delivery of a soft left sectarian agenda — a device which will be discarded or misconstrued whenever the rights articulated do not comply with that agenda.[88]

It may be that the failure of the Government of Victoria to pay proper attention to issues of freedom of conscience would have been the same whether or not the State had a charter. Indeed, the abortion issue could be put forward as an example of why

---

[86] There have been calls for such information to be provided: Committee on the Elimination of Discrimination Against Women, *General Recommendation 24 on Women and Health,* 20th session (1999) (as cited in Ball, above n 84).
[87] Brennan, above n 83, 21.
[88] Ibid 23. See also Ambrose Centre for Religious Liberty, *Submission to 2008 Freedom of Religion and Belief in the 21st Century* (February 2009) [7.5].

a charter might make a difference, at least if properly drafted to protect freedom of religion and conscience to the same extent required by international human rights instruments. After all, the Victorian Government ignored doctors' freedom of conscience in spite of the *Charter of Rights and Responsibilities Act 2006*, not because of it. However, Church submissions opposing a charter of rights did not only argue that it could be ineffectual in protecting freedom of religion and conscience. They also argued that it may operate as a negative.

Would a charter further diminish freedom of religion?

The fundamental issue about a charter of rights is perhaps not whether it would be protective of religious freedom — since a 'neutral' outcome on this issue would be good enough — but whether it could actually do harm to religious freedom. There is a concern expressed in a number of submissions that a charter may add greater legitimacy to a culture in which freedom of religion and conscience is diminished in the name of an equality agenda that involves the coercive imposition of a particular worldview on dissenters, and that in secular liberal interpretations of a charter of rights, anti-discrimination may become the human right that trumps all others. That concern, I argue, is fuelled by the tendency of many secularists to see human rights law as almost synonymous with non-discrimination, perhaps because anti-discrimination is the main work of governmental organizations that are given a watchdog role in relation to human rights.

This seems to have been the case in Britain. The 'human rights culture' promoted by the *Human Rights Act 1998* has led to a serious diminution of the human rights of those who hold dissident viewpoints grounded in their religious faith. Julian Rivers has summarised the precarious state of religious freedom in Britain:

> [A] new moral establishment is developing, which is being imposed by law on dissenters. Those filling public offices are well advised to avoid challenging it, and even the most measured and reasoned public questioning of its truth can trigger formal investigations. This new orthodoxy masks itself in the language of equality, thus refusing to discuss its premises and refusing to articulate its conception of the good ... Churches and religious associations find themselves boxed in by its obligations, benefiting only from narrowly drafted exceptions narrowly interpreted by an unsympathetic judiciary.[89]

Rivers' assessment of the British situation is not dissimilar to Ogilvie's assessment in Canada.[90]

---

[89] Rivers, above n 73, 52.
[90] Ogilvie, above n 71.

The issue of exemptions in Victoria

In the submissions to the National Human Rights Consultation, a particular issue was the threat to religious freedom in Victoria that was seen as being linked to the charter.[91] A number of Christian organizations expressed deep concern about various options being considered to remove or limit exemptions from anti-discrimination laws that have previously been included in those enactments out of respect for freedom of religion and belief.[92] The Committee, which was pre-empted by an announcement from the Attorney-General as to the Government's intentions,[93] later came down on the side of limited reforms which would operate to protect the core exemptions of faith-based groups.[94]

The Presbyterian Church of Australia certainly linked its concerns about religious freedom in Victoria directly to the charter. Its submission to the NHRC stated in bold that 'the charter is employed to produce a set of options that significantly reduce freedom of conscience, thought and religion'.[95]

Frank Brennan sought to argue that a review of the exemptions under the anti-discrimination law was timely whether or not there was a charter,[96] and therefore had nothing to do with the charter debate. The review was wide-ranging and not at all confined to the exemptions that have been enacted to protect religious freedom. However, the review was originally established, according to the Attorney-General, to ensure that the exceptions and exemptions 'are compatible with the charter'.[97]

---

[91] It should be noted that some protection for faith-based organizations is provided in ss 38(4) and (5) of the Victorian Act; however, this only applies to decisions of public authorities.

[92] Scrutiny of Acts and Regulations Committee, Parliament of Victoria, *Inquiry into exceptions and exemptions in the Equal Opportunity Act: Options Paper* (7 May 2009) (available at <http://www.parliament.vic.gov.au/sarc/article/919>).

[93] Melissa Fyfe, 'Government Bows to the Religious Right', *The Age* (Melbourne), 27 September 2009.

[94] Scrutiny of Acts and Regulations Committee, above n 92. The Committee recommended that the religious exceptions be narrowed so that they do not apply to allow discrimination on the basis of the attributes of race, impairment, physical features or age: see recommendations 48–50. Controversy and uncertainty about the way those exemptions were drafted in the *Equal Opportunity Act 2010* led to further amendments being made after a change of government, by the *Equal Opportunity Amendment Act 2011*.

[95] Presbyterian Church of Australia, above n 50, [32].

[96] Frank Brennan, Letter to the Editor, *Sydney Morning Herald* (Sydney) 31 July 2009, 10. See also Frank Brennan, 'The Role Played by Religious Groups in the Australian Bill of Rights Debate' (Paper given at the Conference on Law and Religion: Legal Regulation of Religious Groups, Organisations and Communities, Melbourne, July 2011) 13.

[97] Media Release, Office of the Attorney-General, 'Hulls announces discrimination review', 29 February 2008.

Another concern is that government-funded human rights organizations, dominated, in my view, by people who believe human rights are synonymous with a secular liberal agenda, will fund court cases to persuade judges to that point of view. That is particularly a concern if the domestic human rights charter gives little protection to religious freedom or the rights of ethnic minorities to maintain their culture and identity. In that regard, there is a real concern that certain of the bodies that are entrusted with the protection of human rights in Australian society seem to place very little importance on the human right of religious freedom. *Quis custodiet ipsos custodies?*[98]

The track record of human rights organizations in protecting human rights

How could statutory human rights organizations fail to protect human rights? Is that not their mission? Perhaps, but a true watchdog for human rights has to do more than be concerned about the progressive agendas that are most fashionable at the time. It has to protect unpopular human rights,[99] rights which conflict with a secular liberal worldview, and which may need to be fairly and properly balanced with rights that represent cherished social causes. In this regard, the submissions on the charter show some reasonable grounds for concern.

The issue of a doctor's freedom of conscience in relation to referral for an abortion in Victoria, previously discussed, provides one example raised in several submissions. Another issue was statements made by then members of the Australian Human Rights Commission concerning freedom of political speech.

The AHRC's questioning of freedom of political speech

The Australian Human Rights Commission's discussion paper on freedom of religion raised significant alarm among Christians. One of the questions asked in the discussion paper is, 'Is there a role for religious voices, alongside others in the policy debates of the nation?'.[100] The question was framed neutrally, but given that at present, there are no restrictions on any voice being heard in the public square, and that includes religious voices, the most obvious implication of the question is that

---

[98] This may be translated as 'Who Guards the Guards?'
[99] It may be that human rights organisations would argue that they stand up for many unpopular rights, such as the rights of refugees. However, such rights are usually popular amongst progressive university-educated law graduates and like-minded others who represent the social circle of the organisation's staff.
[100] Australian Human Rights Commission, *Freedom of Religion and Belief in the 21st Century: Discussion Paper* (August 2008) 9.

the Commission was considering whether it remains appropriate for religious voices to be heard in the public square. If not, then presumably the Commission would recommend ways to try to silence those voices within constitutional limits.

That the question should even have been asked at all caused consternation in Christian circles. The NSW Council of Churches, for example, indicated that it would be most interested to learn 'which particular religious voices are to be silenced, and the reasons for such an attack on freedom of conscience, freedom of speech and freedom of religion'.[101]

While it is no doubt possible that there is a benign explanation for this question, Christian concerns about this were heightened as a result of comments reportedly made by AHRC commissioner Tom Calma at the time of the launch of the AHRC inquiry.[102] The ABC reported him as saying that there was a growing fundamentalist religious lobby, in areas such as same-sex relationships, stem-cell research and abortion, and that he argued that there was a need to strike a balance between freedom of religion and not pushing those beliefs on the rest of society. The clear implication of these reported remarks, in my view, was that he thought the rights of people of faith to engage in public policy debates ought to be limited in some way, if they wanted to put forward views with which he disagreed.

Perhaps Calma did not mean this. He has certainly claimed in subsequent public statements that the AHRC inquiry was an open one, asking legitimate and important questions without any preconceptions or agendas.[103] However, taken together with that very odd question in the discussion paper, a perception was created amongst Christians concerned about a charter of rights that the Commission does not think it is right for people of faith to be engaged in debates on public policy, adopting positions informed by their beliefs about when human life commences or about issues of sexual practice.

There are certainly various versions of a liberal view that religious arguments should be excluded from the public square,[104] but there is a big difference between saying that the public square needs a common language — reason — and saying that certain voices should be prohibited from participating in public debate because of the positions for which they reason. Meyerson, for example, considers that arguments based solely on religious convictions should not be offered as reasons for changes to

---

[101] NSW Council of Churches, above n 4, 7.
[102] 'National religious freedom review to be launched' (2008) *ABC News Online* <http://www.abc.net.au/news/stories/2008/09/17/2366511.htm?section=justin> at 9 September 2011.
[103] Tom Calma, 'Religious freedom: what's all the fuss?' (2009) *Online Opinion* <http://www.onlineopinion.com.au/view.asp?article=8798&page=0> at 9 September 2011.
[104] See, eg, the debate in Robert Audi and Nicholas Wolterstorff, *Religion in the Public Square: the Place of Religious Convictions in Political Debate* (1997). See also Meyerson, above n 32, 44.

the law or public policy. However, she makes clear that her position is one about a voluntary approach to be adopted by people of faith. She does not suggest that legal effect should be given to it.[105] Calma's reported comments, by way of contrast, appeared to indicate the need for some kind of legal constraint in the name of 'balancing' rights and interests.

Even the suggestion of silencing certain voices in public life is utterly contrary to democratic principles and the most foundational requirements of international human rights law.[106] Articles 19 and 21 of the UDHR, and articles 19 and 25 of the ICCPR could not be clearer in saying that everyone has a right to participate in the policy debates of the nation whatever their perspectives may be and whatever the influences that may have shaped those perspectives. Bishops, talkback radio hosts and human rights commissioners have equal rights to participate in public debate.

A later conference paper that reported on some of the early findings of the religious freedom project raised further questions about the credibility of the AHRC in this area. Co-authored by Calma and a senior official of the Commission, it began with the remarkable sentence: 'The compatibility of religious freedom with human rights is the subject of the most comprehensive study ever undertaken in Australia in this area'.[107] No doubt, this contrast between freedom of religion and human rights, as if religious freedom was not a human right, was unintended and unconscious, but it is revealing. The title of their paper was not much better. The title, 'Freedom of religion and belief in a multicultural democracy: an inherent contradiction or an achievable human right?', certainly recognizes that religious freedom is a human right. However, the implication within the question contained in the title is that perhaps freedom of religion cannot, or should not, survive in a multicultural democracy. The contrast with the ICCPR could not be more marked. Freedom of religion is a non-derogable human right in international law, not an optional one. Furthermore, as article 27 demonstrates, there is no contradiction between religious

---

[105] Meyerson, above n 32, 44–5.
[106] Secularism is also enshrined in some national constitutions — albeit with a great variety of meanings. See András Sajó, 'Preliminaries to a Concept of Constitutional Secularism' (2008) 6 *International Journal of Constitutional Law* 605. In *Refah Partisi (The Welfare Party) v Turkey* (application nos 41340/98, 41342/98 and 41344/98) ECHR 3003-II, the European Court of Human Rights did uphold the right of the government of Turkey to dismantle a party which was established to promote sharia law. Even this controversial decision cannot support an attack on individual freedom of speech.
[107] Tom Calma and Conrad Gershevitch, 'Freedom of religion and belief in a multicultural democracy: an inherent contradiction or an achievable human right?' (Paper presented at the Unity in Diversity Conference, Townsville, 12–14 August 2009) (available at <http://www.humanrights.gov.au/about/media/speeches/race/index.html>).

freedom and multiculturalism. One is an essential precondition to the other, given the close connection between faith and ethnicity.

Neither Calma nor his co-author on that conference paper were at the Commission by the time the project concluded. In the end, the Commission released a research report made to it by the Australian Multicultural Foundation, rather than publishing its own report and making recommendations.[108] However, at the time of the debate about a human rights Act, the Commission's perceived stance on religious freedom was a significant concern for many of those opposed to such an enactment.

The question of credibility

These were not the only concerns raised in submissions about the track record of human rights organizations. As these submissions demonstrate, there has been at least a perception that human rights commissions, both state and federal, are dominated by people of similar persuasions and values who take a very minimalist view of what respect for freedom of religion, belief and conscience entails. The Ambrose Centre for Religious Liberty, for example, wrote that 'The fundamental human right of religion, belief, conscience, opinion and expression have been addressed by the protagonists for a Charter/Bill of Rights in the flimsiest of manners or not at all'.[109]

Similarly, former Federal Treasurer Peter Costello wrote:

> No one will tell you that the purpose of such a Commonwealth charter [of rights] will be to curtail religious conscience or practice. But it will work out the same way.
>
> Whatever the proponents say, the crusading lawyers will use any new federal charter against those institutions to which they are hostile. They will have sympathetic ears in the equal opportunity commissions. After all, experience in the human rights industry will be a qualification for appointment. The churches and Christian schools will be in the firing line.[110]

Within a few days, Costello was proved right. In evidence before a Parliamentary Committee, Michael Gorton, the Chair of Victoria's Equal Opportunity and Human Rights Commission, argued for severe restrictions on religious freedom. He did so,

---

[108] Gary Bouma, Desmond Cahill, Hass Dellal, and Athalia Zwartz, *Freedom of Religion and Belief in 21st century Australia: A research report prepared for the Australian Human Rights Commission* (2011).

[109] Ambrose Centre for Religious Liberty, *Submission to the National Human Rights Consultation into a Charter/Bill of Rights* (15 June 2009) 6.

[110] Peter Costello, 'Pursuing the churches over human rights is contradictory', *The Age* (Melbourne) 29 July 2009.

emphasizing the importance of reviewing exemptions from anti-discrimination law in light of the charter. In relation to faith-based schools, he said:

> We do not see a need for a religious school to be able to discriminate in relation to the choice of a cleaner or for a religious school to discriminate in relation to the choice of a mathematics teacher who has no contact with the practice of the religion or the profession of faith in that school.[111]

On the relationship between maths teaching and the Christian faith, Gorton could not have been more wrong. From a Christian perspective, mathematics is God's language.[112] It has a central role in the debates about the scientific evidence for a Creator of the universe.[113]

Gorton went on to say:

> I think there are a number of faiths that have some fundamental beliefs that we would not accept as meeting the obligations of the charter and the Act, because some of those fundamental beliefs are, at their core, discriminatory. There are some fundamental beliefs in some faiths that, for example, are absolutely discriminatory against women, that would be not acceptable in our pluralist, secular society.[114]

This appears to imply that in his view Parliament should outlaw any discrimination against women even if it was based on fundamental religious beliefs (for example, about female ordination). On this view, there seem to be few limits on the extent to which even the core activities and practices of faith communities, based upon their most fundamental beliefs, are safe from government interference. The Pope can be Catholic, but not necessarily male.

It is surely little wonder, with such statements from leaders of human rights organisations that appeared to give short shrift even to non-derogable rights under the ICCPR, that many Churches were so deeply concerned about the enactment of a charter of rights. Such a charter would give a lot of influence to these organisations, which could be used negatively to attack the human rights of people of faith.

---

[111] Evidence to Scrutiny of Acts and Regulations Committee, Inquiry into exceptions and exemptions in the Equal Opportunity Act, Parliament of Victoria, Melbourne, 4 August 2009, 5 (M. Gorton).
[112] M Livio, *Is God a Mathematician?* (2009).
[113] John Lennox, *God's Undertaker: Has Science Buried God?* (2007).
[114] Evidence to Scrutiny of Acts and Regulations Committee, above n 111, 7.

Human rights organizations have no credibility if they only champion the causes that are intellectually fashionable, or to which leaders of the organization adhere.[115] When I champion the human rights of my enemy, when I insist on the freedom of speech of someone with whom I profoundly disagree, when I respect the freedom of conscience of someone whose beliefs and values cannot allow her to do what I want her to do, when I demand the freedom for others that may have a prejudicial effect on my interests, then I demonstrate that I really do believe in human rights.

Human rights organizations and lobbyists in Australia do not necessarily stand up very well when measured against that test. It ought to be a matter of grave concern to such organizations if people in the mainstream of Australian society perceive them to lack credibility and to be driven by particular ideological agendas that are antithetical to some human rights. There can be little question that this perception had a real and practical impact on submissions to the National Human Rights Consultation. There are many objections to having a judicially policed charter of rights that would remain important objections even if the human rights to be guaranteed far more faithfully reflected the requirements of international human rights norms. Nonetheless, at least some objections may have dissipated if there was more confidence that watchdog bodies in Australia would be effective and dispassionate advocates for all human rights in a manner consistent with the priorities about what is fundamental and non-derogable, and what is less fundamental, so clearly established in the various basic Declarations and Covenants.

There is value, therefore, in human rights organizations reflecting carefully on the National Human Rights Consultation debates and the negative perceptions that have emerged about their own commitment to human rights. The perception that some human rights organizations, or individuals who represent them, place a low value on freedom of religion or conscience has, I believe, been widely held. The Australian Human Rights Commission has certainly engaged in some fence-mending since that time.[116] Human rights bodies may also need to look at their own employment practices to see whether there is a sufficient diversity of opinion within

---

[115] It is quite possible, indeed likely, that some causes held dear by members and leaders of human rights organizations are not causes that can be given primacy when in conflict with other human rights, according to the priority of rights established in the foundational international human rights doctrines. This point is made, for example, in the submission to the NHRC of the Life, Marriage and Family Centre of the Catholic Archdiocese of Sydney: Chris Meney, *National Human Rights Consultation — Submission from the Life, Marriage and Family Centre of the Catholic Archdiocese of Sydney* (May 2009).

[116] For example, the AHRC President, the Hon Catherine Branson QC, gave a well-received address at the Religion in the Public Square Colloquium in Melbourne, July 23rd 2010 (available at <http://www.humanrights.gov.au/about/media/speeches/speeches_president/2010/20100723_religion.html>).

them, and to ensure that they have people who can challenge the prevailing dogma within the organization in order to ensure better fidelity to human rights. One way of encouraging diversity and fidelity to human rights is to appoint champions for those rights which may not be all that popular within the Commission.

It may also be advisable to separate human rights and equal opportunity commissions into two different bodies, one exercising functions in relation to anti-discrimination laws, and the other having a broader role as an advocacy body for human rights. This may reduce the extent to which 'human rights' are seen as entirely synonymous with non-discrimination.

Governmental human rights bodies play an important role. Human rights organizations need to be generally perceived as part of the solution to human rights concerns in Australia, not part of the problem.

Conclusion

Like all groups in society, there are differences of opinion amongst Christians, and indeed amongst church leaders, about the wisdom of having a charter of rights in Australia. There are valid arguments for and against the protection of human rights by means of establishing vague higher order and abstract standards which courts are meant to interpret and apply. People of great intellect, knowledge and goodwill, equally committed to the protection of human rights, can take quite different stands on such matters. It is no surprise therefore that Christians should also have differing views.

What is clear from the submissions is that at least some Christians who are opposed to a charter of rights or who have serious doubts about it would be less opposed to it if they thought that the legislators and policy-makers would take all human rights seriously, and faithfully protect freedom of religion and conscience in the manner required by article 18 of the ICCPR and other human rights instruments. The suspicion that those advocating for a charter do not take freedom of religion and conscience nearly seriously enough — a concern that has been fuelled by the track record of the human rights lobby and the drafting of the two charters that already exist in Australia — has certainly played a significant part in enlivening opposition to a national charter.

The submissions of the Standing Committee of the General Synod of the Anglican Church of Australia and the Australian Catholic Bishops Conference are really bellwether submissions for Christian opinion. The national body of the Anglican Church would support human rights legislation if it took religious freedom as seriously as international conventions do. It would also support anti-vilification laws that are very carefully drafted. The Australian Catholic Bishops endorse the order of questions raised by the National Human Rights Consultation. Asking what human rights should be protected is a first question. Asking how best to protect them is a secondary one.

Human rights charters cannot just be a vehicle for the promotion of particular ideological agendas. When those who support a charter demonstrate higher standards of fidelity to the cause of all human rights, then they will be better able to persuade at least some doubters to their cause.

8

Apostasy in Islam and the Freedom of Religion in International Law

Asmi Wood

This chapter examines the issue of apostasy in Islam and under the *Shari'a*, and how this understanding can be reconciled with the practical operation of such an understanding for Muslim minorities under 'the freedom of religion' provisions under international law and ultimately under a freedom of religion provision in a putative Bill of Rights.

Apostasy is a question of law under the *Shari'a*. In examining apostasy under the *Shari'a*, I first identify relevant sources of *Shari'a* law and *Shari'a*, particularly from a perspective of apostasy. Submitting to God, that is, becoming a Muslim, is a free, unilateral acceptance of the Muslim Covenant by proclamation of the *shahada*.[1] Apostasy is the free, unilateral repudiation of the *shahada*. This understanding of apostasy is broadly common to many religions. Problems arise with the legal consequences that may still attach to apostasy under some Schools of Islamic law, which in some cases appear to mandate the death penalty for apostasy. If this view is correct, such Islamic law consequences are potentially problematic not only under a bill of rights but also under the general law in Australia, particularly if some Muslims seek to intimidate 'apostates' or to try to implement this interpretation on 'apostates' in Australia.

---

[1] The declaration of faith constitutes the dual declarations (*shahadatain*) that (i) there is but One God and (ii) the acceptance of the apostleship of Mohamed: Izzeddin Ibrahim and Denys Johnson-Davies, *Forty Hadith Qudsi* (1991) 74, 130.

This chapter examines apostasy under the *Shari'a* and whether the Qur'an and *sunna*[2], or other religious texts, support capital punishment. Such an examination first requires setting out the definition and meaning of what constitutes apostasy in the context of the Qur'an and the *sunna*. I conclude that while apostasy is a grave crime under Islamic law, its prescribed punishment is reserved for the Hereafter and, therefore, that temporal authorities do not have jurisdiction over apostasy *per se*. This view, however, is not universally agreed upon.

Shari'a notions on apostasy are sometimes said to be incompatible with international law on the freedom of religion,[3] a criticism likely to be repeated if this right is codified in an Australian bill of rights, an individual, non-derogable right. This characterisation, however, is incomplete. The Qur'an, and thus the *shari'a*, provide for freedom of religion[4] but require individuals to exercise this choice carefully and judicially with respect to Islam, that is, 'to accept Islam wholeheartedly'.[5] Therefore, those who freely accept Islam, unilaterally undertake wholeheartedly to enter Islam, specifically including the clause never to renounce the faith. This is a contractual issue and is not controversial if a person enters freely into the contract. Problems do occur, however, when children who are 'born and raised' as Muslim and are then refused the right to freely adopt another faith or to renounce the faith 'given' to them by their parents, a parental right under international law.[6]

Key terms that circumscribe the notion of apostasy in Islam

Apostates are only one category of people described in the Qur'an. In examining the concept of apostasy and its legal consequences, I first identify and discuss other key categories of people, their legal obligations and the importance that the Qur'an attaches to such categorisation.

---

[2] Sunna broadly means the practice of the Prophet as documented in collections known generically as the hadith.
[3] Art 18, *Universal Declaration of Human Rights*, GA Res 217 A (III) UN GAOR, 3rd sess, UN Doc A/810 (1948) ('UDHR'); *International Covenant on Civil and Political Rights*, opened for signature 16 December 1966, 999 UNTS 171, art 18 (entered into force 23 March 1976) ('ICCPR').
[4] Qur'an 2:256.
[5] Qur'an 49:14.
[6] *International Covenant on Economic, Social and Cultural Rights*, opened for signature 16 December 1966, 999 UNTS 3, art 13(3) (entered into force 3 January 1976) ('ICSCR').

What is Islam? Who is a Muslim?

The word Islam derives from the Arabic root (سلم peace) and means 'to submit'. All Qur'anic Prophets urged humanity to submit to God's Will[7] and by this definition they all taught Islam, and their followers therefore became Muslims, or 'those who submit'. For clarity, however, the Qur'an variously refers to the followers of the earlier Prophets as Jews, Christians or the People of Noah.

In this chapter, Islam is the religion taught by the Prophet Mohammed, contained in the Muslim Covenant and his follower, a Muslim.[8] The Qur'an states that, 'God chose the name "Muslim" [to describe the followers of the Prophet Mohamed]'.[9] The Qur'an, however, makes a key distinction between a Muslim, who merely submits, and a *mu'min*, who truly believes, and this distinction has significant legal implications. The Qur'an describes a believer *inter alia* as one possessing the 'inner' quality of *taqwa* described above.[10]

To become a Muslim, one consciously and freely has to make the 'two declarations', cognisant that this act formally enters one into a binding Covenant with God.[11] The Covenant imposes binding obligations. The main obligation of interest here is a key term of the Covenant, that having freely accepted it, one may never repudiate the Covenant.[12] That is, while acceptance of the Muslim Covenant is voluntary,[13] once adopted, it is unilaterally binding, as with any other unilateral contract.

Muslims collectively: The umma

Muslims collectively are called the *umma*, or the Muslim community,[14] which, according to the Qur'an, forms a single entity[15] of believing men and believing women who are friends/protectors of each other who command good and forbid evil.[16] The Qur'an describes the *umma* as the mid-most community, that is, one that avoids the extremes, *because* it is upright and equitable.[17] The *Sunna* notes further

---

[7] Qur'an 40:75; Qur'an 4:164.
[8] Qur'an 22:78.
[9] Qur'an 22:78.
[10] Qur'an 42:37–39.
[11] See Ibrahim and Johnson-Davies, above n 1.
[12] Qur'an 49:14.
[13] Qur'an 2:256.
[14] Qur'an 2:143; Qur'an 22:41.
[15] Qur'an 49:10; Ibrahim Abdulla al-Marzouqi, *Human Rights in Islamic Law* (2001) 521, *Constitution of Medina* art 2. Noel J Coulson asserts that: 'Islamic political theory rested on the idea of a universal Muslim community or *umma*': *Conflicts and Tensions in Islamic Jurisprudence* (1969) 21.
[16] Qur'an 42:37–39.
[17] Qur'an 2:143. (وسطا *wa sa tha*, midmost). Ahmad Hassan, *The Doctrine of Ijma' in Islam: A Study of the Juridical Principle of Consensus* (2002) 40.

that Islam 'is easy [and consequently], that the *umma* is against extremism of any form'.[18] As An-Naim notes, however, the *umma* is not a 'State'.[19]

The *umma* comprises two broad classes: Muslim and *dhimmi*.[20] Lands in which Muslims hold political power are sometimes referred to as *dar al-Islam* and the rest of the world is divided between *dar al-sulh* (treaty partners)[21] and *dar al-harb* (land of war).[22] The terminology is archaic but is sometimes still employed and for this reason I briefly examine it below.[23]

The political union of Muslims ceased in around 750 AD and was never fully restored.[24] Ford posits that this worldview of a 'unitary theocratic state [that has been succeeded by] multiple fractious states [has] exacerbated a radical bifurcation in Islam between sacred law and secular law'.[25] However, in spite of the break-up of the political union,[26] Muslims sometimes still refer to the term *umma* in aspirational terms.[27] The idealised Muslim nostalgia for a 'golden age', now long past, often takes a sterilised view of history.

---

[18] Coulson, above n 15; Muhammad Al-Mughirah al-Bukhari, *The Translations of the Meaning of Sahih al-Bukhari Vol 1* (1976) 34. [الله يريد اليسر بكم ولا يريد بكم العسر]: Mohammad Hashim Kamali, *Equity and Fairness in Islam* (2005) 24.

[19] According to Abdullahi Ahmed An-Na'im, *Islam and the Secular State: Negotiating the Future of Shari`a* (2008) 271.

[20] N Shah Shahid, *Islamic Terms Dictionary* (1996). A '*dhimmi*' is defined as a non-Muslim living under the protection of a Muslim ruler. Patricia Crone and Michael Cook, describe the Jewish community in Medina as part of the *umma*: *Hagarism: The Making of the Islamic World* (1977) 7.

[21] Majid Khadduri, *War and Peace in the Law of Islam* (1955) 144.

[22] H A R Gibb and J H Kramers (eds), *Concise Encyclopaedia of Islam* (2001) 68.

[23] This terminology of *dar al-Islam* and *dar al-harb* is quite anachronistic but is nonetheless retained here as it is still used, although perhaps less frequently. On questioning the appropriateness of the terms *dar al-Islam* and *dar al-harb*, see Taha Jabir al-Alwani, *Ijthihad* (1993) 28.

[24] Rudolph Peters, *Jihad in Classical and Modern Islam* (1996) 5.

[25] Christopher A Ford, 'Siyar-ization and its Discontents: International Law and Islam's Constitutional Crisis' (1995) 30 *Texas International Law Journal* 499, 500.

[26] Peters, above n 24, 5.

[27] See, eg, *Resolutions On General, Statutory And Organisational Matters Adopted By The Twenty-Fifth Session Of The Islamic Conference Of Foreign Ministers (Session For A Better Future For The Peoples of The Islamic Umma)* Doha, State of Qatar, 17–19 Dhul Quida, 1418H, 15–17 March, 1998; Khaled Ali Beydoun, however, refers to this phenomenon as 'token kinship': 'Dar Al-Islam Meets "Islam as Civilization": An Alignment Of Politico-Theoretical Fundamentalisms And The Geopolitical Realism Of This Worldview' (2004–05) 4 *UCLA Journal of Islamic and Near Eastern Law* 143, 146, This view that the concept of an *umma* was a convenient political ploy is given some credence and supported by Yaroslav Trofimov, *The Seige of Mecca: The Forgotten Uprising in Islam's Holiest Shrine* (2007) 21.

Dar al-Islam — *The domain of peace*

In a geographical sense, *dar al-Islam* comprises the lands ruled by notionally Muslim rulers, ideally where the *Shari'a* is the law of the land and justice prevails. The *umma* is not necessarily identical with *dar al-Islam*, as Islam accepts that Muslims will live in minority situations. Muslims living as minorities are also legitimately part of the *umma*.[28]

Another meaning of *dar al-Islam* that one can construct from the Qur'an is one that lends meaning not so much to a geographical entity but rather a state of spiritual attainment. In this context the (major) *jihad*, which is mandatory on all Muslims,[29] aims primarily at the taming of the animal soul (*nafs al-ammara*).[30] The *Shari'a* provides a path and a discipline by which this animal soul can tame itself.[31] The greater *jihad* properly undertaken begins to elevate the soul to a point of spiritual development where a soul questions its own raison d'être, and becomes *nafs al-lawama*,[32] a self-reproaching soul. As further spiritual development occurs the soul reaches the point of peace and satisfaction (*nafs al-mutmainna*[33]). When souls reach this point of spiritual development they will not want, nor create, mischief and they will be at peace. Hence, the term *dar al-Islam* (the abode of peace) when viewed from this perspective is not confined geographically but is a collective of (disparate) souls at peace with themselves, their surroundings and their Creator and who recognise each other with mutual affection.[34] Therefore, when a soul has exerted itself to the utmost, through prayer, contemplation and spiritual exercise, and has reached a point of feeling love and concern for the broader human family, this soul then encourages others to follow the spiritual path. It does so in order that every soul, including those of *dar al-harb* (the domain of war) — which by definition is at war with, and wrongs, itself[35] — may learn to be at peace with itself and its surroundings and *ipso facto* become part of *dar al-Islam*. The better view, therefore, is that *dar al-Islam* is where a soul can practise faith freely and without hindrance, exercise its God-given right to free will, irrespective of the actual religious persuasion of the leader of or the prevailing orthodoxy of the geographical area in question.

---

[28] Muslims sought sanctuary from Meccan persecution in the Christian Empire of Abyssinia, a practice approved by the Prophet: Adil Salahi, *Muhammad: Man and the Prophet* (2002) 123.
[29] Qur'an 25:52.
[30] Qur'an 12:53.
[31] Qur'an 31:18; Qur'an 25:63.
[32] Qur'an 75:2.
[33] Qur'an 89:27.
[34] Qur'an 8:62–63.
[35] Qur'an 7:23.

Conversely, *dar al-harb* is where Muslims (and others) are persecuted or are unable to practise or reject faith openly, even if that entity is notionally ruled by a Muslim.[36]

Other Qur'anic classes of people

In addition to Muslims and *dhimmis*,[37] the Qur'an *inter alia* refers to believers, Prophets,[38] followers of the previous Prophets[39] (or Scriptuaries[40]), disbelievers (*kafir*), polytheists (*mushrik*), hypocrites (*munafik*) and others. These are all categories that apply to the two species endowed with free will: (1) the *djinn*, genies[41] and (2) *ins(an)*, humanity. I now address briefly the significance of these categories. In practice, the *djinn* are of no particular significance.[42] This multiplicity, particularly of religious traditions, leads to the recognition by Islam of a plurality of legal traditions and has a direct bearing on apostasy. This view of religious legal plurality may *prima facie* be viewed as uncritical acceptance but is in principle no different from the legal plurality that exists within the European Union or, more broadly, the UN.

Dhimmis may follow their own respective Covenants.[43] Historically there was some fluidity in practice, as for example Christians sometimes followed Muslim legal schools in Sufi circles without formally adopting the Muslim Covenant.[44] Further, in practice, customs (*adaat*) of peoples other than Scriptuaries were also allowed to coexist with Islam.[45]

Muslims, 'heresy' and hypocrisy

There does not appear to be either a *Shari'a* or etymological connection between the concepts of Muslim and heresy.[46] The use of arabicised words and concepts

---

[36] Majid Khadduri, *War and Peace in the Law of Islam* (1955) 158.
[37] Above n 20.
[38] The Qur'an 10:47, refers to Prophets as sent to every people. Of these the Quran only names 25 Prophets.
[39] Qur'an 2:62; Qur'an 5:69.
[40] That is: *ahl al-kitab* or, literally, 'the people of the book'.
[41] Qur'an 51:56.
[42] The *djinn* and their antics are an almost inseparable part of the lives of people of some Muslim societies: see generally William Dalrymple, *City of Djinns: A Year in Delhi* (1994).
[43] Qur'an 5:48.
[44] Idris Shah, *The Sufis* (1964) 132.
[45] Qur'an 18:90–92. (The example of the Prophet Zul Quarnain permitting the people to remain in their natural or indigenous state); see also generally M B Hooker, *Adat Laws in Modern Malaya: Land Tenure, Traditional Government and Religion* (1972); Ibrahim Abdulla al-Marzouqi, *Human Rights in Islamic Law* (2001) 523.
[46] E W Lane, *Arabic English Lexicon Volume 2* (1984) 2397.

such as 'heresy'[47] require clarification and elucidation for legitimate use in a *Shari'a* context. The Qur'anic phrase used to describe those who 'submit' but will not submit *wholeheartedly* is that they 'will not believe'.[48] That is, while failure to submit wholeheartedly prevents one from reaching the higher station of a 'believer', one's previous standing as a Muslim nonetheless remains.[49] Further, the Qur'an refers to errant Muslims as *fasik, or violators of Islamic law*,[50] and juxtaposes the spiritual attainment of a believer against that of a *fasik*.[51] That is, it is not easy to displace the status of a person as a 'Muslim'. The significance of these distinctions is that the Qur'an reserves the true knowledge of what is in people's hearts to the Creator and that judgment on matters of 'submission' and 'faith' should find no temporal jurisdiction. This is a significant issue in the legal consideration of apostasy.

The Qur'an defines hypocrites as 'those who say that they believe in God and the last day but [that they] are not at all believers'. Again, the Qur'an juxtaposes and contrasts the absence of spiritual attainment of a hypocrite with that of a believer and not to that of a 'Muslim'.[52] Thus, theologically, while a hypocrite cannot *ipso facto* be considered a believer, he or she can nonetheless claim to be a 'Muslim'.[53] However, individual believers and hypocrites are known (with certainty) only to God.[54] That is, while some of their acts may show hypocrites as such, it is not a matter that humans can decide upon with any degree of certainty,[55] and thus while both apostasy and hypocrisy are serious *Shari'a* crimes they must remain outside temporal jurisdiction.[56]

Takfir

In some cases, the issue of who is or is not recognised by the Muslim community as 'a Muslim' can become an existential, practical temporal issue.[57] This is because some Muslims seek to classify others as heretics/non-Muslims/apostates for various reasons.[58]

---

[47] Milton J Cowan (ed), *The Hans Wehr Dictionary of Modern Written Arabic* (1980). See هرطقة heresy.
[48] The Arabic لايؤمنون is rendered into English as '(they) will not believe'.
[49] Qur'an 49:14.
[50] Lane, above n 46, 2621.
[51] Qur'an 32:18.
[52] Qur'an 2:8.
[53] Adil Salahi, *Muhammad: Man and the Prophet* (2002) 310.
[54] Qur'an 29:11.
[55] Qur'an 9:69.
[56] Salahi, above n 53, 310.
[57] Abdullah Saeed and Hassan Saeed, *Freedom of Religion, Apostasy and Islam* (2006) 50.
[58] See, eg, Brynjar Lia, *Architect of Global Jihad: The Life of al-Qaida Strategist Abu Mus'ab al-Suri* (2007) 159.

One reason is because fighting 'heretics' is religiously more acceptable and this remains true in the contemporary world as it was in the past.[59] The declaration that a person is a non-Muslim is done by a process called *takfir*,[60] and although theologically strongly discouraged,[61] is not uncommon.[62] This process of *takfir* goes back in Islamic history to quarrels between governments and their opponents.[63] Bin Laden, for example, declared the Saudi government as apostate based on Qur'an 5:44[64] because in his view the Saudis 'don't apply the *Shari'a*',[65] although Saudi Arabia's claim that *Shari'a* is the law of the land is not generally disputed. There is an almost universal consensus among Muslims that the Saudis and other Muslim rulers are Muslims. The importance of this somewhat low threshold for (becoming and) remaining a Muslim is that the presumption in favour of the validity of the claim 'of being Muslim' is not easily displaced and is an important issue in the 'declaration' of individuals as apostates.

Wahhabis and neo-salafis

Wahhabism[66] is one of the more puritanical contemporary strains of Islam.[67] Individuals in wealthy Arab nations have at times used their political power and wealth for funding it, indirectly through 'charities'[68] and directly through support for groups such as the Taliban.[69] *Wahhabism's* legitimacy in Saudi Arabia is enhanced

---

[59] Peters, above n 24, 5.
[60] See Lane, above n 46, 2620.
[61] Ibid.
[62] For a description of the *takfiri* ideology see Robert Baer, *The Devil We Know: Dealing With the New Iranian Superpower* (2009) 123–4.
[63] Peters, above n 24, 7. See also the discussion below at 'the *Umma*' of Muslims collectively.
[64] Qur'an 5:44.
[65] Rosalind Gwynne, *Al-Qa'ida and al-Qur'an: The 'Tafsir' of Usamah bin Ladin* (2001) University of Tennessee <web.utk.edu/~warda/bin_ladin_and_quran.htm> at 5 October 2011.
[66] Daryl Champion, *The Paradoxical Kingdom: Saudi Arabia and the Momentum of Reform* (2003) 26n; Khaleed Abou El-Fadl, 'Muslim Minorities and Self-Restraint In Liberal Democracies' (1996) 29 *Loyola of Los Angeles Law Review* 1525, 1527.
[67] Khaleed Abou El-Fadl, *The Great Theft: Wrestling Islam from the Extremists* (2005) 95.
[68] *Saudi Arabia Terrorist Funding Issues*, Report No RL32499, Library of Congress (2004) 2. Saudi Arabia denied this claim (at fn 7)The 9/11 Commission Report 'found no evidence that the Saudi government as institution [...] funded Al Qaeda': 9/11 Commission, *Final Report of the National Commission on Terrorist Attacks upon the United States Authorized Edition*, (2004) 171 (Emphasis added).
[69] The Taliban were recognised as the legitimate government of Afghanistan by only three pro-Western governments — Saudi Arabia, Pakistan and the United Arab Emirates: see *QAAH OF 2004 v Minister for Immigration and Multicultural and Indigenous Affairs* [2004] FCA 1448, [26] (Dowsett J).

by the UK's 'close relationship',[70] the US's 'special relationship,'[71] and Saudi Arabia's dependence on this support.[72] There is thus a perception in the Muslim world that while on one hand the US and its allies condemn 'Islamic fundamentalism', that in practice they favour *Wahhabism*, a form of fundamentalist Islam. This Western support for Saudi Arabia, however, is based on economic and strategic interests rather than for *Wahhabism* as an ideology.[73]

Wahhabism universalised the particular Bedouin culture, initially of the Nejd, but was later developed to include a broader Arab culture, its adherents now claiming to represent 'true Islam'.[74] *The Encyclopaedia of Islam* refers to this process as the 'Arabisation' of Islam. The *Wahhabi* now tend to call themselves *salafi* and the two terms, once quite distinct and different, have since the 1970s come to be used synonymously.[75]

El-Fadl notes that *salafi* groups take a very selective, abusive and restrictive view of the Hanbali School, one that opportunistically concentrates on sections of the works of some great Hanbali scholars but arguably for pragmatic reasons ignores other great Hanbali scholars such as ibn 'Aqil and al-Tufi,[76] rendering *salafi* legal opinions somewhat unbalanced. Bin Laden particularly favoured the works of ibn Taymiyyah[77] and ibn Qudama, who are both great Hanbali scholars.[78] This idiosyncratic use of 'methodology' has allowed the *salafi* selectively to ignore Islamic precedent. Further, this opportunistic use of law has sometimes resulted in the justification of cruel methods for killing not only but principally Muslims, including children, who were first, and illegitimately, declared heretics or apostates.[79]

Disbelievers

A disbeliever is an individual who has 'seen the truth' but is unwilling to enter into a Covenant. Notwithstanding the reasons, those who have not accepted the Qur'anic

---

[70] David Leigh and Rob Evans, '"National interest" halts arms corruption inquiry', *The Guardian* (London), Friday 15 December 2006.
[71] Daryl Champion, *The Paradoxical Kingdom: Saudi Arabia and the Momentum of Reform* (2003) 281 n 275.
[72] Sami Zubaida, *Law and Power in the Islamic World* (2003) 155; James Risen describes the US view of Saudi support for terrorism as being 'in denial': *State of War: The Secret History of the CIA and the Bush Administration* (2006) 173.
[73] Anthony M Cordesman, *Saudi Arabia: Guarding the Desert Kingdom* (1997) 194–96.
[74] Abou El-Fadl, above n 67, 52.
[75] Ibid 75, 79.
[76] Ibid 152.
[77] Bruce Lawrence (ed), *Messages to the World: The Statements of Osama Bin Laden* (2005) 5 fn 7.
[78] Ibid, 60–1, esp 8n.
[79] Abou El-Fadl, above n 67, 55.

Covenant are not bound by its specific terms. In this case, the Prophet's practice was, when necessary, to subject an accused to the individual's own law by judges of that tradition.

Now that I have identified the key Qur'anic categories of people, I examine the significance of these categories with respect to the law of apostasy through the analytical framework of the *Shari'a* view of humanity's raison d'être, the answers that lie in the concept of free will and the obligation of worship.

The centrality of free will and law to the *Shari'a*

The centrality of law to Islam is often acknowledged.[80] However, the following short analysis attempts to demonstrate the centrality of free will to Islam from a *theological* perspective and is crucial to the broader understanding of apostasy.

When David, a Prophet in the Islamic tradition, asked God:[81]

> 'O Lord! Why did you cause creation to come into being?' God replied 'I was a hidden treasure and I wanted to be known, so I created creation'.

Thus, God said 'Be'[82] and the universe (used here as a synonym for creation) began to establish over 'six days'.[83] To be 'known', however, it appears required an uncoerced recognition by a self-aware and free-willed being.[84] To this end, the Qur'an relates how God in turn, offered 'free will' to every created species,[85] an offer that was accepted only by humanity (and the *djinn*);[86] and in foolishly doing so these two species acted unjustly to themselves.[87] Thus, each soul is bound by its ancient acceptance and recognition of God's overlordship.[88] The Qur'an states that God forewarned both species of the horrific consequences of failure and the ecstatic joys of the 'correct' use of free will. From this theological perspective that underpins the *Shari'a* law, apostasy is not a reasonable option because each soul, having individually spoken with God, *ipso facto* cannot legitimately deny God, but similarly, for obvious reasons, is only

---

[80] Sami Zubaida, *Law and Power in the Islamic World* (2003) ii; Wael B Hallaq, 'The Quest for Origins or Doctrine? Islamic Legal Studies as Colonialist Discourse' (2002) 2 *UCLA Journal of Islamic and Near Eastern Law* 1, 1; Joseph Schacht, *An Introduction to Islamic Law* (1975) 1.
[81] Javad Nurbakhsh, *Traditions of the Prophet* (1981) 13.
[82] Qur'an 36:82.
[83] Qur'an 70:54.
[84] Qur'an 7:172.
[85] Qur'an 33:72.
[86] Qur'an 7:30.
[87] Ibid.
[88] Qur'an 7:172.

justiciable by God. This life is not the end but the start of a process. In order to 'test' the use of human free will, God sends humanity down to earth, born as children with no memory of pre-birth. God sends Prophets, however, inter alia to remind humanity of its acceptance of free will and that each individual will be judged on the Day of Judgment.

Thus, some unspecified time later, 'human history' begins. The obligations related to the correct use of free will, the ultimate object of which is freely to recognise the Creator, is a key object of human life on Earth.[89] To this end, life on earth is the 'test' where each individual is allocated a sojourn with the infrastructure necessary (*rizq*) to discharge his or her individual obligations and in doing so to recognise God as Creator.

Individual obligations that discharge this ancient acceptance of free will are formally articulated in the Covenant of each Prophet and enable an individual to achieve this 'ultimate' goal. Thus, a believer choosing to follow Prophets Moses or Abraham will adhere to the Mosaic or Abrahamic Covenant.[90] The Qur'anic reference to a Covenant is similar in function, although perhaps not in content, to the Biblical Covenants.[91] 'Correct' performance against the Covenant of any Prophet leads to 'success'.[92] Human history as we know it will end on the Day of Judgment, when every human is judged as against his or her individual Covenant obligations and the individual's success or failure publicly proclaimed.[93]

Free will

In the beginning there were, broadly speaking, two types of Covenant established. The first Covenant constitutes the immutable physical laws of nature to which every part of creation is subject, containing laws that bind absolutely but separately. It is essential to sustain life in a form that can appear independent of a Sustaining Being. This 'infrastructure' is necessary for the life of each soul in its physical form, and *ipso facto* is not judged.

The second type of Covenant is a Covenant of a Prophet. Each individual who freely adopts this Covenant is required to discharge its obligations. A central part of the Covenant is that a person must sagely exercise his or her free will. Each free-willed individual, however, independently decides the extent of their own (moral) performance based on a free recognition of the Creator. The Qur'an further states

---

[89] Qur'an 7:172.
[90] Qur'an 2:93.
[91] Genesis 9:1–7, eg, God's Covenant with the Prophet Noah and his followers.
[92] Qur'an 2:62, Qur'an 5:69.
[93] Qur'an 36:51.

that God, in mercy, sent revelation through Prophets to warn, to remind and to invite humanity towards fulfilling the binding obligations resulting from its ancient decision to accept free will. Thus, for Muslims, the *Shari'a* of the Prophet, and in its various manifestations, of all Prophets, is the law *necessary* to lead an individual to the 'right way', with respect to the use of free will.

The Omnipotent God who is outside time,[94] by definition knows all outcomes, and this concept is sometimes referred to as *qada wa qadr* (قضاء و قدر).[95] Earthly life, however, is given to humanity freely to play out its individual decisions so that judgment is fair, is accepted as fair by every individual, and will be an identical outcome for each individual no matter how many times this 'experiment' is repeated. While nothing turns on this point, it appears to strike a chord with the sentiment one often hears that 'If I had my life over I would probably make the same choices'.

In 'acting out' free will, humans will interact with the rest of creation. This interaction creates the opportunity for doing both good and wrong. In dealing with 'crimes/wrongs', there is a well known axiom in Islam that God will forgive unstintingly of 'crimes/wrongs' against God although 'crimes/wrongs' committed against others must be settled as between them.[96] Crimes against persons, when proven, may be punished according to the law or forgiven by the injured party (or their legal representative).[97] Apostasy is a crime against God and thus can only be forgiven or punished by God and as required by the Qur'an. It does not find temporal jurisdiction.

What is apostasy in Islam?

Apostasy is the renunciation of faith. Some key questions associated with apostasy under the *Shari'a* are: What does apostasy mean in practice? How is it established and, unless renunciation is done by the individual while free from duress, who is competent to declare apostasy?

As discussed, on becoming a Muslim one undertakes to do so wholeheartedly, consciously and freely, and thereby undertakes not ever to renounce the faith.[98] As Covenant obligations inhere on becoming a Muslim, the question becomes: Other than for the explicit, uncoerced rejection of faith, what level of breach of the Covenant constitutes 'renunciation'?

---

[94] Qur'an 103:1–3. Time is a 'created thing' in Islam and 'time' as we know it will end on the Day of Judgment.
[95] Sami Zubaida, *Law and Power in the Islamic World* (2003) 24.
[96] See, eg, Khaleed Abou El-Fadl, 'Islam and the Challenge of Democratic Commitment' (2003) 27 *Fordham International Law Journal* 4, 51.
[97] Qur'an 17:33.
[98] See above n 12.

Gwynne presents the view of the great Hanbali scholar al-Qurtubi that even if a Muslim commits a major sin (*kabirah*), she or he does not become a disbeliever.[99] The vast majority of contemporary Muslims would consider al-Qurtubi's views correct.[100] To this end, the mere existence of the *Shari'a* concept of *kabirah* or a 'major sin', which constitutes a breach or neglect of a major Covenant obligation such as prayer, fasting or avoiding adultery, clearly distinguishes such breaches from renunciation, and explicitly means that the person in breach is nonetheless a Muslim and not an apostate. There appears to be a consensus among Muslims that only free renunciation of belief in God or the apostleship of Mohamed makes one an apostate.

Freedom of religion: Problems with the practical expression of apostasy laws

The problems of apostasy in Islam do not spring from the concept itself, as all Abrahamic faiths are cognisant of the issue. Each faith also reserves the right to exclude apostates from their communions. That is, the problem arises under the *Shari'a* not so much with the term in the Covenant that requires the surrender of the right of renunciation but that some Muslims believe that apostates must be put to death, as discussed below. Such a penalty is in conflict with international human rights norms since human rights instruments such as the Universal Declaration of Human Rights, the International Covenant on Civil and Political Rights and the International Covenant on Economic, Social and Cultural Rights provide for the freedom of religion. It is certainly problematic in Australia, where such a 'penalty' would reasonably be construed as a death threat. However, the conflation of the two issues is arguably the source of the controversy. It is the death 'sentence' that is problematic. There is no requirement in the international norms that an apostate must continue to receive the privileges of faith within the communion in question or be free from social ostracism.

However, there are further consequences that can arise from the variations in the application of Islamic law and the blurring of lines between Islamic law and, for example, *adaat*[101] in South-East Asia. There appears to be belief in non-Malay communities that a Muslim can never convert from Islam. The term used by non-Malays in the archipelago for conversion to Islam is *masuk Melayu*.[102] This

---

[99] Gwynne, above n 65.
[100] Anne Elizabeth Mayer, 'Islam and the State' (1991) 12 *Cardozo Law Review* 1015, 1026.
[101] *Adaat* is Malay customary law. For the relationship between *adat* and Islam see R F Ellen, 'Social Theory, Ethnography and the Understanding of Practical Islam in South-East Asia' in M B Hooker (ed), *Islam in South-East Asia* (1988) 64.
[102] Ibid 56. *Masuk Melayu* literally means 'to become a Malay' and strictly the term for conversion should be *masuk Islam* or 'to enter into Islam'.

belief in the nexus between Malay culture and Islam must be very strong, as even in secular Singapore, where Islamic law does not apply, and where adherence to the fundamentals of Islam is quite variable, apostasy among Malays is said to be unknown.[103] In Malaysia, for example, it is impossible for a Malay person to convert to another religion, not because of laws against apostasy, but for reasons of definition. The Malaysian Constitution defines Malays as being Muslim.[104] Thus, if a person who was once Malay renounces Islam, then she or he ceases to be Muslim and *ipso facto* ceases to be Malay in the meaning of the Malaysian Constitution. On the other hand, *adaat* is protected by article I(1) of the Declaration of the Principles of International Cultural Co-operation[105], which recognises the value of various traditional cultural practices and may qualify *adaat*, including the version of *Shari'a* that forms part of *adaat*, for separate protection, although arguably with few legal consequences under international law.

The Australian Constitution, for example, does not have a freedom of religion provision although in practice Australians appear to enjoy freedom of religion including the public expressions of faith. Countries such as France have some limits on the free expression of faith. Debates in Australia have also canvassed issues such as the banning the *niqab* (face covering) for Muslim women, although the majority of Australian politicians have not been willing to publicly entertain such a ban. This absence of protection in law for the freedoms, or against curtailing freedoms, as the case may be, do not appear to be viewed as contrary to international law on the freedom of religion. Therefore, 'freedom of religion' under international law is not absolute and does appear to concede limits particularly when they conflict with domestic norms such as secularism or *adaat*.

I note, however, that it would be both unnecessary and patronising to suggest that a sane adult cannot freely enter into a unilaterally binding contract even if it means that he or she is eternally bound. Marriage under some faiths requires a lifetime commitment,[106] and while controversial, is not considered immoral or unlawful when entered into freely. As with marriage, however, while people respect cultural practices, the autonomy of an individual to choose a spouse is recognised under international law,[107] and the free adoption of a religion can be seen as analogous to marriage in the context of an individual's personal autonomy.

---

[103] Ibid 57.
[104] *Malaysia Constitution*, art 160.
[105] 'Each culture has a dignity and value which must be respected and preserved': *Declaration of the Principles of International Cultural Co-operation*, UNESCO General Conference, 14th sess, 4 November 1966, art I(1).
[106] That is, in the context of a marriage until 'death do us part'.
[107] UDHR, above n 3, art 16(2).

There are, however, problems associated with people deemed Muslims by others, such as with children by parents, which can be problematic if the 'Muslim child' when grown up then decides to renounce the faith. That is, the children of Muslim parents 'raised' as Muslims but who have not had the option to choose freely is a source of problems. Further, a problem arises in that international norms give parents the 'right' unconditionally to raise their children according to their own faiths.[108] Islam caters for this problem by requiring that each individual make her or his own choice. A Muslim is also bound to enquire into any obligation or duty before acceptance,[109] and there is a presumption in the Qur'an that a Muslim is cognisant of the Qur'anic warnings with respect to apostasy.

The eponyms required their followers to understand and deliberately accept or reject a School's legal opinion, including those on apostasy, as human legal opinions. Abu Hanifa made this a specific condition for those using his methodology.[110] According to some Muslim scholars, there is a general obligation on a Muslim to enquire[111] whether a legal opinion 'contains God's decree only or includes human opinion'.[112] In the latter case, the Muslim is <u>obliged</u> to consult another independent specialist (*ittiba*').[113]

This raises two further central issues that I now discuss. These are (a) What is the status of a person who did not voluntarily declare the *shahada*, and (b) whether the death penalty is mandated for apostasy under the *Shari'a*.

'Apostasy' by those raised as Muslims

The Prophet stated that all humans were born in *fitra*, that is, born as 'Muslims', with a natural inclination to submit to God and it is the parents or society who 'change' a child's natural inclination.[114] On this argument, therefore, all non-Muslims should be put to the sword because their individual apostasy is clearly apparent, a position for which there is no Qur'anic, *sunna* or jurisprudential support. Therefore, the argument that children born into 'Muslim' families are Muslims through *fitra* is

---

[108] ICESCR, above n 6, art 13(3).
[109] See below discussion of '*ittiba*' or 'the duty to enquire'.
[110] Charles Adams, 'Abu Hanifa' in I Edge (ed), *Islamic Law and Legal Theory* (1996) 381.
[111] This enquiry is clearly only mandatory to the extent of the individual's knowledge and ability: see, eg, Qur'an 2:33; Qur'an 2:286.
[112] Rudolph Peters, 'Idjtihad and Taqlid in 18th and 19th Century Islam' (1980) 20 *Die Welt des Islams* 131, 140.
[113] Ibid; Yaroslav Trofimov, *The Seige of Mecca: The Forgotten Uprising in Islam's Holiest Shrine* (2007) 38.
[114] Shaheen Sardar Ali and Javaid Rehman, 'The Concept of Jihad in Islamic International Law' (2005) 10 *Journal of Conflict and Security Law* 321, 336.

only partly valid as the Prophet conceded the possibility that children will follow their parents' faith (Islam or otherwise) as opposed to adopting the Covenant independently. Islam does not permit such blind faith,[115] for the abrogation of free will.

This raises the specific question of whether a Muslim may change his or her religion. The short answer is yes, a Muslim man or woman may change his or her religion,[116] although as mentioned the Qur'an promises a severe punishment in the Hereafter. In practice, it appears that in the 'stricter' Muslims states,[117] Qur'an 2:256 is interpreted as follows: reversion from Islam is allowed if the original 'conversion' to Islam was effected by force only (that is, by compulsion). Some Muslim states have codified the right to follow a religion of one's choice.[118] However, this right of a person to convert away from Islam is not without its temporal consequences in some expressions of Islamic law or in domestic law, as in Malaysia. However, the right to waive 'future rights' with respect to religion, or re-marriage, does not appear problematic as a matter of law.

The Death Penalty: For Apostasy or Treason?

Apostasy is a *hudud* crime under the *Shari'a*.[119] *Hudud* is a class of *Shari'a* crime that carries a 'fixed' punishment.[120] In this context it means fixed by God and must mean that human agency cannot alter these fixed punishments including extending such punishments to other classes of crimes. This view is supported by the *Hanafi* view[121] that the punishment for consuming grape wine, the only intoxicant explicitly prohibited in the Qur'an, applies to a person intoxicated by grape wine *only* and

---

[115] Qur'an 43:22–24.
[116] Qur'an 2:256.
[117] See, eg, above discussion of Malaysia.
[118] See, eg, *Malaysian Constitution* art 11(1): 'Every person has the right to profess and practice his religion and ... to propagate it'.
[119] Qur'an 4:89.
[120] Sayed Hassan Amin, *Islamic Law in the Contemporary World* (1985) 28. While the punishments are fixed and often severe, in addition to the strict rules of evidence discussed *infra*, there are several excuses that help reduce or mitigate the impact of the severity. For example, Boyle-Lewicki refers to the allowances made for stealing food in poverty, considering alcohol consumption as a sickness etc: Edna Boyle-Lewicki, 'Need World's Collide: The Hudad Crimes of Islamic Law and International Human Rights' (2000) 13 *New York International Law Review* 43, 72; eg, while drug use is prohibited in Islam, drug use is also considered a sickness and is treated as such, meaning that *hudud* punishments are suspended: Norman Swan, 'Female drug users in Iran', *ABC Radio National Health Report*, 17 December 2007.
[121] The Hanafi Islamic School is the largest school in contemporary Islam.

not analogised intoxicants[122] and is the better view in keeping 'God's punishments' separate. The requisite standard of proof for *hudud* crimes is 'certain' (that is, beyond doubt).[123] While non-Muslims (including apostates) are entitled to receive the protection of the *Shari'a* they are not subject to some *hudud* punishments — including, say, for adultery[124] — that draws the death penalty, or if someone is involuntarily declared a non-Muslim they cannot *ipso facto* be subject to *hudud*. The death sentence generally is an unacceptable option in the international plane, although it is still on the statute books in many States including in industrialised States such as the US and Japan.

In part, the death penalty for apostasy continues from biblical tradition,[125] as crimes and punishments not specifically abrogated by the Qur'an or the *sunna* are therefore still in force.[126] While death for apostasy or blasphemy is no longer part of the Canon law, it is in the view of some[127] still part of Islamic law as it was not explicitly abrogated in the Qur'an or the *sunna*, and here arguably lies another source of the controversy.[128] It is a further *Shari'a* requirement, however, that a person must be aware of the punishment for a particular *hadd* crime when committed, for the punishment to be enforceable.[129] Therefore, children who 'chose Islam' for parental pressure but who are not independently aware of its unilaterally and eternally binding nature, cannot be subject to any punishment. Clearly, the subjective knowledge of the child will be a relevant factor in each case.

---

[122] Nisrine Abiad, *Sharia, Muslim States and International Human Rights Treaty Obligations: A Comparative Study* (2008) 25.

[123] Some Malikis permit the use of circumstantial evidence (such as pregnancy) with respect to *zina*: Noel J Coulson, *Conflicts and Tensions in Islamic Jurisprudence* (1969) 62. This, however, is a minority view in conflict with the Qur'an, and should therefore not be considered persuasive.

[124] Matthew Ross Lippman, Seán McConville and Mordechai Yerushalmi, *Islamic Criminal Law and Procedure: An Introduction* (1988) 60. A *hadd* punishment is by definition 'God's right': J Tanzil-ur-Rahman, *Islamic Criminal Laws (Part-I Hudud)* (1982) 35 and arguably, therefore, should not apply to those not voluntarily bound by the Muslim Covenant who should not suffer a sanction for breach of a Covenant obligation or for a Covenant crime.

[125] Death penalty for apostasy is prescribed in the Old Testament, Deuteronomy: 13:6–9 and the death penalty for blasphemy is prescribed in Leviticus 24:16; 1 Timothy 4:1–3; Hebrews 3:12.

[126] Boyle-Lewicki, above n 120, 61. For the political use of apostasy prosecutions see below.

[127] For a survey of various historical and contemporary opinions on the subject, see generally S A Rahman, *Punishment of Apostasy in Islam* (1996).

[128] The discussion of the Qur'anic concept of abrogation itself is a separate issue which is outside the scope of this chapter.

[129] Nisrine Abiad, *Sharia, Muslim States and International Human Rights Treaty Obligations: A Comparative Study* (2008) 22.

Apostasy is a Qur'anic crime, although the Qur'an does not provide for a temporal punishment for apostasy alone[130] but instead warns of a severe punishment in the Hereafter.[131] Further, the Schools agree on the 'death penalty' only for men, and not for women apostates,[132] which *must* mean at least that it is not the 'apostasy' *per se* that draws the death penalty. This interpretation supports the view that God reserves the penalty for apostasy *in* the Hereafter.[133] Al Awzaa'y, who was a great scholar and a contemporary of Abu Hanifa, was of the view that both men and women ought to be left alone, but only if there 'is no plot to take over the State' (that is, treason).[134] In my opinion, this is the better view.

In this context, the *sunna*, which is consistent with the Qur'an,[135] reserves the death penalty for those who apostatised <u>*and* treasonously fought against the Muslims</u>.[136] The *sunna* of the Prophet in the overwhelming majority of cases was to pardon even treason.

The death penalty for apostasy is also problematic because of the unprincipled and instrumental reasons for bringing on charges and accusations of apostasy against individuals for, say, political reasons. For an accused, such a charge is difficult to defend. There is also a view that the evidence and rationale for the death penalty for apostasy by some contemporary scholars such as Maududi (d. 1979) 'is farfetched'.[137] The Prophet also stated that, 'We make judgments on the basis of what is apparent, and God takes charge of hidden things'.[138] One may make the point that apostasy is sometimes indeed apparent. However, in the final analysis, the Prophet said that the worst of all (false) gods worshipped by people is 'our self–love'[139], and it is clearly a matter that is not always apparent — but even when apparent, it is not punished, although this polytheism clearly puts one outside the fold of Islam and is the ultimate crime in Islam.

---

[130] Qur'an 2:217; 5:54; 47:25. Those who apostatise and then fight against Muslims however may be fought: Qur'an 4:89.
[131] Qur'an 3:90; 4:89; 4:137; 63:3. The key point is that even though the Qur'an recognises vacillating faith as a fact of life, which in the Qur'anic view is *ipso facto* for material or worldly reasons, it prescribes no temporal punishment.
[132] Shaheen Sardar Ali and Javaid Rehman, 'The Concept of Jihad in Islamic International Law' (2005) 10 *Journal of Conflict and Security Law* 321, 336.
[133] J Bowker, *What Muslims Believe* (1998) 96; see also Qur'an 7:62–63.
[134] Bowker, above n 133, 96.
[135] Qur'an 4:89.
[136] Adil Salahi, *Muhammad: Man and the Prophet* (2002) 603–32.
[137] Abdullah Saeed and Hassan Saeed, *Freedom of Religion, Apostasy and Islam* (2006) 57.
[138] Bernard G Weiss, *The Spirit of Islamic Law* (1998) 652.
[139] W H T Gairdner, *The Niche for Lights* (1980) 57–161, 151.

Conclusion

Apostasy is a grave crime in Islam and 'Muslim' apostates fall outside the faith, as do apostates in other Abrahamic faiths. For self-declared apostates this is not controversial as they enjoy the right of renouncing the faith and may do so both secretly, in a way that can never be justiciable by temporal authorities, but nonetheless sometimes is used for political reasons.[140] On the other hand, high profile individuals giving open expression to their renunciation with little, if any reaction, is also not unknown.[141] Such renunciation must have some social consequences although the key legal impediments of specific concern are (a) a possible conflict with international norms on the freedom of religion, and (b) the possible death penalty that may attach in the view of some Schools.

Those who accept Islam voluntarily should be aware that non-renunciation is a term of their new faith. A matter of personal autonomy for adults, this is not controversial. For those raised by their parents 'as Muslims' the penal consequences of renunciation can apply only if they freely accepted the faith with knowledge of the terms of the Covenant including the obligation not to renounce the faith. For those who were unaware of the specific terms, *Shari'a* law holds no punishment but is a matter that varies in each individual case depending upon the subjective level of the individual's knowledge.

The most problematic aspect of apostasy in Islam is the death penalty, a view supported by some *Shari'a* scholars. This chapter has argued that only those who freely accept the Muslim Covenant are bound by its specific terms and further that the Qur'an and *sunna* provide no temporal jurisdiction over apostasy *per se*. *Shari'a* punishment can only legitimately apply to those who apostatise, then fight against Muslims and are subsequently found guilty of treason under the *Shari'a* by a competent *Shari'a* judge. Even in these instances, the death penalty is not mandatory, as was shown by the Prophet.

On this analysis, the *Shari'a* does not conflict directly with international law. Freedom 'to choose' must also include the right unilaterally to elect to be forever bound. On the other hand, a parents' right under international law to raise a child in their faith clashes with the *Shari'a's* obligation that each person must individually and freely choose to exercise their free will according to a Covenant. Again, *Shari'a* norms and international norms can be interpreted in a manner that is not inconsistent. That is,

---

[140] For political prosecutions using apostasy as a charge see Boyle-Lewicki, above n 120, 61.
[141] Tariq Ali, a well known, respected and high-profile author and commentator, eg, is a self-confessed atheist and 'cultural Muslim' who lives between the UK and Pakistan: Tariq Ali, *The Clash of Fundamentalisms: Crusades, Jihads and Modernity* (2002) 22.

parents may raise their children in a faith, but for Muslims, the ultimate decision to be eternally bound must remain an individual decision as required by the *Shari'a*.

In the final analysis, Muslims should permit free thought and expression as required under the *Shari'a* as it is only the free expression of one's faith that will satisfy the ancient undertaking given by each human soul to their Creator and is a matter utterly beyond human jurisdiction, competence and perception. It is in this spirit that Muslims should interpret freedom of religion provisions under a bill of rights.

9

Political Culture and Freedom of Conscience: A Case Study of Austria

David M Kirkham

Since the end of World War Two, the speed, breadth and long-term consequences of world events have put human rights high on the international political and legal agenda. The Holocaust, genocides in the former Yugoslavia, Rwanda and Sudan, and too many acts of mass terrorism are some of the events that have placed them there. Some nations — usually inveterate abusers — would just as soon that human rights were not prominent. Others — usually rights respecters — have taken a proactive approach to protecting individual fundamental freedoms by incorporating into their own legal systems all or many of the traditional rights found in the Universal Declaration of Human Rights and other international protective instruments. In fact, protecting human rights has gained sufficient momentum in the international arena that even most countries that do not support such rights at least pay lip service to them and include them — though often with qualifications — in their constitutional laws and charters.

Among the rights at the heart of the debate, rights fundamental to democracy and its institutions, are those of conscience, religion and belief. Touching at the core of what it means to be human, at the very essence of the significance men and women give to their lives and the lives of others, protection of rights of conscience can be found in virtually every human rights charter, bill, and comprehensive code. The importance of these rights permits analysis of their protection as models for the protection of fundamental rights in general. But as nations wrestle with the best ways to protect, preserve and perpetuate these and other fundamental rights, the legal approach is limited to essentially two options: a people can embed them in the constitutional law of the land or protect them through the course of ordinary legislation. Bills of rights, charters, and routine legislation — each approach offers something to gain and something to lose to the nations who undertake them.

Australia and the United Kingdom are two nations with good human rights reputations who have recently debated means by which they can further ensure the fundamental liberties of people within their borders. One of the means both countries are considering is the adoption of a bill of rights (in the UK's case a 'new' bill of rights[1]). Although Australia's initiative seems recently to have ground to a halt and the ultimate outcome remains to be seen in the United Kingdom, part of the debate surrounding these and other bills of rights discussions has centred on the optimal language and best type of instrument to be adopted.

In the case of freedom of conscience, it is generally assumed that laws having constitutional force will strengthen the hands of an independent judiciary and protect religious minorities against the possible tempting tyranny of a parliamentary majority. On the other hand, the argument for a legislative charter or its equivalent states that such a charter will prevent the opposite abuse: legislation 'from the bench', as some think occurs too often by judges in the United States. Regardless of the language used or instrument adopted, we must examine the debate in light of the practices of sovereign violators of freedom of religion or belief, who nonetheless have constitutionally embedded, very clear provisions for religious freedom. What really accounts for the differences between those countries where freedom of conscience is respected and those where it is not? Do religious guarantees in practice depend on whether they are written in a bill as opposed to a charter or a constitutional basic law or are simply scattered throughout various legislative provisions? Henry Kissinger once reportedly said, tongue-in-cheek, 'the illegal we do immediately. The unconstitutional takes a little longer'.[2] Do some countries have genius draftsmen and women who simply 'know the magic words' to guarantee civil liberties? The arguments can become absurd.

The debates over specific language and types of legal instruments sometimes become so volatile as to obfuscate a more fundamental determinant of how well the free conscience of a people are protected: the political culture of a nation. This chapter posits that, when it comes to protections of freedom of religion or belief, political culture is as important, if not more so, than whether those protections find themselves in a charter, a bill, or whether they are somehow constitutionally embedded in a basic law. This does not mean that the words and instruments are not important. They may themselves, however, be reflections of the political culture. More important than the words or type of instrument is the perceived legitimacy conveyed to the words and documents through the drafting and enforcement processes of the country, through

---

[1] Michael Wills, *A Bill of Rights for the UK? Papers and Written Evidence, Memorandum, December 18,* (2008) <http://www.publications.parliament.uk/pa/jt200809/jtselect/jtrights/15/1506.htm#a12> at 26 March 2011.

[2] DuPre Jones, 'The sayings of Secretary Henry', *New York Times* (New York), 28 October 1973.

the perceived authority of the drafters and enforcers, and the attitudes towards the documents, words, processes and persons held by both the political elites and political masses. To begin to test the waters of these assertions, this chapter will look at Austria as a case study. It will ask how the nation's underlying political culture reflects the realities of its constitutional protections for freedom of conscience and other fundamental rights and suggest that, in Austria's case, cultural safeguards could be stronger.

Freedom of religion and illiberal republics

Virtually every national constitution in the world guarantees some kind of freedom of conscience and religious belief. One will find protective provisions in the constitutions of Iran, North Korea, Belarus and Tajikistan, to name only a few countries with less liberal regimes and reputations. These provisions may differ in their wording, or they may resemble provisions in international human rights documents and the liberal constitutions of others, but the words are there, regardless. In each case they give innocent citizens grounds to think their rights are protected — rights to believe or not to believe and to pursue their beliefs on their own or with others within institutional structures. But every country, regardless of its constitutional provisions, does not really guarantee religious freedom in practice. Violations are documented near daily by such organizations as Human Rights Without Frontiers (HRWF) or Forum 18.[3]

Although the Iranian Constitution specifically guarantees freedom of worship only to Muslims and, as 'the only recognized religious minorities', to Zoroastrian, Jewish and Christian Iranians, it nonetheless assures for everyone that 'the investigation of individuals' beliefs is forbidden, and no one may be molested or taken to task simply for holding a certain belief'. It also asserts that 'the government of the Islamic Republic of Iran and all Muslims are duty-bound to treat non-Muslims in conformity with ethical norms and the principles of Islamic justice and equity, and to respect their human rights' — this despite numerous well-documented official Iranian persecutions of members of the Bahá'í faith.[4]

North Korean citizens have constitutionally guaranteed 'freedom of religious beliefs'. The North Korean Constitution notes that, 'This right is granted by approving the construction of religious buildings and the holding of religious ceremonies'.

---

[3] See *Human Rights Without Frontiers International* (2011) Human Rights Without Frontiers <http://www.hrwf.net/> at 26 March 2011; *Forum 18* (2011) Forum 18 <http://www.forum18.org> at 26 March 2011.

[4] *Iranian Constitution* arts 13–4, 23; *Iran Press Watch* (2011) Iran Press Watch <http://www.iranpresswatch.org/> at 26 March 2011.

If it seems potentially restrictive, that religious freedom is further qualified by the provision that 'religion must not be used as a pretext for drawing in foreign forces or for harming the State and social order'. This must presumably have been the case when, if Associated Press reports are correct, a North Korean woman was executed in June 2009 for distributing the Bible.[5]

In Belarus, where the government's approach to freedom of conscience issues is not so draconian but still far from liberal, the constitution provides that 'all religions and faiths shall be equal before the law' and that 'the establishment of any privileges or restrictions with regard to a particular religion or faith in relation to others shall not be permitted'. On the individual level, supposedly 'everyone shall have the right independently to determine his attitude towards religion, to profess any religion individually or jointly with others, or to profess none at all, to express and spread beliefs connected with his attitude towards religion, and to participate in the performance of acts of worship and religious rituals and rites'.[6] And yet HRWF and Forum 18 continue to note abuses in Belarus.

The Constitution of the likewise restrictive Tajikistan is similar. It instructively explains that 'in Tajikistan, social life develops on the basis of political and ideological pluralism', and hence, 'no state ideology or religion may be established'. The implication of that, however, is that 'religious organizations are separate from the state and may not interfere in governmental affairs'. However, here too 'each person has the right independently to determine her or his religious preference, to practice any religion alone or in association with others or to practice no religion, and to participate in the performance of religious cults, rituals, and ceremonies'.[7]

It is clear that protective words regarding freedom of religion or belief in a constitution are no guarantee that this freedom will be respected in practice. Of course, careful framers will argue that words do make a difference — and they do. It can be argued that the constitutions of Belarus and Tajikistan, for example, have somewhat less obtrusive qualifications to their protection of religious rights than do the constitutions of North Korea and Iran, and that the abuses are slightly less egregious in the former two as well. But one finds sometimes the same protective words in the constitutional documents of abuser nations as in those of countries who do a good job of protecting freedom of belief. For example, all forty-seven members of the Council of Europe are held to the same constitutional standards for religious protection laid out in the European Convention on Human Rights and yet some

---

[5] *North Korean Constitution* art 68; Kwang-Tae Kim, *Activists claim Christian executed in NKorea* (2009) *Associated Press* <http://www.breitbart.com/article.php?id=D99KNBDO0&show_article=1> at 26 March 2011.
[6] *Belarussian Constitution* arts 16, 31.
[7] *Tajikistani Constitution* arts 8, 26.

of those countries do a much better job at actually protecting religious rights than others. A review of the eleven article 9 cases dealing with freedom of religion or belief communicated to the European Court of Human Rights during May and June 2009 reveals five cases from Russia and four from Turkey.[8]

It is easy to recognize that some constitutions are completely ineffective in protecting freedom of religion or belief and other fundamental rights. Thus, for modern nations conducting a dialogue on the value of written constitutional provisions, especially a bill of rights, in protecting rights of conscience, it makes little sense to spend too much time analysing the extreme cases. Australia is not Iran. The United Kingdom is not the Democratic People's Republic of North Korea. It makes more sense for countries serious about the protection of human rights to look at nations more closely resembling themselves. A key as to why this is so lies in their political cultures.

Political culture

At least since the 1980s, political scientists have recognized political culture as a useful concept for examination. Definitions vary but find much in common. Lucian Pye states:

> Involving both the ideals and the operating norms of a political system, political culture includes subjective attitudes and sentiments as well as objective symbols and creeds that together govern political behavior and give structure and order to the political process. Nations generally have both elite and mass political cultures, along with further subcultures that are rooted in regional, occupational, class, ethnic, and other differences.[9]

Almond and Verba originally described political culture as societally shared:

> cognitions, perceptions, evaluations, attitudes and behavioral predispositions that permit the members of that polity to order and interpret political institutions and processes and their own relationships with such institutions and processes.[10]

---

[8] *Convention for the Protection of Human Rights and Fundamental Freedoms (as amended by Protocol No. 11, 1998)*, opened for signature 4 November 1950, ETS 5 (entered into force 3 September 1953).

[9] Lucian W Pye, 'Political Culture' in Joel Krieger (ed), *Oxford Companion to Politics of the World* (1993) 712. For Australia, see the discussion in Bede Harris, *A New Constitution for Australia* (2002) ch 2.

[10] Ann L Craig and Wayne A Cornelius, 'Political Culture in Mexico: Continuities and Revisionist Interpretations' in Gabriel A Almond and Sydney Verba (eds), *The Civic Culture Revisited* (1989) 340.

A Canadian definition states that political culture is:

> 1. The sum of attitudes, beliefs, and expectations that constitute particular orientations toward society in general and politics in particular [or] 2. The specifically political orientations — attitudes towards the political system and its various parts, and attitudes toward the role of the self in the system.[11]

In other words, in each of these definitions political culture transcends law to the extent that law emanates from the polity and society. Legal institutions will generally reflect the attitudes, beliefs and expectations of the polity. This is clearly so in a democracy, but when a citizenry accepts passively the will of authoritarian leaders or even actively the pronouncements of theocratic rulers in which it had no say, that too is a reflection of political culture.

When it comes to freedom of religion or belief and other fundamental freedoms, when the political culture reinforces their preservation, these freedoms tend to take root and are sustainable over long periods. The actual words used to preserve those freedoms are not so important if it is widely and insistently understood that such is their intent. On the other hand, where the words seem just right from the standpoint of draftsmanship, but widespread cultural agreement as to the meaning and importance of those words is lacking, fundamental freedoms are less likely to be maintained.

Post-World War Two Austria presents a recent example of a country in which the language of fundamental rights became part of its legal and political institutions before that language reflected some of the realities of the political life of the nation. Austria is a useful case study because the level of its commitment to fundamental rights as reflected by its post-war political controversies was far from apparent at a time when most of Austria's Western contemporaries had made significant steps in adopting the realities of democratic governments and it was presumed that Austria had as well. Many observers were surprised when controversies broke out in the mid-1980s with the election to the presidency of Kurt Waldheim, and again in 1999 when the right-wing Freedom Party, deemed extremist by many observers, came to power in coalition under the leadership of Jörg Haider. Waldheim was a former National Socialist Wehrmacht officer whose service during the war has led to serious criticism; the recently deceased Haider was the son of National Socialists. His statements seemed at times to defend Nazi policies and practices. The elevation to

---

[11] *Canadian Political Culture: The Problem of Americanization: Definitions* (2009) Markville Secondary School <http://www.markville.ss.yrdsb.edu.on.ca/politics/exemplars/meg2.html> at 26 March 2011.

power of Waldheim and Haider called into question for some whether Austria would in fact protect the individual rights guaranteed in its basic law.

Austria: A bit of post-war history

Though democratic principles are acknowledged to have existed in societies ranging from Iroquois Amerindians to African ethnic communities, few would argue that their conceptional development has been largely Western European and American. Western Europe has seemed to be largely immune from the phenomenon dubbed by Fareed Zakaria as the post-Cold War rise of the illiberal democracies, that is, governments democratically elected but nonetheless oppressive to a considerable segment of their population.[12]

The European Union has embraced democracy as a guiding principle and as a condition for membership. Although it almost went without saying that its founding members were established democracies, each potential new member, especially those clamouring for entry from the former Soviet bloc, has been screened and scrutinized for its commitment to the rule of law, protection of human rights, and other 'European' and democratic values.[13]

Nestled in the heart of Europe, Austria is a highly developed, functioning democracy with a market economy. Overall, its citizens enjoy a high standard of living. It is known for cleanliness, quaintness, natural beauty, winter sports and other tourist magnets. As a member of the European Union since 1995, it has only rarely drawn attention to itself in the international media in negative ways.

Since the end of World War Two, however, two events, both surrounding controversial political figures, have given rise in some circles to questions regarding Austria's political culture and its commitment to liberal constitutional values. The first was the election to the Austrian Presidency in 1986 of former UN General Secretary Kurt Waldheim. Facts unknown to most during his tenure at the United Nations, Waldheim had served as a Wehrmacht intelligence officer during the war in Yugoslavia at a location and time that war crimes occurred. These facts came out following his election, with allegations that he at least knew and lied about the commission of these crimes, if he was not more directly complicit in them. He denied wrongdoing and many reputable Austrians came to his defence. In protecting

---

[12] Fareed Zakaria, 'The Rise of Illiberal Democracy' (1997) 76 *Foreign Affairs* 22.
[13] Heather Grabbe, 'European Union Conditionality and the "Acquis Communautaire"' (2002) 23 *International Political Science Review* 249. See also Alselm Skura, *The Eastern Enlargement of the European Union: Efforts and Obstacles on the Way to Membership* (2005).

Waldheim, however, some suggest Austrians were in fact at least deceiving themselves about their own responsibilities for their past experiment with National Socialism.

Austria's political neutrality following the war became a fundamental component of its political culture. Its courtship by both sides in the Cold War allowed Austrians to move forward after the war without ever accounting for their own contribution to Nazi atrocities — something the division of Germany never allowed the Germans:

> In distinguishing Austria from Germany, neutrality ... helped foster Austria's amnesia vis-à-vis its role in the Third Reich. Accepting history's verdict as Nazi Germany's first victim, Austrians could blame the Holocaust's horrors on the 'evil' Germans and avoid the painful process of coming to terms with their own complicitous past. Paradoxically, it was the international controversy surrounding the election of Kurt Waldheim to the Austrian Presidency in 1986 that for the first time led to broad-based debates in Austria about the country's role under National Socialism.[14]

According to historian Gordon Brook-Shepherd, the Waldheim affair forced Austria

> to shed some carefully nurtured delusions and illusions. The Austrians, like Waldheim, had got used to thinking of themselves purely as victims of Nazism, with no regard for the part they had played in its regime of evil, the Holocaust included. Both felt that Hitler's war was safely behind them, shut away in unvisited archives, yellowed newspaper files, and even behind the locked doors of their own memories. Both believed that the outside world felt respect and even affection for them, and it must be said that the outside world had given them every reason for that belief. For four decades after achieving independence, Austria had again become, to most foreign eyes, the sweet land of *The Sound of Music*; of Strauss and Mozart; of Danube steamers and alpine ski-runs.[15]

Austria had made some limited restitution to the victims of the Nazi regime at the end of the war, but in light of Austrians quickly taking up the status of Nazi victimhood, this restitution did not go far materially for those who suffered. More importantly, it did not go far psychologically in transforming the political culture to one firmly planted on liberal values. According to US Department of State reports, many observers were disturbed over time by

---

[14] Andrei S Markovits, 'Austria,' in Joel Krieger (ed), *The Oxford Companion to Politics of the World* (2003) 60.
[15] Gordon Brook-Shepherd, *The Austrians: A Thousand-Year Odyssey* (1996) 439. (Shepherd's discussion of Waldheim incident is at 429–40).

the continuation of the view that prevailed since 1943 that Austria was the 'first free country to fall a victim' to Nazi aggression. This 'first victim' view was in fact fostered by the Allied Powers themselves in the Moscow Declaration of 1943, in which the Allies declared as null and void the Anschluss and called for the restoration of the country's independence. The Allied Powers did not ignore Austria's responsibility for the war, but nothing was said explicitly about Austria's responsibility for Nazi crimes on its territory.[16]

Although the embarrassment caused by the Waldheim affair was the beginning of much public and private introspection among Austrians as to their national identity, it was not sufficient to quell the even greater controversy that would arise in 1999 with the coming to power of the Austrian Freedom Party in the country's ruling coalition.

Beyond the rhetoric: The rise of Austria's Freedom Party

Austria's entrance into the EU in 1995 was largely uncontroversial. Austria was viewed as a liberal democracy that, at the time of its entry, was governed by a coalition of moderately left-wing Social Democrats (SPÖ) and the moderately conservative People's Party (ÖVP). The profile of its government was not therefore remarkably different from that of other EU members. The Austrian Freedom Party (FPÖ) did exist and, in fact, had joined in an earlier partnership with the Social Democrats, but in 1995 its representation in Parliament was limited to 41 members (about 21 per cent) and it was deemed marginalized. The EU clearly did not feel threatened by the existence of a right-wing party in Austria. The EU placed no added conditions on the new member, issued no warnings, raised no outcries, and expressed no fears of a potential upsetting of the EU apple cart by the FPÖ. Indeed, had the thought even occurred, most, if not all EU members had their own extreme right-wing parties to contend with and the scent of hypocrisy would simply have been too strong to restrict Austria's membership on that basis.

Five years later, when the SPÖ and the ÖVP failed to establish their traditional coalition, the rumblings began. EU members menaced younger partner Austria that an ÖVP/FPÖ coalition would bring down the EU's wrath. Indeed, the country's subsequent inclusion of the FPÖ in its government was criticized as a threat to human rights, security and democratic institutions. In the midst of initial protests and concerns voiced in the international community, the loudest and most potentially damaging voices came from EU nations, who promptly cut off bilateral contacts

---

[16] Bureau of European and Eurasian Affairs, *Background Note: Austria* (2010) US Department of State <http://www.state.gov/r/pa/ei/bgn/3165.htm> at 26 March 2011.

with the new government and proceeded on a campaign of embarrassing snubs and boycotts of official Austrian persons and programs.

Concerns centred primarily on Jörg Haider, governor of the Austrian province of Carinthia and the Freedom Party's strong man and de facto leader. Many viewed Haider's comments on a number of occasions as sympathetic to the national socialist policies of Adolf Hitler and, given Austria's historical links with the Third Reich, as a threat to Austrian and European democracy. The main contention was that the FPÖ's fiercely anti-immigration platform reflected the kind of ethnocentrism at the heart of Hitler's National Socialism, which history showed to have relatively quickly spun out of control.

Jörg Haider and Freedom Party politics: Serious threat or mere opportunism?

Despite all the rhetoric against Jörg Haider in 1999, there were many seemingly responsible people outside of Europe, even on the political left, who doubted that Haider was a full-blown neo-Nazi. He made no attempt to hide his Third Reich connections, however. He was born in 1950 to parents with National Socialist ties. His father, a member of the Hitler Youth and the Nazi storm troopers, included Adolf Eichmann among his cohorts. His mother belonged to the Nazi Party's League of German Girls. Jörg studied law in Vienna and became active in Freedom-Party politics in his early twenties. He served in Parliament from 1979-1983 and again beginning in March 1992, and as Governor of the Austrian state of Carinthia from 1989–1991 and 1999–2008. In 1986 he became Freedom Party leader, only to resign after the formation of the ÖVP-FPÖ coalition in March 2000.[17]

Although under Haider the FPÖ saw remarkable growth and electoral success, he was nevertheless a grand contributor to the Freedom Party's troubled and troubling history. He outraged the international community with his provocative comments and challenges: 'Our soldiers were not criminals; at most they were victims', he declared in October 1990 to an audience that likely included former members of the Waffen SS. On another occasion he stated, 'In the Third Reich they had an "orderly" employment policy'. Still on other occasions he referred to concentration camps as 'punishment camps' or said to groups that included ex-SS members that 'there are still decent people of good character who also stick to their convictions, despite the greatest opposition, and have remained true to their convictions until today' and

---

[17] Max Riedlsperger, 'Heil Haider! The Resurgence of the Austrian Freedom Party since 1986' (1992) 4 *Politics and Society in Germany, Austria and Switzerland* 18.

that 'the Waffen SS was a part of the Wehrmacht and hence it deserves all the honor and respect of the army in public life'.[18]

However, Haider provided convenient if not plausible explanations for each of the few comments on which the media focused its attention: he did not know his audience included former SS members when he praised World War Two veterans; his reference to Nazi concentration camps as 'punishment' camps is not unusual in Germany and is subject to various interpretations in the German language; and his brief but positive reference to Third Reich labour policies, which he regretted having made, was part of an awkward attempt to criticize the disorganization of current Austrian labour politics.[19]

Haider's apologies and explanations did little to satisfy his critics, however, and the question remained of the nature of the FPÖ threat and the commitment of a substantial number of Austrians to the less then liberal human rights values the party proclaimed. As with most opposition parties, once in power the FPÖ began to adapt to the practical necessities of rule. Haider himself formally stepped down from party leadership, but continued to pull the strings from behind the scenes until he left the FPÖ in 2003 to form a new right-wing opposition party (the BPÖ) with similar platforms. By 2005, the traditional ÖVP-SPÖ was back in power. However, Haider's influence remained significant until his death in a car accident in 2008.

Haider and the FPÖ undoubtedly reflected an important aspect of Austrian political culture at the turn of the century. The FPÖ and the BPÖ are still important and their platform remains one of anti-immigration. Although the 'extremist' parties have never been in a majority by themselves, the failure of Austrians to wrestle with National Socialism until *after* the Cold War has allowed Austria to slide into the twenty-first century never having entirely reconciled itself to the contradictory aspects of its political culture. It is worth examining here whether the Austrian constitutional structure has the stuff to ward off an extremist threat.

Safeguards for democracy and human rights: The Austrian Constitution

Constitutionally and institutionally, Austria is as much a democratic republic as any of its European neighbours. Its form of government is a federal parliamentary

---

[18] 'Views under Fire; Words That Ignited a Diplomatic Crisis', *New York Times*, 1 February 2000 <http://www.nytimes.com/2000/02/01/world/views-under-fire-words-that-ignited-a-diplomatic-crisis.html> at 2 August 2011.

[19] Andrew Purvis and Angela Leuker, 'Haider's Apology', *Time*, 14 February 2000 <http://www.time.com/time/magazine/article/0,9171,996092,00.html> at 2 August 2011.

republic. Elections are periodic, free, multi-party and deemed fair by human rights organizations. Governmental institutions are replete with checks and balances. The Austrian Constitution is based on the principles of a republican, democratic and federal state, the principle of the rule of law, and the principle of the separation of legislative and executive powers and the separation of jurisdiction and administration.[20]

In word, if not deed, protective provisions within the Austrian system are longstanding. Although the present republican constitution originated in 1920 in the aftermath of World War One and the dissolution of the Austro-Hungarian Empire and was revised in 1929, the empire itself had not been without some legacy of basic rights protection. These provisions, particularly the 'Basic Law of 21 December 1867 on the General Rights of Nationals in the Kingdoms and Laender' and the 'Law of 27 October 1862 on Protection of the Rights of the Home' still nominally guarantee fundamental rights should the current constitution or international human rights treaties fail.[21]

The republican constitution was suspended from 1938-1945 during Austria's membership in Hitler's Third Reich, and then reinstituted after the war. Although the realities of post-war occupation by the 'Big Four' Allies obscured the essence of Austrian commitments to democracy and human rights protection, in 1955 the 'State Treaty for the Re-establishment of an Independent and Democratic Austria' provided recognition by the Allied and Associated Powers of Austria as a 'sovereign, independent and democratic state'. This treaty required that Austria protect the human rights of 'all persons under Austrian jurisdiction, without distinction as to race, sex, language or religion', that Austria 'have a democratic government based on elections by secret ballot' and that it 'guarantee to all citizens free, equal and universal suffrage as well as the right to be elected to public office without discrimination as to race, sex, language, religion or political opinion'.[22]

These principles were enshrined in the post-war, post-occupation revival of the 1920/1929 constitution and its subsequent modifications (for example, the 'Federal Constitutional Law of 29 November 1988 on the Protection of Personal Liberty').

---

[20] *Austrian Constitution*, International Constitutional Law Project <http://www.servat.unibe.ch/icl/au00000_.html> at 2 August 2011.

[21] *Basic Law on General Rights of Nationals in the Kingdoms and Länder represented in the Council of the Realm, 1867* (2011) Austrian Chancellery <http://www.ris.bka.gv.at/Dokumente/Erv/ERV_1867_142/ERV_1867_142.pdf> at 26 March 2011; *Law on Protection of the Rights of the Home, 1862* (2011) Austrian Chancellery <http://www.ris.bka.gv.at/Dokumente/Erv/ERV_1862_88/ERV_1862_88.pdf> at 26 March 2011.

[22] *State Treaty for the Reestablishment of an Independent and Democratic Austria, 1955* (2011) European Navigator <http://www.ena.lu/state_treaty_reestablishment_independent_democratic_austria_vienna_15_1955-020302233.html> at 26 March 2011.

Furthermore, Austria has adopted the European Convention for the Protection of Human Rights and Fundamental Freedoms and given it the status of constitutional law.[23] Although the US 'Country Reports on Human Rights Reports' and Amnesty International's 'Annual Reports' do not give Austria a clean bill of health with regard to human rights protections, neither do they blame their few cited violations on the FPÖ, nor portray Austria as any worse than its most critical EU partners.[24]

Religious freedom in Austria

On paper, Austria has a longstanding tradition of protecting religious freedom and, for the most part, does so in practice. Overall, human rights groups, including the US State Department Office of International Religious Freedom that does an annual international assessment of religious freedom, rate Austria as doing a reasonably good job of protecting the free practice of religion and conscientious beliefs. The Austrian Freedom Party, as part of its party platform, has declared itself a strong proponent of religious freedom. Although, as in many developed countries, Austria sees its share of anti-Semitic and anti-Islamic incidents and abuses of religious minorities, the FPÖ offers a specific declaration on its main website homepage in favour of protecting the rights of Muslims.[25]

It is not uncommon, however, for religious minorities, known in Austria as 'sects', to complain of official 'second-class' treatment. The core of that complaint centres on Austria's practice of conferring differing legal status on different religious groups according to established criteria. The law provides for the classification of religious organizations into three categories: 1) religious societies, 2) religious confessional communities, and 3) associations. The effect of these classifications can be significant when it comes to rights, privileges and societal duties. According to the 2008 US State Department Report on International Religious Freedom:

---

[23] *Federal Constitutional Law on the Protection of Personal Liberty, 1988* (2011) Austrian Chancellery <http://www.ris.bka.gv.at/Dokumente/Erv/ERV_1988_684/ERV_1988_684.pdf> at 26 March 2011; *Convention for the Protection of Human Rights and Fundamental Freedoms*, above n 8.

[24] Bureau of Democracy, Human Rights and Labor, US Department of State, US Government, *1999 Country Reports on Human Rights Practices: Austria* (2000) (available at <http://www.state.gov/www/global/human_rights/1999_hrp_report/austria.html.) That is, if Austria is even as bad; see, eg, the similar reports for France, Belgium and Germany (available at http://www.state.gov/g/drl/rls/hrrpt/1999/c30.htm). For the Austrian reports, see Amnesty International, *Amnesty International Annual Report 2000* (2000), *Austria* (available at <http://www.amnesty.org/en/library/info/POL10/001/2000/en>); Amnesty International, *Amnesty International Annual Report 2009* (2009), *Austria* (available at http://thereport.amnesty.org/>).

[25] See *FPÖ: Die Soziale Heimapartei* (2011) FPÖ <http://www.fpoe.at/> at 26 March 2011.

Recognition as a religious society under the 1874 law [on Recognition of Churches] has wide-ranging implications, such as the authority to participate in the mandatory church contributions program, provide religious instruction in public schools, and bring religious workers into the country to act as ministers, missionaries, or teachers. Under the 1874 law, religious societies have 'public corporation' status. This status permits them to engage in a number of public or quasi-public activities that are denied to confessional communities and associations. The Government provides financial support for religious teachers at both public and private schools to religious societies but not to other religious organizations. The Government provides financial support to private schools run by any of the 13 officially recognized religious societies.[26]

Religious communities do not receive these same financial and educational privileges. They do have the right to apply for religious society status but under stringent criteria that include 'a 20-year period of existence (at least 10 of which must be as a group organized as a confessional community under the 1998 law) and membership equaling at least 0.2 percent of the country's population (approximately 16,000 persons)'.[27]

The 1998 'Law on the Status of Religious Confessional Communities' allows religious groups to apply for the secondary status of a religious community. This confers the privileges, among others, of being able to buy and own real property assets and enter into contracts in the name of the group.

Groups not eligible for status as societies or communities have the option of forming associations. Although this confers some limited protective legal status, associations experience more restrictions in what they can do in their own name as well as in their rights to bring foreign representatives into the country. Religious communities and associations do not receive government funding for religious education, nor do they receive the extremely generous tax benefits afforded religious societies.[28]

One recent case study illustrates particularly well the challenges created by this differential treatment of religious bodies. The European Court of Human Rights (ECHR) is Austria's transcendent human rights protective instrument. A July 2008 case before the ECHR documents some of Austria's struggles for perspective on religious freedom issues. The case of *Religionsgemeinschaft der Zeugen Jehovas and Others v Austria* illustrates the long-term frustrations of the Jehovah's Witnesses in their quest for full recognition in Austria well beyond their general acceptance in most Western nations.

---

[26] *Austria, International Religious Freedom Report, 2008* (2008) US Department of State <http://www.state.gov/g/drl/rls/irf/2008/108434.htm> at 26 March 2011.
[27] Ibid.
[28] Ibid.

Religionsgemeinschaft der Zeugen Jehovas and Others v Austria

Beginning in 1978, the Jehovah's Witnesses in Austria tried for nearly 30 years to achieve status as a religious society. The Federal Ministry for Education and Arts, which had power to grant this recognition, refused to act on the 1978 request, stating not that the Jehovah's Witnesses had no legal right to such recognition but that they did not even have a right to a decision on the matter one way or the other. A similar scenario occurred again in 1987, again with the Ministry failing to grant such recognition and refusing to provide a formal decision. Shortly thereafter the Jehovah's Witnesses launched a series of judicial complaints and proceedings, some of which were decided against them on technical grounds, until finally in June 1995 the Austrian Constitutional Court held that the Jehovah's Witnesses were entitled to either recognition as a religious society or a written decision by the Ministry denying them such. In subsequent proceedings on remand, an Austrian Administrative Court ordered the Ministry to issue a decision one way or the other and in 1997, the Ministry denied Jehovah's Witnesses standing as a religious society,

> because of their unclear internal organisation and their negative attitude towards the State and its institutions. Reference was further made to their refusal to perform military service or any form of alternative service for conscientious objectors, to participate in local community life and elections and to undergo certain types of medical treatment such as blood transfusions.

Following further bureaucratic delay by the Ministry, the Constitutional Court, citing the Ministry's failure to properly investigate the facts of the Jehovah's Witnesses situation in Austria, quashed the Ministry's decision in March of 1998 and handed the case back to the Ministry: 'The Constitutional Court … concluded that the Ministry's decision was arbitrary and violated the principle of equality'.[29]

In January 1998, the *Religious Communities Act* had become law and the Ministry granted the Jehovah's Witnesses recognition as a religious community but not as a society pursuant to their original request. In July, now in this community status, they applied again for recognition as a religious society. In December, the Ministry denied the application, stating that under the new law a religious organization had to exist in Austria as a registered religious community for at least ten years before it could be named a religious society. Since the Jehovah's Witnesses had only been a recognized community since July, they failed to meet this requirement. The Austrian Constitutional Court upheld the Ministry's decision in 2001 and, upon referral of the case back to the Administrative Court, the Administrative Court held likewise.

---

[29] *Religionsgemeinschaft der Zeugen Jehovas & Ors v Austria* (2008) (Application 40825/98) 31 October 2008 [29].

The Jehovah's Witnesses filed a complaint with the ECHR under, among other provisions, articles 9 (Freedom of thought, conscience and religion) and 11 (Freedom of assembly and association) of the European Convention on Human Rights.

Issuing its decision in 2008, the Court held that there had been an interference with the applicants' right to freedom of religion and that that interference was prescribed by law pursuant to the legitimate aims of protecting public order and safety. However, under the circumstances, the restrictions placed on granting recognition to the Jehovah's Witnesses were not necessary in a democratic society. The Court found

> that such a prolonged period [of bureaucratic machinations] raises concerns under Article 9 of the Convention. In this connection the Court reiterates that the autonomous existence of religious communities is indispensable for pluralism in a democratic society and is thus an issue at the very heart of the protection which Article 9 affords … and, given the importance of this right, the Court considers that there is an obligation on all of the State's authorities to keep the time during which an applicant waits for conferment of legal personality for the purposes of Article 9 of the Convention reasonably short.[30]

Thirty years clearly was not reasonably short. (Note in passing, however, that by the time the European Court had issued its decision, the Jehovah's Witnesses would have existed in Austria as a religious community for the requisite ten years to become a society.)

Austria's law or constitution cannot explain the country's treatment of Jehovah's Witnesses. These, especially the European Convention, clearly hold Austria to a higher standard than was manifested by the bureaucratic mistreatment of this religious body. The Jehovah's Witnesses attitudes towards government and other societal institutions have brought official persecution on them in less developed democracies or non-democracies and made them less than favourites of a number of even more liberal regimes. Nevertheless, by the end of the twentieth century, they were an established religion recognized in most nations, having already proven themselves before the European Court on more than one occasion as meriting better treatment. The point is that Austria's constitutional mandates and political culture were not in harmony. The harsh discriminatory realities of the latter continued to smoulder beneath those constitutional mandates, resulting in the denial of fundamental rights to some of the nation's citizens and residents.

In addition to its own constitutional requirements for equality and fair treatment, Austria has been a member of the Council of Europe since 1956, the fifteenth

---

[30] Ibid [78].

member state in fact, and as such has been subject since that time to the provisions of the ECHR. It clearly takes time in many countries for the realities of human rights protection to catch up with proclaimed constitutional values and ideals. As evidenced in a case like Austria's, where real attitudes concerning the political environment were obfuscated by the demands and pressures of the Cold War, a country's political culture can go far in determining how quickly those ideals catch up.

Having said as much, despite the continued influence of the far-right parties, Austria's transition since World War Two and especially since the end of the Cold War from a democratic country in name, with a strong smouldering anti-liberal component to its political culture, to a fully-fledged democracy in practice as well as precept, is nearly complete. It is difficult to prove that this transition has not been the result of the demands of the law as imposed by Austrian and European constitutional instruments. Once again, however, the likes of North Korea, Iran, Belarus and others are clear evidence that liberal-sounding constitutional provisions do not a liberal democracy or republic make. Such documents serve as a guide to law and ideals in a nation where the political culture supports adaptation to the ideals.

Austria's political culture historically included the Third Reich as an important component. Coming out as neutrals from under the Third Reich at the end of the war arguably allowed Austrians ashamed of their complicity the chance to transform that culture to match the liberal values of their Western neighbours, while allowing those nostalgic for the policies of national and ethnic superiority to continue on their way for sometime behind the scenes. Pressures from Europe have contributed to Austria's full compliance and transition to a more liberal state and in turn to Austria's present political culture. Again, the parties may look to constitutional instruments as their guide, but the underlying compatibility of the political culture has been essential to the transformation.

One could tell a different story, but with similar results, of Germany. Countries of the former Eastern Bloc, now members of the EU and Council of Europe, are currently writing their own stories of transition as their cultural practices and beliefs race to catch up with the constitutional instruments they have adopted in the last twenty years.

What are the implications of these stories for nations like Australia and the UK, debating the best ways to go forward in the preservation of human rights? Does Austria's story argue for a bill of rights with constitutional status or for a charter or other instrument on the level of ordinary legislation? The answer at this stage of the argument of this chapter is 'not necessarily one or the other'. The implications are that, more important than the instrument adopted is the reassurance that a society has in place the cultural mechanisms to sustain its commitment to human rights. To this extent, it is true that the instrument adopted may reflect the political culture.

The elevation of a bill of rights to constitutional status may suggest the commitment of a people to making those rights prominent and difficult to amend or abandon. Fears that the judiciary may become too strong in such a case could also reflect liberal values, however, keeping the law in the hands of the citizens as represented in parliament. However, it may also inadvertently communicate less of a commitment of a people to human rights because if ordinary legislation establishes rights, then ordinary legislation can repeal them.

In the end, each nation must decide, hopefully in a lively, informed public debate, whether its particular history calls for stronger legal instruments, and hence stronger cultural symbols, to assure that human rights protection remains central to its way of life. Americans, Austrians, Iranians or North Koreans will not be able to tell Australians and Britons what to do.

10

The Sky is Falling if Judges Decide Religious Controversies! — Or is it? The German Experience of Religious Freedom under a Bill of Rights

Cornelia Koch*

Most modern Western societies operate under a broadly secular system of government. Germany is no exception. Among the fundamental features of a secular polity are State neutrality in questions of faith, the absence of a State religion, the toleration of all beliefs (religious or not) and the guarantee of the individual's freedom to believe or not to believe and to exercise his or her religion.

Despite this fundamentally secular orientation of the State, many people have strong feelings about religious issues. Occasionally, these views can trigger heated, emotive and widespread public debate, particularly when the belief systems of different religious groups or of believers and non-believers come into conflict. An extreme example is the worldwide controversy about the publication of cartoons of the Prophet Muhammad in the international press, which even resulted in violence and a number of deaths.[1] Other examples include the debate on introducing

---

* I thank Laura Grenfell, Anne Hewitt and Richard Arnold for their helpful comments on an earlier draft of this chapter and Anthony Orford and Richard Arnold for their research assistance.

[1] Initially by *Jyllands-Posten* in Denmark on 30 September 2005 and then reprinted in newspapers in over fifty countries. For a timeline of events following the publication see BBC News Online, *Muslim Cartoon Row Timeline* (2006) BBC News Online <http://news.bbc.co.uk/2/hi/middle_east/4688602.stm> at 18 March 2011.

Sharia law² and on the regulation of displaying or wearing of religious symbols or clothing in public settings in Western countries.³

Two questions that touched a nerve in German society were whether the State could require that crucifixes are installed in all primary school classrooms and if a Muslim teacher could wear the Islamic headscarf (*hijab*) while teaching in a public school. Both of these questions are morally and politically highly controversial. They are the type of questions for which there is no easy answer and where every answer given is bound to have its detractors. In a democratic society, which branch of the government is best suited to make these decisions? Some opponents of bills of rights claim that these types of questions are for the elected Parliament alone and are not suitable for determination by courts.

These opponents argue that a bill of rights will inevitably lead to the courts being called upon to rule on morally and politically controversial issues. Doing so makes the courts vulnerable to public criticism because their judgments on these difficult matters will become the object of a wider public debate. In the long run, opponents maintain, this will harm the authority of the courts and in turn the entire legal and political system because the public at large will lose respect for and trust in the courts. The determination of highly controversial issues should therefore be left to the political branches of government, the legislature and the executive. Consequently, a bill of rights is undesirable.⁴

The purpose of this chapter is to challenge the argument that controversial questions of a moral and political nature should not be decided by the courts. The German experience of religious disputes under a bill of rights demonstrates that, even when

---

2   For the debate in Ontario, Canada, see Natasha Bakht, 'Family Arbitration Using Sharia Law: Examining Ontario's Arbitration Act and its Impact on Women' (2004) 1 *Muslim World Journal of Human Rights* Article 7 <http://www.bepress.com/mwjhr/vol1/iss1/art7>; Anne McIlroy, 'One Law to Rule Them All', *Guardian Unlimited Online (UK)* (2005) <http://www.guardian.co.uk/world/2005/sep/14/worlddispatch.annemcilroy> at 4 March 2011. For the Australian context see Peter Costello, 'Worth Promoting, Worth Defending: Australian Citizenship, What it Means and How to Nurture it' (Speech delivered at the Sydney Institute, Sydney, 23 February 2006).

3   In some countries the debate has led to the banning of such clothing and symbols from educational institutions or even from all public spaces.

4   See, eg, Ben Saul, 'Putting Rights Back into the Human Rights Consultation: Why Politicians Have Too Much Power and Judges Need More' (Speech delivered at the NSW Young Lawyers Charter of Rights Conference, Sydney, 9 May 2009) which includes reference to Hon Senator George Brandis SC, 'The Case Against a Statutory Bill of Rights' (Speech delivered at the Queensland Law Society 47th Annual Symposium, Brisbane, 28 March 2009); Bob Carr, 'Only people — not bills protect rights. Power rests with parliament, not the courts', *The Australian* (Sydney), 9 January 2001, 17; John Howard, 'Proposed Charter of Rights' (Speech delivered at the Menzies Lecture, Perth, 26 August 2009).

courts are called upon to determine politically and morally charged issues, a loss in public confidence of the legal system is not inevitable. To support my point, I examine two of the most controversial decisions ever handed down by Germany's highest court, the German Federal Constitutional Court (*Bundesverfassungsgericht*) (FCC). Both concerned religious freedom. They dealt with the two questions outlined above: whether the State can require that crucifixes are installed in all primary school classrooms (the *Classroom Crucifix* case)[5] and if a Muslim teacher can wear the Islamic headscarf while teaching in a public school (the *Teacher Headscarf* case).[6]

My discussion lends support to the first part of bill of rights opponents' argument that such a bill leads to the courts being called upon to decide morally and politically controversial questions. Both the *Classroom Crucifix* and the *Teacher Headscarf* cases illustrate this clearly, and I chose them to support my argument precisely because the issues under review were so highly controversial. The *Crucifix* case also exposed the FCC to fierce public criticism, while the strong attacks on the Court following the *Headscarf* case came mostly from academic commentators. Therefore, as the discussion will show, I fully agree with opponents of bills of rights that under such a bill the courts may be required to rule on very controversial questions and become the target of strong criticism.

However, I strongly disagree with the second part of the argument, that long-term damage to the institution of the courts and the legal and political system as a whole is an inevitable consequence of such public exposure and criticism. The German experience shows that the FCC's reputation and the German legal and political system did not suffer long-term damage, although the Court was required to rule on highly controversial issues and became the target of fierce and widespread public criticism.

The argument developed in this chapter is divided into seven parts. Following the introductory section is an explanation of some fundamental aspects of the German constitutional system, including an introduction to the relevant principles of constitutional law and interpretation. This provides the background to the

---

[5] BVerfGE 93, 1 ('*Classroom Crucifix* case') (available at http://www.servat.unibe.ch/dfr/bv093001.html). An English language translation of excerpts from the judgment can be found at *Foreign Law Translations* (2007) University of Texas at Austin Institute for Transnational Law <http://www.utexas.edu/law/academics/centers/transnational/work_new/german/case.php?id=615> at 30 January 2011.

[6] BVerfGE 108, 282 ('*Teacher Headscarf* case') (available at http://www.servat.unibe.ch/dfr/bv108282.html). An English language translation of excerpts from the judgment can be found at *Foreign Law Translations* (2007) University of Texas at Austin Institute for Transnational Law <http://www.utexas.edu/law/academics/centers/transnational/work_new/german/case.php?id=613> at 30 January 2011.

discussion of the guarantee of religious freedom under the bill of rights and the FCC's approach to this guarantee in part three. The fourth section explores the Court's jurisprudence on the free exercise of religion in public schools, culminating in the *Classroom Crucifix* and *Teacher Headscarf* cases. Then, I portray the public and scholarly debate surrounding these cases. The next section explores empirical research that demonstrates that the FCC's authority and reputation did not suffer long-term damage from being the target of much criticism. Likewise, the legal and political system of the Federal Republic of Germany did not suffer as a consequence of the Court's decisions. The chapter concludes that a mature legal and political system can survive highly charged controversies being decided by the courts unscathed, as demonstrated by the German experience. Therefore, the fact that courts may be drawn into controversial debates and become the object of public criticism is not a valid argument against a bill of rights.

Background: Some fundamental aspects of the German constitutional system

The Constitution of the Federal Republic of Germany, the *Basic Law* (*Grundgesetz*), contains a bill of rights in its first chapter.[7] The guarantees in the Bill constitute limitations on acts of all public authorities, no matter whether they belong to the legislative, executive, or judicial branch of government, and apply at both the Federal and the State level.[8] The most important provision guaranteeing freedom of religion is article 4(1) and (2) of the *Basic Law*. Before considering this guarantee and the FCC's approach to it in detail, I outline some basic rules of German constitutional law and interpretation that underpin the entire jurisprudence of the Court. This jurisprudence forms a vital part of German constitutional law because the FCC is the final arbiter of matters arising under the Constitution.

Two competing ideas strongly influence the interpretation of the guarantees in the bill of rights. On one hand, human rights are understood as individual rights defined by law. In contrast to positivist notions, law is believed to have existed before parliaments and governments. Human rights are rights of the individual and oblige

---

[7] *Grundgesetz für die Bundesrepublik Deutschland* [Basic Law of the Federal Republic of Germany] (the '*Basic Law*'). The Bill of Rights comprises articles 1–19 of the *Basic Law*. An English language translation of the *Basic Law* by Christian Tomuschat and David P Currie, 'Basic Law for the Federal Republic of Germany' (2010) is available at <http://bundesrecht.juris.de/englisch_gg/index.html> at 23 January 2011.

[8] *Basic Law* arts 1(3), 20(3). Religious freedom is also protected under all States' Constitutions. However, those provisions play a minor role because art 4 is directly applicable in the States. See Kay Hailbronner and Hans-Peter Hummel, 'Constitutional Law' in Werner Ebke and Matthew Finkin (eds), *Introduction to German Law* (1996) 50, 64.

the State authorities to justify any infringement.[9] Therefore, there is a presumption in favour of protection of the human right and every law that seems to violate it will be scrutinised by the Constitutional Court. On the other hand, the Court recognises the separation of powers as 'a guiding organisational principle' of the *Basic Law*[10] and notes that this separation places important limitations on the scope of judicial review.

In an attempt to reconcile both of these guiding ideas, the FCC has developed a method of interpretation of individual rights that applies different levels of judicial scrutiny to different types of rights, depending on the danger to individual liberty and depending on what particular activity of the State is being considered. The lowest level of scrutiny is called 'control of evidence' (*Evidenzkontrolle*). Here the Court is reluctant to substitute its own opinion of what a fair and just solution might be for the political decision made by Parliament. This method is used whenever the principle of equality is involved.[11] The parliamentary solution that restricts the human right will be tolerated as long as there are reasonable or at least constitutionally admissible reasons for choosing that solution, even if they are not very convincing.

Stricter is the 'control of reasonableness' (*Vertretbarkeitskontrolle*). In these cases involving, in particular, the right to choose trade, occupation or profession[12] or the right to property,[13] the FCC seeks to understand the logic of the political decision. The decision should be the result of a careful examination of the factual situation. While the Court must be convinced of the application of a solid legislative method in this category, it does not directly question the consequences of the political decision.[14]

The most stringent level of scrutiny is applied if there is a danger of grave violations of fundamental rights. Here the Court uses the method of 'strict control' (*intensivierte inhaltliche Kontrolle*). It examines very closely whether an action by a State authority is justified, or at least tolerated by the Constitution.[15] The cases on freedom of religion belong to this last group, which is indicative of the great significance that religious freedom enjoys in the German constitutional system. Therefore, the Court will always carefully scrutinise the government action that is alleged to have violated a person's right to religious freedom.

---

[9] Bodo Pieroth and Bernhard Schlink, *Grundrechte Staatsrecht II* (10th ed, 1994) 14.
[10] BVerfGE 34, 52 at 59.
[11] *Basic Law* art 3.
[12] *Basic Law* art 12.
[13] *Basic Law* art 14.
[14] See, eg, BVerfGE 25, 1 at 17.
[15] Ernst Benda, 'The Position and Function of the *Bundesverfassungsgericht* (Federal Constitutional Court) in a Reunited Germany' in Edward McWhinney, Jerald Zaslove J and Werner Wolf (eds) *Federalism-in-the-Making* (1992) 29, 32–3.

Another guiding principle of constitutional interpretation developed by the Constitutional Court is that the *Basic Law* forms a unitary system, in the sense that each provision refers to all others and each must be read in the light of the instrument's structural unity.[16] Therefore, all provisions of the Constitution 'must be interpreted in such a way as to render them consistent with the fundamental principles of the *Basic Law* and its order of values'.[17] The Court has explicitly rejected 'value-free legal positivism' as the philosophical foundation for constitutional interpretation.[18]

The next principle governing the interpretation of basic rights concerns the extent to which restrictions can be imposed on them. While some of the provisions in the bill of rights stipulate expressly that they can be limited by law (that is, legislation), others lack such a stipulation. With regard to the latter category, the FCC recognises that certain restrictions on rights must be legitimate because no right is absolute. However, the Court requires that, where the constitutional text makes no provision for limitations, any implied restrictions on the guarantees must spring from the *Basic Law* itself. The guarantee of freedom of religion in article 4 is an example of a right that lacks an express recognition of limitations by law. Therefore, a person's religious freedom cannot be curbed by legislation unless that legislation is justified by another part of the *Basic Law*.[19]

The final concept relevant to this chapter is the principle of proportionality. The Constitutional Court has derived this unwritten standard from the rule of law (*Rechtsstaatsprinzip*), which is regarded as one of the foundations of the German legal system.[20] The proportionality principle requires that the limitation imposed on a constitutionally protected right by the State is proportionate to the objectives pursued by the limitation. Proportionality between the law or act restricting individual rights and the public benefit expected from this intrusion is a principle that dominates all German constitutional and administrative law.[21] It establishes a test for detecting an excessive wielding of power by the State.

---

[16] See Jacques-Yva Morin, 'The Rule of Law and the *Rechtsstaat* Concept: A Comparison' in Edward Mcwhinney, Jerald Zaslove and Werner Wolf (eds), *Federalism-in-the-Making* (1992) 60, 78; Ibid 32.
[17] BVerfGE 30, 1 at 19.
[18] BVerfGE 3, 225 at 232.
[19] See BVerfGE 28, 243 at 260 delivered on 26 May 1970, holding that limitations on the right to conscientious objection to compulsory military service cannot be justified merely by laws, norms or institutions, but rather have to be based on colliding fundamental rights of third parties. See also *Classroom Crucifix* case, BVerfGE 93, 1 at 21; *Teacher Headscarf* case, BVerfGE 108, 282 at 297.
[20] See *Basic Law* art 28. For a comprehensive discussion of that principle see Morin, above n 16, 74.
[21] Morin, above n 16, 75–6.

When applying the proportionality test, the courts undertake a three-step analysis. First, they determine whether the restricting act is *suitable* to protect the community interest. In other words, the act must be capable of achieving its stated aim. Secondly, the courts examine whether the infringing act is *absolutely necessary* to fulfil its aim. This test is satisfied only if the means employed by the public authority is the least restrictive of the basic right. Thus, if the court finds that there is a way that is less injurious to the human right, but is sufficient to achieve the desired objective, it will declare the overly restrictive act unconstitutional. Finally, the act must be *appropriate* to the objective pursued. In this last stage, the courts carry out the actual balancing exercise. They weigh one constitutionally protected right or value against another. The balancing is carried out in accordance with the principle of 'practical harmony' (*praktische Konkordanz*), which requires the courts to reconcile or harmonise the conflicting values as much as possible, infringing each to the least possible extent.[22] These general rules of German constitutional law provide the background for the examination of the guarantee of freedom of religion under the *Basic Law* that follows.

The guarantee of religious freedom under the German Constitution

The most important provision protecting religious freedom in the German constitutional system is article 4(1) and (2) of the *Basic Law*[23], which reads:

(1) Freedom of faith, of conscience, and freedom to profess a religion or a particular philosophy (*Weltanschauung*) shall be inviolable.

(2) The undisturbed practice of religion shall be guaranteed.

What does this provision protect? Paragraph one appears to guarantee, firstly, under 'freedom of faith and conscience', the thinking, the so-called *forum internum*, of religious (faith) and moral (conscience) convictions, and, secondly, under 'freedom to profess a religion or philosophy', the expression of religious and non-religious ideas, the so-called *forum externum*. In contrast, paragraph two seems to protect only *religiously* motivated actions, but not those motivated by moral convictions or a philosophy.[24] The plain meaning of the words thus suggests that the provision

---

[22] Gunther Schwerdtfeger, *Öffentliches Recht in der Fallbearbeitung* (9th ed, 1993) 43–4; Kay Hailbronner and Hans-Peter Hummel, 'Constitutional Law' in Werner Ebke and Matthew Finkin (eds), *Introduction to German Law* (1st ed, 1996), 68.

[23] In addition to art 4, other constitutional provisions protect aspects of religious freedom. However, for the purposes of this chapter it is sufficient to focus on art 4 because it contains the most important principles on freedom of religion in Germany, which were relevant in the *Classroom Crucifix* and *Teacher Headscarf* cases.

[24] Bodo Pieroth and Bernhard Schlink, *Grundrechte Staatsrecht II* (10th ed, 1994) 138–9.

has two distinct 'spheres of protection' (*Schutzbereiche*), one guaranteed by the first paragraph and the other by the second paragraph.

However, diverging from a strict reading of the words, the FCC has found that article 4 has only one uniform sphere of protection. The reasoning leading to this interpretation is as follows: if paragraphs one and two were read separately, the values which article 4 safeguards would not enjoy equal protection. If only religiously motivated actions are guaranteed, as the wording of paragraph two might suggest, then religion is privileged over other consciences and philosophies. The Court regards this as incompatible with the equal treatment of religion, conscience and philosophy in paragraph one. The FCC also maintains that separate treatment would render impossible what conscience and philosophy as well as religion try to achieve: action according to a person's strong belief of what is right. Overcoming these textual problems, the Court holds that the uniform sphere of application of article 4(1) and (2) safeguards the freedom to form and have a certain belief, conscience, religion or philosophy, to express ideas based upon these, and to act in accordance with them. German legal scholars and courts generally accept this interpretation.[25]

In addition to this positive element of religious freedom, article 4 also protects a negative aspect, according to the FCC. This aspect includes the freedom not to believe, not to disclose a belief, or not to take part in religious practices.[26]

As outlined above, the Constitutional Court understands article 4 to guarantee the freedom to form and have a belief or philosophy, to express them, and to act according to them. Religious freedom is encompassed by the concept of freedom of belief.[27] The FCC has held that the term 'belief' has to be interpreted broadly.[28] It defines belief as a (religious, but also non-religious) conviction of the position of human beings in the universe and their relationship to higher powers and other stages of existence.[29] Belief is not restricted to Christian traditions.[30]

The majority of cases heard by the Court under article 4 relate to the freedom to act according to one's belief, as opposed to the freedom to have, form or express a belief.[31] Therefore, in defining the sphere of protection of article 4, the Court mostly

---

[25] Ibid.
[26] BVerfGE 49, 375 at 376; BVerfGE 52, 223 at 238; BVerGE 65, 1 at 39.
[27] BVerfGE 24, 236 at 238.
[28] BVerfGE 35, 376 at 377.
[29] BVerfGE 12, 1 at 3–4.
[30] See, eg, BVerfG NJW 1989, 3269 (judgment of 15 August 1989).
[31] There are two reasons for this. First, it is practically impossible for public authorities to limit the freedom to form or have a belief; what an individual thinks is beyond the control of the State. Secondly, no important cases on the freedom to express one's belief have relied on article 4 because the *Basic Law* protects freedom of speech and expression separately in article 5.

had to determine what sorts of actions fall under the guarantee of free exercise of religion and which kind of behaviour, even if related to religion, falls outside of its scope.

The Court has taken a liberal approach, holding that exercising religion goes beyond the traditional manifestations of a belief, such as prayer or Sunday service. It also includes religious education, ceremonies of non-established religions and other expressions of religious and ideological life.[32] Thus, for example, a Catholic youth group's charitable campaign collecting second hand goods for needy people and the publicising of this campaign at church services was regarded as religious in character because it constituted an active expression of love of one's neighbour.[33] According to the FCC, article 4 generally safeguards the right of the individual to base his or her entire conduct upon the teachings of his or her religion.[34]

While principally taking a broad approach, the Constitutional Court places a number of limitations on the protective scope of article 4. First, the faith or association must indeed be a religion or religious group according to their spiritual ideas and external appearance.[35] Secondly, it is not sufficient that someone merely claims that his or her conduct is religiously inspired and required. Instead, the claim must be plausible. Examples where it was held that religiously inspired conduct is not plausible include a duty of university staff to consider the social consequences of scientific findings,[36] the compulsory requirement to bury urns in cemeteries,[37] and the duty to pay tax even if the monies are used for purposes contrary to the payer's faith.[38] Thirdly, the Court decided that acts that occur only on the occasion of religious functions, but are religiously neutral, must be distinguished from acts motivated by religion. This is exemplified by a constitutional complaint mounted by Scientology, seeking exemption from trade tax, which a lower administrative court had refused to grant to it.[39] The FCC held that, while the organisation of religious meetings is protected by article 4, the sale of food and drink to the members at these functions is not.[40]

Even if a type of behaviour is regarded as an exercise of religion, this does not mean that it cannot be restricted. As explained above, the Constitutional Court recognises that no right is absolute. However, because the wording of article 4 does not explicitly

---

[32] BVerfGE 24, 236 at 247.
[33] BVerfGE 24, 236.
[34] BVerfGE 32, 98 at 106.
[35] BVerfGE 83, 341 at 353.
[36] BVerfGE 47, 327 at 385.
[37] BVerfGE 50, 256 at 262.
[38] BVerfG, NJW 1993, 455 at 455.
[39] BVerfGE 19, 129.
[40] Ibid 133.

provide for the possibility of limitation by law, 'any limitation ... must be rooted in the Constitution. Legislatures are not free to restrict [religious] liberty in the absence of such limiting provisions in the *Basic Law* itself'.[41] In other words, religious freedom can only be restricted if that is justified by a part of the *Basic Law*.

Controversies about the free exercise of religion in public schools: The *Classroom Crucifix* and *Teacher Headscarf* cases

The general rules and concepts explained above underpin the FCC's case law in relation to the free exercise of religion in public, non-faith-based schools that is presently examined. The main focus of my discussion is on the *Classroom Crucifix* and *Teacher Headscarf* cases, dealing with the highly controversial questions of whether the State can require that crucifixes are installed in all primary school classrooms and if a Muslim teacher can wear the Islamic headscarf while teaching in a public school. In order to understand the law relevant to these cases, one must first consider two earlier decisions: the *Interdenominational School* (*Gesamtschule*) case[42] and the *School Prayer* case.[43] All four cases concerned the extent to which the secular German State is under a duty to remain neutral with regard to religion. The constitutionally safeguarded interests that collided in all four of these disputes were similar: the positive freedom of religion of students and teachers, the negative freedom of religion of other students, the State's educational mandate,[44] and the parents' right to the upbringing of their children.[45] Because the *Basic Law* protects all of these interests, it falls to the FCC to strike the constitutionally appropriate balance between them. In doing so, the Court attempts to reconcile the conflicting values as much as possible, infringing each to the least possible extent, in accordance with the aforementioned principle of proportionality.

Pre-*Classroom Crucifix* and *Teacher Headscarf*: The *Interdenominational School* and *School Prayer* cases

The first two times when the Constitutional Court had to decide issues of religious freedom in public schools were in the *Interdenominational School*[46] and the *School*

---

[41] BVerfGE 93, 1 at 21.
[42] BVerfGE 41, 29.
[43] BVerfGE 52, 223.
[44] Contained in art 7(1) of the *Basic Law*: 'The entire education system is under the supervision of the State'.
[45] Provided for in art 6(2) of the *Basic Law*: 'Care and upbringing of children are the natural right of the parents and a duty primarily incumbent on them. The State watches over the performance of this duty'.
[46] BVerfGE 41, 29.

Prayer[47] cases in the 1970s. The *Interdenominational School* case concerned an amendment by the State of Baden-Württemberg of its Constitution, which established Christian interdenominational schools as the uniform type of public school within the State. The complainants were parents of children who attended those schools. They alleged that the amendment violated their children's negative right to religious freedom under article 4 because they objected to any kind of religious or ideological education.

The FCC confirmed that article 4 protected both the negative as well as the positive manifestation of religious freedom against encroachments by the State. It stressed that this freedom was especially important in those areas of life which were 'not left to the free play of social forces but have been taken into the care of the State'.[48] Compulsory school attendance fell within this category. The Court recognised that the complainants' request to shield their children from religious education had to inevitably conflict with the desire of other parents to afford their children such an education.[49] It explained that in such a case 'the individual is limited in the exercise of his or her basic right by the countervailing basic right of persons with different views'.[50]

The Court then determined that in school matters the task of resolving the inevitable tension between negative and positive religious freedom fell to the democratic State legislature rather than the FCC.[51] However, the kind of school created by the legislature had to adhere to the following requirements:

> [T]he legislature must choose a type of school which, insofar as it can influence children's decisions concerning faith and conscience, contains only a minimum of coercive elements. ... Affirming Christianity within the context of secular disciplines refers primarily to the recognition of Christianity as a formative cultural and educational factor, which has developed in Western civilisation. It does not refer to the truth of the belief. ... A school, which permits an objective discussion of all ideological and religious views, even if based on a particular ideological orientation, does not create an unreasonable conflict of faith and conscience for parents and children under constitutional law.[52]

It was held that the schools created by the State of Baden-Württemberg fulfilled these conditions. The parents' constitutional complaint was therefore unsuccessful.

---

[47] BVerfGE 52, 223.
[48] Ibid 34.
[49] Ibid 34.
[50] Ibid 35.
[51] Ibid 35.
[52] Ibid 37.

In the *School Prayer* case[53] the Constitutional Court had to rule on the permissibility of school prayer outside of formal religious instruction, when a pupil's parents object to this practice. The FCC maintained the principles it had developed in the *Interdenominational School* case and held that

> if religious references are permissible in compulsory State schools … then praying in school is not fundamentally and constitutionally objectionable. However, the performance of the prayer must … not violate the individual rights of participants derived from article 4.[54]

The Court found that to ensure its neutrality, the State cannot issue an order for compulsory school prayer, but is entitled to make an offer to conduct prayers, which the school class may accept. However, the FCC emphasised that the State must balance this affirmative freedom to worship with the negative freedom of religion of other parents and pupils opposed to school prayer. In conclusion, the Court saw no constitutional impediments to school prayers as long as the right of a pupil holding another belief to decide freely and without compulsion whether to participate in the prayer was guaranteed by the school.[55]

The principles developed in the two cases previously discussed were tested in the *Classroom Crucifix* case[56] of 1995, about the legality of placing Christian crucifixes in public school classrooms, and the *Teacher Headscarf* case[57] of 2003, on the right of a Muslim women wearing *hijab* to be admitted to a teaching position in a public school. Both of these issues touched a nerve in German society. They constituted two of the most controversial topics that the FCC had been asked to rule on since its inauguration in 1951. The public interest in them was so immense that they sparked several months of debate in the media and led to a number of mass rallies. While the immediate questions before the Court concerned the desirability of religious symbols in schools, these issues also sparked a much broader debate about the limits of religious tolerance in German society. Leading German politicians and public figures, including the German President and Chancellor,[58] voiced their opinion on these issues. The public discussion was wide-ranging and arguments put forward encompassed diametrically opposed points of view, for example that the State should be truly neutral with regard to religion and hence there was no room for either crucifixes or headscarves in State

---

[53] BVerfGE 52, 223.
[54] Ibid 238.
[55] Ibid 249.
[56] BVerfGE 93, 1.
[57] BVerfGE 108, 282.
[58] The Federal President is the German Head of State. The Chancellor is the Head of Government, comparable to the Australian Prime Minister.

schools; that crucifixes should remain in classrooms as an expression of Western culture and civilisation, which has been profoundly influenced by Christianity; and that a woman who believes that wearing *hijab* is her religious duty should be entitled to teach in public schools. Both the *Crucifix* and the *Headscarf* cases also caused a flood of academic discussion.[59] Even inside the Constitutional Court they were controversial and three out of eight Justices dissented in each case. This is unusual in the German judicial culture and further illustrates the divisive nature of the two issues under consideration. I will discuss each case in turn.

The Classroom Crucifix *case*

The *Classroom Crucifix* case involved a Bavarian Primary School Ordinance ('the Ordinance') that required the display of the crucifix in every classroom of all primary schools (*Volksschulen*).[60] The non-Christian parents[61] of children attending one of these schools objected to the display on the basis that the crucifix offended their children's religious beliefs and thus violated article 4. They filed an action for removal of the cross in the Bavarian Administrative Court. The rejection of their motion was sustained on appeal. Consequently, they challenged these decisions and the practice of displaying the crucifix in primary school classrooms in a constitutional complaint. A majority of the FCC found for the applicants, but three Justices dissented. Both the majority judgment and the dissenting opinions relied on the *Interdenominational School*[62] and the *School Prayer*[63] cases.

The majority held that the constitutional complaint was justified. The administrative courts had based their judgments on section 13(1), clause 3 of the Ordinance, which was held to be incompatible with article 4 of the Constitution and thus void. Therefore, the lower courts' rulings violated the *Basic Law*.[64] While their Honours acknowledged that 'in a society that tolerates a wide variety of faith commitments, the individual clearly has no right to be spared exposure to quaint religious manifestations, cultish activities, or religious symbols', they found that 'a different situation arises when the State itself exposes an individual to the influence of a given faith, without giving him or her a chance to avoid such influence, or to the symbols

---

[59] For a list of contributions relating to the *Teacher Headscarf* case see Axel Freiherr von Campenhausen, 'The German Headscarf Debate' (2004) 2 *Brigham Young University Law Review* 665, 671 note 28. For contributions relating to the *Classroom Crucifix* case see Axel Freiherr von Campenhausen and Heinrich de Wall, *Staatskirchenrecht* (3rd ed, 1996) 76.
[60] *Schulordnung für die Volksschulen in Bayern*, 21 June 1983, s 13(1), clause 3.
[61] The family believed in the anthroposophical philosophy of Rudolf Steiner.
[62] BVerfGE 41, 29.
[63] BVerfGE 52, 223.
[64] BVerfGE 93, 1 at 15.

through which such a faith represents itself'.[65] The majority emphasised that article 4 required the State to remain neutral in matters of faith and religion. Otherwise the peaceful coexistence of members of various and even conflicting religious convictions in a society could be jeopardised.[66] Their Honours explained that, in the context of compulsory education, the presence of crucifixes in classrooms amounted to State-enforced 'learning under the cross', with no possibility for non-Christians to avoid seeing the religious symbol.[67] Herein lay the crucial difference between the proceeding before the Court and the *Interdenominational School*[68] case. The majority regarded the cross as 'the most significant symbol of the Christian faith and not only an expression of cultural values that have been influenced by Christianity'.[69] Taking into account that 'the mission of the school is to develop and promote a student's personality and to influence his or her social behaviour' their Honours explained that 'the display of the cross in the classroom takes on critical significance'.[70]

The majority then turned to balance the conflicting interests by applying the principle of practical harmony, explained above.[71] One of the constitutional rights colliding with the negative freedom of religion in article 4 was article 7(1), which confers an exclusive supervision over educational matters on the State. This includes the duty of establishing schools and setting educational goals and courses of study. The majority recognised that these requirements may often conflict with the religious convictions of students and their parents. Accordingly, the Court's task was to find a solution that would preserve, to the greatest extent possible, the values of both article 4 and 7.[72] Their Honours explained:

> On one hand, article 7 acknowledges the role of religious ... influences in education; on the other hand, article 4 mandates ... that religious ... pressures be removed from decisions favouring a certain type of school. Each provision must be interpreted in the light of the other, and the two must be harmonised in such a way as to protect the interests that they were originally designed to safeguard. [73]

In the majority's view, the State, in order to fulfil its educational mission mandated by article 7, had to find an acceptable compromise that resolved the tension

---

[65] BVerfGE 93, 1 at 16.
[66] Ibid 16.
[67] Ibid 18.
[68] BVerfGE 41, 29
[69] BVerfGE 93, 1 at 19.
[70] Ibid 20.
[71] See text accompanying n 22 above.
[72] BVerfGE 93, 1 at 21.
[73] Ibid 22–3.

between negative and positive aspects of religious freedom.[74] Referring to the *Inter-denominational School* and *School Prayer* cases,[75] their Honours repeated that the State legislature is not generally forbidden to introduce Christian values. However, this presupposes that religious coercion is reduced to a minimum.[76] The display of crosses in classrooms of public compulsory schools was held to exceed the limits of permitted State influence and, hence, the practice violated article 4.

Subsequently, the majority addressed the tension between the positive freedom of religion of some parents and students and the negative freedom of others:

> Parents and students who adhere to the Christian faith cannot justify the display of the cross by invoking their positive freedom of religious liberty. All parents and students are equally entitled to the positive freedom of faith not just Christian parents and students. The resulting conflict cannot be solved on the basis of majority rule since the constitutional right to freedom of faith is particularly designed to protect the rights of religious minorities. Moreover, article 4 does not provide the holders of the constitutional right with an unrestricted right to affirm their faith commitments within the framework of public institutions.[77]

As a result, the majority determined that it would be incompatible with the principle of practical harmony to suppress completely the feelings of people of different beliefs in order to enable the students of Christian belief not only to have religious instruction and voluntary prayer in public schools, but also to learn under the symbol of their faith even when instructed in secular subjects.[78] The constitutional complaint was therefore successful.

Like the majority, the three dissenting Justices applied the principle of practical harmony to determine the limits of article 4.[79] Contrary to their colleagues, however, their Honours exercised the balancing in favour of the guarantee in article 7 and the positive aspect of religious freedom in article 4. The dissenters found that article 7 granted to individual States a 'large measure of discretion in determining the nature and organisation of primary schools'.[80] In their opinion, the rule that mandated the display of the crucifix did not exceed that discretion[81] and the display

---

[74] Ibid 22.
[75] BVerfGE 41, 29; BVerfGE 52, 223.
[76] BVerfGE 93, 1 at 23.
[77] Ibid 24.
[78] Ibid 24.
[79] Justice Evelyn Haas further dissented on the procedural ground that the constitutional complaint was inadmissible: BVerfGE 93, 1 at 34–7.
[80] BVerfGE 93, 1 at 28.
[81] Ibid 28.

was from a constitutional perspective not different from voluntary prayer in public schools.[82] It did not constitute an unacceptable burden on the religious conscience of non-Christian students because to them the cross was held not to be a symbol of the Christian faith, but 'of the values reflected in the Christian community school, namely, those values associated with a Western culture deeply rooted in Christian ideas'.[83]

The *Classroom Crucifix* judgment unleashed a storm of controversy in Germany, which involved fierce attacks on the Constitutional Court. This public debate is the focus of the section following the present analysis of the *Teacher Headscarf* case.

The Teacher Headscarf *case*

Fereshta Ludin, a German citizen of Islamic faith who had completed her training as a teacher in the State of Baden-Württemberg, brought the *Teacher Headscarf* case before the Constitutional Court. When she sought employment in this State, she was refused the status of a civil servant by the authorities, a status which was a precondition for becoming a teacher in a public school. A requirement for the appointment of civil servants under Baden-Württemberg legislation was that the applicants are personally qualified (*persönlich geeignet*).[84] The State authorities decided in relation to Ms Ludin's application that a person who insisted on wearing *hijab* while teaching is not qualified in the relevant sense. This decision was upheld by two lower administrative courts and the Federal Administrative Court. Ms Ludin then filed a constitutional complaint in the FCC, alleging that the original decision and the judgments confirming it violated her right to free exercise of religion and her right of access to the public service according to qualification irrespective of religion.[85]

The majority of the Constitutional Court took an unusual course, effectively deferring to the legislature. In short, it determined that the authorities of the State of Baden-Württemberg and the lower courts had infringed the complainant's rights but only because the original determination that Ms Ludin was not fit to become a civil servant had been made by the executive without an express legislative mandate.

---

[82] Ibid 31.
[83] Ibid 32–3.
[84] *Landesbeamtengesetz Baden-Württemberg*, s 11(1) .
[85] See arts 33(2), (3) of the *Basic Law*: '(2) Every German shall be equally eligible for any public office according to his aptitude, qualifications and professional achievements … (3) Neither the enjoyment of civil and political rights, nor eligibility for public office, nor rights acquired in the public service shall be dependent upon religious affiliation. No one may be disadvantaged by reason of adherence or non-adherence to a particular religious denomination or philosophical creed'.

The State authority had interpreted a general norm requiring an applicant for a position of civil servant to be 'personally qualified' to mean that a person wearing *hijab* was not so qualified. This broad provision was held to be insufficient to provide the executive with a mandate to exclude Ms Ludin. However, in the majority's view it was open to Parliament to create a mandate through legislation stipulating unequivocally that wearers of *hijab* were not qualified to become civil servants. Such a law would be constitutionally valid and would not fall foul of article 4.

The reasoning that led the majority to this result was as follows: first, their Honours determined that Ms Ludin's religious freedom had been infringed by the challenged decisions because they put her in the position of having to choose between working in her chosen profession and wearing her religious clothing.[86] The majority restated the general rule that a legitimate limitation on the religious freedom protected by article 4 must stem from the *Basic Law* itself and added that an infringement is only valid if it is based upon a sufficiently specific statutory provision.[87] Their Honours further determined that in addition to article 4, article 33(2) and (3) was also relevant to this case. Under this provision, eligibility for public office is independent of religious denomination and nobody shall suffer a disadvantage as a result of adhering to any creed or belief. The majority explained that, while article 33(2), (3) did not make it impossible to lay down duties which restricted an official's freedom of religion, the restriction had to be strictly justified.[88]

In relation to Ms Ludin's case, the Justices in the majority stipulated that preventing her from becoming a teacher because of her insistence on wearing *hijab* could only be justified if, first, her action conflicted with other constitutionally protected rights and values, and, secondly, the restriction could be based on a sufficiently precise statutory provision. The constitutional values which were in potential conflict with the complainant's positive freedom to exercise her religion in this case were the State's educational function,[89] the parents' right to bring up their children[90] and the negative freedom of religion[91] of the students.[92]

The majority reiterated the rule developed in the *Interdenominational School*[93] and *School Prayer*[94] cases that it falls to the democratically elected legislatures of the States

---

[86] BVerfGE 108, 282 at 297.
[87] Ibid 297.
[88] Ibid 298.
[89] See art 7(1) of the *Basic Law*.
[90] See art 6(2) of the *Basic Law*.
[91] See art 4(1), (2) of the *Basic Law*.
[92] BVerfGE 108, 282 at 299.
[93] BVerfGE 41, 29.
[94] BVerfGE 52, 223.

to resolve the inevitable tension between these conflicting interests.[95] It distinguished the situation in the *Headscarf* case from that in the *Crucifix* case in that, in the latter, the exposure of students to the religious symbol had been instituted by the State while, in the former, it was a consequence of a decision of an individual teacher to dress according to her faith. The teacher's decision was not an expression of the State's own opinion and should not be taken as such. It was true that a teacher wearing *hijab* who stands in front of the class all day may have an effect on the students, who cannot avoid the sight of this religious symbol. But this effect could be weakened if the teacher explains its religious significance to the students.[96]

The majority accepted that there could be a danger that the wearing of religious clothing in class by a teacher could influence the students and lead to conflicts with their parents which could in turn result in a disruption of the peace in the school and make it difficult for the school to perform its educational role. However, their Honours held that this was only an abstract rather than a concrete danger. There was no indication in this case that Ms Ludin would use her presence to influence or convert the students in her charge.[97] Therefore, her choice of religious clothing alone could not establish a sufficient reason for her not to be personally qualified to teach. If her right to the free exercise of religion should be limited in order to guard against the merely abstract danger explained above, this would need a specific statutory basis, which was absent in this case.[98] However, the majority determined that it was constitutionally open to the State Parliament to make laws that prohibit teachers from displaying their religious adherence while at school.[99] Because no such law existed here, their Honours found Ms Ludin's constitutional complaint to be justified.

Three Justices delivered a strong dissent. They criticised the majority for failing to decide the principal question in this case (that is, what were the limits of state neutrality in the educational context of schools) and instead deferring it to the legislature. In their Honours' view, the majority judgment asks the State legislature to carry out a function that is the duty of the Federal Constitutional Court itself: to determine the limitations of freedom of religion. In addition, the minority complained about the lack of guidance provided to the legislature as to what kind of regulation of the issue of religious dress in schools would be constitutionally valid.[100]

---

[95] BVerfGE 108, 282 at 302–303.
[96] Ibid 305–306.
[97] Ibid 307.
[98] Ibid 306–9.
[99] Ibid 309–13.
[100] Ibid 336–8.

In the dissenters' opinion, the decisions taken by the State authority and the lower courts rejecting Ms Ludin's application to be admitted as a teacher were correct because a civil servant does not enjoy fundamental rights in the same way as other citizens. The civil servant belongs to the sphere of the State and therefore has to abstain from displaying an allegiance to a particular religion in schools. He or she would otherwise offend the principle of State neutrality.[101] In this regard there was no relevant difference between a crucifix installed in a classroom and a teacher wearing a headscarf. Both symbols were directly attributable to the State.[102] The minority believed that it was objectively possible for the headscarf to create conflicts in schools and this abstract danger was sufficient to entitle the executive to decide not to employ a teacher.[103]

While Ms Ludin's constitutional complaint was successful, her win was short-lived. Some German States moved quickly to ban teacher headscarves by way of legislation and this included the State of Baden-Württemberg, where Ms Ludin was seeking employment. She ultimately accepted a position in a private Islamic school.

The debates surrounding the *Classroom Crucifix* and *Teacher Headscarf* cases

Before considering in more detail the debates surrounding the *Classroom Crucifix* and *Teacher Headscarf* cases, one important difference between them must be emphasised: while both have in common that the *issue* under review was highly controversial in Germany, causing widespread debate in society, the amount of public attention surrounding the FCC's *judgments* differed significantly. The decision in the *Classroom Crucifix* case became the object of a highly charged public discussion and large sections of society fiercely criticised the Court. In contrast, the judgment in the *Teacher Headscarf* case was much less controversial, probably because politicians from across the political spectrum welcomed it and did not fuel debate to the same degree as they had done when the decision in the *Crucifix* case was handed down.[104] However, while not the focus of as much attention by the public at large, the FCC's *Headscarf* case received a myriad of academic commentary, much of it critical.[105]

---

[101] Ibid 322–5.
[102] Ibid 330.
[103] Ibid 326–9, 331–2.
[104] See, eg, 'Diese Entscheidung gehört in die Parlamente', *Süddeutsche Zeitung Online* (2003) <http://www.sueddeutsche.de/politik/reaktionen-diese-entscheidung-gehoert-in-die-parlamente-1.896993> at 3 March 2011.
[105] For a list of academic contributions on this case see von Campenhausen, above n 59, 671 note 28.

The judgment in the *Classroom Crucifix* case was among the most controversial decisions ever handed down by the Constitutional Court. The ferocity of the reactions that it triggered had not been encountered since the FCC's inauguration in 1951. The Court received 250,000 letters of complaint from citizens, while it had only received 160,000 in total in its forty-four year history prior to the *Crucifix* decision.[106] The reactions in Bavaria were particularly intense. The churches in that State organised mass protest rallies against the judgment that were attended by large crowds of more than 10,000 people.[107] The Premier and government of Bavaria participated in one of these rallies.[108] Leading Bavarian politicians called upon schools to ignore the judgment of Germany's highest court.[109] Such conduct by elected officials was unprecedented in the history of the Federal Republic of Germany.[110] Ultimately, the Bavarian Parliament changed the law under review in the *Crucifix* case, but in a way that undermined the Court's ruling. The new law stipulated that crucifixes would generally remain in Bavarian classrooms but that a compromise would be sought in cases where parents object to their presence.[111] As a result, on the occasion of the one-year anniversary of the *Crucifix* judgment the crosses had only been removed from the classrooms of six Bavarian schools.[112] This new legal situation led to further litigation in lower courts instigated by teachers and students who asked for the crucifixes to be removed from their individual schools.[113]

The *Crucifix* case also featured in the media for months. Germany's major newspapers received so many letters to the editor on this topic that they had to publish special issues in order to cope with the volume of the public response. The amount of media attention for the judgment and the underlying issue whether crucifixes should be placed in schoolrooms of public, non-religious schools was unprecedented and

---

[106] Hannes Burger, 'Nur in sechs Fällen wurde das Kruzifix abgehängt', *Die Welt Online* (1996) <http://www.welt.de/print-welt/article654261/Nur_in_sechs_Faellen_wurde_das_Kruzifix_abgehaengt.html> at 17 March 2011.

[107] For example, a rally organised by the Catholic Church in September 1995 in Munich.

[108] See, eg, Uwe Wesel, 'Die zweite Krise', *Die Zeit* (Hamburg), 29 September 1995, 13, 15.

[109] See, eg, Hans Maier, Interview: 'Purer Unsinn und Übermut', *Focus* (Munich), 14 August 1995, 44. See also Ingo Friedrich as quoted by Beate Schindler in 'Furcht vor Signalwirkung', *Focus* (Munich), 14 August 1995, 42.

[110] Gary S Schaal, 'Crisis! What Crisis? Der "Kruzifix-Beschluss" und seine Folgen' in Robert van Ooyen and Martin Möllers (eds) *Das Bundesverfassungsgericht im politischen System* (1st ed, 2006) 175, 184.

[111] 'Kruzifix-Urteil erzürnt CSU', *Der Spiegel Online Politik* (2002) <http://www.spiegel.de/politik/deutschland/0,1518,175140,00.html>

[112] Burger, above n 106.

[113] See *Der Spiegel Online*, above n 111. But it must be noted that within one year of the judgment only 13 applications were made for crucifixes to be removed in approximately 50,000 classrooms in Bavaria: see Burger, above n 106.

enormous, as demonstrated by the extent of newspaper coverage. The average attention dedicated to decisions of the Constitutional Court in the five leading national newspapers in Germany usually ranges from one article for uncontroversial decisions to up to fifteen articles within a timeframe of a maximum of two weeks for controversial cases. In contrast, both the *Süddeutsche Zeitung* and the *Frankfurther Allgemeine Zeitung* each published almost 100 articles on the *Crucifix* case and hundreds of letters to the editor. The case remained the object of media attention for a period of roughly three months.[114]

Some of the more extreme criticisms made of the Constitutional Court and its Justices included calling them 'criminals' and asking for them to undergo 'psychiatric examinations'.[115] In a media interview, the President of the Court, Jutta Limbach, said about the ferocity of the attacks on the Court that 'the limits of what is bearable have been reached'.[116] The FCC was also accused of having disregarded its alleged duty to 'keep the peace' in society. In other words, the Court was blamed for having caused the fierce and polarised public debate about the crucifix issue.[117] Furthermore, the method of appointment of the Justices of the FCC was questioned, perhaps because the three Catholic Justices hearing the case had all dissented.[118]

In the immediate aftermath of the judgment, many commentators described the situation in which the Court found itself as one of 'crisis'.[119] Among these commentators was a former Justice of the Court who proclaimed that 'the Federal Constitutional Court is no longer what it was until 10 August 1995' (the date of the judgment).[120] Some feared that the *Crucifix* case would do lasting damage to the Federal Constitutional Court as an institution and even to the political culture of the Federal Republic of Germany.[121]

The amount of public interest in the issue under review in the *Teacher Headscarf* case was similar. The question whether a teacher in a State school could wear a headscarf

---

[114] Schaal, above n 110, 179.
[115] See, eg, the letters to the editor cited by Jutta Limbach, 'Interview: "Die Grenzen sind erreicht"', *Der Spiegel* (Hamburg), 28 August 1995, 34.
[116] Ibid.
[117] Schaal, above n 110, 182, citing Edmund Stoiber, *Süddeutsche Zeitung* (Munich), 14 August 1995, 2.
[118] Ibid 181.
[119] See, eg, Wesel, above n 108.
[120] Ernst-Wolfgang Böckenförde, cited in 'Bundesverfassungsgericht steht vor dem Kollaps', *Süddeutsche Zeitung* (Munich), 17 May 1996, 6.
[121] See Schaal, above n 110, 175, 180–1, who identifies not one but three distinct debates in the mass media following the publication of the *Classroom Crucifix* judgment: the first on State neutrality in questions of religion, the second on the FCC as an institution, and the third on the consequences of the first two debates for the German political culture.

triggered a wide debate about the desirability of religious symbols in schools, but also more broadly about the limits of religious tolerance in German society.[122] The applicant, Fereshta Ludin, was for example depicted on the front cover of *Der Spiegel*, probably Germany's most important weekly news magazine.[123] Some commentators attacked the headscarf as a symbol of political Islam.[124] Alice Schwarzer, a prominent German feminist, for example, called the *hijab* the 'flag of the Islamist crusaders' and a 'symbol for separation' and asked whether 'the *sharia* is clandestinely introduced into Germany under the banner of religious tolerance'.[125] In contrast, some well-known public figures, including Johannes Rau, the Federal President of Germany, believed that headscarves should be tolerated because all religious symbols had to be treated equally. Therefore, if the *hijab* was banned from school, then Christian symbols would have to suffer the same fate. This consequence was regarded as undesirable.[126] Gerhard Schröder, the German Chancellor, held a different point of view. Prioritising the principle of State neutrality in questions of religion, he declared that 'headscarves are inappropriate for people who act on behalf of the State and that includes teachers'.[127]

However, as explained above, the FCC's judgment in the *Headscarf* case did not attract as much public and media attention as the *Crucifix* decision had. In contrast, it attracted a myriad of academic treatment not seen since the *Crucifix* judgment had been handed down.[128] The Court was fiercely criticised by academic commentators for not deciding the principal question in issue, but deferring it to the legislature. Critics regarded this as an abdication of the Court's role as the guardian of the Constitution and the final arbiter of disputes arising under it.[129] The Court was

---

[122] A summary of contributions to this debate can be found at *Deutschland: Kopftuch-Urteil des Bundesverfassungsgerichts* (2009) <http://www.migration-info.de/mub_artikel.php?Id=030801>.
[123] *Der Spiegel* (Hamburg), 29 September 2003, cover.
[124] Dominik Cziesche et al, 'Das Kreuz mit dem Koran', *Der Spiegel* (Hamburg), 29 September 2003, 82, 84.
[125] Alice Schwarzer, 'Die Machtprobe', *Der Spiegel* (Hamburg), 23 June 2003, 88.
[126] Hans Maier, former Bavarian Minister for Education, was of the same view. See von Campenhausen, above n 59, 667–71.
[127] 'Schröder unterstützt Kopftuchverbot', *Handelsblatt* (Düsseldorf) (2003) <http://www.handelsblatt.com/politik/deutschland/schroeder-unterstuetzt-kopftuchverbot/2294586.html> at 8 March 2011.
[128] Von Campenhausen, above n 59, 671–672.
[129] For example, Matthias Mahlmann, 'Religious Tolerance, Pluralist Society and the Neutrality of the State: The Federal Constitutional Court's Decision in the *Headscarf Case*' (2003) 4 *German Law Journal* 1099, 1112; von Campenhausen, above n 59, 686–687; Karl-Hermann Kästner, 'Darf eine muslimische Lehrerin im Unterricht das Kopftuch tragen? Anmerkung zum Urteil des BVerfG vom 24.9.2003' (2003) 58 *Juristen Zeitung* 1178, 1179; Georg Neureither, 'Ein neutrales Gesetz in einem neutralen Staat' (2003) 36 *Zeitschrift für Rechtspolitik* 465, 467.

blamed for triggering a charged political debate about the position of Islam in German society and the dangers of a radical version of the religion because of its failure to meet the question head on.[130] The judgment was also criticised because it led to different regulations in different federal States in this highly sensitive area.[131] Furthermore, commentators disapproved of the lack of guidance provided by the Court to legislatures as to what type of legislation would be constitutionally valid.[132] This reaction by academics reveals an important aspect of German legal culture: the FCC is expected to engage with and decide politically and morally difficult questions. If it does not meet this expectation, it is strongly criticised.

Despite the significant difference in the public's reaction to the judgments, the controversies surrounding both the *Classroom Crucifix* and the *Teacher Headscarf* case demonstrate that religious issues can trigger highly charged and polarised debate in society. Of course, I have chosen two of the most controversial issues that the FCC has ever had to rule on in order to illustrate this point. These fierce debates are not the norm, but occur rarely in German society. Nevertheless, the cases show that in a legal system where religious freedom is protected under a bill of rights, it is likely that the Courts will be asked to decide divisive, politically and morally charged questions at times. This can place them in the crossfire of fierce public debate. But is that so bad? Does it really have the grave long-term consequences that bill of rights opponents predict, that is, a loss of the Courts' authority and reputation and even damage to the legal and political system as a whole? As the following part shows, this is not necessarily the case.

Crisis! What crisis?: The long-term consequences of the *Classroom Crucifix* case[133]

After delivering the *Classroom Crucifix* judgment, the Constitutional Court became the target of unprecedented attacks not only from politicians and academics, but also from large sections of society. Judged by the public reaction to it, the decision was the most controversial ever handed down by the FCC. Many commentators believed that the Court was in a state of severe crisis,[134] one which, they feared, had the potential to not only damage the institution of the FCC in the long term, but also the political culture of the Federal Republic of Germany.[135] Therefore, the *Classroom*

---

[130] Von Campenhausen, above n 59, 665–6.
[131] Mahlmann, above n 129, 1112.
[132] Von Campenhausen, above n 59, 698–9; Kästner, above n 129, 1180.
[133] Phrase inspired by Schaal, above n 110.
[134] See, eg, Wesel, above n 108.
[135] Schaal, above n 110, 175, 181 citing Otwin Massing, 'Anmerkungen zu einigen Vorraussetzungen und (nichtintendierten) Folgen der Kruzifix-Entscheidung des Bundesverfassungsgerichts' (1995) 4 *Politische Vierteljahresschrift* 719, 721.

Crucifix case provides the perfect case study for testing the argument of bill of rights opponents. If the most fiercely criticised judgment ever delivered did not cause long-term damage to the FCC and to the broader legal and political system, then this severely undermines the case put forward by bill of rights opponents.

The *Crucifix* judgment was handed down in 1995. Ten years later, political scientist Gary S Schaal investigated whether the decision had really resulted in a long-term loss of authority by and respect for the Constitutional Court, whether it had indeed brought about a state of crisis. Schaal postulates that indicators for a crisis are, first, continuous critical commentary on the FCC in the mass media, secondly, the way in which the political elite interacts with the Court, and, thirdly, the community attitude towards it. Relying on empirical research, he demonstrates that the media returned to treating the Constitutional Court respectfully, even when being critical of specific judgments. Politicians have not seriously repeated calls for boycotts of the FCC's rulings at any time after the *Crucifix* case. It therefore seems that the Court has not lost its institutional authority in the longer term[136] and thus Schaal maintains that it is probably inappropriate to speak of a crisis.[137]

However, there may have been a short-term crisis concerning citizens' perception of the FCC. Schaal shows that the population's attitude towards the Court had changed significantly by the end of 1995, the year when the *Crucifix* case was decided. While the Constitutional Court used to enjoy a much higher trust than all the other political and judicial institutions of the Federal Republic of Germany, the level of trust had dropped significantly, to match that held for these other institutions at the end of 1995. While Schaal recognises that in the same year the Court also dealt with a number of other highly controversial issues and thus this reaction may not have been caused by the *Classroom Crucifix* case alone,[138] he maintains that the *Crucifix* judgment clearly damaged the public image of the FCC.[139] However, this was only temporary. Schaal demonstrates that the trust in the Constitutional Court had increased significantly by 1998 and in 2002 the public trusted the Court as much as it had before the *Crucifix* case. Furthermore, while the positive attitude towards the FCC had plummeted in 1995, the negative attitude against it had not increased dramatically. Only around fifteen per cent of the persons surveyed had a negative opinion of the Court, an increase from roughly eight per cent before the end of

---

[136] Hans Vorländer, 'Der Interpret als Souverän: Die Macht des Bundesverfassungsgerichts beruht auf einem Vertrauensvorschuss, der anderen Institutionen fehlt', *Frankfurther Allgemeine Zeitung* (Frankfurt), 17 April 2001, 14.
[137] Schaal, above n 110, 185.
[138] Schaal, above n 110, 175; see also Wesel, above n 108, 14. The other cases were BVerfGE 93, 266 ('*Soldaten sind Mörder* case'), BVerfGE 92, 277 ('*Markus Wolf* case') and BVerfGE 92, 1 ('*Sitzblockaden II* case').
[139] Schaal, above n 110, 185.

1995. According to Schaal, all of this shows that one cannot speak of a 'continuous' crisis of the Constitutional Court.[140]

Schaal also detects a direct relationship between critical commentary in the mass media and the public's perception of the FCC. According to Schaal, research has shown that the community's trust in the Court tends to falter when a judgment becomes the object of a partisan debate between political parties, which is reported in the media. However, as soon as politicians and thus media coverage move on from the topic, the public's trust in the Constitutional Court returns to its previous high level.[141]

Furthermore, Schaal maintains that critical public debate about the FCC is a direct result of its institutional role in the German legal and political system. Because the Court is the guardian of the Constitution, it is predestined to become the focus of public debate on some occasions. Therefore, when this happens it is not a symptom of a crisis, but rather an inevitable consequence of the institution's role. Schaal predicts that in future the high level of trust that the Court usually enjoys will most likely continue to prevent it from suffering lasting damage after making controversial decisions.[142] In conclusion, Schaal's analysis shows that the handing down of the most controversial judgment in the FCC's history did not do long-term damage to either the Court's authority and reputation or to the German legal and political system.

Conclusion: The sky is not falling if judges decide religious controversies

This chapter shows that while religious issues may trigger emotive discussion in society, a mature legal system can survive such controversies relatively unscathed. The German experience demonstrates that the answer to the question 'Will a bill of rights involve the courts in morally and politically controversial issues and occasionally make them the object of fierce and widespread criticism?' is a resounding 'Yes'. The issues under review in both the *Classroom Crucifix* and *Teacher Headscarf* cases were very controversial and the Court was drawn into heated public debates because it was asked to rule on these issues.

However, the discussion also shows that the answer to the question 'Will this do long-term damage to the courts' reputation and the legal and political system as a whole?' is an equally resounding 'No'. The attacks on the FCC after handing down judgment

---

[140] Ibid 186.
[141] Ibid.
[142] Ibid.

in the *Crucifix* case were incredibly fierce, the worst and most widespread criticism that the Court has ever experienced. However, Gary S Schaal has demonstrated that this did not do lasting damage to the FCC's authority and reputation, let alone to the legal and political system of the Federal Republic of Germany. While the population's trust in the Court did indeed drop shortly after the *Crucifix* judgment was delivered, it increased significantly in the following three years, returning to its normal high level within seven years. This shows that a robust legal and political system can survive such controversies without suffering the adverse consequences predicted by bill of rights opponents. Therefore, it is not a convincing argument against such a bill to say that it will involve the courts in controversial issues that will inevitably result in long-term damage to the courts, the administration of justice and the legal and political system as a whole. It is true that the public image of the German Federal Constitutional Court suffered in the short term after the *Crucifix* decision. However, this is a small price to pay in return for providing individuals whose religious freedom has been violated with an avenue to redress the injustice done to them.

11

Religious Freedom in a Secular Society: The Case of the Islamic Headscarf in France

Nicky Jones

One of the most interesting examples in recent years of a confrontation between secular and religious values occurred in France in the so-called 'affair of the headscarf'. The affair can be traced back to events in 1989, which were followed by a further series of events during the 1990s. It started when a public school in Creil, a town in northern France, expelled three Muslim schoolgirls for refusing to remove the Islamic headscarves they wore to school. The expulsions were widely reported in French and international media and were followed by further expulsions of other Muslim schoolgirls in towns and cities across the country, accompanied by growing community protests.

The affair was controversial for a variety of reasons. For one thing, it revolved around the headscarf, an item of clothing that has historically had strong and sometimes conflicting political, religious, cultural and social connotations. During the events of the affair, the headscarf sent a range of messages that were 'heavy with symbolism',[1] a symbolism which could be powerful, complex and indeed contradictory.

Another important set of reasons for the controversy surrounding the affair was that it struck a social, political and cultural 'nerve': the principal parties in the affair were Muslim schoolgirls, many of whom were the children of immigrant families already likely to experience high unemployment and religious or racial discrimination and to live in poor housing conditions. In addition, the headscarf became associated

---

[1] Françoise Gaspard and Farhad Khosrokhavar, *Le foulard et la République* (1995) 19.

with social policies of integration and assimilation, despite the fact that many of the Muslim girls concerned had been born or had grown up in France. The events also served as a powerful catalyst for conservative political parties and groups who became involved in the public debates to promote an anti-Muslim or anti-immigration agenda and to criticise the apparent failure or unwillingness of the schoolgirls to integrate into mainstream French culture.

However, one of the key issues was the fundamental role of secularism in France. The principle of secularism is a central tenet of French public policy, particularly where public education is concerned. In addition, secularism represents a set of social and cultural values that have profound historical resonances for many French people. The events also revived historical debate over the role of religion and the operation of secularism and secular institutions in public life in France.

This chapter will discuss some of the significant events in the affair of the headscarf, including the 1989 legal opinion delivered by France's highest administrative court, the Conseil d'État, which stated the legal principles to be followed in resolving the disputes, as well as key ministerial circulars issued to explain how the legal opinion was to be applied and the case law from the appeals brought by many of the expelled schoolgirls. The chapter will also consider the development of secularism in France and the notion of rights and duties, which was integral to the doctrine of secularism, as emphasised in the 1989 legal opinion and then applied in the 'headscarf' case law.

Finally, this chapter will consider some lessons that can be learned from the affair of the headscarf in France: should a government legislate against clothing and what issues arise in relation to such legislation? How might religious freedoms be best protected? Should religious protections (or indeed secularism itself) be narrowly or broadly defined? A broadly-defined protection might in practice afford a degree of flexibility which results in greater application and better outcomes for those whom it protects. I also note some events that have occurred in Australia in recent years which raise similar questions to those considered in relation to the French affair of the headscarf: what does secularism mean in a country such as Australia and what might be its implications for cultural and religious freedom and restrictions on such freedom?

The affair of the headscarf in France

Affair of the headscarf in 1989

The first incidents in the affair took place on 18 September 1989, at the start of the new school year. Three Muslim schoolgirls, 14-year-old Fatima, her 15-year-old sister Leila and their 14-year-old friend Samira, came to their lower secondary school in Creil wearing their headscarves. The girls refused to remove the headscarves when asked to do so by the school principal and teachers, who interpreted their refusal as a breach of secularism in public education, and immediately suspended them from the school.

The girls' suspension attracted considerable media attention. Over the following weeks, national newspapers featured front-page stories describing similar incidents taking place in other cities across France, in which other Muslim schoolgirls were also expelled for wearing their headscarves to school.[2] There was heated debate in the media over the principle of secularism and the girls' rights to equality, education and freedom of religious belief.

On 9 October, following departmental intervention, meetings with the parents and mediation on the part of local cultural associations, the three Creil girls returned to school. The negotiations had identified a compromise: the girls could wear their headscarves anywhere they wished within school grounds but would lower the scarves to their shoulders while in classes.

However, 10 days after they had agreed to the compromise, the three schoolgirls breached the agreement by refusing to lower their headscarves in class. It was noted in the media that their actions followed meetings between the girls' fathers and a representative of the Fédération Nationale des Musulmans de France, a Muslim association that was setting itself up in opposition to the more moderate Paris Mosque.[3] The girls were again suspended, removed from their classes and taken to the school library. Their suspension resulted in a five-hour meeting between their teachers and parents, the education authorities and representatives from cultural associations in a vain attempt to reach a new agreement.[4] According to one analysis, this was the point at which 'the dimension of this problem changed' and 'the affair exploded, particularly in relation to the media'.[5]

Clearly, there was considerable confusion over whose responsibility it was to negotiate and resolve the various cases. The father of one schoolgirl in Lille called for clarification of the legal principles underpinning the affair: 'If the State decides that the headscarf is prohibited at school, I will agree. It is the State. But the teachers cannot decide that it is forbidden'. His appeal was supported by Abdsamad Aïfoute, president of the Montpellier section of the Association of Islamic Students in France:

---

[2] Ibid 14–5.
[3] Ibid 15–6.
[4] Élisabeth Chikha, 'Chronologie' (1990) 1129 *Hommes et Migrations* 1, 2.
[5] Fabien Collet, *La Laïcité, une doctrine de l'Éducation nationale* (Diplôme d'Études Approfondies (Administration publique) thesis, Université des Sciences sociales de Grenoble, 1995) 17.

The government must decide its position very soon. This problem concerns all school-age children. It's ridiculous to prevent them from attending school when nothing in the [school rules] forbids them to wear the Islamic headscarf.[6]

On 23 October, the teaching and administrative staff of the Creil school wrote to the Minister for National Education, Lionel Jospin, asking him to 'express a clear opinion on a question which has gone national in order to restore calm to the school'.[7]

On 4 November, Jospin sought the opinion of the Conseil d'État, France's highest administrative court, whose function is to advise the government on legislative and administrative matters,[8] on whether 'the wearing of signs of affiliation to a religious community is or is not compatible with the principle of secularism'.[9]

Legal opinion of the Conseil d'État

After three weeks of deliberations, the Conseil d'État delivered its opinion on 27 November 1989, entitled 'The wearing of signs showing affiliation to a religious community (Islamic headscarf)'. In summary, the Conseil d'État ruled that wearing religious signs such as the Islamic headscarf was 'not by itself incompatible with the principle of secularism, insofar as it constitutes the exercise of freedom of expression and freedom of manifestation of religious beliefs'. Accordingly, students could wear 'signs of religious affiliation' in public schools without compromising the principles of secularism or secular public education, and wearing the headscarf could not, in isolation, lead to a student's suspension or expulsion.

However, the Conseil d'État noted certain restrictions on the exercise of the students' freedoms. The freedoms could be limited if the signs of religious affiliation, by their 'ostentatious or protesting' character or by the conditions in which they were worn, constituted an act of pressure, provocation, proselytism or propaganda, jeopardised the dignity or freedom of the students wearing the signs or of other students or staff, compromised health or safety, disrupted teaching activities or disturbed order and the normal operation of the school.[10] The list of limitations to the students'

---

[6] Monique Glasberg, Vincent Albinet and François Wenz-Dumas, 'Le choc de l'Islam sur l'école de la République', *Libération* (France), 21 October 1989.
[7] Chikha, above n 4, 3.
[8] The Conseil d'État has both a compulsory and an optional consultative function. In accordance with its optional consultative function, the government may seek the Conseil d'État's opinion on a legal problem which it wishes to have clarified, as occurred in relation to the affair of the headscarf: *Conseiller le gouvernement* (2009) Conseil d'État <www.conseil-etat.fr/cde/fr/conseiller> at 29 June 2009.
[9] Conseil d'État Assemblée Générale (Section de l'intérieur), *Port de signes d'appartenance à une communauté religieuse (foulard islamique)*, Avis No 346893, 27 November 1989, 1.
[10] Ibid 5.

freedom of expression and freedom of religious belief established that secularism was to be understood in conjunction with these freedoms. In practice, respect for both secularism and freedom of religion was to be a balancing act and establishing the balance would be one of the most difficult and contentious issues in the affair of the headscarf.

The legal opinion gave no indication of how schools should identify religious signs that might be considered 'by their nature … ostentatious' or the circumstances in which these signs might constitute 'an act of pressure, provocation, proselytism or propaganda'. However, it noted that the attitudes and behaviour of students wearing the religious signs to school were to be important issues in deciding these questions.

The legal opinion also stated that schools were to negotiate these matters on a case-by-case basis, rather than be decided at a national level. In this way, the Conseil d'État clearly indicated its preference for each incident to be resolved at a local level, rather than in accordance with a strict set of national guidelines.

The Conseil d'État's legal opinion was greeted with mixed responses. It was criticised for appearing to support teachers and students alike by affirming the respective positions taken by Education Minister Jospin, the students, school principals and teachers, or at least not contradicting the public position of either side.[11] This, as one article observed, relaunched the 'soap opera' in Creil.[12] There was also some concern that the Conseil d'État had not defined either secularism or terms such as 'ostentatious', 'pressure', 'provocation', 'proselytism' or 'propaganda', despite their importance as criteria by which a religious sign could be assessed.

Not all of the responses to the opinion were negative. English legal academic Sebastian Poulter observed approvingly that the Conseil d'État achieved '[a] balanced and sensible compromise … in a tense and complex situation through the application of legal principles relating to human rights'.[13]

Meanwhile, the three Creil schoolgirls were still isolated in their school library.[14] On 2 December, sisters Leila and Fatima returned to school without their headscarves and without explaining the reversal of their position. It soon became public knowledge that King Hassan of Morocco had approached the girls' family and on the previous

---

[11] Bronwyn Winter, 'Learning the Hard Way: The debate on women, cultural difference and secular schooling in France' in John Perkins and Jürgen Tampke (eds), *Europe: Retrospects and Prospects* (1995) 203, 204.

[12] 'Le foulard à la carte', *L'Humanité* (France), 29 November 1989.

[13] Sebastian Poulter, 'Muslim Headscarves in School: Contrasting Legal Approaches in England and France' (1997) 17 *Oxford Journal of Legal Studies* 43, 59.

[14] Chikha, above n 4, 9.

evening had summoned the two sisters and their father (who was of Moroccan origin) to the consulate in Paris to request that the girls stop wearing their headscarves.[15] The third girl, Samira, whose family was Tunisian, eventually returned to school without her headscarf on 26 January 1990.[16] The first series of events in the affair of the headscarf, at least as far as these three students were concerned, had lasted just four months.[17]

Over the following weeks, the media and public interest in the affair began to subside. In the majority of cases, schools appeared to be dealing with matters on an individual basis and 'a process of dialogue and a spirit of tolerance resulted in agreements which were acceptable to all parties'.[18] It was these sorts of local resolutions that the Conseil d'État had indicated should be the desired outcome of the process of dialogue to be undertaken in each case.

Affair of the headscarf in the 1990s

Following parliamentary elections in March 1993, a conservative coalition government assumed office in the wake of the former Socialist-led government. As one article noted, this electoral victory marked the point at which 'the official attitude toward Muslims ... changed'. Illegal immigrants increasingly became targeted in police 'round-ups' and Algerians and other North Africans suspected of being or sympathising with fundamentalist militants were detained, sometimes without charge.[19]

In September 1994, the new conservative Education Minister François Bayrou '[reignited] the controversy' by announcing in a magazine interview that he intended to ban the wearing of headscarves in public schools.[20] On 29 September 1994, he issued a ministerial circular[21] that bore the unambiguous title of 'Wearing of ostentatious signs in schools'. The circular recommended that schools take a firm stand, warning that the 'secular and national ideal [that] is the very essence of the Republican school' and the foundation of its duty to provide civic education was under threat from

---

[15] Ibid 11.
[16] Luis Cardoso, 'Au Coeur de "l'Affaire": Un Professeur de Creil témoigne' (Paper presented at the 'The Veil' conference, University of North Carolina, 2000).
[17] According to Bloul, this first controversy continued for three months: Rachel Bloul, 'From Moral Protest to Religious Politics: Ethical Demands and Beur Political Action in France' (1998) 9 *Australian Journal of Anthropology* 11, 15.
[18] Poulter, above n 13, 60.
[19] 'Ban on Islamic scarves renews debate', *The Tennessean* (Nashville), 15 September 1994, 3A.
[20] Ibid.
[21] Ministerial circulars are issued to explain and clarify the application of legislation or jurisprudence in the relevant portfolio area.

the presence and the proliferation of signs so ostentatious that their signification is precisely to separate certain students from the common rules of the school. These signs are, in themselves, elements of proselytism, particularly when they accompany challenges to certain classes or certain subjects, when they involve the safety of students or when they lead to disruptions to the collective life of the school.[22]

Bayrou's circular urged school principals to redraft their schools' internal regulations to include a 'prohibition on these ostentatious signs' and provided draft wording to serve as a model for the amended internal regulations. The suggested wording noted that although students were permitted to wear 'discreet signs manifesting their personal commitment to beliefs, notably religious beliefs', they were forbidden to wear 'ostentatious signs, which constitute in themselves elements of proselytism or discrimination'. In addition, certain behaviours were prohibited:

> provocative attitudes, failure to comply with the obligations of participation and safety, and behaviours likely to constitute pressure on other students, disrupt the progress of teaching activities or disturb order in the school.[23]

Although the circular did not refer to specific religious signs, it was widely understood to refer to the Islamic headscarf. Its effect was to 'rebrand' the headscarf, confirming that it could now be regarded as an ostentatious and divisive sign that constituted in itself an element of proselytism and discrimination. In so doing, the circular broadened the potential application of the Conseil d'État's 1989 legal opinion, which had stated that 'the wearing by students of [religious signs] is not by itself incompatible with the principle of secularism'. However, once the signs could be identified as 'ostentatious' or as constituting an act of pressure, provocation, proselytism or propaganda, they could be prohibited.

Bayrou's circular also afforded support for those schools still wishing to ban the headscarf. As became clear from the subsequent legal decisions, a number of schools immediately incorporated the circular's draft wording into their internal regulations and then applied the regulations to expel students wearing the headscarf. For example, in late 1994 two Strasbourg secondary schools amended their internal regulations to incorporate the wording suggested by Bayrou's circular. The schools then requested that all Muslim girls wearing headscarves to school remove them or risk expulsion. Dozens refused and the schools suspended at least 38 girls, many of whom had been wearing the headscarves to school for many months, if not years. After their

---

[22] 'Port de signes ostentatoires dans les établissements scolaires' (1994) 35 *Bulletin officiel de l'Éducation nationale* 2528, 2528–9.
[23] Ibid 2529.

expulsions had been confirmed, 18 of these students commenced appeals against the expulsion decisions in Strasbourg's administrative tribunal.[24]

The 'headscarf' legal cases

During the 1990s, France's administrative courts were starting to hear other appeals brought by expelled schoolgirls. Around half a dozen 'headscarf cases' were heard each year between 1992 and 1995, although by the end of the 1995 school year the controversy 'appeared to have died down and the tide had turned in favour of the Muslim girls'.[25] However, the number of legal proceedings surged in 1996 and 1997, with administrative courts across the country hearing 38 and 21 cases respectively.[26]

The case law shows that the courts consistently ruled that wearing the headscarf was not inconsistent with secularism. More often than not, the cases were decided in the schoolgirls' favour, although for the girls themselves this was sometimes a case of 'winning a battle but losing the war'. The outcomes of the cases heard in the busiest years of 1996 and 1997 are worth noting: in the overwhelming majority (around 83 per cent) of these cases the schoolgirls' expulsions were overturned by the courts, while in the remaining cases (approximately 15 per cent) the expulsions were upheld. However, it should be noted that most of the cases in which expulsion decisions were overturned tended to involve a single student, while those cases in which the expulsions were upheld often involved groups of students. Taking this factor into account, around 60 per cent of the students had their expulsions overturned and were entitled to return to school, while a sizeable minority of the students — 40 per cent — were unsuccessful in their appeals.

The case law provides some examples of judicial reasoning in relation to the wearing of the headscarf in public schools. On the whole, the courts considered and attempted to balance the various competing priorities. A relatively consistent set of principles emerged from the body of case law, based on the Conseil d'État's legal opinion. In the most straightforward cases, a school was not to expel a student simply for wearing the headscarf. So, for example, in one 1996 case, a school principal had expelled a student whose return to school he had opposed while she was wearing the headscarf on the sole basis that 'the wearing of this headscarf is by its nature incompatible with

---

[24] Michel Sousse, 'Le tribunal de Strasbourg annule l'exclusion de 18 lycéennes qui portaient le foulard', *Libération* (France), 21 April 1995.
[25] Cynthia DeBula Baines, 'L'Affaire des Foulards — Discrimination or the Price of a Secular Public Education System?' (1996) 29 *Vanderbilt Journal of Transnational Law* 303, 307.
[26] The cases can be obtained from legal archives on Legifrance, a French government website providing access to legislation and case law.

the principle of secularism'. The Conseil d'État ruled that this reason was incorrect in law and overturned the girl's expulsion.[27]

However, an expulsion could be justified if, in addition to wearing the headscarf, a student had engaged in political acts or activism, disturbed public order or teaching activities in the school by, for example, distributing brochures,[28] circulating petitions or participating in public protests,[29] or had breached her obligations to attend all classes or obey a teacher's instructions.[30] Such acts were considered to have introduced religious or political influences into the school or disturbed public order in the school and accordingly were found incompatible with secularism in public education. The Conseil d'État was particularly likely to uphold the expulsions of students who had attempted to proselytise to other students or who had actively participated in public protests against school prohibitions.

The number of cases heard by the administrative courts dwindled to a handful in the years between 1999 and 2003. No 'headscarf' cases were decided in 2004 or 2005, although the period from 2006–08 saw a moderate surge of 17 cases appear before the courts.

The doctrine of secularism in France

Historical development of secularism

Contrary to some views, the position taken by the French government and public schools was not simply a reflection of anti-Muslim sentiment nor even a recently-devised attempt to target the Islamic headscarf. Rather, it represents a contemporary manifestation of an historical policy of secularism whose original purpose was to prevent religious and political ideologies and activities from influencing public school students and curricula.

Indeed, from an historical perspective, secularism in France was developed to counter the formidable power of the established Catholic Church and to free the State's public services, particularly its public schools, from the involvement and influence of the Church and clergy. Over many centuries, the Catholic Church had traditionally been responsible for education and had played an important role in administering schooling and maintaining public order in France. The Church and political institutions maintained close relations, as part of which Church officials

---

[27] Conseil d'État, No 170343, 20 May 1996.
[28] Cour administrative d'appel de Lyon, No 96LY02608, 19 December 1997.
[29] Conseil d'État, No 170207 170208, 27 November 1996.
[30] Conseil d'État, No 159981, 10 March 1995.

were paid public functionaries, and the institutions of each power supported the other in a liaison of mutual advantage.[31]

In 1789, the events of the Revolution led to the *Declaration of the Rights of Man and the Citizen*, which weakened the power of the Catholic Church as much as other institutions of the Ancien Régime by promoting the sovereignty and equality of the French people. In line with Enlightenment philosophy, the Declaration listed 'inalienable rights' held by citizens by virtue of their being human, including freedom of religious belief, protected by article 10, which states, 'No-one may be disturbed on the basis of his or her beliefs, even religious beliefs, as long as their manifestation does not interfere with the public order established by the law'.[32]

Although relations between the Catholic Church and the State were fraught with conflict over the course of the nineteenth century, the Church continued to play a key role in maintaining social stability and national loyalty in France. Religious education still had a place in the school curriculum under Napoléon and the clergy were salaried employees of the State. Indeed, the move towards secularism in education was prompted by the increasing numbers of clergy teaching in public schools. In 1879, 'on the eve of the great secular laws, out of the 37,000 clerical teachers, half worked in the public primary schools'.[33]

The principal initiator of these secular laws was Jules Ferry, Minister for Public Instruction from 1879–83. His public education reforms, which were carried out in stages to facilitate their acceptance, implemented three main ideals: the equality of all children through the provision of free education; the right of all children to receive an education, which became a compulsory obligation for the students and a corresponding duty imposed on the State; and finally, secularism in public education, replacing 'religious and moral instruction' in the public school curriculum with 'civic and moral instruction'.[34]

Increasingly hostile, Church-State relations in France were brought to a head by the Law of 9 December 1905.[35] This law, which became known as the Separation Law, abrogated the 1801 Concordat negotiated between Napoléon and the papacy that had regulated Church-State relations and the status of religious orders in France for more

---

[31] Carlton J H Hayes, *France: a Nation of Patriots* (1974) 32.
[32] *La Déclaration des Droits de l'Homme et du Citoyen 1789* (Fr) art 10.
[33] Louis Caperan (quoted in Collet, above n 5, 9).
[34] W D Halls, *Education, Culture and Politics in Modern France* (1976) 7.
[35] Relating to the Separation of Churches and State. Ironically, since he is forever associated with French secularism in public education, the 1905 Separation Law was not passed by Jules Ferry (who died in 1893) but by Bienvenu Martin, then Minister for Public Instruction. His full title at the time was Minister for Public Instruction, the Arts *and Religions* (my emphasis): 'Documents Parlementaires — Chambre', 136.

than a century, and introduced a range of administrative and procedural measures which effectively entrenched Church-State separation.[36] The 1905 Separation Law has become incontrovertibly linked with secularism in France, although the word 'secularism' appears nowhere in its provisions. Nonetheless, the law realised Jules Ferry's desire for 'the separation of these two worlds, the civil world and the religious world'.[37]

Rights and duties in secularism

At the time it was adopted, the Separation Law reflected the view of its legislators that the doctrine of secularism entailed more than administrative, financial or political separation from the Church: it was also bound up with rights and duties. Transcripts of parliamentary debates at the time of its adoption reveal heated disagreements dividing the ranks of parliamentarians.[38] It is clear from the debates that concern for fundamental rights and freedoms played an important part in the arguments presented by both sides of Parliament,[39] accompanied by concern for public order and the social unrest which opponents of secularism believed would follow Church-State separation and its 'violent rupture with all … traditional French politics'.[40]

Although it is associated with secularism, the Separation Law also enshrined guarantees of freedom of conscience and belief and freedom of religious expression. However, the law provided that the State could restrict these freedoms in the interests of public order, as is evident from article 1 of the Separation Law: 'The Republic guarantees freedom of conscience. It guarantees the free exercise of religion under the sole restrictions decreed hereafter in the interests of public order'.[41] Thus, from its earliest days, the doctrine of secularism has represented more than the separation of Churches and State — according to one of its foundation documents, it has also expressly upheld the right to religious freedom.

The preamble to the 1946 *French Constitution* (incorporated into the current 1958 *Constitution*) reaffirmed the principle of secularism: 'The provision of free, public and secular education at all levels is a duty of the State'.[42] The 1958 *Constitution*

---

[36] Hayes, above n 31, 99–100.
[37] Speech given by Jules Ferry, Saint-Quentin, 16 November 1871 (quoted in Collet, above n 5, 11).
[38] 'Annales de la Chambre des Députés', 21 March 1905, 1244; also 'Annales de la Chambre des Députés', 3 April 1905, 1494.
[39] Georges Berry in 'Annales de la Chambre des Députés', 21 March 1905, 1238; also Gabriel Deville in 'Annales de la Chambre des Députés', 23 March 1905, 1296.
[40] M Ribot in 'Annales de la Chambre des Députés', 3 April 1905, 1494.
[41] *Law of 9 December 1905 relating to the Separation of Churches and State* (Fr) art 1.
[42] *Le Préambule de la Constitution du 27 octobre 1946.*

later entwined rights and duties, stating in article 1: 'France is an indivisible, secular, democratic and social Republic. It shall guarantee equality before the law of all citizens without distinction according to origin, race or religion. It shall respect all beliefs'.[43]

In 1989, the Conseil d'État stated in its legal opinion that 'the principle of secularism necessarily implies respect for all beliefs', basing this claim on article 10 of the *Declaration of the Rights of Man and the Citizen*. The Conseil d'État also quoted from the Separation Law, which states that 'the Republic guarantees freedom of conscience'. The Conseil d'État further emphasised that freedom of belief 'must be regarded as one of the fundamental principles recognised by the laws of the Republic'. This freedom was to be interpreted and exercised alongside other rights and obligations that were also to be respected. According to the Conseil d'État, these rights and obligations included secularism.

More recently, French Parliaments have legislated to enshrine rights and duties of the State and students respectively in relation to public education.[44] For example, article L141-1 of the 2000 *Code of Education* specifically incorporates and reaffirms the following constitutional principles:

> The State shall guarantee equal access for children and adults to teaching, training and the acquisition of cultural knowledge and skills; the organisation of free, public and secular education at all levels is a duty of the State.

In addition, the *Code* sets out certain rights and responsibilities that attach to public school students. Article L141-2 of the *Code* goes some way towards protecting freedom of religion, although it also provides for the possibility of State limitations to this freedom: 'The State shall make all necessary arrangements to guarantee freedom of religion and religious instruction to public school students'.

Student obligations are stated in article L511-1 as follows: 'The obligations of students consist of carrying out the tasks inherent to their studies; these include participation and respect for the rules regarding the operation and the collective life of schools', while article L511-2 sets out the students' rights:

> In lower secondary and secondary schools, pupils are acknowledged to have, while respecting pluralism and the principle of neutrality, freedom of information and freedom of expression. The exercise of these freedoms must not interfere with teaching activities.

---

[43] *La Constitution de 1958* art 1.
[44] See Law No 89-486 of 10 July 1989 on Direction in Education and Decree No 2000-549 of 15 June 2000, which substantially amended the 1989 law.

Debates over the interpretation of secularism in the affair of the headscarf can tend to overlook these constitutional and legislative guarantees of freedom of conscience and freedom of religious expression. But remember that the Conseil d'État acknowledged these guarantees in its 1989 legal opinion and that even according to its foundation texts, the principle of secularism was intended to encompass respect for freedom of belief.

The 2004 law on secularism

In 2004, the legal regime governing the wearing of the headscarf changed significantly when the French Parliament enacted legislation formally prohibiting the wearing of any religious signs in public schools. The legislation was based on recommendations presented to the government by the Commission to Consider the Application of the Principle of Secularism in the Republic, headed by Bernard Stasi, a former French and European parliamentarian and then-Ombudsman for the Republic. Over six months, the Commission interviewed members of the community during more than 100 public hearings and stimulated widespread debate on 'the question of secularism', before handing down its report in December 2003.

In the report's preamble, the Commission emphasised the fundamental importance of secularism, calling it a 'founding value and essential principle' upon which the Republic was constructed. One recommendation that attracted considerable publicity called for the drafting of a new law on secularism to include the following provision:

> In respect for freedom of belief and for the particular nature of private schools, clothing and signs manifesting a political or religious affiliation shall be prohibited in primary and secondary public schools. Any penalty must be proportionate and applied after the student has been invited to comply with his or her obligations.[45]

The Commission explained that the provision would apply to 'visible signs, such as large crosses, headscarves, or [Jewish skullcaps]' but would not extend to smaller 'discreet signs' such as medallions or pendants consisting of small crosses, stars of David, Hands of Fatima or miniature Qur'ans.[46] The examples of religious signs drawn from the three major religions practised in France — Roman Catholicism, Judaism and Islam — were a clear indication that the law was intended to apply to followers of all religions.

---

[45] *Rapport au Président de la République* (2003) Commission de réflexion sur l'application du principe de laïcité dans la République <www.ladocumentationfrancaise.fr/brp/notices/034000725.shtml> at 27 July 2009.
[46] Ibid.

The draft legislation, entitled 'Bill concerning the application of the principle of secularism, the wearing of signs or clothing manifesting a religious affiliation in public schools, lower secondary and secondary schools', was passed with overwhelming bipartisan support and greeted with applause across the benches. However, extensive protests were held in France and other countries across Europe to mark the concerns of many in the community about the enactment of the new law.[47]

The new law inserted the following provision into the *Code of Education*:

> Art. L. 141-5-1 — In primary, lower secondary and secondary public schools, the wearing of signs or clothing by which students visibly manifest a religious affiliation is forbidden. The internal regulations note that the commencement of disciplinary proceedings shall be preceded by dialogue with the student.[48]

The prohibition applies to all visible signs which make the wearer's religious affiliation immediately identifiable, meaning that the wearing of Islamic headscarves, Jewish skullcaps and oversized Christian crosses is now forbidden in public schools. Students wearing those signs are liable to be suspended or expelled.

French secularism in the European Court of Human Rights

In its report, the Stasi Commission had also considered the possibility that the law on secularism would conflict with article 9 of the Council of Europe's *Convention for the Protection of Human Rights and Fundamental Freedoms* ('the European Convention'),[49] which protects the right to freedom of religion and freedom of religious manifestation. However, it recognised that the European Court of Human Rights tends to acknowledge 'the traditions of each country, without seeking to impose a uniform model for relations between Church and State', and leaves each State a 'margin of appreciation' with regard to Church-State relations. According to the Commission, '[t]he European Court in Strasbourg will protect secularism if it is

---

[47] In January 2004, tens of thousands of Muslims marched in protest against the proposed law on secularism in Paris, Marseille, Lille and other cities across France, while other protests were held in London, Berlin, Stockholm, Brussels, Cairo and Bethlehem: 'Mobilisation contre le projet de loi sur la laïcité', *Le Monde* (France), 17 January 2004; Jean-Paul Dufour, 'Forte mobilisation à Lille', *Le Monde* (France) 19 January 2004; Jon Henley, 'French MPs reappraise plan to outlaw veils', *The Guardian* (UK), 20 January 2004; Jon Henley, 'France steps closer to Muslim headscarf ban', *The Guardian* (UK), 30 January 2004.

[48] Law No 2004-228 of 15 March 2004, art 1: applying the principle of secularism to regulate the wearing of signs or clothing manifesting a religious affiliation in public schools, lower secondary and secondary schools.

[49] *Convention for the Protection of Human Rights and Fundamental Freedoms*, opened for signature 4 November 1950, CETS No 005 (entered into force 3 September 1953).

a fundamental value of the State' and, in addition, 'permits limitations to freedom of expression in the public services, particularly if it is a question of protecting minors from external pressures'.[50]

At this stage, the European Court of Human Rights has not been required to consider whether the 2004 law on secularism might be contrary to the article 9 right to freedom of religion. However, on 4 December 2008, the court delivered its decisions in relation to two French 'headscarf cases',[51] both arising from events that took place before the entry into force of the 2004 law on secularism. In both cases, the court found in favour of the French government and school authorities, confirming the expulsions of the two Muslim schoolgirl applicants because they wore the headscarf.

The two cases arose from similar events that occurred at around the same time and in the same school: two Muslim schoolgirls, aged 11 and 12 years old, wore their headscarves to physical education classes, were asked on a number of occasions to remove them, refused to do so and were expelled from the school. The girls' families appealed against the expulsion until they had exhausted all available domestic legal options. Both girls then complained to the European Court of Human Rights that their expulsions violated article 9 of the European Convention protecting their right to freedom of religious expression and article 2 of Protocol No 1 to the European Convention protecting their right to education.

The court considered the two complaints together. It found that the school's ban on wearing the headscarf during physical education and sports classes and the girls' subsequent expulsions constituted a restriction on the exercise of their right to freedom of religion. However, it noted that article 9(2) of the European Convention provided that a person's freedom to manifest his or her religion might be subject to certain limitations that are 'prescribed by law and are necessary in a democratic society in the interests of public safety, [to protect] public order, health or morals, or for the protection of the rights and freedoms of others'.

After considering the Conseil d'État's 1989 legal opinion, ministerial circulars and the relevant case law, the court accepted that the restriction had a sufficient legal basis in domestic law and so could be regarded as having been 'prescribed by law'. Furthermore, the restriction mainly pursued the legitimate aims of protecting the rights and freedoms of others and protecting public order.[52] The court noted that article 9 of the European Convention did not protect every act motivated or inspired by a religion or belief. In

---

[50] Commission de réflexion sur l'application du principe de laïcité dans la République, above n 45, 20–1, 59.
[51] *Kervanci v France*, No 31645/04, ECHR, 4 December 2008 (volume still unallocated) and *Dogru v France*, No 27058/05, ECHR, 4 December 2008 (volume still unallocated).
[52] *Kervanci v France* and *Dogru v France*, [48], [59–60].

a democratic society in which several religions coexisted in the same population, it might be necessary to restrict religious freedom in order to reconcile the interests of the various groups and ensure that everyone's beliefs are respected.[53]

In the circumstances, the court considered that it was not unreasonable to conclude that wearing the headscarf was incompatible with sports classes for reasons of health or safety. Moreover, the various disciplinary proceedings against the schoolgirls fully satisfied the duty to undertake a balancing exercise of the various interests at stake. Finally, the penalty of expulsion from school did not appear disproportionate. The court found that the question of whether the schoolgirls had overstepped the limits of their right to express and manifest their religious beliefs on the school premises 'falls squarely within the margin of appreciation of the State'.

The court further noted that secularism was a constitutional principle and a founding principle of the French Republic, the protection of which appeared to be of primary importance, particularly in schools. An attitude that failed to respect that principle would not necessarily be covered by the freedom of religious manifestation and would not be protected by article 9 of the European Convention.[54]

Accordingly, having regard to the circumstances of the cases and to 'the margin of appreciation that should be left to the States in this domain', the court concluded that the restriction in question was justified as a matter of principle and proportionate to the aim pursued. As a result, it ruled that there had been no violation of article 9 of the European Convention.[55]

The 2010 law to ban the burqa

The affair of the headscarf, and the profound social and political fragmentation which it both reflected and catalysed, subsided somewhat in 2005. However, the debate over religious clothing in France was not finished. In 2009, President Nicolas Sarkozy announced in a speech to Parliament that the full-face or full-body veil ('voile intégral'), also known as the burqa or niqab, was not welcome in France. The government also announced the formation of a parliamentary commission to examine the practice of wearing the burqa in France.

In January 2010, the commission reported back to the National Assembly. Its report noted conflicting issues such as secular rights and responsibilities in France; Republican nationalism; militant religious fundamentalism; the constraining influences of parents, family and community on some Muslim girls and women; the importance of education; and human and women's rights to equality, free choice

---

[53] Ibid [61–2].
[54] Ibid [72].
[55] Ibid [73–8].

and freedom of movement, as well as the choices and desires of Muslim women themselves with regards to their clothing.

The report also made a number of recommendations, the first of which stated that the burqa should be condemned as contrary to Republican values and that discrimination and violence against women should also be condemned. Other recommendations advised that immigration and refugee laws should be amended to require would-be citizens and refugees to accept values such as equality of the sexes and the principle of secularism and to allow the refusal of residency status and citizenship to religious fundamentalists. Recommendation 13 advocated the adoption of a law which would prohibit the hiding of one's face in public places.[56]

Following this report, both houses of the French Parliament passed a law prohibiting the wearing of clothing which would conceal a person's face in public places. Any breaches of the law may attract a maximum fine of 150 euros or citizenship classes, or both. The law also prohibits anyone from forcing another person to conceal the face, on penalty of one year's imprisonment and a 30,000 euro fine. Both penalties are doubled if the person being so constrained is a minor. The law, which received strong support from both sides of politics and was approved by France's Constitutional council, came into force on 11 April 2011.

Moreover, France is not the only European country to introduce a ban on the burqa: the Belgian government enacted similar legislation in 2010, while parliaments in Italy, Holland, Spain, Germany, Denmark and the UK have also debated the adoption of laws banning the burqa.

Conclusions

Legislating against clothing

One issue that arises in the context of a ban on wearing the headscarf is the practical difficulty of legislating against everyday items such as clothing or jewellery. For example, it is arguably difficult to determine when a headscarf might be a religious or cultural sign, as opposed to an item of clothing with no particular significance.

The question of distinguishing between an Islamic headscarf and a headscarf with no religious characteristics, or indeed between an Islamic headscarf and other religious items of clothing, was raised on a number of occasions in France. For example, one Muslim girl suspended from her school in Avignon for wearing the headscarf noted

---

[56] Mission d'information sur la pratique du port du voile intégral sur le Territoire national, Rapport d'information fait en application de l'article 145 du Règlement, Assemblée Nationale, No. 2262, 26 January 2010, 123–85.

that she had worn it to school since 1982 and that this was the first time she had been penalised for doing so. Her father commented, 'If she had been preaching Islam I would understand, but this, it's just a scarf'.[57] Some Muslims also pointed out that devout Jewish and Christian women wear the headscarf as well, and that the Virgin Mary herself is rarely portrayed without one.[58]

Clearly, in the context of the affair of the headscarf, the headscarf itself functioned as something more than an item of clothing. Its symbolic nature was evident in the compromise solution proposed to the schoolgirls in Creil: their headscarves would be accepted in the school courtyard and corridors on condition that they were lowered to the girls' shoulders during classes.[59] In other words, the powerful symbolism of the headscarf could be countered with a symbolic gesture of equal or greater power.

Sometimes it appeared to depend on what the headscarf looked like. In one school, the principal persuaded a schoolgirl to wear a headscarf '*à la provençale*'. According to one of the girl's teachers, she used to wear 'one [headscarf] with little ducks on it and another with flowers. It was pretty'.[60] Clearly, the schoolgirl's headscarf could be more easily accepted (or overlooked) when it appeared to be a rural-style or fashionable headscarf displaying flowers or animals, rather than a black headscarf that might be construed as consistent with religious and political fundamentalism.

Moreover, how did the headscarf compare with other religious signs or clothing such as the cross or the Jewish kippa, or skullcap? In 1994, Education Minister François Bayrou's circular distinguished between 'discreet signs' worn by students that manifested 'their personal commitment to [religious] beliefs'. It was generally assumed that jewellery displaying a Christian cross or crucifix was likely to be considered discreet and therefore acceptable. Similarly, there was nothing to indicate that the 1994 prohibitions would affect other religious clothing such as the kippa. The Jewish community had been concerned since the early days of the affair that the kippa might constitute an 'ostentatious' sign.[61] They were reassured in 1989 by Education Minister Lionel Jospin, and again in 1994 when Prime Minister Édouard Balladur expressly assured Jewish leaders at a community dinner that the kippa did not have an 'ostentatious character'.[62]

---

57 Chantal Seignoret, '"C'est juste un foulard"', *La Croix* (France), 25 October 1989.
58 'À bas Rushdie, vive le foulard!' *L'Évènement du Jeudi* (France), 19 November 1989.
59 'Quand l'islam fait école', *Le Quotidien de Paris* (France), 21 October 1989.
60 Anne Fohr, 'École: la déchirure', *Le Nouvel Observateur* (France), 6 October 1994, 46.
61 'Le couvre-chef dans le judaïsme', *Les nouveaux Cahiers* (1994) 37 (quoted in Dominique Le Tourneau, 'La laïcité à l'épreuve de l'Islam: le cas du port du "foulard islamique" dans l'école publique en France' (1997) 28 *Revue générale de Droit* 275, 294).
62 Philippe Bernard, 'Marceau Long s'interroge sur la validité de la circulaire Bayrou à propos du foulard islamique', *Le Monde* (France), 20 September 1994; also Henri Tincq, 'De l'autre côté du voile', *Le Monde*, 30 November 1994.

Yet as Marceau Long, Vice-President of the Conseil d'État, asked in 1994, 'How can one say that the headscarf is ostentatious but that the kippa [or] the huge crosses or crucifixes which appear to be fashionable once again are not?'[63]

Such contradictions highlight the difficulty of legislating against the wearing of items of clothing: where are the limits of such legislation and how are they to be monitored or enforced? These questions arose in France when the Stasi Commission handed down its report and recommendations on secularism in 2004. Commenting on the proposed law, Education Minister Luc Ferry speculated that in addition to religious signs, beards or bandanas worn by students might also be prohibited if they appeared to be 'religious': 'As soon as anything becomes a religious sign, it will fall under this law'.[64] The Minister failed to speculate on the practical difficulties of identifying a beard or a bandana that might be a religious sign and of distinguishing them from ones that were not. Moreover, the debate has recently resumed in France over the question of whether to ban Muslim women from wearing the burqa or niqab in public places and whether Muslim women who cover themselves completely in public constitute an assault on secularism and women's rights.[65]

Similar issues have arisen in Australia. In November 2002, a member of the New South Wales Legislative Council, Fred Nile, called for a ban on Muslim women wearing the chador (which consists of the headscarf and a long cloak covering the body) in public places in Australia for fear that they might be concealing weapons beneath their clothing. His call ignored the fact that in practice a range of other everyday clothing including trench coats and ponchos can also conceal weapons. More recently, in July 2009, a Muslim woman wearing a face-veil on a Sydney bus was approached by the bus driver and told to 'remove her mask'. The woman accused the driver of discrimination and asked him what the difference was between what she was wearing and the swine flu masks that many people were then choosing to wear.[66]

Limiting judicial discretion

Another issue is the question of how to construct a legal regime that protects rights and responds to a variety of needs and circumstances. Before 2004, the legal regime in France governing the wearing of the headscarf was based on the Conseil d'État's 1989 legal opinion and its application by the administrative courts in each 'headscarf'

---

[63] Bernard, above n 62.
[64] Jon Henley, 'Veil ban may extend to "religious" beards', *The Guardian* (UK), 21 January 2004.
[65] 'Port de la burka en France: des députés réclament une commission d'enquête parlementaire', *Le Point* (France), 17 June 2009.
[66] Simon Santow, *Muslim woman 'culturally raped' in veil bus row* (2009) ABC News Online <www.abc.net.au/news/stories/2009/07/30/2641498.htm> at 31 July 2009.

case. In its opinion, the Conseil d'État had not ruled definitively either for or against wearing the headscarf. Rather, it had identified relevant constitutional and legislative provisions and extrapolated a set of guiding principles relating to secular public education, freedom of religion and the rights and obligations of students. When the courts applied these principles to the different circumstances of each case, a pattern of judicial responses and indeed protection emerged.

Overall, the 'headscarf' cases reflected an inclination on the part of the courts — and the law which they applied — to protect the education and religious freedom of Muslim schoolgirls wearing the headscarf, while also upholding principles of secularism by protecting the 'public order' which marked the limits of the students' rights.

The courts ruled consistently that a school could not expel a student simply for wearing the headscarf or in the absence of a lawful ground. At the same time, they also applied the obligations that had been imposed on students to respect public order and observe their responsibilities to attend and participate in school classes and activities, and penalised students if these obligations were breached. As a result, as I noted earlier, in those cases where expulsions were upheld, for the most part the students had at least participated actively in the events that led to their expulsion. By incrementally negotiating judicial responses to particular circumstances arising in the affair of the headscarf, the courts were contributing to the construction of a working definition of secularism that encompassed both rights and duties, and were adapting secularism to the specific challenges posed by significant numbers of the population, who, while they were French, were also insisting on their right to be recognised as Muslims.

In practice, the legal cases appeared to function as a practical vindication of the key principles and indeed the flexibility advocated by the Conseil d'État in its 1989 legal opinion. The Conseil d'État had sought to balance a number of priorities, including freedom of religion and secularism, while also providing principles to guide the application of the law in accordance with the circumstances of each case. Its caution and apparent imprecision enabled restrictions to the wearing of religious signs such as the headscarf to be interpreted broadly and applied flexibly. The outcomes of the cases, in which the majority of the students' expulsions were overturned, reflected the equitable nature of the Conseil d'État's legal opinion. A more narrowly-defined definition of secularism prohibiting the display of all religious symbols, such as that proposed by Education Minister Bayrou in 1994, would have fettered the courts' attempts to respect the complex mesh of principles articulated in the Conseil d'État's 1989 legal opinion.

Yet in 2004, the law on secularism effectively redefined secularism in a narrower sense, restricting and penalising students' choices in relation to clothing or signs that might be both visible and religious, with potentially serious consequences for the students' right to freedom of religious expression. In doing so, the law radically changed the previous legal regime, imposing an outright ban on the wearing of visible religious signs and eliminating the degree of judicial discretion and flexibility that administrative courts could exercise in assessing the circumstances of each case and reaching their decisions. Under the new legislation, Muslim girls wearing the headscarf may be expelled from school whether or not they have engaged in political or proselytising activities, disrupted teaching or disturbed public order.

In this way, the 2004 law on secularism changed the delicate judicial balance that French administrative courts, particularly the Conseil d'État, had worked to achieve throughout the 1990s. Furthermore, the law compromises rights which secularism and the Republic are supposed to uphold. As a result, it has significant implications for the doctrine of secularism itself in France.

Forms of secularism

Finally, this chapter returns to the issue of secularism as a formal policy and cultural and community value. Clearly, the affair of the headscarf in France was an opportunity to consider very carefully the operation and institutions of secularism in a modern context. There was broad general agreement that secularism was an important principle in contemporary France, although many people were nonetheless unsure of how to interpret and apply secularism and secular values to the circumstances of the affair of the headscarf.

There was also considerable disagreement over how the doctrine of secularism should be understood and its implications: was it 'hardline' secularism or a flexible variety? 'Hardline' secularism would require that strict neutrality of the public service be respected by prohibiting all public school students from manifesting any religious beliefs and limiting all manifestations of religion to those displays or practices which could take place in the students' private lives or on weekends. In contrast, a more flexible interpretation of secularism would provide a forum in which all religious beliefs could be acknowledged and expressed equally. This variety of secularism would accept all beliefs, recognising that their expression in the form of an outward religious sign — such as the headscarf — was a matter of individual right.[67]

Certainly, there were other factors at play in the affair of the headscarf that meant that it was not simply a conflict between secular values and freedom of religious expression. In 1989, Jospin noted some of these factors: the emergence of 'a powerful anti-Arab feeling' stemming from the Algerian war of independence; the controversial issue of immigration; socio-economic problems such as unemployment and

---

[67] Le Tourneau, above n 61, 289.

inadequate housing for many Muslim people; and, finally, 'the question of French national identity and the place that foreigners can have in it'. According to Jospin, the fact that the French community 'could become so inflamed about [the affair of the headscarf was] most certainly a sign of unease' about issues such as these.[68]

It is worth noting that in 1905, the heated parliamentary debates that took place when the Separation Law was passed were also based on deep concern that Church-State separation would weaken or even destroy the Republic. Perhaps the unease arising from the affair of the headscarf reflected a more contemporary concern that aspects of modern secularism were proving inadequate to the challenges of a modern French Republic.

What does the affair of the headscarf mean for other countries such as Australia? In many ways, the situation in Australia is very different from that in France: Australia has no formal legislative or constitutional separation of Church and State, nor is secularism an important social, cultural and community value in the way that it is in France. Moreover, legislation such as the 2004 law on secularism could not be passed in Australia, since s 116 of the *Constitution* prohibits our Commonwealth Parliament from legislating on matters of religion.

However, like France, Australia has no established or State religion. In the 2006 Census, although the most common religious affiliations reported were Catholic (26 per cent) and Anglican (19 per cent), 19 per cent of the population also stated that they had no religion, an increase from 16 per cent in 2001.[69] Many Australians would feel comfortable with a claim that we are a secular State. Indeed, in 2007, a booklet published by the Australian government to inform aspiring citizens about Australian culture stated that this country has a secular government and that freedom of religion and secular government are important values in modern Australia.[70]

If this is so, how important is the doctrine of secularism to Australian culture and the Australian community? Do we believe that secular values should be protected? If so, how and what would be the extent of any such protection? What form of secularism do we want in Australia? Should it be clearly articulated and understood? Perhaps in practice a complex and abstract principle such as secularism works best when it remains undefined and when it is not restricted by concrete examples of what it is or is not, the circumstances in which it should or should not apply or, as in the affair

---

[68] Lionel Jospin, 'Now or Never' in Anne Corbett and Bob Moon (eds), *Education in France: Continuity and Change in the Mitterand Years, 1981–1995* (1996) 76–7.
[69] Australian Bureau of Statistics, *2006 Census QuickStats: Australia — Religious Affiliation: Main responses for Australia* (2006).
[70] Commonwealth of Australia, *Becoming an Australian citizen* (2007) 5–6.

of the headscarf in France, the particular religious signs with which it is or is not compatible.

Similarly, how can Australia best enshrine freedom of religion in a way that provides meaningful protections to those practising a wide variety of religions and beliefs in the community? What restrictions would Australians impose on the rights to freedom of religion and freedom of religious expression? Should Australian law allow a 'margin of appreciation' to apply to certain manifestations of religious freedom, or to any restrictions on such freedom?

In considering these questions, it may be helpful to look to and learn from the events of the affair of the headscarf in France. Should we regard the affair negatively, as a suppression of the schoolgirls' right to manifest their religious beliefs by wearing the headscarf, or positively, as a protection of pluralism and secular cultural values? In France, these events constituted a modern challenge for secularism, signalling that there were still important questions to ask about the nature and role of contemporary secularism in society. In Australia, just as in France, these are also questions to which the government and the people must respond, and the response must not divide people along lines of religion, ethnicity, socio-economic status or politics in the name of 'social peace and national cohesion'.[71] In Australia and in France, the face of secularism — and religious freedom — must reflect the changing face of the community.

---

[71] 'Dossier d'actualité: Réaffirmer le principe de laïcité', 10 February 2004.

12

Religious Freedom in the UK after the *Human Rights Act 1998*

Ian Leigh*

According to a book title chosen by one commentator on the UK's *Human Rights Act 1998*, Professor Francesca Klug, human rights are *Values for a Godless Age*.¹ No doubt before the events of September 11 2001 the secularization thesis had a certain resonance. The legislation could be seen as a (very faint) shadow of that great hymn of the secular state — the French Declaration of the Rights of Man. Certainly some religious organisations feared that rather than the *Human Rights Act 1998* enhancing their religious freedom it would be used against them and they therefore sought — unsuccessfully — guarantees against litigation in the form of exemptions.² A decade later, the revolutionary fervour has cooled somewhat and an assessment can be made of the treatment of religious liberty under the Act to date. We now know also that the obituary notices for religious faith were premature, even in (comparatively) secular Western Europe: 'God is Back' as another recent book title has it.³ Indeed, the resurgence of a vigorous religious discourse in public life in the UK is perhaps not just a reaction to secularization but in a sense also evidence of a growing human rights culture following incorporation of the European Convention.

---

* I am grateful to Peter Edge for helpful comments on an earlier draft. The usual caveat applies.
1. Francesca Klug, *Values for a Godless Age: The Story of Britain's New Bill of Rights* (1998).
2. Peter Cumper, 'The Protection of Religious Rights under Section 13 of the Human Rights Act' [2000] *Public Law* 254; Ian Leigh, 'Towards a Christian Approach to Religious Liberty' in Paul Beaumont (ed), *Christian Perspectives on Human Rights and Legal Philosophy* (1998) 64-71.
3. John Micklethwait and Adrian Wooldridge, *God is Back: How the Global Rise of Faith is Changing the World* (2009).

The focus in this chapter is on a handful of the more controversial religious liberty claims that have come before the courts since 2000.[4] I have selected these for the range and variety or issues that they raise directly concerned with claims to manifest religious belief.[5] These include whether Christian parents have a right that their children be educated in private schools in accordance with their religious beliefs on discipline; whether a Muslim schoolgirl has the right to wear a jilbab, contrary to the school uniform policy of her (mixed) state secondary school; whether a Hindu community can resist an order for the destruction of a diseased bullock of sacred religious significance to them; and whether orthodox Hindus should be accommodated in their wish for cremation upon an open-air funeral pyre.

In fact, each of these claims ultimately failed (although the funeral pyre decision was successfully appealed on other grounds). Nevertheless, the hurdles that the applicants faced and the reasons for failure yield some important lessons about the treatment of religious liberty claims.

The constraints of the article 9 Strasbourg jurisprudence

The *UK Human Rights Act 1998* is an Act to give further effect to the European Convention on Human Rights ('ECHR') in UK law. It does so by two primary mechanisms: a strong duty on the courts to interpret primary and secondary legislation as far as possible compatibly with Convention rights (section 3)[6] and a duty on public authorities (including the courts) to act in conformity with a person's Convention rights (section 6). In both instances UK courts and tribunals are to 'take account' of the jurisprudence of the European Court of Human Rights concerning the meaning of Convention rights.[7]

---

[4] The *Human Rights Act 1998* (UK) came into force on 2 October 2000.

[5] This is not a comprehensive treatment of all *Human Rights Act 1998* (UK) cases concerning religion. It does not include *R (Pretty) v Director of Public Prosecutions* [2002] 1 AC 800, in which art 9 was raised peripherally if unsuccessfully in a challenge to the law on assisted suicide, or *R (Baiai, Trzcinska, Bigoku & Tilki) v Secretary of State for the Home Department* [2007] 1 WLR 693 where religious discrimination under art 14 of the European Convention (which prevents discrimination in the enjoyment of Convention rights *inter alia* on grounds of religion) was raised in subsidiary argument. Also excluded is discussion of the litigation in which the House of Lords found that a Parochial Church Council of the Church of England was not a public authority within the meaning of the *Human Rights Act 1998* (UK): *Aston Cantlow and Wilmcote with Billesley PCC v Wallbank* [2004] 1 AC 546.

[6] Where this is not possible, the higher courts may issue a declaration of incompatibility drawing Parliament's attention to the inconsistency: *Human Rights Act 1998* (UK) s 4.

[7] *Human Rights Act 1998*, s 2. For a much more detailed general treatment, see Ian Leigh and Roger Masterman, *Making Rights Real: The UK Human Rights Act in its First Decade* (2008).

Among the Convention rights so incorporated into UK law is article 9:

> 1. Everyone has the right to freedom of thought, conscience and religion; this right includes freedom to change his religion or belief and freedom, either alone or in community with others and in public or private, to manifest his religion or belief, in worship, teaching, practice and observance.
>
> 2. Freedom to manifest one's religion or beliefs shall be subject only to such limitations as are prescribed by law and are necessary in a democratic society in the interests of public safety, for the protection of public order, health or morals or for the protection of the rights and freedoms of others.

What use has been made of this provision since October 2000 when the *Human Rights Act 1998* came into force?

Firstly, it is clear that in conformity with their general approach, the UK courts are reluctant to give enhanced protection rights over and above that enjoyed at Strasbourg. This has disappointed one of the hopes for the *Human Rights Act 1998*, that it would lead to British judges giving a confident lead to other jurisdictions and to the European Court of Human Rights itself in the way that, for example, the German Constitutional Court has. If anything, the potential for doing so was greater with religious liberty than other rights since the Strasbourg jurisprudence developed very late (the first major cases were not decided until the 1990s) and the protection is weak by comparison with free speech or privacy.

In practice, however, UK courts have essentially tracked the limitations of the Strasbourg approach, although some domestic judges have voiced occasional misgivings. In *Ullah*, unsuccessful appeals were brought by two failed asylum-seekers, a Pakistani member of the Ahmadhiya faith and a Vietnamese Roman Catholic, who feared persecution if returned to their respective countries. The House of Lords refused to extend the principle under Convention jurisprudence that a deporting or extraditing state is liable for torture or inhuman or degrading treatment at the hands of the state to which a person is removed[8] to cover religious persecution. The European Court of Human Rights had not clearly extended the principle to cover denial of article 9 rights and the appellate committee held that it should not take this step either.[9]

---

[8] *Soering v United Kingdom* (1989) 11 EHRR 439; *Chahal v United Kingdom* (1996) 23 EHRR 413.

[9] Of their Lordships, Lord Caswell came closest to allowing the possibility in a flagrant case (which did not apply on the facts here), as conceptually consistent with the ECtHR's reasoning (*R (on the application of Ullah) v Special Adjudicator; Do v Immigration Appeal Tribunal* [2004] UKHL 26), although in such cases art 3 would probably also be engaged.

As Lord Bingham put it:

> It is of course open to member states to provide for rights more generous than those guaranteed by the Convention, but such provision should not be a product of interpretation of the Convention by national courts, since the meaning of the Convention should be uniform throughout the states party to it. The duty of national courts is to keep pace with the Strasbourg jurisprudence as it evolves over time: no more, but certainly no less.[10]

Similarly, in *Copsey v WWB Devon Clays Ltd*[11] the Court of Appeal found that an employee's freedom to manifest his religion under article 9 of the ECHR was not infringed when he was dismissed for refusing to work on Sundays. Mummery LJ applied the so-called 'non-interference' line of jurisprudence from the European Commission of Human Rights, and held that article 9(1) was not engaged because Mr Copsey was entitled to resign if his employer's work requirements were incompatible with manifesting his religion.[12] He found that, although much-criticised, this line of authority was clear and, in the absence of a change of heart at Strasbourg or a different view from the House of Lords, should apply.[13] Rix LJ stressed that this approach had the virtue of giving primacy to the autonomy of the parties and concluded that he had 'no difficulty with the general thesis that contracts freely entered into may limit an applicant's room for complaint about interference with his rights'.[14] For those who hoped that the UK courts would give a broader interpretation of religious freedom to overcome the limitations of the article 9 jurisprudence, *Copsey* came as a disappointment.[15]

---

[10] Ibid [20] (Lord Bingham).

[11] [2005] EWCA Civ 932.

[12] See especially *Stedman v United Kingdom* (1997) 23 EHHR 168; Rex Ahdar and Ian Leigh, *Religious Freedom in the Liberal State* (2005) 176–179, 298 ff; Gillian Morris, 'Exclusion of Fundamental Rights by Agreement' (2001) 30 *Industrial Law Journal* 49.

[13] *Copsey v WWB Devon Clays Ltd* [2005] EWCA Civ 932 [26-39] (Mummery LJ).

[14] See especially at [52], referring to *Ahmad v ILEA* [1978] QB 36 and *Ahmad v United Kingdom* (1981) 4 EHRR 126 (refusal of time off for Muslim teacher to attend Friday prayers did not violate art 9). Rix LJ went on to find that unfair dismissal legislation could, even disregarding art 9, contain a concept of reasonable accommodation of religion: at [67-73]. Cf the judgment of Neuberger LJ.

[15] A case on similar facts would now be treated as an example of indirect religious discrimination under the *Equality Act 2010* (UK), in which case the question of voluntary acceptance of the limitation is not relevant: see, eg (under earlier legislation), *R (on the application of Watkins-Singh) v Governing Body of Aberdare Girls High School* [2008] EWHC 1865 (Admin).

Testing religious claims

A further major constraint on the development of article 9 comes from Strasbourg jurisprudence in the so-called *Arrowsmith* test.[16] This states that not all actions motivated by religious belief qualify, rather only those 'intimately connected' with the beliefs in question. Arguably, this approach (sometimes referred to as the necessity link or test) puts a gloss on the text of article 9 and has the effect of limiting religious liberty claims at the definitional stage, rather than as the structure of article 9 suggests at the stage of applying the 'necessary in a democratic society' test under article 9(2).

This aspect of the article 9 approach has led domestic courts under the *Human Rights Act 1998* to apply a threshold test to establish whether the beliefs or practices fall within the ambit of article 9 in the first place.[17] Judges in the common law world are aware of course of their lack of competence to rule on theological matters and the danger of interfering in disputes affecting the internal affairs of organized religions. These factors point toward judicial modesty and the hurdles are therefore set low. Even in this weakened form, however, they have tripped some litigants and in practice, some domestic judges appear to be operating a more demanding standard than in Strasbourg (where it is exceptionally rare for the court to rule that a belief that an applicant claims is religious is not in fact[18]).

The clearest example of the application of the threshold comes in *R (on the application of Playfoot) v Governing Body of Millais School*[19] in which a 16-year old schoolgirl challenged the refusal by her school under its policy against the wearing of jewellery of permission for her to wear a 'purity ring'. The ring symbolised her commitment to celibacy before marriage, which she claimed was a manifestation of her religious belief as a Christian in pre-marital sexual abstinence. She argued that the school's refusal violated her right to manifest her belief and was (in view of the school's policy to permit some religious jewellery items) discriminatory contrary to article 14 of the Convention. Michael Supperstone QC (sitting as a Deputy High Court Judge)

---

[16] *Arrowsmith v United Kingdom* Application 7050/75 (1980) 19 *Eur Comm HR* 5.

[17] Art 9 gives an absolute right to freedom of belief (the so-called inner forum: *C v the United Kingdom*, Application 10358/83 (1984) 37 *Eur Comm HR* 142, 147) covering beliefs of all kinds. The right to manifest beliefs is however qualified and only applies to *religious* beliefs.

[18] *Valsamis v Greece* (1996) 24 EHRR 294 is an instance of the ECtHR so ruling. The Court found that participation in a National Day parade did not violate the applicant's pacifist beliefs as Jehovah's Witnesses, despite their claim that it did.

[19] [2007] EWHC 1698. See also *Gallagher (Valuation Officer) v Church of Jesus Christ of Latter-day Saints* [2008] UKHL 56, in which the House of Lords held that the requirement under rating legislation for a place of worship to be open to the public in order to qualify for charitable relief did not violate arts 9 or 14 in the case of a Mormon temple. The majority (Lord Scott dissenting) found that there was no impediment on the right to manifest religion or belief.

found no 'intimate link' between the wearing of the ring and belief in celibacy before marriage for religious reasons. Consequently, it could not be said that in wearing the ring that the claimant was manifesting her religion.[20]

A similar conclusion was reached at first instance in *Williamson* in which Elias J in the High Court[21] and Buxton LJ in the Court of Appeal[22] found (in the context of a challenge brought by a number of Christian independent schools to the statutory ban on the use of corporal punishment) that parental discipline of children was a peripheral concern to Christian belief. This approach was not, however, followed by other members of the Court of Appeal or by the House of Lords.[23] As Lord Bingham's speech argues:

> [I]t is not for the court to embark on an inquiry into the asserted belief and judge its 'validity' by some objective standard such as the source material upon which the claimant founds his belief or the orthodox teaching of the religion in question or the extent to which the claimant's belief conforms to or differs from the views of others professing the same religion … [24]

There is a clear danger in a court's assuming the role of theological arbiter over a litigant's beliefs in this way. Once the sincerity of the plaintiff's beliefs has been accepted then it really should not matter whether the beliefs in question are peripheral or minority ones — they are nonetheless entitled to be considered as *religious* beliefs. (This does not mean, of course, that they are therefore automatically entitled to priority over other interests.)

One alternative is that judges will increasingly be drawn into hearing expert evidence on whether the beliefs in question are orthodox according to the religion in question. An example is the recent claim in *Ghai v Newcastle CC*[25] by orthodox

---

[20] Moreover, in any event she had voluntarily accepted the uniform policy of the school and there were other means open to her to practice her belief without undue hardship or inconvenience. Even had there been an interference it would have been proportionate because of the sound reasons based on promoting school identity, minimising differences of appearance and bullying, and promoting high standards and conduct underlying the school's policy on uniform. Nor was there any evidence of breach of art 14 since although the school had made exceptions to its policy on occasion to accommodate other pupils this was after careful inquiry that wearing the items involved (which included a Kara bracelet in the case of one Sikh pupil) were required by the pupil's religion.

[21] *R (on the application of Williamson) v Secretary of State for Education and Employment* [2001] EWHC Admin 960 [44-5].

[22] Ibid [26-9, 57-8].

[23] [2005] UKHL 15.

[24] Ibid [22].

[25] [2009] EWHC 978 (Admin).

Hindus that they be allowed by Newcastle City Council to hold open-air funeral pyres[26] — a claim supported by a Sikh temple but opposed by the Ministry of Justice, both intervening in the litigation. Cranston J's judgment evaluated the conflicting evidence of four experts submitted by the parties and intervenors as to Hindu and Sikh funeral practices, as well as related academic literature. This included evidence as to Hindu beliefs and practices from a professor at a Hindu university, from a consultant anthropologist, and from a specialist in death and bereavement in the British Hindu communities.

Cranston J concluded that although belief in the need for cremation on an open air funeral pyre was a minority belief among British Hindus generally, in the case of orthodox Hindus like the applicant that the belief in the practice was, nevertheless, central. However, in the case of a Sikh temple that had also intervened in the litigation this was not the case, since open-air funeral pyres were a matter of a tradition rather than belief. Although the judge's survey of funeral rites is fascinating and informative one is nevertheless left wondering about the value of exercise in determining what was supposed to be a cursory threshold check on the sincerity and cogency of the beliefs in question.[27] Ironically, despite this painstaking examination by the judge, the Court of Appeal later concluded that there was no necessary conflict between the applicant's beliefs and the legislation governing cremations.[28]

It is clear, however, that in the light of the approach in *Ghai* that would-be litigants would now be well-advised to first martial their experts. Well-established religions with well-known or widely shared beliefs are clearly at an advantage here.[29] Although it should not matter how widely held the beliefs in question are, plainly where they can be shown to be conventional views this makes the evidential task easier.

---

[26] A claim for judicial review of the Council's refusal to set aside land for open-air funeral pyres for cremation according to orthodox Hindu practice. The law on cremation made it a criminal offence to cremate human remains other than in a licensed crematorium.

[27] Cranston J found that case law compelled him to apply a threshold test and determine whether an open-air funeral pyre fell within core beliefs (at [101]).

[28] *R (on the application of Ghai) v Newcastle CC and the Secretary of State* [2010] EWCA Civ 59. For discussion of further aspects of Cranston J's judgment see below (text at n 39).

[29] In a different context, a former Archbishop of Canterbury (Lord Carey) has suggested that some cases be heard by a panel of judges with greater familiarity and understanding of religious issues: *McFarlane v Relate* [2010] IRLR 872 (unsuccessful religious discrimination claim brought by a counsellor who declined to offer sexual counselling to same-sex couples). The suggestion was robustly rejected by Laws LJ (at [16-7]). See P Parkinson, 'Accommodating Religious Belief in a Secular Age: The Issue of Conscientious Objection in the Workplace' (2011) 34 *University of New South Wales Law Journal* 281, 288–90.

Proportionality and restrictions on religious liberty

Establishing that the beliefs or practice in question are religious is of course only the first hurdle, since religious liberty both under the ECHR and the ICCPR is a *qualified* right, subject to limitation. The 'necessary in a democratic society' test under article 9(2) of the ECHR suggests a high burden of justification on the state but this has often turned out to be illusory in practice. The European Court of Human Rights has not itself been completely consistent: on one occasion, for example, it denied an article 9 claim because the applicants (Orthodox Jews facing considerable difficulty in obtaining meat slaughtered in accordance with their religious dietary requirements) had not shown that it was 'impossible' to do so.[30]

Although some UK judges have expressed dissatisfaction with this approach, in the light of their overall approach to taking into account Convention jurisprudence under section 2 of the *Human Rights Act 1998*, they have felt obliged to replicate it where article 9 cases have arisen in the domestic courts.

In *Begum*, the House of Lords upheld a state secondary school's refusal for a pupil to wear the jilbab (a loose-fitting garment covering the entire body except for the head, face and hands), contrary to the policy on school uniform. The school's policy already permitted Muslim girls to wear the shalwar kameez (comprising a tunic and trousers), and allowed those who wished to do so to wear the hijab (a headscarf). The majority of the House of Lords (Lords Bingham, Hoffmann and Scott) considered that the facts that Shabina Begum had been content to comply with the policy on uniform until her religious views changed, that she had joined the school knowing the policy and that there were other state schools available to her where she could wear the jilbab meant that there was no interference with her rights under article 9.[31] As Lord Hoffmann put it:

---

[30] *Jewish Liturgical Assn Cha'are Shalom Ve Tsedek v France* (Application 27417/95) 27 June 2000.

[31] The approach of the majority in *Begum* was followed in *R (On the application of X) v The Headteacher of Y School* [2007] EWHC 298 (Admin), concerning the refusal of a selective all-girls Grammar school to allow a 12-year-old Muslim girl to wear a niqab veil (a veil which covered her entire face and head except her eyes). Silber J held that art 9 was engaged but that the school had not interfered with the pupil's rights since she had an offer to attend an alternative school where she would be permitted to wear the niqab veil. Even had there been interference, however, Silber J held that it would have been justified under art 9(2). The conclusion was based on the absence of prior rulings from the European Court of Human Rights or domestic courts of interference with art 9 where a claimant could without excessive difficulty manifest or practice their religion as they wished in another place or in another way: at [38].

Article 9 does not require that one should be allowed to manifest one's religion at any time and place of one's own choosing. Common civility also has a place in the religious life.[32]

The minority were more sceptical of this application of the Strasbourg approach, however: Lord Nicholls laid more weight on the costs involved in changing schools and Baroness Hale emphasised that a choice of school was usually made by parents rather pupils. Notwithstanding this difference, all their Lordships found any interference to be justified under article 9(2). Their Lordships considered that the school had done its best to accommodate conflicting beliefs about school dress in a conscientious way. As Baroness Hale argued:

Social cohesion is promoted by the uniform elements of shirt, tie and jumper, and the requirement that all outer garments be in the school colour. But cultural and religious diversity is respected by allowing girls to wear either a skirt, trousers, or the shalwar kameez, and by allowing those who wished to do so to wear the hijab. This was indeed a thoughtful and proportionate response to reconciling the complexities of the situation. This is demonstrated by the fact that girls have subsequently expressed their concern that if the jilbab were to be allowed they would face pressure to adopt it even though they do not wish to do so.[33]

The House of Lords also gave general advice on approaching proportionality claims. In his speech, Lord Hoffmann was particularly critical of the Court of Appeal's suggestion that the school governors should have asked a structured series of questions before finding that the article 9 right could be displaced.[34] This was a misguidedly formalistic approach: what mattered was the substance of the decision not the process for reaching it.

Following this general approach few judgments undertake anything approaching a rigorous analysis of whether it is 'necessary in a democratic society' to restrict the right under article 9(2). An honourable exception, however, was the first instance decision in a case that became a cause célèbre in Wales in 2007. This was the case of Shambo the Sacred Calf, a challenge by way of judicial review by a Krishna Community to the decision of the Welsh Assembly Government to issue a slaughter notice in respect of a bullock that had tested positively for Bovine tuberculosis. At first instance,

---

[32] *R (SB) v Governors of Denbigh High School* [2007] 1 AC 100, [50]. Critics have pointed out that this approach represents an extension of the 'specific situation' principle in the art 9 jurisprudence, which had not been applied by the Strasbourg court to school pupils: Mark Hill and Russell Sandberg, 'Is Nothing Sacred? Clashing Symbols in a Secular World' [2007] *Public Law* 488.
[33] *R (SB) v Governors of Denbigh High School* [2007] 1 AC 100, [98].
[34] See *R (SB) v Governors of Denbigh High School* [2007] 1 AC 100, [68] (Lord Hoffman).

His Honour Judge Hickinbottom (sitting as a Deputy High Court Judge) granted the application because there was no evidence that the government had correctly identified a legitimate public health objective under article 9(2) on which to justify a restriction.[35] His Honour based this conclusion on careful analysis of the relevant policy documents and of the decision to slaughter. The government's position was that it was 'imperative public health objective that the risk of transmission of bTB is entirely eliminated from any bovine which positively reacts to a tuberculin test. That elimination can only occur if the animal is slaughtered'.[36] On the other hand, the Community argued that because of the very great religious significance of Shambo to them, an exception should be made and proposed to isolate the animal and enforce other health safeguards. The judge found that government's policy was framed unduly narrowly and without any explanation of how it served the underlying public health considerations. The government had simply not correctly identified a legitimate objective to be balanced under article 9 in the first place. The Court of Appeal disagreed, however, and found that the minister had public health (rather than rigid policy) in mind as the objective.[37] The government's policy of slaughter and surveillance where infection was discovered was to be regarded as a means rather than an objective in its own right. Moreover, the refusal to make an exception to the policy in the case of the bullock Shambo was proportionate to this broader objective.

Although this may appear to be a semantic difference, the underlying issue of how governmental bodies are required to justify policies that impinge on religious freedom is important. At the one pole — as the House of Lords made clear in *Begum*[38] — it is whether a public body's actions infringe rights rather than the process of reasoning that matters, especially in the case of bodies like school governors which do not have constant and easy access to specialist legal advice. Equally, however, public bodies should not be allowed to 'Convention-proof' their actions though a 'tick-box' exercise and then present the case for restriction of rights in a way that prevents genuine questioning of whether to do so is necessary in a democratic society.

The Hindu funeral pyre litigation is a further cautionary example of the approach to proportionality. In the first instance decision in *Ghai*, Cranston J held that restrictions on open air funeral pyres were justified under article 9(2) as necessary in a democratic

---

[35] *R (on the application of Suryanda) v Welsh Ministers* [2007] EWHC 1376 (Admin).
[36] Ibid [97].
[37] *R (on the application of Suryanda) v Welsh Ministers* [2007] EWCA Civ 893.
[38] See *R (SB) v Governors of Denbigh High School* [2007] 1 AC 100, [68] (Lord Hoffman).

society.³⁹ The government had intervened to defend the policy based on health and environmental considerations and for reasons of public morals. The applicant argued that such concerns could be met by regulation, rather than prohibition: sites could be licensed away from housing and where the public in general would have access, conditions could deal with the possibility of poor weather or atmospheric conditions and so on. The applicant was, however, hampered perhaps by lack of detailed reference to a scheme of licensing elsewhere among Convention states.

Particularly contentious, however, was evidence from the Ministry of Justice — accepted as relevant by the judge — referring to the 'abhorrence' that would be felt by a large proportion of the population at the idea of the disposal of human remains by funeral pyre, invoking the protection of morals. Cranston J ruled that deference was owed to the view of elected representatives' assessment of public offence.

Prohibition on the basis of offence at the very *idea* of the beliefs or practices of others has a familiar ring to it: indeed, ironically, the common law offence of blasphemy was only abolished in 2008 by Parliament in the UK.⁴⁰ Moreover, the state is not required to be consistent — some other religious practices that a significant proportion of the population may well abhor are legally permitted, including male circumcision and animal ritual slaughter.

The Court of Appeal subsequently found that the litigation had in effect wrongly proceeded on the assumption that a Hindu-compliant funeral pyre could not be licensed under existing legislation.⁴¹ It concluded some structures used for Hindu cremations on funeral pyres *could* both comply with the legal requirement that cremation take place in a building and the applicant's religious requirement that fire was used rather than electricity and that sunlight should be able to shine directly on the dead body: they could therefore be licensed under the *Cremation Act 1902*.⁴²

Nevertheless, the High Court decision in *Ghai* stands alongside those in *Begum* and *Suryanda* in demonstrating the approach to proportionality in relation to article 9

---

³⁹ Similarly, there was no violation of art 8 (respect for private and family life) since cremation on a funeral pyre was necessarily a public act rather than an aspect of private life (*R (on the application of Ghai) v Newcastle CC and the Secretary of State* [2009] EWHC 978, [138]). Moreover, even if art 8 did apply to some aspects of funeral arrangements, any interference was justified. Nor was there a violation of art 14 (discrimination in the enjoyment of Convention rights): the applicant had failed to establish that that the Council's refusal had or the policy had a disproportionate impact on Hindus sharing his beliefs. Even if he had done so, however, the policy was capable of objective and reasonable justification in Cranston J's view (at [151]).

⁴⁰ *Criminal Justice and Immigration Act 2008*, s 79(1).

⁴¹ *R (on the application of Ghai) v Newcastle CC and the Secretary of State* [2010] EWCA Civ 59.

⁴² This decision made it unnecessary, in the Court of Appeal's view, to discuss any of the issues decided at first instance by Cranston J: ibid [40].

by UK courts. Although the results are disappointing, certainly by comparison with the more probing and rigorous analysis by South African or Canadian courts of the need for restrictions on religious liberty,[43] this perhaps exemplifies a more general lightness of touch by judges in the UK. The article 9 cases are by no means unique in this regard.[44]

The problems that religious liberty claimants face in first bringing their claims within the scope of article 9 and in overcoming state claims of the need for restrictions lead naturally to them pursuing alternative legal avenues for these claims — in particular, through use of anti-discrimination law.

By-passing the *Human Rights Act 1998*: Discrimination law

In a sense, the restricted approach to article 9 demonstrated in these decisions creates incentives for claimants to bring their challenges within the ambit of discrimination law, rather than human rights law. The advantages of doing so can be seen by comparing the *Begum* case with the successful outcome for the applicant in a comparable challenge brought by a 14-year-old Sikh school girl of Punjabi-Welsh heritage, to the decision of Aberdare Girls' High School to prevent her from wearing a Kara (a religious bracelet) at her school. In *R (on the application of Watkins-Singh) v Governing Body of Aberdare Girls High School*[45] Silber J found that the decision not to grant a waiver from the school's uniform policy to the claimant to permit her to wear the Kara constituted indirect discrimination on grounds of race under the *Race Relations Act 1976* and on grounds of religion under the *Equality Act 2006*. The judge found that there was objective evidence that the wearing of the Kara was 'regarded universally by observant Sikhs as a matter of exceptional importance and it symbolises their loyalty to the teaching of their Gurus'. In view of this Silber J was satisfied that the school's decision placed an observant Sikh like the applicant under a 'particular disadvantage' or 'detriment' (the test under section 1(1)(1)(A) *Race Relations Act 1976* and section 45 (3) *Equality Act 2006*).

The key issue in satisfying the tests in discrimination law was that she genuinely believed for reasonable grounds that wearing the Kara was a matter of exceptional importance to her racial identity or her religious belief and it could be shown objectively to be of exceptional importance to her religion or race as a Sikh. Moreover, the Kara was unobtrusive (it was 50 millimetres wide and could be worn under long-sleeved garments). Silber J stressed that far from allowing an exception to the school's

---

[43] See, eg, *Prince v President of Law Society of Cape of Good Hope* (2002) SA 794; *Multani v Commission scolaire Marguerite-Bourgeoys* [2006] 1 SCR 256.
[44] Leigh and Masterman, above n 7, ch 6.
[45] [2008] EWHC 1865 (Admin).

policy being regarded as somehow discriminatory against pupils who might want to wear other religious symbols (such as crucifixes), the correct approach was to focus on the specific detriment that this pupil would suffer if not allowed to wear the Kara, which would not affect other pupils without her beliefs.

There is a striking contrast in approach here to the *Begum* and *Playfoot* cases. It is plain that by using discrimination law where it is available a litigant may be able to overcome the stilted approach towards manifestation of religion in the Strasbourg jurisprudence.[46] Whereas the article 9 jurisprudence emphasizes voluntary commitments undertaken by a litigant as a reason for denying that religious liberty is even in issue, religious discrimination law effectively turns the scales by putting a duty to accommodate upon the employer or school.[47]

Conclusion

Overall, it is unclear if the introduction of the *Human Rights Act 1998* in the UK has by itself increased litigiousness concerning religion. The picture is a more complex one.

Paradoxically, religious groups were some of the main opponents when the *Human Rights Act 1998* was progressing through Parliament — fearful for the effect of the Act on religious autonomy. It is perhaps ironic, then, that beleaguered religious groups have increasingly turned to human rights law to defend themselves in the face of more visible secularism and increasing pressures to privatise religion in public and social life. The language of human rights has a general resonance and acceptability

---

[46] There are signs that the European Court of Human Rights is moving away from a wide application of the *Arrowsmith* approach. In *Case of Leyla Sahin v Turkey* (Application no. 44774/98, 10 November 2005) the Grand Chamber of the Court considered the compatibility with art 9 of the prohibition on wearing the Islamic headscarf at Istanbul University and found the ban to be justified under art 9.2. The Court found that it was prescribed by law in pursuit of the legitimate aims of protecting the rights and freedoms of others and maintaining public order, in aiming to preserve the secular character of educational institutions, and was proportionate, thus satisfying art 9.2 (at [98-9]). By contrast, in *Karaduman v Turkey* (1993) 74 DR 93 the (former) Commission found *no interference* with a student's art 9 right because of her voluntary acceptance of the rules applicable in a secular university (at 108).

[47] Some later discrimination rulings, however, in effect 'read down' discrimination legislation in light of the courts' approach to art 9: see esp *Islington London Borough Council v Ladele* [2010] 1 WLR 955, [55-8] (Lord Neuberger MR) (council's refusal to accommodate marriage registrar's religious objections to officiating at same-sex civil partnership ceremonies did not constitute religious discrimination). A challenge to *Ladele* is pending at the European Court of Human Rights.

for beliefs and positions that the media and the liberal political and legal elite often otherwise treat as primitive or even distasteful.

In addition, minority religions that feel alienated or disadvantaged in Britain have also attempted to use the Act to 'level-up' their rights, although arguably tailor-made anti-discrimination legislation is a far more effective tool. It is perhaps significant that a number of the cases discussed in this chapter have concerned questions of manifestation of religious belief by what are admittedly minority groups within a mainstream religion. Such claimants face the inevitable difficulty that their beliefs may appear extreme or unorthodox when compared with the majority of adherents of the religion concerned. There is a clear risk that public bodies committed to religious freedom will consider that they have done sufficiently when they have accommodated mainstream opinion. Courts can be prone to a variation of the same approach in judging the extent to which religious liberty is engaged according to the core or central beliefs of the religion in question, with peripheral views accorded less or no respect.

As with the experience of the *Human Rights Act 1998* generally,[48] few of these claims have been ultimately successful. For the most part, courts using the Act have confirmed existing legal positions, albeit with new reasons. Nevertheless, the effect on public and political discourse has been considerable. Some of these developments are legally questionable or at least inconsistent — the Act has been cited, for example, as justification for the Royal Navy for the decision to provide storage space on board ship for the equipment of a practising Satanist and as the rationale for the *removal* of bibles from some hospital wards. In time, however, a new sensitivity towards religious liberty may indeed take root. If so, something of the revolutionary fervour that greeted the legislation may yet be justified.

---

[48] Leigh and Masterman, above n 7.

13

Judicial Interpretation, Neutrality and the US Bill of Rights

Frank S Ravitch*

Neutrality, whether formal or substantive, does not exist in the context of the religion clauses in the United States Constitution. Others have recognized this.[1] Still others have come part way to this conclusion by suggesting that neutrality is inherently dependant upon the baseline one chooses to use in describing it, and thus it does not exist apart from these baselines.[2] Yet claims of neutrality cannot be proven. There is no independent neutral truth or baseline to which they can be tethered.[3] This is important because it means that any baseline to which we attach neutrality is not

---

* A version of this chapter first appeared as chapter two of Frank S Ravitch, *Masters of Illusion: The Supreme Court and the Religion Clauses* (2007).
[1] See, eg, Steven D Smith, *Foreordained Failure: The Quest for A Constitutional Principle of Religious Freedom* (1995) 96–7 ('*Foreordained Failure*'); Alan E Brownstein, 'Interpreting the Religion Clauses in Terms of Liberty, Equality, and Free Speech Values — A Critical Analysis of "Neutrality Theory" and Charitable Choice' (1999) 13 *Notre Dame Journal of Law Ethics and Public Policy* 243, 246–56; Steven D Smith, 'Symbols, Perceptions, and Doctrinal Illusions: Establishment Neutrality and the "No Endorsement" Test' (1987) 86 *Michigan Law Review* 266, 314 ('Symbols, Perceptions, and Doctrinal Illusions'); Cf John T Valauri, 'The Concept of Neutrality in Establishment Clause Doctrine' (1986) 48 *University of Pittsburgh Law Review* 83, 92.
[2] See, eg, Douglas Laycock, 'Formal, Substantive, and Disaggregated Neutrality Toward Religion' (1990) 39 *DePaul Law Review* 993, 1005; Larry Alexander, 'Liberalism, Religion, and the Unity of Epistemology' (1993) 30 *San Diego Law Review* 763, 793; Michael A Paulsen, 'Religion, Equality, and the Constitution: An Equal Protection Approach to Establishment Clause Adjudication' (1986) 61 *Notre Dame Law Review* 311, 333. Cf Steven D Smith, 'The Restoration of Tolerance' (1990) 78 *California Law Review* 305, 319–24 ('Restoration of Tolerance') (critiquing the argument that neutrality requires a baseline, and rejecting neutrality as an empty ideal).
[3] Smith, *Foreordained Failure*, above n 1; Alexander, above n 2; Paulsen, above n 2; Smith, 'Symbols, Perceptions, and Doctrinal Illusions', above n 1.

neutral, and claims of neutrality built on these baselines are by their nature not neutral. This might seem circular — that is, since there is no independent state of neutrality from which to derive neutral rules or applications of rules, there can be no neutral results and no means by which one can prove a given baseline is neutral. Yet examples, even in US Supreme Court opinions, are readily available.[4] The Court has used varying concepts or baselines of neutrality,[5] and in several cases Justices in the majority and dissenting opinions claimed to be relying on the same or similar principles of neutrality, yet they reached opposite conclusions.[6]

This critique of neutrality applies to both the recent Court's use of formal neutrality (a concept explained further below) and to earlier Courts' substantive neutrality or separation as neutrality approaches (also explained further below). This chapter pays much attention to the concept of formal neutrality that seems most pervasive today, at least in cases involving aid to religious entities or individuals, equal access, and free exercise clause exemptions. As will be seen, the critique of neutrality provided herein applies to any claim that a given approach is 'neutral' in regard to the many highly contested questions arising when government and religion interact in our complex regulatory state. In the end, as with interpretive claims based on hard originalism, neutrality requires value choices that are often masked under the cloak of even-handedness or other mostly rhetorical devices.

Steven Smith has explained:

> the quest for neutrality, despite its understandable appeal and the tenacity with which it has been pursued, is an attempt to grasp at an illusion. Upon reflection, this failure should not be surprising. The impossibility of a truly 'neutral' theory of religious freedom is analogous to the impossibility, recognized by modern philosophers, of finding some outside Archimedean point … from which to look down on and describe reality. Descriptions of reality are always undertaken from a point within reality. In the same way, theories of religious freedom are always offered from the viewpoint of one of the competing positions that generate the need for such a theory; there is no neutral vantage point that can permit the theorist or judge to transcend these competing positions. Hence, insofar as a genuine and satisfactory

---

[4] See generally Frank S Ravitch, 'A Funny Thing Happened on the Way to Neutrality: Broad Principles, Formalism, and the Establishment Clause' (2004) 38 *Georgia Law Review* 489.
[5] Ibid.
[6] See, eg, *Mitchell et al v Helms et al*, 530 US 793, 809–11 (plurality opinion), 877–84 (Souter J, dissenting) (2000) ('*Mitchell*') (plurality relied on formal neutrality, and Justice Souter's dissent rejected formal neutrality in favour of a form of substantive neutrality that is not necessarily decisive); *School District of Abington Tp v Schempp*, 374 US 203, 215, 222–7 (majority), 311–3, 317 (Stewart J, dissenting) (1963) (majority equating separation with neutrality and dissent suggesting that accommodation is consistent with neutrality, but coercion is not).

theory of religious freedom would need to be 'neutral' in this sense, rather than one that privileges one of the competing positions from the outset, a theory of religious freedom is as illusory as the ideal of neutrality it seeks to embody.[7]

Others have also acknowledged the illusive and malleable nature of neutrality.[8] The Court's use of the term until recently was often symbolic — not in the sense that William Marshall's fascinating work has used that term[9] — but rather in the sense that the Court was trying to send a message that it was being balanced in its resolution of the issues that it decided.[10] Of course, despite protestations otherwise, this was not always so. Still, the Court did not use neutrality as the 'be all or end all' concept in actually deciding cases. Rather it had to also rely on other principles because neutrality is so malleable — parasitic, Steven Smith has argued.[11] If there is no such thing as neutrality — or at least neutrality as more than a buzzword — this seems a logical state of affairs. The Court suggests that it is acting neutrally, but can only define this neutrality by reference to other principles (which are not neutral).

The current Court, however, has begun to rely on neutrality more directly.[12] Neutrality is no longer a background principle that the Court sees no need to consistently define. Rather, it is an actuating principle that the Court apparently believes must be given a formalistic definition that can be rigidly applied.[13] As will be seen, the Court connects its formal neutrality with what appear to be arguments for formal equality between religion and 'non-religion'.[14] Yet, the current Court's neutrality is no more neutral than past Courts' neutrality. In fact, because of its formalistic nature it is potentially 'less neutral' — if it is possible to be less than something that does

---

[7] Smith, *Foreordained Failure*, above n 3, 96–7; see also Smith, 'Symbols, Perceptions, and Doctrinal Illusions', above n 1, 314.
[8] See generally Ravitch, above n 4.
[9] William P Marshall, '"We Know It When We See It": The Supreme Court Establishment' (1986) 59 *Southern California Law Review* 495, 504 (advocating an approach that is more focused on the symbolic impact of government action than on government involvement with, and support of, religion).
[10] Of course, while the Court may have been trying to send the message that it was being balanced in its Religion Clause decisions, that message presumed that there is a way to be balanced in such cases, and of course many people disagreed that the Court was balanced. See, eg, Frederick Mark Gedicks, *The Rhetoric of Church and State: A Critical Analysis of Religion Clause Jurisprudence* (1995) 26–7; Stephen M Feldman, *Please Don't Wish Me A Merry Christmas: A Critical History of the Separation of Church and State* (1997).
[11] Smith, 'Symbols, Perceptions, and Doctrinal Illusions', above n 1, 268, 325–31.
[12] *Zelman v Simmons-Harris*, 122 S Ct 2460 (2002) ('*Zelman*'); *Mitchell*, 530 US 793 (2002).
[13] In her concurring opinion in *Mitchell*, Justice O'Connor decried the central role of neutrality in the plurality's approach: *Mitchell*, 530 US 793, 837 (O'Connor J, concurring in the judgment) (2002).
[14] See generally *Zelman*, 122 S Ct 2460 (2002).

not exist — because at least potentially if a government action or inaction meets the Court's definition of neutrality (and the element of individual choice discussed below), pesky things such as the effects of the program need not be considered.[15] This is particularly problematic because the Court does not explain why its formal neutrality is neutral given the competing views of neutrality, and the Court uses terms such as 'entirely neutral'[16] and 'neutral in all respects'.[17] By relying on the term in this direct, yet unsubstantiated, manner the Court gives it extra power.

Not to be outdone, the Justices who reject the Court's formal neutrality have begun strenuously arguing for a return to substantive neutrality,[18] or sometimes to separation as neutrality, as the guiding principle.[19] The battle thus joined, the Justices argue the meaning of neutrality, which as I have suggested is like arguing over the real location of Oz. Neither side is forced to confront in any serious way the interpretive presumptions that inform its chosen neutrality position, although the substantive neutrality wing often openly acknowledge their reliance on separation (without, of course, explaining how separation is in fact neutral). As will be seen, substantive neutrality — at least as envisioned by Douglas Laycock — has something important to lend to this debate, but not because it is neutral.

The current Court's formal neutrality approach requires a law or government policy to be facially neutral in regard to religion.[20] In the aid context there is an additional element to the formal neutrality approach.[21] Any benefit or funding that flows to religious entities must do so as the result of the choices of private individuals.[22] As will be seen below, this approach has not been applied in all aid cases, but to the extent it has been applied, the private choice element may have lost its substantive bite.[23]

The current version of neutrality that has become dominant in the aid, equal access, and free exercise contexts is intensely formalistic and it appears to minimize the

---

[15] *Zelman*, 122 S Ct 2460, 2484–5 (Stevens J, dissenting), 2485–6, 2490–7 (Souter J, dissenting), 2507–8 (Breyer K, dissenting) (2002).
[16] Ibid 2473.
[17] Ibid 2467.
[18] Ibid 2485 (Souter J, dissenting).
[19] Ibid 2484 (Stevens J, dissenting).
[20] *Zelman*, 122 S Ct 2460 (2002).
[21] Ibid.
[22] Ibid 2460.
[23] See Ravitch, above n 4, 513–23; Ira C Lupu and Robert W Tuttle, 'Zelman's Future: Vouchers, Sectarian Providers, and the Next Round of Constitutional Battles' (2003) 78 *Notre Dame Law Review* 917, 938.

effects of government programs and actions.[24] Establishment Clause jurisprudence has traditionally been fact sensitive, but the Court's formal neutrality approach lacks the tools to enable it to deal with the many situations to which it will invariably be applied. The more flexible *Lemon* test[25] was much maligned because of the questionable distinctions drawn by the Court.[26] Thirty years from now the Court's apparent move toward a formal neutrality test might be viewed in the same way. Formalism does not necessarily beget clarity. In the end, when the issues that arise are complex and fact-specific the more formalistic the test the less clarity it will likely bring in the long-run, either because it must be contorted to fit the diversity of situations to which it will be applied or because it will ignore context and function somewhat like a bull in a china shop.

The Court's formal neutrality approach reminds me of a quotation from Professor Philip Kurland's classic 1961 article, 'Of Church and State and the Supreme Court',[27] which has influenced the Court's formal neutrality approach. In describing a 'neutral principle' that would 'give the most appropriate scope to the Religion Clauses', Kurland explained:[28]

> This 'neutral principle' has been framed in reliance on the Aristotelian axiom that 'it is the mark of an educated man to seek precision in each class of things just so far as the nature of the subject admits,' rather than the Platonic precept that 'a perfectly simple principle can never be applied to a state of things which is the reverse of simple.'[29]

While it may at first seem an odd thing for a legal academic to state, I am inclined to favour the Platonic precept over the Aristotelian axiom upon which Professor Kurland relied, at least when it comes to formal neutrality. The vast web of factual scenarios involved in funding cases and equal access cases — situations where the Court has already and clearly applied formal neutrality — is indeed the reverse of simple, and formal neutrality is an intensely simple concept (although in no way

---

[24] *Zelman*, 122 S Ct 2460 (2002); Steven K Green, 'The Illusionary Aspect of "Private Choice" for Constitutional Analysis' (2002) 38 *Willamette Law Review* 549.

[25] See *Lemon v Kurtzman*, 403 US 602, 612–3 (1971) (setting forth test is based on earlier cases that required that government action have a secular purpose, a primary effect that neither advances nor inhibits religion, and does not cause excessive entanglement between government and religion).

[26] Michael W McConnell, 'Religious Freedom at a Crossroads' (1992) 59 *University of Chicago Law Review* 115, 127–34; Michael Stokes Paulsen, 'Lemon is Dead' (1993) 43 *Case Western Reserve Law Review* 795, 800–13.

[27] Philip B Kurland, 'Of Church and State and the Supreme Court' (1961) 29 *University of Chicago Law Review* 1.

[28] Ibid 2.

[29] Ibid.

perfect). While Professor Kurland may have advocated a version of formal neutrality, it is unlikely he was advocating the kind of acontextual neutrality toward which the Court has been headed.

Lurking underneath the Court's formal neutrality is the notion that religion has no special status, and thus there is no need to differentiate between religion and non-religion if the government is acting 'neutrally'.[30] A corollary to this notion is the argument that by treating religion differently one is being hostile to religion. Thus, it is discrimination and hostility to religion if religious organizations are not given access to the same benefits as secular organizations,[31] and at the same time there is nothing wrong with failing to provide religious exemptions to 'generally applicable' laws even if those laws interfere with core religious practices.[32] There would be significant problems with the Court's implicit presumptions even if neutrality were a real and attainable concept, but if neutrality is nothing more than an empty construction[33] then the Court's other presumptions are even more problematic.

To understand the Rehnquist Court's notion of neutrality it is useful to explore several of the cases where the Court has used neutrality analysis in varying contexts. Thus, this chapter looks at three cases to see the formal neutrality doctrine in action: *Zelman v Simmons-Harris*,[34] *Good News Club v Milford Central School*,[35] and *Employment Division v Smith*.[36] These cases each represent a major area where the Court has used a version of its neutrality concept, *Zelman* in the government aid to religious schools context,[37] *Good News Club* in the context of equal access to government facilities by religious groups,[38] and *Smith* in the context of exemptions to 'generally applicable' laws under the Free Exercise Clause.[39] Before analyzing these cases, however, it is useful to further answer the question what is neutrality, or at least what does it pretend to be?

The answer to the question — 'What is neutrality?' — is central to the discussion of neutrality's place in religion clause jurisprudence. Thus, the answer that neutrality, at

---

[30] *Zelman*, 122 S Ct 2460, 2467–8 (2002); *Mitchell*, 530 US 793 826–9 (plurality opinion) (2002); Cf *Good News Club v Milford Central School*, 533 US 98, 110–12, 114) (2001) ('*Good News Club*') (addressing viewpoint discrimination).

[31] *Good News Club*, 533 US 98, 118–20 (2001); *Mitchell*, 530 US 793, 826–9 (plurality opinion) (2002).

[32] *Employment Division v Smith*, 494 US 872 (1990) ('*Smith*').

[33] See Ravitch, above n 4, 498–523, 531–44.

[34] 122 S Ct 2460 (2002).

[35] 533 US 98 (2001).

[36] 494 US 872 (1990).

[37] *Zelman*, 122 S Ct 2460 (2002).

[38] *Good News Club*, 533 US 98 (2001).

[39] *Smith*, 494 US 872 (1990).

least in the religion clause context, is a myth, may seem wholly unsatisfying. Yet can there be some use for a concept that is impossible to achieve? Neutrality is nothing more than a variable social construction, and formal neutrality nothing more than a rigid judicial construction. Each relies on a baseline that is not provably neutral, but each has a value because people take solace in the notion of neutrality.[40] Even if objectivity does not exist in contested spaces, there may be value in the perception of objectivity.[41]

This sounds a bit odd at first, but it actually tracks much of what the pre-Rehnquist Court did with the concept of neutrality. Neutrality was mentioned quite a bit in numerous contexts — sometimes the Court used a vague adjective to describe it such as 'benevolent neutrality'.[42] Yet the Court never relied exclusively on the principle, supplementing it with separationism or accommodationism.[43] For those who did not dig too deeply there was always the reassuring tone of neutrality. For those who did dig, it was apparent that the Court could not substantiate its claim to neutrality, but the Court had the other principles to fall back on and one could support or attack those other principles without focusing on whether they were neutral in application or effect.[44] It would not be a reach to read some of these cases and perceive that the Court was essentially saying, 'we are following a separationist principle or an accommodationist principle that we think is more neutral than the alternatives in this context, but neutrality is only the lofty object of the religion clauses, not something we can prove with absolute certainty'.

I do not defend the earlier Courts' use of the term. It was in a sense false advertising, because there is no way to prove that separationism or accommodationism is inherently more neutral than other principles.[45] Yet the implicit message that was at least potentially infused in these earlier decisions — that is, we know that neutrality is

---

[40] Laycock, above n 2, 998; Smith, 'Symbols, Perceptions, and Doctrinal Illusions', above n 1, 313, 329, 331.
[41] Cf Frank S Ravitch, 'Can an Old Dog Learn New Tricks? A Nonfoundationalist Analysis of Richard Posner's The Problematics of Moral and Legal Theory' (2001–02) 37 *Tulsa Law Review* 967, 971 (legal scholarship symposium) ('the social belief in "natural" rights might be useful in a given context, even if they are not objectively natural and are actually contingent on context').
[42] *Walz v. Tax Commission of City of New York*, 397 US 664, 669 (1970).
[43] Douglas Laycock, 'The Underlying Unity of Separation and Neutrality' (1997) 46 *Emory Law Journal* 43 (separation); Michael W McConnell, 'Accommodation of Religion' (1985) *Supreme Court Review* 1, 3–6 (accommodation).
[44] Smith, 'Symbols, Perceptions, and Doctrinal Illusions', above n 1 (suggesting that it would be impossible to prove neutrality so the other principles could not be accurately defined by the neutrality ideal).
[45] It is possible that concepts such as separation and accommodation might serve as baselines for neutrality, which requires the setting of baselines — see Laycock, above n 2, 996, 998, 1004–5 — but there is no place from which one can prove that any such baseline is neutral: Smith, *Foreordained Failure*, above n 1, 96–7.

just a lofty principle and we are only using it to describe the outcome in this case *vis à vis* the alternatives — is less troubling than claims that both the mode of analysis and the results *are* neutral, and that the alternatives are not. The latter is the message of the formal neutrality approach. The current Court has converted neutrality from a lofty, albeit impossible, goal to both the means and ends of religion clause analysis.[46]

The Court's struggle with neutrality over the years reminds me of a conversation I had with my older daughter a few years ago when she was five years old and excited after realizing that her tooth was loose and would soon fall out. She realized that I might be the 'tooth fairy', and asked if the tooth fairy was real or if I was the tooth fairy. I responded that the tooth fairy would leave her a present when she lost her tooth, not wanting to burst her bubble or lie. She responded that she knew I was the tooth fairy but that she wanted the tooth fairy to visit and leave her a present anyway.

This is akin to the struggle for neutrality. Like the tooth fairy, neutrality is just a myth, but like children who want the tooth fairy to visit, we want it to be real or at least for something to stand-in for it to make us believe it is real. Unlike my five-year-old daughter, however, the Rehnquist Court has strenuously argued in essence that the tooth fairy is real, and when confronted with the question of why, the answer seems to be 'because we said so'. The nuance of the stand-in concept — neutrality not as a real thing but a lofty principle that we try to emulate — seems lost.

Of course, even though neutrality as a lofty principle is less problematic than formal neutrality because it is not used to reach or empower outcomes, it is no more neutral. Moreover, in two contexts it has been used to, or argued to, empower results. These two contexts are substantive neutrality and separation as neutrality. As will be seen, one conception of substantive neutrality has some merit, but not because of the neutrality claim. This conception of neutrality is far more nuanced and sophisticated than other neutrality claims. It recognizes that there is no agreement about what neutrality is. I am referring to Douglas Laycock's construction of substantive neutrality.[47] Laycock is not alone in arguing for substantive neutrality. Scholars,[48] as well as Justices of the Supreme Court,[49] have argued for some form of substantive neutrality. Laycock,

---

[46] See *Zelman*, 122 S Ct 2460 (2002).

[47] Laycock, above n 2, 1001–6; Laycock, above n 43, 68–73.

[48] Hugh J Breyer, 'Laycock's Substantive Neutrality and Nuechterlein's Free exercise Test: Implications of Their Convergence for the Religion Clauses' (1994) 10 *Journal of Law and Religion* 467; Stephen V Monsma (2000) 'Substantive Neutrality as a Basis for Free Exercise: No Establishment Common Ground' 42 *Journal of Church and State* 13.

[49] Perhaps the most eloquent plea for substantive neutrality in recent years has come from Justice Souter: see *Zelman*, 122 S Ct 2460, 2490–92 (2002); *Mitchell*, 530 US 7, 877–84 (2002); Liza Weiman Hanks, 'Note: Justice Souter: Defining "Substantive Neutrality" in an Age of Religious Politics' (1996) 48 *Stanford Law Review* 903.

however, provides the best and most succinct conception of substantive neutrality. His substantive neutrality has a lot to recommend it. In fact, it has had a strong influence on the facilitation approach I propose in *Masters of Illusion: The Supreme Court and the Religion Clauses* referenced earlier in this chapter. Still, as I hope to show, substantive neutrality may have a lot of substantive value, but no neutrality.[50] This might seem a bit nit-picky since the approach has a lot to offer, but while Laycock may have made a wise choice among potential baselines, his choice and the resulting baseline are no more provably neutral than the Court's formal neutrality.[51]

The following quote reflects Laycock's formulation of substantive neutrality:

> My basic formulation of substantive neutrality is this: the religion clauses require government to minimize the extent to which it either encourages or discourages belief or disbelief, practice or nonpractice, observance or nonobservance. If I have to stand or fall on a single formulation of neutrality, I will stand or fall on that one. But I must elaborate on what I mean by minimizing encouragement or discouragement. I mean that religion is to be left as wholly to private choice as anything can be. It should proceed as unaffected by government as possible. Government should not interfere with our beliefs about religion either by coercion or by persuasion. Religion may flourish or whither; it may change or stay the same. What happens to religion is up to the people acting severally and voluntarily; it is not up to the people acting collectively through government.[52]

Laycock suggests that neutrality depends on the baseline one sets in defining it, and that there are varying baselines.[53] The baseline approach, however, is problematic because there is no super-baseline to determine whether a given baseline is neutral.[54] Yet the very term neutrality asserts an epistemic (in the sense that it suggests some theory or way to know something is neutral) and arguably a teleological claim. A given baseline might be a useful paradigm for Establishment Clause jurisprudence,

---

[50] This is not because of any flaw in Professor Laycock's reasoning, but rather a result of the epistemological claim inherent in any concept of neutrality: see Smith, *Foreordained Failure*, above n 1, 96–7. Laycock recognizes the epistemic problem with claims to neutrality and addresses the concern by pointing out that neutrality is a function of the baseline one sets for the concept: Laycock, above n 2, 994, 996, 1004–5. Yet, without some way to determine if a given baseline is neutral, the setting of such a baseline cannot make a concept neutral: Smith, 'Restoration of Tolerance', above n 2, 319–24.
[51] Smith, 'Restoration of Tolerance', above n 2, 319–24.
[52] Laycock, above n 2, 1001–2.
[53] Ibid 994, 996, 1004–05.
[54] Cf Thomas S Kuhn, *The Structure of Scientific Revolutions* (1996) (discussing paradigms in the sciences, and asserting that there is no super-paradigm to decide between conflicting paradigms).

but unless one can demonstrate the neutrality of the baseline itself, the baseline cannot support claims of neutrality.[55]

The *Zelman* case is a good example through which to view this. If the Court had held that vouchers are unconstitutional when given for attendance at religious schools, but that districts can maintain vouchers for secular private schools and of course can maintain the secularized public schools without any voucher program, would the result encourage secularism? Would such a limitation advance private choice or would it place burdens only on the private choice of religious individuals because they must choose between a secular education free of charge and their values?[56] Yet, under the Court's holding which allows vouchers to be used at religious schools, there is a powerful argument that religion, and particularly more dominant and well-funded religions, will benefit from an infusion of government funds,[57] and that private choice will be skewed toward sending one's children to schools with whose faith mission one disagrees simply to keep them on a level playing field with other children in the area who may face no such conflict.[58]

Which of these options is neutral? Which encourages or discourages religion the most? These are actually two very different questions. The first is unanswerable in any objective way unless one has a magic key to demonstrate that a contested account of neutrality is actually neutral. Yet the second question is answerable, even if it is not precisely so. More importantly, even though the answer may be contestable, the contestability of the answer is more open to debate when it is not appended to the concept of neutrality. The answer must be debated on its merits, without regard to the unprovable claim that it is neutral,[59] and thus neutrality should have no power in the interpretive process. As Steven Smith has implied, calling a result neutral adds nothing of value to an argument.[60] I would add that doing so may obfuscate the nature and value of other principles that undergird an argument, or may unnecessarily prop those principles up.

---

[55] Smith, 'Restoration of Tolerance', above n 2, 319–24.

[56] This Hobson's choice may be reflective of a larger issue, namely, the possibility that cultural, legal, and political currents favour secularism and may place religious adherents at a disadvantage by inducing them to take part in the dominant secularized culture at the expense of their deeply held religious convictions: see Stephen L Carter, *The Culture of Disbelief: How American Law and Politics Trivialize Religious Devotion* (1993).

[57] See *Zelman*, 122 S Ct 2460, 2484 (Stevens J, dissenting), 2485 (Souter J, dissenting) (2002); Steven K Green, 'Of (Un)equal Jurisprudential Pedigree, Rectifying the Imbalance Between Neutrality and Separationism' (2002) 43 *Boston College Law Review* 1111.

[58] *Zelman*, 122 S Ct 2460, 2494–7 (2002).

[59] Smith, *Foreordained Failure*, above n 1, 96–7; Smith, 'Symbols, Perceptions, and Doctrinal Illusions', above n 1, 314.

[60] Smith, 'Symbols, Perceptions, and Doctrinal Illusions', above n 1, 268, 325–31.

Yet, as will be seen, this does not destroy the force of Laycock's principle.[61] Significantly, the fact that divorcing Laycock's substantive principle of religion clause jurisprudence from neutrality does not undermine that principle demonstrates the lack of import the neutrality concept has. As between formal neutrality and substantive neutrality, substantive neutrality is the better option, not because it is more neutral — neither option is neutral — but because it is still useful even when divorced from its neutrality claim. The Court's formal neutrality hinges too much on neutrality as a real concept, or at least on formal equality as neutrality,[62] and while a more sophisticated and consistently applied version of the equality principle could have independent value,[63] the formal equality as formal neutrality version has little to offer since its claim to neutrality (and its implicit claim of equality) cannot be proven.

Separation as neutrality is another concept of neutrality that has at times been linked to substantive neutrality. The separation as neutrality approach was used in early cases such as *Everson*, *McCollum* and *Schempp*, and is currently favoured by a minority of Justices.[64] Of course, it is no more neutral than formal or substantive neutrality. Consider both arguments in *Everson*.[65] The majority held that funding the transportation of students to parochial schools did not violate the separation principle because it simply demonstrated neutrality between religion and non-religion.[66] The dissenting opinions argued that neutrality mandated a separationist outcome, and thus the funding was unconstitutional.[67]

Assume the funding is constitutional as the Majority held. How is it neutral? Putting aside for the moment that as Justice Jackson pointed out in his dissenting opinion the funding only went to Catholic school students and not to other parochial or secular private school students,[68] the bulk of the funds going into private hands for

---

[61] See Ravitch, above n 4, 544–58.
[62] See generally *Zelman*, 122 S Ct 2460 (2002).
[63] See Christopher L Eisgruber and Lawrence G Sager, 'Equal Regard' in Stephen M Feldman (ed), *Law and Religion: A Critical Anthology* (2000); Cf Alan E Brownstein, 'Interpreting the Religion Clauses in Terms of Liberty, Equality, and Free Speech Values — A Critical Analysis of "Neutrality Theory" and Charitable Choice' (1999) 13 *Notre Dame Journal of Ethics and Public Policy* 243, 246.
[64] *Everson v Board of Education*, 330 US 1 (1947) ('*Everson*'); *State of Illinois ex rel McCollum v Board of Education*, 333 US 203 (1948); *School District of Abington Tp v Schempp*, 374 US 203, 215, 222–27 (1963). The most prominent proponent of separation as neutrality is Justice Stevens: See *Van Orden v Perry*, 125 S Ct 2854, 2882–8 (Stevens J, dissenting) (2005). Moreover, Justice Souter's substantive neutrality approach seems to reflect the separation as neutrality principle, although not by itself: *Zelman*, 122 S Ct 2460, 2485 (Souter J, dissenting) (2002).
[65] See generally *Everson*, 330 US 1 (1947).
[66] Ibid.
[67] Ibid 19 (Jackson J, dissenting), 29 (Rutledge J, dissenting).
[68] Ibid 20–1 (Jackson J, dissenting).

transportation will go to those attending religious schools. The Court noted that parochial schools were the primary venues for private school students in that area and even if the program allowed transportation funding to all private schools,[69] the denominations with the largest number of schools would receive the largest benefit.

The reasons the Court gave for upholding the program, save one, make some sense. That one — that the funding regime and its practical outcome are neutral — is simply not true. The funding could provide additional encouragement for families to send their kids to private school, and especially to parochial schools, which were the largest constituency of private schools in Ewing Township. Admittedly, this is not a huge windfall for religion, and in fact, it would be allowed under the facilitation test that I have proposed, which considers whether government has substantially facilitated or discriminated against religion, but speaking of neutrality simply covers over the real world impact of such a funding regime given religious and private school demographics.

The dissents' position, however, would be no more neutral, because to deny funding under the facts in the case would give added encouragement to send one's children to the public schools. For those who chose not to do so because of their religious convictions, the denial of funding would add an additional cost (in addition to property taxes to support the public schools and parochial school tuition) not borne by those who decide to send their children to the secularized world of the public schools. This *may* be justifiable under the separation principle, but it would end up discouraging religion. Neutrality talk adds nothing to the analysis except perhaps a rhetorical justification (as it did for the majority).

Issues surrounding government interaction with religious entities have become increasingly complex as over the last hundred years or so government, both state and federal, has grown and become involved in many areas of life where there was traditionally little or no government participation or regulation.[70] It is hard for government to act 'neutrally' when its actions or failure to act in the same situation can have massive repercussions.[71] This creates problems for any 'neutrality' test that must be applied to this massive web of government action and inaction. At the theoretical level, such a test can make no absolute claim to neutrality because there

---

[69] *Everson*, 330 US 1, 4–6, 16–8 (1947).

[70] Carl H Esbeck, 'The Establishment Clause as a Structural Restraint on Governmental Power' (1998) 84 *Iowa Law Review* 1; Noah Feldman, 'From Liberty to Equality: The Transformation of the Establishment Clause' (2002) 90 *California Law Review* 673, 679–80; Ira C Lupu, 'The Lingering Death of Separationism' (1994) 62 *George Washington Law Review* 230; McConnell, above n 43, 14, 23–4.

[71] Smith, 'Symbols, Perceptions, and Doctrinal Illusions', above n 1, 329–31. This is also reflected in the differences between the majority and dissenting opinions in *Zelman*: see *Zelman*, 122 S Ct 2460 (2002).

is no principle of super-neutrality that can be used to demonstrate its neutrality, and thus contested perspectives necessarily enter the process of developing such a test.[72] It would solve the problem if one could prove neutrality by looking at the effects of a court's approach, but as the above examples demonstrate this is impossible to do without presuming that a certain baseline is neutral and using the presumed baseline to justify the neutrality of outcomes.[73]

Take another example: a creation science advocate applies to the National Science Foundation (NSF) for a grant.[74] To make this hypothetical even more interesting, let us assume that the creation scientist is not an advocate of 'intelligent design theory', which makes a greater attempt to assume the mantle of mainstream science,[75] but is a traditional advocate of creation science. Moreover, the creation scientist is applying on behalf of a creation science centre, and not a specific church or religious organization, and the centre has no direct connection to any religious entity. The applicant and his team all have PhDs in biology or chemistry, some from evangelical universities. Their proposed project consists of proving that spontaneous evolution in lower organisms proves that evolution could have happened in a much shorter period of time than is currently accepted, and that it is limited to certain organisms. They argue that the period of time would be between six and seven thousand years, and that humans are not among the organisms that have evolved. In fact, they suggest Australopithecus, Homo erectus, and Homo habilis were all simply spontaneous mutations from great ape species that never took hold and died out.

The NSF rejects their proposal because the creation scientists have not supported their hypothesis with adequate testable data. The scientists sue, claiming that NSF's decision demonstrates hostility to religion in a program open to secular scientific debate and that NSF undervalued their empirical data. How do we address this situation based on formal and substantive neutrality?

The natural answer is to say that the scientists were not qualified to participate in the program because they were unwilling or unable to produce adequate scientifically acceptable data to support their hypothesis and their hypothesis was unscientific,

---

[72] Cf Kuhn, above n 54 (making similar argument about the lack of a super paradigm in the sciences that would allow one to select between various contested scientific paradigms).
[73] Laycock, above n 2, 994, 996, 1004–5.
[74] The idea for the NSF hypothetical was sparked by the implications of *Zelman* in combination with *Witters v Washington Department of Services for the Blind*, 474 US 481 (1986) ('*Witters*') and *Zobrest v Catalina Foothills School District*, 509 US 1 (1993) ('*Zobrest*') in regard to a statement made in Dhananjai Shivakumar, 'Neutrality and the Religion Clauses' (1998) 33 *Harvard Civil Rights — Civil Liberties Law Review* 505, 544.
[75] For an excellent discussion of the relationship, and differences, between creationism and intelligent design theory, see Robert T Pennock, *Tower of Babel: The Evidence Against the New Creationism* (1999).

yet the program from which they sought funding was a scientific program. This is of little help, however, because the creation scientists can simply charge that the whole selection process, including the reliance on secular scientific 'theories' and 'adequate scientific' data, is biased against faith-affected approaches, which are put at a disadvantage because they can not compete for funding on an equal basis even if they engage in some empirical research. They would assert that the NSF's definition of science as requiring use of the scientific method is not neutral as between religion and irreligion.

Based on the formal neutrality approach it would appear that the program discriminates against faith-based entities,[76] or at the very least against faith-based 'scientific' viewpoints trying to compete with secular scientific theories in the marketplace of ideas.[77] To the extent it requires applicants to adhere to the scientific method preferred by secular science, it is not neutral as between religion and secularism. It prefers secular hypothesis and methods over religiously derived hypothesis, even when the 'religious scientists' engage in some empirical research.

Perhaps the most obvious argument in NSF's favour would be that in this case, government is funding the research through a competitive process and on its own behalf, and by analogy to the free speech cases, government can 'selectively fund a program to encourage activities that it believes are in the public interest'.[78] The problem with the competitive process aspect of this argument is that the creation scientists are in essence arguing that the process is only competitive for those holding secular scientific views. It would be as if the NEA in *Nat'l Endowment for the Arts v Finley*[79] had said it would only allow artists to compete if their styles were influenced by secular art or artists. The problem with the government as speaker aspect of the argument is that the government does not necessarily endorse all the scientific research that arises from NSF grants, and indeed it seems to be creating a 'funding forum' for the exploration of scientific ideas (thus it might be a designated public forum open to 'scientists'). This might make the situation more like that in *Rosenberger*

---

[76] *Zelman*, 122 S Ct 2460 (2002); *Good News Club*, Good News Club, 533 US 98, 117–20 (2001); *Mitchell*, 530 US 793 (2002); *Zobrest* 509 US 1 (1993); see also *Davey v Locke*, 299 F.3d 748 (9th Cir 2002) ('*Davey*') (denial of funding to student wishing to pursue theology degree under broad funding program violates Free Exercise Clause and state interest in not funding religious instruction is not compelling after *Zelman*).

[77] *Good News Club*, 533 US 98, 117–20 (2001); *Rosenberger v Rector and Visitors of the University of Virginia*, 515 US 819, 835–7, 839, 842–6 (1995) ('*Rosenberger*').

[78] *Davey* 299 F.3d 748, 752 (9th Cir 2002); see also *National Endowment for the Arts v Finley*, 524 US 569 (1998); *Rust v Sullivan*, 500 US 173 (1999); *Regan v Taxation With Representation*, 461 US 540 (1983).

[79] 524 US 569 (1998).

v Rector and Visitors of the Univ. of Va.,[80] where the University of Virginia's system for funding student organizations was deemed a limited public forum,[81] although the competitive nature of NSF funding could still be a distinguishing factor. It is, of course, quite possible that a court would analyse the situation presented in this hypothetical under *Finley* or the government speech cases, but let us presume for the moment that as in *Rosenberger* it does not, and the applicable analysis is the Court's neutrality analysis. Would a decision favouring the creation scientists be neutral?

The answer to this question must be separated from the question of whether it would be good policy or good science. After all, neutrality, like objectivity, makes a universal claim that cannot be addressed based on one's policy preferences. One could argue that allowing creation scientists access to NSF funding is not neutral, because it gives religion a preferred status over other scientific theories that are not in the scientific mainstream. This begs the question for the other side, which could argue that not including religiously affected theories would give secularism and secular science preferred status and benefits over religiously affected theories.[82] The claim that the latter theories are not scientific or that the evaluators who make the scientific decisions reject those theories as unscientific is inadequate to address this concern under formal neutrality, because the creation scientists can argue that they included empirical data in their proposal and that the NSF policies and definition of science are hostile to religiously affected theories, and therefore the denial of funding puts those accounts at a disadvantage when compared to the secular scientific accounts.

Moreover, once this argument is made, other religious groups — for example a UFO cult that believes humans were placed here by aliens from the planet Zermac — would also be able to challenge the use of secular scientific standards in the NSF selection process. To avoid discriminating against religion by favouring secular scientific standards in a government funded program open to private applicants, the

---

[80] 515 US 819 (1995).
[81] Ibid.
[82] *Zelman*, 122 S Ct 2460 (2002) leaves this possibility open, especially when one considers it in connection with cases that have found programs that exclude religiously affected beneficiaries from government funds based on their religious perspectives to be unconstitutional. See *Rosenberger*, 515 US 819 (1995); *Davey*, 299 F.3d 748 (9th Cir 2002). The fact that the program in question is a scientific program does not alter this under a formal neutrality/exclusion as hostility to religion approach, because scientific standards are simply one perspective under such an approach, and the exclusion of religious voices from the marketplace of ideas because they do not meet the secular standards would seemingly violate the formal neutrality approach. The fact that many in the secular community see the exclusion of such voices as obvious could be used to prove the point that religious views have been skewed out of the debate by massive government funding supporting the secular scientific view. The notion that the secular community may view a situation as obvious and fair, while a religious community may see discrimination and hostility in the same situation is not new: see, eg, Gedicks, above n 10, 26–7.

only neutral process for selection among those willing to include empirical data in their proposals might be a first-come, first-served system or a lottery system. The creation science scenario is not a huge leap under the Court's formal neutrality approach.[83]

How would the creation scientist fare under a substantive neutrality approach? One could argue that giving government funds to creation scientists certainly encourages religion, both because of the financial aid and because of the credibility that NSF funding might lend to creation scientists. One could also argue, however, that by funding only secular scientific theories government increases the ability of secular science to replace religion-based theories, and puts religion at a competitive disadvantage in the marketplace of ideas. Laycock foresaw this tension between secular programs and religion, and recognized a caveat to his substantive neutrality approach, namely, that government is not encouraging or discouraging religion by funding secular social activities.[84] I do not disagree with his caveat, but with or without the caveat his substantive principles are not neutral. Either side could argue the result is not neutral if the other side wins. Thus, whatever the independent merits of the substantive neutrality approach, the term 'neutrality' is a misnomer.

While Laycock's theory is highly useful in the religion clause context, the Court has unfortunately chosen to pursue the formal neutrality approach in regard to a number of issues. I now consider some of these issues by exploring three landmark cases, each applying a version of the formal neutrality approach.

Zelman v Simmons-Harris

Zelman is a significant case for several reasons. It is the first US Supreme Court case to uphold a government-funded educational voucher program, and thus it is quite significant from the education policy perspective as well as the law and religion perspective. Additionally, a majority of the Court affirmed the use of formal neutrality, holding that if a program is neutral on its face and functions through

---

[83] See Ravitch, above n 4, 513–28. *Rosenberger*, 515 US 819 (1995) and *Davey*, 299 F.3d 748 (9th Cir 2002) demonstrate that exclusion of religious viewpoints from a general program of funding violates the Constitution. Add to this *Zelman*, 122 S Ct 2460 (2002) and *Good News Club*, 533 US 98 (2001), which would apparently allow access by religious groups to almost any government program or forum that is neutral on its face — see Ravitch, above n 4, 513–23 — and it appears that religious entities and individuals have the potential right to access broad ranging government programs and will be able to claim that exclusion is hostile to religion and unnecessary under the Establishment Clause if they are excluded based on their religious viewpoints or government preference for secular viewpoints.

[84] Laycock, above n 2, 1003.

'true private choice' then it is constitutional.[85] Finally, while the majority opinion purports to consider whether private individuals who channel the government money to religious schools had real choices, the opinion expands the pool of 'choices' to include public magnet and charter schools, leaving open the possibility that the comparison group could be further expanded to include all public schools, at least in districts that have open enrolment or public school choice programs.[86]

The *Zelman* Court ostensibly followed the *Lemon* test as modified in *Agostini*.[87] The Court first held that *Zelman* did not present a secular purpose issue, because the goal of providing a better education to students in the Cleveland School District was an adequate secular purpose[88] — indeed, at least in government aid and equal access cases, it is hard to imagine a situation where there would not be an adequate secular purpose. Thus, the case centred on the effects of the program,[89] as have several other funding cases.[90]

Yet there is a significant catch. The two factors that determine whether an indirect aid program meets the *Zelman* test are that the program must be neutral on its face and the money must flow through individuals who have 'true individual choice' regarding where to direct the aid.[91] If a program is neutral on its face between religious and non-religious entities it is highly unlikely it would ever fail the secular purpose test, nor is there a significant distinction between direct and indirect aid, since so long as the government entity drafting the program relates the aid that flows to religious institutions to the number of individuals who choose to use the private service it does not matter whether the government writes the check directly to the religious institution.[92] It is not a stretch to say that at least in cases of government aid to religious institutions the test is one of facial neutrality plus a private 'circuit breaker' — that is, the money ostensibly flows to the religious institution because of the choices of private individuals.[93] Significantly, the 'circuit breaker' element is connected to the Court's broader neutrality analysis. It is the private individual 'choice' that makes a facially neutral program 'entirely neutral'.[94]

---

[85] *Zelman*, 122 S Ct 2460, 2466–8, 2473, 4476–7 (O'Connor J, concurring) (2002).
[86] Ibid 2491 (Souter J, dissenting).
[87] Ibid 2465–6, 2476 (O'Connor J, concurring).
[88] Ibid 2465.
[89] Ibid.
[90] This is especially true since the Court rolled the entanglement prong of the *Lemon* test into the effects prong: See *Agostini v Felton*, 521 US 203 (1997).
[91] *Zelman*, 122 S Ct 2460, 2467, 2473 (2002).
[92] *Mitchell*, 530 US 793, 816 (plurality opinion) (2002).
[93] Ibid; *Zelman*, 122 S Ct 2460, 2467–8 (2002).
[94] *Zelman*, 122 S Ct 2460, 2473 (2002).

This begs the question, however, about what constitutes 'true private choice' under the Court's analysis. The Court's answer to this question is significant, because it involved a statistical slight of hand that could potentially make all public schools the relevant comparison group to religious schools for purposes of government aid programs. This would be so even in areas with no secular private schools or where such private schools cannot afford to take voucher students, so long as secular private schools would be included in the program if they existed.[95] This makes the Court's new test an exercise in almost pure formalism.[96] If a program is neutral on its face — it does not specify religious entities as beneficiaries — and there is some government or non-religious private entity that the recipients could conceivably choose to go to for service, the test is met because the program is neutral on its face and provides 'true private choice',[97] even if virtually all funding going to private organizations goes to religious organizations.[98]

If this really was neutral, and neutrality was an appropriate actuating principle under the Establishment Clause,[99] the Court's approach would be perfectly acceptable. Conversely, if the Court's approach is not neutral, calling it neutral should give it no further power and it should be adequately supported by some other principle. In fact, if it is not neutral, having the Court pronounce its neutrality is especially dangerous because the Court would simply be placing the label of neutrality on analysis that is neither neutral nor likely to lead to 'neutral' results and using the label to validate its approach. The Court could call its undergirding principle 'Ralph' and it would have the same descriptive accuracy.[100] In fact, Ralph might be more descriptively accurate because one would still have to determine what the essence of Ralphness is, and the nature of the term does not suggest that it has any extra power or reality until defined.

---

[95] Ibid 2491 (Souter J, dissenting).
[96] Ibid 2486 ('verbal formalism').
[97] Ibid 2473 (using term 'true private choice').
[98] Ibid 2491–3 (Souter J, dissenting).
[99] See Ravitch, above n 4, 502–13 (suggesting that neutrality is not appropriate as a central actuating principle under the Establishment Clause).
[100] I am reminded of Alfred Kahn's famous juxtaposition of the term 'recession' with the word 'banana' (he later used 'Kumquat') after President Carter had asked advisors not to use the term 'recession' (Kahn was a member of the Carter administration): Peter Carlson, 'Yes, We Have No Banana', *Newark Star-Ledger* (Newark), 11 February 2001, 1. Of course, the distinction between that brilliant and comical juxtaposition and the one suggested herein (aside from the latter not being brilliant) is that there was at least some 'objective' definition of the term recession that economists agree upon, levels in certain economic indicators that mean we are in a recession: William Neikirk, 'Economy Remains Largely Stagnant, Jobless Rate Up as Payrolls Show Second Straight Dip', *Chicago Tribune* (Chicago), 1 November 2002, 1.

This might seem tongue-in-cheek, and it is to a point, but it demonstrates the serious problems with claims to neutrality. Since there is no neutral foundation or baseline that can be used to prove that something is 'truly' neutral, neutrality is nothing more than a buzzword and a dangerous one at that, because it implies that the supposedly neutral approach should be taken more seriously because it is actually neutral.[101] Legal tests and definitions of neutrality do not make an approach neutral — they are simply tests or definitions and neutrality is nothing but extra baggage.[102] As I explained above, this does not mean that conceptions of neutrality — such as Laycock's substantive neutrality[103] — are not useful tools, but it does mean that they are not neutral and should gain no additional validity from the use of that term.[104]

This suggests that the Court's formal neutrality approach is especially dangerous, because the formalistic approach leaves little room for introspection, and its very nature makes it less likely to account for nuances or context. Supporting such a rigid regime with a concept that cannot be proven is particularly dangerous, since once the formalistic test controls outcomes there will be little opportunity to adapt to varied circumstances without sacrificing the clarity such formalistic tests are intended to create. Thus, courts applying the test must either rigidly apply a test that has never adequately justified itself because it is based on a non-existent principle, attempt to modify the test in its application to varied circumstances without the help of a useful guiding principle, or, in the case of the Supreme Court, abandon *stare decisis* and either overturn the decisions giving rise to the approach or apply the approach in a manner that goes against its underlying purpose.[105]

A response to this line of reasoning might be that none of this is relevant if the Court's approach is 'truly' neutral. I will respond to this argument here in three parts. First, I will look at whether the individual beneficiaries of the program in *Zelman* had 'true private choice'.[106] Second, I will examine whether the notion of a private circuit breaker can make a government funding program 'neutral' where that program ultimately gives a disproportionate amount of public money meant for private entities to religious institutions. As will be seen, the answer to this question is related to the first question, even if one accepts the notion that neutrality exists and that it consists of treating both religious and nonreligious individuals and institutions the same. Finally, I will explore whether the 'facial neutrality' of a law — the fact

---

[101] See Ravitch, above n 4, 502–13.
[102] Smith, 'Symbols, Perceptions, and Doctrinal Illusions', above n 1, 325–31.
[103] Laycock, above n 2, 1001–6.
[104] See Ravitch, above n 4, 502–13.
[105] Some would argue that is exactly what the Court did in *Mitchell* and *Zelman*: see *Mitchell*, 530 US 793, 837 (O'Connor J, concurring), 899–900 (Souter J, concurring); *Zelman*, 122 S Ct 2460, 2473 (Souter J, concurring) (2002).
[106] *Zelman*, 122 S Ct 2460, 2473 (2002).

that a law does not distinguish between potential recipients within the broad class of recipients eligible for aid[107] — has anything to do with neutrality as an actuating principle for Establishment Clause jurisprudence.

In *Zelman*, the Court found that the parents of the students in the Cleveland School District, the private 'circuit-breakers', had real individual choice regarding where to send their children.[108] In finding this 'true' choice the Court went beyond the private school options the parents had, and included several public school options.[109] Thus, government-run programs became part of the field of options the Court considered. Arguably, a program would be neutral and parents would have 'true' choices even if 100 per cent of the money going to private entities went to religious entities or if the only private choices parents had were religious.[110] This would seemingly be so even if the resulting government-funded regime put non-religious private programs at a competitive disadvantage and led to religious institutions funded by a single sect taking over a market for services.[111]

One argument in favour of so expanding the comparison group is that government is so pervasive that to exclude government-run programs — which are by their nature secular — from the comparison group, would be to put religion at a disadvantage in the marketplace of ideas and programs.[112] Yet this argument is something of a red herring. For example, religious groups have not generally had equal access to compete to run police or fire services, nor would one have thought (prior to *Zelman*) that religious organizations could compete to take over road services or state-run children and family services. Moreover, religious organizations could not administer a public school or a charter school that relies on public funds for its existence. The relevant comparison group in the context of a voucher program is thus private schools.[113] Such schools are the only relevant entities that are not government-run, wholly reliant on government funds, or subject to pervasive government regulation and oversight.

---

[107] This might be called 'verbal neutrality' and contrasted with actual neutrality, that is, with provable neutrality, if there is such a thing. Similarly, Justice Souter has used the term 'verbal formalism' to describe the Court's approach: *Zelman*, 122 S Ct 2460, 2486 (Souter J, dissenting) (2002).

[108] See generally *Zelman*, 122 S Ct 2460, 2473 (O'Connor J, concurring) (2002).

[109] Ibid 2470–71 (majority opinion), 2473–4 (O'Connor J, concurring).

[110] Ibid 2491 (Souter J, dissenting).

[111] Cf Green, above n 24, 559–60 (suggesting that the market will favour more established faiths with existing schools over less established faiths, and that adherents of the former will have more options than adherents of the latter).

[112] But see Laycock, above n 2, 1003 (secular programs should not be considered when determining whether government encourages or discourages religion simply because they are secular. The relevant comparison is between religious and anti-religious government action).

[113] *Zelman*, 122 S Ct 2460, 2491–4 (Souter J, concurring) (2002).

The relevant statistics regarding private schools in the Cleveland area were skewed such that the bulk of the money passing through the voucher program into private hands went to religious schools, and parents who participated in the voucher aspect of the Cleveland program had few non-religious options.[114] Over 3,700 students participated in the voucher program, and of those, 96 per cent enrolled in religious schools.[115] Forty-six of the 56 private schools participating in the program were religious schools.[116] Moreover, the non-religious private schools were generally small and had fewer seats for voucher students.[117] These figures are not unusual because religious schools make up a significantly larger proportion of private schools nationally than non-religious schools.[118]

Rather than rehashing the debate regarding this data — a debate that played out between the various opinions in *Zelman* and in the law review literature — I focus on the Court's characterization of the Cleveland program as an 'entirely neutral' program of 'true private choice'.[119] Assume for the moment that the Court's statistical slight of hand was a valid comparison of apples to apples, and thus in addition to the 3,765 voucher students in the program, we can consider the 1,400 students who stayed in public school and received subsidized tutorial aid, the 1,900 students enrolled in publically funded community schools, and the 13,000 enrolled in public magnet schools.[120] The percentage of students attending religious schools drops to below twenty per cent when the reference group shifts from 3,765 students to 20,000 students.[121] In fact, if we were to include the entire Cleveland schools system in the comparison group using the *Zelman* Majority's approximate figure of 75,000,[122] the percentage going to religious schools under the voucher program

---

[114] Ibid 2494–5 (Souter J, dissenting).
[115] Ibid 2464 (majority opinion). As Justice Souter points out in dissent, the exact statistic is 96.6 per cent (at 2494).
[116] Ibid 2464 (majority opinion).
[117] Cf ibid 2495 (Souter J, dissenting) (of the more than 3,700 participating voucher students only 129 attended participating non-religious private schools, and all such schools combined had a total of only 510 seats between kindergarten and eighth grade, which of course includes seats for their non-voucher students).
[118] Ibid 2469–70; see also Joseph M O'Keefe SJ, 'What Research Tells us About the Contributions of Sectarian Schools' (2001) 78 *University of Detroit Mercy Law Review* 425 (2001).
[119] *Zelman*, 122 S Ct 2473 (2002).
[120] Ibid 2464–5.
[121] Ibid 2470–1.
[122] Ibid 2463.

would be approximately 4.85 per cent.[123] The 75,000 figure would represent all the 'choices' parents in the Cleveland District had (or could have assuming open enrolment at all Cleveland public schools).[124]

Yet if parents choose to take advantage of the voucher program because of dissatisfaction with all public school options (including community schools), or the inability to get into a magnet school or failure to win a lottery slot at a community school,[125] the parent may have little choice but to send his or her children to religious schools or forego the voucher option entirely.[126] If parents in the area do not subscribe to the faith of any participating religious school, as is likely for non-believers and many religious minorities, they can make the same 'choice' as their neighbours who participate in the voucher program and who subscribe to one of the represented faiths, only by sending their children to a religious school that may indoctrinate the children in a faith with which the family disagrees or at the very least does not believe in. This choice hardly seems neutral. Nor does the Court's assurance that the program is neutral since it provides everyone with 'true private choice' and does not discriminate on its face, provide much solace to a parent who desperately wants to provide the best education possible for her children but who is afraid that her children will be confronted daily with lessons and choices that are alien to the family's faith.[127]

This is the problem with neutrality. One person's neutrality is another's discrimination or favouritism, and if a court proclaims something to be neutral there is no way of proving the proclamation to be true. The Rehnquist Court relies on 'true private choice' and facial neutrality as the basis for demonstrating that a program is 'entirely neutral',[128] yet it is easy to dispute the availability of 'true private choice', and the

---

[123] This figure was obtained by comparing Justice O'Connor's figure of 3,637 students attending private religious schools under the voucher program — *Zelman*, 122 S Ct 2460, 2473 (O'Connor J, concurring) (2002) — to the overall number of 75,000. 4.85 per cent would represent 3,637.5 out of 75,000 students.

[124] The majority also mentions that suburban school districts could have participated in the program, but none chose to: ibid 2463–4. There are significant financial disincentives for suburban districts wishing to participate in the program because the districts would only receive a per-pupil amount equalling the voucher amount plus the state's normal contribution, but this would not cover the per-pupil expenditures in such districts since a significant amount of their funding comes from local property taxes: at 2496 fn 17 (Souter J, dissenting).

[125] Ibid 2464 (noting that admission to community schools is by lottery).

[126] Ibid 2494–5 (Souter J, dissenting).

[127] The fact that children may be exempted from religious classes does not alter the sectarian messages and pedagogy that pervade (appropriately so) many religious schools, or the possible discrimination that outsider children may face in such environments. Cf Frank S Ravitch, *School Prayer and Discrimination: The Civil Rights of Religious Minorities and Dissenters* (1999) 7–18.

[128] *Zelman*, 122 S Ct 2460, 2473 (2002).

facial neutrality of a program does not mean that the program is neutral or even that it was not designed to discriminate against religious minorities or to favour dominant religious groups in a given area.[129]

Even if the Court were correct that parents had a choice of multiple, equally viable non-religious options, the program is not neutral. The overwhelming amount of money flowing into private hands (that is, not *initially* dependant on government for survival) flows to religious schools as does the overwhelming number of students.[130] Unless the Court explains how the existence of 'true private choice' under such circumstances is neutral, especially in light of the inequity in same-sect options between the denominational 'haves' and 'have nots', there is no reason to take the Court's word for it. The Court's reasoning is circular — neutrality equals private choice and facial neutrality because if a program is facially neutral and provides private choice it is neutral. The neutrality claim remains unsubstantiated, yet without the claim to neutrality the Court is left having to justify why religion is indistinct as a matter of constitutional law and why excluding only religion from the voucher program (as a contrary holding could require) might be unconstitutional. The claim that the program is neutral allows the Court to evade significant doctrinal and conceptual problems.

What if on the other hand, a voucher program included a large number of non-religious private schools.[131] Would this program be neutral? Where would the line be drawn if private choice is the *sin quo non* of neutrality so long as a program is neutral on its face? Seventy-five per cent religious schools? Fifty per cent? Forty per cent? What if 70 per cent of the 40 per cent of participating schools that are religious belong to one denomination? What if one 100 per cent belong to one religion? These questions can be answered — although not perfectly — but not by claiming the programs or the answers to the questions are neutral.[132] If there were a real range of choices available to parents within the voucher option, as was the case with the programs in *Zobrest v Catalina Foothills Sch. Dist.*[133] and *Witters v Wash. Dept of Servs. for the Blind*,[134] the program would be constitutional, not because the private choice makes an otherwise biased program neutral but rather because the effects of such a program do not give religion a disproportionate and substantial benefit.[135]

---

[129] Cf *Church of the Lukumi Babalu Aye v City of Hialeah*, 508 US 520 (1993).
[130] *Zelman*, 122 S Ct 2460, 2491–5 (2002).
[131] Justice Souter suggests the constitutionality of such a program in his dissenting opinion in *Zelman*, but only if it provides a range of choices compatible with that in *Witters*, a highly unlikely and expensive possibility: see *Zelman*, 122 S Ct 2460, 2496 (2002).
[132] See Ravitch, above n 4, 544–73.
[133] *Zobrest*, 509 US 1 (1993).
[134] *Witters*, 474 US 481 (1986).
[135] See Ravitch, above n 4, 544–73.

Good News Club v Milford Central School

Good News Club presents another version of the Court's formal neutrality, again grounded in the notion that treating religion differently would be hostile to religion.[136] *Good News Club* derives from a long line of equal access cases that at least arguably have a more consistent pedigree than the aid cases.[137] Equal access cases are those where a religious organization seeks access to government-owned facilities or government-funded fora that non-religious entities have access to.[138] The primary difference in *Good News Club* is that the forum to which the religious group sought access was a central school that included an elementary school.[139]

I will note at the outset that I think all of the equal access cases up to *Good News Club* were correctly decided, and that *Good News Club*, while a closer call, was also correctly decided, but not because the analysis or results were neutral or because religion should automatically be treated the same as non-religion. In fact, by automatically connecting exclusion of the religious group with hostility to religion and thus non-neutrality,[140] the Court makes another leap that it fails to adequately support.

Good News Club is in many ways a straightforward speech case.[141] School district policy allowed a variety of non-curricular student groups access to school facilities when school was not in session.[142] Both parties agreed that the district provided a limited public forum for a variety of groups at the school.[143] The religious club was denied access because the religious character of its meetings were the equivalent of religious instruction.[144] The district argued that the denial of access under such circumstances was in compliance with New York law.[145] It was specifically the group's deeply religious mission, as well as its proselytizing nature, that gave the school

---

[136] *Good News Club*, 533 US 98, 114, 118–20 (2001).
[137] Examples of these cases include *Rosenberger*, 515 US 819 (1995); *Lamb's Chapel v Center Moriches Union Free School District*, 508 US 384 (1993); *Board of Education of Westside Community Schools v Mergens*, 496 US 226 (1990); *Widmar v Vincent*, 454 US 263 (1981). See also *Capitol Square Review and Advisory Board v Pinnette*, 515 US 752 (1995) ('*Capitol Square*').
[138] *Good News Club*, 533 US 98, 106–7 (2001).
[139] The school building includes students from kindergarten to twelfth grade: ibid 118.
[140] Ibid 114, 118–20.
[141] Ibid 106–112.
[142] Ibid 102, 108.
[143] Ibid 108 (the district, however, disputed the scope of the forum).
[144] Ibid 103–4.
[145] N.Y. Educ. Law § 414 (McKinney 2000) (stating purposes for which schools may be opened for public use).

district pause.¹⁴⁶ Thus, from a free speech perspective, the issue was one of viewpoint discrimination rather than content discrimination.¹⁴⁷

Content discrimination occurs when government discriminates against or excludes an entire subject, but viewpoint discrimination occurs when the government discriminates against speech based on the specific viewpoint involved. Thus, it would be content discrimination to exclude all religious speech from a public forum, but it would be viewpoint discrimination to exclude only speech from a Jewish perspective. Claims of content discrimination in a public forum give rise to strict scrutiny,¹⁴⁸ and thus the district would need to demonstrate a compelling governmental interest and that its action was narrowly tailored to serve that compelling interest.¹⁴⁹ The Court has suggested that viewpoint discrimination in a public forum is presumed unconstitutional,¹⁵⁰ but the Court did not answer this question in *Good News Club*¹⁵¹ and there is some support for applying strict scrutiny to viewpoint discrimination, albeit especially strict scrutiny.¹⁵² Regardless, the line between content and viewpoint discrimination is somewhat blurred.

The district argued that its compelling interest was compliance with the Establishment Clause, because the group was intensely religious, believed in proselytizing, was run by outside adults, and, most importantly, was geared for elementary school students who are young and impressionable.¹⁵³ Thus, this case had the potential to directly confront the issue of whether religion is constitutionally different from other aspects of life, but the majority passed on the opportunity to deeply analyze this question. Instead, the Court presumed that treating religion differently was hostile to religion, and would send a message of hostility to students in the same way the school feared the group's meetings would send a message of endorsement of religion to non-believing students.¹⁵⁴

---

[146] *Good News Club*, 533 US 98, 103–4, 137–9 (Souter J, dissenting) (2001).
[147] Ibid 107–110.
[148] *Capitol Square*, 515 US 752, 761 (1995); see also *Church on the Rock v City of Albuquerque*, 84 F.3d 1273, 1279 (10th Cir 1996) ('*Church on the Rock*').
[149] Ibid.
[150] *Rosenberger*, 515 US 819, 829–30 (1995).
[151] *Good News Club*, 533 US 98, 112–3 (2001).
[152] *Bartnicki v Vopper*, 532 US 514, 544 (Rehnquist J, dissenting) (2001) (implying discrimination based on viewpoint is subject to strict scrutiny); *Church on the Rock*, 84 F.3d 1273, 1279 (10th Cir 1996). The fact that the Court in *Good News Club* refused to decide whether viewpoint discrimination might be justified in order to prevent violations of the Establishment Clause in rare circumstances at least leaves the question open: *Good News Club*, 533 US 98, 112–3 (2001).
[153] *Good News Club*, 533 US 98, 113–6, 137–9 (Souter J, dissenting) (2001).
[154] Ibid 118–20.

As the dissent points out, the group was connected to a national organization that focuses on getting a foothold with elementary aged children precisely because they are young and impressionable.[155] The majority argued that religious organizations are the same as other organizations, and to deny them the same rights as other organizations is to discriminate against religion or religious viewpoints — that is, it is not neutral.[156] Differential treatment is not mandated by the Establishment Clause and indeed might violate that clause.[157]

Once again, the analysis boils down to formalism — this time with the aid of the Free Speech Clause. If religion is treated differently in a limited public forum, even in a sensitive context like an elementary school, this is viewpoint or content discrimination (depending on whether a specific viewpoint(s) or category of speech is focused upon).[158] Yet treating religion differently in a forum neutrally open to all student groups is never a compelling government interest, because such differential treatment is not required by the Establishment Clause since that clause requires religion to be treated the same as non-religion.[159] By assuming that religion must be treated the same as non-religion the Court both sets up the claim of viewpoint discrimination and answers the compelling interest defence to that claim.[160] Beyond asserting that differential treatment in this context is hostility to religion, the Court never explains why religion should be treated the same as non-religion, and why differential treatment in this context is automatically hostile and non-neutral.[161] This is reminiscent of a longstanding critique of the Court's formal equality doctrine under the Fourteenth Amendment: is treating differently situated groups the same equality?[162] The Court's formal neutrality-different treatment as hostility argument presumes that a differently situated (both textually and historically) classification — religion — is the same as every other classification for purposes of religion clause analysis.[163]

---

[155] The mission of the club is reflected in the format of the club's meetings as described by Justice Souter in his dissenting opinion. Ibid 137–9 (Souter, J, dissenting).

[156] Ibid 111–2, 114, 118–20.

[157] Ibid 118–20.

[158] Ibid 106–12.

[159] This is certainly implicit in *Good News Club:* ibid 112–20.

[160] Ibid.

[161] Ibid.

[162] Cf Alexander T Aleinikoff, 'A Case for Race Consciousness' (1991) 91 *Columbia Law Review* 1061, 1087–8; Frank S Ravitch, 'Creating Chaos in the Name of Consistency: Affirmative Action and the Odd Legacy of *Adarand Constructors, Inc. v Pena*' (1997) 101 *Dickinson Law Review* 281, 292–3; David A Strauss, 'The Myth of Colorblindness' (1986) *Supreme Court Review* 99, 105–6.

[163] See Daniel O Conkle, 'The Path of American Religious Liberty: From the Original Theology to Formal Neutrality and an Uncertain Future' (2000) 75 *Indiana Law Journal* 1, 25 (2000).

Yet, I think the general result in *Good News Club* was correct. How is it possible to reach this conclusion without at least accepting the idea that government needs to treat religion the same as non-religion in the equal access context? My reasoning is that the policy allowing a variety of student groups to meet does not substantially facilitate religion as compared to non-religion. If it did, it would be perfectly acceptable to treat religion differently because of Establishment Clause concerns. Additionally, the facilitation approach I have proposed would not preclude the school from preventing completely equal access — that is, the school can limit the group's ability to advertise in the classroom (as opposed to bulletin boards) or could limit announcements over a generally available public address system to basic information about meeting times and locations, even if other groups are not so limited (and so long as all religious student groups have the same limitations).[164] Perhaps most importantly, if the group begins to interfere with the rights of other students through organized proselytization or by overreaching in recruitment efforts, the school can revoke access. Additionally, if the school favoured the group, students (through parents) could bring an 'as applied' challenge to the access policy.

The key is that the *Good News Club* result is correct not because it is inherently neutral — many religious minorities might not have the numbers or the desire to form such clubs, and thus the result may favour religions with greater numbers or a greater will to proselytize[165] — but because the free speech concerns cannot be rebutted under the facts of the case. Thus, precluding the group is not automatically hostile to religion and allowing them to meet does not automatically favour religion. The concepts of hostility and favouritism, like neutrality, are quite manipulable and can vary depending on who is evaluating the claim.

Employment Division v Smith

Smith demonstrates the application of the formal neutrality principle in the Free Exercise Clause context. Two members of the Native American Church were denied unemployment benefits after being fired from their jobs at a substance abuse rehabilitation centre.[166] They were fired because they had used peyote, an illegal substance under Oregon law, during religious rituals.[167] Oregon law stated that being fired for misconduct — which is how the firing was characterized — precludes the

---

[164] Ibid.
[165] Cf Green, above n 24, 559–60 (suggesting that vouchers will favour groups with larger numbers and established schools over those with fewer numbers and lower support for sectarian schools).
[166] *Smith*, 494 US 872, 874 (1990).
[167] Ibid.

receipt of unemployment benefits.[168] Neither member had abused peyote and there was no evidence that they used it anywhere other than in religious ceremonies.[169] In fact, it would violate the tenets of the Native American Church to use peyote outside of appropriate religious rituals because the substance has significant religious import for members of the faith.[170] Oregon, unlike many states and the federal government, did not have a religious exemption for Native American peyote use under its general drug laws.[171] Thus, the Court had to decide whether the two men denied unemployment benefits had a constitutional right to an exemption to the drug laws given the religious nature of their peyote use.[172] An exemption would preclude the denial of unemployment benefits based on misconduct.[173]

The backdrop of legal precedent seemed to favour the men, but that precedent — contrary to popular belief — was anything but clear or terribly helpful to religious minorities. The precedent many thought would be key to the decision was *Sherbert v Verner*,[174] which held that a state must have a compelling governmental interest for denying unemployment benefits to a person who was fired for refusing to work on her Sabbath.[175] Relevant, but not decisive on my reading of the *Sherbert* opinion, was the fact that the state unemployment laws contained a number of exemptions for nonreligious reasons.[176]

Another decision, *Wisconsin v Yoder*,[177] was also potentially relevant. In *Yoder*, the Court held that Amish families with high school age children were entitled to exemptions from the state's compulsory education laws in the absence of a compelling state interest.[178] The court looked at the Amish community's track record of good citizenship, hard work, and the success of its young people within the community to demonstrate that the state had no compelling interest for denying the exemption.[179]

---

[168] Ibid.
[169] See Respondents' Brief at 1–5, *Employment Division v Smith*, 485 US 660 (1988) (Nos. 86–946, 86–947), 1987 WL 880316; Garrett Epps, 'To An Unknown God: The Hidden History of *Employment Division v Smith*' (1998) 30 *Arizona State Law Journal* 953, 962–3, 981–5.
[170] Garrett Epps, 'What We Talk About When We Talk About Free Exercise' (1998) 30 *Arizona State Law Review* 563, 583; see also *Smith*, 494 US 872, 913–6 (Blackmun J, dissenting) (1990).
[171] See generally *Smith*, 494 US 872 (1990).
[172] Ibid.
[173] Ibid.
[174] 373 US 398 (1963).
[175] Ibid.
[176] Ibid 406; see also Douglas Laycock, 'The Remnants of Free Exercise' (1990) *Supreme Court Review* 1, 50.
[177] 406 US 205 (1972).
[178] Ibid.
[179] Ibid 209–12, 216–8, 222–7, 235–6.

There have been some serious criticisms of the Court's approach in *Yoder*,[180] but for present purposes this basic overview of the Court's holding is adequate.

Given this precedent, most people believed that the battle lines in *Smith* would be drawn over whether the state had an adequate compelling governmental interest.[181] In fact, Oregon's attorney general at that time later pointed out that the state never argued for disposing of the compelling interest test,[182] but rather argued that compliance with the state's drug laws satisfied the burden under that test, especially in light of post *Sherbert* and *Yoder* case law.[183] Subsequent case law suggested that *Sherbert* and *Yoder* were primarily paper tigers, at least in the US Supreme Court.[184]

Between *Yoder* and *Smith*, the Court decided a string of free exercise exemption cases, with the exception of a few unemployment cases the person seeking the exemption never won.[185] In some cases the nature of the government institution, that is, the military or prisons, served as a basis for not applying the compelling interest test.[186] In others, the relief requested was decisive in not applying the compelling interest test. For example, cases where the government entity involved would have had to change its policies to grant an exemption.[187] Finally, there were cases where the court ostensibly applied the compelling interest test, but in a manner that made it

---

[180] *Wisconsin v Yoder*, 406 US 205, 241–2 (Douglas J, dissenting) (1972); Stephen M Feldman, 'Religious Minorities and the First Amendment: The History, the Doctrine, and the Future' (2003) 6 *University of Pennsylvania Journal of Constitutional Law* 222, 252–6; see also Richard J Arneson and Ian Shapiro, 'Democratic Autonomy and Religious Freedom: A Critique of *Wisconsin v. Yoder*' in Ian Shapiro and Russin Hardin (eds), *Political Order* (1996) 365–8; Ira C Lupu, 'Reconstructing the Establishment Clause: The Case Against Discretionary Accommodation of Religion' (1991) 140 *University of Pennsylvania Law Review* 555, 563 fn 17.

[181] See Garrett Epps, above n 169, 1015; and at 956–7 fns 11–2 (citing many legal and journalistic commentators criticizing *Smith* soon after it was decided).

[182] See Brief for Petitioners, *Employment Div. v Smith* 494 US 872 (1990) (No. 88-1213), 1989 WL 1126846; Garrett Epps, above n 169, 1010–5. This was also confirmed in a conversation I had with former Oregon Attorney-General Dave Frohnmayer in Kyoto, Japan in 2001, when we both spoke at a forum addressing the free exercise of religion at Doshisha University (Frohnmayer was speaking as the President of the University of Oregon, and I was a Fulbright Scholar at the Faculty of Law at Doshisha University).

[183] Ibid.

[184] See below ns 193–4 and accompanying text.

[185] In fact, no non-Christian has ever won a Free Exercise Clause exemption case before the United States Supreme Court and even most Christians have lost such cases: Mark Tushnet, 'Of Church and State and the Supreme Court: *Kurland* Revisited' (1989) *Supreme Court Review* 373, 381.

[186] See, eg, *Goldman v Weinberger*, 475 US 503 (1986) (military setting); *O'Lone v Estate of Shabazz*, 482 US 342 (1987) (prison setting).

[187] *Bowen v Roy*, 476 US 693 (1986).

anything but strict scrutiny.[188] Note, however, that *Sherbert* and *Yoder* did influence the outcomes of some lower court cases.[189]

The *Smith* Court relied on the post-*Yoder* decisions, as well as some pre-*Sherbert* decisions, to hold that *Sherbert* is limited to the unemployment context where there is generally a variety of exemptions built into the unemployment laws.[190] Furthermore, the claim in *Smith* was different from earlier free exercise cases granting exemptions to unemployment laws because the claimants in *Smith* sought an exemption based on illegal conduct while the claimants in the earlier cases sought an exemption based on religious conduct that was otherwise legal.[191] *Yoder* was harder to distinguish, but the Court created the concept of hybrid-rights, that is, cases in which the Free Exercise Clause right is connected to some other important right (in *Yoder* parental rights).[192] This theory works well to distinguish several earlier cases that involved freedom of expression as well as free exercise concerns,[193] but to characterize *Yoder*, as a hybrid rights case was a stretch.

This stretch would be more troubling if the traditional story of Free Exercise Clause jurisprudence was accurate, but the reality is that *Sherbert* and *Yoder* were never the

---

[188] *United States v Lee*, 455 US 252 (1982).

[189] Lower court cases went both ways after *Sherbert* and *Yoder*, and while many denied the claimant's exemptions, a number did not: see, eg, *Dayton Christian Schools, Inc v Ohio Civil Rights Commission*, 766 F2d 932 (6th Cir 1985) (school's free exercise rights violated by application of civil rights laws); *McCurry v Tesch*, 738 F2d 271 (8th Cir 1984) (enforcement of state order against operation of church school in violation of state law infringed church's free exercise rights); *Warner v Graham*, 675 F Supp 1171 (DND 1987) (Free Exercise Clause violated where plaintiff lost her job because of sacramental peyote use); *United States v Lewis*, 638 F Supp 573 (WD Mich 1986) (rule requiring government to consent to waiver of a jury trial violated defendants' free exercise rights); *United States v Abeyta*, 632 F Supp 1301 (DNM 1986) (*Bald Eagle Protection Act* violated defendant's free exercise rights); *Equal Employment Opportunity Commission v Fremont Christian School*, 609 F Supp 344 (ND Calif 1984) (same); *Congregation Beth Yitzchok of Rockland, Inc v Town of Ramapo*, 593 F Supp 655 (SDNY 1984) (regulations interfering with congregation's operation of its nursery school violated free exercise rights); *Chapman v Pickett*, 491 F Supp 967 (CD Ill 1980) (free exercise rights of Black Muslim prisoner were violated by his punishment for refusal to follow order to handle pork); *Geller v Secretary of Defense*, 423 F Supp 16 (DDC 1976) (regulation denying Jewish chaplain right to wear facial hair violated his free exercise rights); *Lincoln v True*, 408 F Supp 22 (WD Ky 1975) (denial of unemployment compensation to claimant who terminated employment for religious reasons infringed her free exercise rights); *American Friends Service Commission v United States*, 368 F Supp 1176 (ED Pa 1973) (tax withholding statute violates plaintiffs' free exercise rights); *Nicholson v Board of Commissioners*, 338 F Supp 48 (ND Ala 1972) (statutory oath required of applicant for admission to state bar infringed on applicant's free exercise).

[190] *Smith*, 494 US 872, 883–4 (1990).

[191] Ibid 874–5, 878.

[192] Ibid 881–2.

[193] Ibid.

panacea they have been made out to be.[194] The idea of a compelling interest test held a lot of promise, but in the hands of shifting majorities on the Court that promise was never realized — although it was sometimes realized in the lower courts.[195]

Divorcing *Smith* from all the important — but for present purposes irrelevant — baggage regarding *stare decises* and so on, we are left with the basic notion that the Free Exercise Clause does not require exemptions to generally applicable (today the Court might say facially neutral) laws. The argument seems to be that because these laws are religion neutral the Free Exercise Clause has no impact on them except through the political process.[196] This is, of course, a claim of formal neutrality. But how is facial neutrality 'neutral' in this context? One might ask this in the language of *Smith*: how can a law be generally applicable in this context? The concurring and dissenting opinions essentially ask this question and answer that the laws are neither neutral nor generally applicable for free exercise purposes.[197]

Here there may be a dichotomy between claims of neutrality and general applicability. The law without religious exemptions is not neutral, whether viewed from the perspective of free exercise or from that of the legal regime as a whole. The Court admits as much in suggesting that no one is entitled to a religious exemption and religious minorities might be at a disadvantage when attempting to get exemptions through the political process.[198] Whatever baseline one sets for neutrality in this context, neither the result nor the baseline can be proven neutral. Yet, one might set two different baselines for general applicability in this case, one that views general applicability without regard to the nature of the claim and one that views general applicability specifically in the free exercise context. From the latter perspective, the law is not generally applicable because it places a significant burden on those whose religious practices require a violation of the law. From the former perspective, the

---

[194] Frederick Mark Gedicks, *The Rhetoric of Church and State* (1995) 90–9; John Thomas Bannon, Jr, 'The Legality of the Religious Use of Peyote By the Native American Church: A Commentary on the Free Exercise, Equal Protection, and Establishment Issues Raised by the *Peyote Way Church of God* Case' (1998) 22 *American Indian Law Review* 475, 484 (1998); Christopher L Eisgruber and Lawrence G Sager, 'Why the Religious Freedom Restoration Act is Unconstitutional' (1994) 69 *New York University Law Review* 437, 446–7; Lino A Graglia, 'Church of the Lukumi Babalu Aye: Of Animal Sacrifice and Religious Persecution' (1996) 85 *Georgia Law Journal* 1, 16); Marci A Hamilton, 'The Religious Freedom Restoration Act: Letting the Fox Into the Henhouse Under Cover of Section 5 of the Fourteenth Amendment' (1994) 16 *Cardozo Law Review* 357, 385 fn 101; Ira C Lupu, above n 70, 237; Robert W Tuttle, 'How Firm A Foundation? Protecting the Religious Land Uses After *Boerne*' (2000) 68 *George Washington Law Review* 861, 871–2 (2000).

[195] Ibid.

[196] See generally *Smith*, 494 US 872 (1990).

[197] Ibid 891 (O'Connor J, concurring), 907 (Blackmun J, dissenting).

[198] Ibid 890.

law is generally applicable because it applies to all citizens, even if it may have a differing impact on some. This, of course, simply begs the question.

How does one choose between these baselines? Certainly, the choice should not based on the tortured use of precedent by both the Majority and dissenting opinions. So what really allowed the Justices to choose? We will never know for sure, but it seems the Majority presumed that it is religion-neutral to analyze the general applicability of the law without regard to the nature of the claim.[199] Otherwise, the Court's reasoning makes no sense. If the law was not religion neutral in the free exercise context than it is not generally applicable because it would apply differently to different religious groups. The Court's approach is one of formal neutrality because it is concerned only with the facial neutrality of the law and not with its practical effects. The concurring and dissenting opinions seem to assume that the law is not generally applicable or religion neutral in the context of a free exercise claim.[200] Thus, for purposes of the present discussion I focus on the majority opinion.

Whether the decision in *Smith* is a valid interpretation of the Free Exercise Clause (I suggest elsewhere that it is not) cannot be determined based on the implicit neutrality claim or on the presumption regarding the general applicability of the law. Rather, we must look elsewhere. The governing precedent was mixed, although it does seem the Majority opinion took some liberties with precedent. In the end the Court had to answer the question, as the *Sherbert* Court tried to do, what does the Free Exercise Clause mean and how should it be applied to exemptions from laws that are not directly aimed at religion? By relying on general applicability and facial neutrality, the Court never seriously engages this question. The answer is presumed — general applicability/neutrality are determinative because that is what the Free Exercise Clause requires. Why? Because generally applicable laws cannot burden free exercise in a constitutionally significant way. Why? Because we said so. The Court might be able to justify this approach with an appropriate mode of religion clause interpretation, but neutrality is not such a mode and the court uses general applicability as a stand in for neutrality. Even if one were to argue that general applicability has meaning separate from its implicit neutrality claim one is left trying to determine if the laws of general applicability approach used by the Court is adequately supported by an appropriate mode of religion clause interpretation. Neutrality is used here to avoid carefully answering the tough question of what the Free Exercise Clause requires and why.

---

[199] See generally ibid 886 fn 3.
[200] Ibid 891 (O'Connor J, concurring), 907 (Blackmun J, dissenting).

14

Protecting Religious Freedom: Two Counterintuitive Dialectics in US Free Exercise Jurisprudence

Brett G Scharffs

This chapter focuses on what is usually described in the United States as the problem of religious exemptions. Imagine that you have religious reasons for resisting the requirements of a state or federal law. Perhaps you are a conscientious objector to military service, having religious (or philosophical) grounds against taking up arms. Perhaps you are a member of a church that uses peyote or other banned substances in your sacramental rituals. Perhaps you seek an exemption from having to work on Saturday, your Sabbath. How does — and how should — the law go about determining whether or not you are entitled to an exemption from generally applicable laws?

From the perspective of equality, an exemption may not be warranted, if the law treats everyone the same, with perhaps the additional requirement that the law, even though it appears general and neutral on its face, was written to specifically target a particular set of unpopular religious beliefs. From the perspective of liberty, an exemption might be warranted, as long as the burdens on religious exercise are real and the burdens on the state for accommodating the religious exemption are not unduly onerous. The problems of balancing the individual's interest in an exemption against the state's interest in enforcing its laws may be difficult, but this is a type of analysis with which the law is familiar and adept.

Thus, one important question will be whether we see the question of exemptions as presenting a problem that should be viewed primarily through the prism of equality, or through the prism of freedom. In most situations, freedom and equality will both be present as values a court will acknowledge, but it may be that one of these values takes precedence.

Conceptualizing the freedom-equality dialectic

There are a variety of ways that we can conceptualize the tension that arises between freedom and equality when examining a request for a religious exemption. One common way of conceptualizing the problem is that we are balancing values. We could say that freedom and equality should be afforded equal weight, with one consideration to be balanced against the other.

On this way of looking at the problem, it is one of correctly balancing the requirements of freedom, which might weigh in one direction, with the requirements of equality, which might weigh in another direction. But sometimes when we are dealing with multiple values the task is not simply one of balancing, since the values may be incommensurable — that is to say they cannot be traded back and forth in terms of some common denominator of value. It is also difficult to balance a specific individualized minority interest in an exemption (which although important to the individual may be quite small on a societal scale) against a general societal interest in enforcing the laws (which at a high degree of generality always looks very large).

An alternative metaphor would conceive of freedom and equality as different lenses through which we might view a problem. Here we might imagine a pair of eyeglasses with one lens focused upon freedom and the other lens focused upon equality. By shifting from eye to eye, we could alternate between seeing a problem as one primarily involving freedom and viewing it as something primarily involving equality. This can be useful, and can help us develop empathy for the various interests at stake, but it is not particularly helpful in helping us prioritize when each approach suggests a different outcome. Also, it can be disorienting to look through glasses with different magnifications in the different lenses.

This metaphor does illustrate the commonplace truth that often how things look will depend upon the lens through which we view an issue. When we view a problem through the lens of equality it may look one way, whereas when we view it through the lens of freedom it may look quite different.

When we look through an equalitarian lens, we may view an issue in terms of neutrality, non-discrimination, and equal treatment. These are important baseline values. A legal system that promotes or tolerates discrimination, which treats people differently based upon their religious status — whether in education, legal status, family law such as adoption and inheritance, in economic and professional opportunities, or most egregiously in overt religious persecution — violates the basic baseline requirements of equal treatment. Many religious freedom problems, especially egregious problems such as discrimination or more extreme types of hostility or violence towards religious or other minorities are really problems of equality.

But even when baseline equality exists, when we look at problems through a lens of freedom, we may be more attuned to the special needs of religious groups, especially those who find themselves as minorities in a particular legal system. From the perspective of freedom, sometimes special treatment or accommodation is needed in order for religious liberty to be possible. Whereas an equalitarian perspective may look suspiciously upon religious exemptions from general and neutral laws, when a situation is viewed through a lens of freedom we may be much more sensitive to the need to accommodate and make space for religious beliefs and actions that depart from majoritarian norms.

Sometimes it can be difficult to shift perspectives between freedom and equality. But it can be disorienting to look through glasses with different magnifications in the different lenses, or when the lenses are different colours. We might compare the difficulty to the experience of shifting perspectives when wearing bifocal (or as my ophthalmologist kindly termed them when I turned 40, 'progressive') lenses. Each part of bifocal glasses have a specific purpose, either viewing things at a distance, or viewing things up close. At first it can be somewhat disorienting to try to shift perspectives between the two different magnifications.

When looking at issues at the intersection of law and religion, usually concerns of both freedom and equality are present and bear upon our analysis, although often one of these values is in the foreground and the other lies in the background of our thinking. One way that Professor Cole Durham and I have previously tried to illustrate the way in which our perspective of what belongs in the foreground and what is in the background may shift is illustrated by drawing analogy to the 'Necker Cube,' an optical illusion first published in 1832 by Louis Albert Necker, a Swiss crystallographer.

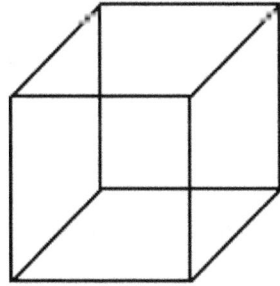

The shifting ways that the Necker Cube is perceived represents in an oversimplified way the notion of a paradigm shift that I am trying to describe. To some viewers, the square at the bottom left of the Necker Cube will naturally appear in the forefront, whereas to other viewers, the square at the top right will appear to be the front face of the cube. Shading different faces of the cube, as shown below, makes it easier to see the alternatives.

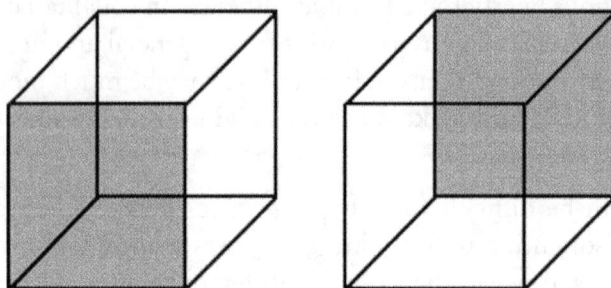

One needs an adroit ability to shift perspectives in order to move easily back and forth between the two ways of viewing the cube.

Although the phenomena involved in perceiving legal issues or relationships will be much more complex, something similar happens when we see things in a way that places either freedom or equality in the front or dominant position on the cube. Imagine that the words 'freedom' and 'equality' are each written on the face of one of the squares that make up the front and back of the cube.

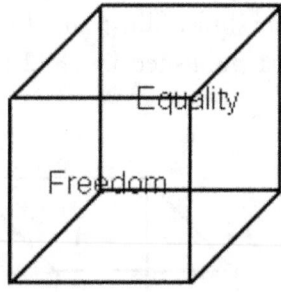

From one perspective, freedom is in front and equality is on the back side of the cube, whereas from another perspective, equality is in front and freedom is in the background.

It is easier to see this shift when one of the square planes is highlighted and one value, freedom or equality, is thrust to the forefront, and the other value is pushed to the background. Indeed, one value could receive such heavy shading that the other value is largely obscured from view.

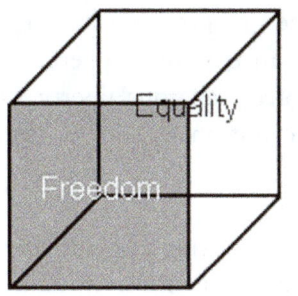 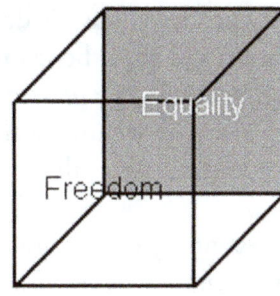

When thinking about an issue involving law and religion, one important question is whether the problem is one primarily involving an issue of equality or an issue of freedom. The approach we take to solving the problem will vary significantly based upon what kind of problem we understand it to be.

Another way of imagining (or imaging) how one of these values can be viewed as dominant and the other as secondary or distant is to think of a long road disappearing towards the horizon. One of these values might appear quite large, like a car in the foreground, while the other value might appear quite small, like a car at a distance. Both cars (or values) may in fact be the same size, but our perspective may make one appear larger and the other smaller. One value may be held so close that it dominates our entire field of vision, while the other may recede to what artists call the vanishing point, where the road meets the distant horizon.

Freedom and equality in US Establishment Clause and Free Exercise jurisprudence

Since the end of World War II, the US Supreme Court has decided over a hundred cases directly interpreting the religion clauses of the First Amendment, and other federal and state courts have decided thousands of cases. To a large extent the history of Free Exercise and Establishment Clause jurisprudence can be seen as a struggle for dominance between an approach that emphasizes freedom as the predominant value and an approach that emphasizes equality as the more important value.

One popular way of viewing the two religion clauses in the First Amendment of the US Constitution is to see the Establishment Clause as providing for equal treatment among different religions and between that which is religious and not religious,[1]

---

[1] The Supreme Court has often stated that the Establishment Clause forbids laws 'which aid one religion, aid all religions, or prefer one religion over another': see, eg, *Everson v Board of Education*, 330 US 1, 15 (1947); *Epperson v Arkansas*, 393 US 97, 104 (1968) ('the First Amendment mandates government neutrality between religion and religion, and between religion and nonreligion').

whereas the Free Exercise Clause is designed to promote freedom for religion. An alternative reading urges that the clauses must be read together as essentially one provision, the purpose of which is to protect religious liberty. For example, The Williamsburg Charter, an ecumenical declaration signed by numerous religious, legal and political leaders, states that:

> the clauses are essentially one provision for preserving religious liberty. Both parts, No establishment and Free exercise, are to be comprehensively understood as being in the service of religious liberty as a positive good. At the heart of the Establishment Clause is prohibition of state sponsorship of religion and at the heart of Free Exercise Clause is the prohibition of state interference with religious liberty.

The move from freedom to equality in Establishment Clause jurisprudence

In the past twenty years, equality has trumped freedom as the predominant value in the Supreme Court's interpretation of the Establishment Clause.

Freedom as the dominant interpretive principle

The Establishment Clause, which might more accurately be referred to as the 'non-establishment clause,' has experienced profound shifts in meaning over the course of its history. When initially adopted, it was part of the general compromise that endowed the federal government with certain limited powers, and retained most power for the states.[2] In this setting, the First Amendment's pronouncement that '*Congress* shall make no law respecting an establishment of religion'[3] was designed to make it clear that the federal government was not authorized to meddle with established churches that continued to exist in several of the states.[4]

Originally, the non-establishment principle was conceived fundamentally as a limitation on public power. It was designed to promote liberty by preventing the growth of the governmental institutions that had posed the greatest hazard to religious freedom in the past. Following the demise of established churches, the idea of non-establishment was eventually rooted in the constitutions of the various states. Indeed, the idea has become so deeply entrenched that it comes as a surprise to most

---

[2] Steven D Smith, *Foreordained Failure: The Quest for a Constitutional Principle of Religious Freedom* (1995) 17–34; *United States Constitution* amend X.
[3] *United States Constitution* amend I (emphasis added).
[4] For an account of the history of disestablishment between the time of the adoption of the First Amendment in 1791 and the demise of the last established church in Massachusetts in 1833, see Carl H Esbeck, 'Dissent and Disestablishment: The Church-State Settlement in the Early American Republic' (2004) *Brigham Young University Law Review* 1385.

Americans to learn that the Establishment Clause was originally designed to protect state establishments.

In the founding era, the 'establishment of religion' was understood to 'refer to a church which the government funded and controlled and in which it used its coercive power to encourage participation, like the Anglican Church in England or the Roman Catholic Church in southern Europe'.[5] Historians note that there were three primary concerns that drove the adoption of the Establishment Clause. First, there was concern about the church exercising the coercive power of government, including the power to enforce criminal laws that reflected the church's denominational and moral requirements.[6] Second, early Americans worried about direct financial support of the church in aid of its worship, rituals, and other denominational activities, through general tax revenue.[7] Third, they were also concerned with control by the state over the church, particularly in its definition of doctrine and selection of leaders.[8]

Concern for the freedom, or autonomy, of both churches and of the state is at the heart of each of these concerns.[9] Early Establishment Clause jurisprudence was in large measure an attempt to work out the contours of these freedom interests. The dominant ideal became 'separation of church and state'. Indeed, even today the typical American is surprised to learn that the phrase 'separation of church and state' does not appear in the First Amendment.

The ideal of separation is reflected most prominently in the metaphor of a wall, which is strewn through Establishment Clause cases. The wall of separation is supposed to divide church and state into their proper spheres, with as little interaction, interference and overlap as possible.[10] The 'wall of separation' metaphor is usually traced to Thomas Jefferson, who used the phrase in a letter to the Danbury Baptist

---

[5] Frederick Mark Gedicks, 'A Two-Track Theory of the Establishment Clause' (2002) 43 *Boston College Law Review* 1071, 1091 (citing Thomas J Curry, Farewell to Christendom (2001) 16, 37, 109); see also Thomas J Curry, *The First Freedoms: Church and State in America to the Passage of the First Amendment* (1986) 191–2.

[6] Gedicks, above n 5, 1098.

[7] Ibid.

[8] Ibid.

[9] Brett G Scharffs, 'The Autonomy of Church and State' (2004) *Brigham Young University Law Review* 1217.

[10] Separationists argue that 'the original purpose of the establishment clause was to create an absolute separation of the spheres of civil authority and religious activity by forbidding all forms of government assistance or support for religion': Derek Davis, *Original Intent: Chief Justice Rehnquist and the Course of American Church/State Relations* (1991) 47–8.

Association that he wrote when he was President.[11] But it can also be found in the writings of Roger Williams, the founder of Rhode Island.[12] Jefferson and Williams represent two major strands in the American separationist tradition.[13] Williams, who lived a century earlier, urged separation primarily to protect religion from the risks of corruption, apathy and distortion of mission that flow from the religious quest for state power. He wanted to protect the garden of the church from the wilderness of the state.[14] Jefferson, in contrast, was much more a figure of the French Enlightenment, and was concerned to protect the state from control by the forces of organized and often unenlightened religion. Significantly, freedom is a primary focus for both of these early strands of separationist thought. Separation is not an end in itself, but an institutional means of protecting religion and the state from each other in the interest of promoting freedom.

Everson v Board of Education: Freedom and equality as competing visions of the Establishment Clause

While the Establishment Clause dates back to the earliest days of the American republic, most of the case law under the Establishment Clause has been decided since 1947, when the Supreme Court handed down *Everson v Board of Education*[15] and held for the first time that the federal Establishment Clause was applicable to

---

[11] See Thomas Jefferson, in Adrienne Koch and William A Peden (eds), *The Life and Selected Writings of Thomas Jefferson* (1944) 332. For commentary on Jefferson's 'wall of separation', see, eg, Daniel L Dreisbach and John D Whaley, 'What the Wall Separates: A Debate on Thomas Jefferson's "Wall of Separation" Metaphor' (1999) 16 *Constitutional Comment* 627; Stephen J Safranek, 'Can Science Guide Legal Argument? The Role of Metaphor in Constitutional Cases' (1994) 25 *Loyola University Chicago Law Review* 357.

[12] Roger Williams was concerned about protecting the garden of religion from the wilderness of the world: Roger Williams, 'Mr Cotton's Letter Lately Printed, Examined and Answered' in M Howe, *The Garden in the Wilderness* (1965) 5–6.

[13] These two broad streams have long represented major positions in American thought. Other sources of support for the separation principle come from (1) groups who fear assimilation or simply being submerged in the dominant culture; (2) those committed to equalitarian pluralism or multiculturalism, and; (3) committed secularizers for whom secularism represents a political ideal that should be implemented as an end in itself. These various streams intermingle, invoke each other's arguments, and often have rather different positions on how the boundaries between religion and state should be structured.

[14] Ibid.

[15] 330 US 1 (1947).

the states.[16] The competition between the freedom and equality paradigms that has occupied much of the subsequent Establishment Clause litigation is already prefigured in *Everson*. The question in that case was whether a school board could subsidize school bus transportation for children attending private religious schools.

After quoting the religion clauses, the Court began its analysis by stating, 'These words of the First Amendment reflected in the minds of early Americans a vivid mental picture of conditions and practices which they fervently wished to stamp out in order to preserve liberty for themselves and their posterity'.[17] Liberty, or freedom, is clearly the analytical starting point. The Court continues, 'In the words of Jefferson, the clause against establishment of religion by law was intended to erect "a wall of separation between Church and State"'.[18] The Court states, 'No tax in any amount, large or small, may be levied to support any religious activities or institutions, whatever they may be called'.[19] Indeed, the Court insists, the wall of separation 'must be kept high and impregnable. We could not approve the slightest breach'.[20] This strong separationist language emphasized the importance of freedom and the independence of church and state, and the Court appeared ready to apply the principle of strict separation to strike down the county reimbursement program.

But instead, the Court changed direction and turned its attention to the equality principle, noting that this was a 'general program' that reimbursed the parents of all children, 'regardless of their religion'.[21] The Court stated that it 'must be careful … that we do not inadvertently prohibit New Jersey from extending its general State law benefits to all its citizens without regard to their religious belief'.[22] The Court likened the reimbursement program to the provision of general government services such as police and fire protection, and concluded that if the parents of children who attended religious schools were excluded, the program would not be neutral.[23] The Court concluded that the First Amendment 'requires the state to be neutral in

---

[16] Ibid 16. This is spoken of in technical jargon as 'incorporation' of the Establishment Clause into the right to substantive due process under the Fourteenth Amendment of the US Constitution. Following several scholars, Justice Thomas contends that the text and history of the Establishment Clause argue against the theory of its 'incorporation' against the states — *Van Orden v Perry*, 545 US 677, 692 (Thomas J, concurring) (2005); *Elk Grove Unified School District v Newdow*, 542 US 1, 46 (Thomas J, concurring in the judgment) (2004); *Zelman v Simmons-Harris*, 536 US 639, 677–80 (Thomas J, concurring) (2002) — but his resistance to this constitutional fait accompli has not found supporters among other members of the Supreme Court.
[17] Ibid 8.
[18] Ibid 16.
[19] Ibid.
[20] Ibid 18.
[21] Ibid.
[22] Ibid 16.
[23] Ibid 17–8.

its relations with groups of religious believers and non-believers; it does not require the state to be their adversary'.[24]

In permitting the reimbursement program, the Court shifted emphasis from a freedom principle, emphasizing separation, which would seem to render the program unconstitutional, to an equality principle, which allowed the program because it is general and neutral. The dissenting opinion complained that 'the undertones of the opinion, advocating complete and uncompromising separation of Church from State, seem utterly discordant with its conclusion yielding support to their commingling in educational matters'.[25] Thus, in *Everson* we see side-by-side an early articulation of both the freedom paradigm and the equality paradigm that become and remain the primary competing principles in Establishment Clause jurisprudence.

In the quarter century following *Everson*, Establishment Clause cases were largely about determining how high and impregnable the wall of separation of church and state was required to be. The Court held that 'release time' religion courses were impermissible if held on public school premises,[26] but could be allowed if held 'off-site'.[27] A firestorm of public controversy was unleashed in the early 1960s by decisions that held school prayer[28] and Bible reading[29] to be unconstitutional. In 1970, however, the Court held that the wall was not so high as to invalidate the deeply entrenched practices of allowing tax deductions and tax exemptions for religious organizations.[30]

Separation and the *Lemon* test

The Supreme Court wove the holdings of these cases together in the 1971 case *Lemon v Kurtzman*[31] to formulate what has become known as the three-prong *Lemon* test for evaluating Establishment Clause violations. Under this test, in order to withstand Establishment Clause scrutiny, state action must have a secular purpose, it must have a primary effect that neither advances nor inhibits religion, and it may not create excessive entanglement between church and state.[32]

---

[24] Ibid 18.
[25] Ibid.
[26] *McCollum v Board of Education*, 333 US 203 (1948).
[27] *Zorach v Clauson*, 343 US 306 (1952).
[28] *Engel v Vitale*, 370 US 421 (1962).
[29] *Abington School District v Schempp*, 374 US 203 (1963).
[30] *Walz v Tax Commission*, 397 US 664 (1970).
[31] 403 US 602 (1971).
[32] Ibid 612–3.

The *Lemon* test has often been criticized for its incoherence, and for the crazy-quilt pattern of results it has spawned.[33] But on reflection, this is a not-unexpected consequence of *Lemon*'s effort to fuse the freedom and equality paradigms into a single test. The anti-entanglement prong is clearly aimed at protecting freedom,[34] as is that portion of the primary effect prong that focuses on 'inhibiting' religion. Primary effects that 'advance' religion, on the other hand, typically have more to do with privileging some or all religions, and in this sense they typically raise equality issues (although they may bring greater government regulation in tow). The secular purpose prong is more ambiguous, though it is at core a requirement of state neutrality, which reflects equality concerns in the main. In short, the problem at the core of the *Lemon* test is that it papers over the tension between equality and freedom paradigms.

In the 1970s and 1980s, the *Lemon* test was utilized to reach separationist outcomes in a wide variety of cases, especially in public schools, where the Court has invalidated moments of silence,[35] prayer at extra-curricular activities,[36] graduation prayer,[37] posting of the Ten Commandments,[38] many forms of government funding of private religious schools,[39] and has banned many displays of religious symbols on public property.[40]

---

[33] See, eg, Wanda I Otero-Ziegler, 'The Remains of the Wall: From *Everson v Board of Education* to *Strout v Albanese and Beyond*' (2000) 10 *Temple Political and Civil Rights Law Journal* 207, 241; Michael W McConnell and Richard A Posner, 'An Economic Approach to Issues of Religious Freedom' (1989) 56 *University of Chicago Law Review* 1, 25–6.

[34] Avoidance of entanglement and the corresponding protection of religious autonomy has been a key factor in several Establishment Clause cases: see, eg, *NLRB v Catholic Bishop of Chicago*, 440 US 490 (1979) (holding that church-run schools were exempt from national law requiring schools to recognize labor unions in light of risks of excessive entanglement); *Corporation of Presiding Bishop v Amos*, 483 US 327, 345–6 (1987) (non-profit religious organization allowed to engage in preferential hiring of believers in its sponsoring faith, and the exemption from employment discrimination laws that permitted this was justified on the grounds that it would 'avoid the entanglement and the chill on religious expression that case-by-case determination would produce').

[35] *Wallace v Jaffree*, 472 US 38 (1985).

[36] *Santa Fe Independent School District v Doe*, 530 US 290 (2000).

[37] *Lee v Weisman*, 505 US 577 (1992).

[38] *Stone v Graham*, 449 US 39 (1980).

[39] *Levitt v Committee for Public Education & Religious Liberty*, 413 US 472 (1973); *School District of Grand Rapids v Ball*, 473 US 373 (1985); *Aguilar v Felton*, 473 US 402 (1985). As described below, the Ball and Aguilar cases were overruled in the late 1990s as part of the recent reformulation of Establishment Clause doctrine: see below ns 71–76 and accompanying text.

[40] *Stone v Graham*, 449 US 39 (1980); *McCreary County v ACLU of Kentucky*, 545 US 844 (2005); *Van Orden v Perry*, 545 US 677 (2005); *Capitol Square Review & Advisory Board v Pinette*, 515 US 753 (1995); *Lynch v Donnelly*, 465 US 668 (1984).

Equality as the dominant interpretive principle

Alternatives to the Lemon *test*

In the years since *Lemon*, the power of the equality paradigm has become more and more evident. This has taken many forms. For example, many cases over the past quarter century have been willing to move away from strict separationist models and to allow various kinds of 'accommodations' between religion and the state. Accommodationists argue that governmental aid to religious institutions is permitted as long as it is imparted in a non-discriminatory fashion.[41] In this view, equal treatment and non-discrimination are the primary Establishment Clause values. Accommodationists explicitly qualify or reject the wall of separation metaphor. Many of them would share Justice Jackson's view that Jefferson's 'wall of separation' has become 'as winding as the famous serpentine wall' he designed at the University of Virginia.[42] Dissenting in *Wallace v Jaffree*, Chief Justice Rehnquist went further and wrote, '[t]he "wall of separation between church and state" is a metaphor based on bad history, a metaphor which has proved useless as a guide to judging. It should be frankly and explicitly abandoned'.[43] Accommodation is sympathetic with a degree of interplay and cooperation between church and state. Accommodationists emphasize non-discrimination and neutrality, values that reflect a concern for equality among religious and secular viewpoints. This position has led to a number of decisions that have accorded greater flexibility with respect to tax exemption and deduction schemes,[44] grants to higher education institutions that are not pervasively religious,[45] funding for secular tasks at religious institutions,[46] and granting religious

---

[41] See Peter J Weishaar, 'School Choice Vouchers and the Establishment Clause' (1994) 58 *Albany Law Review* 543, 545: 'The "nonpreferential accommodationists" … claim that the religion clauses of the Constitution permit various forms of nonpreferential government support for religion. They argue that government may aid all religions, as long as it does not prefer one religion over another'. For a leading articulation of the accommodationist position, see Michael W McConnell, 'Accommodation of Religion' (1985) *Supreme Court Review* 1.

[42] *McCollum v Board of Education*, 333 US 203, 238 (Jackson J, concurring) (1948). But see *Committee of Public Education and Religious Liberty v Nyquist*, 413 US 756, 761 (Powell J) (1973) (rejecting the serpentine wall image and claiming that 'the broad contours of our [Establishment Clause] inquiry are now well defined').

[43] 472 US 38, 107 (Rehnquist CJ, dissenting) (1985) (criticizing a decision that struck down a state statute authorizing a moment of silence in public schools).

[44] *Mueller v Allen*, 463 US 388 (1983) (upholding deductions for private school tuition).

[45] *Roemer v Board of Public Works*, 426 US 736 (1976); *Hunt v McNair*, 413 US 734 (1973); *Tilton v Richardson*, 403 US 672 (1971).

[46] *Committee for Public Education and Religious Liberty v Regan*, 444 US 646 (1980) (upholding state payments for costs of administrative and recordkeeping costs associated with state-required tests); *Wolman v Walter*, 433 US 229 (1977) (upholding state-administered tests rendered off-site for private school students).

organizations equal access to public facilities.[47] This accommodationist impulse has helped paved the way for revision of the *Lemon* test, as described below.[48]

Another significant development has been the emergence of the so-called 'endorsement' approach to Establishment Clause analysis. In 1984, in a concurring opinion in *Lynch v Donnelly*,[49] Justice O'Connor suggested an alternative to the *Lemon* test, which focused on whether state action impermissibly 'endorsed' religion. In *Lynch*, the Court upheld a city-owned holiday display that included a nativity scene, but also included depictions of Santa Claus, reindeer, and other Christmas figures. While the majority applied the *Lemon* test, and held that the display did not have the purpose or effect of advancing religion, Justice O'Connor applied her new test, focusing upon whether the government action, in purpose and effect, communicates a message of 'endorsement or disapproval of religion'.[50] An endorsement, in her view, 'sends a message to nonadherents that they are outsiders, not full members of the political community, and an accompanying message to adherents that they are insiders, favored members of the political community'.[51]

In shifting the focus of enquiry to endorsement, Justice O'Connor subtly shifted the focus of the *Lemon* test from freedom to equality. The endorsement approach emphasizes the equalitarian dimension of the first two prongs of the *Lemon* test by narrowing the issue from whether there is a secular purpose and a primary effect that advances religion to the narrower question of endorsement. The latter pays more attention to issues of discrimination and lays stress on whether there is state preference for or identification with religion. Moreover, by ignoring *Lemon*'s 'entanglement' prong and the 'inhibits religion' half of the primary effect prong, the endorsement test jettisoned those aspects of the *Lemon* test most attuned to the freedom paradigm. The endorsement test has attracted increasing support over time, with a majority of the Court applying it in cases involving holiday season symbols[52] and prayers at high school sports events.[53] Not altogether unsurprisingly, it has seemed more relevant in religious symbol cases than in those involving financial aid in religious settings.

---

[47] *Board of Education v Mergens*, 496 US 226 (1990) (sustaining *Equal Access Act*, 20 USC §§ 4071–74 (1984)); *Rosenberger v Rector and Visitors of the University of Virginia*, 515 US 819 (1995); *Lamb's Chapel v Center Moriches Union Free School District*, 508 US 384 (1993).
[48] See below ns 71–76 and accompanying text.
[49] 465 US 668, 688 (O'Connor J, concurring) (1984).
[50] Ibid 688.
[51] Ibid.
[52] *County of Allegheny v American Civil Liberties Union*, 492 US 573 (1989).
[53] *Santa Fe Independent School District v Doe*, 530 US 290 (2000).

In general, as the Court's use of the tests it has crafted for Establishment Clause analysis has seemed uneven and unpredictable.[54] Sometimes it has ignored such tests altogether. Thus, in *Marsh v Chambers*[55] the court sustained legislative prayer by a paid chaplain on the grounds that the 1791 Congress that adopted the First Amendment engaged in the same practice. In other cases it invokes *Lemon* as if there had never been a question of its applicability. For its critics, the *Lemon* test has been a recurring nightmare: '[l]ike some ghoul in a late-night horror movie that repeatedly sits up in its grave and shuffles abroad, after being repeatedly killed and buried'.[56] In still other cases, the endorsement test bears the burden of analysis. Despite the zigzag quality of the resulting case law, the general trend has been toward giving greater weight to equalitarian concerns.

Restructuring Lemon*: Recent aid cases*

In recent years, the two primary areas of controversy involving the Establishment Clause have been, first, the presence of religious speech and symbols in public places, and, second, government funding that indirectly benefits religious bodies. On their face, the trend in each of these areas appears to be moving in opposite directions. With respect to public religious expression, religion appears to be losing ground, as reflected in recent Supreme Court decisions prohibiting prayer before football games[57] and at graduation ceremonies,[58] a Court of Appeals decision holding that the words 'under God' in the Pledge of Allegiance violate the Establishment Clause,[59] and in the recent cases involving public displays of the Ten Commandments.[60]

---

[54] See, eg, *Van Orden v Perry*, 125 S Ct 2854, 2860–61 (2005).
[55] 463 US 783 (1983).
[56] *Lamb's Chapel v Center Moriches Union Free School District*, 508 US 384, 398–9 (Scalia J, concurring) (1993).
[57] *Santa Fe Independent School District v Doe*, 530 US 290 (2000).
[58] *Lee v Weisman*, 505 US 577 (1992).
[59] *Newdow v United States Congress*, 292 F.3d 597 (9th Cir, 2002). This case reached the Supreme Court in *Elk Grove Unified School District v Newdow*, 542 US 1 (2004), but the Supreme Court did not reach the merits of the case, holding instead that the Appellate Court's ruling had to be reversed, because the father who brought suit was not the primary custodial parent of the child supposedly offended by the pledge of allegiance practice, and he therefore lacked standing to bring the case.
[60] *McCreary County v ACLU of Kentucky*, 545 US 844 (2005) (ruling unconstitutional courthouse displays of Ten Commandments on grounds that there was no legitimate secular purpose for displaying them and that the displays violated the neutrality principle); *Van Orden v Perry*, 545 US 677 (2005) (permitting stone Ten Commandments display on grounds that the display is a passive acknowledgement of the historical role religion has played in American life and not an active endorsement of religion).

On the other hand, in cases involving the extent to which public funds can be used in ways that indirectly benefit religion, religion appears to be gaining ground. Whereas in earlier state aid cases decided under the *Lemon* test, aid was restricted to separable secular functions,[61] new cases began to emphasize neutrality and equal treatment between religious and non-religious uses. Thus, in 1986, in *Witters v Washington Dep't of Services for the Blind*,[62] the Supreme Court held that the Establishment Clause did not prohibit the state from providing aid to a blind student eligible for academic support just because he proposed to use this aid to study for the ministry at a Christian Bible college. A series of further cases began chipping away at what had been an ironclad rule against direct subsidies to religious groups.[63]

This culminated in 1997 in a major revamping of the *Lemon* test. The vehicle for this revision was the case of *Agostini v Felton*.[64] In that case, the Supreme Court reconsidered its earlier decision in *Aguilar v Felton*,[65] which had invalidated on Establishment Clause grounds a federal aid program that involved sending public school teachers and employees into religiously affiliated schools to provide remedial instruction and other specialized secular services. The bureaucratic structures developed to respect the 'wall of separation' had proven to be costly and inefficient, and the religious schools continued to have a particularly effective track record in dealing with the economically deprived students the federal program was designed to benefit. More significantly, the series of cases that found that rigid application of the 'no aid' principle discriminated against religious groups had undermined some of the premises on which the *Lemon* test was based.

Accordingly, the Court revised its approach to Establishment Clause jurisprudence by reinterpreting the secular purpose and primary effect tests, and folding 'entanglement' analysis back into the primary effect test.[66] That is, in assessing a potential Establishment Clause violation, it continued to invoke the first two prongs

---

[61] See, eg, *Committee for Public Education & Religious Liberty v Regan*, 444 US 646 (1980) (upholding state payments for the administrative and recordkeeping costs associated with state-required tests); *Wolman v Walter*, 433 US 229 (1977) (upholding state-administered tests in private schools).
[62] 474 US 481 (1986).
[63] See, eg, *Zobrest v Catalina Foothills School District*, 509 US 1 (1993) (federal assistance to disabled students could be used to pay for a sign language interpreter for a deaf student at a private religious high school without violating Establishment Clause); *Rosenberger v Rector and Visitors of University of Virginia*, 515 US 819 (1995) (Establishment Clause does not prohibit a state university from providing financial assistance magazine published by a Christian student group when such assistance was being provided to a wide array of student publications).
[64] 521 US 203 (1997).
[65] 473 US 402 (1985).
[66] Ibid 203–35.

of the *Lemon* test by assessing (1) whether the state action in question has the *purpose* of advancing or inhibiting religion (or whether, on the contrary, its purpose is secular), and (2) whether the state action has the *effect* of advancing or inhibiting religion. However, the Court concluded that the criteria for assessing impermissible effect had changed. No longer would the Court presume 'that the placement of public employees on parochial school grounds inevitably results in the impermissible effect of state-sponsored indoctrination or constitutes a symbolic union between government and religion'.[67] Since it was this presumption that had forced the erection of a bureaucratic wall of separation in *Aguilar*, the change in criteria allowed the wall to come down.

With respect to entanglement, the Court took the position that since 'the factors we use to assess whether an entanglement is "excessive" are similar to the factors we use to examine "effect"',[68] entanglement analysis could be recombined with effect analysis. Not surprisingly, since Justice O'Connor wrote the opinion for the Court, the effect of this reinterpretation of the *Lemon* test was to make it coincide much more closely with Justice O'Connor's endorsement test. Entanglement, with its freedom component, is deemphasized. Individual choice remains relevant only in assuring that government aid does not have the effect of inculcating and thus advancing religion.[69] Government aid that steers choice, through incentives or other forms of endorsement is impermissible, but aid channelled to religious schools or other religious entities by voluntary choice is permissible. But freedom in this picture is overshadowed by the fundamental equalitarian step: the state may not discriminate among programs it funds merely because religious groups carry out some of them.

Agostini paved the way for a number of further decisions that appear to widen the doors open to cooperation between the state and religion. *Mitchell v Helms*[70] applied the *Agostini* precedent to reverse the earlier Establishment Clause ban on a federal program that loaned secular instructional materials and equipment to religious schools. Then, in a landmark 2002 case, *Zelman v Simmons-Harris*, the Court upheld a program involving vouchers from the government that parents could use to pay for their children's educations, including at religious schools.[71] In a 5–4 decision, the Court upheld the argument on the basis that religious schools were afforded treatment no less favourable than non-sectarian schools, and based on the fact that the program reflected private choice and was permissible. Like *Agostini*, *Zelman* involved unique needs in an economically distressed environment, but it

---

[67] Ibid 203.
[68] Ibid 232.
[69] Ibid 225–6.
[70] 530 US 793 (2000).
[71] *Zelman v Simmons-Harris*, 536 US 639 (2002).

appears to point to a channel through which massive public financial cooperation could be steered from government via private choice to religious institutions. Only time will tell the extent to which state legislatures will attempt to pursue this option.

Today, the question remains somewhat unsettled whether the same rationale will be applied to permit 'faith-based initiative' programs. But there are indicators pointing in this direction. In 2003, for example, the Seventh Circuit Court of Appeals permitted a pervasively Christian halfway house to serve as a rehabilitation centre under a state prison-parole program.[72] More generally, the Supreme Court's increased concern with prevention of discrimination against religious service providers in the allocation of government support, as signalled by Justice O'Connor's reformulation of the *Lemon* test, has led to a dramatic increase in public funding of religiously affiliated organizations that provide social services. In 2004 the federal government granted 1,968 grants to faith-based organizations totalling over $1.3 billion. Compared with 2003 this marks a 20 per cent increase in grants given and a 14 per cent increase in total spending.[73]

Religious symbols

Shifting from funding to religious symbol cases, the latest decisions involve cases about displays of the Ten Commandments in public settings. These cases provide a glimpse of the structure of Establishment Clause argumentation in its latest iteration. Like the various faces of the Necker Cube, the ascendancy of one paradigm seldom means the total eclipse of another. In fact, one sees the paradigms of liberty and equality playing off against each other in judicial disagreements about contested issues.

The Supreme Court decided the cases in question in June 2005. The cases involved public displays of the Ten Commandments from different parts of the United States. An older display from Texas was held to be permissible in *Van Orden v Perry*.[74] In this case, involving a large stone display of the Ten Commandments on the state capitol grounds in Texas, the Court ruled 5–4 that the display did not violate the Establishment Clause, emphasizing that the display was one among many other statues and monuments in a park-like setting, that the display had been donated by a private group, and that it had been in place for over 40 years without causing

---

[72] *Freedom from Religion Foundation v McCallum*, 324 F 3d 880 (7th Cir 2003).
[73] *Grants to Faith-Based Organizations Fiscal Year 2004* (2005) White House Office of Faith-Based and Community Initiatives <http://www.whitehouse.gov/government/fbci/final-report.pdf> at 5 April 2011.
[74] *Van Orden v Perry*, 125 S Ct 2854 (2005).

controversy.⁷⁵ In contrast, in *McCreary County v ACLU*,⁷⁶ the Court reached the opposite conclusion in another 5–4 decision, holding that Ten Commandment displays in two Kentucky courthouses violated the Establishment Clause, on the grounds that the displays had the non-neutral purpose of promoting one religious viewpoint over others.

The key difference in the two outcomes was the vote of Justice Breyer, who concurred in the respective results but not the reasoning of the respective majority opinions. Justice Breyer criticized the view espoused by the justices who thought that the displays violated Establishment Clause principles according to which 'neutrality' was the proper standard. He was not opposed to neutrality, he just thought it did not constitute a workable judicial standard. In his view:

> Where the Establishment Clause is at issue, tests designed to measure 'neutrality' alone are insufficient, both because it is sometimes difficult to determine when a legal rule is 'neutral,' and because 'untutored devotion to the concept of neutrality can lead to invocation or approval or results which partake not simply of that noninterference and noninvolvement with the religious which the Constitution commands, but of a brooding and pervasive devotion to the secular and a passive, or even active, hostility to the religious.'⁷⁷

The key factor for Justice Breyer was not an illusory or generalized ideal of neutrality, but a context-sensitive legal judgment based on a variety of factors, including assuring the fullest possible scope of religious liberty and tolerance, demonstrating secularity of purpose, and avoiding divisiveness.⁷⁸ The long undisturbed history of the Texas display helped distinguish it from the more politicized efforts to introduce new displays in Kentucky. In effect, Justice Breyer's practical and contextual approach protected countless older memorials from sandblasting or removal, but made it very difficult for newer, politically motivated memorials to survive Establishment Clause scrutiny.

While the Breyer opinion was outcome determinative, the other opinions in the two cases are more helpful in laying bare the core disagreements between different members of the Court. Thus, the anti-display plurality in *McCreary* (the dissent in *Van Orden*) emphasizes the concept of neutrality and concludes that neither the Kentucky nor the Texas displays are neutral. For example, Justice Souter begins his

---

⁷⁵ Ibid.
⁷⁶ *McCreary County v ACLU of Kentucky*, 125 S Ct 2722 (2005).
⁷⁷ 125 S Ct 2854, 2868 (Breyer J, concurring) (2005) (quoting *Abington School District v Schempp*, 374 US 203, 306 (1963)).
⁷⁸ Ibid 2868.

dissent in *Van Orden* by noting that 'although the First Amendment's Religion Clauses have not been read to mandate absolute governmental neutrality toward religion, the Establishment Clause requires neutrality as a general rule'.[79] Justice Souter then concludes that, 'A governmental display of an obviously religious text cannot be squared with neutrality, except in a setting that plausibly indicates that the statement is not placed in view with a predominant purpose on the part of government either to adopt the religious message or to urge its acceptance by others'.[80] Similarly, Justice Stevens concludes that the Texas monument is an endorsement of religion and is 'flatly inconsistent' with 'this Nation's resolute commitment to neutrality with respect to religion'.[81] The paradigm of equality could not be more evident.

In contrast, the pro-display plurality opinion in *Van Orden* disclaimed the usefulness of the *Lemon* test in dealing with a passive monument,[82] and instead said that analysis should be driven by the monument's nature and the nation's history.[83] It cited the country's 200-year history of official acknowledgment by the government of religion's role in American life, and concluded that the Texas display is typical of such acknowledgments.[84] The Court emphasized that the Texas display was no more prominent than numerous other non-religious displays.[85]

By emphasizing traditional practice, the plurality in effect identified with the older freedom paradigm approach. By emphasizing the 'rich American tradition of religious acknowledgements',[86] the plurality implicitly differentiated the Texas display from impermissible endorsement of religion, thereby opening public space for certain types of religious displays.

The freedom paradigm is even more evident in concurrences by the more conservative justices on the Court. Justice Scalia, joined by Justices Rehnquist and Thomas, argues vigorously on the basis of historical tradition that the Establishment Clause has not required strict neutrality when it comes to favouring religion over non-religion, or traditional monotheism over other views.[87] In his view, the original meaning of 'establishment' was understood 'necessarily [to] involve actual legal coercion'.[88] In this more conservative view, an impermissible establishment occurs only when

---

[79] Ibid 2892.
[80] Ibid.
[81] Ibid 2877.
[82] Ibid 2861.
[83] Ibid.
[84] Ibid 2861–2.
[85] Ibid 2862–3.
[86] Ibid 2863.
[87] *McCreary County v ACLU*, 125 S Ct 2722, 2750–3 (Scalia J, dissenting) (2005).
[88] Ibid 2865 (citing *Elk Grove Unified School District v Newdow*, 542 US 1, 52 (Thomas J, concurring in the judgment) (2005); *Lee v Weisman*, 505 US 577, 640 (Scalia J, dissenting) (1992).

state action coerces religious orthodoxy or practice. A display whose maximal impact was to offend those walking by would not violate the Establishment Clause as viewed through the freedom-based conceptual filter.

Justice O'Connor's concurring opinion is also noteworthy. In one of her last opinions before retiring from the Court, and after a career in which she often turned to principles of neutrality and endorsement in Establishment Clause cases, Justice O'Connor departed the Court with a ringing endorsement of the concepts of freedom and liberty, which in her case entailed votes against both the Texas and Kentucky Ten Commandments displays:

> The First Amendment expresses our Nation's *fundamental commitment to religious liberty* by means of two provisions — one protecting the *free exercise of religion*, the other barring establishment of religion. They were written by the descendents of people who had come to this land precisely so that they could *practice their religion freely*. Together with the other First Amendment guarantees — of *free* speech, a *free* press, and the rights to assemble and petition — the Religion Clauses were *designed to safeguard the freedom* of conscience and belief that those immigrants had sought. They embody an idea that was once considered radical: *Free people are entitled to free and diverse thoughts*, which government ought neither to constrain nor direct.
>
> Reasonable minds can disagree about how to apply the Religion Clauses in a given case. But the goal of the Clauses is clear: to carry out the Founders' plan of *preserving religious liberty* to the fullest extent possible in a pluralistic society.[89] (emphases added)

It may seem paradoxical that after two decades of favouring an equalitarian paradigm in analyzing Establishment Clause cases, Justice O'Connor sounded a resounding endorsement of freedom as the first principle in the interpretation of the religion clauses in her farewell Establishment Clause decision.

The Establishment Clause in retrospect

Looking back over Establishment Clause developments, a few concluding points are in order. First, while the trends with respect to public religiosity and public funding of religion seem to be going in different directions, in reality both trends illustrate the ascendance of the equality paradigm. When religion is excluded from public life, it is done largely in the name of equality and neutrality, to avoid the impermissible purpose or effect of endorsing or promoting a particular religious

---

[89] *McCreary County v ACLU of Kentucky*, 545 US 844, 881-2 (O'Connor J, concurring) (2005) (emphases added).

viewpoint. Similarly, recent cases eroding the 'no aid' principle have justified major flows of public funding to religious organizations through programs involving vouchers, scholarship programs, or other social service programs on the grounds that excluding religious organizations or schools would discriminate against them vis-à-vis secular service organizations, and equality forbids such discrimination.

Part of the explanation of the shifting understanding of the Establishment Clause has to do with transformation of the background institutions of state and society. In the early republic, when the scale of government institutions was small and government services were limited, baseline social expectations from government were limited. In the founding era, it was widely assumed that the best way to promote freedom was to impose sharp constraints on governmental power. As the size of the state has expanded, the benchmarks against which citizens measure equal treatment have changed. For example, now we assume that the state will provide public education. Refusal to aid the private educational sector, which in an earlier day would have seemed completely normal, increasingly looks like discrimination against those who for reasons of conscience support the public schools through taxation and their private school through tuition. If the state provides assistance to the deaf and blind, it now appears discriminatory to preclude them from using this assistance at religious schools. Similar arguments can be made across the entire domain of faith-based initiatives. In an earlier day, a 'no aid to religion' policy would have simultaneously averted state entanglement and provided equal treatment. In a world in which state-supported social programs are the norm, denial of access to funding increasingly seems hostile rather than neutral.

Thus, while in the early years of the American Republic, public expressions of religious sentiment were widespread and largely uncontested as a reflection of religious freedom, and public funding of religion was one of the primary evils that the Establishment Clause was meant to prohibit, today there has been a substantial reversal. Equality has replaced freedom as the dominant interpretive value, and in the effort to treat everyone equally, the wall of separation has been significantly eroded. This is not to say that the reinterpreted Establishment Clause allows anything like the level of cooperation in the form of direct subsidies to religion that are common in Europe. But it does recognize that there has been considerable equality-driven convergence toward European models. Religious viewpoints that are not shared by everyone are often suppressed in public settings because of fears of endorsement and unequal treatment, and public funding that benefits religion is allowed on a scale that would have been unimaginable even a generation ago. Both of these trends reflect the rise of the equality paradigm.

There is some irony in these developments. Politically, one would have expected the pressure for greater equality to come from the left, since in American society it is typically left-leaning politicians who emphasize equalitarian arguments. Yet pressure for greater cooperation with religion has and continues to come in significant measure from the religious and political right. This is matched by political alignments on the Supreme Court. The new equalitarian arguments often come from the more conservative Justices. It is as though the right has appropriated the rhetoric of equality and turned it against the left. Though the left tends to oppose the cooperationist results, it is hard-pressed to deny the equalitarian arguments that the right has begun to deploy. This paradoxical situation is one further evidence of the ascendancy of the paradigm of equality: even those who favour the paradigm of freedom as a matter of substance find themselves invoking the paradigm of equality as a matter of argumentative strategy.

Freedom and equality in US Free Exercise jurisprudence

The history of the interpretation of the meaning of the Free Exercise Clause reflects a similar move from viewing freedom as the dominant value at stake, to viewing Free Exercise in a way that emphasizes equality. If anything, the move towards an equalitarian paradigm is even more striking than in the Establishment Clause context. This is all the more remarkable because on its face the *Free* Exercise Clause announces itself as concerned with freedom. Thus, it is nothing short of remarkable, if not alarming, that the Free Exercise Clause has come to be viewed by the Supreme Court primarily as an equality principle, protecting against overt discrimination and requiring only that laws burdening religion be 'general and neutral'.

<u>The early emphasis on freedom</u>

The Free Exercise Clause began as essentially a limit on federal power. The Free Exercise Clause of the First Amendment to the US Constitution provides that '*Congress* shall make no law ... prohibiting the free exercise [of religion]'. Originally, the emphasis was on the limits placed on Congress. For the first century and a half of its existence, the Free Exercise Clause was not even applied to the states. Initially, it was understood as a rule of law constraint, analogous to the 'prescribed by law' constraint in modern limitation clauses that define the outer limits of religious freedom. The basic idea was that religious freedom was promoted by constraining federal power per se.

The Free Exercise Clause was first applied to the states, as opposed to the federal government, in 1940.[90] In the 1960s and 1970s, the Supreme Court used what

---

[90] The Free Exercise Clause was first applied to the States in *Cantwell v Connecticut*, 310 US 296 (1940), a case in which a Connecticut statute requiring a Jehovah's Witness engaged door-to-door proselytizing to obtain a state license was struck down as a violation of the Free Exercise Clause.

is known as the compelling state interest test to evaluate claims for an exemption from laws that burden religious freedom. The 1963 case *Sherbert v Verner* involved a woman who was a Seventh-day Adventist who lost her job because she refused to work on Saturday, her Sabbath day.[91] The state denied her application for unemployment benefits on the grounds that she had refused to accept suitable work 'without good cause'. The Supreme Court held that denying her unemployment benefits violated the Free Exercise Clause. The Court explained that in denying the benefits the state had placed a 'substantial burden' on Mrs Sherbert's religious exercise, and had imposed on her a constitutionally impermissible decision, requiring her to choose between losing her benefits or violating a cardinal tenet of her faith. Such an imposition could be justified, the Court said, only if the state had a 'compelling' or 'paramount' interest and, even then, only if the state could demonstrate that there was no 'alternative form of regulation' that would avoid infringing on Mrs Sherbert's ability to exercise religious freedom. The Court ruled that the state had failed to demonstrate such a compelling state interest. This standard of review had the effect of creating a powerful presumption in favour of religious liberty, unless the government could establish a particularly strong reason for a rule that placed a burden on religion.

This strong defence of religious freedom was reinforced by the Supreme Court's 1972 decision in *Wisconsin v Yoder*,[92] where the Supreme Court granted Amish School children an exemption based upon freedom of religion from a state law requiring compulsory education until the age of sixteen. The Court focused on whether the exemption in question was based upon religious belief or more general cultural factors, and concluded that the Amish objection to compulsory education beyond the eighth grade was based upon religious belief. The Court then said that laws that impose burdens on religious belief must be subject to heightened scrutiny.[93] As in *Sherbert*, this was held to mean that the state had to show a compelling state interest in order to justify such burdens and, further, that the state has employed the least restrictive available means of effectuating the state interest. In *Sherbert*, the Court held that the State had not met this burden of proof, so it granted the religious exemption.

The compelling state interest test played a formidable role in protecting freedom of religion, albeit not necessarily at the level of Supreme Court adjudication. By creating a strong presumption in favour of religious freedom, it gave those claiming religious freedom rights substantial leverage in negotiating with lower level officials in various government bureaucracies who might otherwise have refused to

---

[91] *Sherbert v Verner*, 374 US 398 (1968).
[92] 406 US 205 (1972).
[93] Ibid 210–1.

accommodate religion in the course of carrying out their programs. Moreover, the 'least restrictive means' test provided important protections for religious groups. While constitutional analysis often focuses on the balancing of religious freedom rights against other weighty government interests, the focus on 'alternatives' often points the way towards solutions that work for both religious groups and for the state. As a practical matter, the 'least restrictive means' tests (or variations on this theme that insist on a narrow tailoring of means to governmental ends) may be one of the most significant aspects of the 'strict scrutiny' test and its proportionality counterparts elsewhere.

The erosion of the freedom paradigm

Since the 1970s, constitutional developments in the United States have seen a shift from an emphasis on freedom to an emphasis on equality in Free Exercise jurisprudence.[94] While neither value has ever completely eclipsed the other, there has been a notable and, over time, dramatic shift, with equality replacing freedom as the dominant interpretive paradigm. This tendency to see things predominantly in equalitarian terms has transformed the Free Exercise Clause from a guarantor of religious liberty into a narrow principle that emphasizes neutrality and primarily guards against religious discrimination and the explicit targeting of religion.

At the level of Supreme Court adjudication, the strength of religious freedom protections began to be eroded by a series of cases in the 1980s. In *United States v Lee*,[95] the Court rejected a claim that religious beliefs exempted an Amish farmer from paying social security taxes for his employees. The Court found that the state's interest in mandatory participation was indispensable to the fiscal vitality of the system, and that this constituted an overriding interest sufficiently compelling to outweigh

---

[94] A similar shift has taken place in the Supreme Court's interpretation of the Establishment Clause, which was originally viewed as a limit on the Federal Government's ability to sponsor a state church, which protected the freedom of all churches. In early post-World War II cases through to the 1970s, the dominant metaphor in Establishment Clause cases was the 'wall of separation,' designed to divide church and state into their proper spheres, with as little interaction, interference and overlap as possible. This separation was to serve the dual purposes of protecting the freedom interests of churches from state interference and to protect the freedom interests of the state from religious interference. This chapter will focus on the Free Exercise context rather than the Establishment Clause context. For an analysis of the trend from freedom to equality in US Establishment Clause jurisprudence, see W Cole Durham, Jr and Brett G Scharffs, 'State and Religious Communities in the United States: The Tension Between Freedom and Equality', in *Church and State: Towards Protection for Freedom of Religion*, Proceedings of International Conference on Comparative Constitutional Law, 2005 (The Japanese Association of Comparative Constitutional Law, 2006) (317–61, Japanese version) (362–406, English version).

[95] 455 US 252 (1982).

what the court recognized as a bona fide religious claim. In *Goldman v Weinberger*,[96] the Court sustained military regulations that prohibited the wearing of headgear while indoors against a claim by an orthodox Jewish officer asserting the right to wear a yarmulke. Here, as in various prison cases,[97] the Court dealt with the unique demands of specially restricted environments. Congress reversed this regulation in short order, crafting a legislative exemption for religious apparel that was 'neat and conservative' and did not 'interfere with the performance of the member's military duties'.[98] Another significant case rejected Native American claims that a national forest service road construction policy interfered with the use of space that various Indian tribes viewed as sacred and used for religious rituals.[99] Here the unique issue was that the land was owned by the government in a proprietary capacity, and the Court believed that even though the federal policy 'could have devastating effects on traditional Indian religious practices',[100] the government 'simply could not operate if it were required to satisfy every citizen's religious needs and desires'.[101]

This succession of cases showed that protection of religiously motivated conduct was never as absolute as the strong language of the compelling state interest test suggested, but the test itself nonetheless created a strong presumption in support of the freedom paradigm, which had significant effects at the level of practical governmental interaction with religious groups. Freedom remained the baseline from which analysis began.

Equality as the dominant interpretive principle

General and neutral laws: Employment Division v Smith

In 1990, in *Employment Division v Smith*,[102] the Supreme Court took a big step towards viewing Free Exercise jurisprudence through an equalitarian lens, jettisoning the compelling state interest test in favour of a test that defers to legislative policy except where there is intentional discrimination against religion. In short, it replaced a test designed to afford maximal protection to religious freedom with a test limited to protecting religious equality.

In *Smith*, two drug rehabilitation counsellors were fired from their jobs after ingesting peyote, a hallucinogenic drug used in sacramental ceremonies of the

---

[96] 475 US 503 (1986).
[97] See, eg, *O'Lone v Estate of Shabazz*, 482 US 342 (1987) (sustaining prison policies that prevented prisoners from attending weekly Muslim service for security reasons).
[98] Pub L No 100-180 (1987) (amending 45 USC § 774).
[99] *Lyng v Northwest Indian Cemetery Protective Association*, 485 US 439 (1988).
[100] Ibid 451.
[101] Ibid 452.
[102] 494 US 872 (1990).

Native American Church of which they were members. There was no doubt that the religious use in question was sincere and had a long history, but the state of Oregon denied them unemployment benefits on the basis that they had been fired for work-related misconduct, and maintained that its decision was supported by a compelling state interest.

The majority opinion, written by Justice Scalia, ignored or distinguished earlier precedent and discarded the compelling state interest test. The majority held that a law that burdens religion may override religious freedom claims, so long as it is general and neutral, and does not specifically target religious belief.[103] Thus, government action that restricts religious freedom is permissible, unless there is evidence of intentional discrimination and unequal treatment against the burdened religion. In the view of the *Smith* majority, unless a law is not general or neutral, or unless it specifically targets religion, the government need not provide an exemption to a law that burdens religious exercise.[104] Justice Scalia's approach views free exercise as an equality norm. If laws are general and neutral (that is, they treat religions equally and religion and non-religion equally), and as long as the laws to not specifically target religion (that is, treat different religions unequally), then a law survives Free Exercise scrutiny.

In her concurring opinion, Justice O'Connor pointed out that the Court could easily have decided the case without rendering such a sweeping decision. In her view, the state had a compelling state interest in combating illegal and dangerous drugs. Thus, Justice O'Connor argued, the Court could have retained the compelling interest test, and concluded that the state's interests were sufficiently compelling in the particular case to override the religious freedom claim that was being asserted. But this path was not taken.

From Justice Scalia's perspective as a judicial conservative, the motivation for the decision may have been to increase judicial deference to the legislative branch by reducing the range of circumstances in which the judiciary could carve out exemptions to protect religious freedom. In so holding, however, the Court shifted the analytical starting point in free exercise jurisprudence from freedom to equality. Rather than requiring a compelling state interest and narrow tailoring to justify burdens on religious practice, laws that burden religion are permitted if they are general and neutral. Furthermore, the version of equality selected is formal and defective.

---

[103] Ibid 878.
[104] In Church of the *Lukumi Babalu Aye, Inc v City of Hialeah*, 508 US 520 (1993), the Supreme Court held that a city ordinance that prohibited the ritual slaughter or sacrifice of animals violated the Free Exercise Clause under the *Oregon v Smith* standard, because although the ordinance did not specifically mention the Santeria religion, there were so many exceptions for other types of killing of animals, it discriminated against the Santeria religion.

Formal equality means that all addressees of legislation are treated exactly the same. A suitable substantive conception of equality recognizes that an individual's religion is a factor justifying differential treatment where there is not a compelling reason of sufficient weight to override the religious freedom claim, or where the state's interest can be achieved in some less burdensome way.

Discriminatory laws, hybrid rights, and church autonomy

The *Smith* decision left open the possibility of some narrow grounds for recognizing religious claims for an exemption from laws that negatively affect religious exercise. First, laws that are not general and neutral would still provide a basis for a free exercise claim. Second, so-called hybrid rights, free exercise claims that implicate other important Constitutional rights, including First Amendment rights such as freedom of speech or freedom of association, could still be evaluated under the compelling state interest standard. Third, the case cited positively and thus left undisturbed the set of Supreme Court cases dealing with religious autonomy.

The first possibility, laws that target religion even though they appear to be general and neutral, was tested in *Church of the Lukumi Babalu Aye v City of Hialeah*, 508 US 520 (1993), a case involving a city regulation that forbade the ritual slaughter of animals. The Court concluded that these ordinances were specifically targeted at the practices of a particular religious group, Santeria, an Afro-Caribbean religion, and that they were therefore not general or neutral. Although the ordinances did not specifically mention the Santeria religion, there were exceptions for 'almost all killings of animals except for religious sacrifice', including hunting, slaughter of animals for food, eradication of pests, and euthanasia. Having concluded that the ordinances were discriminatory, the Court applied 'the most rigorous scrutiny' and held that the stated reasons for the ban — preventing cruelty to animals and protecting public health — were unavailing since those reasons applied to the other types of killing that were permitted under the ordinances. *Lukumi* is significant because it makes clear that even after *Employment Division v Smith*, laws that in fact single out religiously motivated conduct are not neutral and generally applicable. Particularly where statutory schemes provide a variety of exceptions, the Court will look beyond the surface of the law to determine whether there is in fact religious discrimination, and if there is, the compelling state interest will be applied to determine whether there is a Free Exercise violation.

The second exception to the general and neutral law test articulated in *Smith* would apply in cases involving 'hybrid' claims that combined a free exercise claim with other constitutional rights. Although the Supreme Court has yet to decide a case that explicitly relies on the 'hybrid rights' theory, the Court has decided cases involving constitutional claims that implicate Free Exercise rights. In *Boy Scouts of America v*

Dale, 530 US 640 (2000), the Supreme Court relied upon Freedom of Association to uphold the right of the Boy Scouts to remove an assistant scoutmaster who was openly gay. The Court held that the Boy Scouts had expressly disapproved of homosexual conduct and that their ability to communicate that message would be significantly impeded if they were required to have an openly gay scoutmaster. This might be an example where hybrid rights theory would apply. In general, the hybrid rights theory has not found much traction, because either the other supporting right is sufficiently strong to be effective on its own, in which case it is redundant to assert the hybrid religious claim, or the other right is not sufficient on its own, in which case adding a religious claim probably will not help. This appears to be a case in which two half rights do not add up to a whole.

The third exception involves cases implicating the religious autonomy rights of churches. The idea of the judiciary avoiding decisions about religious doctrine undergirds one of the main arguments for *Smith's* neutral and generally applicable rule. The Supreme Court wrote that the judiciary lacks the authority to 'question the centrality of particular beliefs or practices to a faith, or the validity of particular litigants' interpretations of those creeds'.[105]

Congress's attempt to reassert freedom in Free Exercise jurisprudence

The public reaction to the *Smith* case was overwhelmingly negative. A broad coalition of religious and civil liberty groups, both conservative and liberal, pressed Congress to enact a statute reinstating the compelling state interest test. Congress responded by nearly unanimously passing the *Religious Freedom Restoration Act of 1993* ('RFRA').[106] RFRA provided that the government may not substantially burden one's exercise of religion, even through rules of general applicability, unless it can show that the burden furthers a 'compelling governmental interest' and is 'the least restrictive means' of furthering that interest.[107] RFRA sought to restore the compelling state interest standard set forth in *Sherbert* and *Yoder* in free exercise cases as a matter of legislation. The basic idea was that Congress could impose a higher 'floor' on religious freedom than the Supreme Court required.

---

[105] 494 US 872, 887 (1990).
[106] *Religious Freedom Restoration Act of 1993*, Pub L No 103-141, 107 Stat 1488 (1993) (codified as amended at 42 USC §§ 2000bb, 2000bb-1 to 2000bb-4 (2000)), invalidated by *City of Boerne v Flores*, 521 US 507, 511 (1997). RFRA was adopted in the House of Representatives by unanimous vote and in the senate by a vote of 97 to 3, and President Clinton promptly signed the legislation: Peter Steinfels, 'Clinton Signs Law Protecting Religious Practices', *New York Times*, 17 November 1993, A18.
[107] Ibid RFRA, §3.

But in *Boerne v Flores*,[108] the Supreme Court ruled that RFRA was unconstitutional, at least as applied to state and local government actions, on the grounds Congress lacked the power to pass the legislation in question. Remember that the Constitution grants Congress only certain enumerated powers. RFRA had been enacted on the basis of Section 5 of the Fourteenth Amendment, which empowers Congress to enact legislation designed to 'enforce' Fourteenth Amendment protections of the rights to 'life, liberty, and property'.

Defenders of RFRA contended that the Act fell within the range of measures Congress could enact to enforce religious freedom protections, but the Court disagreed, at least to the extent that Congress was thereby imposing a level of religious freedom protection on the states that went beyond that required by the Supreme Court. In the Court's view, section 5 of the Fourteenth Amendment gives Congress power to 'enforce the provisions' of the Fourteenth Amendment 'by appropriate legislation', but not to make 'a substantive change in constitutional protections'.[109] This upset at least the balance between federal and state power, if not that between the Court and Congress as well.

Post-Boerne developments: Reasserting a freedom paradigm

Although the *Boerne* decision struck a blow for those who believe Free Exercise cases should be viewed through a prism of freedom, a number of subsequent developments have reasserted freedom as an important Free Exercise value. These responses have taken several forms, including state RFRAs, state constitutional law jurisprudence, subsequent Congressional actions, and the Application of RFRA to the federal government.

State RFRAs

As my colleagues Cole Durham and Bob Smith have noted, since the Supreme Court invalidated RFRA in the *Boerne* decision, no less than fifteen states have passed either statutes or state constitutional amendments enacting so-called state RFRAs: Alabama, Arizona, Connecticut, Florida, Idaho, Illinois, Louisiana, Missouri, New Mexico, Oklahoma, Pennsylvania, Rhode Island, South Carolina, Tennessee and Texas.[110] These State Religious Freedom Restoration Acts re-institute the compelling state

---

[108] 521 US 507 (1997).
[109] Ibid 519.
[110] William W Bassett, W Cole Durham, Jr, and Robert T Smith, *Religious Organizations and the Law* (updated annually, forthcoming edition 2011). §§ 2:63–64 (2011).

interest test for cases decided in courts of that state.[111] This represents a significant reassertion of the freedom paradigm in Free Exercise cases.

State supreme court interpretations of state constitutional provisions protecting religious freedom

A number of state supreme courts have held that the level of protection to religious freedom under their state constitutions requires a higher level of protection from religious freedom than that afforded by the Supreme Court's interpretation of the Free Exercise Clause. Some state supreme courts have maintained the compelling state interest test under their state constitutional provisions protecting religious freedom.[112]

State supreme courts have shown surprising indifference to *Smith*. According to Durham and Smith:

> To date, only three state high courts —Maryland, New Jersey, and Wyoming — have followed the *Smith* line of reasoning in interpreting their state constitutions. However, the Court of Appeals case applying *Smith* in Maryland applied strict scrutiny under one of the *Smith* exceptions, making the court's departure from pre-*Smith* free exercise analysis less pronounced. Six other states — Iowa, Mississippi, Montana, Nebraska, Nevada, and Virginia — have shown some inclination to follow *Smith*. But this number may actually be overstating these courts' reliance on *Smith*, as the relevant decisions from Nebraska, Nevada, and Virginia, do not turn on an interpretation of state constitutional law and thus may simply be following *Smith* in applying the federal Free Exercise Clause to matters arising within their jurisdictions.[113]

---

[111] Courts of at least eleven states have held that their state constitutions provide broader protection for religious exercise than the federal *Smith* rule: see, eg, *Fortin v Roman Catholic Bishop of Portland*, 871 A 2d 1208, 1227-8 (Maine 2005); *Larson v Cooper*, 90 P 3d 125, 131 (Alaska 2004), *cert denied*, 546 US 1140 (2006); *City Chapel Evangelical Free Inc v City of South Bend*, 744 NE 2d 443, 445-6 (Indiana 2001); *Humphrey v Lane*, 728 NE 2d 1039 (Ohio 2000); *Open Door Baptist Church v Clark County*, 140 Wash 2d 142, 995 P 2d 33, 39 (2000); *McCready v Hoffius*, 459 Mich 131, 586 NW 2d 723, 729 (1998) (applying strict scrutiny but finding no free exercise violation), *op vacated in part*, 459 Mich 1235, 593 NW2d 545 (1999) (vacating earlier decision that *Civil Rights Act* did not violate free exercise provisions of federal and state constitutions and remanding for determination of this issue); *Korean Buddhist Dae Won Sa Temple v Sullivan*, 87 Haw 217, 247 (Haw 1998); *State v Miller*, 549 NW 2d 235, 240-1 (Wis 1996); *Attorney General v Desilets*, 636 NE 2d 233 (Mass 1994); *Rourke v New York State Department of Corrective Services* 603 NY S 2d 647 (NY Sup Ct 1993), affirmed 615 NY S 2d 470 (NY App Div 1994); *State v Hershberger*, 462 N W 2d 393 (Minn 1990).

[112] Bassett, Col Durham, Jr and Smith, above n 110, § 2:63 (citations omitted).

[113] Ibid.

In contrast, at least eleven states — Alaska, Hawaii, Indiana, Maine, Massachusetts, Michigan, Minnesota, New York, Ohio, Washington, and Wisconsin — 'have interpreted their state constitutions' free exercise clause to require strict scrutiny analysis',[114] while 'An additional four states — California, Colorado, Utah, and Vermont — have expressly declined the opportunity to follow *Smith* and have deferred this decision until a future case'.[115]

Eleven other states — Arkansas, Delaware, Georgia, Kansas, Kentucky, New Hampshire, North Carolina, North Dakota, Oregon, South Dakota, and West Virginia — 'have not yet determined whether they will follow *Smith* or employ strict scrutiny to state free exercise claims. However, in many of these jurisdictions, precedents that antedate *Smith* and applied strict scrutiny are arguably still binding, though the fusion of federal and state standards in many of these cases leaves some uncertainty as to the applicable standard in a post-*Smith/Boerne* setting'.[116]

Durham and Smith conclude:

> The bottom line is that only a handful of states have expressly followed *Smith*, and of those, some have done so only in cases in which no state free exercise claims were asserted or where strict scrutiny protections were still available because of the applicability of one of the *Smith* exceptions. In contrast, a total of twenty-six states have expressly rejected *Smith* and retain a strict scrutiny requirement — fifteen by statute or constitutional amendment, and eleven by judicial enactment. Pre-*Smith* precedents in many of the states that have not squarely faced the issue still point toward a strict scrutiny approach. This means that only 4.9% (14.9 million) of the U.S. population live in states that expressly follow *Smith*, whereas 62.2% (189 million) live in the twenty-six states that have expressly rejected *Smith*.[117]

What is remarkable is that state courts in a variety of ways have been quite resistant to the *Smith* equality paradigm, and have in large measure found mechanisms for asserting under a state law rubric a freedom paradigm that utilizes the compelling state interest test.

Congressional efforts to reassert freedom of religion

At the Congressional level, options have been more limited. After *Boerne* stripped Congress of its ability to invoke section 5 power, at least to impose an across-the-board compelling state interest test that would put limits on all federal and state action,

---

[114] Ibid.
[115] Ibid.
[116] Ibid.
[117] Ibid.

Congress has been limited to passing much more limited pieces of legislation based on specific enumerated powers. Nevertheless, Congress has been quite persistent and active in reasserting the freedom paradigm notwithstanding the Supreme Court's holdings in *Smith* and *Boerne*. There have been at least three significant Congressional efforts to increase the level of protection of religious freedom above *Smith's* requirement that laws affecting religion be general and neutral.

Most directly related to *Smith*, in 1994 Congress passed the *American Indian Religious Freedom Act Amendment* (AIRFAA), a federal law designed to make the religious use of peyote by Native American church members lawful, specifically overturning the results in *Smith*.[118] This is a post-RFRA frontal response to the Supreme Court's holding in the *Smith* case.

Another such action was based on federal bankruptcy power. After *Smith*, several bankruptcy courts began to interpret the federal *Fraudulent Conveyances Act* in a way that caused significant difficulties for religious organizations. Specifically, the *Fraudulent Conveyances Act* provided that bankruptcy courts could recapture transfers made to third parties without consideration during the three months prior to declaration of bankruptcy. Several courts reasoned that donations to religious organizations were made 'without consideration', and began to require churches to return tithing and other religious contributions that had been made by a debtor within the statutory three month period. Congress responded by passing the *Religious Liberty and Charitable Donation Act of 1998* (RLCDPA), which provides that 'a transfer of a charitable contribution to a qualified religious or charitable entity or organization shall not be considered a transfer [in fraud of creditors]'.[119]

Far more significant on a national scale was Congress' passage in 2000 of the *Religious Land Use and Institutionalized Persons Act* (RLUIPA).[120] Congress passed RLUIPA as a direct response to the Supreme Court holding RFRA unconstitutional in *Boerne*. This was a further attempt by Congress to reinstate the compelling state interest standard, although in a narrower range of situations involving religious challenges to land use regulations such as zoning and historic preservation laws, and to regulations involving 'institutionalized persons' in settings such as prisons and mental hospitals. Each of these areas have been the subject of numerous Free Exercise challenges, for example by churches that want to expand their buildings in the face of restrictive zoning regulations, and by prisoners who wish to engage in religious worship or receive special diets based upon religious conviction in the face of unaccommodating prison policies.

---

[118] Pub L No 103-344, 108 Stat. 3125 (1994) (codified at 42 USC § 1996a (2007)).
[119] Pub L 105-183 (1998), revising among other provisions 11 USCA §§ 544, 548(2)).
[120] 114 Stat 804 (2000).

In May 2005, the Supreme Court decided *Cutter v Wilkinson*,[121] which involved an Establishment Clause challenge to RLUIPA. A group of prisoners in Ohio sued the state, asserting that the state violated RLUIPA by failing to accommodate their religious exercise in prison. The State responded by arguing that section 3 of RLUIPA, which reinstituted the compelling state interest standard in cases involving prisoners, violated the Establishment Clause by improperly advancing religion. In a unanimous decision, the Supreme Court held that section 3 of RLUIPA does not violate the Establishment Clause. Noting that the statute does not differentiate among bona fide religious faiths, does not confer privileged status on any particular religious sect, and does not single out any bona fide faith for disadvantageous treatment, the Court concluded that the provision merely removed government imposed burdens on religious exercise. This, in the Court's view, constituted a permissible accommodation of religion, rather than an impermissible advancement or endorsement.

The *Cutter* decision is significant in confirming that a narrow legislatively crafted religious exemption can withstand Establishment Clause scrutiny. This is not surprising, since the Court has long recognized that there is sufficient play in the constitutional joints to assure that legislation passed in the interest of protecting Free Exercise does not violate the Establishment Clause. As a practical matter, the case is not likely to have broad new implications. The legislative history of RLUIPA indicates that particularly in the prison setting, Congress anticipated that courts would apply the Act's standard with 'due deference to the experience and expertise of prison and jail administrators in establishing necessary regulations and procedures to maintain good order, security and discipline, consistent with consideration of costs and limited resources'.[122] Prisons would appear to be a context where compelling government interests are quite likely to justify the state not meeting broad demands for religious accommodations. Thus, prisoners are not heavily favoured by RLUIPA. Nevertheless, the *Cutter* case represents an acknowledgment that there is 'some space for legislative action neither compelled by the Free Exercise Clause nor prohibited by the Establishment Clause'.[123] RLUIPA confirms that some limited portions of the protection lost under *Smith* and *Boerne* can be protected legislatively.

RFRA as applied to the federal government

While RFRA was declared unconstitutional with respect to state and local government action in *City of Boerne*, as yet, the Supreme Court has not squarely faced the issue

---

[121] 544 US 709 (2005).
[122] Ibid 716, citing 'Joint Statement of Senators Hatch and Kennedy', 146 *Congress Records* 16698, 166999 (2000).
[123] Ibid 719.

of whether as applied to the federal government RFRA is constitutional or not. However, the preliminary hints are that it is. As noted above, in *Cutter v Wilkinson*, 544 US 709 (2005), the Court held that RLUIPA did not violate the Establishment Clause. Of course, RLUIPA is much more narrowly drafted than RFRA, but the basic rationale of the case, according to which increasing the level of protection of a prisoners religious freedom rights does not violate the Establishment Clause, would seem to apply in the federal RFRA setting.

In 2006, the US Supreme Court decided a case very much like the peyote case, *Employment Division v Smith*, but this time the case involved hoasca tea, which contained a hallucinogenic substance illegal under US drug laws and international treaties. Moreover, although the issue of the constitutionality of the 'federal RFRA' was not formally before the Court in *Gonzales v O Centro Espirita Beneficente Uniao Do Vegetal*,[124] the fact that the Supreme Court applied RFRA in a manner that allowed religious plaintiffs claiming an exemption from federal drug laws to prevail with no intimation that there might be a constitutional problem that needed to be considered on remand suggests that the Supreme Court is not likely to strike down RFRA's federal reach.

The case involved O Centro Espirita Beneficente Uniao do Vegetal (UDV), a Christian spiritist sect based in Brazil, with an American branch of approximately 130 members. The Church members received communion by drinking a sacramental tea brewed from plants unique to the region in Brazil where the religion originated, which contains a hallucinogen regulated by the Federal Government under the *Controlled Substances Act*. The government conceded that this practice is a sincere exercise of religion, but nevertheless sought to prohibit the use of the drug by members of the Church in the United States on the ground that it violated the *Controlled Substances Act*.

The religious group responded by arguing that RFRA applied to this case and that it prohibited the Federal Government from substantially burdening a person's exercise of religion unless the Government 'demonstrates that application of the burden to the person' represents the least restrictive means of advancing a compelling state interest. The Government argued that it had a compelling state interest in the uniform application of the drug laws and that no exception to the ban on hallucinogenic drugs could be made to accommodate the sect's sincere religious practice. The Supreme Court applied RFRA and concluded that the Government failed to carry its burden of proving that it had a compelling state interest in barring the Church's sacramental use of hoasca tea. The Court rejected the government's categorical approach of looking to 'broadly formulated interests justifying the general

---

[124] 546 U.S.418 (2006).

applicability of government mandates', and focused instead on the harm posed by not granting an exemption.[125]

The Court also rejected the Government's sweeping claim that it had a compelling interest based upon its obligation to comply with the 1971 United Nations Convention on Psychotropic Substances, a treaty signed by the United States that calls upon signatories to prohibit the use of hallucinogens, including DMT.[126]

In conclusion, the Court notes that even though the balancing required by RFRA is difficult, it is what Congress has mandated the courts to do in cases such as this.[127]

Because the case came before the Court on an appeal from the grant of a preliminary injunction, it has now been remanded to lower courts for adjudication on the merits. As indicated above, however, the Court's opinion contains no hint that the statutory language of RFRA, which the Court carefully applied, suffers from any constitutional defects in the federal setting. As a practical matter, neither religious claimants nor federal officials are likely to challenge federal RFRA — the claimants because they seek the most favourable possible protection, and federal officials, because although federal prosecutors might be interested in asserting such a challenge, the top level federal officials charged with making such decisions (the Attorney General and the Solicitor General) have a duty to defend rather than attack federal legislation, and they are particularly unlikely to attack legislation that is as politically popular as RFRA.

<u>Some reflections on US Free Exercise jurisprudence</u>

The struggle concerning the fate of legislative exemptions designed to accommodate freedom of religion has been the central drama of free exercise jurisprudence over the past 20 years. The US Supreme Court has promoted an equalitarian position, focusing upon whether a law is general and neutral, and whether legislation was specifically targeted at burdening religion. The response of Congress, state courts, and state legislature has in large measure been to reassert freedom as a predominant Free Exercise value. They have done this by reasserting the compelling state interest test. These efforts are a kind of counter-insurgency to re-establish the role of freedom in free exercise cases.

---

[125] Ibid 430.
[126] Ibid 437–8.
[127] Ibid 439.

The institutional dialectic: Legislative and judicial role reversal

As Michael McConnell noted in a conference at BYU Law School, the history of the protection of religious freedom is a complete reversal of our normal expectations about the tendencies of legislatures and the assumptions we make about courts. McConnell describes what he calls the 'political science model' of the roles of legislatures and courts:

> Basic political science courses often describe judicial review as fundamental to the protection of individual interests from majority rule. The ability to challenge governmental action in court gives non-majoritarian interests an avenue to overcome the majoritarian pronouncements of the legislatures. The democratic institutions of government represent majority rule, while the courts in our system — or in any system with judicial review — are more amenable to protecting minority interests.[128]

In other words, the political science model posits that legislatures will represent the interests of powerful majorities, and courts are necessary to protect the rights of minorities. According to this model, as Professor McConnell explains, 'we would expect to find laws passed by majoritarian legislatures that violate the free exercise of religion, followed by court decisions protecting religious minorities'.[129]

The interesting irony is that the history of the protection of religious freedom in the United States tells a story that is almost the exact opposite of what the political science model would suggest.[130] For at least the last 20 years, and even previously, in the US, courts, including (or perhaps especially) the US Supreme Court has been an extremely ineffectual institution for protecting religious freedom claims. The legislature, in contrast, has been quite active in trying to assert religious freedom rights, not just for majority religious groups, but for minority groups as well. Indeed, much of the litigation over the past 20 years has been about the constitutionality of Congressional attempts to expand the scope of religious freedom protection.

---

[128] Michael W McConnell, 'Religious Freedom, Separation of Powers, and the Reversal of Roles' (2001) *Brigham Young University Law Review* 611, 612.

[129] Ibid.

[130] McConnell observes, 'And yet, when we look at the actual record of democratic institutions versus the courts in the United States, it turns out that reality does not conform to the political science model we have been taught. It is very nearly the opposite. Legislatures have shown a remarkable degree of solicitude for minority religious interests, and courts in the United States have repeatedly — not always, but frequently — struck down the efforts of legislatures to protect minority religious groups as unconstitutional.' Ibid 612–3.

15

Walking the Tightrope: The Struggle of Canadian Courts to Define Freedom of Religion under the Canadian Charter of Rights and Freedoms

Barbara Billingsley

*Render to Caesar the things that are Caesar's
and to God the things that are God's.*[1]

How should the laws of the state be balanced against the precepts of religion? In Canada, this age-old question has received renewed attention since the 1982 adoption of the *Canadian Charter of Rights and Freedoms*, which constitutionally guarantees freedom of 'conscience and religion' to every person in the country.[2] Like most modern Western democracies, Canada does not have a state religion and the Canadian polity is comprised of individuals holding a wide range of religious views.[3] This means that, in order to comply with the Charter's guarantee of religious freedom,

---

[1] *King James Bible*, Gospel of Mark, 12:17.
[2] *Canadian Charter of Rights and Freedoms* (Canada) s 2(a) (being Schedule B to the *Canada Act 1982* (UK) c 11 ('the Charter')).
[3] The reference to religious views is broad and is intended to include the views of individuals who belong to organized religions, individuals who believe in a deity or hold spiritual beliefs outside of organized religions, and individuals who are areligious (that is, agnostics and atheists).

law-makers must consider the impact of legislation on a wide range of religious beliefs and practices.[4] To ensure that legislators take proper account of religious freedom, the Canadian constitution empowers the courts to nullify any law that unjustifiably infringes upon Charter rights.[5] This casts Canadian courts as the arbiters of any conflict between positive law and religious freedom. In order to fulfil this role, the courts have been forced to conceptualize and articulate a meaningful definition of freedom of religion and to set parameters on the constitutional protection of freedom of religion so as to accommodate other competing, but legitimate, social concerns.[6]

In this chapter, my primary intention is to explain how 'freedom of religion' operates as a constitutional right under the Charter and to outline the scope of this right as it has been defined thus far by Canadian case law. By way of background, I begin with a brief discussion of the role played by 'freedom of religion' in Canadian law prior to the adoption of the Charter. Next, I offer a three-part consideration of freedom of religion under the Charter. First, I outline the Charter provisions that offer religious protection and summarize the process of judicial review authorized by the Charter. Second, I discuss the current judicial understanding of 'freedom of religion' under the Charter, as defined by the Supreme Court of Canada. Third, in order to demonstrate the practical impact of Canada's constitutional guarantee of freedom of religion on contemporary legislative initiatives, I briefly review the leading Canadian Charter cases that have addressed conflicts between state action and freedom of religion. Finally, I conclude with some brief comments on the current state of the law regarding the Charter's protection of freedom of religion and on possible directions for the future.

As a backdrop to this discussion, readers should remember that Canada's constitution in general, and the Charter in particular, apply to the actions of government rather than to the actions of individuals. In large part, Canada's constitution empowers government by establishing the country's federal parliamentary system and by dividing legislative authority between the country's federal and provincial governments.[7] The Charter, however, constrains the powers of government by placing specified

---

[4] Of course, even without the Charter, lawmakers would likely be compelled by political forces to consider the impact of their legislative choices on the wide spectrum of religious interests in Canada. The Charter, however, makes such consideration a legal imperative because courts can nullify legislation that does not accord with Charter values.

[5] *Constitution Act 1982* (Canada) s 52 (being Schedule B to the *Canada Act 1982* (UK) c 11).

[6] As noted in Chief Justice McLachlin (Canada Supreme Court) 'Freedom of Religion and the Rule of Law: A Canadian Perspective' in D Farrow (ed), *Recognizing Religion in a Secular Society: Essays in Pluralism, Religion and Public Policy* (2004) 31.

[7] See the *Constitution Act 1867*, 30 and 31 Vict, c 3 (reprinted in RSC 1985, App II, No 5).

individual rights and freedoms above the laws of the state.[8] Accordingly, I direct my comments at the concept of religious freedom as a limitation on government action.[9]

A further limitation on the scope of this discussion relates to the philosophical or social value of the Charter's protection of freedom of religion. The Charter presumes that freedom of religion is an important and worthy value in a democratic society. I do not question that notion. Commensurate with the approach taken by Canadian courts in applying the Charter, my focus is on discussing the meaning and scope of the right to freedom of religion as it presently exists in Canada's constitution. Accordingly, except as necessary to deal with the interpretation and application of the Charter's guarantee of freedom of religion, I do not discuss the philosophical, social or legal merits of recognizing freedom of religion as a constitutional right.[10]

Background: Freedom of religion prior to the Charter

As noted above, the Charter was enacted in 1982, giving unprecedented constitutional force to the rights and freedoms that it itemizes, including the freedom of religion. This is not to say, however, that religious rights were not recognized or protected by Canadian law prior to the advent of the Charter. For example, since Canada's inception as a nation in 1867, the constitution has provided for the establishment and preservation of denominational schools as a means of protecting minority Catholics and Protestants from assimilation.[11] Since the 1960s, the federal and provincial governments have established and maintained human rights legislation (including

---

[8] Section 32 of the Charter expressly restricts the Charter's application to government, and not private, activity. Canadian courts have interpreted this provision to mean that the Charter applies to legislation and regulations enacted by government and to certain other government actions. See Peter W Hogg, *Constitutional Law of Canada* (2007) ch 37.2. For the sake of convenience, I will use the term 'laws' or 'legislation' to encompass statutes, regulations and all other government actions that may be subject to Charter review.

[9] In Canada, protection of religious freedom against limitations imposed by private parties is provided by human rights legislation enacted by the federal and provincial governments within their respective areas of jurisdiction.

[10] There is a good deal of academic literature dealing with these issues. For example, a short summary of commonly expressed reasons for protecting freedom of religion as a fundamental right is provided by J E Buckingham, 'The Fundamentals of Religious Freedom: The Case for Recognizing Collective Aspects of Religion' in G Mitchell, I Peach, D E Smith and J D Whyte (eds), *A Living Tree: The Legacy of 1982 in Canada's Political Evolution* (2007). For a further discussion of the reasons that freedom of religion is valued in a democratic society, see also A Dorfman, 'Freedom of Religion' (2008) 21 *Canadian Journal of Law and Jurisprudence* 279.

[11] *Constitution Act 1867*, 30 and 31 Vict, c 3, s 93 (reprinted in RSC 1985, App II, No. 5).

bills of rights) to recognize and protect freedom of religion.[12] Moreover, even prior to the passage of such legislation, Canadian courts upheld freedom of religion as an implicit and fundamental right in a democratic society. For example, in *Saumur v City of Quebec*,[13] the Supreme Court of Canada held that a city by-law that prohibited distribution of books and pamphlets without the permission of the Chief of Police could not be relied upon to prevent Jehovah's Witnesses from disseminating their religious publications. Similarly, in *Roncarelli v Duplessis*,[14] the Supreme Court held that the premier of Quebec acted improperly when he cancelled the liquor license of a Montreal restaurant owner as retribution for the owner's decision to post bail for several Jehovah's Witnesses charged with violating a municipal by-law. In short, individual freedom of religion has long been recognized as a basic of Canada's legal tradition. Accordingly, much of the Charter jurisprudence regarding the definition and scope of freedom of religion is built upon this tradition.

Prior to the enactment of the Charter, however, Canadian courts had limited tools to protect individuals' freedom of religion from interference by the state. Since bills of rights are ordinary statutes without constitutional status, the courts were reluctant to liberally apply the rights identified in such legislation as a means of judging the validity of other legislation. The express inclusion of individual rights and freedoms in Canada's constitution gave Canadian courts the authority to more robustly evaluate government action in light of these rights and freedoms, including the right to freedom of religion.

Freedom of religion under the Charter

The protection offered by the Charter

There are five provisions of the Charter that expressly or implicitly raise the issue of religion:

- the preamble states that 'Canada is founded upon principles that recognize the supremacy of God and the rule of law'

- s 2(a) states that 'Everyone has the following fundamental freedoms: ... freedom of conscience and religion'

---

[12] See, eg, the *Canadian Bill of Rights*, RSC 1970, App III, s 1. These statutes remain in place today but they are rarely relied on as a means of protecting individuals from government action because such claims are typically now brought under the Charter. Other legislation protects individuals against discrimination in certain private or civil law relationships.

[13] [1953] 2 SCR 299.

[14] [1959] SCR 1921.

- s 15(1) states that 'Every individual is equal before and under the law and has the right to the equal protection and equal benefit of the law without discrimination and, in particular, without discrimination based on race, national or ethnic origin, colour, religion, sex, age or mental or physical disability'
- s 27 states that 'This Charter shall be interpreted in a manner consistent with the preservation and enhancement of the multicultural heritage of Canadians'
- s 29 states that 'Nothing in this Charter abrogates or derogates from any rights or privileges guaranteed by or under the Constitution of Canada in respect of denominational, separate or dissentient schools'.

Of these five provisions, s 2(a) is the strongest legal guardian of religious rights because it is the only Charter provision that provides a substantive and generally applicable right to religious freedom. The preamble and s 27 of the Charter offer the courts guidelines for interpreting Charter rights but do not provide an express protection of religious or other freedoms. Further, by acknowledging the supremacy of God alongside the rule of law, the preamble recognizes the country's commitment to both of these values but provides no basis for resolving a conflict between them. Section 29 is another interpretive provision, designed to ensure that the court's application of Charter rights does not interfere with the denominational school system provided for elsewhere in the constitution.[15] The equality guarantee in s 15 offers more generally applicable protection against religious discrimination, but, because equality is necessarily a comparative concept, this provision applies only where the impugned legislation has a greater negative impact on the complainant than on people with other religious views.

The appearance of 'freedom of religion' as the first fundamental freedom listed in the Charter speaks to its primacy as a value of Canadian society. As is the case with all Charter rights, however, the freedom guaranteed under s 2(a) is not absolute. Section 1 of the Charter expressly states that the rights and freedoms set out in the Charter are subject to 'such reasonable limits prescribed by law as can be demonstrably justified in a free and democratic society'. This limitation provision necessarily requires Canadian courts to apply a two-part process to determine whether government action unconstitutionally violates a Charter right.

---

[15] Canada's pre-Confederation history involved considerable conflict between French-speaking Catholics and English-speaking Protestants. One initiative that was adopted to help resolve this conflict promised denominational schools to Catholic or Protestant minority groups within the Canadian provinces. This system was subsequently guaranteed by s 93 of the *Constitution Act 1867*, 30 & 31 Vict, c 3, (reprinted in RSC 1985, App II, No 5). The Supreme Court has made clear that government funding decisions made in accordance with the denomination school system provided for in s 93 cannot constitute a violation of freedom of religion under s 2(a) of the Charter: see *Re Bill 30* [1987] SCJ 44 and *Adler v Ontario* [1996] SCJ 110.

First, the court must determine whether the government action infringes on the protected right. In the context of s 2(a) of the Charter, this question requires the court to define 'freedom of conscience and religion' and to evaluate the impugned law against that definition. At this stage of the analysis, the complainant bears the burden of proving, on a balance of probabilities, that the Charter right is violated. Notably, it is not necessary for the complainant to prove that its own Charter right is limited by the challenged law, only that someone's Charter right is violated by the law.[16] For example, while a corporation cannot hold a religious belief or an atheist by definition does not hold a religious belief, it is open to a corporation to challenge a law on the basis that the law violates an individual's right to freedom of religion. As stated by the Supreme Court of Canada:

> A law which itself infringes religious freedom is, by that reason alone, inconsistent with s. 2(a) of the Charter and it matters not whether the accused is a Christian, Jew, Muslim, Hindu, Buddhist, atheist, agnostic or whether an individual or a corporation. It is the nature of the law, not the status of the accused, that is in issue.[17]

Second, if a rights intrusion is found in step 1, the court must determine whether the intrusion is justifiable. At this point, the onus shifts to the government to prove, on a balance of probabilities, that the rights infringement is justifiable. This burden is proven in accordance with the criteria set out by the Supreme Court in *R v Oakes*[18] and which are now known as the 'Oakes Test'. The Oakes Test requires the government to demonstrate (1) that the objective of the impugned government action is sufficiently pressing and substantial to warrant overriding the Charter right, and (2) that the means employed to achieve the stated goal are proportional to that goal. To meet the proportionality requirement, the government must show that the challenged law is rationally connected to the legislative objective; that the challenged law impairs the Charter right no more than is necessary to achieve the objective; and that the effect of the measure is not disproportionately severe given the objective and the benefits of the law.

Applying this analysis, if a court concludes that a challenged law infringes on freedom of religion but does so in a manner that is justifiable under s 1, then the law remains valid because the interference with freedom of religion is constitutionally

---

[16] However, only someone who has standing is entitled to bring constitutional questions before the court. For an explanation of these standing rules, see Hogg, above n 8, ch 59.2.
[17] *R v Big M Drug Mart* [1985] SCJ No 17, [41] ('*Big M*').
[18] [1986] SCJ No 7. With only subtle modifications (see, eg, *Dagenais v Canadian Broadcasting Corporation* [1994] SCJ No 104) the Oakes Test remains the paradigm for applying s 1 of the Charter.

insignificant. If, however, a court concludes that a law's violation of freedom of religion is not justifiable under s 1, then the court can nullify the offending portion of the law.[19]

'Freedom of religion' defined

The Supreme Court of Canada first defined the Charter's protection of 'freedom of religion' in *R v Big M Drug Mart*.[20] The principles enunciated in this seminal case remain the touchstone for judicial consideration of s 2(a)'s protection. In *Big M*, the Supreme Court dealt with two fundamental issues relating to the scope and meaning of 'freedom of religion' under the Charter. First, the court considered the methodology to be applied in assessing the constitutionality of legislation under s 2(a) of the Charter. Should this analysis focus on the purpose of the challenged legislation or on its effects? Second, the court discussed the meaning and scope of freedom of religion as a constitutional right. What state action is limited by this right and what activities are protected from state intervention? The court's treatment of these two issues has resulted in an expansive protection of religious freedom, unprecedented in Canadian law prior to the advent of the Charter.

On the methodology issue, the Supreme Court was cognizant of the fact that, in pre-Charter jurisprudence dealing with freedom of religion under the Canadian Bill of Rights, Canadian courts had focused only on the effects of the impugned legislation. In *Big M*, Chief Justice Dickson (as he then was) rejected this narrow approach and adopted instead the American model of considering both the purpose and effect of legislation. Justice Dickson stated that:

> Both purpose and effect are relevant in determining constitutionality; either an unconstitutional purpose or an unconstitutional effect can invalidate legislation. All legislation is animated by an object the legislature intends to achieve. This object is realized through the impact produced by the operation and application of the legislation. Purpose and effect respectively, in the sense of the legislation's object and its ultimate impact, are clearly linked, if not indivisible. Intended and actual effects have often been looked to for guidance in assessing the legislation's object and thus, its validity.

---

[19] If this happens, the government can respond by abandoning the legislative initiative or by rewriting the law so that it does not run afoul of the Charter's religious rights protection. Pursuant to s 33 of the Charter, the government also has the power to override, or avoid, the court ruling by expressly rendering the law temporarily operable notwithstanding its inconsistency with the Charter. This authority, however, is rarely relied upon by Canadian law-makers. See B Billingsley, 'Section 33: The Charter's Sleeping Giant' (2002) 21 *Windsor Yearbook of Access to Justice* 331.

[20] [1985] SCJ No 17.

Moreover, consideration of the object of legislation is vital if rights are to be fully protected. The assessment by the courts of legislative purpose focuses scrutiny upon the aims and objectives of the legislature and ensures they are consonant with the guarantees enshrined in the Charter. The declaration that certain objects lie outside the legislature's power checks governmental action at the first stage of unconstitutional conduct. Further, it will provide more ready and more vigorous protection of constitutional rights by obviating the individual litigant's need to prove effects violative of Charter rights. It will also allow courts to dispose of cases where the object is clearly improper, without inquiring into the legislation's actual impact.[21]

Building upon this understanding that legislative purpose and effect are both relevant to a freedom of religion analysis, Justice Dickson went on to formulate a two-step process applying s 2(a) of the Charter.

At the first step, the court must determine whether the purpose of the challenged legislation violates s 2(a) of the Charter. At this stage of the analysis, the court's focus is on the objective of the legislation at the point of enactment only; the court does not take account of the fact that the purpose of a law may have transformed or shifted over time.[22] If the law has a religious purpose, a violation of freedom of religion is established without a need to proceed to the second step. If the law does not have a religious purpose, then the court moves on to the second step. This step requires the court to determine whether the effects of the legislation violate freedom of religion despite the validity of the legislative purpose. As summarized by Chief Justice Dickson:

In short, the effects test will only be necessary to defeat legislation with a valid purpose; effects can never be relied upon to save legislation with an invalid purpose.[23]

Although this two-tiered purpose and effect approach to the freedom of religion analysis was not unanimously supported by the panel of Supreme Court justices who heard *Big M*,[24] the Supreme Court has followed it in subsequent cases and it presently stands as the governing methodology for s 2(a) Charter analysis.

The Supreme Court was unanimous, however, in its conceptualization of freedom of religion in *Big M*. On behalf of the court, the Chief Justice broadly defined freedom

---

[21] Ibid [80–8].
[22] Chief Justice Dickson held that accepting a shifting legislative purpose as being relevant to the freedom of religion analysis would run contrary to Canadian legal tradition: Ibid [89–91].
[23] Ibid [88].
[24] In a separate but concurring judgment, Justice Wilson took issue with the two-step analysis outlined by the Chief Justice, arguing that only the effect of the legislation is relevant to the s 2(a) analysis. See ibid [152–64].

of religion, holding that s 2(a) of the Charter endows all people not only with the right to hold religious beliefs but also with the right to practice religious beliefs:

> The essence of the concept of freedom of religion is the right to entertain such religious beliefs as a person chooses, the right to declare religious beliefs openly and without fear of hindrance or reprisal, and the right to manifest religious belief by worship and practice or by teaching and dissemination.[25]

Chief Justice Dickson went on to find that freedom of religion is 'characterized by the absence of coercion or constraint'[26] such that s 2(a) of the Charter prevents the state from prohibiting religious belief or practice and from compelling religious practice:

> One of the major purposes of the Charter is to protect, within reason, from compulsion or restraint. Coercion includes not only such blatant forms of compulsion as direct commands to act or refrain from acting on pain of sanction, coercion includes indirect forms of control which determine or limit alternative courses of conduct available to others. Freedom in a broad sense embraces both the absence of coercion and constraint, and the right to manifest beliefs and practices. Freedom means that, subject to such limitations as are necessary to protect public safety, order, health, or morals or the fundamental rights and freedoms of others, no one is to be forced to act in a way contrary to his beliefs or his conscience.[27]

With this broad interpretation of freedom of religion, the court recognized that the fundamental goal of the rights and freedoms set out in the Charter, including the protection of freedom of religion, is to safeguard minority interests 'from the threat of "the tyranny of the majority"'.[28]

Chief Justice Dickson supported the court's expansive definition of freedom of religion by relying upon the status of the Charter as a constitutional guardian of individual rights. He pointed out that, unlike the Canadian Bill of Rights, which recognizes and affirms listed rights, the Charter provides legally enforceable protection against state interference with the listed rights and freedom. The constitutional status of the Charter merits a purposeful interpretation of Charter rights. Justice Dickson went on to state that a purposeful definition of freedom of religion is one which recognizes the Charter's focus on 'respect for individual conscience and the valuation

---

[25] Ibid [94].
[26] Ibid [95].
[27] Ibid.
[28] Ibid [98].

of human dignity' and the 'emphasis on individual conscience and individual judgment … [that] lies at the heart of our democratic political tradition'.[29]

Justice Dickson also rejected the argument that the protection of freedom of religion under the Charter should be narrowly defined because the Charter lacks an 'establishment' clause (that is, a clause which expressly prohibits the establishment of a state religion).[30] The argument was that 'freedom of religion' under the Charter should be narrowly interpreted as protecting only the free exercise of religion and not as prohibiting state support for a religious practice. Justice Dickson held, to the contrary, that:

> the applicability of the Charter guarantee of freedom of conscience and religion does not depend on the presence or absence of an 'anti-establishment principle' in the Canadian Constitution, a principle which can only further obfuscate an already difficult area of the law.[31]

The court held that the absence of an establishment clause in the Charter does not implicitly authorize the state to compel religious compliance, and that 'whatever else freedom of conscience and religion may mean, it must at the very least mean this: government may not coerce individuals to affirm a specific religious belief or to manifest a specific religious practice for a sectarian purpose'.[32]

In the end, Justice Dickson summarized the court's understanding of the Charter's protection of freedom of conscience and religion in *Big M* as follows:

> The values that underlie our political and philosophic traditions demand that every individual be free to hold and to manifest whatever beliefs and opinions his or her conscience dictates, provided inter alia only that such manifestations do not injure his or her neighbours or their parallel rights to hold and manifest beliefs and opinions of their own.[33]

This definition clearly establishes that freedom of religion, as protected by the Charter, is to receive a broad, purposeful interpretation. The definition also gives rise

---

[29] Ibid [121–2]. Note that the court in *Big M* was relying on a principle of purposeful interpretation of the Charter which had already been established by the court in *Canada (Combines Investigation Acts, Director of Investigation & Research) v Southam Inc* [1984] 2 SCR 145.
[30] The comparative reference here is to the first amendment of the American Bill of Rights, which provides that 'Congress shall make no law respecting an establishment of religion, or prohibiting the free exercise thereof'.
[31] *Big M* [1985] SCJ No 17, [109].
[32] Ibid [123].
[33] Ibid.

to several questions that the Supreme Court of Canada has subsequently addressed and which I discuss below. Generally, the answers that the court has provided to these questions underscore, once again, the wide scope that the Canadian judiciary has given to the right to freedom of religion under s 2(a) of the Charter.

How is freedom of religion limited by practices which cause harm to others?

One question arising from *Big M* relates to Chief Justice Dickson's acknowledgement that freedom of religion is limited by a 'harm principle'. This principle states that the Charter's guarantee of freedom of religion does not permit anyone to manifest religious belief in a way that would 'injure his or her neighbours or their parallel rights'.[34] How does this harm principle fit into a judicial analysis of an alleged infringement of s 2(a) of the Charter? In particular, does the harm principle function as an intrinsic limit on the concept of freedom of religion (such that a court must consider the real or potentially harmful elements of religious practice at the s 2(a) stage of analysis), or does the harm principle relate to an externally imposed limitation on freedom of religion (so as to merit consideration only at the s 1 stage of analysis)? This question has implications for the conceptual or theoretical understanding of freedom of religion as protected under s 2(a) of the Charter. The question also has practical implications because a complainant bears the burden of proof in the s 2(a) analysis, while the burden of proof shifts to the government under s 1.

Prima facie, Chief Justice Dickson's comments in *Big M* appear to suggest that the protection offered by s 2(a) of the Charter is intrinsically limited by the 'harm principle'. In subsequent cases, however, the Supreme Court has made clear that the 'harm principle' is, in general, more properly considered as part of the s 1 justification analysis.[35] As noted by one of Canada's pre-eminent constitutional law scholars:

> The idea that freedom of religion authorizes religious practices only so far as they do not injure others has been abandoned by the Supreme Court of Canada in favour of an unqualified right to do anything that is dictated by a religious belief.[36]

Accordingly, at present, once a complainant demonstrates that a challenged law restricts religious practice under s 2(a), the burden ordinarily shifts to the government to prove that the limitation on freedom of religion is justified, pursuant to s 1 of the Charter, in order to prevent harm to others. The Supreme Court has also recognized, however, that a detailed s 1 analysis may not be necessary where the legislative impact

---

[34] Ibid [123].
[35] See, eg, *B(R) v Children's Aid Society of Metropolitan Toronto* [1994] SCJ No 24, [108–11] ('*B(R)*') and *Ross v New Brunswick School District No 15* [1996] SCJ No 40, [72–5] ('*Ross*').
[36] Hogg, above n 8, 42–8.

on freedom of religion is obviously trivial given the nature of the legislation[37] or where 'a proper delineation of the rights involved would make it possible to avoid any conflict' between the religious right being advanced and another Charter right which is alleged to be harmed.[38]

How does a claimant prove a religious belief or practice?

Another issue raised by the definition of freedom of religion set out in *Big M* relates to a complainant's obligation to prove that his/her freedom of religion has been restricted. How does a complainant prove that an activity that is being limited by the state constitutes a religious belief or practice? Does the belief or practice have to be a recognized tenet of an organized religion or can it be a personally held religious or moral belief? The Supreme Court of Canada resolved this question in *Syndicat Northcrest v Amselem*.[39]

Amselem concerned a freedom of religion claim brought by four orthodox Jews who were each co-owners of units in a condominium building. The building by-laws, signed by each of the claimants when they purchased their units, prohibited the placement of decorations or constructions on the condominium balconies. The claimants each wanted to construct 'succahs', or temporary shelters, on their condominium balconies in order to fulfil a religious obligation to live in small, enclosed temporary huts during the nine-day Jewish religious festival of Succot. Syndicat Northcrest, the co-ownership syndicate for the building, refused to allow the succahs to be built on the balconies, but offered to allow the complainants to set up a communal succah in the condominium garden. The claimants refused the communal succah arrangement on the basis that they believed that their religion mandated the use of personal succahs. The claimants brought the matter to court, arguing that Syndicat Northcrest was violating their freedom of religion, as protected by the *Quebec Charter of Rights and Freedoms*.[40]

The Supreme Court of Canada divided on the result of the case. Of the nine justices hearing the case, a majority of five found that the condominium by-laws violated freedom of religion as protected by the Quebec Charter because the by-laws

---

[37] For example, in *B(R)* [1994] SCJ No 24, (at 111).
[38] *Multani v Commission Scolaire Marguerite-Bourgeoys* [2006] SCJ No 6, [28]. See also at [25–31] for the Court's discussion of its preference to consider limitations on the freedom of religion as part of the s 1 justification analysis rather than as part of the s 2(a) conceptualization of freedom of religion.
[39] [2004] SCJ No 46 ('*Amselem*').
[40] RSQ, c C-12 (the 'Quebec Charter'). This is a provincial statute (not a constitutional document) that aims to provide human rights protection in the context of private relationships. The claimants had to rely on the Quebec Charter because there was no 'government action' involved in the case that would trigger the application of the Canadian Charter of Rights and Freedoms.

unjustifiably interfered with the claimants' sincerely held religious belief. Three of the four dissenting justices held that the by-laws did not interfere with freedom of religion because the evidence did not support the claimants' allegation of a sincere belief that their religion required the construction and use of personal succahs. The evidence of religious experts stated that, while the use of personal succahs was preferable, communal succahs were an acceptable alternative.[41] Another dissenting justice held that claimant's freedom of religion under the Quebec Charter was not violated because the claimants had agreed to forego the use of personal succahs on their balconies when they signed the condominium agreement, which expressly prohibited the erection of structures on the condominium balconies.

Although this case was decided on the basis of the Quebec Charter, the Supreme Court specifically stated that its findings regarding the content of freedom of religion are applicable to the *Canadian Charter of Rights and Freedoms*.[42] Writing for the majority of the court, Justice Iacobucci held that the 'religious' component of freedom of religion is commonly understood as relating to the belief in a divine or spiritual power:

> In order to define religious freedom, we must first ask ourselves what we mean by 'religion'. ... Defined broadly, religion typically involves a particular and comprehensive system of faith and worship. Religion also tends to involve the belief in a divine, superhuman or controlling power. In essence, religion is about freely and deeply held personal convictions or beliefs connected to an individual's spiritual faith and integrally linked to one's self-definition and spiritual fulfilment, the practices of which allow individuals to foster a connection with the divine or with the subject or object of that spiritual faith.[43]

Relying on previous Supreme Court commentary on Charter matters, Justice Iacobucci went on to note that the Charter recognises and protects such belief as a profoundly personal matter for every individual. The Charter therefore protects not only the practices mandated by organized religion, but also religious beliefs and practices undertaken by an individual outside of the requirements of an established religion. As summarized by Justice Iacobucci:

> our Court's past decisions and the basic principles underlying freedom of religion support the view that freedom of religion consists of the freedom to undertake

---

[41] In *Syndicat Northcrest v Amselem* [2004] SCJ No 46, [162], Justice Bastarache summarized the conclusions of the dissenting justices on this point.
[42] *Amselem* [2004] SCJ No 46, [37, 105].
[43] *Amselem* [2004] SCJ No 46, [39].

practices and harbour beliefs, having a nexus with religion, in which an individual demonstrates he or she sincerely believes or is sincerely undertaking in order to connect with the divine or as a function of his or her spiritual faith, irrespective of whether a particular practice or belief is required by official religious dogma or is in conformity with the position of religious officials.

But, at the same time, this freedom encompasses objective as well as personal notions of religious belief, 'obligation', precept, 'commandment', custom or ritual. Consequently, both obligatory as well as voluntary expressions of faith should be protected under the Quebec (and the Canadian) Charter. It is the religious or spiritual essence of an action, not any mandatory or perceived-as-mandatory nature of its observance, that attracts protection.[44]

This finding led the majority of the court to further conclude that a claimant seeking the protection of s 2(a) of the Charter is not required to prove that the restricted religious practice is required by the tenets of an established religion. Instead, in order to establish that freedom of religion is implicated, the claimant must establish only that the impugned legislation is directed at or impacts upon the claimant's sincerely held religious belief.[45]

Justice Iacobucci was careful to point out that the court's assessment of the sincerity of a claimant's belief relates only to the honesty of the claimant's belief. The court is not to involve itself in an evaluation of the reasonability or of the merits of the belief:

the court's role in assessing sincerity is intended only to ensure that a presently asserted religious belief is in good faith, neither fictitious nor capricious, and that it is not an artifice. Otherwise, nothing short of a religious inquisition would be required to decipher the innermost beliefs of human beings.[46]

As a practical matter, Justice Iacobucci noted that the sincerity of the claimant's belief is a question of fact that can be determined by a wide range of criteria, including the credibility of the claimant as a witness, the consistency of the proclaimed belief with the claimant's other religious practices, and possibly, but not necessarily, the consistency of the proclaimed belief with the requirements adhered to by other members of the claimant's religion. Justice Iacobucci also cautioned against assessing the sincerity of the claimant's belief by looking to the claimant's past practices because personal

---

[44] *Amselem* [2004] SCJ No 46, [46–7].
[45] It is worth noting that, in addition to protecting religious freedom, s 2(a) of the Charter also protects 'freedom of conscience'. To date, this aspect of s 2(a) has received scarce attention from Canadian courts as distinct from freedom of religion.
[46] *Amselem* [2004] SCJ No 46, [52].

faith has a 'vacillating nature' such that '[a] person's connection to or relationship with the divine or with the subject or object of his or her spiritual faith, or his or her perceptions of religious obligation emanating from such a relationship, may well change and evolve over time'.[47]

Given this view of religious belief and practice as a fundamentally personal matter, the majority of the court concluded that, in order to trigger s 2(a)'s protection of freedom of religion, a claimant must satisfy two criteria. First, the claimant must prove that the subject of the claim is a belief or practice having a nexus to religion. The religious nexus may be proven:

> either by being objectively or subjectively obligatory or customary, or by, in general, subjectively engendering a personal connection with the divine or with the subject or object of an individual's spiritual faith, irrespective of whether a particular practice or belief is required by official religious dogma or is in conformity with the position of religious officials.[48]

Second, the claimant must satisfy the court that his or her belief is sincere. This is a question of credibility for the court.

The court's conclusion that the nexus between a practice and religion can be subjectively proven arguably supports the characterization of s 2(a) as an individual, rather than a collective, right. This characterization was recently endorsed by the majority of the Supreme Court of Canada in *Alberta v Hutterian Brethren of Wilson Colony*.[49] Writing for a majority of four of seven justices, Chief Justice McLachlin held that, while 'religious freedom has both individual and collective aspects',[50] the protection offered by s 2(a) of the Charter focuses on freedom of religion as an individual right, such that the impact which the legislative restriction of an individual's freedom of religion may have on a religious community is properly considered under the s 1

---

[47] *Amselem* [2004] SCJ No 46, [53]. A related question is whether an individual's claim to freedom of religion can be hindered by a past intention to waive this right or by a pre-existing contract which binds the claimant to act in a manner which conflicts with the religious right now being advanced. This question has not been answered with regard to the right to freedom of religion under the Charter, however, in *Abselem* [2004] SCJ No 46 and in *Bruker v Marcovitz* [2007] SCJ No 54, the Supreme Court of Canada rejected claims to freedom of religion under the Quebec Charter of Rights and Freedoms in part because the claimants had willingly entered into contracts which implicitly required them to forego the religious activity at issue.

[48] *Amselem* [2004] SCJ No 46, [56]. Three of the dissenting judges objected to the notion that a religious nexus could be subjectively proven and insisted on proof of an objective connection between a claimant's personal beliefs or practices and accepted precepts of an organized religion.

[49] [2009] SCJ No 37.

[50] *Alberta v Hutterian Brethren of Wilson Colony* [2009] SCJ No 37, [31].

justification analysis. As stated by the Chief Justice, '[c]ommunity impact does not … transform the essential [individual] claim … into an assertion of a group right'.[51] Note, however, that this view is not without controversy within the court. Indeed, in *Hutterian Brethren*, the dissenting members of the court emphasized the collective aspects of freedom of religion. Justice LeBel, for example, described the freedom of religion as follows:

> the framers of the Charter thought fit to incorporate into the Charter an express guarantee of freedom of religion, which must be given meaning and effect.
>
> That decision reflects the complex and highly textured nature of freedom of religion. The latter is an expression of the right to believe or not. It also includes a right to manifest one's belief or lack of belief, or to express disagreement with the beliefs of others. It also incorporates a right to establish and maintain a community of faith that shares a common understanding of the nature of the human person, of the universe, and of their relationships with a Supreme Being in many religions …
>
> Religion is about religious beliefs, but also about religious relationships.[52]

In the end, the divergence of views within the court as to the conceptualization of religious freedom as an individual or a collective right did not impact on the court's s 2(a) analysis in *Hutterian Brethren* because both the majority and dissenting justices found a violation of freedom of religion. The court divided, however, on whether the legislative intrusion on freedom of religion could be justified under s 1. The dissenting justices criticized the majority's justification of the impugned legislation for failing to adequately take into account the importance of the collective aspects of religious freedom.

<u>Are trivial intrusions on freedom of religion protected by s 2(a)?</u>

Finally, the broad definition of freedom of religion outlined in *Big M* gives rise to a concern that every law that has the effect of restricting religious practice, even in the smallest way, may run afoul of the Charter. Does s 2(a) prohibit all interference with religion? Since *Big M*, the Supreme Court has answered this question by holding that laws that have an incidental and trivial impact on religious practice do not violate s 2(a) of the Charter. In particular, legislation that mandates conduct that incidentally conforms to a religious precept does not run afoul of the Charter. As stated by the Supreme Court in *R v Edwards Books*:

---

[51] Ibid.
[52] Ibid [180–2].

Section 2(a) does not require the legislatures to eliminate every minuscule state-imposed cost associated with the practice of religion. Otherwise the Charter would offer protection from innocuous secular legislation such as a taxation act that imposed a modest sales tax extending to all products, including those used in the course of religious worship. In my opinion, it is unnecessary to turn to s.1 in order to justify legislation of that sort. ... The Constitution shelters individuals and groups only to the extent that religious beliefs or conduct can reasonably or actually be threatened. For a state-imposed cost or burden to be proscribed by s. 2(a) it must be capable of interfering with religious belief or practice. In short, legislative or administrative action which increases the cost of practising or otherwise manifesting religious beliefs is not prohibited if the burden is trivial or insubstantial.

...

Religious freedom is inevitably abridged by legislation which has the effect of impeding conduct integral to the practice of a person's religion. But it is not necessarily impaired by legislation which requires conduct consistent with the religious beliefs of another person. ... I cannot accept, for example, that a legislative prohibition of criminal conduct such as theft and murder is a state-enforced compulsion to conform to religious practices, merely because some religions enjoin their members not to steal or kill. Reasonable citizens do not perceive the legislation as requiring them to pay homage to religious doctrine.[53]

Beyond the coercion scenario, the court has defined a trivial or insubstantial interference as one that 'does not threaten actual religious beliefs or conduct'.[54] It is difficult to ascertain, however, how this definition applies in practice when the impugned legislation restricts the claimant's ability to practice a chosen religion instead of coercing conduct that coincidentally matches a religious precept. While the notion that trivial interference with religion does not violate s 2(a) remains the theory, in practice the Supreme Court generally finds that s 2(a) is breached whenever legislation negatively impacts on a claimant's ability to partake in their own religious practices, even if the impact is minor.[55] In such cases, the court then turns to s 1 of the Charter as a means of justifying the minor legislative intrusion on freedom of religion.

---

[53] [1986] SCJ No 70, [97, 99].
[54] *Alberta v Hutterian Brethren of Wilson Colony* [2009] SCJ No 37, [32].
[55] A notable exception is *R v Jones* [1986] SCJ No 56 ('*Jones*'), in which four of seven justices held that the effect of the challenged legislation on the claimant's freedom of religion was too minimal to support a finding that s 2(a) was breached.

Leading cases balancing law and freedom of religion

As outlined earlier, the Supreme Court has broadly defined freedom of religion for the purposes of s 2(a) of the Charter. This means that, as with other Charter rights, Canadian courts hold freedom of religion in high regard as a constitutional value. Given the two-step process involved in Charter analysis, however, the broad definition of s 2(a) means that the functional or practical scope of the Charter's protection of freedom of religion is usually determined in the s 1 justification analysis. A detailed discussion of the jurisprudence on s 1 of the Charter is beyond the scope of this chapter. Nevertheless, the following brief review of the most salient Charter cases on freedom of religion demonstrates that, as much as the Supreme Court has been willing to liberally define freedom of religion, it has also been willing to accept state-imposed limits on that freedom. Overall, the cases show that the Charter provides no tolerance for legislation mandating specified conduct for religious purposes,[56] limited tolerance for legislation restricting religious conduct,[57] but considerable tolerance for legislation mandating conduct for important secular purposes, even if the required conduct means that some people must act contrary to their religious beliefs or must choose between following their religious views or obtaining a secular benefit.[58] Cases of the latter type, where the legislation at issue requires an individual to act in a manner that is contrary to his or her religious beliefs, seem to be the most problematic for the court. These cases require the court to walk a tightrope, balancing precariously between society's interests in protecting freedom of religion and society's interests in maintaining social order and security.

Sunday closing legislation

The Supreme Court of Canada considered the validity of legislation restricting commercial activity on Sunday in *Big M*[59] and in *Edwards Books*.[60] The legislation at issue in Big M was the *Lord's Day Act*,[61] a federal statute that, with limited exceptions,

---

[56] See, eg, *Big M* [1985] SCJ No 17. A similar position was taken by the Ontario Court of Appeal in *Zylberberg v Sudbury Board of Education* [1988] OJ No 1488 ('*Zylberberg*'), and in *Canadian Civil Liberties Association v Ontario* [1990] OJ No 104 (ONCA).

[57] See, eg, *Ross* [1996] SCJ No 40; *Multani v Commission Scolaire Marguerite-Bourgeoys* [2006] SCJ No 6, and *Congregation des Temoins de Jehovah de St Jerome-LaFontaine v LaFontaine (Village)* [2004] SCJ No 45.

[58] See, eg, *R v Edwards Books* [1986] SCJ No 70; *Jones* [1986] SCJ No 56; *Young v Young* [1993] SCJ No 112 ('*Young*'); *B(R) v* [1994] SCJ No 24; *Alberta v Hutterian Brethren of Wilson Colony* [2009] SCJ No 37; and *AC v Manitoba (Director of Child and Family Services)* [2009] SCJ No 30 ('*AC*').

[59] *Big M* [1985] SCJ No 17.

[60] *R v Edwards Books* [1986] SCJ No 70.

[61] RSC 1970, c L-13.

prohibited commercial businesses from operating on Sunday. The court unanimously struck down the legislation as an unjustifiable restriction on freedom of religion because the purpose of the legislation was to promote Christian values by compelling observance of the Christian sabbath. This objective inherently offended freedom of religion and therefore could not be justified as a pressing and substantial objective under s 1. In *Edwards Books*, however, six of seven Supreme Court justices upheld the constitutionality of provincial Sunday closing legislation.[62] In this case, the court was satisfied that the purpose of the legislation was to ensure fair labour conditions. Although the mandated day of rest coincided with the Christian sabbath, the court found that the purpose of the statute was not to promote religious views. Four of the six majority justices also held that, while the legislation had the effect of infringing the freedom of religion of non-Christians, it contained sufficient exemptions so as to be a reasonable limit on the s 2(a) right within the meaning of s 1 of the Charter.[63]

Medical treatment of children

In Canada, provincial legislation ordinarily empowers the courts to declare a child to be a ward of the state if the child's health or safety is at risk. Such legislation also permits the court to order medical treatment for the child if such treatment is in the 'best interests of the child'. This means that the courts have the discretion to order medical treatment of the child over the religiously-based objections of the child's parents or of the child (depending on the age limitation set out in the statute). The Supreme Court of Canada considered the constitutionality of legislation empowering the courts to make such orders in *B(R) v Children's Aid Society of Toronto*[64] and in *A C v Manitoba Director of Child and Family Services*.[65] In both cases, the courts favoured concerns for the 'best interests of the child' over the s 2(a) protection of freedom of religion.

In *B(R)*, the parents of an infant challenged the constitutionality of a court order that permitted the administration of a blood transfusion to their daughter. The parents were Jehovah's Witnesses who objected to the blood transfusion on the basis of their religious beliefs. A full, nine-member panel of Supreme Court justices rejected the parents' Charter argument. A majority of five justices held that, while s 2(a) protects a parent's right to choose the medical treatment of their child in accordance with the parent's religious beliefs, the statutory scheme which permitted a court to decide whether the child should be made a temporary ward of the state and whether the best interests of the child required medical treatment was a justifiable limit on the

---

[62] The legislation at issue was the *Retail Business Holidays Act*, RSO 1980, c 453.
[63] The other two justices who concurred with the majority in the result held that the legislation did not negatively effect the freedom of religion of persons having a non-Christian sabbath.
[64] [1994] SCJ No 24.
[65] [2009] SCJ No 30.

parent's freedom of religion. The dissenting members of the court held that s 2(a) was not violated because a parent's freedom of religion, which includes the right to educate and rear his or her children according to the parent's religious beliefs, is intrinsically limited by the child's right to life and health. In other words, a parent's freedom of religion stops short of imposing conduct or practices on a child that put the safety or health of the child at risk.

In *A.C.*, a similar court order was challenged, but this time the claimant was a fourteen-year-old Jehovah's Witness who had received a court-ordered blood transfusion against her wishes. The claimant challenged the validity of a provincial statute which permitted the court to issue a treatment order for an individual under the age of sixteen if the court concluded that the order was in the 'best interests' of the child, taking into account various factors including the child's religious beliefs and maturity level. In this case, the treatment order had been issued notwithstanding the fact that psychiatric assessments of the claimant concluded that she was mentally competent and fully understood the potential medical ramifications of refusing treatment. Six of seven Supreme Court justices held that, while the legislation infringed on the claimant's right to freedom of religion, the infringement was justified under s 1 of the Charter because the legislation served an important goal of protecting children and provided for an individualized assessment of the child's best interests, taking into account the child's maturity and religious values. As the sole dissenting voice, Justice Binnie held that the statutory violation of freedom of religion was not justifiable because the statutory scheme was not proportionate to the legislative goal of protecting children who lacked capacity to make their own medical choices.

Education

In the context of education, freedom of religion has been raised in Canadian courts in two main scenarios. The first scenario concerns restrictions on the ability of parents or teachers to communicate religious lessons to children. This Supreme Court considered this situation in *R v Jones*,[66] *Young v Young*[67] and in *Ross v New Brunswick*.[68] The second scenario addresses the ability of a public school to require students to participate in religious conduct. The leading Canadian cases on this issue are *Zylberberg v Sudbury Board of Education*[69] and *Canadian Civil Liberties Association v Ontario*,[70] both decisions of the Ontario Court of Appeal.

---

[66] [1986] SCJ No 56.
[67] [1993] SCJ No 112.
[68] [1996] SCJ No 40.
[69] [1988] OJ No 1488.
[70] [1990] OJ No 104 ('*CCLA*').

In *R v Jones*, the pastor of a fundamentalist church wished to home school his own, and other, children. The claimant pastor objected to the provisions of the provincial School Act that required him to obtain an exemption from the province excusing him from the statutory requirement that all children attend public school. The purpose of the exemption was to satisfy the government that children educated outside of the public school system would obtain the same standard of education as children in the public schools. The claimant argued that obtaining the exemption would contravene his religious belief that the final authority over the education of children lies with God and not with the government. In the result, the court unanimously rejected the claimant's argument and upheld the legislation, despite holding that a parent's freedom of religion includes the right to educate his or her child in accordance with the parent's religious beliefs. Four members of the court held that the impact of the statutory requirements on the claimant's religious views was minimal, such that s 2(a) was not infringed. The remaining three justices held that any infringement of s 2(a) was justified given the purpose of the legislation and the minimal impact on the claimant's religious freedom.

In *Young*, a court order issued pursuant to the federal *Divorce Act* placed a restriction on a divorced father's access to his children that prohibited the father from discussing his religious beliefs with his children. The father, a Jehovah's Witness, argued that his Charter right to freedom of religion was violated by the statutory provision that authorized the court to grant such orders if required for the 'best interests of the child'. Only four Supreme Court Justices found the Charter to be applicable and they held that the father's freedom of religion was not violated because this right is restricted to conduct which does not harm a child — that is, conduct that a court characterizes as being in the best interests of the child.

In *Ross*, the Supreme Court considered the constitutional validity of an order of the New Brunswick Human Rights Commission disciplining a teacher who, during his off-duty time, had been publicly making racist comments against Jews. The court order directed the school board to place the teacher on a leave of absence, to offer him a non-teaching position if possible, and to terminate his employment immediately if he publicized anti-Semitic views while on leave or while employed in a non-teaching role. The teacher challenged the court order on the grounds that it violated his freedom of religion by preventing him from asserting his opinions about a religious belief. He argued that '[a]ll of the invective and hyperbole about anti-Semitism is really a smoke screen for imposing an officially sanctioned religious belief on society as a whole'.[71] The Supreme Court unanimously held that the claimant's freedom of religion was unjustifiably infringed because the order of the Human Rights Commission restricted the claimant's ability to profess his views

---

[71] *Ross* [1996] SCJ No 40, [70].

even when in a non-teaching role. While the court order served the pressing and substantial objective of rectifying discrimination in the educational environment, the limitations the order imposed on the claimant exceeded the means necessary to achieve this objective.[72]

Zylberberg involved a constitutional challenge to a provision of a provincial education Act that required public schools to have prayers read in class at the beginning or end of each school day. The Ontario Court of Appeal unanimously found that this provision unjustifiably violated the Charter's guarantee of freedom of religion by compelling children to manifest a Christian religious practice. Although the statute provided for exemptions that allowed students to excuse themselves from participating in the prayers, the court found that these exemptions did not practically mitigate the statutory compulsion to participate in the religious exercise. As stated by the court:

> the right to be excused from class, or to be exempted from participating, does not overcome the infringement of the charter freedom of conscience and religion by the mandated religious exercises. On the contrary, the exemption provision imposes a penalty on pupils from religious minorities who utilize it by stigmatizing them as nonconformists and setting them apart from their fellow students who are members of the dominant religion.[73]

The court also rejected the argument that the statutory infringement on religious freedom was insubstantial or trivial.

Following *Zylberberg*, another s 2(a) challenge to required public school practices came before the Ontario Court of Appeal. This time the challenge related to a provincial regulation that required public schools to teach religious education for two periods per week. Once again, although the legislation provided for parents to exempt their children from religious education, the Ontario Court of Appeal found that the regulation unjustifiably violated freedom of religion. The court applied the reasoning from *Zylberberg* to find that the regulation compelled religious conduct.

Public safety

In *Multani v Commission Scolaire Marguerite-Bourgeoys*,[74] the Supreme Court of Canada considered the constitutional validity of a Quebec school board order that prohibited a student from wearing a kirpan (a ceremonial religious dagger) to school

---

[72] The Supreme Court of Canada dealt with similar considerations is *Trinity Western University v College of Teachers (British Columbia)* [2001] SCJ No 32.
[73] *Zylberberg* [1988] OJ No 1488, [40].
[74] [2006] SCJ No 6.

on the grounds that the dagger posed a safety risk to other students.[75] Multani was a member of the Orthodox Sikh religion and believed that his religion required him to wear a kirpan at all times. The court was satisfied, on the evidence presented, that the elements of the orthodox Sikh religion required members of the religion to wear a genuine kirpan at all times and that the claimant father and son sincerely believed in this precept. The court also found that the interference was not trivial because the prohibition essentially deprived the claimant of the ability to attend public school (Multani had enrolled in private school as a result of not being allowed to wear the kirpan in a public school). The court therefore readily concluded that the school board's prohibition violated the claimants' freedom of religion. Moving to the s 1 analysis, the court concluded that the restriction on Multani's freedom of religion was not justifiable because the safety concern (which was pressing and substantial) could be met in less obtrusive ways, such as by requiring Multani to wear the dagger in a manner that would keep it safe from other students.[76]

In *Hutterian Brethren*,[77] a four to three majority of the Supreme Court upheld legislation that required all holders of provincial driver's licenses to have their pictures taken and affixed to their licenses. Members of the Wilson Colony of Hutterian Brethren argued that the law unjustifiably violated their freedom of religion by requiring them to have their photos taken when their religion taught them that to do so violated the Second Commandment. The court unanimously held that the law infringed upon the claimants' freedom of religion but the justices divided on the justification analysis. A bare majority of the court characterized the law as a reasonable limitation on freedom of religion because the law was aimed at the pressing and substantial objective of ensuring safety and security of important government issued identification and because the limit on freedom of religion was proportional to this objective, particularly given that the decision to obtain a driver's licence was a matter of personal choice. The dissenting justices, however, found that the impact on freedom of religion was not proportional to the legislative objective. These judges held that the legislation effectively required the members of the Hutterian Brethren to choose between following their religious beliefs or following the law, because the obtaining of a driver's licence was a practical necessity given the Hutterian Brethren's lifestyle as a self-sufficient agricultural community.

---

[75] The school board's decision constituted a government action because the school board was empowered to make the ruling by the province's education statute.
[76] Note that these findings were made by the six members of the court who decided the case on Charter grounds. Two of the justices did not address the Charter at all, preferring to resolve the case on the basis of administrative law principles.
[77] [2009] SCJ No 37.

Property zoning

In *Congregation des Temoins de Jehovah de St. Jerome-LaFontaine v LaFontaine (Village)*,[78] a congregation of Jehovah's Witnesses argued that the Charter guarantee of freedom of religion was unjustifiably infringed by a municipality's refusal to grant the congregation's application for re-zoning of the municipal by-laws so as to allow the congregation to build a church on a particular parcel of land. The majority of the court decided the case on administrative law grounds, ultimately requiring the municipality to reconsider the application. Four dissenting justices, however, considered the Charter argument and held that the municipality's decision did not offend freedom of religion because land that was approved for church use was available elsewhere in the municipality. The denial of the re-zoning request therefore did not prevent the claimant from building a house of worship. With regard to the municipality's obligation to comply with s 2(a) of the Charter, the dissenting justices stated:

> As the municipality is required to be neutral in matters of religion, its by-laws must be structured in such a way as to avoid placing unnecessary obstacles in the way of the exercise of religious freedoms. However, it does not have to provide assistance of any kind to religious groups or actively help them resolve any difficulties they might encounter in their negotiations with third parties in relation to plans to establish a place of worship. … Although the very nature of the zoning by-law means that the appellants do not have absolute freedom to choose the location of their place of worship, this limit is necessary to protect safety and order, and ensure proper land use, in the municipality and does not constitute a violation of freedom of religion. Neither the purpose nor the effect of this by-law has been to infringe the appellants' freedom of religion.[79]

Marriage

Historically, the institution of marriage has been variously understood as being a matter of religion and a matter of civil law. This dual nature of marriage has brought unique challenges to Canadian courts analyzing the constitutionality of legislation relating to the formation and dissolution of marital unions. The courts have struggled to draw an appropriate line between the civil and the religious aspects of marriage while taking account of the fact that laws relating to marriage as a civil union may impact on religious freedom. For example, in *Halpern v Toronto (City)*,[80] the Ontario

---

[78] [2004] SCJ No 45.
[79] *Congregation des Temoins de Jehovah de St Jerome-LaFontaine v LaFontaine (Village)* [2004] SCJ No 45.
[80] [2003] OJ 2268.

Court of Appeal rejected the argument that a provincial statute that barred same-sex marriages interfered with the freedom of religion of a church wanting to perform such unions. The court found that, while the provincial statute did not recognize same-sex marriages for legal purposes, the statute did not restrict the performance of same-sex marriages as a religious ritual. The court stated that:

> this case does not engage religious rights and freedoms. Marriage is a legal institution, as well as a religious and a social institution. This case is solely about the legal institution of marriage. It is not about the religious validity or invalidity of various forms of marriage. We do not view this case as, in any way, dealing with or interfering with the religious institution of marriage.[81]

The Ontario Court of Appeal did find, however, that the prohibition of same-sex marriage discriminated against homosexuals and therefore unjustifiably violated the Charter's protection of equality rights.

The *Halpern* decision, along with similar decisions by other provincial courts,[82] led the federal government to pass the *Civil Marriage Act*[83], which legalized same-sex marriage in Canada while specifically stating that officials of religious groups could refuse to perform marriages that were not in accordance with their religious views. Prior to the passage of the *Civil Marriage Act*, the government of Canada sought the Supreme Court's opinion as to the constitutional validity of the proposed statute. In *Reference re Same-Sex Marriage*,[84] the court held that the statute's acceptance of same-sex marriage did not prima facie violate freedom of religion. Freedom of religion would be violated, however, if the state compelled officials to perform same-sex marriages against their religious beliefs or compelled the use of sacred places for the celebration of such marriages.

Outside of the same-sex marriage context, the Supreme Court also considered the relationship between civil marriage and religious marriage in *Bruker v Marcovitz*.[85] The case involved the divorce of a Jewish couple. As part of the civil divorce proceedings, the husband agreed to obtain a Jewish divorce known as a 'get' immediately upon the granting of the civil divorce. According to the Jewish faith, a husband and wife remain married unless a 'get' is obtained and a wife cannot obtain a 'get' unless

---

[81] *Halpern v Toronto (City)* [2003] OJ No 2268, [53].
[82] See, eg, *Hendricks v Quebec* [2002] JQ No 3816 (QCSC); *Egale v Canada* [2003] BCJ No 994 (BCCA); *Dunbar v Yukon* [2004] YJ No. 61 (YKSC); *Vogel v Canada* [2004] MJ No 418 (MNQB); *Boutilier v Nova Scotia* [2004] NSJ No 357 (NCSC); and *NW v Canada* [2004] SJ No 669 (SKQB).
[83] SC 2005, c 33.
[84] [2004] SCJ No 75.
[85] [2007] SCJ No 54.

her husband agrees to give it. Fifteen years after the granting of the civil divorce, the husband still had not obtained the 'get' and the wife sued him for damages for breach of contract. The husband argued that his right to freedom of religion under the *Quebec Charter of Human Rights and Freedoms*[86] prevented the court from compelling him to obtain a 'get' and from having to pay damages for failing to do so.

Seven of nine Supreme Court justices held that the husband's right to freedom of religion did not shield him from the need to comply with his divorce agreement. The court held that the validly formed legal agreement was not rendered injusticiable by the fact that the purpose of the agreement was to remove religious barriers to re-marriage. Moreover, the husband's right to freedom of religion had to be balanced against the wife's right to equality and autonomous choice in marriage and divorce. In this case, the latter considerations outweighed the former:

> The public interest in protecting equality rights, the dignity of Jewish women in their independent ability to divorce and remarry, as well as the public benefit in enforcing valid and binding contractual obligations are among the interests and values that outweigh Mr. Marcovitz's claim that enforcing [the divorce agreement] would interfere with his religious freedom.[87]

In dissent, two Supreme Court justices refused to enforce Mr Marcovitz's promise on the grounds that it pertained to a religious, and not a civil, obligation. The dissenting justices held that, as a matter of civil law, the claimant wife was able to re-marry as she had obtained a legal divorce. The court should not use civil law to enforce the claimant's entitlement to religious remarriage or to enforce the husband's religious or moral undertaking to obtain a 'get'. According to the dissenting justices, this hands-off approach is necessary to ensure that the courts remain neutral arbiters of civil, and not religious, law.

Conclusion

There is no doubt that, since the enactment of the Charter, the Supreme Court of Canada has embraced the opportunity to reinvigorate the nation's commitment to the protection of individual religious freedom. The broad definition of freedom of religion which has emerged from the court's post-Charter jurisprudence makes clear that s 2(a) protects the fundamental right of every person in Canada to choose his

---

[86] The *Canadian Charter of Rights and Freedoms* did not apply because the court case was brought to compel compliance with a private agreement, not to challenge government action. Nonetheless, the court's comments on freedom of religion are instructive for Charter interpretation.

[87] *Bruker v Marcovitz* [2007] SCJ No 54, [92].

or her own system of religious beliefs and to act in accordance with those beliefs, without law-makers or the courts evaluating the merits of those beliefs. The clear message from the courts is that Canadian society values religious diversity and that Canadian law-makers must respect religious diversity. This message is critical because the pervasive nature of religion in our society means that there are a multitude of circumstances that may give rise to a conflict between positive law and religious freedom:

> Whether in the context of Sunday closing laws, education, medical procedures, same-sex marriage, religious marriage, or by-law enforcement, the broad acceptance of the principle of religious freedom as demonstrated through court decisions plays an important role in defining Canada and Canadians. For a nation that prides itself on tolerance, respect for the freedom of religion is integral to welcoming a broad spectrum of religions and cultures. In this way, the courts have given effect to the national consciousness and imbued Canada with a deep and fundamental respect for multiculturalism and diversity by fiercely protecting religious beliefs and practices.[88]

In short, the Supreme Court rulings culminate in an understanding that every sincere belief or practice, having a nexus with religion, is worthy of constitutional protection under s 2(a) of the Charter.

Having broadly defined freedom of religion under s 2(a), however, the Supreme Court has set itself a difficult task when it comes to applying s 1 of the Charter. The court's characterization of religion as a personal and subjectively proven system of beliefs or practices puts into sharp relief the application of an objective standard to determine whether a legislative limitation on freedom of religion is justified under s 1. While the Supreme Court rulings provide clear tests or criteria for determining what action or behaviour fall within the scope of s 2(a)'s protection, the cases do not provide much guidance as to what legislative action is constitutionally acceptable as a limitation on the freedom of religion. While it is certain that laws having the purpose of promoting or restricting religious activity cannot be justified under s 1 of the Charter, it is much less clear whether laws incidentally restricting religious activity or incidentally requiring conduct prohibited by religious belief can be 'saved' under a s 1 analysis. The validity of such laws still has to be determined on a case by case basis, which, in effect, means that the practical parameters of the Charter's protection for religious freedom remains somewhat nebulous.

---

[88] B P Elman, 'Freedom of Conscience and Religion', in L I Rotman, B P Elman, and G L Gall (eds), *Constitutional Law: Cases, Commentary and Principles* (2008) 923.

In the end, it may be inevitable that some certainty about the practical extent of the Charter's protection of freedom of religion under s 1 has to be sacrificed in exchange for a robust recognition of the scope of that freedom under s 2(a). It is paradoxical to say that, while a religious belief or practice is a purely personal conviction, there is a logical national or social consensus as to appropriate restrictions on that conviction. Given the jurisprudence to date, however, this is the paradox that Canadian law-makers and Canadian courts must continue to negotiate in future cases as they struggle to balance the religious interests of individuals and the secular interests of Canadian society.

16

Quo Vadis the Free Exercise of Religion? The Diminishment of Student Religious Expression in US Public Schools

Charles J Russo

The US Supreme Court 'bristles with hostility to all things religious in public life'.[1]

The first sixteen words of the First Amendment to the United States Constitution, according to which 'Congress shall make no law respecting an establishment of religion, or prohibiting the free exercise thereof', contains an inherent conflict between its clauses that has generated more litigation at the Supreme Court than any education-related topic in its history.[2] In other words, while Americans are free to believe in what they wish, the US Supreme Court and other courts have interpreted the First Amendment as not permitting the government from taking any actions, such as aiding religious institutions or permitting prayer in state-sponsored activities such as public schools, for fear of establishing a state religion. At the same time, although the Federal Constitution forbids Congress from establishing religion, since the Supreme Court extended the same prohibition to state governments,[3]

---

[1] *Santa Fe Independent School District v Doe*, 530 US 290, 318 (Rehnquist CJ, dissenting) (2002) ('*Santa Fe*') (striking down student led prayer at a high school football game).
[2] Desegregation is the second most commonly litigated issue involving public schools in the US:
[3] *Cantwell v Connecticut*, 310 US 296 (1940) (striking down the convictions of Jehovah's Witnesses for violating a statute against the solicitation of funds for religious, charitable, or philanthropic purposes without prior approval of public officials). But see in *Barron v Mayor and City Council of Baltimore*, 32 US 7 (1833) (holding that the Bill of Rights was inapplicable to the states since its history revealed that it was limited to the federal government).

individuals have the same rights against the federal or state governments with regard to religion in the public marketplace (state constitutions typically include similar provisions).

When disputes arise under the First Amendment with regard to prayer and religious expression by students in public schools, the lack of judicial clarity, coupled with what can be interpreted as judicial hostility, has led to the near banishment of many student-led religious activities in many public schools.[4] This unhappy state of affairs with regard to the Religion Clauses resulted in large part by the Supreme Court's inability to create separate and distinct standards when dealing with the Establishment and Free Exercise Clauses. Initially, the Justices created a two-part test in *School District of Abington Township v Schempp* and *Murray v Curlett*[5] to review the constitutionality of prayer and Bible reading in public schools. However, the Court subsequently expanded this two-part measure into the tripartite Establishment Clause test in *Lemon v Kurtzman* (*Lemon*),[6] a dispute involving government aid to religiously affiliated non-public schools.

When the Supreme Court applied the so-called *Lemon* test in cases involving both aid and religious activity, its failure to explain how, or why, it had become a kind of 'one-size fits all' measure that addresses issues of both Free Exercise and Establishment, created confusion for lower courts, lawyers, commentators, and school officials who sought judicial clarity, if not consistency. This confusion is exacerbated because as membership on the Court changes, its collective jurisprudence on the status of the Establishment and Free Exercise Clauses is impacted. The Court's jurisprudence has also been subject to modification through the creation of two later tests. In the earlier of these two tests, *Lynch v Donnelly*,[7] a non-school case, the Court upheld the inclusion of a Nativity scene in a Christmas display on public property pursuant to what Justice O'Connor described as the endorsement test when dealing with religious activity in public settings. Then, in *Lee v Weisman*,[8] a case prohibiting

---

[4] The *Equal Access Act*, enacted in 1984, is an exception. Among its many provisions, the Act provides that public secondary schools that receive federal financial assistance and permit non-curriculum related student groups to meet during non-instructional time cannot deny access to groups due to the religious, political, philosophical, or other content of their speech. The Act also allows officials to exclude groups if their meetings materially and substantially interfere with the orderly conduct of school activities: *Equal Access Act*, 20 USC A §§ 4071 et seq. The Supreme Court upheld the constitutionality of the Act in *Board of Education of Westside Community Schools v Mergens* ('*Mergens*'), 496 US 226 (1990).
[5] 374 US 203 (1963).
[6] 403 US 602 (1971).
[7] 465 US 668 (1984).
[8] 505 US 577 (1992) ('*Lee*').

prayer at public school graduation ceremonies, the Court enunciated the so-called psychological coercion test when addressing prayer in schools.

In light of ongoing conflicts over the place of student prayer and religious activity in public schools in the US, with the result that the free exercise rights are arguably diminishing, this chapter includes three substantive sections. After a brief prolegomena, the first part sets the stage by reviewing the tests that the Supreme Court created. The second section examines four cases where the courts have demonstrated hostility towards Christianity. The third section reflects on where the Court's jurisprudence with regard to students' free exercise of religion in public schools may be headed.

Prolegomena

This chapter takes the position that the Supreme Court has set a judicial tone that is largely hostile to religion, Christianity in particular. In so doing, the Court has seemingly aligned itself with those who oppose religion[9] in the ongoing culture war[10] that has swept the US in excluding prayer and most religious activity from public schools to the detriment of the free exercise rights of students. As such, this chapter reflects on how the judiciary, and school officials, have misapplied and misunderstood the so-called *Lemon* test,[11] the Court's quintessential standard for dealing with religious matters in public education, discussed below, in essentially adopting an attitude that is hostile to religion in the public marketplace of ideas.

At the outset, it is important to note that this chapter does not advocate the inclusion of sectarian prayer and religious activities in public schools. Rather, this chapter maintains that the courts, and educators, should adopt a more even-handed approach to religion, especially Christianity, when evaluating the constitutionality of such activities under Establishment Clause analysis, recognizing that allowing individuals the freedom to express their faiths is not the same as imposing a state religion.

---

[9] For evidence of this recent trend wherein intellectuals have promoted atheism over belief, see, eg, such popular bestselling books as Richard Dawkins, *The God Delusion* (2006), Sam Harris, *Letters to a Christian Nation* (2006), and Daniel Dennett, *Breaking the Spell: Religion as a Natural Phenomenon* (2006).

[10] In an admittedly different factual context, Justice Scalia decried the fact that the Court has taken sides in the culture war. See *Lawrence v Texas*, 539 US 558, 602–3 (Scalia J, dissenting) (2003) (striking down a state statute that made it a crime for two persons of the same sex to engage in specified intimate sexual conduct).

[11] See below n 31 et seq, and accompanying text, for a discussion of *Lemon v Kurtzman*, 403 US 602 (1971) ('*Lemon*').

Setting the stage

As noted, according to the religion clauses of the First Amendment to the US Constitution, 'Congress shall make no law respecting an establishment of religion, or prohibiting the free exercise thereof'. While this part of the First Amendment contains two religion clauses, Establishment and Free Exercise, much of the Court's school-related jurisprudence has essentially blurred the line between the two, treating both as basically one, often relying on what is referred to as its Establishment Clause analysis.

The Jeffersonian metaphor of the 'wall of separation'[12] between church and state that is at the heart of the Supreme Court's First Amendment jurisprudence, words that are not in the text of the Constitution, entered its educational lexicon as a kind of Trojan horse in *Everson v Board of Education* (*Everson*).[13] In *Everson*, the Court, in a judgment by Justice Hugo Black, a former member of the Ku Klux Klan and its virulently anti-Catholic attitudes,[14] upheld a statute from New Jersey that allowed local school boards to reimburse parents for the cost of transporting their children to religiously affiliated non-public schools.[15] In other words, while upholding the program, an argument this chapter believes in light of his attitude towards Roman Catholicism, Black sowed the seeds for the erection of the 'wall of separation' between church and state in declaring that '[i]n the words of Jefferson, the clause against establishment of religion by law was intended to erect "a wall of separation between Church and State"'.[16] The Court would rely on this fateful phrase repeatedly over the next sixty years and more.

Unlike its jurisprudence with regard to state aid to religiously affiliated non-public schools, which has allowed more or less assistance primarily depending on the

---

[12] The metaphor of the 'wall of separation' comes from Thomas Jefferson's letter of January 1, 1802, to Nehemiah Dodge, Ephraim Robbins, and Stephen S Nelson, 'A Committee of the Danbury Baptist Association: Thomas Jefferson', in A Andrew (ed), *Writings Of Thomas Jefferson* (1903) 281. Jefferson wrote: 'their legislature should "make no law respecting an establishment of religion, or prohibiting the free exercise thereof," thus building a wall of separation between church and state'.

[13] 330 US 1 (1947), *Rehearing denied*, 330 US 855 (1947).

[14] See, eg, Ira C Lupu and Robert W Tuttle, 'Federalism and Faith' (2006) 56 *Emory Law Journal* 19, fn 120 (citing Philip Hamburger's *Separation of Church and State* (2002) for Black's prior connections to the Ku Klux Klan and its anti-Catholicism).

[15] The Supreme Court first used the term in *Reynolds v United States*, 98 US 145, 164 (1878) wherein it rejected a Free Exercise Clause challenge to a federal polygamy statute.

[16] *Everson v Board of Education* (*Everson*), 330 US 1, 16 (1947).

composition of the High Court Bench,[17] the Justices have consistently opposed any kind of state-sponsored prayer and/or religious activity in schools. Beginning[18] with *Engel v Vitale*,[19] its first case on prayer in public schools, the Supreme Court has invalidated prayer and Bible reading,[20] the posting of the Ten Commandments in classrooms,[21] a moment of silence,[22] and graduation prayer.[23] The Court also struck down student-led prayer at school sponsored activities such as high school football games.[24] In fairness, note also that the Court has upheld student-organized prayer and Bible study clubs under the *Equal Access Act*[25] and allowed outside religious groups to use school facilities if they are available to other, non-religious, groups.[26]

---

[17] The Court's modern Establishment Clause jurisprudence with regard to state aid in the context of K-12 education evolved through three phases. During the first stage, which began with *Everson*, and ended with *Board of Education v Allen*, 392 US 236 (1968) (upholding a state law mandating the loans of text books in secular subjects for students in religiously affiliated non-public schools), the Court enunciated the Child Benefit Test. The years between *Lemon*, 403 US 602 (1971), and *Aguilar v Felton*, 473 US 402 (1985) (striking down the on-site delivery of Title I services to students in their religiously affiliated non-public schools) were the low point as to the Child Benefit Test as the Court refused to move beyond the limits it created in *Everson* and *Allen*. However, with *Zobrest v Catalina Foothills School District*, 509 US 1 (1993) (permitting the on-site delivery of special education services to a student in his religiously affiliated non-public high school) the Court reinvigorated the Child Benefit Test.

[18] Earlier, in *People of State of Illinois ex rel McCollum v Board of Education of School District No 71, Champaign County*, 333 US 203 (1948), the Court invalidated a program that permitted members of the Jewish, Roman Catholic, and Protestant faiths to offer religion classes in public schools to children whose parents agreed to have them take part in the program. In its only other pre-*Vitale* case involving religion, *Zorach v Clauson*, 343 US 306 (1952), the Court upheld a program in New York City that allowed school officials to release students early from their public schools so that they could attend religious classes at other locations on the basis that this was similar to accommodating parental wishes by granting excused absences for children who were absent for religious reasons.

[19] 370 US 421 (1962).

[20] *Abington Township v Schempp* and *Murray v Curlett*, 374 US 203 (1963).

[21] *Stone v Graham*, 449 US 39 (1980), *Rehearing denied*, 449 US 1104 (1981), *On remand*, 612 SW 2d 133 (Ky 1981).

[22] *Wallace v Jaffree*, 472 US 38 (1985) (invalidating a statute from Alabama on the ground that it lacked a secular purpose since its sponsors hoped that it would lead to a return to school prayer).

[23] *Lee*, 505 US 577 (1992).

[24] *Santa Fe*, 530 US 290 (2002).

[25] *Equal Access Act*, 20 USC A §§ 4071.

[26] See *Lamb's Chapel v Center Moriches Union Free School District* ('*Lamb's Chapel*'), 508 US 384 (1993), *On remand*, 17 F 3d 1425 (2d Cir 1994) (permitting a religious group to show a film series on child-rearing in a school facility); *Good News Club v Milford Central School* ('*Milford*'), 533 US 98 (2001) (allowing a non-school-sponsored club to meet during non-class hours so that members and moderators could discuss child-rearing along with character, and moral development from a religious perspective since officials permitted other groups to address similar topics from a secular perspective).

In addition to the cases discussed below, lower federal courts, often affirming the actions of educational officials, have struck down a wide array of religious, specifically Christian, activities in schools. Among these instances, courts permitted educators to prohibit a student from writing a biography about Jesus as a historical figure since she failed to follow her teacher's directions in completing the assignment,[27] finding that educators did not violate a second-grade student's First Amendment rights to freedom of religion in preventing her from showing a videotape of herself singing a religious song to classmates during show-and-tell.[28] Courts have also allowed school officials to direct a high school student to remove Christian religious messages from a mural she painted as part of a school-wide beautification project,[29] and to prevent a child from placing a religious poster on a school wall.[30]

Constitutional difficulties over the place of prayer and/or religious activity in schools can most directly be traced to *Lemon v Kurtzman* (*Lemon*),[31] the Court's most significant case in the history of church-state relations. In *Lemon*, the Court vitiated statutes from Pennsylvania that called for the purchase of secular services and Rhode Island that basically provided salary supplements for teachers in religiously affiliated non-public schools. In its far-reaching opinion, the Court relied on two of its then recent decisions in creating the seemingly ubiquitous tripartite *Lemon* test. The Court combined the two-part purpose and effect test that it created in *School District of Abington Township v Schempp* and *Murray v Curlett*,[32] invalidating the constitutionality of prayer and Bible reading in public schools by adding the excessive entanglement test from *Walz v Tax Commission of the City of New*,[33] wherein it upheld New York's practice of providing state property tax exemptions for church property that is used in worship services. The Court wrote that:

---

[27] *Settle v Dickson County School Board*, 53 F 3d 152 (6th Cir 1995), *cert. denied*, 516 US 989 (1995). While the teacher certainly had the authority to set the parameters for assignments, she might have turned the event into a teachable moment, rather than litigation, had she pointed out that in addition to the Bible, the First Century Roman historians Pliny and Tacitus reported on the existence of Jesus. For a commentary on this case, see Ralph D Mawdsley and Charles J Russo, 'Religious Expression and Teacher Control of the Classroom: A New Battleground for Free Speech' (1996) 107 *Education Law Reporter* 1.

[28] *DeNooyer v Livona Public Schools*, 799 F Supp 744 (ED Mich 1992), *Affirmed sub nom Denooyer v Merinelli*, 1 F3d 1240 (6th Cir 1993), *Rehearing denied, opinion superseded without published opinion*, 12 F 3d 211 (6th Cir. 1993), *cert. denied*, 511 US 1031 (1994).

[29] *Bannon v School District of Palm Beach County*, 387 F 3d 1208 (11th Cir 2004), *Rehearing and rehearing en banc denied*, 125 Fed Appx 984 (11th Cir 2004), *cert. denied*, 126 S Ct 330 (2005).

[30] See also *Peck ex rel Peck v Baldwinsville Central School District*, 426 F 3d 617 (2d Cir 2005).

[31] 330 US 1 (1947), *Rehearing denied*, 330 US 855 (1947).

[32] 374 US 203 (1963).

[33] 397 US 664 (1970).

Every analysis in this area must begin with consideration of the cumulative criteria developed by the Court over many years. Three such tests may be gleaned from our cases. First, the statute must have a secular legislative purpose; second, its principal or primary effect must be one that neither advances nor inhibits religion; finally, the statute must not foster 'an excessive government entanglement with religion.'[34]

The difficulty with *Lemon* results in part from the fact that it is something of a mixed metaphor that traces its origins to cases involving both the free exercise and establishment of religion. More specifically, since, as noted, *Lemon*'s first two parts were developed in the context of a dispute concerning prayer and Bible reading in public schools and the third in a disagreement over tax exemptions, essentially governmental aid, to religious institutions. Even so, the judiciary applies the *Lemon* test widely, almost indiscriminately, in an array of disputes involving both aid to religious institutions and prayer and religious activities and public schools.

Perhaps the greatest challenge that the *Lemon* test presents, particularly from the point of view of this chapter, arises under its second prong. Under this standard, any governmental action must have a 'principal or primary effect ... that neither advances nor inhibits religion'.[35] Yet, in focusing on avoiding the advancement of religion, and largely ignoring practices that have the practical effect of inhibiting religious freedom, the courts have contributed significantly to attempts to exclude religion improperly from a wide array of educational activities. Moreover, despite the Court's occasional dissatisfaction with the *Lemon* test as the primary vehicle for evaluating prayer and religious activity in public schools, having refused to rely explicitly on Justice O'Connor's proposed endorsement test[36] or Justice Kennedy's psychological coercion test,[37] the Justices have yet to eschew this increasingly unworkable standard in favour of a more manageable test.

---

[34] *Lemon*, 403 US 602, 612–3 (1971). In reviewing entanglement and state aid to religiously affiliated schools, most often in the context of providing aid, the Court identified three additional factors that must be taken into consideration: 'we must examine the character and purposes of the institutions that are benefitted, the nature of the aid that the State provides, and the resulting relationship between the government and religious authority' (at 615).

[35] Ibid.

[36] Writing in a concurring opinion in *Lynch v Donnelly*, 465 US 668, 687ff (1984), a non-school case upholding a display including a creche among secular symbols, Justice O'Connor's endorsement test asked whether the purpose of a governmental action is to endorse or approve of a religion or religious activity.

[37] In the majority opinion in *Lee*, 505 US 577 (1992), Justice Kennedy's opinion invalidated school-sponsored prayer on the basis that such governmental activity could result in psychological coercion of students.

Difficulties with the Court's Establishment Clause jurisprudence arise because its separationist wing, Justices Stevens,[38] the recently retired Souter,[39] and Ginsburg,[40] often joined by Justice Breyer, demonstrated a talisman-like obeisance for the tired, if not failed, Jeffersonian metaphor. The separationists, sometimes joined by Justice Breyer, consistently voted to exclude religion, whether aid, or activity, in public schools. These Justices' reliance on the wall metaphor led Stevens, for example, to reveal a deep-seated animosity to religion in any form based on his voicing his almost paranoid fear that providing poor children in failing urban schools with vouchers might turn the US into a nation that demonstrates the same misuse of religion as occurs in parts of the world that are replete with ethnic-religious strife.[41]

The dominance of the separationists[42] may, however, be coming to an end with the addition of Chief Justice Roberts and Justice Alito as they join the reliably

---

[38] Since joining the Court, Justice Stevens voted against permitting prayer or religious activity in public schools in all but two cases, both of which involved access to educational facilities and which essentially treated religion as a subset of speech: *Widmar v Vincent*, 454 US 263 (1981); *Lamb's Chapel*, 508 US 384 (1993). In all other instances, he voted against religious liberty. See, eg, *Wallace v Jaffree*, 472 US 38 (1985) (striking down a moment of silence); *Edwards v Aguillard*, 482 US 578, 610 (1987) (striking down a statute that prohibited the teaching of 'evolution-science' in public schools unless accompanied by instruction on 'creation-science'); *Mergens*, 496 US 226, 270 (Stevens J, dissenting) (1990); *Lee*, 505 US 577 (1992); *Santa Fe*, 530 US 290 (2002); *Milford*, 533 US 98 (2001); *Newdow v US Congress*, 542 US 1 (2004) ('*Newdow*') (refusing to address whether the words 'under God' could remain in the Pledge of Allegiance), *Rehearing denied*, 542 US 961 (2004).

[39] Since being appointed to the Court in 1990, Justice Souter voted against religious activity in the three cases in which he participated: *Lee*, 505 US 577 (1992); *Santa Fe*, 530 US 290 (2002); *Milford*, 533 US 98 (2001); *Newdow*, 542 US 1 (2004).

[40] During her time on the High Court, Justice Ginsberg also opposed religious activity in the cases in which she was involved: *Santa Fe*, 530 US 290 (2002); *Milford*, 533 US 98 (2001); *Newdow*, 542 US 1 (2004).

[41] In *Zelman v Simmons-Harris*, 536 US 639, 686 (2002), Justice Stevens wrote, 'I have been influenced by my understanding of the impact of religious strife on the decisions of our forbears to migrate to this continent, and on the decisions of neighbors in the Balkans, Northern Ireland, and the Middle East to mistrust one another'.

[42] An imprecise science at best, patterns tend to reflect how the Justices tend to vote. For example, one study reported that in a mathematical analysis of patterns over the then past eight years, covering 468 cases, Justices Scalia and Thomas voted together more than 93 per cent of the time while Justices Ginsburg and Souter voted the same way more than 90 per cent of the time. See Erica Klarreich, 'Ideal Justice', (2009) 163 *Science News* 405; Jack Kilpatrick, 'Justices don't fit into predictable ideological boxes', *Deseret News* (Salt Lake City) 4 August 2003, A9.

accommodationist Justices Scalia[43] and Thomas,[44] often aided by the moderate Justice Kennedy,[45] because the newest members of the High Court bench are expected to adopt more moderate, accommodationist perspectives. It will be interesting to observe whether these new Justices shift the Supreme Court's First Amendment jurisprudence more in the direction of accommodation or whether they will leave the situation basically unchanged. Time will undoubtedly tell.

The Court recently demonstrated how confused its Establishment Clause jurisprudence is in a pair of admittedly non-school cases over the propriety of public displays of the Ten Commandments. For example, in *McCreary County, Kentucky v American Civil Liberties Union of Kentucky (McCreary County)*[46] and *Van Orden v Perry (Van Orden)*[47] the Court handed down a pair of conflicting five-to-four rulings, in which seven of the nine Justices penned opinions,[48] with only Justice Breyer switching allegiances, joining the majorities in both cases.[49] With Justice Souter continuing his unbroken streak of voting to maintain the 'wall of separation' between church and state, he relied on the *Lemon* test in striking struck down public displays of the Ten Commandments in courthouses in *McCreary County*. Conversely,

---

[43] Justice Scalia has also upheld religious freedoms in school settings: *Edwards v Aguillard*, 482 US 578, 610 (Scalia J, dissenting) (1987); *Mergens*, 496 US 226 (1990); *Lee*, 505 US 577, 631 (Scalia J, dissenting) (1992); *Lamb's Chapel*, 508 US 384 (1993); *Santa Fe*, 530 US 290 (2002); *Milford*, 533 US 98 (2001). Justice Scalia did not participate in *Newdow*. For a discussion of *Newdow* and Justice Scalia's non-participation, see Charles J Russo, 'The Supreme Court and Pledge of Allegiance: Does God Still Have a Place in American Schools?' (2004) 2001 *Brigham Young University Education and Law Journal* 301.

[44] *Lee*, 505 US 577 (1992); *Lamb's Chapel*, 508 US 384 (1993); *Santa Fe*, 530 US 290 (2002); *Milford*, 533 US 98 (2001), *Newdow*, 542 US 1 (2004).

[45] Justice Kennedy voted in favour of religious freedom in *Mergens*, 496 US 226 (1990), *Lamb's Chapel*, 508 US 384 (1993), *Milford*, 533 US 98 (2001). But see *Lee*, 505 US 577 (1992); *Santa Fe*, 530 US 290 (2002); *Newdow*, 542 US 1 (2004).

[46] 545 US 844 (2005) ('*McCreary County*').

[47] 545 US 677 (2005) ('*Van Orden*').

[48] In *McCreary County*, 545 US 844 (2005), Justice Souter's majority opinion was joined by Justices Stevens, O'Connor, Ginsburg, and Breyer. Justice O'Connor also authored a separate concurrence. Justice Scalia's dissent was joined by Chief Justice Rehnquist along with Justices Thomas and Kennedy (as to parts II and III). In *Van Orden*, 545 US 677 (2005), Chief Justice Rehnquist's majority opinion was joined by Justices Scalia, Kennedy, and Thomas. Justice Breyer concurred in the judgment. Justices Scalia and Thomas also authored separate concurrences. Justice Stevens' dissent was joined by Justice Ginsburg. Justice Souter's dissent was joined by Justices Stevens and Ginsburg.

[49] For a commentary on these cases, see Charles J Russo, 'Religious Neutrality in Public Schools and Elsewhere: An Assessment of the Supreme Court's Approach to Posting the Ten Commandments in Public Places in the US' (2006) 7 *Education Law Journal* 21.

a plurality[50] opinion by Chief Justice Rehnquist explicitly eschewed the *Lemon* test in affirming the constitutionality of a monument to the Commandments that was situated on the grounds of the Texas State Capitol in *Van Orden*. As such, the next part of this chapter examines three recent cases that demonstrate how courts, in an attempt to bolster the sagging wall have misplaced primacy on the second prong of the *Lemon* test and demonstrated hostility to the free exercise rights of students in American public schools.

Judicial hostility toward religion

Four relatively recent federal cases in particular stand out as demonstrating what this author describes as overt hostility to Christianity, ignoring *Lemon's* directive that governmental action can neither 'advance nor inhibit religion'. This hostility is all the more apparent in light of the fact that the courts seemed to be willing to protect religious expression of faiths other than Christianity, in the second and third of these four cases, belying a lack of even-handedness, often aided and abetted by school officials. While readily conceding that there are some cases where the courts did display even-handedness,[51] their systemic failure to adopt such a perspective consistently reflects judicial attitudes toward religion in public schools.

C H ex rel Z H v Oliva (C H),[52] a case from New Jersey that made its way to the Third Circuit, reveals an appalling lack of understanding of the Establishment Clause by both school officials and the judiciary.[53] The controversy started when the child was in kindergarten and lasted until he was in second grade. The Third Circuit affirmed that school officials could not be liable for prohibiting a student from reading a religious story, 'A Big Family', an adaptation of the story of the reconciliation of the Biblical story of Jacob and Esau, and, in a Thanksgiving exercise, from hanging a

---

[50] In a plurality, less than a majority of justices agree on the same rationale for a decision. In such a case, the earlier judgment remains in place for the parties but is not binding on other litigants or in other jurisdictions.

[51] *Hansen v Ann Arbor Public Schools*, 293 F Supp 2d 780 (ED Mich 2003) (ruling in favour of a student who sued school officials after they refused to permit her to participate in a panel discussion involving clergy and religious leaders on homosexuality and religion because they disagreed with her religious message).

[52] 226 F 3d 198 (3d Cir 2000), *Certiorari denied sub nom Hood v Medford Township Board of Education*, 533 US 915 (2001). Future member of the Supreme Court, Justice Samuel Alito, then on the Third Circuit, dissented from the majority's opinion: *CH ex rel ZH v Oliva CH*, 226 F 3d 198, 204 (Alito J, dissenting) (3d Cir 2000) ('*CH*').

[53] But see *Peck ex rel Peck v Baldwinsville Central School District*, 426 F 3d 617, 621 (2d Cir 2005) (maintaining that officials did not have to display a child's poster with a religious theme because it was not responsive to the assignment).

poster that he drew expressing his thanks for Jesus. Although the court affirmed the actions of school officials largely on procedural grounds, it is perplexing to imagine how educators could have viewed the actions of a child, even if he were encouraged to act by his mother, as involving state action.

In *Skoros v City of New York*, (*Skoros*),[54] the Second Circuit reached a puzzling result in upholding a policy from the Board of Education with regard to holiday displays. The court ruled that the board policy, which permitted December 'holiday' displays that included a menorah commemorating Chanukah and the star and crescent celebrating Ramadan in public schools but which excluded nativity scenes of the Baby Jesus on the basis that the Christian displays were wholly religious, was constitutional.[55] While conceding that a nativity scene is indeed religious, it is amazing that the court acted as a kind of religious tribunal in determining that the other objects were entirely secular.[56] Moreover, one can only marvel how the Second Circuit's serving as arbiter of the relative significance of the religious symbols involved did not violate either *Lemon's* excessive entanglement clause or violate the Free Exercise of religion clause.

Perhaps the most outrageous decision was the Ninth Circuit's affirmation of the dismissal of a claim filed by the parents of a seventh-grader who challenged their school board's use of Islamic-friendly curricular materials in *Eklund v Byron Union School District* (*Eklund*).[57] Here school officials included a simulation unit on Islamic culture in a social studies course that, among other things, required students to wear identification tags displaying their new Islamic names, dress as Muslims, memorize and recite an Islamic prayer that has the status of the Our Father or Lord's prayer in Christianity as well as other verses from the Qur'an, recite the Five Pillars of Faith, and engage in fasting and acts of self-denial.[58] Without addressing the merits of the

---

[54] 437 F 3d 1 (2d Cir 2006), *Certiorari denied*, 2007 WL 506033 (Feb 20, 2007).

[55] For a discussion of *Skoros v City of New York*, 437 F 3d 1 (2d Cir 2006) ('*Skoros*') and its implications, see Charles J Russo, 'Of Baby Jesus and the Easter Bunny: Does Christianity Still Have a Place in the Educational Marketplace of Ideas in the United States?' (2006) 16 *Education and Law Journal* 61.

[56] For a similar case in a school setting, see *Sechler v State College Area School District*, 121 F Supp 2d 439 (MD Pa 2000) (rejecting a challenge from a youth minister where school officials permitted a 'Winter Holiday' display that included information on Chanukah and Kwanza, but nothing on Christmas on the basis that the display did not offend the Establishment Clause by favouring one religion over another). For a similar case in a non-school setting, see *Spohn v West*, 2000 WL 1459981 (SDNY 2000) (dismissing the claim of a Christian worker in a public hospital that a display of Jewish, but not Christian, religious symbols during the December holiday season violated his First Amendment rights under the Establishment Clause).

[57] 154 Fed Appx 648 (9th Cir 2005), *Certiorari denied*, 549 US 942 (2006).

[58] *Eklund v Byron Union School District*, 2006 WL 1519184 (Appellate Petition, Motion and Filing) (US May 31, 2006); *Petition for a Writ of Certiorari* (NO 05-1539), 3–13.

objecting parents' underlying claims, the Ninth Circuit summarily affirmed that the activities at issue 'were not ... "overt religious exercises" that raise Establishment Clause concerns'.[59] One can only imagine the outroar that might have resulted, particularly from selected corners of the 'mainstream media', had school officials distributed rosary beads to students or required them to dress as Roman Catholic priests or nuns.

Most recently, in *Corder v Lewis Palmer School District No 38*,[60] the Tenth Circuit affirmed that school officials in Colorado did not violate a student's First Amendment and Equal Protection rights in requiring her to make an e-mail apology to those who had been in attendance for ignoring the principal's instructions by delivering a speech during graduation that mentioned her Christian faith and encouraged listeners to explore Christianity before she could receive her diploma. The court held that educators did not impinge or burden the student's right to free exercise of religion because they had the authority to regulate school-sponsored speech. The court added that a state law protecting the free expression rights of students applied only to written publications such as school newspapers and that even if the statute had been ambiguous, it could not have been interpreted as prohibiting officials from regulating speech that could violate the Establishment Clause. The court maintained that since the student graduated, her equal protection claim was moot. While one could seek to distinguish this case away from the others on the basis that the student was speaking at a school-sponsored, rather than a public, event, one can only wonder whether officials would have been as quick to discipline her had she spoken on a politically correct topic with which they, and perhaps the audience, agreed.

Reflections

When considering judicial hostility to prayer and/or religious activities in public schools, three interrelated issues, raised by cases in the densely populated, and judicially influential, Second, Third, and Ninth Circuits, in particular, can help to transform the debate over the constitutionality of these events from a contentious exercise to a teachable moment to unite communities. The way in which educators and the judiciary clarify the place of prayer and/or religious activity in schools will have a major impact on the US because the way in which this debate is played out

---

[59] *Eklund v Byron Union School District*, 154 Fed Appx 648 (9th Cir. 2005) (quoting *Brown v Woodland Joint Unified School District*, 27 F 3d 1373, 1382 (9th Cir 1994)) (affirming that a curricular program which asked children to discuss witches or create poetic chants and pretend they were witches or sorcerers did not require them to practice the 'religion' of witchcraft in violation of Establishment Clause or California Constitution).

[60] 566 F 3d 1219 (10th Cir 2009).

will reveal whether the nation still cherishes the underlying values of freedom of religion that contributed so greatly to its foundation.

The first question involves the effect prong in *Lemon*. More specifically, if the US is to continue to foster ongoing dialogue about diversity of perspectives, it is imperative that the Supreme Court provide guidance for the remainder of the federal judiciary as well as school officials in order to avoid the appearance of inhibiting religion, especially in the aftermath of recent cases that have been less than favourable to expressions of religious belief. For example, it is unclear how ordering the removal of a child's drawings or permitting him to read a religious story in *C H* or permitting symbols that are closely associated with Islam and Judaism, but not Christianity, in *Skoros* or having children act as if they were Islamic in *Eklund*, are anything but inconsistent, if not hostile to Christianity, since they display a lack of even-handedness, to say the least.

The decision in *C H* is particularly troubling because it is unclear how school officials could have reached the conclusion that a young child's desire to read a religious story to classmates, even if spurred on by his mother, could somehow have been attributed to the school board as an arm of the state. Further, how the Second Circuit in *Skoros*, backed by attorneys and other school officials from the New York City Board of Education, could claim that both the menorah and star and crescent are wholly secular is nothing short of astounding, rejecting the religious significance that these objects have long held. *Skoros* demonstrates a clear lack of even-handedness in addressing religious symbols and is exacerbated by the fact that the court took it upon itself to be the arbiter of the meaning of the iconographic images at issue, compounding the educators' lack of religious understanding that was evidenced in the board's wrong-headed policy. As Justice Scalia noted in Lee, one cannot help but wonder whether secular jurists 'cannot disguise the fact that the[y have] gone beyond the realm where judges know what they are doing',[61] in acting essentially as religious arbiters in passing judgment in areas well beyond their competence.

Lip service over the importance of respect for differences of opinion aside, educators and the courts must allow educational leaders in schools to practice what they preach and do more than merely talk about inculcating different values. At a time when values occupy a prominent role in public debate, one can only wonder what message children receive in their classrooms when the courts have permitted school officials to ensure that their schools are virtually sanitized of references to prayer and religion other than 'appropriate' discussions in history or English classes. By imposing a wall of silence that prevents believers from exercising their constitutional rights, educators and the courts risk sending out the unmistakable message to children and

---

[61] *Lee*, 505 US 577, 636 (Scalia J, dissenting) (1992).

parents that freedom of religion is little more than a pious platitude that can be freely ignored without consequence.

A second, closely related question concerns the paradox of how a democratic society that was founded on religious principles but continues to preserve the Jeffersonian metaphor by maintaining the 'wall of separation' between church and state with regard to prayer and/or religious activities, can respect the rights of both the majority and minority. In other words, while certainly agreeing with Justice O'Connor's salient observation that 'we do not count heads before enforcing the First Amendment',[62] in protecting the rights of the minority with regard to such potentially contentious matters as prayer and religious activity in schools, it remains to be seen how the courts can avoid the tyranny of the minority. Therefore, finding an acceptable middle ground is essential.

When the Supreme Court struck down school-sponsored graduation prayer in *Lee v Weisman*, the majority spoke of a 'mutuality of obligation' that safeguards the rights of minorities.[63] If this 'mutuality of obligation' is to have any meaning, then public school officials and the courts must find a way to accommodate the viewpoints of all, rather than stifle the religious expression of believers. One can only question how educators expect to foster an appreciation of diversity in all of its manifestations beyond such demographic characteristics as race, gender, and socio-economic status if school officials cannot tolerate expressions of religious beliefs that may not be shared by all members of an audience or community.

It is ironic that in a nation that values freedom of religion, the US courts have been unable to reach a consensus on the appropriateness of public prayer and religious activity. Further, protestations to the contrary notwithstanding, schools teach values regularly, whether informing children not to cheat, to study and work hard, not to fight, and to drink their milk. While readily conceding that the inculcation of religious values is a familial obligation that is best done at home, one can only wonder what message students, especially those from the homes of believers, receive when they are told that they cannot discuss religion in school. This chapter stands for the proposition that reasonable observers cannot help but to think that the message is of one rejecting religion. The notion that there can be no discussion of religion in schools is dubious at best, disingenuous at worst in light of dicta in *School District of Abington Township v Schempp* and *Murray v Curlett* that:

> It certainly may be said that the Bible is worthy of study for its literary and historic qualities. Nothing we have said here indicates that such study of the Bible or of

---

[62] *McCreary County*, 545 US 844, 884 (O'Connor J, concurring) (2005).
[63] *Lee*, 505 US 577, 591 (1992).

religion, when presented objectively as part of a secular program of education, may not be effected consistently with the First Amendment.[64]

Judicial inability to formulate a measure that respects the rights of diverse groups of believers is frustrating where educators have, as in *Lee*, included well-reasoned safeguards such as selecting a religious leader from a different faith each year and providing broad-based guidelines under which prayers may be offered. The Supreme Court's failure to respond adequately to Justice Scalia's salient dissent in *Lee* that silence in response to public prayer does not necessarily mean assent has further exacerbated the situation.[65] By silently listening to and perhaps even reflecting on whatever prayer is being offered, or if a different point of view is being presented, listeners can develop a deeper respect for perspectives other than their own, thereby enhancing the presence of intellectual diversity in schools (and other locales). If students can learn to maintain such a respectful stance, whether in silence as at the graduation, or by engaging in appropriate discussion should such matters arise in classroom settings, when exposed to ideas with which they disagree, then it could be that they, and the adults present, may have learned a valuable lesson in tolerance.

The third question relates to the nature of the prayers specifically. One can only wonder whether Americans risk trivializing the profound relationship between believers and their God about the nature of the 'prayers', in particular, at graduations and other public events. To this end, it could be that these 'prayers' run the risk of being reduced to mere formalities, words uttered to bring a gathering to order, essentially reducing God to little more than a theological rabbit's foot, a mantra to hope that events will go well. If this is the case, then perhaps individuals could rely on selections from books of poetry that can have the same effect in order to avoid the fear of 'coercing' listeners by 'forcing' them to maintain silence.

In other words, if one views prayer as being, in some way, shape or form, a type of communication with, or, a lifting of the heart and mind to God, then these discussions on prayer at graduations may be a variation on the theme of reduction to the absurd. In other words, an argument can be made that it is unfair to claim that a few brief words from scriptures, among many others, run the risk of 'establishing' a state religion. Alternatively, it may be that the erection of the 'wall of separation' runs the risk of mocking believers while turning them into second class citizens. By relegating prayer and religious activities to kinds of afterthoughts, the courts and

---

[64] 374 US 203, 225 (1963). In his concurring opinion, the separationist Justice Brennan added that '[t]he holding of the Court today plainly does not foreclose teaching about the Holy Scriptures or about the differences between religious sects in classes in literature or history…' (at 300).

[65] *Lee*, 505 US 577, 637 et seq (Scalia J, dissenting) (1992).

school officials may be setting a precedent that undermines the very foundation on which the US was founded.

Conclusion

If anything, the ongoing public discourse over the place of prayer and religious activity in public schools is a revealing barometer of how deeply conflicted American attitudes are on this important topic. As the US grows increasingly pluralistic and as multicultural groups that have previously been marginalized move into the mainstream, new and novel issues involving the place of religion in schools will arise. Perhaps a case raised by one of these groups that formerly have been disenfranchised will serve as the spur that energizes the Supreme Court to re-evaluate its stance and set a different tone for the remainder of the judiciary and school officials. At the same time, it is important to recognize that the Court does not run the risk of establishing a state-sponsored religion by permitting prayer at public school graduation ceremonies or other forms of religious activity. Rather, by acknowledging the legitimate place of prayer and religious activity in public schools, the Court can assume a leadership role in truly fostering a climate wherein diversity of opinions and beliefs are both appreciated and celebrated by all Americans regardless of their personal beliefs.

17

Freedom from Discrimination on the Basis of Religion

Kris Hanna

Broad, noble claims of a right to freedom of religion seem, prima facie, unobjectionable, but, that said, 'a right which is not recognised by law is nothing but a pious hope'.[1] Allowing people to be discriminated against on the basis of their religious beliefs or practices limits their right to freedom of religion, if indirectly. In any bill of rights that may be introduced, freedom of religion could be included. In my view, however, this would need to be supported by specific and appropriately crafted equal opportunity legislation to afford realistic protection of cultural and religious practices (subject to the constraints of the law generally). Thus, in July 2009 I introduced into the South Australian House of Assembly amendments to the *Equal Opportunity Act 1984* to ban discrimination on the basis of religion. My effort was unsuccessful, but I think this is a discussion worth continuing.

In this chapter, I discuss the amendments I proposed, and the reasoning behind them. With reference to State and Territory legislation, International Treaties and bills of rights of other countries, I consider how the proposed amendments would protect the freedom to hold, express, declare and practice religious beliefs and values. I then discuss some objections to this proposal. Finally, I discuss how such provisions might relate to a bill of rights, taking account of concerns expressed by some academics and commentators, who believe that a bill of rights is not the best avenue for such protection.

---

[1] Julian Burnside, 'It's Time. A Bill of Rights for Australia' (Speech delivered at the 2008 International Human Rights Day Address, Bob Hawke Prime Ministerial Centre, University of South Australia).

My proposed amendments to the *Equal Opportunity Act 1984* (SA) sought to forbid discrimination on the basis of religion — in relation to employment, associations/clubs, education, the provision of goods and services, and accommodation. Specific exemptions operate throughout each of these provisions to strike a balance between, on the one hand, protecting individuals and groups against unjustified discrimination on the basis of their religious beliefs, and, on the other, the genuine requirements of individuals and institutions operating in good faith according to the precepts of their particular religion.

Under the proposed amendments, discrimination would be unlawful if directly or indirectly based on a person's religious beliefs, religious characteristics or the attributes or circumstances of a relative or associate of the person. The prohibition on discrimination against workers applies to applicants, employees, agents, independent contractors, contract workers and within partnerships. Exemptions are provided for cases where: a worker could not perform the required duties or respond adequately in an emergency; if there is a genuine occupational requirement for the person to be of a specific religion (for example, the role of an imam or rabbi); or if the discrimination is made by an educational or other institution operating under the precepts or auspices of a particular religion (for example, a Catholic school or monastery).

Following the existing categories of the *Equal Opportunity Act 1984* (SA), other areas for prohibition of discrimination would include associations (with an exception for associations for persons of a particular religion), educational institutions in relation to students (except for educational institutions administered in accordance with the precepts of a particular religion), disposing of an interest in land (with an exception for gifts and testamentary dispositions), the provision of goods and services (with an exception for services involving access to a place of worship), accommodation (except where accommodation is to be shared with the decision-maker) and bodies that recognise training/educational qualifications.

I suggest further exemptions for charitable instruments (for example, trust deeds) conferring benefit wholly on persons of a particular religion. Importantly, the proposed amendments also provide an exemption for religious bodies to train and ordain ministers, priests and members, without offending the religious susceptibilities of the adherents of that religion. A further key exemption in Section 50(C) was expressed as follows:

> other practice of a body established for religious purposes that conforms with the precepts of that religion or is necessary to avoid injury to the religious susceptibilities of the adherents of that religion.

This would allow, for example, refusal of the Eucharist or some other sacrament to one considered not of the faith (whichever faith or spiritual tradition that might be).

The proposed amendments would offer protection to someone denied a job, or service in a shop, because of their religious beliefs. Under the broad exemptions, religious schools and institutions would still be able to employ only those who adhere to their faith if they wish.

South Australia, New South Wales and the Commonwealth are the only Australian jurisdictions that have thus far failed to legislate to include religion as an unlawful ground for discrimination.[2] Section 116 of the Australian Constitution gives little ground for the claim that we have 'freedom of religion' in Australia.[3] This constitutional safeguard only prohibits religious discrimination in respect of public office.

If a religious group can also be classified as an 'ethnic' group, they may be protected by the *Racial Discrimination Act 1975* (Cth). Courts have found Jews and Sikhs to be 'ethnic groups', but my research discloses no cases where Muslims, Hindus or Christians have been judicially considered 'ethnic groups' per se,[4] so the protection afforded by this legislation is insufficient.

Article 18(1) of the International Covenant on Civil and Political Rights[5] ('ICCPR') encompasses freedom from discrimination on the basis of religion, freedom to profess and practice religion and freedom to manifest religion and belief individually or with others, in public or in private.[6] At present, the South Australian, New South Wales and Commonwealth jurisdictions do not meet Australia's obligations under this International Covenant. Indeed, in the 1990s, State and federal Parliaments throughout Australia legislated to ensure that we are not bound domestically by these international documents, even though we as a nation are signatories!

The rights protected by a modern bill of rights would reflect the sort of rights addressed in the Universal Declaration of Human Rights, which Australia adopted in 1948. The amendments I proposed in the House of Assembly would bring the South Australian equal opportunity legislation in line with our obligations under the ICCPR, by promoting equality before the law without discrimination on the basis

---

[2] Anne Hewitt, '"It's not because you wear Hijab, it's because you're Muslim" — Inconsistencies in South Australia's Discrimination Laws' [2007] *QUT Law and Justice Journal* 4.
[3] *Australian Constitution* s 116.
[4] See *King-Ansell v Police* [1979] 2 NZLR 531 (Jews), *Mandla v Dowell-Lee* [1983] 2 AC 548 (Sikhs), *Racial & Religious Discrimination Factsheet* (2004) Public Interest Advocacy Centre <http://www.piac.asn.au/publications/pubs/Race%20and%20Religion.doc> at 18 June 2009.
[5] *International Covenant on Civil and Political Rights*, opened for signature 16 December 1966, 999 UNTS 171 (entered into force 23 March 1076).
[6] Ibid arts 18, 26, 27.

of religion[7] and protecting the right of minority groups to practice and profess their own religion.[8] The proposed amendments would also bring the legislation in line with Australia's obligations under the Religious Declaration[9] and the International Labour Organisation's *Discrimination (Employment and Occupation) Convention 1958*.[10] I would expect any proposed bill of rights for Australia to include many of these norms recognised in international documents recognising human rights.

I consulted with a number of religious associations about the proposed amendments, many of whom were supportive. However, I also received many emails and letters from interested parties opposing the amendments. Many of these responses, mainly from Christian groups, expressed concern that the legislation would prohibit religious institutions from operating effectively, or inhibit free speech concerning religious preaching and so on. In fact, most of these concerns appear to either result from incorrect interpretations of the provisions, or are completely unfounded. Under the amendments, and in particular under the exemptions, religious groups and educational institutions administered on the precepts of religion are able to operate in good faith in accordance with their religion. The amendments do not prevent members of a religion 'freely preaching and practising their religion and from seeking to convert others'.[11]

Many academics and other commentators, including Cardinal George Pell,[12] Bob Carr, Justice Keith Mason[13] and the Australian Human Rights Group[14] argue that a bill of rights is not the best avenue for this sort of protection for a number of reasons. These reasons include that changes may need to be made over time, that it would upset the existing balance between parliament and the courts, that they give disproportionate power to minority groups, and that they do not work.[15] The claim that a bill of rights gives power to minority groups is accurate: 'whilst a bill of rights

---

[7] Ibid art 26, EO Amendments s 65A.
[8] Ibid art 27. Visible in most exceptions within the EO Amendments.
[9] *Declaration on the Elimination of All Forms of Intolerance and of Discrimination Based on Religion or Belief*, GA res 36/55, UN GAOR, 36th sess, 55th plen mtg, UN Doc A/36/684 (1981), 171.
[10] *Discrimination (Employment and Occupation) Convention* (ILO No 111), 362 UNTS 31 (entered into force 15 June 1960).
[11] Jeremy Roberts, 'Christian Pressure Kills off Bias Ban', *The Australian* (Sydney), 20 November 2006.
[12] Cardinal George Pell, 'Four fictions: An argument against a Charter of Rights' (Speech delivered at Address to the Brisbane Institute, 28 April 2008).
[13] Keith Mason, 'Law and Religion in Australia' (Speech delivered at National Forum on Australia's Christian Heritage, Canberra, 7 August 2006).
[14] *FAQs* (2009) Australian Human Rights Group <www.humanrightsact.com.au> at 18 June 2009.
[15] Burnside, above n 1.

protects the rights of all, its primary use is to protect the rights of the weak because the strong are already safe'.[16]

Bills of rights, both statutory and constitutional, which include provisions for the right to freedom against discrimination based on religion, have been enacted in New Zealand,[17] Brazil,[18] South Africa,[19] Canada,[20] Hong Kong,[21] Greece[22] and the People's Republic of China.[23] One of the most exemplary seems to be that of the Constitution of South Africa, enacted to 'outlaw many forms of discrimination that remain[ed] after the official end of Apartheid'.[24] Section 9, entitled 'Equality', explicitly prohibits direct or indirect discrimination on the basis of religion (among other broad categories of grounds) by the state or by an individual. Importantly, it also expressly provides that national legislation must be enacted to prevent or prohibit unfair discrimination. In South Africa, this constitutionally-entrenched right has been supported by the *Promotion of Equality and Prevention of Unfair Discrimination Act 2000*, in which religion is one of the prohibited grounds for discrimination. Although the Act provides for some exemption in the determination of whether the discrimination has been unfair, it does not provide specific exemptions as I have drafted to ensure it is clear that religious groups can continue operating in good faith.

Australia is currently the only western democracy that has not enacted a bill of rights, and it is time we did so. The Model Statutory Human Rights Bill[25] ('the Model bill'), drafted by the Australian Human Rights Group, includes religion as a ground for unlawful discrimination in accordance with Australia's obligations under the ICCPR. It also includes specific provisions to protect the right to freedom of religion and the right to practice religion. These provisions are useful, but particularly in relation to discrimination, the South African provision seems more comprehensive as it explicitly includes direct and indirect discrimination from both the State and individuals. The Model bill would also benefit from carefully constructed exemptions.

---

[16] Ibid.
[17] *Bill of Rights Act 1990* (NZ).
[18] Brazil Constitution, art 5.
[19] South Africa Constitution, ch 2.
[20] Canada Constitution, pt 1, ss 2, 15.
[21] Hong Kong Bill of Rights Ordinance, arts 15, 22.
[22] Greece Constitution, Pt 1.
[23] People's Republic of China Constitution, art 36.
[24] Greg Barrow, 'South Africa bans discrimination' (2000) *BBC News Africa Online* <http://news.bbc.co.uk/2/hi/africa/619337.stm> at 19 June 2009.
[25] *Model Human Rights Bill 2009* (2008) Australian Human Rights Group <http://www.humanrightsact.com.au/2008/about-the-campaign/#bill> at 19 June 2009.

I used to think that our common law tradition gave sufficient protection to individuals in Australia. Anxiety about terrorism in the post-9/11 world, combined with populism reigning in parliaments across the land, has led me to think that Australia needs a firmer security for fundamental freedoms. At minimum, a human rights Act should be introduced, including a broad provision prohibiting discrimination on the basis of grounds including religion. A strong, constitutionally entrenched bill of rights would be far preferable, as Parliament could not readily disregard rights.

18

Ruminations from the Shaky Isles on Religious Freedom in the Bill of Rights era

Rex Tauati Ahdar*

In modern New Zealand, public interest, debate, or for that matter, consternation over matters religious is rare: religion, God, and 'all that church stuff' is not a pressing concern in the lives of most of its 4.4 million citizens. In one sense the widespread cultural disinterest in organized religion that typifies much of New Zealand history may be viewed as a positive thing. It can hardly be a cause for regret that it has, by and large, not witnessed the large-scale and bitter religious turmoil that has beset many nations.[1]

New Zealand's largest religious affiliation is Christian, and within Christianity, the largest denominations are Anglicans, Roman Catholics and Presbyterians. Unspecified numbers of Pentecostals and Evangelicals are a rapidly growing sector within Christianity as well. The actual level of churchgoing is significantly less than the official census figures, with the latest International Social Survey Programme report (in 2009) recording that some 20 per cent indicated that they attended church service at least once a month.[2] Notably, the 'no religion' sector has grown significantly in each six-yearly census period since the 1970s, and the latest census,

---

*   This chapter is a revised version of an essay first published in (2010) 29 *University of Queensland Law Journal* 279. I am indebted to Nicholas Aroney for his valuable comments on an earlier draft.
[1] For a fuller discussion, see G A Wood, 'Church and State in the Furthest Reach of Western Christianity' in John Stenhouse (ed), *Christianity, Modernity and Culture: New Perspectives on New Zealand History* (2005) 207.
[2] Massey University, *Religion in New Zealand* (2009).

in 2006, recorded that some 34 per cent of New Zealanders identified themselves in this way.

Against this all too brief thumbnail sketch we turn now to the legal landscape. The *New Zealand Bill of Rights Act 1990* ('NZBORA') recently celebrated its twentieth anniversary. This chapter seeks to draw some lessons from the last two decades. Specifically, it considers how one significant right, the right of religious freedom, has fared in the early years of New Zealand's Bill of Rights era.

The chapter then outlines the genesis of the NZBORA and tightens the focus by recounting the opposition in New Zealand by one major and particularly vociferous opponent to it, conservative religionists. It is no coincidence — given their broadly similar cultural and religious topography — that Australian conservative Christian voices also feature prominently in the opposition to a proposed Bill of Rights in that country. In his comprehensive analysis, Patrick Parkinson notes:

> The divisions about a Charter of Rights were seen in all parts of the community. … There is … one quite prominent sector of Australian society in which opposition to a charter has been rather more evident than support for it. That is in the churches. …
>
> Submissions to the NHRC [National Human Rights Consultation] that are critical of a charter, apart from the Australian Christian Lobby, include those from the Presbyterian Church of Australia, the Baptist Union of Australia, the Anglican Diocese of Sydney, the Life, Marriage and Family Centre of the Catholic Archdiocese of Sydney, and the Ambrose Centre for Religious Liberty (a body that has an advisory council that includes senior figures from a number of different faiths). …
>
> While the Catholic Bishops collectively did not take a stand either way, Cardinal George Pell, the Church's most prominent leader, has been an outspoken critic of a charter.[3]

What were — and, in contemporary Australian political discourse, what are[4] — their particular concerns? This chapter considers what has happened since the NZBORA came into force and comments upon the relatively meagre number of religious freedom cases decided post-1990. Finally, this chapter offers some conclusions and

---

[3] Patrick Parkinson, 'Christian Concerns About An Australian Charter of Rights', chapter 7 of this volume. A previous version of Parkinson's chapter appeared in the (2010) 15 *Australian Journal of Human Rights* 83. On religious opposition, see, eg, Nicola Bercolvic, 'Churches unite over human rights charter', *The Australian* (Sydney), 3 October 2009. As with New Zealand, liberal Christians in Australia — the Uniting Church, for instance — support the charter.

[4] See Parkinson, above n 3, for a full account.

speculations. In effect, the chapter endeavours to answer three broad questions about the New Zealand experience: What was the concern? What transpired? What are the lessons?

The genesis: What was eating Hone and Temepara Smith?[5]

The first thing to note is that the NZBORA is not a 'strong' entrenched, supreme-law type Bill of Rights like the US one or the Canadian Charter of Rights and Freedoms. It is an interpretive or statutory Bill of Rights that requires the courts to interpret ordinary legislation consistently with the NZBORA.[6] The NZBORA expressly states that New Zealand courts do not have the power to strike down legislation that infringes the rights set out therein.[7] In the view of two leading New Zealand constitutional law academics, 'The decision not to pass a supreme law bill of rights was the right one in 1990, and it is the right one today'.[8]

The Fourth Labour Government, led by David Lange, in its 1985 'White Paper' floated an entrenched Bill of Rights, one substantially modelled on the Canadian Charter of Rights and Freedoms 1982 and the International Covenant on Civil and Political Rights 1966.[9] The White Paper proposal attracted much criticism from a diverse range of groups, including some religious ones. Whilst the Christian community was divided on the issue — as it is on most contemporary controversies, such as abortion, euthanasia, same-sex unions, corporal punishment of children — conservative Christians were adamantly opposed to it.[10] For the purposes of our discussion, let us call our ordinary, but socially-aware, Kiwi conservative Christians, 'Hone and Temepara Smith'. The term 'conservative Christian' denotes a Christian who shares several interrelated characteristics and convictions, in brief: deference to authority, whether that be the Bible (typically, but not invariably, read literally) or the Church; moral and ethical absolutism, in that there are universally applicable and timeless standards of right and wrong; restorationist tendencies, insofar as modern society must be renewed to reflect a more Christian conception of nationhood,

---

[5] With apologies to the 1993 film, starring Johnny Depp, Leonardo Dicaprio et al, *What's Eating Gilbert Grape?*
[6] S 6.
[7] S 4.
[8] Grant Huscroft and Paul Rishworth, '"You Say You Want a Revolution": Bills of Rights in the Age of Human Rights' in David Dyzenhaus et al (eds), *A Simple Common Lawyer: Essays in Honour of Michael Taggart* (2009) ch 7, 125.
[9] *A Bill of Rights for New Zealand: A White Paper*, Appendices to the Journals of the House of Representatives 1985, A6 ('White Paper').
[10] For a comprehensive analysis of the conservative Christian response to the White Paper, see Rex Ahdar, *Worlds Colliding: Conservative Christians and the Law* (2001) ch 5.

and; opposition to the prevailing (permissive and degenerating) ethos or *zeitgeist* of contemporary culture.[11]

While the opponents of the Bill were many and varied (including, for instance, the New Zealand Law Society), Sir Geoffrey Palmer, the principal architect of the White Paper, later singled out conservative Christians for special opprobrium: '[e]xtensive submissions from fundamentalist Christian groups did not help' the cause.[12] In the Parliamentary debates, some Government members pilloried Hone and Temepara Smith, and their *whanau* (extended family*)*, as 'the looney Right'.[13]

The concerns raised by many conservative Christians coincided with those raised by others lodging submissions upon the Bill. Hone and Temepara also harboured, however, some distinctive misgivings.

Transfer of power to an unsympathetic judiciary

The principal reason for opposition to the Bill of Rights proposal from the entirety of the submissions was the transfer of power from the elected Parliamentary representatives to the unelected judiciary.[14] The grant of wide-ranging power to determine social and political matters to a select few (that is, judges) and the resulting politicization of the judiciary were concerns for conservative Christians too. But there was a special fear expressed by Hone and Temepara here. They doubted that judges had any sympathy for the Christian worldview. The Reformed Churches of New Zealand argued:

> It is clear that the Bill of Rights will involve the courts in determining matters of social policy ... If we may posit for the moment that there is a liberal humanist world-and-life-view, and a traditional-conservative world-and-life-view it is reasonable to expect that the Cabinet and Parliament, insofar as it has jurisdiction, will appoint

---

[11] For a fuller explanation, detailing the necessary qualifications and exceptions to this broad-brush essentialist depiction of ethnically-diverse religionists that occupy a range of theological, denominational, political and other positions, see Ahdar, see above n 10, ch 2.

[12] Geoffrey Palmer and Matthew Palmer, *Bridled Power: New Zealand Government under MMP* (1997) ch 15, 268.

[13] See, eg, the Hon Bill Jeffries, Minister of Justice — 'Much of the opposition to the Bill was led by the looney Right; it does not have any merit': (1989) 502 *New Zealand Parliamentary Debates* 13044.

[14] See *Interim Report of the Justice and Law Reform Select Committee: Inquiry into the White Paper — A Bill of Rights for New Zealand*, 9 July 1987, Appendices to the Journals of the House of Representatives 1987, 1.8A, 8–9 ('Interim Report'). The then Prime Minister, Geoffrey Palmer, acknowledged this in his Introduction speech to the New Zealand Bill of Rights Bill: (1989) 502 *New Zealand Parliamentary Debates* 13038.

judges that reflect the dominant social consensus of the Government of the Day. This is exactly the situation in the United States.[15]

Secular humanistic foundation

Many conservative Christians (numbering some 25 submissions) were dismayed that there was no explicit acknowledgement of God as the source of rights, as in the Canadian Charter and many other national constitutional instruments. For Hone and Temepara, New Zealand still was a 'Christian nation'. They sought to thwart any further erosion of the *de facto* or cultural Christian establishment (as I have called it) — a situation where public policy and law generally and implicitly reflects Christian values and principles, notwithstanding the lack of any official, *de jure* acknowledgment of Christianity as the state religion.[16]

The Reformed Churches' submission again provided the fullest theological critique:

> [W]e believe that the Bill fails because it does not acknowledge Almighty God as the Source and Bestower of human rights. We believe that as soon as fundamental rights are decreed from an immanent source, immanent in creation, the work of interpretation, administering, applying, or defining those laws must be given to some institution or body which will hold awesome powers … This means that any fundamental law to protect freedoms and rights, which is grounded in the creation, will inevitably remove freedoms and take away rights, for it will concentrate infallible power in one or some governmental institutions. They will function as the supreme authority, and will have absolutist prerogatives over the community.[17]

This was 'a true irony'[18] given that one of the avowed aims of the Bill of Rights was to restrain governmental power.[19] For this submission, the only real check upon tyranny

---

[15] White Paper Submission No 62, 4 (These unpublished public submissions are on file with the author).
[16] See Rex Ahdar, 'A Christian State?' (1998–1999) 13 *Journal of Law and Religion* 453.
[17] White Paper Submission No 62, 5. On the Reformed view that human authority in all its forms is divinely delegated authority, see eg Nicholas Wolterstorff, 'Abraham Kuyper' in John Witte Jr and Frank S Alexander (eds), *The Teachings of Modern Christianity on Law, Politics and Human Nature*, vol 1 (2006), ch 10, esp 310–17; Aad van Egmond, 'Calvinist Thought and Human Rights' in Abdullahi An-Na'im et al (eds), *Human Rights and Religious Values: An Uneasy Relationship?* (1995) ch 14.
[18] White Paper Submission No 62, 5.
[19] See ibid 5 and [4.19].

was the divine one: 'Only by acknowledging Almighty God, to whom all human courts are subject, can effective limits be placed upon courts and parliaments'.[20]

Some noted that there was a conspicuous absence in the NZ Bill of the theistic acknowledgement found in the Canadian Charter, the model for the Bill (the Charter Preamble begins, 'Whereas Canada is founded upon principles that recognize the supremacy of God and the Rule of Law'). The lack of reference to the Deity in the White Paper stood in stark contrast to such a reference in the ill-fated NZ Bill of Rights 1963 a generation earlier and its Preamble which began 'Whereas the people of New Zealand uphold principles that acknowledge the supremacy of God'.[21]

The Select Committee's response to the Preamble issue was to say that theistic or Christian reference would be unfair to non-Christians: 'In our view it would be inconsistent with Articles 6 and 8 [which eventually became sections 13 and 15 respectively of the NZBORA] to acknowledge the supremacy of God. These two articles would protect the beliefs and practices of those who reject the Christian God'.[22] To the Committee, exclusion of reference to God was neutral; to Hone and Temepara, it was a rejection of the traditional theocentric foundation of New Zealand's cultural Christian establishment and its substitution with a humanist one.

A downgrading of Christianity

The corollary of a failure to give God His due in the Bill was the relegation of Christianity to mere equality with all other religions. The Mount Maunganui Baptist Church, for example, decried the fact that 'not only does the Bill ignore Christian values but gives equal pre-eminence to values which may be totally foreign to our society. To be extreme, the values of a Satanic cult or mind-bending group are given equal status to those of a Christian group'.[23]

Not only would Christianity be placed on an even par with other religions, some submissions argued that certain religions — conservative or traditional ones especially — would not even receive that. They predicted that religions challenging the supreme values inherent in the Bill of Rights would fare poorly.

---

[20] Ibid.
[21] The 1963 Bill is reproduced in Tim McBride, *New Zealand Civil Rights Handbook* (1980) 593–9.
[22] Interim Report, above n 14, 24.
[23] White Paper Submission No 266W, 2.

Disestablishment ramifications

The Coalition of Concerned Citizens was concerned that the religious freedom provisions of the proposed Bill of Rights might be given an anti-establishment reading. This might seem odd, for the Bill contained no express anti-establishment provision — such as the opening clause in the First Amendment of the US Constitution, which stipulates that 'Congress shall make no law respecting an establishment of religion, or prohibiting the free exercise thereof'. The decision not to include an anti-establishment provision in the Bill was deliberate. The White Paper explained:

> That provision [the First Amendment] was designed to prevent the creation of a state or official religion. That does not appear to be a real question to address in New Zealand. The American provision moreover has been used to deny state aid to religious schools — a practice long followed in New Zealand — and even voluntary prayers or bible readings in schools. The Covenant [International Covenant on Civil and Political Rights 1966] and the Canadian Charter contain no such provision. Accordingly it has not been included in the above text.[24]

Some White Paper submissions were highly critical of the absence of a non-establishment clause. Two academic lawyers argued that, while the question of a state religion was not a contentious question at the present time, it might become one in the future, and they asked was it 'not the very purpose of the Bill of Rights to attempt to foresee and prevent future abuses?' They suggested the insertion of an explicit unambiguous provision worded, 'There shall be no official State religion in New Zealand'. Without such a provision, they considered religious freedom was not really protected.[25] The Auckland Ethnic Council, New Zealand Jewish Council, Society for the Protection of Public Education and the New Zealand Rationalist Association shared this view.[26]

In its Interim Report two years later, the Select Committee reaffirmed the view expressed in the White Paper that the establishment of a State religion did not loom as a 'real question', adding, somewhat curtly, that inclusion of an anti-establishment provision would be 'inappropriate'. Further, there was no need either for an express recognition that freedom from religion was protected since the Bill did 'not give any greater protection to persons holding a religious belief than it gives to those who do not'.[27] Interestingly, the submission of the subcommittee of the Auckland

---

[24] White Paper, above n 9, 81.
[25] Their submission was published in book form: Jerome B Elkind and Anthony Shaw, *A Standard for Justice: A Critical Commentary on the Proposed Bill of Rights for New Zealand* (1986) 51.
[26] Interim Report, above n 14, 143–5.
[27] Ibid 45–6.

District Law Society predicted that the breadth of the language of the religious liberty provisions in the draft Bill meant that 'an establishment of religion type approach was quite probable'.[28]

The judgment of the Canadian Supreme Court in *R v Big M Drug Mart Ltd*[29] (published soon after the release of the White Paper) was cited by the subcommittee as an example of the 'havoc' that could be wreaked upon New Zealand's trading hours legislation were an anti-establishment reading to be given to the religious liberty provisions. Concerns about possible challenges (on the same basis) to the tax deductibility of contributions to churches and religious charities were also expressed.[30]

Canadian case law on the religious freedom provision in the Charter (s 2(a)) — which is worded solely in terms of free exercise and contains no express anti-establishment prohibition — has interpreted that provision to proscribe governmental establishment of religion as well as restrictions upon the expression of religion.[31] In short, freedom *of* religion includes freedom *from* religion. In *Big M*, the Supreme Court observed:

> The essence of the concept of freedom of religion is the right to entertain such religious beliefs as a person chooses, the right to declare religious beliefs openly and without fear of hindrance or reprisal, and the right to manifest belief by worship and practice or by teaching and dissemination. But the concept means more than that. Freedom can primarily be characterized by the absence of coercion or constraint. If a person is compelled by the State or the will of another to a course of action or inaction he would not otherwise have chosen, he is not acting of his own volition and he cannot be said to be truly free …
>
> Coercion includes not only such blatant forms of compulsion as direct commands to act or refrain from acting on pain of sanction, coercion includes indirect forms of control which determine or limit courses of conduct available to others. Freedom in a broad sense embraces both the absence of coercion and constraint, and the right to manifest beliefs and practices. Freedom means that, subject to such limitations as are necessary to protect public safety, order, health, or morals or the fundamental rights and freedoms of others, no one is to be forced to act in a way contrary to his beliefs or his conscience.[32]

---

[28] Ibid 152.
[29] (1985) 18 DLR (4th) 321.
[30] Interim Report, above n 14, 152.
[31] See, eg, Margaret H Ogilvie, 'Between liberté and egalité: Religion and the state in Canada' in Peter Radan, Denise Meyerson and Rosalind F Croucher (eds), *Law and Religion: God, the State and the Common Law* (2005) ch 6.
[32] (1985) 18 DLR (4th) 321, 353–4 (Dickson J).

The passage adopts an expansive notion to 'coercion', a concept that, in the Supreme Court's view, embraces subtle, indirect efforts to prescribe religious and other behaviour. In *Big M*, the Court held that a law prohibiting Sunday trading worked 'a form of coercion inimical to the spirit of the Charter and the dignity of all non-Christians. In proclaiming the standards of the Christian faith, the [Lord's Day] Act creates a climate hostile to, and gives the appearance of discrimination against, non-Christian Canadians'.[33] Non-Christians — whether Jews, agnostics, atheists or Muslims — were not required or compelled to observe the Christian Sabbath in the sense that they were compelled to attend Church or pray that day. But they were required to 'remember the Lord's day of the Christians and keep it holy' insofar as they were 'prohibited for religious reasons from carrying out activities which are otherwise lawful, moral and normal'.[34] If preserving the religious sensibilities of others precludes one from doing an everyday activity (working, shopping, playing sport), a form of coercion is arguably occurring. One is being indirectly forced to observe a religious practice — a practice that may directly offend one's own conscience.[35] The 'arm of the State'[36] ought not to do this. Early Canadian Charter experience thus provided some basis to the Coalition's anxiety that an anti-establishment interpretation, moreover one that secularized the public sphere, might be given to the Bill's religious liberty provisions.

The Reformed Churches predicted that 'almost certain[ly] all references to the Lord, and to the institutionalizing of Christianity in our national life would be removed'.[37] The National Anthem, Speaker's Prayer and other instances of what Americans dub 'ceremonial deism' would be eradicated. Perhaps, 'it could even get down to local Governments being forbidden to take part in Christmas festivities or put up nativity scenes, as has happened in the United States'.[38]

'Establishment', however, is an elastic, highly contestable term,[39] and the way a particular nation's prohibition upon 'establishments' of religion is interpreted, and hence its actual cultural impact, may vary widely. In Australia, for example, the more than century-old presence of an anti-establishment prohibition has not given rise to a widespread secularization of the public sphere. Section 116 of the Constitution

---

[33] Ibid 354.
[34] Ibid.
[35] Sunday closing trading laws can, of course, be justified on non-religious grounds such as the pragmatic need for regular periods of rest and the social utility of the creation of space for family life and collective leisure pursuits.
[36] Ibid.
[37] White Paper Submission No 62, 10.
[38] Ibid.
[39] On the meaning of 'establishment' of religion, see Rex Ahdar and Ian Leigh, *Religious Freedom in the Liberal State* (2005) 75–84.

provides that, 'The Commonwealth shall not make any law for establishing any religion'. The Establishment Clause, as this part of the section has been dubbed, has had a negligible effect upon religious practice in Australia.[40] Certainly, its impact has been nothing like the sustained secularizing effect that its American First Amendment counterpart (upon which s 116 was, in part, modelled)[41] has had. First, s 116 places no restriction upon the States when it comes to legislative measures regarding religious matters and it is only a limitation upon 'the Commonwealth', or Federal Parliament, in this respect.[42] Second, the High Court in the leading, indeed only, case on the anti-establishment provision to reach it, *Attorney-General of Victoria, ex rel Black v Commonwealth* (the DOGS Case),[43] gave the clause a narrow reading. The Establishment Clause prevents the Federal Legislature from purposefully creating a national church or religion. It does not, as the appellants, the Defence of Government Schools ('DOGS') organization contended, preclude the Federal Government from passing legislation providing for financial assistance to be given to non-governmental religious schools. Mason J explained:

> The first clause in the section forbids the establishment or recognition (and by this term I would include a branch of a religion or church) as a national institution. ... To constitute 'establishment' of a 'religion' the concession to one church of favours, titles and advantages must be of so special a kind that it enables us to say that by virtue of the concession the religion has become established as a national institution, as, for example, by becoming the official religion of the State.[44]

An expansive reading was expressly rejected: s 116 'cannot readily be viewed as the repository of some broad statement of principle concerning the separation of church and state, from which may be distilled the detailed consequences of such separation'.[45] Further, 'The separationist view of establishment ... [did] not sit well with the form of s. 116, addressed as it [was] only to the Commonwealth Parliament'.[46] Murphy J dissented, charging that the majority's narrow reading was tantamount to interpreting

---

[40] See generally Reid Mortensen, 'The Unfinished Experiment: A Report on Religious Freedom in Australia' (2007) 21 *Emory International Law Review* 167, 170, 173–5; Tony Blackshield, 'Religion and Australian Constitutional Law' in Radan, above n 31, ch 4, 85–6, 98–101.
[41] See *DOGS Case* (1981) 146 CLR 559, 621 (Murphy J); Mortensen, above n 40, 169.
[42] See *DOGS Case* (1981) 146 CLR 559, 652 (Wilson J).
[43] (1981) 146 CLR 559.
[44] Ibid 612. See similarly at 582 (Barwick CJ), at 597, 604 (Gibbs J), at 634 (Aickin J, agreeing with Gibbs and Mason JJ).
[45] Ibid 609 (Stephen J).
[46] Ibid 654 (Wilson J).

s 116 as a mere 'clause in tenancy agreement'⁴⁷ and 'ma[d]e' a mockery of s.116'.⁴⁸ For him, a narrow reading 'would deny that s. 116 [was] a guarantee of freedom from religion as well as of religion'.⁴⁹ Murphy J's was a lone voice, however.

What transpired

Following the widespread opposition to a Bill of Rights having the force of supreme law, Sir Geoffrey Palmer, by now Prime Minister, was forced to set his sights lower. An interpretive Bill of Rights, having the status of an ordinary statute, was the result.

With the notion of a supreme law abandoned, most conservative Christians (including Hone and Temepara) lost interest. Fears of an unsympathetic judicial elite instigating humanistic social engineering had dissipated. Few Christian individuals or organizations made submissions on the diluted Bill that was now proposed. The Seventh-Day Adventist Church alluded in its submission to the danger of later Parliamentarians easily altering the Bill to become entrenched.⁵⁰ In parliamentary debate, conservative Christian MP, Graeme Lee, emphasized this point: 'It will just be a matter of time until the Bill will move from being ordinary law — albeit *de facto* supreme law — to being the bench-mark for all New Zealand law: the original objective'.⁵¹

In the last 20 years, the religious freedom provisions of the Act have seldom been mentioned or invoked, nor have they excited much controversy — either in or outside legal circles. As Paul Rishworth observed in an important recent article, 'there has been remarkably little religious freedom litigation in New Zealand'.⁵²

The explanation for this, as Rishworth notes, is multifaceted: the NZBORA is not a supreme law and thus winning plaintiffs cannot succeed in scuttling infringing legislation; the absence of strong, well-organized religious (or secular) pressure groups; a less litigious culture and a sense that litigation would be unproductive; and a more tolerant, live-and-let-live atmosphere coupled with a 'prevailing egalitarianism' amongst New Zealanders.⁵³ On the last point, the Human Rights Commission in its 2004 human rights 'report card' observed:

---

47 Ibid 623.
48 Ibid 633.
49 Ibid 625.
50 Seventh-Day Adventist Church, Submission No 5W.
51 (1990) 510 *New Zealand Parliamentary Debates* 3471. Richard Northey, in the third reading debate, dismissed this 'Trojan horse' thesis: (1990) 510 *New Zealand Parliamentary Debates* 3763.
52 Paul Rishworth, 'The Religion Clauses of the New Zealand Bill of Rights' [2007] *New Zealand Law Review* 631, 632.
53 Ibid 633, 636.

The Commission's complaints data, the Action Plan consultation and other research reveals *widespread acknowledgement of, and appreciation for, the high level of religious freedom and tolerance generally experienced in New Zealand.* Of 2,559 complaints received by the Human Rights Commission in 2002–2003, only 105 (4.1 per cent) claimed discrimination on the basis of religious or ethical belief and, of those, 33 were outside jurisdiction. A further 47 were discontinued either by the complainant or by the Commission. Of the remaining 33, 14 have been resolved.[54]

In its 2010 update, the Human Rights Commission noted that New Zealand was 'generally tolerant of religious diversity'[55] borne out to the extent that '[o]f 1405 complaints of discrimination received by [it] in 2008-09, only 66 (4.7 per cent) claimed discrimination on the basis of religious or ethical belief'.[56] This fairly 'benign' state of affairs may not continue and the NZBORA may yet prove to be more frequently utilized and have more 'bite' than it has to date. I will return to this in 'The Lessons' (below).

New Zealand's religious freedom jurisprudence, to cite Rishworth again, 'is found principally in the record of the legislative and executive branches, and has not been exclusively, or indeed hardly at all, the province of the judiciary'.[57] The core of religious liberty is located not in flowing rhetoric emanating from high-profile court cases, but 'the harsh particularities of legislation and practice in various discrete fields'.[58] Historically, the Legislature and Executive[59] have primarily overseen and undertaken preservation of religious freedom, and this continues to be the pattern post-1990.

In the Bill of Rights era, New Zealand continues to see legislative 'accommodation' made for religious practice. Before 1990, Parliament had carved out exceptions for religionists who might otherwise be caught by the application of the general law of the land. For example, Parliament granted a conscientious exemption to medical personnel from participation in abortion and sterilization procedures, and religious employers were permitted to deny access to union officials to their workplaces.[60] After 1990, the same approach continues. For instance, New Zealand anti-discrimination

---

[54] Human Rights Commission, Parliament of New Zealand, 'The Right to Freedom of Religion and Belief' in *Human Rights in New Zealand Today* (2004) ch 9 (emphasis added) (available at <http://www.hrc.co.nz/report/downloads.html>).

[55] Human Rights Commission, Parliament of New Zealand, *Freedom of Religion and Belief: Draft for Discussion* (2010) 11 (available at < http://www.hrc.co.nz/hrc_new/hrc/cms/files/documents/19-Mar-2010_10-28-25_Status_Report_Freedom_of_Religion_and_Belief_1_.pdf>).

[56] Ibid 8.

[57] Rishworth, above n 52, 634.

[58] Ibid 649.

[59] Ibid.

[60] See respectively the *Contraception, Sterilisation and Abortion Act 1977* (NZ), s 46 and the *Employment Relations Act 2000* (NZ) ss 23–24.

laws contain carefully crafted exemptions excepting religious employers and institutions from the usual prohibitions on sex and religious discrimination in employment, training, education and so on.[61]

The prior parliamentary scrutiny of bills in New Zealand has yet to detect any provisions of pending legislation that appear to infringe the protections for religious freedom in the NZBORA. There has yet to be an instance where the Attorney-General, pursuant to his or her obligation under s 7 of the NZBORA, has found any potential contravention of religious liberty.[62] It may be, as Grant Huscroft contends, that the main significance of the s 7 duty is its salutary impact on the policy development and legislative drafting processes.[63] So, for example, by the time the Coroners Bill 2004 was introduced, it already, as the Attorney-General's report recorded, 'recognize[d] and accommodate[d] religious and cultural beliefs' in terms of its 'procedures for viewing, touching or remaining near the body'[64], and thus any potential violation of religious liberty was averted.

What, then, of the cases that dealt with the NZBORA's religious freedom provisions? These provisions are, in brief, the right to freedom of conscience, thought, religion and belief,[65] the right to manifest one's religious beliefs in worship, observance, practice and so on,[66] and the right of religious minorities to enjoy their religion.[67]

---

[61] Religious institutions are allowed to discriminate on the basis of sex or religion when appointing persons to positions of leadership: *Human Rights Act* (NZ) s 28(2). Other religious exemptions are found, for instance, in s 27(2)(domestic employment) and s 39(1)(qualifying bodies).

[62] For the most recent reports on the consistency of pending legislation with s 15 of the NZBORA (the right to manifest one's religious beliefs), see the NZ Ministry of Justice website: *Ministry of Justice Tāhū o te Ture* (2011) Ministry of Justice <http://www.justice.govt.nz/policy-and-consultation/legislation/bill-of-rights/@@view_by_section#section-15> at 18 April 2011.

[63] G Huscroft, 'The Attorney-General's Reporting Duty' in Paul Rishworth et al, *The New Zealand Bill of Rights* (2003) ch 6, 213.

[64] See Attorney-General, *Legal Advice: Consistency with the New Zealand Bill of Rights Act 1990 (ATT114/1299)* (2011) Ministry of Justice < http://www.justice.govt.nz/policy-and-consultation/legislation/bill-of-rights/coroners-bill> at 18 April 2011. This particular provision is now s 25 of the *Coroners Act 2006* (NZ).

[65] Section 13 provides: 'Everyone has the right to freedom of thought, conscience, religion, and belief, including the right to adopt and to hold opinions without interference': *NZBORA 1990* (NZ) s 13.

[66] Section 15 provides: 'Every person has the right to manifest that person's religion or belief in worship, observance, practice, or teaching, either individually or in community with others, and either in public or in private': *NZBORA 1990* (NZ) s 15.

[67] Section 20 provides: 'A person who belongs to an ethnic, religious, or linguistic minority in New Zealand shall not be denied the right, in community with other members of that minority, to enjoy the culture, to profess and practice the religion, or use the language, of that minority': *NZBORA 1990* (NZ) s 20.

To reiterate, there have been relatively few cases. I do not propose to systematically go through them all.[68] In summary, New Zealand has had cases on such disparate matters as:

- parental refusals to allow potentially life-saving medical treatment to be administered to their children based on the parents' religious beliefs. The Jehovah's Witness parents' refusal to permit life-saving blood transfusions for their three-year-old child was over-ridden by doctors with the courts' approval[69]
- the longstanding ban on shop trading at Easter weekend. The Good Friday shop-trading ban survived the attempt by a Wanaka bookshop to secure a 'declaration of inconsistency' (a pronouncement that the NZBORA has been contravened) from the court[70]
- the wearing of a burqa by a Muslim witness in an insurance case. The devout Afghani woman was required to unveil in court, but only before the judge, counsel and female court staff[71]
- an exorcism that resulted in the death of a church member. The Korean Pentecostal pastor was not able to hold up the shield of religious faith in defence of a manslaughter conviction for a disastrously botched exorcism[72]
- a resident who sought to justify a large painted spotlit swastika on the wall of his house on religious grounds. The bigoted urban dweller's Nazi symbols were removed pursuant to an abatement notice ordered by the Wellington City Council despite his spurious quasi-religious objections[73]
- parents of minority religions whose faith is raised as a negative factor in child custody and access disputes. Family court judges have tried not to be swayed by

---

[68] For analysis and commentary, at least up to the mid-2000s, see Paul Rishworth et al, *The New Zealand Bill of Rights* (2003) ch 11; Andrew Butler and Petra Butler, *The New Zealand Bill of Rights Act: A Commentary* (2005) ch 14.

[69] *Re J (An Infant): Director-General of Social Welfare v B and B* [1996] 2 NZLR 134 (CA). See also *Auckland District Health Board v AZ and BZ*, HC Auckland, Civ 2007-4-4-2260, 27 April 2007 (Baragwanath J); *Waikato District Health Board v L*, HC Hamilton, Civ 2008-419-1312, 23 Sept 2008 (Stevens J).

[70] *Department of Labour v Books and Toys (Wanaka) Ltd* (2005) 7 HRNZ 931 (DC).

[71] *Police v Razamjoo* [2005] DCR 408 (DC). See further David Griffiths, 'Pluralism and the Law: New Zealand Accommodates the Burqa' (2006) 11 *Otago Law Review* 281; Erich Kolig, 'New Zealand Muslims: The Perimeters of Multiculturalism and its Legal Instruments' (2005) 20 *New Zealand Sociology* 73.

[72] *R v Lee* [2006] 3 NZLR 42 (CA).

[73] *Zdrahal v Wellington City Council* [1995] 1 NZLR 700 (HC). See Bede Harris, 'Viewpoint Neutrality and Freedom of Expression in New Zealand' (1996) 8 *Otago Law Review* 515.

embattled spouses of Jehovah's Witnesses, Exclusive Brethren and other believers playing the 'religion card' in custody and access battles[74]

- a Rastafarian who invoked religious freedom in the face of a marijuana charge. The court disregarded the Rastafarian's religious liberty plea in response to his conviction for cannabis cultivation and supply[75]

- an erstwhile leader of a 'New Age' religious community who complained the government did nothing to prevent the community's dissolution following the jailing of its founder and other leaders (for child molestation). The court held that state had no positive duty to ensure the survival of an embattled faith community[76]

- an offender who wished to be excused attendance at the periodic detention induction program run on his Sabbath day. The Seventh-Day Adventist offender was still required to complete the court-directed periodic detention induction program on his day of rest, namely, Saturday[77]

- a church official who granted false charitable donations receipts to enable parishioners to claim a tax rebate. The Tongan Anglican Mission Church official's optimistic appeal to religious and cultural matters to excuse his tax fraud was to no avail.[78]

The outcome of the cases has been rather predictable. I submit that all these outcomes were just as likely without a Bill of Rights. The statutory right of religious freedom was not determinative of the specific final result in these decisions and one would be hard-pressed to say that the right was decisive to, or even played a significant part in, the conclusions reached. In most of the cases, the religious freedom arguments were a mere makeweight and were treated as such by the court — as evidenced by the cursory analysis and discussion of the meaning and scope of the Act's religious freedom provisions. As Rishworth observes:

> One particular feature of the New Zealand landscape has been the relatively low-level resolution of many rights controversies in the religion field. Instead of culture-changing legal precedents, we tend to get ad hoc and unreasoned, but generally satisfactory settlements. A debate about school prayer or religion classes in school ... might flare in the newspapers and on television for a few days, but it is informally

---

[74] See Rex Ahdar, 'Religion in Custody and Access: The New Zealand Experience' (1996) 17 *New Zealand University Law Review* 113.
[75] *R v Anderson*, Court of Appeal, CA27/04, 23 June 2004.
[76] *Mendelssohn v AG* [1999] 2 NZLR 268, 273 (CA).
[77] *Feau v Department of Social Welfare* (1995) 2 HRNZ 528 (HC).
[78] *Tahaafe v CIR*, High Court Auckland, CRI 2009-404-102, 10 July 2009 (Chisholm J).

resolved (or fades away altogether) with no necessary determination of how such issues should be resolved for the future.[79]

In those decisions where the religious liberty plea was more central to the case, the courts have not taken a very sympathetic or generous stance to the meaning or breadth of the right of religious freedom.

Take *Re J*, for example, a case concerning devout Jehovah's Witness parents who refused to permit a blood transfusion for their three-year-old child suffering from a severe and potentially life-threatening nosebleed. The Court of Appeal said that the particular right of religious freedom at issue ought to be defined at the outset to exclude certain kinds of conduct (an approach known in constitutional law parlance as 'definitional balancing').[80] This means that the state is not required to justify limits upon the right, but rather, the right is limited by the state (the court) under the guise of defining the right. In *Re J* it meant that the Jehovah's Witness parents' right to determine their child's medical treatment in accordance with their faith was defined to exclude any exercise of the parental rights of religious upbringing and medical decision-making that endangered the child's health or life. The other, and, in my opinion, better approach (called 'ad hoc balancing')[81], would be initially to define the right broadly and then require the state to justify its restriction. This approach ensures the state carries the onus of establishing that a fundamental civil right really warrants restriction rather than, with definitional balancing, the state not being put to the task of the discharging the onus by the virtue of a court's initial defining away of the disputed scope of the right. In the present case, ad hoc balancing would translate into saying that parents have a broad right to determine their child's medical treatment (including the right to refuse the administration of blood transfusions), but the state may veto this if it discharges its onus of establishing that the overriding of parental consent was fully justified here. On the facts of *Re J*, the different approaches did not make any material difference to the outcome, but the choice of methodology might well do so in other instances.

In *Mendelssohn v Attorney-General*[82] the plaintiff, Mendelssohn, a senior member of a small and highly controversial 'New Age' religious community called Centrepoint,

---

[79] 'Human Rights and the Reconstruction of the Moral High Ground' in Rick Bigwood (ed), *Public Interest Litigation: New Zealand Experience in International Perspective* (2006) 115, 124–5.
[80] [1996] 2 NZLR 134, 145–6.
[81] See further Ahdar and Leigh, above n 39, 184; *R v Oakes* [1986] 1 SCR 103; *Multani v Commission Scolaire Marguerite-Bourgeoys* [2006] 1 SCR 256, [43]; Sidney Peck, 'An Analytical Framework for the Application of the Canadian Charter of Rights and Freedoms' (1987) 25 *Osgoode Hall Law Journal* 1; Andrew Butler, 'Limiting Rights' (2002) 33 *Victoria University of Wellington Law Review* 537, 541–4.
[82] [1999] 2 NZLR 268 (CA).

argued that the Attorney-General had been negligent in failing to protect the group's religious liberty. Centrepoint had been structured in the form of a trust. It experienced considerable disruption following the successful prosecution of its leader Herbert (Bert) Potter in 1992 for indecently assaulting minors living in the community. In 1995, Mendelssohn wrote to the Attorney-General seeking action to restore the operation of the Trust to its proper purposes. The Attorney-General declined to do so. Quite the opposite: he ordered an independent inquiry into the affairs of the Trust that ultimately resulted in the Public Trustee being substituted for the existing trustees.[83]

Mendelssohn viewed the Attorney-General's conduct as in breach of what Mendelssohn asserted was a positive duty to take steps to protect his, and other Centrepoint followers', religious freedom. The Court of Appeal rejected his claim. The plaintiff had misunderstood the nature of the right to religious freedom contained in various provisions of the NZBORA: 'The short answer to [Mr Mendelssohn's] submission is that in their essence those provisions do not impose positive duties on the state, at least in any sense relevant to this case'.[84]

In *Director of Human Rights Proceedings v Catholic Church of New Zealand*,[85] the High Court had to decide whether the Roman Catholic Church was caught by the *Privacy Act 1993*'s disclosure regime. A woman had complained after the Church had refused her request for personal information pertaining to the annulment of her marriage by the Catholic Tribunal. The Church contended that compelled release of personal information would impede the institution's religious freedom: the future adjudication of annulment and divorce proceedings would be hampered if sensitive confidential statements supplied by others (such as an estranged spouse) were circulated more widely. The Court, however, could not see how the Church's right of religious liberty under s 15 of the Act was 'threatened in any way'[86] by the *Privacy Act*'s disclosure requirements.

Perhaps the only case where the right to religious freedom had any 'traction' was *R v Lee*, the case involving the Korean pastor's disastrous exorcism. There, the Court of Appeal recognized that the right to manifest religious belief in s 15 of the NZBORA included the right to conduct exorcisms (and consent to undergo

---

[83] The Court of Appeal dismissed a challenge by Mendelssohn to this appointment: *Mendelssohn v Centrepoint Community Growth Trust* [1999] 2 NZLR 88.
[84] [1999] 2 NZLR 268, [14] (italics in original).
[85] [2008] 3 NZLR 216 (HC).
[86] Ibid [68] (Cooper J).

the same) and rejected the argument that only 'mainstream' methods of performing exorcisms were included within the right.[87]

One trend might appear to negate my argument. An increasingly significant sector of New Zealand society, Māoridom, has fared better in the Bill of Rights era than before. Not so long ago, government and legal recognition of Māori religious and spiritual concerns was unthinkable; now it is virtually *de rigeur*.[88] Here, however, we must be alert not to confuse correlation with causation. The state recognition of Māori religious interests began *prior* to the NZBORA and it can hardly be said that the passing of the Act has been the principal catalyst for Māori spirituality's 'comeback'. Rather, it has ridden on the coat tails of the broader cultural renaissance of, and political solicitude towards, *Māoritanga* (the Māori culture, customs, language and the Māori 'way' in general) that began in the 1980s. Hone and Temepara's cousins, Rangi and Ngaire, are much happier these days that their firm traditional religious beliefs in *taniwha* (spiritual guardians or monsters), *mauri* (life-force), *kaitiakitanga* (spiritual guardianship), *tohunga* (faith healers /priests), *waahi tapu* (sacred sites) and the like, are taken seriously by civil tribunals in environmental, bioethical and other decision-making contexts.

The lessons

New Zealanders' enjoyment of the right to religious freedom fared fairly well prior to the NZBORA, and continues to do so. However, it is possible that the relatively calm religious landscape and the paucity of religious freedom cases might not continue. There are several reasons why this might be so.[89]

First, there is the increase in 'rights consciousness'. Second, there is the growth in non-Christian faiths, an expansion driven by recent immigration. Third, the law continues to penetrate deeply into the private sphere: the re-design of church buildings to meet contemporary liturgical needs clashes with preservation of historic places legislation, a religious body's policy to ordain only heterosexual clergy clashes

---

[87] [2006] 3 NZLR 42, [326]–[330] and [345]. The Court quashed Pastor Lee's conviction for manslaughter and ordered a new trial on the basis that the High Court had erred in not allowing the defence of consent to go to the jury.

[88] See, eg, the *Resource Management Act 1991*, ss 6–8; *Friends and Community of Ngawha Inc v Minister of Corrections* [2002] NZRMA 402 (HC). See further Rex Ahdar, 'Indigenous Spiritual Concerns and the Secular State: Some New Zealand Developments' (2003) 23 *Oxford Journal of Legal Studies* 611; Fiona Wright, 'Law, Religion and Tikanga Maori' (2007) 5 *New Zealand Journal of Public and International Law* 261.

[89] See again Rishworth, above n 52, 633, and also his earlier essay: Paul Rishworth, 'Coming Conflicts over Freedom of Religion' in Grant Huscroft and Paul Rishworth (eds), *Rights and Freedoms* (1995) ch 6.

with human rights norms that mandate no discrimination by training or licensing bodies based on a candidate's sexual orientation, Hone and Temepara's desire to physically discipline their three children clashes with children's rights laws, and so on. Fourth, New Zealand society and the governing elite are becoming more secular. Consequently, situations where conflict may arise between the state and religious groups, especially traditionalist or conservative ones, are increasing. Believers such as Hone and Temepara, who belong to the Pentecostal Destiny Church (perhaps the most disliked and vilified religious body in modern New Zealand), are the type of religionists' whose practice of their faith is coming under closer state scrutiny.[90] The last point merits greater explanation.

New Zealanders are becoming a more secular lot. Each successive census reveals an increase in those who indicate that they have 'no religion'. The latest 2006 Census recorded some 1.297m New Zealanders (32.2 per cent) who identified themselves as squarely in the non-religious fold.[91] Furthermore, the cultural sway of organized religion is waning. The decreasing numbers of adherents formally affiliated to churches leads one to anticipate (other things being equal) a corresponding decline in their social and political influence. Thus, opposition to the abolition to the residual public symbols and rituals of Christianity is likely to be less incisive in 2009 than in 1989, or certainly in 1969.

For example, there was minimal fuss when the Prime Minister refused to allow the saying of grace at the Commonwealth Heads of Government banquet attended by Queen Elizabeth II in 2002.[92] Admittedly, there was an the outcry by Christians (and Muslims) over the screening in 2006 of an episode of *South Park*, the American satirical television cartoon show, which showed a statue of the Virgin Mary menstruating over the Pope. The then Prime Minister, Helen Clark (a self-acknowledged agnostic), denounced the screening of the episode as 'quite revolting'.

---

[90] See 'Protesters hold up Destiny Church march', *New Zealand Herald* (Auckland), 7 March 2005.

[91] See Statistics New Zealand, 'Religious Affiliation', 2006 Census. For a lively discussion see Caroline Courtney, 'Religion: Who needs it?', *North and South* (April 2007) 67. But there are still high levels of belief about life after death, heaven, reincarnation, astrology, fortune tellers, and so on: see Massey University, above n 2, 2.

[92] 'Lack of grace leaves no trace', *Otago Daily Times* (Otago), 9 March 2002, A7. The Prime Minister, Helen Clark, defended: 'There was no grace for the same reason as there is none now in New Zealand, because we're not only a society of many faiths, but we're also increasingly secular. In order to be inclusive, it seems to me to be better not to have one faith put first. We haven't had the grace at state banquets for the last two years.'

However, the Broadcasting Standards Authority found no violation of the TV Broadcasting Code's standards of taste and decency.[93]

Finally, the disestablishment potential of the Act has yet to be realized. The freedom *from* religion interpretation has seldom exerted itself, at least in the courts. The pressures just mentioned could yet see the NZBORA have a similar secularizing impact to the Canadian Charter. In the view of a leading church-state academic, Margaret Ogilvie, 'the courts have "protected" religious freedom by erasure of religion from public institutions, public spaces and the public law. The first twenty years of Charter religious jurisprudence is the story of the use of the Charter to remove Christianity from its legally privileged status in Canada'.[94] In Britain, the much briefer experience of a bill of rights has seen a growth in legal challenges to the privileged status of Christianity in that nation[95] and in turn increasingly strident complaints that Christians are becoming last amongst equals in the clashes between religious rights and other human rights guaranteed in the *Human Rights Act 1998*.[96]

The warning signs in New Zealand are there. Thus, New Zealanders have witnessed:

- a dispute over a Corrections Department decision to rigidly uphold its alcohol ban and not allow communion wine to be given to prisoners[97]

- a complaint about a Marlborough high school's refusal to let girls wear crosses around their neck (despite Māori symbols being allowed)[98]

---

[93] Broadcasting Standards Authority Decision No 2006–022 (26 June 2006). The High Court affirmed the BSA decision in an appeal launched by the NZ Catholic bishops: *Browne v CanWest TV Works Ltd* [2008] 1 NZLR 654 (HC). See further Rex Ahdar, 'The Right to Protection of Religious Feelings' (2008) 11 *Otago Law Review* 629.

[94] Ogilvie, above n 31, 160.

[95] See, eg, H Blake, 'Atheists launch bid to outlaw prayer at council meetings,' *Daily Telegraph* (London), 4 May 2010. The National Secular Society has sought judicial review of the Bideford Town Council's opening council prayers on the ground that they breach art 9 of the *European Convention on Human Rights* (UK), the religious freedom guarantee.

[96] See, eg, A Alderson, 'Church leaders head for showdown with top judges over bias against Christians,' *Daily Telegraph* (London), 11 April 2010. For further examples and analysis, see Christian Institute, *Marginalising Christians: Instances of Christians Being Sidelined in Modern Britain* (2009); Roger Trigg, *Free to Believe? Religious Freedom in a Liberal Society* (2010).

[97] Following the Minister of Corrections' intervention, the Department stated it would allow communion wine in prisons: see 'Government wants review of ban on communion wine', *New Zealand Herald* (Auckland), 26 April 2007; 'Catholic Bishop praises Corrections Dept for reversing decision', *The Tablet* (Otago), 17 June 2007, 6.

[98] 'Marlborough Girls school board stands by dress code', *New Zealand Herald* (Auckland), 18 February 2004: see Butler and Butler, above n 68, 421.

- questioning of the propriety of the Speaker of Parliament's Prayer[99]
- public agitation about the proposal to remove the large illuminated cross atop the municipal clocktower in Palmerston North — a debate that abated once the wind blew the cross down![100]
- a complaint about a voluntary, non-teacher-led, lunch-time evangelical Christian 'KidsKlub' at a Wellington primary school[101]
- Human Rights Commission mediation between warring parents over the 52-year-old practice of saying the Lord's Prayer at an Auckland primary school's weekly assembly[102]
- a Ministry of Education guidelines questioning of the continuance of the longstanding voluntary 'Bible in Schools' program and religious observances in state primary schools[103]
- successive private member's bills to abolish the Good Friday and Easter Sunday retailing bans.[104]

Some of the disputes that are currently resolved by a fortuitous mixture of quiet, behind the scenes compromise by the state — or tactful retreat by the religionists (or atheists) concerned — may instead, in the future, go to court. Admittedly, New Zealand does not have the equivalents to the US's renowned rights pugilists such as

---

[99] Letter from Matt Robson, Progressive Party MP, to Jonathan Hunt, Speaker of the New Zealand House of Representatives, May 6, 2003 (quoted in Allan Davidson, 'Chaplain to the Nation or Prophet at the Gate? The Role of the Church in New Zealand Society' in John Stenhouse (ed), *Christianity, Modernity and Culture* (2005) 312, 314).

[100] Patrick Goodenough, *City riled by dispute over cross* (2003) Crosswalk <http://www.crosswalk.com/1222304/> at 27 April 2011.

[101] Stewart Dye, 'School Split over Religion Club Ban', *New Zealand Herald* (Auckland), 10 June 2005; 'School gives way on lunchtime Bible study', *Dominion Post* (Wellington), 7 July 2005. See further Rex Ahdar, 'Reflections on the Path of Religion-State Relations in New Zealand' [2006] *Brigham Young University Law Review* 619, 639–41.

[102] 'School in trouble over Lord's Prayer', *Otago Daily Times* (Otago), 19 December 2005; 'Prayers for school to decide' (editorial), *New Zealand Herald* (Auckland), 22 December 2005; Paul Rishworth, 'Religious Issues in State Schools' in John Hannan et al, (eds), *Education Law* (2006) 87.

[103] 'Guidelines on religion in schools stun some', *Otago Daily Times* (Otago), 25 August 2006; Rex Ahdar, 'Review better than rows over religion in school', *Otago Daily Times* (Otago), 1 September 2006.

[104] See, eg, the Shop Trading Hours (Easter Trading Local Exemption) Bill 2004 (No 168-1), sponsored by Doug Wollerton MP; the Easter Sunday Shop Trading Amendment Bill 2006 (No 42-2) (sponsored by Jacqui Dean MP); and the Shop Trading Hours 1990 Repeal (Easter Sunday Local Choice) Amendment Bill 2009 (No 104-1) (sponsored by Todd McClay MP). Waitaki MP Jacqui Dean promised to take another private members' Bill to Parliament: 'Easter trading bill in offing,' *Otago Daily Times* (Otago), 19 January 2010.

the ACLU (American Civil Liberties Union) and the Rutherford Institute, or the United Kingdom's Christian Institute, and awareness of one's civil rights is hardly second-nature.

The picture just painted may be misleading. There may not be any great increase in religious liberty controversies and attendant litigation, and the disestablishment potential of the NZBORA may not be realized. Nonetheless, if Hone and Temepara were to ask, 'Do you think our ability to live out our faith is likely to get easier or more difficult?', a New Zealander fully versed in church and state matters would be slow to respond that 'there is no cause for concern' in respect of both the growth in litigation and its likely erosion of longstanding Christian observances and practices.

19

Indigenous Peoples and Bills of Rights

Paul Rishworth*

Proponents of a bill of rights — whether of the constitutional or statutory type — will usually have a vision of what bills of rights can accomplish. Indeed, there may be competing visions. Some will see a bill of rights as affirming a core set of civil and political rights against the possibility of future erosion — essentially 'process' rights such as liberty and speech without which a democracy cannot flourish. Others may seek to include new rights that, as they see it, have not been so well reflected in the legal system, or at least not seen as within the province of judges to rule upon. For them, a bill of rights will be designed to transform targeted areas of law and policy, not just to affirm and protect the existing order. Social and economic rights, for example, may be advocated. The aim will be to set new standards to which the state can be held to account.

For countries with Indigenous peoples, the idea of Indigenous peoples' rights will assuredly be on the agenda when a bill of rights is mooted. But are these part of the core civil rights, or are they new and developing? Are they affirmatory or aspirational? Is it enough that every person, including every Indigenous person, enjoys the basic rights of participation essential to democracy? Or are there particular rights to which Indigenous peoples are entitled, rights that protect the vitality and autonomy of their group, their worldview, their way of life, and set a new standard against

---

* With grateful thanks for the research assistance of Max Harris and Sean Kinsler MA (Hons), LLB (Hons), University of Auckland. Usual disclaimer applies. Some of this chapter draws on Paul Rishworth, 'New Zealand', in D Oliver and C Fusaro (eds), *How Constitutions Change* (forthcoming 2011).

which a state's laws and actions may be measured and, perhaps, found wanting?[1] There is certainly a strong view that this is the case, evidenced internationally by the adoption in the United Nations of the (non-binding) Declaration on the Rights of Indigenous Peoples.[2] Even so, and despite that Declaration, there is not yet a well-settled understanding of what Indigenous peoples' rights comprise, still less of the likely effect of affirming them in a domestic bill of rights enforced by judges. The initial opposition of both Australia and New Zealand, as well as Canada and the United States, to the Declaration has dissipated,[3] but that still leaves each state to work out how the affirmed rights should be reflected in its domestic law.

A certain amount of caution is therefore unsurprising in drafting rights for Indigenous peoples in a bill of rights. What, exactly, would the rights to autonomy and self-determination in articles 3 and 4 of the Declaration mean in practice? Even so, the sentiment that something rather than nothing should be included is likely to be very strong. This chapter seeks to make the modest contribution of chronicling New Zealand's experience with protecting Indigenous rights through a Bill of Rights, in the hope that this may be relevant to Australia if and when an Australian bill of rights becomes a possibility.

New Zealand has had a statutory bill of rights for 21 years, formally titled the *New Zealand Bill of Rights Act 1990*. It is important to note that New Zealand's Indigenous people, the Māori, enjoy all the individual rights that the Bill of Rights bestows on every person, through its use of standard bill of rights-language such as 'Everyone has the right to freedom of expression' or 'No one shall be deprived of life'. But this chapter is about the impact of the Bill of Rights on Māori as a *people*, or, more accurately, as a collection of *iwi* (tribes) and *hapu* (sub-tribal groupings). The Bill of Rights does not mention Māori as such, but one particular right is especially relevant

---

[1] In speaking of a 'standard' set by a bill of rights I intend to remain neutral as between bills of rights that are 'constitutional' (and potentially involve judicial invalidation of enactments), and those that are 'statutory' (and allow, perhaps, judicial declarations of incompatibility). Both models imply a standard for measuring law and actions, the differences effectively being about the consequence of a departure from the standard. And both models can involve pre-enactment scrutiny and political consequences for non-adherence to the legislated or constitutional standard. See Paul Rishworth, 'The Inevitability of Judicial Review under "Interpretive" Bills of Rights: Canada's Legacy to New Zealand and Commonwealth Constitutionalism' in G Huscroft and I Brodie (eds), *Constitutionalism in the Charter Era* (2004) 233.

[2] *United Nations Declaration on the Rights of Indigenous Peoples*, GA Res 61/295, UN GAOR, 61st sess, 107th plen mtg, UN Doc A/RES/61/295 (2007).

[3] The Government of Australia indicated on 3 April 2009 it would support the Declaration. The New Zealand Government indicated likewise on 19 April 2010.

to preservation of group rights. It is s 20 of the Bill of Rights, derived from article 27 of the International Covenant on Civil and Political Rights.[4] It provides:

> **Rights of minorities**–A person who belongs to an ethnic, religious, or linguistic minority in New Zealand shall not be denied the right, in community with other members of that minority, to enjoy the culture, to profess and practise the religion, or to use the language, of that minority.

This is a right for persons in minority groups, accessible only by persons in such groups. If Australia enacted a bill of rights that drew similarly on the ICCPR, it may well end up with something like New Zealand's s 20.

In that sense, the ICCPR's article 27 (and the domestic counterparts that it may inspire in national bills of rights) may be like a 'default setting' for Indigenous rights. Purpose-built Indigenous rights clauses may be seen as too complex, too uncertain, or too contentious. Attempts to specify the detail of what is involved in the rights to religion, language and culture for Indigenous minorities may be unsuccessful or, conversely, turn out to be too lengthy and complex for a document intended (as bills of rights generally are) to state pithy and general principles. But because Indigenous peoples are generally also minorities in their state, and because minority rights are likely to be included in a bill of rights if the ICCPR is taken as a guide, then minority rights will provide a measure of protection for Indigenous peoples (but will benefit non-Indigenous minorities as well).

This chapter concludes that the New Zealand Bill of Rights and its minority rights section has had relatively little impact in the field of Māori issues. This may seem a paradox, because on most measures the Māori dimension of New Zealand life and law has grown significantly during the 21 years that the Bill of Rights has been in force. But the lack of recourse to the Bill of Rights on Māori issues is, on examination, readily explicable. As with most civil rights, the right of minorities to enjoy their culture, speak their language and practise their religion is affirmed in the Bill of Rights as an abstract and 'high-level' principle. It sets a standard for law and practice to meet. But the real work of rights-protecting and advancing, the work of meeting that standard, is performed by ordinary statutes, by regulatory regimes, and by the policies and actions of governments and their agents. When, as has been the case in New Zealand since the mid-1980s, there is general political will for advancing

---

[4] Art 27 reads: 'In those States in which ethnic, religious or linguistic minorities exist, persons belonging to such minorities shall not be denied the right, in community with the other members of their group, to enjoy their own culture, to profess and practise their own religion, or to use their own language': *International Covenant on Civil and Political Rights*, opened for signature 16 December 1966, 999 UNTS 272 (entered into force 23 March 1976).

Māori interests through ordinary law and policy, one should not expect significant recourse to the higher level abstractions of a Bill of Rights. Not, at least, when the day-to-day laws and policies are crafted with a concern for the Māori dimension of New Zealand life, and themselves grapple with the balancing that is often involved between rights of Indigenous persons and wider social and national interests. In those circumstances, an appeal to the higher level of principle (in a Bill of Rights) will likely replicate the recognition and balancing that is already immanent in the legal system.

Indeed, the most important cases about Māori rights over the 21 years of New Zealand's Bill of Rights turn out to have been based not on the Bill of Rights at all, but on the common law or on statutory affirmations of the principles of New Zealand's founding treaty, the Treaty of Waitangi (1840). There is only sporadic invocation of the Bill of Rights in a Māori context. Significantly, in the few cases where there is such recourse, it turns out that the standard set by s 20 of the Bill of Rights (read in light of the international human rights law that lies behind it, as interpreted by the Human Rights Committee in cases about article 27 of the ICCPR) is understood in terms of *process*. That is, s 20 and article 27 are taken to require consultation and good faith by Government in relation to Māori when Māori interests are affected. This replicates well-settled domestic understandings about Government-Māori relations, already reached independently through domestic law in Waitangi Tribunal opinions and judicial decisions in administrative law cases. These understandings are based on the Treaty of Waitangi itself and preceded, and hence were not dependent in any way, on the Bill of Rights.

In short, the Bill of Rights in this field has not added much to what was happening anyway. The language of Indigenous or Māori rights in New Zealand remains 'Treaty rights', not 'Bill of Rights-rights' nor even 'human rights'. If anything, the Bill of Rights and human rights have at times been regarded as being in a slight tension with Māori rights, especially when special recognition of Māori interests or cultural understandings is argued to involve discriminatory impact on others, so needing justification under the rubric of discrimination law. That said, there has been no significant court finding to this effect, only rumblings in the community. At this stage, the Bill of Rights neither helps nor hinders Māori interests. So far as Māori are concerned, the Bill of Rights is something of a sideshow to the main event, which is the Treaty of Waitangi and its influence upon the formulation of policy and law. To put it another way, the New Zealand Bill of Rights is largely affirmatory of Treaty understandings.

The salience of this for Australia and any bill of rights it may enact must turn, of course, on local Australian factors. Critical amongst them will be the extent to which current policy and legislation is reckoning with Indigenous peoples' rights and whether it needs to be called to account against higher level principles set out in a bill of rights. If so, what should those principles be? If there is difficulty in precisely defining them, will recourse be had, as in New Zealand, to the generic formula of the ICCPR on minorities? And if so, what might be expected, given that the choice for a bill of rights (over *not* having a bill of rights) necessarily involves some degree of judicial empowerment to articulate the impact of legislatively-affirmed standards in particular cases and rule on whether they have been attained? Will the result be to entrench or transform?[5]

This chapter now seeks to answer these questions. It begins with the New Zealand experience to date.

Evolution of the Māori dimension of New Zealand law

The Treaty of Waitangi in English

The Treaty of Waitangi signed in February 1840 looms large in contemporary debate about issues affecting Māori. As will be seen, its text has proved quite serendipitous, neatly articulating critical issues of concern to Māori and indeed to all Indigenous peoples in once-colonised countries. This is serendipity indeed, given the speed with which the Treaty's amateur drafters settled the text in 1840.[6]

The Treaty's origin lies in the decision of the United Kingdom Government to seek a cession of sovereignty from Māori chiefs, as a prelude to annexing New Zealand as a colony. Captain William Hobson was despatched to secure that cession. Within days of his arrival, and apparently without the benefit of any suggested draft or precedent, Hobson had prepared and obtained the first signatures on the treaty now known as the Treaty of Waitangi. It was drafted in English but, for obvious reasons, translated into Māori — by then a written language due to the efforts of missionaries over previous decades.

The Treaty in English comprises three brief 'articles'. By article 1 the Māori cede their sovereignty to Queen Victoria; by article 2 the Crown guarantees Māori the continued enjoyment of their 'lands, estates, forests, fisheries and other properties' for so long as they wish to retain them; and by article 3 Māori are guaranteed equal

---

[5] This probably presents the choice a little starkly. A fuller treatment would make the point that even purported affirmations of existing rights still lend themselves to progressive or radical interpretations by successive generations of judges (and indeed legislators).

[6] For the authoritative account of the signing of the Treaty of Waitangi, see C Orange, *The Treaty of Waitangi* (1987) 28–9. For a comprehensive treatment of the history of the Treaty's relationship with the New Zealand legal system, see M Palmer, *The Treaty of Waitangi in New Zealand's Law and Constitution* (2008).

rights along with British subjects. It is essentially, therefore, an early form of human rights treaty, an affirmation of Māori property rights and a general right to equality — albeit as quid pro quo to a cession of sovereignty. (An oral addendum at Waitangi, not written into the text but still regarded as important, added a guarantee of religious liberty.)

Colonisation then began apace. English-style institutions were created — a legislature, an executive and a judiciary — delivering essentially English-style outcomes through English-style processes. For their part, Māori came to be regarded as susceptible to the entirety of English law, ameliorated in the early period so far as enforcement of criminal law was concerned. Chiefly authority remained in a de facto sense, given the relativities in numbers and the geography of the country. But this authority was soon to be undermined by the universality of English law, by land sales and by the new economy. There was some recognition of Māori customary law, by means of the common law's 'custom-recognising' window. But that recognition withered and largely disappeared in the early twentieth century, both because many Māori were integrated into European life but also because of the onslaught of legal positivism that held that legally-cognisable rights could be produced only by legislation.[7] By such means Māori fishing rights, for example, disappeared as a legal concept for nearly a century, despite the Treaty's apparent affirmation of them. A 1985 court case 'rediscovered' customary fishing rights as a common law right (part of the Australian and Canadian renaissance of Indigenous land rights happening at much the same time).[8]

As things stand, the English dimension of New Zealand's constitution is well understood. For most of New Zealand's history, the Treaty has been understood as a *foundational* document — deserving pride of place in the national archive yet not a document to which constant recourse is required and not formally a part of the law. It could quite reasonably be thought to need no specific implementation in positive law. After all, one might say, English common law already delivered the promises of respect for Māori property rights and equality in articles 2 and 3. Certainly, successive New Zealand governments down to about the mid-1980s did not regard the Treaty as a significant political fetter on their power, nor as speaking with particularity to contemporary situations. All the same, the Treaty has always been prominent in New Zealand's history and self-description, and governments through the decades since 1840 would never have thought to disavow it. Indeed, they would aver that they were implementing or at least acting consistently with it. But as to that averment

---

[7] Notably *Wi Parata v Bishop of Wellington* (1877) 3 NZ Jur (NS) 72 (NZSC), and *Waipapakura v Hempton* (1914) 33 NZLR 1065 (NZSC).

[8] *Te Weehi v Regional Fisheries Officer* [1986] 1 NZR 680 (NZHC). In Australia, momentum was building for the celebrated *Mabo v Queensland (No 2)* (1992) 175 CLR 1, and in Canada there had been *Calder v Attorney-General of British Columbia* (1973) 34 DLR (3d) 145.

there was no ultimate judge. Being a treaty, and not law, it was not susceptible to authoritative interpretation by a body superior to Parliament. And that is still so.

But a Māori dimension to New Zealand's public life and law has evolved, steadily and powerfully. This has given the Treaty significantly greater political and sometimes legal traction. The progressive resolution of historic land grievances over the last 20 years has seen substantial inflows of money for many Māori tribes and subtribes. Those that have reached settlements will often have a significant economic base, and increasingly seek a measure of influence and autonomy over matters affecting them. And, in this renaissance, the Māori version of the Treaty has been, if not literally influential, then at least emblematic of the progress made. It is evidence that the deal struck in 1840 aligns closely with contemporary aspirations of Māori: to participate in the governance of their historic lands. How has this come about?

The Māori Treaty, Te Tiriti o Waitangi

Virtually all signatories signed the Māori version of the Treaty of Waitangi, both at Waitangi and subsequent signings elsewhere. In that sense, its text carries the moral weight. It turns out that the Māori version is not a literal translation of the English. When translated back into English, it is capable of being understood as a blueprint for a different type of constitutional arrangement from the one we have. One cannot at this distance be sure whether this was intended, but it is assuredly the reason why the Treaty remains so enduring.

In Māori, article 1 of the Treaty is not obviously a cession of Māori sovereignty. Rather, Māori cede to the Queen 'governorship',[9] not inconsistent with a continuing role for themselves in the new order alongside the Governor. The Māori article 1 does not self-evidently envisage the English Crown monopolising law-making power and control. Meanwhile, and consistently with Māori article 1, article 2's promise of continuing Māori ownership reads, in Māori, as a promise of continuing *chieftainship*[10] over their possessions. That, it is now commonly said, is more than mere ownership; it implies political control and some degree of immunity from the control of another. Further, amongst the concepts signified by the Māori word *taonga*, chosen to translate the English word 'properties' in article 2, are intangibles

---

[9] The word used is *kawanatanga*, a transliteration of the English word 'governor', in use by 1840 to denote the office of Pontius Pilate in the New Testament and of Governor Gipps in New South Wales, each of whom answered to a higher authority. This point was first made by R M Ross, 'Te Tiriti o Waitangi: Texts and Translations' (1972) *New Zealand Journal of History* 129, 140 (cited in M Palmer, above n 6, 63 and fn 164).

[10] The word is *rangatiratanga*, derived from *rangatira* or chief, denoting chieftainship. The treaty term is actually *tino rangatiratanga*, the former word being an intensifier denoting absolute chieftainship.

such as language and culture. So the Crown's promises in the Māori version include a promise to recognise Māoridom's chiefly authority over tangible and intangible properties including language and culture — indeed, it is now said, Māori institutions and way of life.

The Māori version, te Tiriti o Waitangi, is, as a result, very close to the set of aspirations that modern Indigenous people have in the once-colonised nations. If the English version is like a Māori bill of rights, then the Māori version is closer, even, to the Declaration on the Rights of Indigenous Persons that it anticipated by 167 years. It can be read as envisaging continuing self-determination and autonomy; some sort of equal place, or at least *a* place, in the constitutional order. It is no surprise, then, that the Treaty has been central to Māori concern about the structure of the New Zealand state and the way their interests ought to be regarded.

An overview of the place of the Treaty in New Zealand law and practice

The fact is, however, that New Zealand's legal history — or much of it — was premised on the English version of the Treaty. It remains the position that the Treaty gives no legally enforceable rights, unless and to the extent it is embodied in legislation.[11] And no legislation has ever incorporated the Treaty into the law of New Zealand in any global sense.[12] The real problem is that, as with most human rights treaties, the Treaty of Waitangi, even when read in light of its Māori text and associated aspirations, is vague and general, potentially applying across the whole field of governmental endeavour, from immigration, health and education to transport, leisure and welfare. The crucial questions become: what does it really *mean* to protect and treat Māori equally in health, education, in licensing intellectual property, in applying the rules for protecting the environment and entering free trade agreements with other states? Such questions demand practical answers, and often the allocation of significant resources. Answers given will also depend on the times in which they

---

[11] The authority for this proposition, as applied to the Treaty of Waitangi, is *Te Heu Heu Tukino v Aotea District Māori Land Board* [1941] NZLR 590; [1941] AC 301 (PC). Intriguingly, in *New Zealand Māori Council v Attorney-General* [1987] 1 NZLR 641, Cooke P commented that this was orthodoxy, 'at any rate from a 1941 standpoint' (at 667), thereby hinting at potential judicial revision. In a modest sense, that revision has come: eg, in oral argument in *Te Runanga o Wharekauri Rekohu v Attorney-General* [1993] 2 NZR 301 (CA), Cooke P observed that, even in the absence of a statutory reference to the Treaty, the Crown could not argue that its actions in seeking to settle Māori grievances over fisheries were somehow free of Treaty of Waitangi considerations. The applicants lost that case for unrelated reasons.

[12] The *Supreme Court Act 2003* (NZ) provides in s 13 that, for the purposes of gaining leave to appeal to the Supreme Court, a significant issue relating to the Treaty of Waitangi is a matter of general or public importance. But this is far from a general provision that the Treaty may be called by a Court as a source of rights when addressing any legal question.

are given. They are the stuff of politics. It is conceivable that such questions could be consigned to the courts. But without a statute that so consigns them, the courts have had only a marginal role to play.

In this state of affairs, the real work is done at the political level. The question is what the Treaty requires or precludes in this or that field. While Māori have consistently sought to advance their interests in political life, it is only in recent times that such arguments have fared prominently and relatively successfully in political debate. For example, in education, there is provision for state-funded Māori immersion schools at all levels, a requirement that all schools must emphasise Māori culture and make Māori language available for those that wish, and for all tertiary institutions to recognise a commitment to the Treaty of Waitangi. In the important fields of conservation, natural resources and the environment, the relevant legislation is similarly explicit in requiring consultation with Māori *iwi* (tribes) in the development of planning controls, and also in requiring that regard be had to Māori cultural and spiritual concerns. The place of the Treaty in the constitutional order is indicated by the requirement, laid out in New Zealand's Cabinet Office Manual and accepted by successive governments, that, before being adopted as a government measure, any proposed legislation must be certified by the responsible Minister as being consistent with the Treaty.[13]

Māori electoral success, especially since the advent of the proportional representation electoral system in 1993, has contributed to this sea change. Māori members have been elected to Parliament in significant numbers and have been influential in most of the minority governments since 1996. The current National Administration has a 'Confidence and Supply Agreement' with the Māori Party.

But, of course, not all political struggles are won. There is not space here for any detailed account but in general terms the pattern of recent New Zealand law has been this: a search by Māori and their lawyers for a legal basis upon which to make claims to courts in order to assert their customary rights to fisheries, forests, land, culture, language and political participation. Māori have also sought influence in domestic politics and in the development of national, regional and local policies. Finally, there has been continuing pressure to redress the injustice of the loss of Māori land, some of which was lost by sharp practices but much of it by 'reforms' and legal structures that made its transfer out of traditional Māori ownership easy and hence inevitable.[14]

---

[13] See New Zealand Government, *Cabinet Office Manual* (2008) [7.60(a)].
[14] See the excellent book by Stuart Banner, *Possessing the Pacific* (2007), especially the evocative chapter titles relating to New Zealand (chapter 2 is entitled 'Conquest by Contract' and chapter 3 'Conquest by Land Tenure Reform').

For much of the twentieth century, then, there was only occasional meaningful regard to the implications of the Treaty. But by the mid-1970s political traction for change had occurred to the point that the *Treaty of Waitangi Act 1975* was enacted. This Act allowed Māori to make claims, to the newly-constituted Waitangi Tribunal, that the Crown had acted (or was proposing to act) inconsistently with the 'principles of the Treaty of Waitangi'. The Tribunal was empowered to make findings and recommendations, but not binding judgments. Initially the Tribunal could inquire only into post-1975 issues. In 1984 the jurisdiction of the Tribunal was extended so as to enable it make findings, and recommendations, about governmental actions dating right back to 1840. Any Māori person may complain about a past or planned action of the Crown.

The Tribunal's jurisdiction therefore has the Treaty as its centrepiece. Because its statutory function is to report on inconsistencies with 'the principles of the Treaty of Waitangi' and not its literal text, the Tribunal has been free to blend the English and Māori texts to provide a contemporary explanation of New Zealand's situation. Its solution is not overtly radical and revolutionary, but constitutional in import. The Tribunal has held that the Treaty principles require a process by which the Crown (by which is meant successive governments) and Māori must relate: that there should be consultation, good faith, cooperation and so on. The Tribunal accepts, as realistically it must, that the Crown is sovereign, but says that this sovereignty rests on the basis that Māori interests be accorded an appropriate priority in matters that relate to and affect them. In this way Māoridom as a whole and each Māori tribe are bestowed a sort of quasi-constitutional status. This comes about because, through the medium of abstracted Treaty principles, New Zealand's founding document is taken to require consultation and solicitation for Māori interests in a way that is somehow different from the general political duty owed by governments to their citizenry. And obligations of consultation necessarily imply the existence of entities with which to consult, and hence the continuing vitality of these entities' own mechanisms for generating internal leadership and authority. In short, it implies a dynamic Indigenous culture within the broader national culture.

A related development was that from around 1986 onwards it became common for Parliament to impose, in legislation, these same 'principles of the Treaty' as a mandatory consideration in the making of statutory decisions, or as a limit on executive power in certain discrete fields (for example, in environmental or conservation decisions). By this means, the substance of the Treaty of Waitangi was made justiciable in those fields. It thus became a part of the domain of administrative law and judges, and not just the Waitangi Tribunal.

The first and most far-reaching example was the *State-owned Enterprises Act 1986*, which contained in s 9 a general proviso that 'nothing in the Act' permitted the Crown 'to act in a manner that is inconsistent with the principles of the Treaty of Waitangi'. This produced landmark litigation: *New Zealand Māori Council v Attorney-General*.[15] For the first time the Court of Appeal of New Zealand needed to articulate the Treaty principles and decide whether the Crown had acted consistently with them. Agreeing with the Waitangi Tribunal, the Court held that those principles included the need for good faith between the Treaty partners and fiduciary-like obligations for the Crown to consult and to consider Māori interests when policies and actions affecting Māori are determined. On the facts of the case, the Court held that the Crown would breach the Treaty principle of 'redress' for past breaches were it to proceed (as it proposed) to transfer a huge proportion of state-owned land to the new 'corporatized' state trading enterprises. (This was because transferring the land would make it impossible for the Crown to return any land that the Waitangi Tribunal might subsequently recommend for return to Māori on the ground it had been wrongly taken in the past.)

The chronology of events so far brings us to 1987. By this time, New Zealand was reckoning with the idea of a Bill of Rights. We need to go back to 1985 for the beginning of the Bill of Rights idea, just before the Treaty was being kick-started back into life by the policies of the 1984–90 Labour Government and the series of judicial decisions of which the *Māori Council* case just mentioned was the first. The timing was significant.

The White Paper proposal for a New Zealand Bill of Rights

On Waitangi Day in 1984, Geoffrey Palmer announced that a future Labour government would include the Treaty of Waitangi in a Bill of Rights. Following the change of government in 1984, the *White Paper: A New Zealand Bill of Rights* was tabled in April 1985. Article 4 would have included the Treaty (along with other civil and political rights provisions) as supreme law.

As with much of the proposed Bill of Rights, Article 4 drew inspiration from the Canadian Charter of Rights and Freedoms. As to the Treaty, it would have said:

> 4. (1) The rights of the Māori people under the Treaty of Waitangi are hereby recognised and affirmed.
>
> (2) The Treaty of Waitangi shall be regarded as always speaking and shall be applied to circumstances as they arise so that effect may be given to its spirit and true intent.
>
> (3) The Treaty of Waitangi means the Treaty as set out in English and Māori in the Schedule to this Bill of Rights.

---

[15] [1987] 1 NZLR 641 (CA).

The term 'recognised and affirmed' was borrowed from the Canadian Charter of Rights and Freedoms.[16] There it was designed neatly to avoid the difficulty that there was no consensus on the rights Canada's Aboriginal peoples enjoyed. The Charter lobbed that issue into the courts. That would have been the outcome in New Zealand too.

But, as it happened, the White Paper proposal for a Bill of Rights in New Zealand proved unpopular with the citizenry and did not proceed.[17] The article 4 Treaty proposal was particularly unpopular with Māori. This seems puzzling now, given that a Treaty clause in a supreme law would have been, one might think, a vast improvement over a non-justiciable Treaty.

The dominant Māori view, however, was that a justiciable Treaty would be susceptible to restrictive judicial interpretation. Further, because of the way the Bill of Rights had been drafted, article 4 was subject to article 3, meaning that Treaty rights, like all rights, would be potentially subject to such 'reasonable limits' as were 'demonstrably justified in a free and democratic society'. Māori opinion leaders judged it better to keep the Treaty outside the legal system, where it could be invoked through the ages to critique that system — if not formally through litigation, then at least through political debate and activism. Handing the Treaty over to (then as now) largely non-Māori judges within the system did not seem wise, given the way Māori cases had generally turned out to that point.

Māori distrust was understandable. In 1985, Māori had not had the measure of litigation success that came from 1987 onwards when the then-Labour Government began to insert Treaty references into legislation. The *New Zealand Māori Council* case mentioned above was the first, but more followed. They all had much the same pattern: when the government of the day was privatising or restructuring a new sector of state enterprise, the applicable legislation generally the 'Treaty clause' that restrained executive power and made it an administrative law question whether the principles of the Treaty had been observed in the decision-making process. This

---

[16] Canada Constitution s 25.
[17] An overview of the Bill of Rights proposal and how it eventually resulted in the New Zealand Bill of Rights Act 1990 is to be found in Rishworth, 'The Birth and Rebirth of the Bill of Rights' in Huscroft and Rishworth (eds), *Rights and Freedoms* (1995) ch 1.

occurred in the power generation sector,[18] television[19] and radio broadcasting,[20] mining,[21] forests[22] and fisheries.[23]

These cases were not all successful, but they signalled the potential applicability of Treaty principles, and Māori aspirations for involvement, across the whole spectrum of public activities. They showed the role the courts might play, and they showed how the Treaty actually spoke to most areas of public activity and enterprise. But in 1985 all this lay in the future. In the result, the White Paper proposal did not proceed. Five years later, a statutory bill of rights, the *New Zealand Bill of Rights Act 1990*, was enacted instead.

The *New Zealand Bill of Rights Act 1990* and minority rights

The *New Zealand Bill of Rights Act 1990* was seen as a retreat for the then Government. A supreme law Bill of Rights having been rejected by the citizenry, the Labour Government used its voting majority to enact a statutory bill of rights with (so far as the rights were concerned) essentially the same text. But, in recognition of Māori concerns, the Treaty clause was excised. In the Bill of Rights as enacted there is no mention of Treaty rights, only the 'minority rights' in s 20, based upon article 27 of the ICCPR.

Plainly, s 20 inured for the benefit of all minorities, not just Māori. But because Māori make up less than 50 per cent of the population they are undeniably a minority and entitled to whatever protection it offers. The question arose in New Zealand, therefore, whether s 20 might make justiciable, as minority rights, controversies that were otherwise mere non-justiciable Treaty claims. This seemed a possibility, especially in relation to the right to enjoy the 'culture' of the minority. That denoted customary rights and control over historic resources, including lucrative and important resources such as fisheries, rivers and forests.

---

[18] *Te Runanganui o Te Ika Whenua Inc Soc v Attorney-General* [1994] 2 NZLR 20 (CA).
[19] *New Zealand Māori Council v Attorney-General* [1994] 1 NZLR 513 (PC).
[20] *New Zealand Māori Council v Attorney-General* [1991] 2 NZLR 129 (CA).
[21] *Tainui Māori Trust Board v Attorney-General* [1989] 2 NZLR 513 (CA).
[22] *New Zealand Māori Council v Attorney-General* [1989] 2 NZLR 142 (CA).
[23] *Te Runanga o Muriwhenua Inc v Attorney-General* [1990] 2 NZLR 641 (CA).

There was indeed some early support for the idea, at least in academic articles.[24] The argument was that s 20 effectively incorporated the Treaty in the Bill of Rights: one writer suggested that it was as if there were a right to have the Treaty observed. This seemed a big claim to make, and the argument suffered a little from the weakness that it read s 20 as requiring that things had to be done *for* Māori, rather than, as was usual for bills of rights, a restraint on the power of the state (s 20 is, after all, expressed as a duty not to deny the right to culture). Even so, in human rights law it is possible that largely negative rights will have some measure of positive content.[25] That is, there may be occasions when the state's inaction might itself constitute a denial of a right to culture, language or religion, and positive measures are then effectively required to prevent a breach.

But the main problem with the argument was that s 20 would be an amazingly subtle way of incorporating the Treaty of Waitangi into the Bill of Rights, and there was nothing in its legislative history that supported the argument in any way. Still, one could not rule out the possibility that s 20 went at least some of the way toward producing what a Treaty clause might have produced.

Another difficulty in regarding s 20 as a Trojan Horse containing the Treaty of Waitangi was the likely unwillingness of Māori to embrace the idea that a section aimed at minorities — at *all* minorities — had any special significance for them. The strongly expressed, and understandable, Māori view is that they are no mere minority in New Zealand. Rather, together with the Crown, they are a founding partner.[26] All this said, such sentiments have not, as we shall see, totally precluded invocation of s 20 by Māori individuals and groups.

In the end, the question whether observing s 20 equates to observing the Treaty of Waitangi depends upon what we regard as 'observing the Treaty' and whether that properly satisfies the standards implied by s 20. By the 1990s, as we have seen, the Treaty was increasingly seen as requiring a certain type of 'process — good faith, consultation and so on — in relation to Māori. Intriguingly, as we shall see next,

---

[24] A Blades, 'Article 27 of the ICCPR: A Case Study on Implementation in New Zealand' [1994] 1 *Canadian Native Law Reporter* 1, and E Durie, 'Constitutionalising Māori' in G Huscroft and P Rishworth (eds) *Litigating Rights; Perspectives form Domestic and International Law* (2002) 241, 251–2.

[25] See, eg, *Platform 'Artze Fur Das Leben' v Austria* (1991) 13 EHRR 204. The key point is that protecting freedoms may require positive action where governments have knowledge that a citizen's rights are endangered by other citizens and the means to protect them.

[26] As put recently in a debate about immigration law by Māori Party MP Hone Harawira, but paraphrasing Māori academic Dr Ranginui Walker, '[the Treaty] was the guarantee of a developing social contract. It was a partnership of the two cultures, with, at its very core, the expectation that Māori, as a Treaty partner, would be consulted on every aspect concerning people who want to come here': (29 October 2009) 658 *New Zealand Parliamentary Debates* 7648.

this resonated with the impact of article 27 (s 20's ICCPR counterpart) on matters affecting Indigenous peoples in other parts of the world.[27]

The Bill of Rights and advancement of Māori claims

In the main, Māori litigation in the Bill of Rights-era has not been based on the Bill of Rights. Even when s 20 could offer assistance, as in several major cases aimed at the protection of the Māori language,[28] that section has not been mentioned by judges and (one assumes) not pressed by the litigants. The reason is not hard to discern: there was agreement that government was under a statutory duty, imposed by ordinary legislation, to have regard to Treaty principles and that one such principle required protection of the Māori language. The cases turned only on whether, on the facts, there was a breach of these principles. Putting these arguments in terms of s 20 of the Bill of Rights would, at best, have been another way of addressing the same issue.

But there are cases in which Māori have invoked s 20 of the Bill of Rights when there was no other statutory 'peg' on which to hang their claim. It is to these cases I now turn, for they exemplify the manner in which the imperatives that underpin s 20 are operating in other dimensions of New Zealand law — in the common law and in politics — and producing outcomes that are consistent with s 20.

Māori values in environmental law

An early Bill of Rights case indicated the potential use of s 20. In *New Zealand Underwater Association Inc v Auckland Regional Council*[29] a Māori tribe objected when the Auckland Port company obtained permission to dump harbour dredgings onto the sea floor at an outlying part of Auckland's Hauraki Gulf. The claim was that this was deeply offensive to their culture and religion, which regarded the waters of the Hauraki Gulf as sacred. Dumping these dredgings — actually accumulated sediment from the city's stormwater drains — was said to be desecration.

The Auckland Port company had received consent to dump the dredgings, conferred by the council under a statutory power. The objectors' argued that a broad statutory power could never be used to infringe their s 20 rights. The argument was sound as a matter of form, but weak on its merits.[30] The idea that mere *offence* to religious

---

[27] (2001) 8 IHRR 372.
[28] *New Zealand Māori Council v Attorney-General* [1994] 1 NZLR 513; [1994] 1 AC 466.
[29] New Zealand Planning Tribunal, 16 December 1991.
[30] The legal reasons given would now be understood as wrong. The reasoning was that a statutory power could not be read down in light of rights in the Bill of Rights. See now *Drew v Attorney-General* [2002] 2 NZLR 58 (CA).

and cultural sensibilities denied a tribal right to culture was problematic. (It might be different if the claim were that the dumping would impede actual cultural practices.)

But what is more significant for present purposes is that there have been no more similar cases. And the reason is because of a law reform that made such arguments unnecessary. The harbour dredgings case was in the dying days of the old legislation about water rights. The incoming *Resource Management Act 1991* specifically incorporated Māori spiritual and other concerns into the environmental planning regime. No recourse was thereafter required to the general provisions of the *New Zealand Bill of Rights Act 1990*. Māori concerns, including spiritual concerns, were mainstreamed into the ordinary operation of the law, and not made a Bill of Rights matter. This is not to say that they will always prevail, but they are now seen as proper and routine considerations and there are indeed cases where they do prevail.[31]

The Sealord litigation and the off-shore fisheries

The next, and still the most significant, s 20 case was the 1992 fisheries litigation in *Te Runanga o Wharekauri Rekohu Inc v Attorney-General*[32] and its sequel — a complaint by some Māori tribes to the Human Rights Committee under the Optional Protocol to the ICCPR that New Zealand had breached article 27, on which s 20 was based.

The background was that by 1985, Māori had succeeded in a series of fishing rights cases in the High Court, establishing that it was possible for Māori to assert customary (pre-1840) Māori fishing rights as a defence to fisheries prosecutions. Further, it was readily accepted that these rights could be exercised with modern fishing equipment and in relation to commercial fishing. The implication of these victories was considerable, and by 1992 not yet fully explored.

On one view, the wording of the (then) *Fisheries Act* affirmed that Māori had a legal claim to customary fishing rights — including, perhaps, even (to quote the Māori version of the Treaty) rangatiratanga or 'chiefly authority and control' — over the lucrative offshore fisheries resource of New Zealand worth millions of dollars. Litigation with these implications was pending. It had prospects of success, because the *Fisheries Act* contained this ominous provision: 'Nothing in this Act shall affect any Māori fishing rights'. Once it had been accepted, in 1985 as a result of *Te Weehi v Regional Fisheries Officer*, that customary Māori fishing rights actually existed, this phrase had real bite, and especially in the architecture of the fisheries management system. Government had been busy allocating fishing quota *under* the *Fisheries Act*

---

[31] One such case is *TV3 Network Services Ltd v Waikato District Council* [1998] 1 NZLR 360, holding that a regional council did not err when, to recognize Māori spiritual and cultural views, it refused consent to the erection of a television translator device on top of a mountain.

[32] *Te Runanga o Wharekauri Rekohu Inc v Attorney-General* [1993] 2 NZLR 301 (CA).

— and doing so without proper regard to Māori rights and potential claims — yet the Act affirmed that Māori fishing rights were not to be affected.

The ensuing litigation was resolved by way of a major 'pan-Māori' settlement in which the Government paid $150 million to a newly created Māori entity (the Treaty of Waitangi Fisheries Commission). The settlement became known as the 'Sealord Deal' because the settlement sum was intended to be used (and was indeed used) to purchase for the Commission a 50 per cent share in a major fishing company, Sealord Products Ltd. That shareholding, together with further fishing quota issued to the Commission, would place a considerable share of the New Zealand fishing industry in Māori control. In exchange, Māori for their part agreed to the enactment of legislation that would remove their right to make customary (or, much the same thing, Treaty of Waitangi-based) claims to the fisheries resource. In effect, Māori were mainstreamed into the fishing industry, and received a substantial share of it, on the basis that they surrendered their customary (and Treaty) rights to fisheries.

Some tribes dissented from this settlement and challenged it in the courts. Seeking a cause of action, they based their claim on s 20 of the *New Zealand Bill of Rights Act 1990* — the right of a minority to 'enjoy' its 'culture'. Māori, said these tribes, were a fishing people with a fishing culture. The proposed settlement, said the tribes, would force them to abandon these cultural rights with only the promise of a share in a pan-Māori settlement as compensation. The Crown was, they argued, acting unlawfully in seeking to implement a deal that contravened s 20 of the Bill of Rights.

The dissenters lost their challenge. The Court of Appeal ruled that because the settlement was to be implemented by legislation, the Courts could not rule the promised legislation unlawful nor preclude any bill from going to Parliament. For this reason the merits of the Māori tribes' argument were not justiciable. But the Court hinted that, in its view, the Sealord Deal was a very good one for Māori.

Meanwhile, several Māori groups commenced a claim in the Waitangi Tribunal seeking a declaration that the proposed settlement was inconsistent with the principles of the Treaty of Waitangi. The Tribunal, too, gave the Sealord Deal its general approval as a positive step for Māori, albeit that it criticised the 'lawyerly' tone of the settlement deed and made some recommendations (not in fact taken up by Government).[33] The settlement proceeded, and it does indeed appear to have been successful in delivering returns for Māori from commercial fishing.

But the present interest lies in what the dissenting tribes did after losing their court challenge. They took their case to the Human Rights Committee under the Optional Protocol to the ICCPR. There the argument centred, as it had to, on article 27. And

---

[33] Waitangi Tribunal, *The Fisheries Settlement Report* (1992).

in that forum the focus was on the merits of the settlement, and whether it denied Māori their right to culture.

In fact, however, the Human Rights Committee also dismissed the challenge to the Sealords Deal (*Mahuika v New Zealand*).[34] The Committee readily accepted that the claimant tribes enjoyed a fishing culture and that the effect of the Sealord settlement was to bring an end to their traditional rights, replacing them with an entitlement to share in the Sealord settlement and to fish under New Zealand law. But, the Committee ruled, this was *not* a denial of their right to culture. The Committee emphasised the extensive consultation that had taken place between Government negotiators and representatives of Māori tribes. That there was some dissent could not obscure the fact of widespread consultation leading to agreement, with the wisdom and fairness of the deal appreciated by the majority. Citing its decision in *Kitok v Sweden*[35] the Committee said:[36]

> it may consider whether the limitation in issue is in the interests of all members of the minority and whether there is reasonable and objective justification for its application to the individuals who claim to be adversely affected.

This was essentially to apply, as principles of article 27 of the ICCPR, the same principles of good faith and consultation as the New Zealand institutions (the courts and the Waitangi Tribunal) had held to be required by the principles of the Treaty of Waitangi.

This was a significant finding for Treaty law and practice in New Zealand. It meant that the requirements of international human rights law largely replicated the position that had evolved by way of developing 'Treaty principles': the requirements of good faith, consultation and so on. In a variety of fields including health, conservation, education, resources, hazardous substances control, and law reform, New Zealand law does contain provisions that direct the attention of decision-makers to Māori interests. If properly executed, that law ought to result in outcomes that are consistent with article 27 as it has been interpreted by the HRC in cases such as *Mahuika* and *Länsman v Finland*.[37]

So in these two cases, s 20 has not in fact added anything to that which is produced by Treaty principles. The Bill of Rights has not advanced Māori interests beyond the point they reach when advanced as Treaty rights. What has really counted, then, is the readiness of successive governments to give meaning to Treaty rights, a readiness

---

[34] (2001) 8 IHRR 372 (HRC).
[35] Comm No 197/1985, 27 July 1988.
[36] *Mahuika v New Zealand* (2001) 8 IHRR 372 (HRC), [9.6].
[37] Comm No 511/1992, 8 November 1994.

assisted by judicial decisions in those cases where the substance of the Treaty has been made justiciable in a particular field.

Dogs that didn't bark: cases in which s 20 is conspicuous by its absence

In several cases, the salient point about s 20 is that it is not mentioned at all, even though it was, on its own terms, relevant. This suggests that the operation of ordinary law is effectively serving interests that s 20 promotes.

One such case was the landmark one of *Ngati Apa v Attorney-General*[38] in which the Court of Appeal, overruling a 1963 decision of its own,[39] held that it was possible for Māori to advance claims to customary ownership of the seabed and foreshore around New Zealand. Previously, that was thought impossible as the seabed and foreshore was vested by various statutes in the Crown. But customary title, said the Court of Appeal, could co-exist and was not ousted by the Crown's own title.

Section 20 played no part in the reasoning: it was essentially a case about the common law of 'aboriginal title'. Still, the outcome, that Māori could advance customary claims to specific pieces of foreshore and seabed, was consistent with their right to enjoy their culture.

There was a dramatic sequel, however. In a climate fuelled by speculation that Māori tribes might gain exclusive title to beaches and then exclude New Zealanders from access to them, the Government introduced legislation to prevent Māori claims to the foreshore and seabed going to the Māori Land Court. Instead, a different process was to be instituted to compensate Māori for their claims, to make various other provisions for their cultural practices, and to exclude the possibility of any claim for exclusive customary title. This was duly enacted as the *Foreshore and Seabed Act 2004*.

The central thrust of that legislation was to deny Māori recourse to the courts to press their property rights. That made the legislation unattractive, in human rights terms, from the outset. But there is no right to property in the New Zealand Bill of Rights and the new legislation could not be criticised on that account. There is, however, the right to culture and a right against discrimination. Both were implicated here.

Section 7 of the Bill of Rights required that the Attorney General signify to the House of Representatives, on introduction of the Foreshore and Seabed Bill, whether any provision was inconsistent with a protected right. But she did not. She issued a legal opinion giving her view that the Bill did not deny the right to culture in s 20, saying she was unaware of any Māori cultural practice that required *exclusive* possession

---

[38] [2003] 3 NZLR 643 (CA).
[39] *Re the Ninety Mile Beach* [1963] NZLR 461 (CA).

of seabed and foreshore. She went on to say that the bill was *not* discriminatory, reasoning that the national interest in attaining certainty over ownership of seabed and foreshore was a compelling objective, and that discrimination against Māori (in precluding only Māori from asserting claims to foreshore and seabed)[40] was rationally and proportionately related to that end. The fact that the AG signed this 'no breach' opinion personally — in contrast to the practice, in other cases, of lawyers in the Crown Law Office or Ministry of Justice signing them — perhaps carries an inference that the Attorney-General's view was not shared by her own advisers.

But a further sequel is significant. The Labour Government's promotion of the *Seabed and Foreshore Act* was deeply unpopular with Māoridom and with many of its Māori members. It led to the defection of a Māori member of Parliament, and formation of the Māori Party. In 2008, the Government changed. The incoming National government formed a relationship with the Māori Party. It quickly established a task force to review the *Foreshore and Seabed Act*, and that Taskforce recommended its repeal and replacement.[41] That has now occurred.[42] This is an instance, then, of the ordinary political process ultimately delivering rights-consistent outcomes to Māori, even in circumstances where the Bill of Rights was powerless (both because it could not accomplish a repeal or annulment of legislation and because the Attorney-General had not seen the 2004 Act as discriminatory or as inimical to minority rights).

Looking at the Foreshore and Seabed saga more broadly, its genesis was largely bound up with Māori aspirations for marine farms, and so the saga takes its place in the series of cases that involved Māori claims for recognition of their rights when public assets are being allocated for private benefit. Subsequently, a political settlement of Māori claims to aquaculture has been reached, not unlike that reached for sea fisheries in the Sealord Deal, whereby 20 per cent of new aquaculture space is allocated for the benefit of Māori tribes.[43]

Māori custom and custody of a body for burial

A recent High Court judgment, *Clarke v Takamore*,[44] has also illustrated the extent to which the common law (independent of any statutory bill of rights) is able to reckon with the customs of Indigenous peoples. The case concerned the funeral arrangements for the body of James Takamore, a Māori man who lived most of his

---

[40] For historical reasons it appeared that some New Zealanders, who could have been of any race, did in fact hold title to areas of seabed and foreshore and the bill was not aimed at them, but only at Māori claiming customary title.
[41] Ministerial Review Panel, *Report of the Ministerial Review Panel* (2009 [7.6.2]).
[42] Marine and Coastal Area (Takutai Moana) Act 2011 (NZ).
[43] See *Māori Commercial Aquaculture Claims Settlement Act 2004* (NZ).
[44] High Court, Christchurch, CIV 2007-409-001971, 29 July 2009 (Fogarty J).

life in the South Island but whose tribal affiliations were with two North Island tribes. He had spent his adult life living away from his tribal grouping. In his will he expressed a wish to be buried, not specifying where. His wife (and executor) duly made arrangements for the funeral service to be held on a *marae* (Māori ceremonial meeting area) and for the body to be buried at a Christchurch cemetery. But the night after Mr Takamore's death, his extended family arrived from the North Island seeking to retrieve his body and return it to the Tuhoe tribal area in accordance with claimed Māori custom. The following day, after heated discussions, the Takamore family removed Mr Takamore's body against his wife's wishes, taking it north.

The High Court (this being the first instance superior court in New Zealand) traversed three issues: first, the extent of an executor's common law power to determine where a body is to be buried; second, whether the *tikanga* (customary law) of Tuhoe Māori should be recognised as part of that common law, and; third, how any clash between the executor's rights and Māori customary law should be resolved in the specific case. On the second issue, the Court adopted much of the evidence of customary practice provided by counsel for the tribe. Relevant Māori custom *did* involve the possibility of a tribe's wishes about burial of a member prevailing over those of a surviving spouse. The Judge then canvassed the case law, suggesting that New Zealand common law was open to adaptation in light of Indigenous customary law.[45] It noted the flexibility of Indigenous custom, and pointed out that 'this approach by the common law of recognising customary internal self-government for resolving disputes, as this tikanga does, is not undermined by any statute'.

As to the case in front of it, however, the Court was reluctant to allow Tuhoe custom to prevail. Mr Takamore, he pointed out, had effectively ceased to identify with his tribe. Applying a three-part test from an early case about Māori custom[46] — which required Courts to examine the existence of a custom, the consistency of a custom with statute law, and whether a custom is reasonable — the Court found the first two ingredients of the test were satisfied but held that the Māori custom was unreasonable to the extent that it claimed to apply to a person who had chosen to live apart from his tribe.

The Court drew on Article 3 of the Treaty of Waitangi, which accords Māori rights as British subjects, to hold that some middle ground needed to be found between customary law and the common law. Recognising the collective right of Tuhoe funeral practices would in this case impose too great a restriction on individual freedom for the custom to be applied. Consequently, the actions of Mr Takamore's North Island family were found to be unlawful.

---

[45] Citing cases such as *Nireaha Tamaki v Baker* [1901] AC 561 and *Attorney-General v Ngati Apa* [2003] 3 NZLR 643 as support for this proposition.
[46] *Public Trustee v Loasby* (1908) 27 NZLR 801.

This is significant for our discussion of statutory bills of rights and their role in advancing Indigenous interests. If it is clear that, where there is a will to make it so, the common law is moving organically to recognise customary rights as well as broader interests (as *Takamore* implies), a straitjacketed 'right to culture' might be not just unhelpful but counter-productive in the way in which it could narrow the number of Indigenous interests capable of recognition by the Courts. The common law itself contains sufficient resources, without needing the help of a statutory bill of rights, to advance the causes of Indigenous rights and interests — at least this is what the New Zealand experience would suggest. But the right of a minority to enjoy its culture is the principle that lies behind such decisions.

In that sense s 20 gives voice to a principle that is intrinsic to common law as it reckons with Indigenous peoples. Perhaps it serves as an impetus to advance recognition of minority rights to culture. But it is surely significant that there is not one mention of s 20 in the *Takamore* judgment. When the applicable principles are seen as embedded in the law, recourse to the Bill of Rights is not necessary.

Has the Bill of Rights impaired Māori interests?

The issue to consider here is whether legislation or policies designed to advance Māori interests might be conceived as discriminatory in relation to other racial groups whose interests are not similarly advanced. This requires a consideration of s 19 of the Bill of Rights, which gives rights against discrimination on various grounds, and the *Human Rights Act 1993* (which does the same but in relation to private sector discrimination).

Significantly, the *Human Rights Act 1993*, which established an anti-discrimination code along with a Human Rights Commission to educate, advise and report on human rights generally, did not initially contain any reference to Māori and the Treaty of Waitangi. The interaction of Treaty-observing and anti-discrimination law began to attract attention in the late 1990s and early 2000s, when a small backlash began to develop about so-called 'special measures' for Māori (affirmative action in state employment and universities, for example, and provision for Māori seats in local government). The question was asked: might Treaty-honouring provisions in legislation and policy be precluded by anti-discrimination law? It was true that the *New Zealand Bill of Rights Act 1990* and the *Human Rights Act 1993* each contained special clauses designed to facilitate affirmative action schemes. But this came at the cost of making it look like Treaty-honouring was some sort of dishonourable exception to a general principle of equality. There was particular controversy about a proposal to put a Treaty clause into the New Zealand Public Health Bill in 2000: some took the point that a Bill about public health should surely focus on the health needs of individuals, and not send signals that the race or ethnicity of a sick person was somehow relevant. To the argument that taking race into account might in fact be necessary for effective delivery of health care to minority groups, the rejoinder was that this applied for all races and not just Māori. The result was a Solomonic backdown for the Treaty clause in that case. At the policy level, Māori health organisations would continue to be funded and consulted about delivery of health services to their people, but similar arrangements might be made for Pacific people and Somalis, for example.

A *Human Rights Amendment Act of 2001* mentioned the Treaty of Waitangi for the first time. By this Act, the Human Rights Commission was given a new statutory function:

> (d) to promote by research, education and discussion a better understanding of the human rights dimensions of the Treaty of Waitangi and their relationship with domestic and international human rights law.

As I wrote at the time:

> That addition appears to have been prompted by a combination of factors. In various ways, the time to hitch Treaty rights to the wagon of human rights seemed to have come. As s 5(2)(d) makes clear, the aim was for a 'better understanding' of what all this might mean. That may be a reference to a growing public concern in 2001 over whether, in fields like public health, Treaty rights should mean special or even different arrangements for Māori. Sorting out the interaction of human rights and Treaty rights needed some work. So, while 'Treaty clauses' had become common in other statutes, often requiring decision-makers to have regard to the 'principles of the Treaty of Waitangi', the clause chosen for the Human Rights Act was somewhat more tentative. This time it is not Treaty principles, but Treaty 'dimensions'. No one is bound by them, but there is to be a research, education and discussion about them.[47]

So what has been the record in relation to Māori and the provisions of the Bill of Rights and the *Human Rights Act 1993*? In fact, there has been remarkably little litigation, but the following cases and events will give the flavour.

---

[47] Paul Rishworth, 'The Treaty and Human Rights' [2003] *New Zealand Law Review* 381, 382.

Affirmative action schemes

It is not uncommon for New Zealand universities that offer limited-entry tertiary level courses such as Law and Medicine to set aside a quota of places for groups perceived as educationally disadvantaged and under-represented. In the main, these schemes have not been tested against the criteria set out for them in the *Human Rights Act 1993*. On their face, they necessarily discriminate against potential students who are not included in the scheme, and who must therefore compete for a lesser number of places. Depending on the type of scheme, it is almost certain that there will be non-admitted persons with a higher grade point average than targeted students who qualify for preferential admission.

The ability to offer such schemes is assured by s 73 of the *Human Rights Act 1993* and s 19(2) of the Bill of Rights. These are broadly equivalent to s 15(2) of the Canadian Charter — a statement that special measures that take race into account to ensure equality will not violate the prohibition on discrimination.

There has only been one decided case, an undefended first instance tribunal decision with little precedential value. Responding to government funding incentives, a regional polytechnic institute had set aside for Māori *all* available places in a fishing industry training course. A local fishing company complained that it could not enrol its own non-Māori cadet in the course. The polytechnic had no interest in defending its action. The undefended complaint was upheld, on the ground that no evidence had been led to satisfy the statutory test for such schemes: that Māori 'may reasonably be supposed to need assistance or advancement in order to achieve an equal place with other members of the community'.

There has been no other case, and targeted assistance schemes involving quotas are not uncommon in universities. This state of affairs, and the likelihood that they will be upheld if able to be demonstrated as rational and proportionate, suggests that the anti-discrimination principle is not a hindrance to Treaty-driven or needs-driven favourable treatment for Māori. Note, of course, that the reasons why Māori might be favoured under special admissions schemes — a history of educational disadvantage — could be applicable to other minorities: it is not necessarily a Treaty-inspired policy.

Discrimination in favour of Māori to accommodate Māori representational interests

The issue of Bill of Rights consistency comes up in relation to the passage of 'Treaty-implementing' bills that potentially discriminate on the grounds of race. This will be when Māori institutions are created, or Māori representation is desired on national or regional institutions.

At the level of the national parliament, New Zealand has a long history of Māori representation. This goes back to 1867 when four dedicated Māori seats in the House of Representatives were created. These are seats representing Māori electorates, whose voters, having some degree of Māori ancestry, have opted to be on the Māori electoral roll. More recently, when proportional representation was introduced in 1993, the number was increased and is now dictated by a formula driven by the number of Māori electors on the Māori electoral roll — presently there are seven seats.[48] The continuation of Māori seats is criticised in some quarters, including on the ground that it is discriminatory.[49]

Māori representation (by way of dedicated seats elected by voters on the Māori roll) has been made possible at the level of municipal government,[50] but, controversially, was ruled out of contention for the 'super-city' of Auckland that was created in late 2010. But a noteworthy feature of political debate about that proposal was that no-one pressed the argument for Māori representation on the basis of rights in the Bill of Rights (although some who oppose it do so on the basis that there should be no racial qualifications, and hence no racial discrimination, in electoral law).

That raises the question of what the courts might say if they were empowered to rule on whether the creation of Māori seats in municipal government infringe the rights of others to be free of discrimination. Some hint at the Crown Law Office's views is evident in legal advice given on a related issue. In the Historic Places Amendment Bill 2004, provision was made for four persons to be appointed to the Māori Heritage Council on the basis of, amongst other things, their being Māori. If the Bill was discriminatory, then s 7 of the Bill of Rights required the Attorney-General to report that fact to Parliament on introduction of the Bill.

But the advice provided to the Attorney-General concluded that the racial qualification was not unlawful discrimination because it was (in terms of s 5 of the Bill of Rights) a 'justified' limitation (on the right of potential candidates of other races to be considered).[51] That advice stressed that making appointments to the Council solely on the basis of a person's qualification and experience *without* reference to Māori ethnicity would affect the credibility and *mana* of the Trust. This would in turn undermine the ability of the Trust and the Board to understand the concerns of and speak with Māori constituents about the protection of Māori culture. This legislation therefore did not result in a s 7 report. Note that this was an instance of

---

[48] See *Electoral Act 1993* (NZ) s 78.
[49] Philip A Joseph, *The Māori Seats in Parliament* (2008).
[50] See *Bay of Plenty Regional Council (Māori Constituency Empowerment) Act 2001* (NZ), ss 5–6.
[51] Advice provided to the Attorney General: *Historic Places Amendment Bill* (2004) Ministry of Justice <http://www.justice.govt.nz/policy/constitutional-law-and-human-rights/human-rights/bill-of-rights/historic-places-amendment-bill> at 9 September 2011.

the actual appointees needing to be Māori, and not simply a case of a dedicated seat to which Māori electors would appoint (where, as with the Māori parliamentary seats, the candidate need not necessarily be Māori — although in practice has been).

Looking at it more broadly, a likely judicial resolution of Māori representation issues seems to be this. Representational advantages bestowed on Māori through creating a Māori electoral roll and special seats are a form of political discrimination representing the current interpretation of the deal struck by the Treaty of Waitangi. It is not racial or ethnic discrimination, since it implements a deal made with Māori *political* entities in 1840. This is the approach of the United States Supreme Court in rejecting a discrimination challenge in the case of *Morton v Mancari*,[52] which concerned hiring preferences for Indigenous North Americans in the Bureau of Indian Affairs. The essential point is that obligations assumed in (or agreed to be implicit in) a Treaty between two political entities will not too readily be taken as impossible of performance due to a generalized anti-discrimination code.

Reflections on the New Zealand experience and implications for Australia

While New Zealand has a Bill of Rights with no written constitution, Australia has a written constitution and no bill of rights.[53] For New Zealand the future will see continuing calls for a formal constitution. Indeed, at the time of writing (February 2011) the country is in the early days of a 'constitutional review process', one that was stipulated by the Māori Party as the quid pro quo for its entering into a governance arrangement with the National Party in 2008. It is plain enough that no issue will be more difficult to resolve than how any new constitution reckons with the Māori dimension of New Zealand, and of course no new constitution will be possible without that resolution. The debate will not simply be about the Treaty of Waitangi as a basis for ex post facto review by judges of the actions of other branches of government, as is made possible by bills of rights. Rather, it will also be about devising structures that ensure an appropriate degree of Māori political influence in all branches of government (perhaps, say, a second legislative chamber with dedicated Māori seats). The likelihood, in other words, is that a new constitution will be seen as the occasion for deciding what a nation founded on the Treaty should be *like*. That is a different thing from simply regarding the Treaty of Waitangi as a fetter on the powers of the state, in its continued form, to legislate and act. For Māori, that

---

[52] 417 US 535 (1974).
[53] New Zealand does have its *Constitution Act 1986* (NZ), but this is simply descriptive of its constitutional arrangements, and not constitutive of them. There is scarcely ever any recourse to it in litigation.

type of restraint would probably still be seen as too uncertain in its impact, even if not as uncertain as it was in 1985.

Australia's written constitution does not traverse anything approaching Indigenous peoples' rights. A Bill of Rights might therefore be seen as the occasion to introduce Indigenous peoples' rights, but cannot accomplish greater structural change. A bill of rights can rule some acts and policies out of contention, but does not compel any particular act or policy. In the main, a bill of rights is a reason for not doing things, rather than doing them. The truth is that advancement of Indigenous interests requires political will and action. What does the New Zealand experience mean for Australia as it considers whether to have a bill of rights, and what a potential text for Indigenous rights might be? My essential point has been that recourse to s 20 is not frequent in New Zealand because ordinary law, achieved through the political process, is serving those same values — of protecting Māori rights to language and culture (religion has not yet featured as such but is embraced in the recognition given to sacred sites as a factor in environmental decision-making). This may not always be so, and so mine is not an argument against putting in place something like s 20. It is just an argument that it need not be seen to have revolutionary consequences. The real work has happened elsewhere in the executive and legislative branches and is in no small measure due to Māori political activity and influence.

What might this mean for Australia? If the New Zealand experience is anything to go by, Indigenous rights will not be subverted or aggressively advanced through judicial reasoning. The site of advancement will continue to be the political realm. However, we should ask: is the New Zealand experience in fact anything to go by? Are there factors that might differentiate Australia?

Differences in political culture

Australia has a different history to New Zealand in relation to Indigenous rights. First and foremost, it was not founded on a treaty, still less a treaty whose text serendipitously expresses contemporary aspirations of an Indigenous race and which cannot easily be disregarded as out of date. Much might have changed in 170 years, but the principles the Treaty of Waitangi embodies (or, by mutual consent, are now taken to embody) are capable of application in a new age. Australia lacks any such overarching and evocative treaty as a focal point. This may well have hindered the advancement of Indigenous claims through the political process.

In saying this, one must not overstate the effect of New Zealand's Treaty of Waitangi. If there had been no such treaty, we would still be having much the same debates as we do. But the Treaty of Waitangi supplies the language for that debate. Importantly, its prominence as a part of New Zealand's founding narrative means that it has a considerable salience as the Māori 'Bill of Rights'. In those circumstances, a second bill of rights has not seemed as important to Māori as it might otherwise have been. Without the Treaty of Waitangi, we probably would have had a very different Bill of Rights debate. This suggests Australia will have a different sort of debate too.

A second difference between Australia and New Zealand is geography and resources. The degree of interaction and intermingling between the Indigenous and settler communities seems to have been much greater in New Zealand. This is assuredly a consequence of New Zealand's relatively compact geography and, relatedly, of noticeable Māori entrepreneurialism and economic participation. That has set up a dynamic in which Māori have achieved considerable successes though political participation allied with the moral suasion of the Treaty. Given different historical and contemporary relationships between Indigenous and non-Indigenous peoples in Australia, an Australian bill of rights might carry more weight, at least in its symbolic recognition of the Indigenous peoples. They might take up the opportunity of litigating their claims in the courts with greater enthusiasm borne of greater need. Courts, too, may feel the need to fill a gap to a greater extent than in New Zealand. But the recognition of this possibility will serve also to focus careful attention on just what a bill of rights should say on Indigenous peoples' rights.

Conclusion

New Zealand's Bill of Rights signified no particular aims in relation to the Māori dimension of New Zealand life. The Treaty of Waitangi was and remains the centrepiece for Māori aspiration, and Māori opinion has generally been against incorporating the Treaty into law if this means in practice that its meaning and effect becomes the province of judges. Those, at least, were the sentiments that led to the enactment of a New Zealand Bill of Rights in 1990 that only incidentally reached Māori concerns, doing so through s 20 and its general right for all minorities, Māori and others, to enjoy their culture, speak their language and practice their religion. But recourse to s 20 is sporadic and not particularly consequential. This is because, in practice, the general law of New Zealand has been solicitous for recognition of Māori culture, language and religion, a position that has come about through Māori political participation. The operation of that general law, I have suggested, meets the standard set by s 20 and so there has not been occasion for courts to hold it inconsistent or for Māori to bring claims arguing that it is so.

What has really counted, then, is Māori political success in ensuring that ordinary law accommodates Māori concerns and interests. Significantly, it has actually been the core civil and political rights — the right to vote, and the freedoms of expression, association and assembly — that underpin these political successes. But, equally, there has been the influence of the Treaty of Waitangi, the nation's founding document, that symbolises the coming together of the English Crown (and the settlers whose entry and governance the Treaty made possible) with the Indigenous occupants of New Zealand.

Australia has, of course, equal capacity to accommodate the concerns of Indigenous persons through its ordinary law and ordinary political processes. It does not have an overarching treaty carrying the symbolic weight and value of New Zealand's. In that state of affairs, the inclusion of Indigenous rights in a bill of rights will likely carry more expectations. An Australian bill of rights, with Indigenous rights within it, may serve as a high level set of principles to which recourse is constantly made both by executive government as it chooses how to act, by law-makers as they legislate, and by the courts when called upon to determine the consistency of governmental actions and omissions with those principles. An Australian bill of rights presents an opportunity for a grand symbol, one that serves for Australia in the same way as the Treaty of Waitangi has served New Zealand. This, of course, raises the stakes in negotiations over the wording of the relevant rights.

But it may also be that a comprehensive statement of Indigenous peoples' is left for another day and another document. If that were so, but minority rights to language, culture and religion were included in a bill of rights as they were in New Zealand, then an Australian Bill of Rights might still have considerable impact for Indigenous peoples. That has not been New Zealand's experience, but this is explicable for the reasons given: that Māori concerns have been integrated into the fabric of many major enactments and are required to be taken into account by decision makers. The critical question, then, is whether the detail of Australian law, as it impacts upon Indigenous peoples, incorporates their rights to culture, religion and language or whether, instead, that law may fall to be judged as inconsistent with those rights. How significant such a measure then becomes will likely hinge on more general questions about the impact of a bill of rights — on questions about judicial interpretation of rights and deference to legislative choices and, perhaps most importantly, about whether the judiciary perceives a mandate to take the general idea of minority rights into the realm of rights for Indigenous peoples.

TABLE OF LEGISLATION AND INTERNATIONAL INSTRUMENTS

Afghanistan
Legislation
Afghanistan Constitution

Australia
Legislation
Abortion Law Reform Act 2008 (Vic)
Anti-Discrimination Act 1991 (Qld)
Anti-Discrimination Act 1998 (Tas)
Australian Constitution
Broadcasting Act 1942 (Cth)
Broadcasting Services (Transitional Provisions and Consequential Amendments) Act 1992 (Cth)
Charter of Human Rights & Responsibilities Act 2006 (Vic)
Classification (Publications, Films and Computer Games) Act 1995 (Cth)
Crimes Act 1900 (NSW)
Customs (Cinematograph Films) Regulations 1979 (Cth)
Customs (Prohibited Imports) Regulations 1956 (Cth)
Defamation Act 2005 (NSW)
Equal Opportunity Act 1984 (SA)
Human Rights Act 2004 (ACT)
Mental Health Act 1986 (Vic)
Racial Discrimination Act 1975 (Cth)
Sex Discrimination Act 1984 (Cth)

Cases
Andreyevich v Kosovich and Publicity Press (1938) Pty Ltd (1947) 47 SR(NSW) 357
Attorney-General (Vic) ex rel Black v Commonwealth (1981) 146 CLR 559
Australian Broadcasting Corporation v O'Neill (2006) 227 CLR 57
Ayan v Islamic Co-ordinating Council of Victoria Pty Ltd and ors [2009] VSC 119 (3 April 2009)
Bashford v Information Australia (Newsletter) Pty Ltd (2004) 218 CLR 366

Bennette v Cohen (2005) 64 NSWLR 81
Bennette v Cohen [2009] NSWCA 60
Catch the Fire Ministries Inc & Ors v Islamic Council of Victoria Inc [2006] VSCA 284
Cattanach v Melchior [2003] HCA 38
CES v Superclinics (1995) 38 NSWLR 47
Church of the New Faith v Commissioner for Pay Roll Tax (Vic) (1983) 154 CLR 120
Coco v The Queen (1984) 179 CLR 427
Consolidated Trust Co Ltd v Browne (1948) 49 SR (NSW) 86
David Syme & Co v Canavan (1918) 25 CLR 234
Davis v Commonwealth (1988) 166 CLR 79
Deen v Lamb [2001] QADT 20
Ettingshausen v Australian Consolidated Press (1991) 23 NSWLR 443
Evans v NSW [2008] FCAFC 130
Fletcher v Salvation Army Australia [2005] VCAT 1523
Gardner; Re BWV (2003) 7 VR 487
Haddon v Forsythe [2011] NSWSC 123 (8 March 2011)
Islamic Council of Victoria v Catch the Fire Ministries Inc [2004] VCAT 2510
Jackson v TCN Channel 9 [2001] NSWCA 108
Kracke v Mental Health Review Board [2009] VCAT 646 (23 April 2009)
Lange v Australian Broadcasting Corporation (1997) 189 CLR 520
Mabo v Queensland (No 2) (1992) 175 CLR 1
Mann v Medicine Group Pty Ltd (1992) 38 FCR 400
McBain v Victoria (2000) 99 FCR 116
Members of the Board of the Wesley Mission Council v OV and OW (No 2) [2009] NSW ADTAP 57
Mundey v Askin [1982] 2 NSWLR 369
Obermann v ACP Publishing Pty Limited [2001] NSWSC 1022
Pell v Council of Trustees of the National Gallery of Victoria (1998) 2 VR 391
Pell v Council of Trustees of the National Gallery of Victoria [1997] VSC 52
Plenty v Dickson [2009] SASC 9 (19 January 2009)
QAAH OF 2004 v Minister for Immigration and Multicultural and Indigenous Affairs (2004) [2004] FCA 1448
R v Jones (Unreported, NSW Supreme Court Quarter Sessions, Simpson J, 18 February 1871)
Random House Australia Pty Ltd v Abbott [1999] FCA 1538, (1999) 94 FCR 296
Re an application under the Major Crime (Investigative Powers) Act 2004, [2009] VSC 381 (7 September 2009)
Re The Christian Institute's and others' Application for Judicial Review [2008] NI 86
RJE v The Secretary to the Department of Justice [2008] VSCA 265

Roberts v Bass (2002) 212 CLR 1
Trad v Harbour Radio Pty Ltd [2009] NSWSC 750
Trad v Harbour Radio Pty Ltd [2011] NSWCA 61 (22 March 2011)
Wik Peoples v Queensland (1996) 187 CLR 1

Austria
Legislation
Austrian Constitution
Basic Law on General Rights of Nationals in the Kingdoms and Länder represented in the Council of the Realm, 1867 (Austria)
Federal Constitutional Law of 29 November 1988 on the Protection of Personal Liberty (Austria)
Federal Constitutional Law on the Protection of Personal Liberty, 1988 (Austria)
Law of 27 October 1862 on Protection of the Rights of the Home (Austria)
Law on Protection of the Rights of the Home, 1862 (Austria)
State Treaty for the Reestablishment of an Independent and Democratic Austria, 1955

Belarus
Legislation
Belarus Constitution

Brazil
Legislation
Brazil Constitution

Canada
Legislation
Canada Constitution
Canadian Bill of Rights, RSC 1970, App III, s 1
Canadian Charter of Rights and Freedoms (Canada)
Lord's Day Act, RSC 1970, c L-13
Retail Business Holidays Act, RSO 1980, c 453

Cases
AC v Manitoba (Director of Child and Family Services) [2009] SCJ No 30
Adler v Ontario [1996] SCJ 110
Alberta v Hutterian Brethren of Wilson Colony [2009] SCJ No 37
B(R) v Children's Aid Society of Metropolitan Toronto [1994] SCJ No 24
Bai v Sing Tao Daily Ltd (2003) 226 DLR (4th) 477

Boutilier v Nova Scotia [2004] NSJ No 357 (NCSC)
Bruker v Marcovitz [2007] SCJ No 54
Calder v Attorney-General of British Columbia (1973) 34 DLR (3d) 145
Canada (Combines Investigation Acts, Director of Investigation & Research) v Southam Inc [1984] 2 SCR 145
Canadian Civil Liberties Association v Ontario [1990] OJ No 104
Congregation des Temoins de Jehovah de St Jerome-LaFontaine v LaFontaine (Village) [2004] SCJ No 45
Dagenais v Canadian Broadcasting Corporation [1994] SCJ No 104
Dunbar v Yukon [2004] YJ No. 61 (YKSC)
Egale v Canada [2003] BCJ No 994 (BCCA)
Gauthier v Toronto Star Daily Newspapers Ltd (2004) 245 DLR (4th) 169
Halpern v Toronto (City) [2003] OJ No 2268
Hendricks v Quebec [2002] JQ No 3816 (QCSC)
Malette v Shulman (1990) 67 DLR (4th) 321
Multani v Commission scolaire Marguerite-Bourgeoys [2006] 1 SCR 256
NW v Canada [2004] SJ No 669 (SKQB)
Police v Razamjoo [2005] DCR 408 (DC).
R v Big M Drug Mart [1985] SCJ No 17
R v Edwards Books [1986] SCJ No 70
R v Jones [1986] SCJ No 56
R v Oakes [1986] 1 SCR 103
R v Oakes [1986] SCJ No 7
Re Bill 30 [1987] SCJ 44
Reference re Same-Sex Marriage, [2004] SCJ No 75
Roncarelli v Duplessis, [1959] SCR 1921
Ross v New Brunswick School District No 15 [1996] SCJ No 40
Saumur v City of Quebec, [1953] 2 SCR 299
Syndicat Northcrest v Amselem, [2004] SCJ No 46
Trinity Western University v College of Teachers (British Columbia) [2001] SCJ No 32
Vogel v Canada [2004] MJ No 418 (MNQB)
Young v Young [1993] SCJ No 112
Youssoupoff v Metro-Goldwyn-Mayer Pictures Ltd (1934) 50 TLR 581

China

Legislation
People's Republic of China Constitution

France

Legislation
Decree No 2000-549 of 15 June 2000 (France)
La Constitution de 1958 (France)
La Déclaration des Droits de l'Homme et du Citoyen 1789 (France)
Law No 2004-228 of 15 March 2004 (France)
Law No 89-486 of 10 July 1989 on Direction in Education (France)
Law of 9 December 1905 relating to the Separation of Churches and State (France)
Le Préambule de la Constitution du 27 octobre 1946 (France)

Cases
Conseil d'État, No 159981, 10 March 1995
Conseil d'État, No 170343, 20 May 1996
Conseil d'État, No 170207 170208, 27 November 1996
Cour administrative d'appel de Lyon, No 96LY02608, 19 December 1997

Germany

Legislation
Grundgesetz für die Bundesrepublik Deutschland (Germany)
Landesbeamtengesetz Baden-Württemberg (Germany)
Schulordnung für die Volksschulen in Bayern, 21 June 1983 (Germany)

Cases
BVerfG NJW 1989, 3269 (judgment of 15 August 1989)
BVerfG NJW 1993, 455
BVerfGE 108, 282 ('*Teacher Headscarf* case')
BVerfGE 12, 1
BVerfGE 19, 129
BVerfGE 24, 236
BVerfGE 25, 1
BVerfGE 28, 243
BVerfGE 3, 225
BVerfGE 30, 1
BVerfGE 32, 98
BVerfGE 34, 52
BVerfGE 35, 376
BVerfGE 41, 29BVerfGE 47, 327
BVerfGE 49, 375
BVerfGE 50, 256
BVerfGE 52, 223

BVerfGE 83, 341
BVerfGE 92, 1 ('*Sitzblockaden II* case')
BVerfGE 92, 277 ('*Markus Wolf* case')
BVerfGE 93, 1
BVerfGE 93, 1 ('*Classroom Crucifix* case')
BVerfGE 93, 266 ('*Soldaten sind Mörder* case')
BVerGE 65, 1

Greece
Legislation
Greece Constitution

Hong Kong
Legislation
Hong Kong Bill of Rights Ordinance

Cases
Ng Ka Ling and Chan Kam Nga v Director of Immigration (1999) 2 HKCFAR 82
Yeung May Wan v HKSAR (2005) 8 HKSAR 137

Indonesia
Legislation
Penal Code 1952 (Indonesia)

Iran
Legislation
Iran Constitution

Ireland
Legislation
Defamation Act 2009 (Ireland)
Ireland Constitution

Malaysia
Legislation
Administration of Islamic Law (Federal Territories) Act 1993 (Malaysia)
Malaysia Constitution
Syariah [Sharia] Criminal Offences (Federal Territories) Act 1997 (Malaysia)

New Zealand

Legislation

Bay of Plenty Regional Council (Māori Constituency Empowerment) Act 2001 (NZ)
Bill of Rights Act 1990 (NZ)
Constitution Act 1986 (NZ)
Contraception, Sterilisation and Abortion Act 1977 (NZ)
Electoral Act 1993 (NZ)
Employment Relations Act 2000 (NZ)
Māori Commercial Aquaculture Claims Settlement Act 2004 (NZ)
Marine and Coastal Area (Takutai Moana) Act 2011 (NZ)
Resource Management Act 1991 (NZ)
Supreme Court Act 2003 (NZ)
Treaty of Waitangi 1840 (NZ)

Cases

Attorney-General v Ngati Apa [2003] 3 NZLR 643
Auckland District Health Board v AZ and BZ, HC Auckland, Civ 2007-4-4-2260 (27 April 2007)
Broadcasting Standards Authority Decision No 2006-022 (26 June 2006)
Brooker v Police [2007] 3 NZLR 91
Browne v CanWest TV Works Ltd [2008] 1 NZLR 654 (HC)
Department of Labour v Books and Toys (Wanaka) Ltd (2005) 7 HRNZ 931 (DC)
Director of Human Rights Proceedings v Catholic Church of New Zealand [2008] 3 NZLR 216 (HC)
Drew v Attorney-General [2002] 2 NZLR 58 (CA)
Feau v Department of Social Welfare (1995) 2 HRNZ 528 (HC)
Friends and Community of Ngawha Inc v Minister of Corrections [2002] NZRMA 402 (HC)
Human Rights Commission v Eric Sides Motors Co Ltd (1981) 2 NZAR 447
King-Ansell v Police [1979] 2 NZLR 531
Mendelssohn v AG [1999] 2 NZLR 268, 273 (CA)
Mendelssohn v Attorney-General [1999] 2 NZLR 268 (CA)
Mendelssohn v Centrepoint Community Growth Trust [1999] 2 NZLR 88
Network Services Ltd v Waikato District Council [1998] 1 NZLR 360
New Zealand Māori Council v Attorney-General [1987] 1 NZLR 641
New Zealand Māori Council v Attorney-General [1989] 2 NZLR 142 (CA)
New Zealand Māori Council v Attorney-General [1991] 2 NZLR 129 (CA)
New Zealand Māori Council v Attorney-General [1994] 1 NZLR 513 (PC)
Public Trustee v Loasby (1908) 27 NZLR 801
R v Anderson, Court of Appeal, CA27/04 (23 June 2004)

R v Lee [2006] 3 NZLR 42 (CA)
Re J (An Infant): Director-General of Social Welfare v B and B [1996] 2 NZLR 134 (CA)
Re the Ninety Mile Beach [1963] NZLR 461 (CA)
Tahaafe v CIR, CRI 2009-404-102 (10 July 2009)
Tainui Māori Trust Board v Attorney-General [1989] 2 NZLR 513 (CA)
Te Heu Heu Tukino v Aotea District Māori Land Board [1941] NZLR 590; [1941] AC 301 (PC)
Te Runanga o Muriwhenua Inc v Attorney-General [1990] 2 NZLR 641 (CA)
Te Runanga o Wharekauri Rekohu Inc v Attorney-General [1993] 2 NZLR 301 (CA)
Te Runanganui o Te Ika Whenua Inc Soc v Attorney-General [1994] 2 NZLR 20 (CA)
Te Weehi v Regional Fisheries Officer [1986] 1 NZR 680 (NZHC)
Waikato District Health Board v L, HC Hamilton, Civ 2008-419-1312 (23 Sept 2008)
Waipapakura v Hempton (1914) 33 NZLR 1065 (NZSC)
Wi Parata v Bishop of Wellington (1877) 3 NZ Jur (NS) 72 (NZSC)
Zdrahal v Wellington City Council [1995] 1 NZLR 700 (HC)

North Korea

Legislation
North Korean Constitution

Pakistan

Legislation
Pakistan Penal Code 1860 (Pakistan)

South Africa

Legislation
Promotion of Equality and Prevention of Unfair Discrimination Act 2000 (South Africa)
South Africa Constitution

Cases
Prince v President of Law Society of Cape of Good Hope (2002) SA 794

Tajikstan

Legislation
Tajikistan Constitution

United Kingdom

Legislation
Canada Act 1982 (UK) c 11, sch B pt 1
Constitution Act 1867, 30 & 31 Vict, c 3 (reprinted in RSC 1985, App II, No 5)
Criminal Justice and Immigration Act 2008 (UK)
Equality Act 2006 (UK)
Equality Act 2010 (UK)
Human Rights Act 1998 (UK)
Human Rights Act 2000 (UK)
Public Order Act 1986 (UK)
Race Relations Act 1976 (UK)
Racial and Religious Hatred Act 2006 (UK)

Cases
A Children [2000] 4 All ER 148
Ahmad v ILEA [1978] QB 36
Ahmad v United Kingdom (1981) 4 EHRR 126
Airdale NHS Trust v Bland [1993] AC 789
Aston Cantlow and Wilmcote with Billesley PCC v Wallbank [2004] 1 AC 546
Berkoff v Burchill and anor [1997] EMLR 139
Choudhury v UK (1991) 12 HRLJ 172
Collins v Willcox [1984] 3 All ER 374
Copsey v WWB Devon Clays Ltd [2005] EWCA Civ 932
Gallagher (Valuation Officer) v Church of Jesus Christ of Latter-day Saints [2008] UKHL 56
Ghai v Newcastle CC [2009] EWHC 978
Hammond v DPP [2004] EWHC 69
Islington London Borough Council v Ladele [2010] 1 WLR 955
Knupffer v London Express Newspaper, Ltd [1944] AC 116
London Borough of Islington v Ladele and Liberty [2009] IRLR 154
Mandla v Dowell-Lee [1983] 2 AC 548
McFarlane v Relate [2010] IRLR 872
Nireaha Tamaki v Baker [1901] AC 561
Parmiter v Coupland (1840) 6 M&W 105
R (Baiai, Trzcinska, Bigoku & Tilki) v Secretary of State for the Home Department [2007] 1 WLR 693
R (on the application of Ghai) v Newcastle CC and the Secretary of State [2010] EWCA Civ 59
R (on the application of Ghai) v Newcastle CC and the Secretary of State [2009] EWHC 978

R (on the application of Playfoot) v Governing Body of Millais School [2007] EWHC 1698
R (on the application of Suryanda) v Welsh Ministers [2007] EWCA Civ 893
R (on the application of Suryanda) v Welsh Ministers [2007] EWHC 1376 (Admin)
R (on the application of Ullah) v Special Adjudicator; Do v Immigration Appeal Tribunal [2004] UKHL 26
R (on the application of Watkins-Singh) v Governing Body of Aberdare Girls High School [2008] EWHC 1865 (Admin)
R (on the application of Williamson) v Secretary of State for Education and Employment [2001] EWHC Admin 960
R (On the application of X) v The Headteacher of Y School [2007] EWHC 298 (Admin)
R (Pretty) v Director of Public Prosecutions [2002] 1 AC 800
R (SB) v Governors of Denbigh High School [2007] 1 AC 100
R v Gott [1922] 16 Cr App R 87
R v Lemon (Denis) [1979] AC 617
R v Taylor (1676) 1 Vent 293; 86 ER 189

United States of America

Legislation
Alabama Constitution
American Indian Religious Freedom Act Amendment, Pub L No 103-344, 108 Stat. 3125 (1994)
Arizona Revised Statues, Annotated §§ 41-1493
Connecticut General Statutes, Annotated § 52-571b (West 2003)
Controlled Substances Act (US)
Equal Access Act, 20 USC §§ 4071-74 (1984)
Florida Statutes, Annotated §§ 761.01-761.04 (West 2003)
Idaho Code §§ 73-401 et seq (Supp 2002)
Illinois Compiled Statues, Annotated §§ 35/1-35/99 (West 2002)
New Mexico Statutes, Annotated §§ 28-22-1 – 28-22-5 (Michie 2002)
NY Educ Law § 414 (McKinney 2000)
Oklahoma Statutes, Annotated tit 51, §251 (West 2003)
Pennsylvania Consolidated Statutes, Annotated 2401
Pub L 105-183 (1998)
Pub L No 103-344, 108 Stat. 3125 (1994) (codified at 42 USC § 1996a (2007))
Religious Freedom Restoration Act of 1993, Pub L No 103-141, 107 Stat 1488 (1993)
Religious Liberty and Charitable Donation Act of 1998, Pub L 105-183 (1998)
Restatement (Second) of Torts 1977 s 566

Rhode Island General Laws §§ 42-80.1-1 – 42-80.1-4 (2001)
South Carolina Statues, Annotated § 1-32-10 (Law Co-op 1999
Texas Civil Practice and Remedies Code §§ 110.001 (West 2003)
United States Constitution
US Declaration of Independence, 4 July 1776
Vernon's Annotated Missouri Statutes §§ 1.302, 1.307 (West 2004)

Cases
Abington School District v Schempp, 374 US 203 (1963)
Agostini v Felton, 521 US 203 (1997)
Aguilar v Felton, 473 US 402 (1985)
American Friends Service Commission v United States, 368 F Supp 1176 (ED Pa 1973)
Attorney General v Desilets, 636 NE 2d 233 (Mass 1994)
Bannon v School District of Palm Beach County, 387 F 3d 1208 (11th Cir 2004)
Barron v Mayor and City Council of Baltimore, 32 US 7 (1833)
Bartnicki v Vopper, 532 US 514 (2001)
Beauharnais v Illinois, 343 US 250, 258 (1952)
Board of Education of Westside Community Schools v Mergens, 496 US 226 (1990)
Board of Education v Allen, 392 US 236 (1968)
Board of Education v Mergens, 496 US 226 (1990)
Boerne v Flores, 521 US 507 (1997)
Bowen v Roy, 476 US 693 (1986)
Bowers v Hardwick, 478 US 186 (1986)
Boy Scouts of America v Dale, 530 US 640 (2000)
Brown v Woodland Joint Unified School District, 27 F 3d 1373, 1382 (9th Cir 1994)
Cantwell v Connecticut, 310 US 296 (1940)
Capitol Square Review & Advisory Board v Pinette, 515 US 753 (1995)
CH ex rel ZH v Oliva CH, 226 F 3d 198 (3d Cir 2000)
CH ex rel. ZH v Oliva, 226 F 3d 198 (3d Cir 2000)
Chapman v Pickett, 491 F Supp 967 (CD Ill 1980
Church of the Lukumi Babalu Aye v City of Hialeah, 508 US 520 (1993)
Church on the Rock v City of Albuquerque, 84 F 3d 1273, 1279 (10th Cir 1996)
City of Boerne v Flores, 521 US 507 (1997)
Committee for Public Education & Religious Liberty v Regan, 444 US 646 (1980)
Committee of Public Education and Religious Liberty v Nyquist, 413 US 756 (1973)
Congregation Beth Yitzchok of Rockland, Inc v Town of Ramapo, 593 F Supp 655 (SDNY 1984)
Corder v Lewis Palmer School District No. 38, 566 F 3d 1219 (10th Cir 2009)
Corporation of Presiding Bishop v Amos, 483 US 327 (1987)

County of Allegheny v American Civil Liberties Union, 492 US 573 (1989)
Cutter v Wilkinson, 544 US 709 (2005)
Davey v Locke, 299 F 3d 748 (9th Cir 2002)
Dayton Christian Schools, Inc v Ohio Civil Rights Commission, 766 F 2d 932 (6th Cir 1985)
DeNooyer v Livona Public Schools, 799 F Supp 744 (ED Mich 1992)
DeNooyer v Merinelli, 1 F3d 1240 (6th Cir 1993)
Dworkin v Hustler Magazine Inc 867 F 2d 1188, 1200 (9th Cir App) (1989)
Edwards v Aguillard, 482 US 578 (1987)
Eisenstadt v Baird, 405 US 438 (1972)
Eklund v Byron Union School District, 154 Fed Appx 648 (9th Cir 2005)
Eklund v Byron Union School District, 2006 WL 1519184 (Appellate Petition, Motion and Filing) (US May 31, 2006)
Eklund v Byron Union School District, 154 Fed Appx 648 (9th Cir 2005)
Elk Grove Unified School District v Newdow, 542 US 1 (2004)
Employment Division v Smith, 485 US 660 (1988)
Employment Division v Smith, 494 US 872 (1990)
Engel v Vitale, 370 US 421 (1962)
Epperson v Arkansas, 393 US 97 (1968)
Equal Employment Opportunity Commission v Fremont Christian School, 609 F Supp 344 (ND Calif 1984)
Everson v Board of Education, 330 US 1 (1947)
Filartiga v Pena-Irala, 630 F 2d 876, 882 (2d Cir App 1980)
First Covenant Church of Seattle v City of Seattle, 840 P 2d 174 (Wash 1992)
Freedom from Religion Foundation v McCallum, 324 F 3d 880 (7th Cir 2003)
Geller v Secretary of Defense, 423 F Supp 16 (DC 1976)
Gertz v Robert Welch, Inc, 418 US 323, 339 (1974)
Goldman v Weinberger, 475 US 503 (1986)
Gonzales v O Centro Espirita Beneficente Uniao Do Vegetal, 546 US 418 (2006)
Good News Club v Milford Central School, 533 US 98 (2001)
Griswold v Connecticut, 381 US 479 (1965)
Hansen v Ann Arbor Public Schools, 293 F Supp 2d 780 (ED Mich 2003)
Hood v Medford Township Board of Education, 533 US 915 (2001)
Humphrey v Lane, 728 NE 2d 1039 (Ohio 2000)
Hunt v McNair, 413 US 734 (1973)
In re Browning, 476 SE 2d 465 (NC 1996)
Joseph Burstyn, Inc v Wilson, 343 US 495, 529 (1952)
Lamb's Chapel v Center Moriches Union Free School District, 508 US 384 (1993)
Lawrence v Texas, 539 US 558, 602-3 (2003)
Lee v Weisman, 505 US 577 (1992)

Lemon v Kurtzman, 403 US 602 (1971)
Levitt v Committee for Public Education & Religious Liberty, 413 US 472 (1973)
Lincoln v True, 408 F Supp 22 (WD Ky 1975)
Lynch v Donnelly, 465 US 668 (1984)
Lyng v Northwest Indian Cemetery Protective Association, 485 US 439 (1988)
Marbury v Madison, 5 US 137 (1803)
McCollum v Board of Education, 333 US 203 (1948)
McCreary County v ACLU of Kentucky, 125 S Ct 2722 (2005)
McCreary County v ACLU of Kentucky, 545 US 844 (2005)
McCurry v Tesch, 738 F.2d 271 (8th Cir 1984)
Milkovich v Lorain Journal Co, 497 US 1 (1990)
Mitchell et al v Helms et al, 530 US 793 (2000)
Mitchell v Helms, 530 US 793 (2000)
Mueller v Allen, 463 US 388 (1983)
Murray v Curlett, 374 US 203 (1963)
National Endowment for the Arts v Finley, 524 US 569 (1998)
Newdow v United States Congress, 292 F 3d 597 (9th Cir, 2002)
Newdow v US Congress, 542 US 1 (2004)
Nicholson v Board of Commissioners, 338 F Supp 48 (ND Ala 1972)
NLRB v Catholic Bishop of Chicago, 440 US 490 (1979)
O'Lone v Estate of Shabazz, 482 US 342 (1987)
Peck ex rel Peck v Baldwinsville Central School District, 426 F 3d 617 (2d Cir 2005)
People of State of Illinois ex rel McCollum v Board of Education of School District No 71, Champaign County, 333 US 203 (1948)
Poe v Ullman, 367 US 497 (1961)
Regan v Taxation With Representation, 461 US 540 (1983)
Reynolds v United States, 98 US 145 (1878)
Roe v Wade, 410 US 113 (1973)
Roemer v Board of Public Works, 426 US 736 (1976)
Rosenberger v Rector and Visitors of the University of Virginia, 515 US 819 (1995)
Rourke v New York State Department of Corrective Services 603 NY S 2d 647 (NY Sup Ct 1993)
Rupert v City of Portland, 605 A 2d 63 (Me 1992)
Rust v Sullivan, 500 US 173 (1999)
Santa Fe Independent School District v Doe, 530 US 290 (2000)
School District of Abington Tp v Schempp, 374 US 203 (1963)
School District of Grand Rapids v Ball, 473 US 373 (1985)
Sechler v State College Area School District, 121 F Supp 2d 439 (MD Pa 2000)
Settle v Dickson County School Board, 53 F 3d 152 (6th Cir 1995)
Sherbert v Verner, 374 US 398 (1968)

Skoros v City of New York, 437 F 3d 1 (2d Cir 2006)
Spohn v West, 2000 WL 1459981 (SDNY 2000)
St John's Lutheran Church v State Compensation Insurance Fund, 830 P 2d 1271 (Mont 1992)
State of Illinois ex rel McCollum v Board of Education, 333 US 203 (1948)
State v Evans, 796 P 2d 178 (Kan 1990)
State v Hershberger, 462 N W 2d 393 (Minn 1990)
State v Miller, 549 NW 2d 235 (Wis 1996)
Stone v Graham, 449 US 39 (1980)
Swanner v Anchorage Equal Rights Commission, 874 P 2d 274 (Alaska 1994)
Tileston v Ullman, 318 US 44 (1943)
Tilton v Richardson, 403 US 672 (1971)
United States v Abeyta, 632 F Supp 1301 (DNM 1986)
United States v Lee, 455 US 252 (1982)
United States v Lewis, 638 F Supp 573 (WD Mich 1986)
Van Orden v Perry, 125 S Ct 2854 (2005)
Van Orden v Perry, 545 US 677 (2005)
Wallace v Jaffree, 472 US 38 (1985)
Walz v Tax Commission of City of New York, 397 US 664 (1970)
Warner v Graham, 675 F Supp 1171 (DND 1987)
Widmar v Vincent, 454 US 263 (1981)
Wisconsin v Yoder, 406 US 205 (1972)
Witters v Washington Dep't of Services for the Blind, 474 US 481 (1986)
Wolman v Walter, 433 US 229 (1977)
Zelman v Simmons-Harris, 122 S Ct 2460 (2002)
Zobrest v Catalina Foothills School District, 509 US 1 (1993
Zorach v Clauson, 343 US 306 (1952)
Zylberberg v Sudbury Board of Education [1988] OJ No 1488

United Nations and International Materials

Treaties and Legislative Instruments
Charter of the United Nations
Combating intolerance, negative stereotyping and stigmatization of, and discrimination, incitement to violence and violence against, persons based on religion or belief, HRC Res 16/18, Human Rights Council, 16th sess, UN Doc A/HRC/RES/16/18 (2011)
Convention for the Protection of Human Rights and Fundamental Freedoms (as amended by Protocol No. 11, 1998), opened for signature 4 November 1950, ETS 5 (entered into force 3 September 1953)

Convention for the Protection of Human Rights and Fundamental Freedoms, opened for signature 4 November 1950, CETS No 005 (entered into force 3 September 1953)

Discrimination (Employment and Occupation) Convention (ILO No 111), 362 UNTS 31 (entered into force 15 June 1960)

International Convention for the Protection of All Persons from Enforced Disappearance, opened for signature 20 December 2006, A/RES/61/177 (entered into force on 1 December 2010)

International Convention on the Protection of the Rights of All Migrant Workers and Members of their Families, opened for signature 18 December 1990, A/RES/45/158 (entered into force on 1 July 2003)

International Covenant on Civil and Political Rights, opened for signature 16 December 1966, 999 UNTS 171(entered into force 23 March 1976)

Little Treaty of Versailles, opened for signature 28 June 1919 (entered into force 10 January 1920)

Universal Declaration of Human Rights, GA Res 217 A (III) UN GAOR, 3rd sess, UN Doc A/810 (1948)

Cases

Arrowsmith v United Kingdom Application 7050/75 (1980) 19 *Eur Comm HR* 5
Case of Leyla Sahin v *Turkey* (Application no 44774/98, 10 November 2005)
Chahal v United Kingdom (1996) 23 EHRR 413
Dogru v France, No 27058/05, ECHR, 4 December 2008 (volume still unallocated)
Jewish Liturgical Assn Cha'are Shalom Ve Tsedek v France (Application *27417/95*) *27 June 2000*
Karaduman v Turkey (1993) 74 DR 93
Kervanci v France, No 31645/04, ECHR, 4 December 2008 (volume still unallocated)
Kokkinakis v Greece [1993] ECHR 20
Leyla Sahin v Turkey, Application No. 44774/98, 29 June 2004
Mahuika v New Zealand (2001) 8 IHRR 372 (HRC)
Platform 'Artze Fur Das Leben' v Austria (1991) 13 EHRR 204
Raihon Hudoyberganova v Uzbekistan, Communication No 931/2000
Religionsgemeinschaft der Zeugen Jehovas & Ors v Austria (2008) (Application 40825/98) *31 October 2008*
Soering v United Kingdom (1989) 11 EHRR 439
Stedman v United Kingdom (1997) 23 EHHR 168
Valsamis v Greece (1996) 24 EHRR 294

INDEX

This book is available as a fully searchable PDF at www.adelaide.edu.au/press
References in this index include footnotes

Afghanistan 87
Ahdar, Rex Tauati 65, 80, 137, 371
Ahmadhiya 241
Alabama 313
Ambrose 118
Ambrose Centre for Religious Liberty 137, 147, 372
Anglican Church of Australia 118, 136, 150
Arizona 313
Association of Christian Schools 118, 128
Australia 117, 119, 120, 121, 127, 132, 135, 137, 139, 146, 149, 150
Australian Capital Territory xiii, xv, 119
Australian Catholic Bishops Conference 118, 130, 150
Australian Christian Lobby 117, 118, 120, 132, 137, 372
Australian Constitution xi, xiii, xiv, xv, 165, 367
Australian Human Rights Commission vii, xxii, 118, 144, 149
Australian Human Rights Group 368, 369
Australian Medical Association 140
Australian Multicultural Foundation 147
Australian Quarantine Service 82
Austria 172, 174, 177, 178, 179, 180, 181, 182, 183, 184, 185, 186, 187, 188, 189

Babie, Paul ix, 1
Baden-Württemberg 200, 205, 208
Badiou, Alain 52, 53, 54, 55, 56, 57, 58, 59, 60, 61
Barth, Karl 30, 38

Bavaria 209
Bayrou, François 221, 222, 233, 235
Bedouin 160
Belarus 174, 175, 188
Billingsley, Barbara ix, 321
Bland, Anthony 19, 20
Blitt, Robert C ix, 86
Brazil 318, 369
Brennan, Frank 8, 141, 143
Britain 45, 123, 137, 142, 252, 390
Buddhism 10

Cadwallader, Alan ix, 51
Caesar 12, 36, 321
Calma, Tom 145, 146, 147
Canaan 35
Canada 134, 138, 142, 321, 324, 325, 339, 345, 346, 347, 369
Canadian Charter of Rights and Freedoms 5, 321, 333, 373, 403, 404
Catholic Church 12, 17, 18, 26, 69, 127, 130, 224, 225, 291, 387
Catholic doctrine 18
Catholic Film Office 51
China xv, 110, 369
Church 47
Church of England 40, 92
Cold War 179, 182, 188
Connecticut 313
Cornhill, Lord Bingham of xvi
Council of Europe 175, 187, 188, 229
Crouch, Colin xvii

Dahl, Nils 54
Declaration of Independence 30, 43

Declaration of the Rights of Man 225, 227, 239
Declaration on the Rights of Indigenous Peoples 394
Denmark 232
Durban Review Conference 109

Egypt 34, 35
Eichmann, Adolf 181
European 187
European Convention on Human Rights xiv, 114, 124, 175, 240
European Court of Human Rights xx, 176, 185, 229, 230, 240, 241, 246
European Union 9, 87, 101, 106, 157, 178

Fédération Nationale des Musulmans de France 218
Fish, Stanley 123
Fitzgerald, Tony QC xviii
Florida 313
Foster, Neil ix, 63
France 46, 127, 165, 216, 217, 218, 223, 224, 225, 226, 227, 228, 229, 231, 232, 234, 236, 238
French Constitution 226

George III 30
German Federal Constitutional Court 192, 215
Germany 33, 46, 179, 182, 188, 190, 205, 208, 209, 210, 211, 232
Greece 369

Haider, Jörg 177, 178, 181, 182
Haldane, John 18
Haneef, Mohammed xviii, xxi
Hanifa, Abu 166, 169
Hanna, Kris ix, 365
Hauraki Gulf 407
Hewlett, Nick 54
Hicks, David xviii, xxi

High Court of Australia x, xi, xv, 21, 68
Hindu 240, 245, 248, 249
Hinduism 10
Hitler, Adolf 179, 181
Hobbes, Thomas 32
Holocaust 172, 179
Hong Kong xiv, xv, 369
Hooker, Richard 39
House of Lords 20, 67, 75, 124, 241, 242, 244, 246, 247, 248
Human 414
Human Rights Commission vii, 116, 118, 141, 144, 149, 341, 381, 382, 391, 415
Human Rights Council 102, 110
Human Rights Watch 99
Human Rights Without Frontiers 174

Idaho 313
Indonesia 99, 100
International Covenant on Civil and Political Rights xii, 71, 105, 119, 367, 373, 377, 395
International Labour Organisation 368
Iran 174, 175, 176, 188
Ireland 94, 113, 114, 140
Islamic Council 65, 66, 97, 98, 115
Israel 34, 35, 60

Jefferson, Thomas 43, 291, 292, 293, 296, 352, 356
Jehovah's Witnesses 185, 186, 187, 324, 339, 344, 385
Jesus Christ vii, 35, 36, 38, 44, 95, 128
John Paul II 36, 37, 38
Jones, Nicky ix, 216
Jospin, Lionel 219, 220, 233, 236, 237

Kaye, Bruce ix, 29
Keane, John xvii
Kirkham, David M ix, 172
Koch, Cornelia ix, 190
Krishna 247

Index

Leigh, Ian x, 239
Lemon test 257, 269, 294, 295, 296, 297, 298, 299, 300, 301, 303, 350, 351, 354, 355, 357, 358
Levinas, Emmanuel 60
Limbach, Jutta 210
Lloyd, John xvii, xviii
Locke, John 32
Luther, Martin 56

Malaysia 97, 98, 100, 165, 167
Māori 10, 388, 390, 394, 395, 396, 397, 398, 399, 400, 401, 402, 403, 404, 405, 406, 407, 408, 409, 410, 411, 412, 413, 414, 415, 416, 417, 418, 419, 420, 421
Mason, Sir Anthony vii, x, xi
Missouri 313
Mohammed 154
Morocco, King Hassan of 220
Moses 34, 35, 162

Naffine, Ngaire x, 12
Nanos, Mark 57, 58, 59
Napoléon 225
National Human Rights Consultation Committee xxiii, 3
Nazareth 38, 40
New Mexico 313
New South Wales 30, 31, 93, 112, 117, 234, 367
New Zealand xiii, xiv, xv, xix, 2, 4, 5, 9, 10, 87, 94, 137, 369, 371, 372, 373, 375, 376, 381, 382, 383, 384, 385, 388, 389, 390, 391, 394, 395, 396, 397, 398, 399, 400, 401, 402, 403, 404, 405, 406, 407, 408, 409, 410, 411, 413, 414, 415, 416, 417, 418, 419, 420, 421
Northern Territory 52
North Korea 174, 175, 176, 188

Oklahoma 313

Organization of the Islamic Conference 100

Pakistan 96, 97, 100, 101, 106, 110
Parkinson x, 65, 69, 372
Pennsylvania 313, 354
Poole, Thomas xx
Punjabi 250

Queensland xviii, 65, 80
Queen Victoria 397
Qur'an 153, 154, 156, 157, 158, 159, 160, 161, 162, 163, 166, 167, 168, 169, 228

Rau, Johannes 211
Ravitch, Frank x, 253
Rawls, John 125
Rhode Island 292, 313, 354
Rishworth, Paul x, 381, 382, 385, 393
Rochow, Neville x, 1
Roman Catholic 29, 36, 37, 47, 69, 241, 360, 371
Rudd Labor government xxiii
Rushdie, Salman 93
Russia 75, 110, 176
Russian Orthodox Church 110
Russo, Charles x, 349
Rwanda 172

Scharffs, Brett x, 285
Schröder, Gerhard 211
Section 116 xi, 31, 367, 379
South Africa 87, 250, 369
South Australia 367
South Carolina 313
South Island 413
Soviet Union 87
Standing Committee of the National People's Congress xv
St Paul 51, 52
Sudan 172

Tajikistan 174, 175
Tasmania 65, 80
Ten Canoes 51
Texas 301, 302, 303, 304, 313, 358
Third Reich 179, 181, 182, 183, 188
Treaty of Waitangi 396, 397, 399, 400, 401, 402, 403, 406, 409, 410, 413, 414, 415, 418, 419, 420, 421
Treaty of Westphalia 46
Turkey 176

United Kingdom xiii, xiv, xv, xvii, xix, xx, xxi, xxii, 2, 4, 9, 173, 176, 392, 397
United Nations 36, 91, 100, 107, 319, 394
United Nations General Assembly 36, 102
United States 2, 7, 30, 173, 281, 285, 301, 308, 318, 319, 320, 375, 379, 394, 418
Uniting Church 119

Universal Declaration of Human Rights 1, 36, 51, 61, 67, 86, 120, 140, 164, 172, 367

Victoria 65, 67, 80, 111, 112, 133, 134, 137, 140, 141, 143, 144

Waitangi Tribunal 396, 402, 403, 409, 410
Waldheim, Kurt 177, 178, 179, 180
Wales 247
Wessel, Margit van xviii
Western Australia xxii
White Australia Policy 42
Wolterstorff, Nicholas 29, 33, 34, 36, 37
Wood, Asmi x, 152
World War Two 137, 172, 177, 178, 182, 188
World Youth Day 68

Žižek, Slavoj 52, 54, 56, 60

Index

Leigh, Ian x, 239
Lemon test 257, 269, 294, 295, 296, 297, 298, 299, 300, 301, 303, 350, 351, 354, 355, 357, 358
Levinas, Emmanuel 60
Limbach, Jutta 210
Lloyd, John xvii, xviii
Locke, John 32
Luther, Martin 56

Malaysia 97, 98, 100, 165, 167
Māori 10, 388, 390, 394, 395, 396, 397, 398, 399, 400, 401, 402, 403, 404, 405, 406, 407, 408, 409, 410, 411, 412, 413, 414, 415, 416, 417, 418, 419, 420, 421
Mason, Sir Anthony vii, x, xi
Missouri 313
Mohammed 154
Morocco, King Hassan of 220
Moses 34, 35, 162

Naffine, Ngaire x, 12
Nanos, Mark 57, 58, 59
Napoléon 225
National Human Rights Consultation Committee xxiii, 3
Nazareth 38, 40
New Mexico 313
New South Wales 30, 31, 93, 112, 117, 234, 367
New Zealand xiii, xiv, xv, xix, 2, 4, 5, 9, 10, 87, 94, 137, 369, 371, 372, 373, 375, 376, 381, 382, 383, 384, 385, 388, 389, 390, 391, 394, 395, 396, 397, 398, 399, 400, 401, 402, 403, 404, 405, 406, 407, 408, 409, 410, 411, 413, 414, 415, 416, 417, 418, 419, 420, 421
Northern Territory 52
North Korea 174, 175, 176, 188

Oklahoma 313

Organization of the Islamic Conference 100

Pakistan 96, 97, 100, 101, 106, 110
Parkinson x, 65, 69, 372
Pennsylvania 313, 354
Poole, Thomas xx
Punjabi 250

Queensland xviii, 65, 80
Queen Victoria 397
Qur'an 153, 154, 156, 157, 158, 159, 160, 161, 162, 163, 166, 167, 168, 169, 228

Rau, Johannes 211
Ravitch, Frank x, 253
Rawls, John 125
Rhode Island 292, 313, 354
Rishworth, Paul x, 381, 382, 385, 393
Rochow, Neville x, 1
Roman Catholic 29, 36, 37, 47, 69, 241, 360, 371
Rudd Labor government xxiii
Rushdie, Salman 93
Russia 75, 110, 176
Russian Orthodox Church 110
Russo, Charles x, 349
Rwanda 172

Scharffs, Brett x, 285
Schröder, Gerhard 211
Section 116 xi, 31, 367, 379
South Africa 87, 250, 369
South Australia 367
South Carolina 313
South Island 413
Soviet Union 87
Standing Committee of the National People's Congress xv
St Paul 51, 52
Sudan 172

Tajikistan 174, 175
Tasmania 65, 80
Ten Canoes 51
Texas 301, 302, 303, 304, 313, 358
Third Reich 179, 181, 182, 183, 188
Treaty of Waitangi 396, 397, 399, 400, 401, 402, 403, 406, 409, 410, 413, 414, 415, 418, 419, 420, 421
Treaty of Westphalia 46
Turkey 176

United Kingdom xiii, xiv, xv, xvii, xix, xx, xxi, xxii, 2, 4, 9, 173, 176, 392, 397
United Nations 36, 91, 100, 107, 319, 394
United Nations General Assembly 36, 102
United States 2, 7, 30, 173, 281, 285, 301, 308, 318, 319, 320, 375, 379, 394, 418
Uniting Church 119

Universal Declaration of Human Rights 1, 36, 51, 61, 67, 86, 120, 140, 164, 172, 367

Victoria 65, 67, 80, 111, 112, 133, 134, 137, 140, 141, 143, 144

Waitangi Tribunal 396, 402, 403, 409, 410
Waldheim, Kurt 177, 178, 179, 180
Wales 247
Wessel, Margit van xviii
Western Australia xxii
White Australia Policy 42
Wolterstorff, Nicholas 29, 33, 34, 36, 37
Wood, Asmi x, 152
World War Two 137, 172, 177, 178, 182, 188
World Youth Day 68

Žižek, Slavoj 52, 54, 56, 60

www.ingramcontent.com/pod-product-compliance
Lightning Source LLC
Chambersburg PA
CBHW060520300426
44112CB00017B/2747